PRAISE FOR *Rebel Yell*

"In *Rebel Yell*, Mr. Gwynne's easy, loping style wraps itself effortlessly around the particulars of Stonewall Jackson's life, from his back-of-the-mountain upbringing to the outburst of military genius in the Civil War. The result is a narrative vivid with detail and insight."

—*The Wall Street Journal*

"In the magnificent *Rebel Yell*, one of the year's best biographies, writer S. C. Gwynne brings Jackson ferociously to life. . . . His battle scenes are marvels of description and kinetic action. [He] brings a deep humanity to his portrayals of Jackson, his fellow Confederate generals, and their Union adversaries. . . . Gwynne's pages fly by, brimming with excitement and terror."

—*Newsday*

"Gwynne stirringly re-creates the bloody, error-plagued battles of the early war and argues that Jackson's legend galvanized the South, outmanned and outgunned, to keep fighting."

—*The New Yorker*

"I believe that the mark of a great biography is a book that helps you understand someone who might be entirely different from you, the reader. The subject might be confounding. Unlikable. Even infuriating. For this twenty-first-century reader, such was the case with S. C. Gwynne's compelling new biography—the story of Confederate general Thomas J. 'Stonewall' Jackson."

—*The Seattle Times*

"An engaging narrative with a pace that never flags . . . Gwynne accomplishes a great deal in his clear and highly readable book. . . . If you read everything about the Civil War—or if you have read very little about the Civil War—*Rebel Yell* is an excellent addition to your reading list."

—*The Huffington Post*

"I've reviewed many books on the Civil War, and this is far and away the best biography of a Civil War general that I've read. . . . If you're a Civil War buff—as I am—or if you're just interested in wonderful biographies—as I am—*Rebel Yell* is a must-read book. It reads like a novel, but it's based on extensive-beyond-belief research."

—*The Huntington News*

"Gwynne's portrait of Jackson is comprehensive, stirring, compelling. . . . This well-researched portrait of a well-studied figure of the Civil War defies the odds and measurably adds to the scholarship surrounding Jackson and the conflict that defined him. . . . The book is hard to put down."

—*The Dallas Morning News*

"Profoundly enlightening . . . The difference in *Rebel Yell* is . . . the historical sweep, the small touches, and the quality and clarity of the writing. . . . Those sorts of little touches, page after page after page, set this book apart. . . . Gwynne's *Rebel Yell* delivers what readers want and deserve—a brave, headlong charge into American history."

—*Chicago Tribune*

"A worthy book that does much to present the general in a realistic, critical, and evenhanded manner. . . . Gwynne writes with style. . . . He creates vivid word pictures and descriptions that keep the reader engaged. *Rebel Yell* is a worthy addition to the shelves of those who study and read about the American Civil War."

—*Washington Independent Review of Books*

"S. C. Gwynne provides a comprehensive portrait of a complex man who triumphed on the battlefield—but remained an enigma . . . a joy to read."

—*Civil War Times*

"[Gwynne's contribution] lies in capturing Jackson's character, personality, and historical significance. He interprets Jackson as a discipline- and God-obsessed social bore, one of the fiercest fighters and most brilliant minds in American military history . . . a 'living myth' . . . Jackson ascended rapidly from nerdy artillery and physics professor at Virginia Military Institute to Lee's audacious and seemingly invincible lieutenant."

—*The Raleigh News & Observer*

"A stimulating study of Confederate general Stonewall Jackson . . . Gwynne reveals him to have been an early master of modern mobile warfare and a clear-eyed interpreter of what modern 'pitiless war was all about.' . . . Readers are likely to agree that, without Jackson, Lee 'would never again be quite so brilliant,' while even in the North Jackson was considered, rather than a rebel, a 'gentleman and . . . fundamentally an *American*.'"

—*Publishers Weekly* (starred review)

"Spry prose and cogent insight . . . Showing Jackson's exploitation of speed and deception, Gwynne's vivid account of his Civil War run, which ended with his death in the 1863 Battle of Chancellorsville, is a riveting, cover-to-cover read for history buffs."

—*Booklist* (starred review)

"In a sea of Civil War books Gwynne's book stands out for its beautiful writing, its highly personalized research accomplishments, and its lush detail . . . a masterful work of popular history."

—*The Wichita Eagle*

"September's most scintillating read may be a 640-page biography of Thomas 'Stonewall' Jackson. . . . S. C. Gwynne's riveting retelling of the canny Confederate whose strategies shaped the early years of the Civil War is just that good."

—*Kirkus Reviews*

"It's hard to imagine an author breaking new ground with another Jackson biography. But S. C. Gwynne does just that in *Rebel Yell*. . . . Readers will come away from *Rebel Yell* with an understanding of the man that goes beyond his military exploits. Gwynne's masterful storytelling makes *Rebel Yell* an absorbing choice for general readers and Civil War buffs alike."

—*BookPage*

"VERDICT: This popular history is recommended for all readers interested in the Civil War."

—*Library Journal*

"*Rebel Yell* breathes contemporary insight and fresh energy into the life of an authentic American legend. In this crackling narrative, S. C. Gwynne gives us the bold tactics, the eccentric thinking, and the wicked genius of one of history's most brilliant—and unconventional—military minds."

—Hampton Sides, author of *Blood and Thunder: The Epic Story of Kit Carson and the Conquest of the American West* and *In the Kingdom of Ice: The Grand and Terrible Polar Voyage of the USS* Jeannette

"Powerfully told, richly detailed, but also deeply human in timeless ways, *Rebel Yell* unmasks General Stonewall Jackson, one of American history's most enduring legends (and yet most private of men). This is history at its best."

—Michael Duffy, coauthor of *The Presidents Club: Inside the World's Most Exclusive Fraternity*

"With the reporter's eye for the revealing vignette and the storyteller's ear for the rhythm of human striving, S. C. Gwynne gives us a beautifully penetrating account of the meteoric rise and tragic death of the most legendary of Civil War soldiers."

—H. W. Brands, author of *The Man Who Saved the Union: Ulysses Grant in War and Peace*

"*Rebel Yell* is the best biography of Stonewall Jackson I have ever read. The scholarship is exemplary, the narrative riveting and richly textured. With a rare combination of unflinching objectivity and genuine compassion, *Rebel Yell* unraveled for me the enigma of Stonewall Jackson. A magnificent achievement, *Rebel Yell* represents a milestone in Civil War literature."

—Peter Cozzens, author of *Shenandoah 1862: Stonewall Jackson's Valley Campaign*

"The great tragedy of modern historiography is that more historians don't write like S. C. Gwynne. In this book on Stonewall Jackson's Civil War career, Gwynne has fashioned a fast-paced narrative of a man complex and enigmatic, awkward and exceptional. Gwynne has taken on a giant figure of quirks and brilliance who demands both restraint and a facile pen, and he delivers in vivid form."

—John Hennessy, author of *The First Battle of Manassas: An End to Innocence* and *Return to Bull Run: The Campaign and Battle of Second Manassas*

ALSO BY S. C. GWYNNE

Empire of the Summer Moon:
Quanah Parker and the Rise and Fall of the Comanches,
the Most Powerful Indian Tribe in American History

REBEL YELL

The Violence, Passion, and Redemption
of Stonewall Jackson

❧

S. C. GWYNNE

SCRIBNER

New York London Toronto Sydney New Delhi

For my wife, Katie,
and my daughter, Maisie

SCRIBNER
An Imprint of Simon & Schuster, Inc.
1230 Avenue of the Americas
New York, NY 10020

First Scribner trade paperback edition October 2015

SCRIBNER and design are registered trademarks of The Gale Group, Inc.,
used under license by Simon & Schuster, Inc., the publisher of this work.

For information about special discounts for bulk purchases,
please contact Simon & Schuster Special Sales at 1-866-506-1949
or business@simonandschuster.com.

The Simon & Schuster Speakers Bureau can bring authors to your live event.
For more information or to book an event contact the Simon & Schuster Speakers Bureau
at 1-866-248-3049 or visit our website at www.simonspeakers.com.

Manufactured in the United States of America

1   3   5   7   9   10   8   6   4   2

The Library of Congress has cataloged the hardcover edition as follows:
Gwynne, S. C. (Samuel C.).
Rebel yell : the violence, passion, and redemption of
Stonewall Jackson / S. C. Gwynne. —First Scribner hardcover edition.
pages   cm
Includes bibliographical references.
1. Jackson, Stonewall, 1824–1863. 2. Generals—Confederate States of America—Biography.
3. Jackson, Stonewall, 1824–1863—Military leadership. 4. Virginia—History—Civil War,
1861–1865—Campaigns. 5. United States—History—Civil War, 1861–1865—Campaigns.
6. Confederate States of America. Army—Biography. I. Title.
E467.1.J15G85 2014
973.7'3092—dc23
[B]   2014010046

ISBN 978-1-4516-7328-9
ISBN 978-1-4516-7329-6 (pbk)
ISBN 978-1-4516-7330-2 (ebook)

And yet the only man of those men who pass
With a strange, secretive grain of harsh poetry
Hidden so deep in the stony sides of his heart
That it shines by flashes only and then is gone.
It glitters in his last words.
— Stephen Vincent Benét,
"John Brown's Body"

He bowed the heavens also, and came down with thick darkness
    under His feet. . . .
He made darkness His hiding place, His canopy around Him,
Darkness of waters, thick clouds of the skies.
— Psalm 18

CONTENTS

PART THREE

VALLEY OF THE SHADOW OF DEATH

PART FOUR

STIRRINGS OF A LEGEND

PART FIVE

ALL THAT IS EVER GIVEN TO A MAN

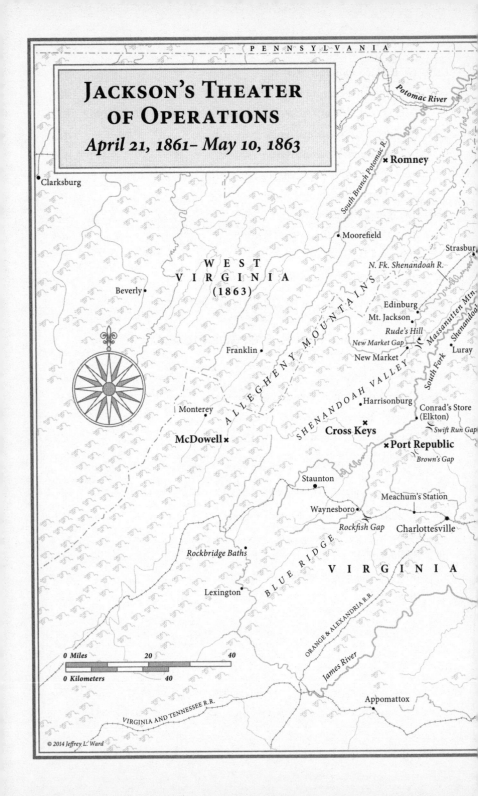

JACKSON'S THEATER OF OPERATIONS
April 21, 1861– May 10, 1863

PENNSYLVANIA

Potomac River

South Branch Potomac R.

× **Romney**

• Clarksburg

• Moorefield

Strasbur×

N. Fk. Shenandoah R.

WEST
VIRGINIA
(1863)

Beverly •

Edinburg •
Mt. Jackson •

Rude's Hill

New Market Gap

New Market •

Massanutten Mtn.

Shenandoa

• Luray

South Fork Shenandoah

Franklin •

ALLEGHENY MOUNTAINS

Harrisonburg •

Conrad's Store
• (Elkton)

| Monterey •

SHENANDOAH VALLEY

Swift Run Gap

McDowell ×

× **Cross Keys**

× **Port Republic**

Brown's Gap

Staunton •

Meachum's Station •

Waynesboro •

Rockfish Gap

Charlottesville •

Rockbridge Baths •

BLUE RIDGE

VIRGINIA

Lexington •

ORANGE & ALEXANDRIA R.R.

| 0 Miles | 20 | 40 |

| 0 Kilometers | 40 |

James River

VIRGINIA AND TENNESSEE R.R.

Appomattox •

© 2014 Jeffrey L. Ward

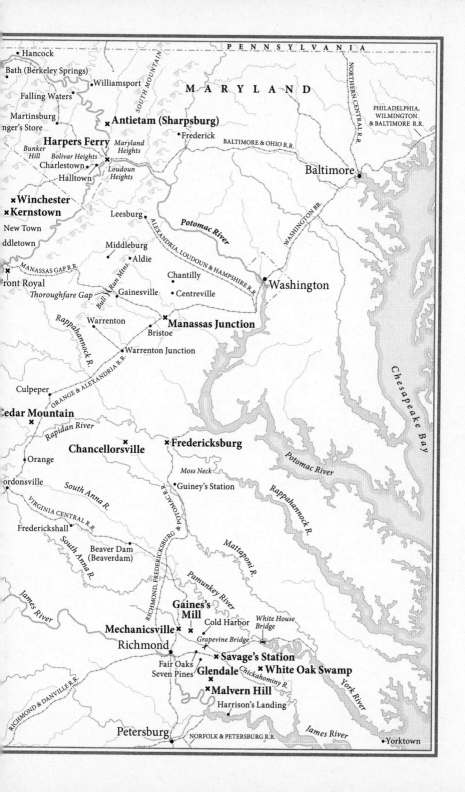

LEGENDS OF SPRING

On the brilliantly clear afternoon of June 19, 1862, in the second year of the great Civil War, a well-dressed, bespectacled Confederate congressman with a trim beard named Alexander Robinson Boteler stood on a platform at the train station in Charlottesville, Virginia. He was on war business, traveling under the personal orders of General Robert E. Lee. He had just arrived from Richmond, having made the seventy-mile journey by rail across the blossoming, river-cut hills of the Piedmont country. Now, as he gazed about him, Boteler realized that something quite unusual was happening. The normally sleepy college town of Charlottesville, he observed, "was in a fever of excitement." There was noise and commotion everywhere, though to no particular purpose. Some sort of large-scale military movement was under way, but no one, neither citizens nor soldiers, could say exactly what it was. Theories abounded. A dozen empty trains had passed mysteriously through the station earlier that day, all headed west, toward the Blue Ridge Mountains and the Shenandoah Valley.[1] None had returned. A cordon of gray-uniformed soldiers had virtually sealed the town off from the outside world—for security reasons, presumably—though what knowledge any of its citizens could possibly have imparted to the enemy was hard to say. All anyone knew was that whatever was taking place was a very large secret. Lee's orders to Boteler, in fact, had simply been to "stop at Charlottesville and await orders," which seemed as cryptic as everything else that was happening that day.[2]

Boteler thought he knew what was happening—he was one of perhaps five people on earth who could make that claim—and, watching the excitement build around him in the warm spring air, he had a clear sense that he stood at one of the pivot points of the war. "Great events," as he put it later, "were on the gale."[3] He was in a position to know. He was a new breed of Southern politician, spawned entirely by the exigencies of war. A former US congressman from western Virginia, he had been one of the last representatives from a Southern state to abandon the Union, and then had promptly been elected to the First Confederate Congress. Soon he was wielding power in a way he never had in Washington—indeed, in a way that had never been done before in American politics or anticipated by the men who had designed the country's democratic systems. Genial, persistent, and charismatic, Boteler acted as liaison between Confederate armies in the field and the capital at Richmond. He moved easily between the two worlds, an insider in both. He occupied himself with issues of military supplies and munitions, with the devastations of war on the towns in his district, even of the movements of Union armies. He had become a sort of wartime public relations officer and courier, the link between the generals and the politicians.

That was the work he was performing that day on the train platform in Charlottesville. But he was doing it now under more perilous conditions than the new Confederate nation had ever experienced. The Richmond he had left that morning was a changed city, a shaken city where it seemed that, if all hell was not yet breaking loose and full panic not quite abroad in the city's streets, both soon would be. In spite of the Confederacy's conviction—bordering on absolute certainty—that the war would be brief, relatively bloodless, heroic, and victorious, the new nation suddenly found itself on the brink of an undreamed-of disaster. Just east of Richmond spread the campfires of an enormous Union army. With 120,000 soldiers, it was the largest military force in the Western Hemisphere and one of the greatest concentrations of sheer firepower in human history.[4] Its sole purpose, pursued doggedly through the mud and swollen streams of the York-James Peninsula for more than three months, was to conquer and occupy the city of Richmond. Confederate troops, some 50,000 of them under General Joseph E. Johnston, had fallen steadily back to the capital in a soggy, dispiriting retreat, fighting rearguard actions but unable to challenge the enemy's crushing numerical superiority.

And now that same Union army, under the guidance of the estimable General George B. McClellan, had bivouacked so close to Richmond that its soldiers could hear the city's church bells. Measured in raw military muscle, the confrontation was a grotesque mismatch: 65,000 Confederates (including the city's defense force) with inferior weaponry against this moon tide of blue-coated troops equipped with the most sophisticated martial hardware in the world. Worse still, the Confederate Army of Northern Virginia was now commanded by a man with at best a shaky reputation as a fighter: Robert E. Lee. He had assumed command of the army just two and a half weeks before, succeeding the wounded Johnston. Though he was a veteran of the Mexican-American War, had once held the job of superintendent at West Point, and was admired within military circles, this new war had already demonstrated with cruel clarity that dusty military laurels were no guarantee of victory. In the fifth month of the war, Lee had lost a campaign at Cheat Mountain in western Virginia, where his retreat had earned him the nickname Evacuating Lee. He had other less than flattering sobriquets, too. Officers who considered him a bit fussy and cautious for army work called him Granny Lee. The soldiers who had obeyed his orders to dig breastworks around Richmond in anticipation of McClellan's attack—finding this an inglorious task for men whose purpose was to stand up and fight—had dubbed him the King of Spades. He had spent most of the war in an office in Richmond as a sort of glorified military sidekick to the West Point–educated Jefferson Davis, a former US secretary of war who had himself fought in Mexico.[5]

The Confederate capital, moreover, was more than just the seat of government. It represented a huge component of the South's industrial and financial might. Its Tredegar Iron Works were the largest of their kind in the South, supplying half of all artillery in the Confederacy, much of its munitions, and most of its locomotive-building capacity. Its warehouses had become the main source of military supply for the war's eastern theater. Richmond was also the source of Confederate currency and the repository of the gold that backed it. The government was so worried about this that, as McClellan's army had muscled closer to the city, the Treasury's gold reserves had been loaded onto a special train whose boilers held a full head of steam at all times, ready to depart at short notice. Without the gold, Confederate dollars were worthless, and if they were worthless, then the Confederate government would be unable to pay for its war.[6] Preparations had already been made to ship military papers and government archives to Columbia, South Carolina, while Virginia legislators had voted to burn Richmond rather than surrender it to the Yankees.[7] As though to underscore just how close Richmond was to falling, President Davis had sent his wife and children south, to Raleigh, out of harm's way.[8]

Northern newspapers were already crowing about what seemed certain victory. The math was inescapable. And citizens of the North could now, finally, after fourteen bloody and frustrating months of war, look forward to Richmond's fall with grim satisfaction, and comfort themselves that a long overdue moral lesson was about to be administered to the traitorous enemy. "It is believed in town," wrote Washingtonian Elizabeth Blair Lee to her husband in the Union navy, "that Virginia will be evacuated without a fight."[9] Others were convinced that the war itself would be over by July Fourth. As panic and resignation seeped through the streets of Richmond, many Southerners seemed to be of the same mind. "I am ready to sink with despair," wrote Jefferson Davis's niece to her mother on May 7.[10]

It was in this explosive climate that Alexander Boteler had made his train trip west from Richmond. On the platform, he heard the scream of an engine and then watched in some amazement as an unscheduled eastbound train "came thundering into the station," as he later put it, and groaned to a stop, trailing great clouds of smoke. The train was a bizarre sight, so overloaded with Confederate troops—some two thousand of them jammed inside the cars and on their roofs—that, as Boteler observed, they "seemed to cover them all over like a cluster of bees."[11]

Then he spotted, amid the roar and the hubbub on the station platform, the lone figure seated on a bench in the postal car, behind the tender. Considering what the man looked like, it was amazing that Boteler—or anyone else, for that matter—noticed him at all. He wore a tattered, faded, and mud-flecked uniform whose shoulders had been bleached yellow by the sun, large artillery boots, and a soiled cap pulled down across the bridge of his nose so that much of his face was obscured. His hair was long and his beard unkempt.[12] He was what most of the thousands of people who saw him and later recorded their observations might have called nondescript.

The distinction was his coat's star-emblazoned collar. The rumpled man was a major general in the Confederate army. His name was Thomas J. Jackson, though most Southerners already knew him as Stonewall, a nickname he had earned at the Battle of Manassas, eleven months earlier. Boteler was, in fact, a part-time member of Jackson's staff. Since the beginning of the war, he had been the general's political eyes and ears in Richmond. He was Jackson's PR man, Jackson's courier and factotum, Jackson's lobbyist, and Jackson's political confidant, and it was on Jackson's behalf that Boteler ran most of his errands, including several direct appeals to the legislature.[13] He had been instrumental in getting Jackson appointed to his command in the first place. And he was even now carrying a personal letter for Jackson that Robert E. Lee had given him the night before.[14]

Jackson recognized Boteler, waved him aboard, and the two men shook hands. Jackson asked him if he had a pencil and paper. Boteler replied that he did. "Then sit down please," Jackson said, "and write as I shall dictate to you."[15] For the next few minutes, while the overstuffed train rested at the platform, and the citizens of Charlottesville tried in vain to understand exactly what they were seeing, Jackson spooled out a string of high-speed orders, dictating details of the complex eastward transfer of his 18,500-man army by train and by road, a sort of layered, hopscotching mechanism and a method of troop transfer new to the ways of war in North America.

Jackson finished, and said good-bye to Boteler, who stepped back onto the platform. The train slipped away from the station, vanishing amid swirls of smoke into the rolling forest of the Virginia Piedmont. An hour later, at the junction town of Gordonsville, the same train startled troops from the 4th North Carolina Regiment, who were on guard duty at the time. They had been told nothing about a troop train bearing several thousand soldiers, heading *east*. "This arrival came on us like a thunderclap," wrote one in a letter. "There is some important movement on hand but no one can even surmise what it is."[16] They were even more surprised when, a few moments later, they received another astonishing piece of information in the form of the "very ordinary looking," "shabbily dressed," yet unmistakable officer whose face flashed by them in the windows of the train.[17]

The reason that the soldiers had known nothing about their commander's whereabouts and intentions was because great pains had been taken, under Jackson's strict orders, to conceal them. His own generals had no idea where he was. They complained loudly about it, too, unable to understand how such absurd levels of concealment could possibly advance the cause of the Confederacy. Two days before, Jackson had instructed his cavalry chief to send all dispatches directly to him—thus bypassing all normal channels of command—and also to meet him secretly, specifying only that "I will be on my horse at the north end of town" and asking that the officer "not inquire after him" since he did not want his own soldiers to know where he was.[18] His own top lieutenant, General Richard Ewell, had been under the false impression that his army was moving *north*, and when he received his orders they merely told him to march in the direction of Charlottesville, his ultimate destination unknown.[19] Jackson's peculiar deceptions had worked brilliantly on the enemy, too: the Union army's best intelligence placed him with up to forty thousand men at five separate locations within a hundred-mile radius, one of which was at, or near, the Potomac River boundaries of Washington, DC.[20] Until Boteler saw the train pull in, even he had had no idea exactly where Jackson and his army were. And of course the common soldier, as usual, knew nothing at all. "I do not know whether we are going to march north, south, east, or west, or whether we are going to march at all," complained one of them who was camped in the area, "and that is about all I will ever know of Jackson's plans."[21]

But at least one thing was certain. Something very big was under way. *Jackson* was going east.

It is a matter of record that, a mere fourteen months earlier, the man everyone from Charlottesville to Washington was so breathlessly concerned about had been an obscure, eccentric, and unpopular college professor in a small town in rural Virginia. He had odd habits, a strangely silent manner, a host of health problems, and was thought by almost everyone who knew him to be lacking in even the most basic skills of leadership. To call him a failure is probably too harsh. He just wasn't very good at anything; he was part of that great undifferentiated mass of second-rate humanity who weren't going anywhere in life. And yet on that bright June day in Charlottesville the oddball science teacher had just completed a military campaign in Virginia's Shenandoah Valley that made him the most famous military figure in the Western world. In a matter of months he had undergone a transformation of such speed and magnitude that it stood out in a war that made a specialty of such changes. Ulysses S. Grant, the most famous of these war-induced transformations, was a washout from the army and a failure in business. When the war began he was employed as a clerk in his father's leather store in Galena, Illinois. William Tecumseh Sherman, a failed banker who had landed at a tiny military academy in Louisiana, was another. Jackson's rise to fame, power, and legend was every bit as deep and transfiguring as that of the two Union generals. But it happened much faster, and his ascent was much steeper.

His metamorphosis began in the first year of the war, with his brilliant performance in the Confederate victory at Manassas. But it was rooted mainly in an extraordinary campaign that had begun on March 23 and ended on June 9, 1862. What Jackson did in those seventy-eight days, in a small and dazzlingly beautiful theater of war bounded by mountain ranges on either side, redefined the conflict and made him the most celebrated field commander in the war. Though the particulars of each battle or skirmish could be quite complex, their significance, seen collectively, was strikingly clear and simple. Using a combination of speed, deception, and sheer audacity, Jackson, with 17,000 men (and often far fewer), had taken on and beaten Union forces that, though never united, totaled more than 52,000. He marched his men at a pace unknown to soldiers of the day, covering an astounding 646 miles in 48 days, fighting five major battles, and skirmishing almost daily. He made flashing strikes in unexpected places, falling on the enemy from behind mountain ranges and out of steep passes. With his small force he had driven four Union armies from the greater part of the Shenandoah Valley, inflicting 5,000 casualties, capturing 3,500 prisoners, an immense quantity of stores and supplies, and seizing 9,000 small arms. He had evaded a massive pincer movement designed by Abraham Lincoln himself to catch him. Then, in the most stunning maneuver of all, he had turned on both jaws of the pincer—two Union armies—and beaten them in succession. In a war where the techniques of marching and fighting were being reinvented almost literally hour by hour, Jackson's intelligence, speed, aggression, and pure arrogance were the wonders of North and South alike. They were the talk of salons in London and Paris.

Jackson's success was all the more striking because it had come amid so many Confederate defeats, just as that feeling of despair that Jefferson Davis's niece described had begun to descend on the entire beleaguered South. Confederates had lost major battles that spring at Shiloh and Forts Donelson and Henry in Tennessee. New Orleans had surrendered. Most of Kentucky and Tennessee were lost, as was part of the Carolina coast. News of what Jackson had done in the valley was rolling off Southern presses at the very moment that McClellan's giant army was shouldering its way up the York-James Peninsula toward Richmond. Jackson's victories not only drove the enemy from a large part of Virginia; his successes had also frozen in place and then diverted another army, some 40,000 troops camped near Fredericksburg, Virginia, that had been ready to move against Richmond.[22] If those troops had arrived on the city's undefended west side—complementing the 120,000 on the east—Richmond would have had little choice but to surrender. That had been the Union's grand plan, and Jackson had laid waste to it. In that sense, he had already saved Richmond, or at least he had bought it time. More than anything else, perhaps, he had given Southern morale a tremendous lift in its darkest hour; he had shown that an undermanned Confederate army could outmarch, outmaneuver, and outfight much larger and better equipped Yankee forces. He had even proven—the math works out almost perfectly—the old Southern chestnut that one rebel was worth at least three cowardly Yanks. (That ratio was probably not random or accidental: in the larger war, some 2.1 million Union soldiers eventually took up arms against 880,000 Confederates.[23])

By the time Jackson passed through Charlottesville that day, a mere ten days after the closing battle of his valley campaign, Confederate papers were already hailing him as the new national idol. The *Richmond Whig* asserted that "he wears the sword of the Lord of Gideon" and proclaimed that "he has been . . . chawing up Yankees by the thousands as if they were so many grains of parched popcorn."[24] The *Richmond Daily Dispatch* called him simply "The Hero of The War," hailing him as a "decisive genius" and comparing his "rapid marches, profound calculations, [and] energetic attack" to the legendary Italian campaign of Napoléon Bonaparte.[25] The North, meanwhile, had gotten the notion that Jackson was a Southern version of the abolitionist John Brown, a man who worshipped a grim, Old Testament God of vengeance, a holy warrior who wielded a strange and powerful influence over his men. Some said he was simply a remorseless killer, nearly as hard on his own troops as he was on the enemy. But no one really knew. Not yet. Jackson, the dusty, rumpled man on the train, was still almost completely shrouded in mystery.

He was traveling east by train that day because Robert E. Lee, a man with whom he would soon develop a partnership that changed the course of the Civil War, had summoned him. And because Lee was about to launch a hazardous—many would have deemed it suicidal—attempt to drive McClellan's army away from the gates of the capital, and he wanted Jackson in its vanguard. Though it would take several days for this closely guarded information to spread through the rank and file, the reaction when it came was one of almost delirious joy. "Jackson is coming!" was the rumor that swept through the Confederate regiments in front of the city.[26] "In our sultry, squalid camps along the Chickahominy," wrote one soldier who was bivouacked in the swampy lowlands east of Richmond, "the news had reached us of the brilliant Valley campaign, and in the midst of destitution and depression and doubt, with the enemy at the very gates of the capital, [Jackson's victories] read like a fairy tale. . . . With feverish interest we devoured the accounts of rapid marches, of sudden appearances where least expected, which had frustrated every combination of the enemy."[27] To them, Jackson's movement east with his vaunted Army of the Valley meant that he was coming to save Richmond, which meant that he was coming to save the Confederacy. And the soldiers of the beleaguered Army of Northern Virginia believed to the bottom of their ragged, malnourished rebel souls that he was going to do precisely that.

PART ONE

THE UNIMAGINED WAR

WAR

CHAPTER ONE

AWAY TO RICHMOND

※

For Thomas J. Jackson the war started precisely at 12:30 p.m. on the afternoon of April 21, 1861, in the small Shenandoah Valley town of Lexington, Virginia. As beginnings go, it was grand, even glorious. Fort Sumter had fallen to the rebels on April 13. Virginia had seceded on the seventeenth, and since then its citizens had been in the grip of a sort of collective delirium that had sent them thronging into the streets. It was that way everywhere in the country, North and South. Though no one could say what was going to happen next, or where it might happen, and very few knew what it might be like to actually shoot another human being, Americans everywhere felt a new and joyous sense of clarity and purpose. War would be the way forward, not the old-fashioned idea of war as horror and heartbreak but a new and heady notion of grand adventure and impending glory. And so Lexington, a quiet, picturesque college town of 2,135 on a hilltop at the southern end of the valley, was being turned into an armed camp, in the happiest possible sense of that term.[1] Volunteer companies were organized in the streets; militiamen marched to and fro; students from Washington College drilled under their Greek teacher; ladies sewed regimental flags and mended socks; lunches were packed; old squirrel guns and fowling pieces and muskets from the War of 1812 were dragged out of storage, cleaned, and oiled. There was an atmosphere of picnic and parade. As one Confederate soldier recalled, those days were "the only time we can remember when citizens walked along the lines offering their pocketbooks to men whom they did not know; that fair women bestowed their floral offerings and kisses ungrudgingly and with equal favor among all classes of friends and suitors; when the distinctions of wealth and station were forgotten, and each departing soldier was equally honored as the hero."[2]

Meanwhile, across town at the Virginia Military Institute, the South's oldest military college, the cadets were embarking on a solemn mission. Three days before, their superintendent had received orders from the governor to send them immediately to Richmond to help drill the raw recruits who were arriving in large numbers. Now, in the warm sunshine of the Sabbath morning of April 21, on a promontory high above the North Branch of the James River and with the mountains rising in the distance, they were preparing to do just that. Around noon, 176 of them were in line in front of their castellated barracks, young, fresh-faced, and deliberately serious, with "their cheeks aglow, and their eyes sparkling with the expectation of the military glory awaiting them," as one observer recalled.[3] They wore short-billed kepis and shell jackets with brass buttons. They stood at attention: four small companies in eight immaculate lines. Flanking them was their baggage train, wagons loaded with equipment, and drivers, mounted, whips in hand, waiting for the command to move out.[4] It was a grand and inspiring scene—for little Lexington, anyway—and a crowd of people had gathered on Institute Hill to watch it.

In front of the cadets stood their commander, the unimposing Major Thomas J. Jackson. He was thirty-seven years old, trim, bearded, a bit gaunt, and a shade under six feet tall. You would have noticed his pale, blue-gray eyes; his high, wide forehead; and his thin, bloodless lips, which always seemed tightly pressed together. For the occasion he had worn his very best uniform: a faded, dark-blue, double-breasted coat with a major's epaulets, blue trousers with gold piping, a sword, sash, and forage cap.

It is worth taking inventory of him at the moment he rode off to war. Though he held himself ramrod straight on the parade ground, his bearing seemed odd, even to a casual observer: more awkward than military, more graceless than dignified. He had large hands and feet, and seemed not to know quite what to do with them. And this strangely stiff posture suggested exactly how these cadets saw him: as a perfect martinet, a humorless, puritanical, gimlet-eyed stickler for detail, a strict enforcer of every rule and regulation. He was such a literalist when it came to duty that he had once, while in the army, worn heavy winter underwear into summer because he had received no specific order to change it. Once, when seated on a camp stool with his saber across his knees, he was told by VMI's superintendent to "remain as you are until further orders." The next morning the superintendent found him seated on the camp stool in the same position, because, according to Jackson, "you ordered me to remain here."[5] He insisted that his students obey his orders just as unquestioningly. He was as painfully formal in conversation as he was in class.

Worse still, from the students' point of view, he not only taught the school's toughest and most loathed course, "Natural and Experimental Philosophy"—essentially what we call physics, though it included math and such other disciplines as optics and astronomy—he was also, by universal acclaim, VMI's worst teacher. Though he was presumed to understand the dreaded *Bartlett's Optics* textbook that he taught, he was unable to impart that wisdom to his students. He insisted on rote recitation; he explained little or nothing. He had survived an attempt led by the school's alumni six years before to get rid of him, for all of those reasons.[6] Jackson also taught artillery drill, at which he seemed only marginally more competent than he was as a science teacher.

He seemed in other ways to be a man who had at least found his place in the world. He had been born in modest circumstances in Clarksburg, in northwestern Virginia (now West Virginia), orphaned at seven, and raised mainly by his uncle, who owned a gristmill and farm. In spite of a poor childhood education, he had somehow made it through West Point. Though he was childless, he was said to be happily married. He was known to everyone as a devout Christian. He was a deacon in the Presbyterian Church, to which he devoted a good deal of his time. He had a very decent brick house in town, and a small farm in the country, and owned six slaves.

Those who knew him well could also have told you that he was a victim of a host of physical ailments, real and imagined, and that he traveled long distances in search of water cures that involved both drinking and soaking in supposedly healing waters. That his diet was odd, too, often consisting of water and stale bread or buttermilk and stale bread and he was so resolute about this that he carried his own stale bread with him when invited out to dinner. As he stood by the barracks inspecting his troops that day, he might have been charitably described as a comfortable mediocrity: a decent enough man, a harmless eccentric, an upstanding Christian and good citizen who, unfortunately, was an inept teacher. It is worth noting that the preceding description is far from complete. There was a good deal more to him even then than most of his students or colleagues ever suspected—more, indeed, of what made him great later on.

He held his secrets close. He was never what he seemed to be, not in Lexington, not later in the war.

There was, however, one item that stood out on Major Jackson's curriculum vitae as of that bright April afternoon. That was his conspicuous and, to many, uncharacteristic record in the Mexican-American War in 1847. Though he seemed to most of his acquaintances in Lexington to have the personality of neither warrior nor leader, it was said that he had exhibited great bravery in battle and that the commanding general Winfield Scott himself had singled out the young Jackson for praise. Students and faculty at VMI had heard the story, though it made no particular sense to them. Jackson seemed the furthest thing from a hero. Whether this brief, anomalous glory held any meaning in the year 1861, no one could yet say.

A little after noon, Jackson removed his cap and called out loudly, "Let us pray." The pastor of the local Presbyterian church, the Reverend Dr. William S. White, piped up with a short prayer, followed by a collective "Amen." It was time to go. Or it would have been if someone other than Jackson had been commanding. Though the battalion was ready to move out—in fact, the cadets were dying with joy and anticipation—Jackson insisted that it depart precisely at 12:30, as planned. Jackson was a fanatic about duty, and duty dictated punctuality, and he was not, merely for the sake of this romantic war that everyone seemed to want, going to waive his rules. When his second in command, Raleigh Colston, a teacher of foreign languages, approached him and said, "Everything is ready, sir. Shall I give the command forward?," Jackson's answer was a clipped "No." They would wait. Jackson sat on a camp stool, unmoving, while the minutes ticked by.[7]

Finally, as the college bells rang 12:30, Jackson mounted his horse, wheeled toward the cadets, then shouted, "Right face! By file left, march!"[8] As the young men marched, Jackson remained motionless and expressionless. One cadet later recalled "how stiffly he sat on his horse as the column moved past him."[9] Thus they went off to war, to the sound of fife and drum, Jackson somewhat awkwardly shepherding the small column that contained the sons of some of the South's most prominent families. A mile away, across the small bridge that spanned the river, lay the carriages, wagons, and stagecoaches that would take them to the town of Staunton, where they would board a train for Richmond. The moment was sweetly sad, as were moments like this that were taking place across the country. It would have been sadder still if the assembled onlookers had known that Jackson and many of his ruddy-cheeked charges would never see Lexington again.

Behind the pomp and circumstance lay the curious fact that the stern, inelegant man leading the column had done everything in his power to prevent the war that he was now marching off to fight. He hated the very idea of it. His conviction was in part due to his peculiar ability, shared by few people who landed in power on either side—Union generals Winfield Scott and William Tecumseh Sherman come prominently to mind—to grasp early on just how terrible the suffering caused by the war would be, and just how long it was likely to last.[10] The detail-obsessed physics professor's embrace of such a large abstraction is perhaps an appropriate introduction to the man himself: Jackson's brilliance was that he understood war. He understood it at some primary, visceral level that escaped almost everyone else. He understood it even before it happened.

In the months leading up to the war Jackson had remained a confirmed Unionist. He opposed secession. Though he was a slave owner, he held no strident, proslavery views. Indeed, his wife, Anna, wrote that she was "very confident that he would never have fought for the sole object of perpetuating slavery."[11] He had attended West Point, had been in combat under the flag of the United States of America, and had later served in the country's peacetime army. He was a patriot, in the larger sense of the word. As a Christian he was shocked by what he saw as the ungodly and inappropriate enthusiasm on both sides to settle their differences by fighting. "People who are anxious to bring on war don't know what they are bargaining for," he wrote to his nephew.[12]

In February 1861, the failure of a Virginia-sponsored peace conference in Washington made Jackson so fearful of war that he called upon his pastor, the Reverend White, to talk about what might happen. "It is painful to discover with what unconcern they speak of war, and threaten it," Jackson told him. "They do not know its horrors. I have seen enough of it to make me look upon it as the sum of all evils."[13] His wife, Anna, offered a striking summary of his beliefs in those early days. "I have never heard any man express such an utter abhorrence of war," she wrote. "I shall never forget how he once exclaimed to me, with all the intensity of his nature, 'Oh, how I deprecate war!'"[14] But there was more to it than that. According to his sister-in-law, Maggie Preston, who was perhaps his closest friend, Jackson also recoiled physically at war's violence. "His revulsions at scenes of horror, or even descriptions of them," she wrote, "was almost inconsistent in one who had lived the life of a soldier. He has told me that his first sight of a mangled and swollen corpse on a Mexican battlefield . . . filled him with as much sickening dismay as if he had been a woman."[15]

And now he was prepared to do what he could to stop the imminent horror. His chosen form of activism was characteristic of the man: prayer. He would pray. He would petition God, and God would stop the madness. When he had thought about it some more it occurred to him that he could do even more than that. So he went to the Reverend White with a proposal. "Do you not think that all the Christian people of the land," he asked White, "could be induced to unite in a concert of prayer to avert so great an evil? It seems to me that if they would thus unite in prayer, war might be prevented and peace preserved." Jackson believed in the power of prayer; now he was proposing to harness the entire nation to that power, a gigantic, country-sweeping petition sent up to God: *a national day of prayer to overturn the political idiocies of the past half century.* White encouraged him, and Jackson did what he could to make it happen. Since none of his correspondence on the subject has survived, we don't know how far he got with the plan. We do know that other Christians in other churches, perhaps sharing his sense of desperation, had proposed the same thing. He pursued it as best he could, writing letters to clergymen in the North and South. His name eventually appeared on several communications from Northern churches supporting the day of prayer.[16] The event never came to pass. Jackson prayed ardently over it anyway. When he was called on in church to lead prayers, the wish he invariably expressed was "that God would preserve the whole land from the evils of war."[17]

That did not mean he was not fully prepared to do his duty when the orders came down from Richmond. His main regret, it seemed, was that he was losing his precious Sabbath, the day appointed for the march. On the eve of his departure, he had told Anna that he hoped that "the call to Richmond would not come before Monday," which would allow him to spend the Sabbath quietly and "without any mention of politics, or the impending troubles of the country."[18] When those orders came anyway, Jackson knelt somberly with her in their bedchamber on Sunday morning. In a quavering voice he read from Corinthians and committed them both to the protection of God. "His voice was so choked with emotion that he could scarce utter the words," wrote Anna. "One of his most earnest petitions was that, 'if consistent with His will, God would still avert the threatening danger and grant us peace.'" Jackson still hadn't given up. He was ready to die for Virginia and for the South, but he still did not believe God was going to let this happen.

If Jackson could seem at times like a Quaker pacifist in a country that was lunging eagerly toward war, there was also a hint, in a letter written in January 1861 to his nephew Thomas Jackson Arnold, of a darker, more complex view. In it he repeated his desire to avert war, but added a qualifier that Arnold found so disturbing that he later edited it out of his own reverent biography of Jackson. "I am in favor of making a thorough trial for peace," wrote Jackson, "and if we fail in this and the state is invaded to defend it with terrific resistance—even to taking no prisoners."[19] *Taking no prisoners.* That idea was well outside the mainstream of American political and military thought at the time; no one in a position of power on either side was seriously considering a "black flag" war in the spring of 1861. Jackson went on to say that if "the free states . . . should endeavor to subjugate us, and thus excite our slaves to servile insurrection in which our Families will be murdered without quarter or mercy, it becomes us to wage a war as will bring hostilities to a speedy close."[20] By that he meant making war so brutally expensive for both sides that they would quickly sue for peace. He meant instant, total war. Amid Jackson's ardent peace prayers, these harder-edged, less charitable thoughts dwelt also.

CHAPTER TWO

THE IMPERFECT LOGIC
OF WAR

❦

Thus the contented, domestic man who did not want to leave his home to fight a war and, until the very last minute, did not think he would have to. In the end, he chose war because he believed Virginia had no choice and, like most people in the United States of America in the year 1861, Jackson's first loyalty was to his home state.

What, then, had sent the professor and his cadets marching down the hill on that pleasant spring day? The answer is maddeningly complex, partly because Jackson's reasons for fighting had little to do with what had propelled the two sections into the war in the first place. Nor were they the same reasons the seven states of the lower South had seceded in late 1860 and early 1861. Virginia—with the most industry, the most manpower, and by far the most military talent in the Confederacy—had its own ideas, its own political logic, and its own destiny to fulfill. Jackson, quintessentially Virginian, must be seen in that light.

What had driven the nation to the brink of war—as opposed to what Jackson and his VMI charges were thinking about that day—was a bitter and often bloody, half-century-long clash over the question of the expansion of slavery. For most of that time, the abolition of slavery in the states where it existed had been a marginal issue. Radical Northerners such as William Lloyd Garrison and Henry Ward Beecher advocated it; the mainstream of the Republican Party, including Abraham Lincoln, did not. But what Lincoln and Republicans and Free Soilers and abolitionists of various stripes in the North absolutely did agree on—and were prepared to risk a good deal to get—was the severe restriction, if not the complete prohibition, of slavery in the nation's *new* territories and *new* states. All other political questions, such as those of states' rights, protective tariffs, and a national banking system, were subservient to this primal, paradigm-shattering, nation-defining question. The antislavery zealot John Brown arose from its darker places, as did the tortured legal arguments of the Dred Scott case. The argument and eventually the war were thus about the future, not the past. They were about the failure, on a grand scale and drawn out over five decades, of Americans to agree on what to do with their westward-booming nation's three prodigious land acquisitions—the Louisiana Purchase in 1803, the annexation of the Oregon Territory from Britain in 1846, and the Mexican Cession that followed the Mexican-American War in 1848. Together these acquisitions had added more than 1.7 million square miles of territory to the United States of America, dwarfing the 375,000 square miles of the original thirteen colonies. They accounted for most of the land west of the Mississippi.[1]

The moral and political debate entailed an inevitable calculus of power: whichever side, slave or free, added more states to its roster, the more its representational power grew, and with it the ability to determine the laws of the land. For the South, failure to add new states meant that its parochial interests would be slowly, surely, choked to death. For the North, failure meant living in a nation of slaves, a possibility made frighteningly real by the Supreme Court's Dred Scott decision in 1857, ruling, in effect, that Congress had no authority to prohibit slavery in the territories. Neither outcome was remotely acceptable to the nation as a whole. The great political accommodations of the age—the Missouri Compromise of 1820, which prohibited slavery north of latitude 36'30" with the exception of Missouri; the Compromise of 1850, a package of bills that admitted California as a free state, allowed the New Mexico and Utah territories to decide the slavery question by popular vote, and preserved slavery in Washington, DC; and the Kansas-Nebraska Act of 1854, which opened those territories to slavery based on popular vote, effectively repealing the Missouri Compromise—represented ever more shrill and ever more desperate attempts to level an unlevelable playing field.

Those were the reasons the politicians, the statesmen, the newspaper editors, the lawyers, and the intellectuals went to war, anyway. But they did not explain why the average soldier fought. They were not the reasons Virginians such as Jackson and his cadets would have given for wanting to fight Yankees. Jackson had remained generally aloof from national politics.

As a slaveholder, he was aware of the congressional debate over slavery in the territories, but not deeply versed in it. He was like many ordinary Virginians of his day: a moderate states'-rights Democrat who favored keeping Washington's nose out of Virginia's business and working within the Union to resolve differences. He had no ideology; he was a Virginian.[2] The cadets he taught, moreover—part of that great mass of young men who would do most of the war's fighting—would have had little understanding of the freakish political complexity of the Compromise of 1850, for example, which attempted to settle the question of slavery in what was essentially the entire American Southwest, plus California. Most would have been unable to parse the meaning of "states' rights" in the federal Constitution, or fully grasp the reasons for the disastrous splintering of the Democratic Party in 1860—a carefully planned conspiracy intended to inspire Southern secession—which had guaranteed the victory of Abraham Lincoln.[3] Virginians were not stupid; they just had more provincial and personal views of the world than the men who rode to battle in the halls of Congress.

Nor were the Virginians inclined as a whole to buy the idea, hawked loudly by the states of the lower South, that Lincoln's election meant that the federal government was going to free the slaves and forcibly mix the two races. Lincoln had denied this categorically in his inaugural address. "I have no purpose, directly or indirectly," he said on March 4, 1861, little more than a month before the Confederate attack on Fort Sumter, "to interfere with the institution of slavery in the states where it exists. I believe I have no lawful right to do so, and I have no inclination to do so." Neither Jackson nor most of his fellow citizens in Lexington believed that the war was about staving off the immediate abolition of slavery. By and large, they abhorred the idea of secession.

What made Jackson and his cadets want to fight, amid all this swirl of rhetoric, belief, ideology, and implicit threat, were events much closer to home.

The first of those events was an invasion of the state of Virginia. It took place on October 16, 1859, a year and a half before the war's official start, when the radical abolitionist John Brown and twenty-one of his followers seized the Federal arsenal at the river-junction town of Harpers Ferry in northern Virginia.[4] Brown's object had been to secure muskets and use them to arm local slaves. He then planned to start a guerrilla war whose object was to free all 491,000 slaves in Virginia.[5] Having accomplished that, he would then head south, replicating his success in other states. The vision was vast, apocalyptic, and, on its face, ridiculous. The raid was so poorly organized that it looked like a planned martyrdom. Brown never made it out of Harpers Ferry, nor did he even appear to have a plan for escaping, let alone arming hundreds of thousands of slaves. His raiding party managed to kill seven townspeople and wound ten others. Then a group of eighty-six US marines under army colonel Robert E. Lee arrived from Washington, stormed the building where Brown and his men were barricaded, and put a fast and violent end to Brown's gambit. Ten of the raiders were killed; Brown was captured and turned over to Virginia authorities, who, to avoid a lynching, brought him speedily to trial. On November 2, 1859, he was convicted of treason, conspiring with slaves to rebel, and murder, and sentenced to be hanged on December 2 in nearby Charlestown.

Rumors, meanwhile, swept the countryside: armed abolitionists were on the march; slaves were rising up; antislavery radicals were coming to Brown's rescue. None of it was true, but that hardly mattered. Brown's attack had been implausible enough. What fresh horrors would now descend on the South? In the days following Brown's sentencing, Virginia governor Henry A. Wise summoned some 1,500 Virginia militiamen to Charlestown. They were put under the command of Colonel Francis H. Smith, Jackson's boss and the superintendent of VMI, who would supervise the execution itself.[6] As additional security, Wise also ordered 85 cadets from VMI to Charlestown. In charge of them were Major William Gilham, commanding an infantry unit of 64 cadets, and Major Thomas J. Jackson, commanding an artillery unit of 21 cadets.[7] On November 25 they traveled by stagecoach to Staunton and from there took trains to Washington and on to Charlestown. The *Richmond Daily Dispatch* called them "the best drilled troops on the ground."[8] Upon arrival, Jackson wrote his wife, Anna, that "there are about one thousand troops here, and everything is quiet." He added that "seven of us slept in the same room."[9]

On the day of Brown's execution, the cadets, armed and uniformed in gray trousers and red flannel shirts crossed by two white belts and looking quite dashing, were stationed near the scaffold. Jackson's artillery unit was about forty yards in front of it.[10] His two howitzers—light, short-barreled cannons that were likely loaded with canister, turning them into the equivalent of large, sawed-off shotguns—were ready to sweep the field. Jackson, who had been an artillerist in the US Army, attended to even the smallest details. He was ready for whatever might come. At 11:00 a.m. Brown was led to the gallows.

One of the best accounts of what followed comes from Jackson himself, who recorded the event in a letter to his wife on the day of the execution. "He behaved with unflinching firmness," wrote Jackson, noting that Brown "ascended the scaffold with apparent cheerfulness," and, when asked if he wished to be signaled when the trapdoor was about to drop, "replied that it made no difference, provided he wasn't kept waiting too long." Jackson then described the death itself: "Brown fell through about five inches, his knees falling on a level with the position occupied by his feet before the rope was cut. With the fall his arms, below the elbows, flew up horizontally, his hands clinched; and his arms gradually fell, but by spasmodic motions. There was very little motion of his person for several moments, and soon the wind blew his lifeless body to and fro. His face, upon the scaffold, was turned a little east of south, and in front of him were the cadets, commanded by Major Gilham." Jackson was clearly mesmerized by what he saw, fascinated by both the means of death and Brown's stoic behavior. "I was much impressed with the thought that before me stood a man in the full vigor of health, who must in a few moments enter eternity. I sent up the petition that he might be saved. Awful was the thought that he might in a few minutes receive the sentence, 'Depart, ye wicked, into everlasting fire.' I hope that he was prepared to die, but I am doubtful. He refused to have a minister with him."[11]

Thus Jackson, a firm believer in the punishments of hell, had sent up a prayer for the salvation of the soul of John Brown, a condemned murderer whom Jackson saw—incorrectly—as a godless man. In fact, Brown, who had modeled himself on biblical patriarchs and believed he had been called by God to rid the world of slavery, was every bit as devout as Jackson.[12] Jackson could not see him that way, of course. He considered Brown a murderer. It is noteworthy that the two men would later be compared by Northerners, who, in their attempt to understand Jackson's character, found important similarities between them. And indeed, in the broadest sense, they were not altogether wrong. Both John Brown and Thomas Jackson were hard, righteous, and uncompromising men, religious warriors in the tradition of Oliver Cromwell, the ardently Christian political and military leader in the English Civil War. Both believed beyond doubt that God was on their side. Both believed that they were agents of God and that by killing the enemy they were doing His work. Jackson would have bridled at any such comparison. He saw murder—as opposed to killing men in an official war—as violating God's law. Though his armies later sent many Yankee soldiers to their graves, there is never any evidence that Jackson, a stickler for duty and obedience, knowingly broke any law.

What happened in the weeks and months after Brown's trial and execution amounted to an almost instant revision of history, and it changed entirely the meaning of his raid in the minds of everyone in slave and non-slave America. The first perceptions of Brown and his attack on Harpers Ferry were easily categorized: he may have thought he was working to abolish slavery, but in fact he was delusional, perhaps even insane. And it followed that Brown and his cohort were only a tiny splinter group of radicals and did not represent the way most abolitionists in the North actually felt. That was certainly the quickly expressed view in the North. The antislavery *Worcester Spy*, in Massachusetts, called it "one of the rashest and maddest enterprises ever." Archabolitionist William Lloyd Garrison thought that, though it might have been "well intended," it was also "misguided, wild, and apparently insane."[13]

But at his trial Brown had surprised everyone. He was not only coolly rational but also remarkably eloquent. "I deny everything but what I have all along admitted," he said,

> of a design on my part to free the slaves. . . . Had I interfered in the manner which I admit . . . in behalf of the rich, the powerful, the intelligent, the so-called great . . . every man in this Court would have deemed it an act worthy of reward rather than punishment. This Court acknowledges, too, as I suppose, the validity of the law of God. I see a book kissed, which I suppose to be the Bible, or at least the New Testament, which teaches me that all things whatsoever that men should do to me, I should do so even to them. . . . Now, if it is deemed necessary that I should forfeit my life for the furtherance of the ends of justice, and mingle my blood further with the blood of my children and with the blood of millions in this slave country whose rights are disregarded by wicked, cruel, and unjust enactments, I say, let it be done.[14]

Brown's words—and his self-possession in the courtroom—changed everything. These were not the words of a madman and a murderer, as Northerners now saw it, but of a principled religious man who insisted that his purpose had not been to incite rebellion but simply to arm slaves for their self-defense. The change of perception swept quickly through the nonslave states in the days following the trial. The day he was executed, church bells had tolled in many Northern towns and cities; guns fired salutes; sermons were preached on the purity and correctness of his motives; and people all over the North prayed for the soul of this martyr to liberty. Brown's death was no longer an oddity. It was suddenly a *sensation*. Henry David Thoreau called him a "crucified hero." William Dean Howells, a leading Northern intellectual, wrote that "Brown has become an idea, a thousand times purer and better and loftier than the Republican idea."[15] Everyone was suddenly talking about the grandeur and nobility of the man, the rightness of what he had done.

The reaction of Southerners to such Northern expressions of sympathy was horror mixed with disbelief that their brethren could possibly wish upon them the fate that Brown had planned. To Southerners and particularly to Virginians, whose state had been invaded, Brown was a terrifying figure, the dark, avenging side of the antislavery movement that had been on view for five years in the bloody civil war in Kansas—where Brown and his Free State volunteers had murdered five men in 1856. He had, after all, intended to arm slaves and set them free, which presumably meant setting them upon their masters, which meant that people in Connecticut and Massachusetts were now endorsing the violent deaths of white men, women, and children all over the South. "This mad attempt by a handful of vulgar cutthroats, and its condign punishment," wrote the Reverend Robert Lewis Dabney, an important Presbyterian leader in the South and later chief of Jackson's staff, "would have been a very trivial affair to the Southern people, but for the manner in which it was regarded by the people of the North. Their presses, pulpits, public meetings and conversations, disclosed such a hatred of the South and its institutions, as to lead them to justify the crime, involving though it did the most aggravated robbery, treason and murder; [and] to exalt the bloodthirsty fanatic who led the party, to a public apotheosis."[16]

Those sentiments were replicated all over the South, and the complaints became more grievous as more became known about the wealthy Northern benefactors who had helped Brown finance his enterprise. Wrote Henry Kyd Douglas, a Virginian and another member of Jackson's staff in the war: "There is nothing in the history of fanaticism, its crimes and follies, so strange and inexplicable as that the people of New England, with all their shrewdness and general sense of justice, should have attempted to lift up the sordid name of that old wretch and . . . to exalt him among the heroes and benefactors of this land. . . . Why they should have sent him money and arms to encourage him to murder the white people of Virginia is beyond my comprehension."[17]

Though some Northern politicians tried to blunt the effect of the Northern response, the damage—and it was very deep, emotional damage—had been done. The reaction to the event now loomed larger than the event itself. "The Harper's Ferry invasion has advanced the cause of disunion more than any event that has happened since the formation of the government," wrote the *Richmond Whig* and the *Richmond Enquirer* under a single byline. "Thousands of men who, a month ago, scoffed at the idea of a dissolution of the union . . . now hold the opinion that its days were numbered."[18] In Jackson's letter to his nephew in January 1861, in which he had put forward the disturbing idea of a "black flag" war, his pointed reference—"if the free states . . . excite our slaves to servile insurrection in which our Families will be murdered without quarter or mercy"—was to John Brown's raid. It had apparently changed Jackson's way of thinking about his Northern brethren, too.

Still, Jackson had remained—like the town of Lexington—"strong for the Union." Indeed, most of the state of Virginia, in spite of this new sense of vulnerability, remained in favor of the Union. But all this would change, with astounding speed, over the course of three days in the month of April 1861.

There had been a sort of giddiness in the air anyway that winter and spring. Lincoln's election on December 20, 1860, had prompted the immediate secession of seven Southern states: South Carolina, Mississippi, Florida, Alabama, Georgia, Louisiana, and Texas. Society in the Old Dominion and other "border" states trembled with anticipation, of what nobody quite knew, though perhaps it was simply the possibility of moral clarity, after so much political bombast. Whatever the cause, an odd sort of social intoxication seemed to grow in direct proportion to the bitterness and fatalism of the political debate, and it took the outward form of happiness. "The winter of 1860–1861 was with us one of unprecedented gaiety," wrote Confederate memoirist Charles Minor Blackford of the town of Lynchburg, though he could have been describing many other Virginia towns. "The spirit of fun and frolic seemed to take possession of our people both young and old, and for months entertainments were given. Party after party succeeded each other in rapid succession."[19] Though Virginia remained within the Union, secession flags were being raised all across the state, including on the campuses of VMI and Washington College. In one instance, Major Jackson had discovered a piece of cloth hanging from a flagpole where the American flag usually hung. It turned out to be a crude secession flag with the words "Hurrah for South Carolina" written in shoe blacking. Jackson ordered it removed.[20] Public debates had, meanwhile, grown more and more strident: Jackson's father-in-law, for example, Dr. George Junkin, president of Washington College, was strongly critical of anyone who supported secession. He became a fixture at the increasingly common public gatherings, once arguing that secession was "the essence of all immorality."[21]

The issue of secession came to a head for Lexington—and for Jackson—on the evening of April 13. VMI cadets who supported secession marched from campus into town, where they were greeted by a hostile, overwhelmingly pro-Union crowd consisting mostly of members of a local militia company.[22] There was some pushing and shoving, and a few threats were issued; but peace held, and the secessionists soon hoisted their fifteen-star flag of the Southern Confederacy, with the motto "Union of the South," from a pole erected near the courthouse.[23] Speeches were made, including several by VMI faculty members.[24] Pleased with its success, the secessionist group started to disperse. The Unionist group stepped forward and raised the Stars and Stripes on its own pole. But the cadets had managed, the night before, to sabotage the pole, which snapped and fell. The cadets cheered.

At that point, the mood of the assembled crowd changed. Taunts were made, blows exchanged.[25] An intoxicated militiaman drew a revolver and knife on several cadets. When one cadet returned to the institute and announced that cadets were being assaulted by Unionists, "the effect was instant and magical," wrote former cadet Charles Copland Wight. "Everyone rushed for his gun and a cartridge box and then all rushed pell mell for town."[26] Almost two hundred of them arrived, loaded their muskets, fixed bayonets, and prepared to charge the militiamen, who seemed fully prepared to stand their ground.

Into the incipient battle now strode Colonel Francis H. Smith, the school's superintendent, along with several faculty members, including Jackson. He insisted that he was their commander and that if they were going to fight it would be under his command. With Jackson's help, he managed to stop them and persuade them to return to their barracks. It is unclear exactly what Jackson did, but according to the local Presbyterian minister, were it not for his intervention, "blood would have been shed."[27] When the cadets got back to the institute, still in high spirits, Smith berated them for being "unwise and unsoldierly." Then two other professors stepped forward with their own, more gentle remarks. As they spoke, however, cries went up through the hall—no one was sure if they were serious or joking—for "Old Jack" to address the crowd. Considering who Jackson was, what the cadets apparently thought of him, and the gravity of the situation, it was a strange request. Still, Smith seemed to think it was a good idea, too. He turned to Jackson, who was seated next to him. "I have driven the nail in," he said, "but it needs clinching. Speak with them."

To the surprise of many of the cadets, Jackson mounted the rostrum. For those who witnessed it, what happened next was an astounding transformation, one that many would talk about for decades to come. "Military men make short speeches," Jackson began, in a tone of voice unfamiliar to his charges, "and as for myself I am no hand at speaking anyhow." There was something about his voice that caught the cadets' attention, a hint that the man on the rostrum was no longer their eccentric professor, a man they sometimes called Tom Fool, the object of teasing and jokes around the institute. Jackson continued: "The time for war has not yet come, but it will come, and that soon. And when it does come, my advice is to draw the sword and throw away the scabbard."

That was all. *Draw the sword and throw away the scabbard.* Perhaps it was the simplicity of those words, or their saber-thrust directness. But as Jackson turned and stepped to his seat, the room, until now tense and murmurous, erupted in a series of cheers, one after another, that rang through the barracks. The force of his words—their sheer implausibility— had shocked and dazzled the young men. Instead of the awkward physics teacher, what they saw before them was a soldier and, watching his flashing eyes and intent expression, they were reminded of those stories of the Mexican-American War they had heard. "Hurrah for Old Jack!" they shouted, themselves amazed that they were hurrahing the eccentric major, and continued shouting it long after the meeting was dismissed. And they never forgot it. Fifty years later, one of them wrote, "The thrilling effect of those words is felt by the writer to this day. They touched the heart of every boy who heard them, and men now gray will tell of the enthusiastic cheers which drowned all further speeches."[28]

Now the tide of secession and war began to sweep in quickly. What settled the matter for Virginians—with the same galvanizing speed with which the attack on Sumter had united the North—was a proclamation, issued on April 15 by Abraham Lincoln, calling on the states that had not seceded to provide 75,000 troops "to maintain the honor, the integrity, and the existence of our National Union," and also "to execute the laws of the Union, [and] suppress rebellions." Virginians knew what this meant: armed coercion. It meant that 2,340 sons of Virginia (the state's quota) were going to be used as a military force against the sons of Georgia and Texas and other Confederate states. If Lincoln was calling for war on the Confederate States of America, the subtext was also clear: these troops would be used against *any* state that left the Union.

The reaction in Virginia was swift and, this time, sure. Governor John Letcher, a pragmatist who had opposed secession, now cabled furiously back to Washington on the sixteenth. "I have only to say that the militia of Virginia will not be furnished to the powers at Washington for any such use or purposes as they have in view," he wrote. "Your object is to subjugate the Southern states, and a requisition made upon me for such an object . . . will not be complied with. You have chosen to inaugurate civil war."[29]

On April 17, Virginians learned that their militia had already been dispatched to seize both the federal armory at Harpers Ferry and the enormous naval yard at Norfolk. That same day the state convention voted 88 to 55 to secede from the Union (though Jackson's Shenandoah Valley voted 12 to 5 against secession).

If the cadets who marched to Richmond with Thomas Jackson four days later had been asked why they were doing it, few would have replied that it was because of their convictions about slavery, or their beliefs about state sovereignty or any of the other great national questions that had been debated for so long. They would have told you then—as most of Stonewall Jackson's soldiers in the army of the Confederate States of America would have told you later—that they were fighting *to repel the invaders, to drive the Northern aggressors from their homeland.* That was why Virginia went to war. The great and complicated political reasons for secession, thundered about in Congress and in the state legislatures, were not their reasons, which were more like those expressed by a captive Confederate soldier, who was not a slaveholder, to his puzzled Union captors. "I'm fighting because you're down here," he said.[30] To Jackson, Lincoln had launched a war of aggression against sovereign states. That was why he fought, why he believed that God could not possibly be on the side of the aggressor. The Northern response to John Brown's raid had proven beyond a doubt the North's malign intent. Now, finally, soldiers were coming. "Had [Lincoln] not made war upon the South, Virginia would not have left the Union," wrote William Thomas Poague, who would fight as a gunner under Jackson, and whose view was typical of Virginians in the war. "The North was the aggressor. The South resisted her invaders. History will vindicate her course."[31]

CHAPTER THREE

FATE INTERVENES

◆◗◲◆

They traveled north, thirty-eight rough miles through the green brilliance of the Shenandoah spring, through drifts of dogwood blossoms so thick they looked like snow on the ground. At Staunton they took a special train east, crossing the Blue Ridge Mountains and then dropping down across the river-and-stream-crossed plateau of the Piedmont country, watching as the flawless farms, timbered hillsides, and swelling meadows floated by in the windows of the train. Though none of them could have known it then, this was one of the last glimpses they would ever get of the old South, a place as yet unvexed by war and unmarked by the ravages of sprawling, rapacious armies. That was all to come. Soon it would be impossible to find even a small corner of Virginia that had not been deeply scarred. When Major Thomas J. Jackson and his 176 charges arrived on the night of April 22, 1861, Richmond, a steepled brick city of forty thousand that rose sharply from the banks of the James River, was already in the embrace of this great change.

The city, in fact, was swarming with recruits. They had been streaming in, day and night, since Virginia's secession. They were conspicuous for their almost complete lack of understanding of military methods and protocols, their fondness for alcohol, their idiosyncratic and often brilliantly colored uniforms, their plumed and sashed commanders, and the atrocious and obsolete weapons they carried—when they carried them at all.[1] Many had ancient smoothbore flintlocks that literally could not have hit a barn door at fifty paces. Some carried butcher knives, as though those might be enough to frighten the Yankees back to Maine or Ohio. They were undiscouraged: they marched and countermarched, bivouacked where they could, and looked for someone in authority who could somehow make sense of all this or tell them where they ought to go.

Into this happy swirl of confusion came Jackson and his cadets, arriving unheralded at the Richmond station. They were desperately needed. Soldiering, as it turned out, was all about drilling and discipline and such inconveniences as adherence to a strict schedule. The cadets, as it happened, knew something about these things. (The usual repository of such skills, the militias, were relics of a bygone era, more like social clubs than functioning military units; though they were supposed to perform three perfunctory drills a year, few did even that.[2]) Jackson delivered his charges to the Virginia authorities, who put them briefly on review, then put them immediately to work instructing the new recruits. They were just boys, really. But they looked crisp and soldierly and possessed specialized knowledge that was suddenly critical to the war effort—often to the annoyance of the volunteers and militiamen, many of whom saw indignity in the whole idea. "To get up at dawn to the sound of fife and drum . . . to be drilled by a fat little cadet, young enough to be my son, of the Virginia Military Institute, that, indeed, was misery," wrote a thirty-three-year-old recruit. "How I hated that little cadet!"[3] (The cadets would eventually train some 15,000 recruits that year in Richmond.[4])

Having done his duty, Jackson was now curiously adrift, without a command. No new orders had awaited him on his arrival. No one in authority had any immediate plans for him. This was despite the fact that, of 1,200 West Point graduates who were fit for military service at the beginning of 1861, only 300 were in the South, and thus in great and immediate demand in a new country that was planning to repel an invader.[5] Overlooked, too, were Jackson's regular army credentials—four years in the service, including a brief, distinguished stint in the Mexican-American War—that ought to have been highly valued in the chaotic, protomilitary world of Richmond. Jackson left no record of his reaction to this apparently deliberate oversight, though he cannot have been pleased. It appeared that, in some parts of the Southern hierarchy anyway, his reputation as an eccentric martinet had preceded him.

While he harbored plenty of ambition and earnestly believed he could help the Confederacy's war effort, he was not the sort of man to push himself on state politicians. "He knew that the estimate formed of his powers by the major part of the people and the authorities was depreciatory," acknowledged his friend and later chief of staff Robert Lewis Dabney. "But he disdained to agitate, or solicit for promotion."[6] His fate, he believed, was in God's hands, as was the whole of this incomprehensible war, and he preferred to leave it that way.

Jackson managed to make himself useful anyway. Duty was duty, after all. He volunteered to be an artillery drillmaster, joining other former US Army officers on a training ground at Richmond College.[7] His immediate supervisor was the flamboyant John B. Magruder, who had been Jackson's commander in the Mexican-American War. For the next two days, Jackson, rejoined by twelve of his cadets, instructed recruits in the rudiments of artillery.

But there was no getting around it. Jackson was, for the moment, lost in the crowd. And a bumptious, jostling crowd it was in that unruly spring, jammed with self-seekers and self-promoters and name-droppers and people with political connections who were clamoring for colonelcies or captaincies or whatever they fancied. "He was not the recipient of any special attention," wrote one officer who met Jackson at camp. "[He] was very quiet and reticent, having little to say to anyone."[8] Jackson's dress, especially amid the plumage of the militia officers, was plain verging on shabby, starting with his weather-beaten cap. "From its faded looks it would be fair to judge that he bought it when he became a member of the faculty in 1851," wrote his friend John Lyle. "His blue cloth coat had no advantage of the cap in smartness of appearance and was, no doubt, of the same age . . . a stranger would not have picked out the man in the faded blue uniform."[9] In these early days Jackson was the man everyone expected him to be: plain, shy, tight-lipped, polite to everyone yet never eager to chat or make small talk; a modest man of apparently modest talents who smiled but never laughed.[10]

In this uncertain state, he fended off his wife's offer to come and join him. "The scene here, my darling pet, looks quite animated," he wrote Anna on April 25, in an upbeat tone that almost certainly did not match his mood. "Troops are continually arriving. Yesterday about seven hundred came in from South Carolina. . . . I received your precious letter, in which you speak of coming here in the event of my remaining. I would like very much to see my sweet little face, but my darling had better remain at her own home, as my continuance here is very uncertain."[11] Indeed, it was so uncertain and his time so unoccupied that at one point he spent the better part of the day teaching a raw recruit—a corporal of the guard—every detail of the man's new position, accompanying him through the whole circuit of sentry posts, patiently teaching him the various salutes and challenges, and instructing him in his duty.[12] Jackson was not only unwanted and unneeded; he was bored, too.

That same day his orders finally came through. They were a crushing disappointment. They confirmed whatever feelings he had that he was being slighted. He had been made a major in Virginia's topographical engineers, an appointment that his wife said he found "distasteful," which was probably a graceful understatement.[13] It was more like an insult. That was first because Jackson was no engineer, a job that involved "drawing"—essentially the rendering of terrain, buildings, and fortifications. It had been his worst subject at West Point. Far worse was the implied lack of respect for him as a soldier. The job was likely to be behind a desk in Richmond rather than on the front lines. And at a time when colonelcies and field commands were being given out liberally to men with less experience or no experience at all, Jackson would now enter the army at the same rank he had won by brevet fourteen years before.[14] As the great surge of war thrummed about him in the streets of Richmond, he was, in effect, being buried in a desk job for which he had little aptitude.

Fortunately for Jackson, he was not the only one who saw the absurdity in placing someone with wartime experience behind a desk in a fledgling nation full of people who did not have the slightest idea how to fight a war. As it happened, an old friend from his childhood days in northwestern Virginia named Jonathan Bennett was working in Richmond as state auditor. Bennett had been surprised to hear about Jackson's assignment, and took his concern immediately to Virginia governor John Letcher, another Jackson friend from Lexington, where the former had practiced law. Letcher quickly intervened, and by April 26 had secured for Jackson an appointment as colonel of the Virginia volunteers. The next day he summoned Jackson to his office and announced what must have seemed an astounding turn of luck, giving Jackson what Jackson himself later said was the best possible appointment he could have received. Not only was it a colonelcy; he would soon receive orders to take command at Harpers Ferry, the northernmost outpost of the Confederacy and a place of great strategic value that contained an armory and was located on one of the Union's key railroad lines.

Jackson was elated. He left that night. Along the way, he received his actual orders from Major General Robert E. Lee, the ranking army officer of the Confederacy. "You will proceed without delay to Harper's Ferry, Virginia . . . and assume command of that Post," wrote Lee. "After mustering into the service of the state such companies as may be accepted under your instructions, you will organize them into regiments or battalions, uniting as far as possible companies from the same section of the state."[15] Jackson already liked and admired Lee, and wrote Anna that he regarded him as "a better officer than Gen. [Winfield] Scott," the highest-ranking Union commander. Jackson had met both men in the Mexican-American War.

The location of his assignment at the edge of the mountainous and Union-tilting northwestern section of the state (today it is the state of West Virginia) was not coincidental. Jackson, who had grown up in those mountains, had so many relatives there that, in Bennett's words, "almost every second man is his kinsman."[16] In a directive to Letcher, Lee stated that "great confidence is placed in the personal knowledge of Major Jackson in this regard. If deemed expedient, he can assemble the volunteer forces of the northwest."[17]

Thus Jackson's commission had been given him as much for political reasons as for any perceived notion of his military abilities. But there was nothing wrong with that. The early days of the war were a sort of golden age for "political" generals and colonels and other officers—men who were given appointments for the constituencies they represented or the allies they brought with them and not for their military experience. The ranks of both sides were already full of them, and it would take several years to weed out the worst of them. Because he had been to West Point and had fought in Mexico, Jackson would never be grouped with such people. Still, he was seen as someone who might be politically useful in the western regions of Virginia. Either way, he got the job. It was a small event that would have astonishing consequences.

CHAPTER FOUR

DISCIPLINE AND OTHER NOVEL IDEAS

The chaos Jackson found at Harpers Ferry was very like the chaos he had found at Richmond, with one important distinction. He was now in command of it. Here was the same motley assortment of volunteers and militiamen, the same rawboned recruits with the same naive, self-fulfilling notions of what the war was going to be like; the same lack of order; the same wild exuberance. Some 2,500 men, mostly from the Shenandoah Valley, had assembled in the warming Appalachian spring in the tiny, picturesque mountain town on a tongue of land at the confluence of the Potomac and Shenandoah Rivers. It was lovely, outsized country: broad-shouldered mountains falling abruptly into sparkling, muscular rivers. If this notch in the mountains seemed to the recruits a perfect place to have a sort of extended social picnic, punctuated with parades, they could hardly be blamed. There had been no one, in the two weeks since secession, to tell them otherwise. "Society was plentiful," wrote a young recruit who was there, "for the ranks were filled with the best blood of Virginia; all its classes were there. Mothers and sisters and other dear girls came constantly to Harper's Ferry and there was little difficulty in seeing them. Nothing was serious yet; everything much like a joke."[1]

In charge of all this were four generals of the militias, a colorful set of men even by the standards of the early war. They dressed the way they believed generals ought to dress: cocked hats and feathers, epaulets and ceremonial sashes, gleaming sabers and pistols. They looked quite grand, the more so since they went about like pashas, with entourages that included aides-de-

camp, adjutants, inspectors general, personal servants, and various super-
numeraries. They served whiskey liberally to friends and colleagues. They
liked ceremony and spectacle, and provided plenty of both. They owed their
positions to their prominence in their hometowns and counties; the ranking officer, for example, sixty-year-old Major General Kenton Harper, was
the mayor of Staunton, Virginia, and the editor of the town's newspaper.
He presided over what, by military standards, was an organizational disaster: there was no medical facility, no commissary or quartermaster, no chief
of ordnance. The limit of military organization was the hundred-man company. There was little equipment or ammunition, and many of the men
had no rifles.[2] But no one in command seemed terribly exercised about the
shortages. Life rolled on, reviews were held, speeches made, and everyone
seemed quite happy in anticipation of the excitement that was surely to
come.

Amid such pomp and visions of martial glory, the new commanding
colonel who arrived on the evening of April 27 was a sorry disappointment. He was, in fact, the opposite of anyone's idea of what a leader was
supposed to look like, and his somber, uncourtly, and undashing manner
did nothing to change that impression. He had only two assistants: Assistant Adjutant General John Preston, a personal friend, founder of VMI,
and a leading businessman in Lexington; and Inspector General James
Massie, a VMI faculty member. The new commander had no prancing
steeds and not a thread of gold trim on his uniform. Bearded, solemn, and
unexceptional, he walked with long awkward strides through the camps,
wearing his faded blue VMI uniform and a beaten-up cadet cap that he
pulled down so far over his nose that it obscured the upper part of his face.
"The Old Dominion must be sadly deficient in military men, if this is the
best she can do," wrote one newspaper correspondent who spent some
time with him. "He is nothing like a commanding officer."[3]

Jackson, meanwhile, felt *exactly* like a commanding officer. This was
what he had wanted, and he believed without any doubt that he was equal
to the task. He took a modest room at a little wayside hotel near the railroad bridge, where he sat with Preston at a small pine table—often under
a tree in the yard—reviewing the rolls of troops.[4] His self-assurance was
immediately tested. On the day he arrived, Virginia governor Letcher
had informed state militias in Harpers Ferry and elsewhere that officers
above the rank of captain would be relieved of duty the moment a state-
designated commanding officer arrived. Jackson's first job was to enforce

this order, which meant dismantling most of the military command structure in Harpers Ferry. Predictably, the idea that the imperial generals were being ousted in favor of this shabbily dressed, socially inept professor seemed disgraceful, both to the officers and to the men who served under them. "The deposed officers . . . left for home or for Richmond in a high state of indignation," wrote a member of a Staunton regiment. "The men were deeply attached to their field officers, and regarded the ordinance of the convention as an outrage on freemen and volunteers."[5] Jackson thus began his tenure in an atmosphere of outright hostility and insubordination. Many of the militia officers had stormed off to Richmond to plead their cases, unable to believe that it could possibly be in the interest of the state or the Confederacy to replace them. Some militiamen simply left in disgust.

Jackson, unfazed by any of this public contempt—one of his great strengths, and weaknesses, was that he cared little about the opinions of others—now moved quickly to reorganize the troops. He began by asking some of the militia officers to stay and help him, thus buying goodwill with a number of companies. Working late into the night and sometimes through until morning—his one complaint to his wife in otherwise happy letters was his lack of sleep—he slowly but firmly stripped the militia companies of their independence and hammered them together into regiments, recruiting many VMI graduates into command positions. He got rid of the whiskey and instituted a rigorous and unforgiving program of drill and instruction, which began at 5:00 a.m. and continued for the next seventeen hours and included up to seven hours of marching. Sometimes the days did not end even there: on May 2 Jackson ordered his troops to sleep on their weapons, and scheduled a full inspection for 1:30 a.m.

Drilling came in different forms. There were marching drills, which taught the men how to walk together in formation and how to transform themselves from a marching column, two or four abreast, into a two-man-deep battle line—and then how to reverse that action. The idea was to be able to move a five-hundred-to-one-thousand-man regiment in an orderly way to, from, and around a battlefield; how to advance, how to retreat, how fast to march, how to dress ranks, how not to shoot at friendly troops. Weapons drills involved instruction in the nine separate actions required to fire a musket. There was instruction on all sorts of other skills, too, from military protocol to making camp to the handling and cooking of rations. To help him with this, Jackson had procured the services of ten cadets from

VMI. Since there was virtually no training for officers in the South—who often sat up late at night in their tents reading printed manuals—the cadets' expertise was crucial to the early war preparations of the Confederacy.[6]

Within a week Jackson had, to the amazement of local observers, quietly rebuilt the entire military operation at Harpers Ferry. Though the troops were still alarmingly green in many cases, "The presence of a mastermind was visible in the changed conditions of the camp," wrote John D. Imboden, an artillerist from Staunton. "Perfect order reigned everywhere. Instruction in the details of military duty occupied Jackson's whole time."

Many of the militia officers who had left in a huff had thought better of it and had quietly returned, taking their places in the new volunteer army, now squarely under the command of the peculiar professor. What had emerged from the anarchy and disarray of that week was, in fact, a distinct and unusual style of command. It began with rigid discipline and adherence to the strictest military code. Jackson would not tolerate disobedience, insubordination, tardiness, or neglect of duty. "Once or twice some willful young officer made experiment of resisting his authority," wrote Dabney, "[but] his penalties were so prompt and inexorable that no one desired to adventure another act of disobedience."[7] Punishments were doled out fairly and evenhandedly, without passion or prejudice. Duty was duty. You shirked it at your own peril, and there was nothing personal about what happened to you—arrest and the guardhouse—if you did. Jackson—the new Jackson, anyway—was all about scrupulous honesty, meticulous accountability, and cool professionalism. Soldiers quickly learned that quiet and unconversational did not mean irresolute.

Everyone who had known him before noted the change. "It occurred to us at the time that Jackson was much more in his element here as an army officer than when in the professor's chair at Lexington," wrote John Gittings, a former student who saw him in Harpers Ferry. "His manner had become brusque and imperative; his face was bronzed from exposure, his beard was now of no formal style, but was worn unshorn."[8] He was already a very different creature from the professor he had been just a few weeks before. He had discovered a new competence, something he had never done before on this scale but was exceptionally good at. The men could feel it, and perceptions changed. The martinet's obsession with petty detail now came to be seen as evidence of an iron will. "The only moments of relaxation we enjoyed were those we spent at meal times, but here we were met by the grave, solemn countenance of our Commanding Colonel," wrote recruit Charles Grattan. "All were afraid of him, for none knew how kindly and genial a heart beat in his bosom. . . . We ate silent as mutes, ever and anon casting a healthy eye upon the Colonel to see if he ate like other men, or bolted raw meat and gnawed bloody bones."[9]

Men who performed their duty to Jackson's specifications quickly discovered the other side of their commander. "He was a rigid disciplinarian, yet as gentle and kind as a woman," wrote Imboden. "He was the easiest man in the army to get along with pleasantly so long as one did his duty. He was as courteous to the humblest private who sought an interview for any purpose as to the highest officer in his command."[10] As an instructor, he was patient, forbearing, and tolerant of mistakes, provided his students were trying diligently to learn.

Jackson proved to be good at pure logistics as well. After his arrival in Harpers Ferry he had been tasked by Lee with the removal of the rifled-musket fabricating machinery from the former Federal armory to Richmond. Within a week, Jackson had informed an amazed Lee that two-thirds of it had already been moved—a remarkable feat, considering that the complicated machines and their water-powered gearing had to be carefully dismantled before shipment.[11] When he discovered that a wagon shortage had occurred because local merchants were paying twice the government rate, he seized the rolling stock. Local businessmen screamed in protest. Jackson ignored them.[12] Unwilling to wait for Richmond to ship him the ammunition cars he wanted, he put blacksmiths and carpenters to work converting commercial wagons to caissons. Impatient with the military bureaucracy on his requisition of horses, he dispatched his quartermaster to horsey Loudon County to impress or purchase them. Realizing that Confederate railways were low on rolling stock, he conceived and carried out an ingenious plan that siphoned off locomotives and cars from the Baltimore and Ohio Railroad, an important Union lifeline to Washington and points east, and took them south into Virginia.[13]

By May 11, Jackson had seen his command grow to 4,500 soldiers, and his transformation of the large, disorderly encampment into the rudiments of an effective military force had not gone unnoticed. Lee was certainly aware of it.[14] "[I] am gratified at the progress you have made in the organization of your command," he noted in a letter to Jackson on May 9.[15] By May 21 Jackson would have fully 8,000 men—7,000 of them armed—a number that included infantry and cavalry from Virginia, Mississippi, Alabama, Kentucky, and Maryland.[16] They were still woefully underequipped.

"Words cannot express to you our deplorable condition here," wrote Major Kirby Smith on May 29 in a blast directed at his inept state government. "[We are] unprovided, unequipped, unsupplied with ammunition and provisions."[17] In Harpers Ferry, as in the rest of the South, soldiers drilled in whatever they could muster: frock coats, swallowtails, jackets, and shirt-sleeves. They carried their own carbines and fowling pieces until someone put an official weapon—likely a smoothbore musket—into their hands. (Indeed, Jefferson Davis was still complaining to Brigadier General Joseph Johnston more than a month later: "I have not arms to supply you."[18]) In spite of that, Jackson's sheer organizational prowess inspired plenty of optimism. A report from an inspector general of the army in late May was surprisingly upbeat. He pointed out shortages of clothing and equipment, inadequate ground for drilling, and the rawness and inexperience of the soldiery. But the inspector also noted that "a fierce spirit animates these rough-looking men," and credited Jackson with assembling "force enough here to hold this place against any attack."[19]

While Jackson was laboring to create a fighting force, making do with a scant few hours of sleep each night, he also managed to write a steady stream of affectionate letters to his wife, expressing his love, and advising her on such matters as closing up the house, finding places for the slaves, and moving to her parents' house in North Carolina. "I just love my little business woman," he wrote. "Let Mr. Tebbs have the horse and rockaway at his own price; and if he is not able to pay for them, you may give them to him, as he is a minister of the Gospel. . . . My habitual prayer is that our kind Heavenly Father will give unto my darling every needful bless-ing."[20] He wrote of his military progress, too: "I am strengthening my position, and if attacked shall, with the blessing of Providence, repel the enemy. I am in good health, considering the great amount of labor which devolves upon me, and the loss of sleep to which I am subjected. . . . Colonels Preston and Massie have been of great service to me. Humanly speaking, I don't see how I could have accomplished the amount of work I have done without them. . . . Oh, how I would love to see your precious face!"[21]

Jackson enjoyed other, less visible successes as well. He had, as it turned out, an exceptional eye for talent, particularly when it was attached to sober, hardworking, Christian men. He had assembled the core of what would become one of the most talented staffs in either army: John A. Harman, a loud, profane stagecoach operator from Staunton, would become one of the most effective quartermasters in the Confederacy. Wells J. Hawks, a stagecoach builder from Charlestown who had been one of that community's leading citizens, became chief commissary—the man in charge of the food; the brilliant Hunter McGuire, a doctor destined for national prominence after the war, who was so young-looking that Jackson checked his credentials, became medical director on his staff; finally there was the whip-smart Alexander S. "Sandie" Pendleton, not yet twenty-one, and the son of William Nelson Pendleton, the Episcopal rector in Lexington, who became Jackson's chief of artillery. The highly competent Pendleton quickly became one of Jackson's favorites, starting out as an ordnance officer and ending up as assistant adjutant general (the chief administrative officer), and doing a good deal of the critical military work on Jackson's staff. Jackson would have some forty staff officers in his Civil War career. But these four would always remain at the heart of his operations.

Jackson was, moreover, blessed with not one but two exceptional cavalry officers. There was James Ewell Brown Stuart, known as Jeb, a loud, joyous, irrepressible twenty-eight-year-old West Pointer who had spent his previous military career with the mounted rifles and cavalry in the West. He was an odd combination of flamboyance and puritanically strict personal habits: he wore oversized gloves, a yellow sash, and a feathered hat, went about singing and reciting poetry, and practiced a devout form of Christianity. Implausibly, considering how utterly different they were, Stuart and Jackson became close and even affectionate friends; Stuart was the only man in the army who could make Jackson laugh, the only one who could kid him and get away with it. There was also the thirty-seven-year-old Turner Ashby, a born leader of men who was almost recklessly brave and already a legend in his home state of Virginia. He had courtly manners, a flowing beard, and, while sorely lacking in administrative skills, had astounding abilities as a rider and fighter. He was perhaps the purest example of the South's early, overwhelming dominance in cavalry. Jackson's earliest personnel crisis involved both men. It was brought about by his own appointment of Stuart as head of cavalry. Facing an incipient revolt by Ashby, Jackson settled the matter by splitting the cavalry command in two, and preserving the loyalty of both men. Stuart and Ashby would loom large in Jackson's future campaigns.

So would a smallish, gaunt sorrel gelding that Jackson acquired for his wife during his Harpers Ferry posting and named Fancy. The horse turned out to have extraordinary endurance; a gentle, rocking gait that Jackson liked; and the ability, later on, to doze peacefully in the middle of the hottest fights. To everyone else in the war the horse was known as Little Sorrel. He became Jackson's principal mount for the rest of his life.

The point of all this frenetic organization and reorganization was, of course, defense against the Northern invasion. Harpers Ferry was not only the South's northernmost military post, a knob jutting into the sovereign lands of Maryland; it was also a gateway to the Shenandoah Valley, the long, mountain-walled corridor that sat on Washington's western flank, and to the still-disputed lands of northwestern Virginia. But the town's main strategic value was as a transportation hub. The Baltimore and Ohio Railroad, the largest railroad network in the United States and a key lifeline to Washington, ran through it, and the 185-mile-long Chesapeake and Ohio Canal hugged the banks of the Potomac, just across the river.

Harpers Ferry was also one of the least defensible strategic sites in Virginia, if not the entire South. The problem was classically military: the town occupied conspicuously low ground. There were large mountains on three sides of it. Artillery placed on those heights could annihilate within hours whatever army was camped in the town. With troops and guns enough to occupy those heights, of course, Harpers Ferry could be held. But Jackson had nothing like that.

There was the thorny problem of political geography, too: Maryland was a slave state that had not seceded. But the belief persisted that it *might* yet secede—indeed, many Southerners believed that it would—meaning that any actions that might annoy Marylanders, such as military occupation of their lands, was thought to be a bad idea. The highest of the heights overlooking Harpers Ferry, as it happened, were on the Maryland shore of the Potomac.

On May 6, Jackson, who seemed unimpressed by such political considerations, wrote Lee that he had "occupied the Virginia and Maryland Heights" and was fortifying them.[22] Lee, as President Jefferson Davis's chief military adviser, responded immediately, and with some alarm: "In your preparation for the defense of your position it is considered advisable not to intrude upon the soil of Maryland unless compelled by the necessities of war."[23] As it happened, at that very moment Maryland was objecting strongly to the Union's "invasion" of its sovereign land.[24] Might not Maryland consider Jackson an invader as well?

But Jackson, an artillery officer who understood the tactical implications of his position, was pushing ahead on his own. He wrote Lee on May 7 that he had finished reconnoitering Maryland Heights and had "determined to fortify them at once, and hold them, as well as the Virginia Heights and the town, be the cost what it may." *Be the cost what it may.* In case he had not made himself perfectly clear, later in the same letter he stated, "I am of the opinion that this place should be defended with the spirit which actuated the defenders of Thermopylae."[25] His reference was to the 480 BC battle in which 7,000 Greeks held off 100,000 or more invading Persians for seven days before succumbing. Jackson's carefully chosen image is strikingly bloody, epic, and absolute in a war that had seen very little bloodshed. On May 9 Jackson wrote Lee again to report that he had placed five hundred troops on Maryland Heights, prompting this scolding retort from Lee: "I fear you have been premature," he told Jackson. "The true policy is to act on the defensive and not invite attack. If not too late you might withdraw until the proper time." Lee also pointed out the political repercussions of Jackson's rash moves: "Your intention to fortify the heights of Maryland may interrupt our friendly arrangements with that state, and we have no right to intrude on her soul unless under pressing necessity for defense."[26]

In any case, it was too late. The troops would stay. But Jackson, after proving his mettle as an administrator, had now begun to build a reputation as something less desirable—an officer who was overeager and required close watching by a superior officer, and who, above all, needed to be reined in. In his movement into Maryland he was completely at odds with the political climate in Richmond and with individual politicians such as Jefferson Davis, who were deeply suspicious of him.

This was in part Jackson's own fault. He was motivated by the belief that, for the South to win against obvious industrial and numerical odds, it would have to win quickly. That meant hitting the enemy's green troops hard and soon, and not paying attention to such political niceties as state boundaries. That meant burning Baltimore and Philadelphia and making Northerners understand on a visceral level what this war was going to cost them. As early as the week after secession, Jackson had proposed to Virginia governor John Letcher the idea he had mentioned in the letter to his nephew in January: a war of invasion in which the South would fly the "black flag"—meaning that all Union prisoners would be summarily executed. He even proposed to set the example himself.[27]

Though his plan sounded bloody, brutal, and un-Christian, as Jackson saw it there was clear and practical logic behind it. "He affirmed that this would in the end be the truest humanity," wrote Robert Dabney, "because it would shorten the contest, and prove economical of the blood of both parties. . . . This startling opinion he calmly sustained in conversation, many months after, [saying that since] the Confederate Authorities had seen fit to pursue the other policy, he had cheerfully acquiesced."[28] But he still believed it. As for his then-radical idea for a war of invasion, he was simply ahead of his time. By the second year of the war, Robert E. Lee would come to the same conclusion. He would eventually invade the North twice. Jackson's notion of total war, meanwhile, would soon define the entire conflict on both sides. The final campaigns of Union generals Grant, Sherman, and Sheridan in 1864 and 1865 were the fulfillment of Jackson's ideas.[29] For now, however, they were seen as wildly aggressive, if not outright crazy.

CHAPTER FIVE

A BRILLIANT RETREAT

Jackson's one-man show in Harpers Ferry was not destined to last. Upper Virginia was too important, and Jackson was a mere colonel, a largely unknown quantity. On May 23, the twenty-sixth day of his command, Brigadier General Joseph E. Johnston arrived to replace him. The transition was perfectly characteristic of the scrupulous, by-the-book Jackson. Since he had not been informed by either Lee or Letcher of the change of command, Jackson politely but firmly refused to relinquish it until Johnston—whose staff was dumbfounded by Jackson's stubbornness—could produce proof of his appointment. Johnston was not just any officer. When the war started, he was quartermaster general of the US Army and the highest-ranking officer to join the Confederacy. He was considered by several high-ranking officers on both sides—notably Longstreet and Sherman—to be the equal of Robert E. Lee. When warned by Johnston's staff officer Chase Whiting, Jackson's supercilious upper-class tutor at West Point, that he might be arrested for his behavior, Jackson stated calmly, "I consider my duty clear." He was never impolite. He even took Johnston on a tour of the camps. But he was insensitive to peer pressure, and he did not waver. Johnston, who managed to maintain his soldierly bearing and understood the military rule that officers should not relinquish command on verbal assurance alone, soon located a telegram with Lee's endorsement. Jackson immediately gave way, with no hard feelings. For anyone who was paying attention, it was another signal that Jackson was not like other officers in the Confederacy. Though he was clearly ambitious, he would not extend even this small, rule-bending courtesy to one of the Confederate army's most important officers and the man who would be in a position to promote him.

Johnston, meanwhile, brought a radically different approach to the defense of Harpers Ferry. Where Jackson had preached the spirit of Thermopylae and as good as invaded Maryland to set his defenses, Johnston's first thought was to fall back. "This place cannot be held against an enemy who would venture to attack it," he wrote to Lee. He offered a lengthy list of reasons why this was so, including lack of men, lack of ammunition, the presence of a hostile populace, and an inability to guard river fords. Lee, who regarded Harpers Ferry as a critical part of his strategy in northern Virginia, protested strongly in a letter to Johnston, writing, "The abandonment of Harpers Ferry will be depressing to the cause of the South." Johnston immediately fired back, "Would not the loss of five or six thousand men be more so?"[1]

On June 14, with reluctant approval from the Davis administration—and against Jackson's wishes, too, though he did not air his objections—Johnston evacuated Harpers Ferry. His pretext was the presence of a large Union force in the town of Romney, sixty miles to the east. It would later turn out that no such force existed. Johnston ordered Jackson to arrange the evacuation, which meant taking with them whatever equipment and matériel they could, burning what they could not, and looking after sick men and military records. This included setting fire to much of the town, and blasting to bits the magnificent nine-hundred-foot B & O Railroad bridge over the Potomac. Three days later, Jackson systematically destroyed the sprawling B & O Railroad shop complex. He hated doing it. All he could see was the destruction of key wartime assets.

In spite of the awkward transfer of power, Johnston and his duty-obsessed subordinate managed to get along. Johnston appreciated Jackson's talents immediately, retaining him as commander of the Virginia regiments and thus making him his top lieutenant. Though he had insisted on retiring from Harpers Ferry, Johnston was anything but a coward. He had graduated from West Point in the Class of 1829, ranking thirteenth out of forty-six cadets, had fought with distinction in the Mexican-American War (where he was twice wounded) and in the Seminole wars, and had attained a higher rank in the regular army than his West Point classmate Robert E. Lee. Confederate general and war historian Richard Taylor pronounced him the "beau ideal of a soldier," an officer who "gained and held the affection and confidence of his men."[2]

It was under Johnston that Jackson—known to his men by the name he had been called at West Point and the name he would be called for the rest of the war, Old Jack—saw his first combat experience as a commanding officer. On July 2, he was encamped with 2,300 men and four cannons north of Martinsburg, a town about fifteen miles northwest of Harpers Ferry in what is now West Virginia, when he received word that Union troops had crossed the Potomac River and were coming toward him. Jackson, whose standing orders from Johnston were to retire if the enemy approached him "in force," could not tell exactly how many soldiers he was facing, though he knew that a large Union force under Major General Robert Patterson had been camped on the Maryland side. So he decided to find out in the most aggressive way possible, conducting what was known in military jargon as a "reconnaissance in force"—an attack whose purpose is to make the enemy reveal himself.

Issuing precise orders in a soft voice that carried an accent from the western mountains of Virginia, Jackson ordered one of his four regiments—the 5th Virginia—to advance accompanied by a single piece of artillery. The 2nd and 4th Virginia Regiments were to act as reserves, in a state of full readiness; the 27th Virginia loaded the brigade's baggage and equipment onto wagons. Less than half an hour after he had gotten the news from Stuart's courier, Jackson's men were on the move. The Federals were moving, too. When Jackson's force of 380 advanced on them at 9:15 a.m., at a place called Falling Waters, Union troops were about 3,000 strong. Jackson swung his men immediately into action, sending one of his companies on a flanking movement to the right. "The enemy soon advanced, also deployed, and opened their fire," wrote Jackson in his battle report. His skirmishers returned fire, driving the enemy back.[3] The Federals came on a second time, and were again repulsed. But that was the end of whatever tactical advantage Jackson enjoyed. He was clearly outnumbered, and now he could see just how bad the mismatch was. Federal guns began to rake his position, while enemy soldiers appeared in a battle line that was two regiments wide—enough to flank and even envelop Jackson's small group. Jackson gave the order to fall back. Before he did, his battery chief, William Pendleton—who less than three months before had been the Episcopal rector of Grace Church in Lexington—fired a cruelly efficient volley of solid shot that, in Jackson's words, "entirely cleared the road in front."[4]

Jackson handled the retreat masterfully. It was the first real sign of his talent as a field commander. He held his command together as it executed the difficult and nerve-racking task—even for veterans—of falling back three miles under fire before an enemy that held an eight-to-one numerical advantage. Under Jackson's calm, self-possessed guidance—he was on horseback, in the middle of the fight—the regiment withdrew slowly and deliberately, constantly checking the Federal troops, who, Jackson wrote, "were advancing through the fields in line and through the woods as skirmishers, endeavoring to outflank me."[5] It was, in other words, a fight all the way. Throughout it, as bullets and shells buzzed about them, Jackson, seated on his horse and moving constantly in front of his troops, had seemed fearless. In midfight he stopped by the side of the road to write a note to Johnston. While he was writing, according to an artillery corporal who witnessed it, "A shot from a Federal battery struck centrally, ten feet from the ground, a large white oak that stood in the fence corner close to Jackson and knocked a mass of bark, splinters and trash all over him and the paper on which he was writing. He brushed it all away with the back of his hand, finished the dispatch without a sign that he knew anything unusual was going on, folded it, handed it to the courier and dismissed him courteously: 'Carry this to General Johnston with my compliments, and see that you lose no time on the way.' "[6]

In his first test Jackson had performed well. By the tactical standards of the early war, he had done exceptionally well. He had conducted an aggressive reconnaissance in force, had inflicted damage on the enemy, and then, obeying the letter of Johnston's orders, had conducted a disciplined retreat, contesting ground all the way. He was so effective that Union general Patterson estimated Jackson's total strength at 3,500 men, ten times what he actually had on the field. Most gratifying of all to Jackson was the performance of his men, all of whom he had trained personally and almost none of whom had seen combat before. "My officers and men behaved beautifully," Jackson wrote Anna. Then, lest it seem that he was giving them too much credit, he added, "I am very thankful that an ever-kind Providence made me an instrument in carrying out General Johnston's orders so successfully."[7] This was no figure of speech, no trope of the era: Jackson believed that he was merely God's instrument, a crude tool in God's hands. All credit for victory belonged to God, and to no one else.

He had also benefited from the brilliant debut of Jeb Stuart, whose Virginia cavalry had been instrumental in making the retreat an orderly one. At one point Stuart and his men daringly swept around the Federal right flank and captured an entire company of Union soldiers—a neat trick considering how badly Stuart and Jackson together were outnumbered. "Col. Stuart and his command merit high praise," Jackson reported, "and I may here remark that he has exhibited those qualities which are calculated to make him eminent in his arm of the service."[8] Though estimates of the numbers of killed, wounded, and captured at the Battle of Falling Waters vary widely, it is likely that each side suffered several dozen killed and wounded, in addition to the forty-nine Union prisoners taken by Stuart and the ten rebels captured by the Union.

Johnston was quick to realize what Jackson had accomplished. He was a combat veteran and knew a talented field commander when he saw one. On July Fourth, he wrote the War Department in Richmond to recommend that Jackson "be promoted without delay to the grade of brigadier-general."[9] But General Lee had already come to that conclusion himself, in spite of whatever reservations his associates in Richmond had about Jackson's rash behavior. In a letter to Jackson dated July 3, Lee wrote, "My dear general, I have the pleasure of sending you a commission of brigadier-general in the Provisional Army, and to feel that you merit it. May your advancement increase your usefulness to the State."

Jackson was elated. "My promotion was beyond what I anticipated, as I expected it to be in the volunteer forces of the state," he wrote Anna, proudly enclosing the letters from Lee and Johnston.[10] What he meant was that his commission no longer came from the state of Virginia. His appointment as brigadier general was to something entirely new: the *Provisional Army of the Confederate States of America*. He would be a general in the *Confederacy*, an organization that was slowly but steadily assuming authority over the states. Still, not everyone in Richmond was convinced that his promotion was a good idea. When President Jefferson Davis announced it, according to one Richmond insider, "it provided laughter among those who thought they knew him well."[11]

Jackson knew nothing about what well-dressed men in Richmond salons and offices were thinking. He knew only that he had come very far in a very short time, and he had no doubt that God had made it happen, or that he deserved it. Though he did not say so, it must have thrilled him to realize that only two and a half months had passed since he had arrived, unheralded, unappreciated, and without a commission, in the teeming streets of Richmond.

CHAPTER SIX

MANEUVERS,
LARGE AND SMALL

⊰⊱

The real war was coming. There was no doubt about it now. It would be here with the summer's heats and would be fought somewhere in the state of Virginia by large numbers of men, and the resolution would be Armageddon-like in its clarity. There was very little disagreement about that. "Everyone seemed to think one battle would settle it," wrote Confederate officer William Blackford, "and those in authority, who had brought on all the trouble, who ought to have known better, thought so too."[1] The world would be sorted out, and there would be glory in the sorting.

Above all, nobody wanted to miss the show.

Witness, then, the 1st Virginia Brigade, 2,300 men in four regiments under the command of newly minted brigadier general Thomas J. Jackson, restive in its camps in early July in the heretofore peaceful and prosperous town of Winchester, at the northern end of the Shenandoah Valley, sixty miles west of Washington, DC. (This is also known, counterintuitively, as the *Lower* Valley because it is farther downstream on the Shenandoah River.) The past month had not exactly been glorious. The men had been ordered, much against their will and that of their commander, to retire from their base at Harpers Ferry in mid-June. They had been warned, in late June, not to engage the enemy if the enemy was in force, had engaged him anyway at Falling Waters, and had retreated under orders to the hamlet of Darkesville, just south of Martinsburg. They had waited there for a battle that never materialized, and then on July 7, to their anger and disbelief, they had retreated yet again under orders, this time into the safety of Winchester.

There was a clear theme here. Flight. Joe Johnston's Army of the Shenandoah Valley was moving inexorably west and south. The action and glory, meanwhile, as everyone knew, almost certainly lay to the north and east. It seemed to be a war of maneuver, and they were losing it. Union commander Robert Patterson, inching down upon them from the north with eighteen thousand men, was certainly of that opinion. Crowing about his occupation of Harpers Ferry and Martinsburg, on the Virginia side of the Potomac, he observed that "we will thus force the enemy to retire and recover, without a struggle, a conquered country."[2]

Even more unsettling, word had arrived that a Confederate force in western Virginia had been soundly beaten and its commanding general killed by a thirty-four-year-old military genius and foursquare Union hero named George Brinton McClellan. The men of Jackson's 1st Virginia Brigade had been told they were already greatly outnumbered by the Union forces in Maryland. Now, with a victorious Union army apparently running roughshod over the northwestern part of Virginia, it seemed likely that Patterson would be coming with even more men, which would mean more caution, more retreat. It all seemed quite dispiriting. Jackson, irritated and restless, chafing at this enforced passivity, could do nothing about it. "I want my brigade to feel that it can itself whip Patterson's whole army," he wrote in a letter, "and I believe we can do it."[3] That was about the last thing Joe Johnston or Jeff Davis or anyone else was going to let him do.

So Jackson's men settled, somewhat sullenly, into camp life, where they were relentlessly drilled by their stern commander and awaited whatever sort of war might descend upon them. They also discovered the first of war's horrors, the sort that affected both armies equally and would eventually claim two soldiers' lives for every one lost on the battlefield: disease. Epidemics of mumps, measles, and smallpox swept through the valley army in the late spring and early summer, adding to the misery already caused by the inevitable, intractable camp illnesses: diarrhea, dysentery, malaria, and typhoid. Jackson's brigade was especially hard hit by measles and typhoid. Men who had never seen a battlefield were already dying painful deaths, and the number of soldiers on the sick list in Johnston's army rose to a remarkable 1,700 as of mid-July, nearly 20 percent of his force. Much of the sickness came from the galling sanitary conditions in the camps. The mid-nineteenth century had seen many technological advances, but they did not yet include an understanding of bacteria or microbes. One of the key causes of disease in camp was the contamination of the water supply from what passed for latrines, which were nothing more than patches of ground, usually next to a watercourse, that were covered with fresh earth once a week.[4] But men with severe dysentery and explosive diarrhea often did not make it to the appointed area, and so the soldiers were literally eating, sleeping, and drilling in a murk of infectious germs. Diarrhea, especially (which was also a symptom of typhoid and dysentery), was one of the major killers of the war. Even in the relatively controlled conditions of Richmond hospitals, more than 10 percent of all diarrhea cases resulted in death, usually from severe depletion of bodily fluids.[5]

Jackson, meanwhile, was getting used to the idea of command. His new rank had changed the fundamental nature of his relationship with the world around him. VMI cadets who had been his students, including those who had mocked and teased him, and former colleagues who now served under him could feel it. Behind every word, order, or request now rested the full weight of a brigadier general in the Provisional Army of the Confederate States. His obsessions with duty and detail now, in the perilous life of a large army, took on a different cast. Jackson, taking it all in stride, ignored the heat and the dust, which were plentiful, and the epidemics that were engulfing his tents (which included fleas), and ordered six drill sessions per day, punctuated by camp duties, roll calls, and meals. He did not limit himself to daytime work. The men marched at night, too. Often for half the night. "Jackson is considered rigid to the borders of tyranny by the men here," wrote one captain in his brigade. But that same captain also said he believed that Jackson "enjoyed the entire confidence of his command."[6] Jackson, in turn, was immensely proud of them.

As many of his soldiers noted, then and later, as hard as Jackson could be, he was also solicitous of his troops' welfare, sometimes almost motherly in his concern for their well-being. He was, as any of his friends from Lexington who knew him well could tell you, a strange mixture of sternness, severity, and deep kindness. What his wife—who saw him clearly most of the time—called "this mingling of tenderness and strength" was on display in a remarkable letter he wrote to one of his officers who had requested an extension of a furlough to visit gravely ill and dying family members:

> *My Dear Major—I have received your sad letter, and wish I could relieve your sorrowing heart; but human aid cannot heal the wound. From me you have a friend's sympathy, and I wish the suffering condition*

of our country permitted me to show it. But we must think of the living and of those who are to come after us, and see that, with God's blessing, we transmit to them the freedom we have enjoyed. What is life without honor? Degradation is worse than death. It is necessary that you should be at your post immediately. Join me tomorrow morning.

Your sympathizing friend, T. J. Jackson.[7]

His tenderness was very real, but it was also merely a sentiment; he would not allow it to interfere with what he considered to be his duty, and he would not budge in his insistence that the officer leave his stricken family.

The men were getting used to his idiosyncratic ways, too. Jackson was no less eccentric than he had been at VMI, though his behavior was now on display in a much larger arena, before thousands of men. He had his peculiar way of walking; his peculiar, ungraceful way of riding Little Sorrel, who seemed to be an extension of his personality; his dirty uniform and odd way of wearing his hat so that you could barely see his eyes; and his tendency to walk away abruptly in the middle of a conversation. He dined on cornbread and water, slept on "the floor of a good room" in a house with little or no furniture in Winchester, though he also found that he liked sleeping outside and spent several weeks sleeping outdoors on the ground, saying that it "agreed with me well, except when it rained, and even then it was but slightly objectionable."[8] And, of course, he prayed and read his Bible and consecrated every act of his life, every thought he had, to God. He did this consciously, every day. The blessings of his life—and in the month of July in the year 1861, Jackson believed he was in a high state of grace—all came from the hand of God. At least part of his devotion involved reminding himself constantly of just that.

Some 60 miles away, across the valley, through the towering ramparts of the Blue Ridge and the river-crossed lands of the Piedmont, the enemy was busy preparing for the war that the Northern newspapers, with rising shrillness, were demanding. The central—and somewhat bizarre—characteristic of the war was that the capital cities of the two enormous nations—the Confederacy alone encompassed 750,000 square miles and 3,000 miles of coastline—were just 90 miles away from each other. And so while recruits since mid-April had been swarming into large towns and cities across the country, in places such as St. Louis and Columbus and Atlanta and New Orleans, organizing themselves into regiments and brigades to fight the

the inescapable reality was that the first big fight was going to be—had to be—close to the power centers of the two nations, if only because losing one capital or the other would likely end the war almost before it started. "On to Richmond!" was the battle cry in the Northern newspapers. It was a catchy slogan and communicated a simple idea: Richmond, an easy and close target, would fall, and the South would lose whatever credibility it had as a military power, both at home and with such potential allies as France and England. Peace, on Union terms, would follow.

Thus by mid-July, a mere three months after the surrender of Fort Sumter, three Union armies confronted three Confederate armies in the Virginia theater, along the most likely routes of invasion. Across the Potomac River from Washington camped a Union army of 35,000 men, commanded by Irvin McDowell. Facing it, some thirty miles to the west, at a strategic railroad junction called Manassas, was a Southern army of 20,000, commanded by Pierre Gustave Toutant Beauregard. To the west, in the Shenandoah Valley, Joe Johnston's 11,000 at Winchester faced Robert Patterson's 18,000, and on the Chesapeake Bay coast at Fortress Monroe, John B. Magruder's 5,000 Confederates squared off against Benjamin Butler's 15,000. Thus the underdog Confederacy began the war outnumbered and outgunned at every point in Virginia: 68,000 to 36,000.

But there was plenty of reason for hope. Though the war had barely begun, the South had already found in Beauregard a hero for the ages, a five-foot-seven-inch bantam with an erect military carriage, piercing eyes, and a magnificent Van Dyke. He was a Creole from an important family in Louisiana. Like many other highborn sons of the South, the army had seemed a natural vocation. He had attended West Point and performed splendidly there, graduating second in the Class of 1838. In the Mexican-American War he had served as an engineer on General Winfield Scott's staff, alongside Robert E. Lee and George McClellan. At the battle for Mexico City, he was wounded three times on the same day, and finished the war with the brevet rank of major. For the next thirteen years he mostly rebuilt and repaired forts in the South. In January 1861 he assumed the superintendency of West Point, only to be asked to resign soon afterward because of his pro-secessionist sentiments.

All that gave him a record as accomplished as most officers in either army. But what made the dapper little man with the hair-trigger sense of dignity famous—indeed, an instant legend—was the Battle of Fort Sumter. It was Beauregard, as commanding officer in Charleston, South Carolina, who had demanded the surrender of Union troops. And it was Beauregard who had ordered and supervised the thirty-four-hour artillery attack on the fort. It had not been his idea to shell the fort, and in the "battle" that followed the only casualties occurred when, as Union forces were firing a hundred-gun salute before lowering the American flag, a cannon misfired, killing two Union soldiers and wounding four. And, indeed, the fort he was pounding into submission was, for all practical purposes, defenseless, and was about to run out of food anyway. Virtually any officer could have given the same orders.

None of that made any difference, nor did the fact that Beauregard was not an especially engaging personality. The war was commenced, and Beauregard, the brave and audacious soldier who had ordered the first shot, was an instant hero.[9] The Southern press portrayed him as a Napoleonic figure—that part was hard to miss in a compact, French-speaking soldier with grand ambitions—and when he traveled north in late May to assume command of the Confederate Army of the Potomac in front of Washington, throngs turned out to meet his train, cheering rapturously. When he arrived, Carolina troops who had served under him roared, "Old Bory's Come!"[10]

The North, as yet, had only McClellan to pit against Beauregard, and he was off in the mountains of western Virginia, still largely unknown. Beauregard's opposite number, commanding the Union forces in front of the capital, was Brigadier General Irvin McDowell, an army lifer who had never actually commanded troops in combat. A large, plain-looking man with a doughy countenance, a large, square head, a square jaw, and a squarish beard to go with it, he had, like so many general officers in the war, attended West Point, where he graduated in 1838, eight years before Jackson. His subsequent career had been spent on various military staffs, starting as an aide-de-camp in the Mexican-American War and ending in the War Department in Washington, where he served under Winfield Scott and Joseph E. Johnston, among others. Though he had pursued a solid, unspectacular career, he was earnest, intelligent, self-confident, and politically well connected, most notably to Lincoln's Treasury secretary, Salmon P. Chase. On May 14, 1861, McDowell, still a brevet major, was vaulted over many officers who were superior in rank and length of service and made brigadier general. Soon he was given the most important command in the Union army.

He was in many ways a hard man to like. Stiff, formal, and aloof, a poor listener who often drifted while others were speaking—unless the subject was fishing—he had a singular inability to remember names and faces. Even his friend Salmon Chase thought him a bit distant. "He is too indifferent in manner," Chase wrote. "His officers are sometimes alienated by it. . . . There is an apparent hauteur—no, that is not the word—rough indifference expresses better the idea, in his way towards them, that makes it hard for them to feel any warm personal sentiment towards him."[11] He was a strict and unforgiving disciplinarian, which made him unpopular with the volunteers. He was also a massive eater, so much so that, while in the midst of a meal, he often paid little attention to the people around him. "At dinner he was such a Gargantuan feeder and so absorbed in the dishes before him that he had but little time for conversation," wrote a Union officer who attended formal dinners with him. "While he drank neither wine nor spirits, he fairly gobbled the larger part of every dish within reach."[12] Nevertheless, he would be the one to fight the big, definitive battle that would decide the fate of the nation.

If McDowell seemed to be a minor sort of man—in talent and career achievements—his immediate supervisor, Winfield Scott, was in most ways larger than life. Scott was the nation's preeminent soldier. He was, as it happened, actually older than the United States itself. Virginia-born in 1786, he had been a hero as a young man in the War of 1812, became general in chief of the US Army in 1841, and was the chief architect of its stunning victory in the war with Mexico. He ran as the Whig Party candidate, and lost, in the presidential election of 1852. He was everyone's idea of what a general ought to look like. A massive six feet five inches tall, with splendid side-whiskers and hair swept back from a noble brow, and dapper in his blue uniform, he was, as his subalterns said in Mexico, a magnificent man.

But by the time the war began, those days were over. He was seventy-four years old now. In addition to his towering height, he was now massively, almost comically fat. He lurched about, had trouble standing for long periods of time, and could no longer ride a horse. He was vain, and prone to fits of temper, as he had always been.[13] Still, after Robert E. Lee turned Lincoln down for the job, there was no one else in the North with quite Scott's military stature.

And it was Scott who, quite sanely and reasonably, as a military man who knew what war was all about, had come up with a grand scheme for a relatively bloodless victory. Derided in Northern newspapers as the "Anaconda plan," the metaphor was nonetheless apt. The idea was to envelop the Confederacy from without, blockade its Gulf and Atlantic ports, and send a force of sixty thousand men down the Mississippi to choke off its commerce and in effect split the South in two, bottling it up in what would then be a useless, and valueless, sea of cotton. The idea was to squeeze the South to death. It had merit—and indeed would be revisited by the Union later in the war. But Scott's plan would take time—time to build or acquire ships, time to train troops for the Mississippi expedition—and time was something no one seemed to have. Passive, slow-burning solutions were not what the times—or the bellicose press of both sides—called for. Public opinion in the North was overwhelmingly in favor of crushing the rebellion *now*. Lincoln himself favored an immediate invasion. There was even a timetable of sorts, if one believed what one read in the papers. On June 26, Horace Greeley's influential *New York Tribune* began running an editorial page slogan that read, "The Nation's War Cry! Forward to Richmond! Forward to Richmond! The Rebel Congress Must Not Be Allowed To Meet There On The 20th Of July! By That Date The Place Must Be Held By The National Army."

So the armies were gathered up and sorted into their camps, where they waited in the rising summer heat for politicians and generals to decide exactly who would strike first and when the blow would fall. There was a strange, dreamlike quality to these weeks of waiting that many soldiers commented on. Except for the diseases that seemed inevitable when soldiers were crammed twenty-men-deep into white canvas Sibley tents, life for the Southern soldiery on the Alexandria line was not so bad. It could even seem languorous. "The country people are all staying at their farms and are now cutting wheat and the darkeys and the old red hills look as natural as can be," wrote young officer Edward Porter Alexander to his wife on July 5, 1861. "The country girls come around here every morning to see the parades and it looks a good deal like West Point." The war still seemed distant. "I candidly do not believe that any attack will be made on us for at least a long time," Alexander wrote, "nor that Beauregard intends to advance on Washington within a month at least."[14]

Thirty miles away, across the Potomac, their Union counterparts, many seeing a big city for the first time, had become earnest and enthusiastic tourists. They tromped through all the public and government buildings, including the Smithsonian, the Post Office, and even the White House. The most popular place of all was the Patent Office, which displayed a large array of the latest gadgets and inventions.[15] Those were the more tame diversions, anyway. The streets, badly cut and rutted by army wagons, now teemed afternoon and night with drunken, quarrelsome troops.

Hotels and boardinghouses were filled to overflowing. Soldiers jammed the saloons, slugged down juleps and gin slings and whiskey skins and brandy smashes, and brawled in the streets, often brandishing revolvers and bayonets. Sanitary conditions were nightmarish. The Washington Canal, running through the middle of the city, became an open toilet, a receptacle for all the city's sewage—human, equine, and otherwise. It all found its way to the Potomac and, according to a government report, "spread out in thinner proportions over several hundred acres of [tidal] flats immediately in front of the city, the surface of which is exposed to the action of the sun at intervals during the day, and the miasma from which contaminates every breath of air which passes."[16] The stench was everywhere, inescapable. Thus the men waited for their unimaginable war. They would not wait much longer.

Johnston's army, meanwhile, was rapidly becoming the key strategic pawn in the looming battle that, at its core—as with all Civil War battles—was a numbers game, one played with both real and imaginary figures. McDowell knew that he had about 35,000 men in four roughly equal divisions. He estimated Beauregard's strength at 35,000. This was grossly inaccurate, as many early war assessments were, particularly by Union generals. Beauregard had barely 20,000. But McDowell's number nevertheless dictated strategy and, in particular, one excruciatingly obvious piece of that strategy: if the numbers in Manassas were going to be roughly equal, then, at all costs, *Johnston must be prevented from joining Beauregard*. And it was equally true that in Confederate war councils, where they were absolutely aware of their strength along the "Alexandria line" in front of Washington, and their likely disadvantage in number of troops, number of regular army soldiers, and ordnance, there was a growing conviction that *Beauregard could not win without Johnston*.

With the fate of the nation apparently hanging on the whereabouts of Joseph E. Johnston, what followed in the Shenandoah Valley in the second and third weeks of July was one of the great military blunders of the Civil War. It very likely altered the course of the war and, in any case, profoundly changed the lives of Thomas J. Jackson and his Virginia brigade. It starred Major General Robert Patterson, a sixty-nine-year-old Pennsylvanian who had fought in the War of 1812, had been a major general of volunteers in the Mexican-American War, and later became quite wealthy as the owner of cotton mills and a sugar plantation. Though he was brilliant at business, and prominent in the politics of Pennsylvania, what he experienced at the head of an army in unfamiliar country with massive supply requirements and an enemy of unknown strength was more like paralysis. It was Patterson who had moved timidly with his army from Chambersburg, Pennsylvania, to occupy an abandoned Harpers Ferry on June 16, and Patterson whose forces had crossed the Potomac River from the Maryland side on July 1 and then engaged Jackson at Falling Waters. The Confederate force had then fallen back again, while Patterson marched unopposed into the town of Martinsburg, announcing by wire to Winfield Scott that he was "in hot pursuit" of Johnston. But instead of driving south to meet the enemy, Patterson now paused to wait for supplies. He would not attack before he was certain that he had absolutely everything he needed. "As soon as provisions arrive," he told Scott, "I shall advance to Winchester to drive the enemy from that place, if any remain."

He would do no such thing. Patterson, as would soon be apparent, was scared. He was in enemy territory in Virginia and surrounded by a hostile populace. His supply lines were, implicitly, threatened. He worried, above all, that he did not have enough men, and this worry took the form of an uncritical willingness to believe the mostly wildly exaggerated reports about the size of the enemy's force. How, he wondered, could he be expected to bring his eighteen thousand men against twenty-six thousand men in enemy territory? At Martinsburg he waited, and urgently requested more troops, which Scott sent to him: five regiments.

Still, Patterson dithered and worried. He complained about lack of transportation, about the ninety-day enlistments that were soon to expire, making the men unwilling to fight, and, again, of being in an exposed position in enemy country. He worried that the reason Johnston did not attack him was that Johnston was luring him into a trap. Had Scott himself not warned him a month before that "a check or drawn battle would be a victory to the enemy" and that he should "attempt nothing without a clear prospect of success"?[17] Patterson, an old warhorse, was not necessarily afraid of violence; like so many inept generals early in the war, he was afraid of the *responsibility*, and of the shame and embarrassment that would follow any defeat or disaster that had resulted from his orders. His attitude is worth noting because it would become so common among general officers on both sides. It is visible in Patterson's hedged response to Scott, who was trying, in late June, to coax Patterson to cross the Potomac into Virginia. "I would not, on my own responsibility, cross the river and attack without artillery a force so much superior in every respect to my own," Patterson wrote, "but would do so cheerfully and promptly if the general-in-chief would give me explicit orders to that effect."[18] In other words, he would happily sacrifice his army if only Scott shouldered the responsibility. It was all about blame.

On July 16, Patterson, goaded by Scott, finally ordered a reconnaissance in force of Johnston's army, which had by now fallen back to the town of Winchester. Patterson had been told that McDowell was marching that day on Manassas, and so the purpose of this demonstration was to make sure Johnston and his Confederate force did not go anywhere. That was the main idea: prevent the two Confederate armies from uniting. So a small body of Union infantry and cavalry went forward and briefly engaged Colonel Jeb Stuart's cavalry. But Patterson, now only a few miles in front of Johnston's smaller force, suddenly became frightened by reports that Johnston had thirty thousand to forty thousand or even more troops in front of him, with sixty pieces of artillery. Patterson and his officers reasoned that, since Johnston had already been prevented from joining Beauregard, why risk fighting? So instead of advancing, they retreated. On July 17, eighteen thousand Union troops marched seven miles back to Charlestown, near Harpers Ferry, the Potomac River, and the soil of Maryland.

That night Patterson received a wire from an impatient and exasperated Scott in Washington, who did not yet know that the cautious Pennsylvanian had retreated. "Do not let the enemy amuse and delay you with a small force in front whilst he reinforces the junction [Manassas] with his main body," said Scott, who evidently still expected Patterson to move against Winchester. Patterson was behaving badly, and he knew it. When he was advised by a staff member that if he did not move against Winchester he would be "a ruined man" and that "in the event of a misfortune in front of Washington the whole blame will be laid to your charge," Patterson summoned up his courage and decided that he would advance the next day. Incredibly, he lost heart again. He never moved. He gave many reasons for this, chief among them that parts of his army, whose ninety-day enlistments were up, and who were weary of the promised advances that never happened, would not serve an hour past their time.

Unfortunately for Patterson, Johnston's troops, under orders from Beauregard and with Jackson's brigade in the vanguard, were already marching toward a pass in the Blue Ridge Mountains and to the train depot that lay beyond the mountains, on their way to fulfilling Winfield

Scott's worst nightmare. Patterson and his officers, in their secure camps in Charleston, saw none of this. That was because Jeb Stuart, executing one of the war's first great cavalry screens, had rendered him blind. While Johnston and Jackson slipped away, Stuart's dashing horsemen were thrown forward between the two armies to create dust and confusion and general mischief and to make sure no Union scouts got through.

Scott, increasingly suspicious, now demanded angrily of Patterson: "Has he [Johnston] not stolen a march and sent reinforcements toward Manassas Junction?" To which the hapless, doomed Patterson replied, even as Jackson was marching, undetected, east toward the mountains: "The enemy has stolen no march upon me. I have kept him actively employed, and by threats and reconnaissance caused him to be reinforced. I have accomplished in this respect more than the General-In-Chief asked or could well be expected, in face of an enemy far superior in numbers."[19]

He soon discovered how disastrously wrong he was. He finally acknowledged this two days later in a telegram to Scott: "With a portion of his force Johnston left Winchester by the road to Millwood on the afternoon of the 18th," he wrote. "His whole force was about thirty-five thousand two hundred."[20] Patterson could not resist a final lie, and one with phony filigree to boot: the "two hundred" made the false intelligence sound precise. (It was only a "portion," moreover, because Johnston left 1,700 sick soldiers behind in Winchester.[21]) In any case, the war was over for Patterson. On July 22 Scott ordered him relieved of his command.[22]

Jackson had struck his tents and marched through Winchester and out the other side of town while a frightened and disheartened citizenry looked on. He hated to leave them. He had fallen in love with Winchester, and now believed that he was likely abandoning it to the enemy. For his 2,600 men, who had not been told where they were going, the orders to move out were the worst thing they had heard yet. After a full month of retreating and then languishing in their disease-ridden camps, they were skulking away from the enemy yet again. As they moved out along the long, dusty, winding pike, toward the looming blue haze of mountains, they chafed and grumbled. Then, an hour and a half out of Winchester, under orders from Johnston, regimental adjutants read them a communiqué:

General Beauregard is being attacked by overwhelming forces. He [Johnston] has been ordered by the government to his assistance. . . . General

Patterson and his command have gone out of the way to Harper's Ferry, and are not in reach. Every moment is precious, and the General hopes that his soldiers will step out and keep closed, for this march is a forced march to save the country.

The reaction was immediate and thunderous. "At this stirring appeal the soldiers rent the air with shouts of joy," Jackson wrote to Anna, "and all was eagerness and animation where before there had been only lagging and uninterested obedience."[23] They waded across the waist-high Shenandoah, arrived at the small town of Paris, six miles from the Piedmont Station on the Manassas Gap Railroad, at about two o'clock in the morning. They would take the train to Manassas Junction the next day. The exhausted men slept. Jackson, meanwhile, joined the other sentinels and kept watch.

The next day was remembered later by many soldiers as one of those sweet, soft intervals that occurred in the early days of the war, before the fighting began to take its fearful toll. Because there were not enough trains and cars to transport the troops all at once, some of the regiments had simply to wait their turn, passing time in the pleasant countryside until midafternoon. "We had a regular picnic," recalled John Casler, a member of Jackson's brigade. "[There was] plenty to eat, lemonade to drink, and beautiful young ladies to chat with. We finally got aboard, bade the ladies a long farewell, and went flying down the road."[24] Actually, they labored down the road, behind a single, struggling locomotive; the thirty-four-mile trip took a full eight hours. But the rumbling, snail-like pace had at least some benefits. Along the way crowds gathered to wish them well, ladies waved handkerchiefs, and food was handed through the windows. The picnic was not quite over. As humble as the journey was, Jackson's brigade was engaged in one of the first large-scale transfers of soldiers to battle by railroad in history.

CHAPTER SEVEN

ALL GREEN ALIKE

❧

How astonishing, at first glance, that this unprepossessing little patch of ground in the middle of nowhere was something that large numbers of men would fight and die for. Jackson and his brigade arrived at their destination in the early evening of July 19, 1861, having first been packed into freight and cattle cars like so many "pins and needles," as one man put it, then carried on a rattling, bumping, and excruciatingly slow journey into a nondescript northern Virginia country of wheat- and cornfields and pastures broken by pine woods and farmhouses that suggested prosperity but not wealth.[1] The land was, in all ways, unexceptional. So was the little knot of frame buildings—a tallow factory, telegraph office, hotel, and a few railroad workshops—scattered around the depot where the soldiers of the 1st Virginia Brigade detrained and stood awaiting orders, gazing about as though to gather in the significance of the place, or its relationship to the glorious battle they were going to fight. They were a motley group, as unimpressive to look at as their brigadier. Some wore gray uniforms, some wore blue, some wore what looked to be civilian dress with a bit of military trim.[2] They sported a bewildering variety of hats, and carried mostly outmoded smoothbore muskets. They were Jackson men all, some of them former students from VMI or neighbors from Rockbridge County, drilled to the limits of their patience in camps from Harpers Ferry to Winchester, bent to the will of their surprising new master, and tested exactly once, in the brief fight at Falling Waters. Though they did not look like much, in a young war full of puffed-up amateurs they passed for a well-trained fighting unit, and Jackson was extremely proud of them. The hot, flat crossroads where they now found themselves, thirty miles west of Washington,

DC, would, within two days, become one of the most famous places in the Western world. It was called Manassas Junction.

There were exactly two reasons why anyone cared about the little junction that summer. First, it marked the point where the 148-mile-long Orange and Alexandria Railroad, the principal north–south line in Virginia, crossed the Manassas Gap Railroad, a 77-mile-long line that linked the fertile lower Shenandoah Valley with the rest of northern Virginia. This made Manassas Junction the most important strategic site north of Richmond and the inevitable target of a Union advance. Second, the Confederacy had decided, at all costs, to defend it. This meant placing its largest army between Manassas Junction and McDowell's Union army, which had moved west from its camps near the Potomac to the tiny town of Centreville, a small cluster of buildings that included several taverns, tanyards, and a squat stone church seven miles to the northeast. It had also meant fortifying the land around the junction itself: trenches had been dug and stockades erected. Amazingly, in the middle of those works was a giant, three-ton naval cannon that had somehow been dragged into place and would hurl thirty-two-pound balls, though it was difficult to imagine, just then, at what or at whom such a massive projectile was going to be thrown.[3]

Jackson disembarked, obtained directions to army headquarters, then rode off to receive his new orders. When he arrived, General Beauregard was holding a meeting with a group of pipe-smoking generals and colonels bedecked with an assortment of epaulets, sashes, and sabers and seated on the shaded lawn in front of a farmhouse belonging to a man named Wilmer McLean. They were deep in conversation when Jackson, unimposing in his rumpled blue VMI uniform and stiff as ever, approached, saluted, and reported that he had just come from the Shenandoah Valley with 2,600 men, the vanguard of Johnston's army. Instead of a warm welcome—or even a perfunctory welcome—from Beauregard, Jackson was greeted with a mixture of shock and surprise, the general gist of which was: What on earth was he doing there? Unbeknownst to Jackson, Beauregard had the day before suggested to Joe Johnston—he could not issue an order because Johnston outranked him—a grand plan of battle in which Johnston, instead of coming to Manassas Junction, would take his army on a wide swing to the north through the Bull Run Mountains, then head east and fall upon the flank and rear of the Federal force at Centreville. Beauregard, meanwhile, would attack the army in front, creating a viselike movement that would send the Yankees reeling back to

Washington. Beauregard had thought the plan ingenious, and was quite pleased with it.

Johnston had found it foolish. "I did not agree to the plan," he wrote later, and charitably, "because, ordinarily, it is impracticable to direct the movements of troops so distant from each other, by roads so far separated, in such a manner as to combine their action on a field of battle. . . . I pre-ferred the junction of our armies at the earliest time possible."[4] The prob-lem was that either he had never bothered to tell Beauregard that or his message had not gotten through.

Beauregard had been describing this ambitious flanking movement to his officers, explaining that Johnston was crossing the Blue Ridge that very day and would attack the enemy's right flank the next morning, when Jackson walked in to announce that a significant portion of Johnston's army, at least, was doing no such thing. And now Jackson was the target of unfriendly questioning. Was Johnston planning to march with the rest of his army on the enemy's flank? Beauregard demanded.[5] Jackson, who was tight-lipped anyway in the presence of other general officers, now replied, in formal tones, that as far as he knew such a flanking march was not likely, since Johnston was coming east with his column on the same train Jack-son had taken. Beauregard found Jackson so lacking in credibility, such a worthless officer, that he simply refused to believe him. He told the brig-adier where to camp his brigade, and dismissed him.[6] Jackson returned to the junction and marched his weary men three miles through pouring rain to a pine thicket near a creek called Bull Run.

Beauregard, meanwhile, resumed addressing his officers as though this inconvenient interruption had not happened. "The information received from General Jackson was most unexpected," wrote Jubal Early, then a brigade commander, "but General Beauregard stated that he thought Jack-son was mistaken, and that he was satisfied General Johnston was march-ing with the rest of his troops and would attack the enemy's right flank as before stated. . . . He stated that the effect would be a complete rout, a perfect Waterloo, and that we would pursue, cross the Potomac and arouse Maryland."[7] Jackson was, of course, right: the Creole general would very quickly be disabused of these plans for a second Waterloo.

Beauregard's plan had indeed been a bad idea, coming at a time when green armies with neophyte officers could barely execute a ten-mile march at route step on a clear road, let alone a fifty-mile turning maneuver through unknown terrain, out of touch with the main body of the army, where the timing of the attacks would be everything. But Beauregard, as it turned out, the dashing hero of the South, the man who had brought Sumter to its knees, was full of bad ideas. On July 14 he had sent an emissary to the Confederacy's first council of war, held at the Spotswood Hotel in Richmond, where he had presented a plan for a slashing offensive against the North that was Napoleonic in its grandeur and ambition. Beauregard would begin by uniting with Johnston and his "20,000" men. They would fall upon the Federals in front of Washington and, as Beauregard put it, "thus exterminate them or drive them into the Potomac."[8] Johnston would then return to the Shenandoah Valley with his original 20,000, plus another 10,000 from Beauregard's army, and destroy the smaller Union army under Robert Patterson, all within a week. After a side trip to eliminate McClellan's irksome 12,000-man column in western Virginia, Johnston would turn, march through Maryland, and attack Washington from the rear, while Beauregard assailed what remained of its defenses in front. The result: in what Beauregard confidently asserted would be a campaign of fifteen to twenty-five days, the South would not only win a crushing victory, but would then, in effect, dictate peace to a beaten and bereft Lincoln in the White House.

In its breathless optimism, and its assumption that the Federal armies would happily cooperate with the Confederate plan, Beauregard's scheme—the product of a restless, energetic, impulsive nature—managed to sound less like a calculated military strategy than something a child might concoct on his bedroom floor with toy soldiers. His proposal was heard by President Jefferson Davis, his military assistant Robert E. Lee, and Adjutant General Samuel Cooper, all of whom found it ridiculously impractical, starting with Beauregard's wishful assumption that Johnston had twenty thousand men. This rejection had a larger meaning, too, for the opening gambit of the war. Beauregard's proposal, vainglorious and overblown though it was, had been *offensive* in nature. But the Confederate approach to this first big test of strength, as developed by Davis and Lee, would be fundamentally *defensive*. They would wait for McDowell to come out of his camps in front of Washington; then they would protect their land and their country with everything they had.

Having been ignored first by Davis and Lee, and then by Johnston, Beauregard finally proceeded to do what his bosses wanted him to do, which was to put in place the first large-scale defensive position of the war, an eight-mile-long line made up of the bulk of his 32,000 troops along the lethargic, debris-clogged Bull Run, which wound, snakewise, in a northwest-to-southeast arc roughly perpendicular to a straight line between Manassas Junction and Centreville. It was here, Beauregard had said, that he would make his "desperate stand." He had moved all of his troops back from forward positions nearer to Washington, and now his line extended from the Warrenton Pike and its stone bridge on the north, and the Orange and Alexandria's bridge at Union Mills on the south. Between those two points were seven fords, only one of which was considered easy to cross. On July 18 these defenses had been tested halfheartedly by a Union reconnaissance in force at a place called Blackburn's Ford, and the attack had been sharply and convincingly rebuffed. But neither side had gained any tactical advantage. In any case, by July 20, reinforced by Johnston's brigades from Winchester, including Jackson's, Beauregard had his line fully in place.

McDowell, meanwhile, had more to worry about than the constant indigestion he was suffering from eating his multicourse meals. As he saw it, he was being goaded into attacking the Confederacy, quite against his will, by what seemed a vast alliance of howling news editors, congressmen, cabinet officers, rank-and-file soldiers, and Lincoln himself, and he was feeling more and more uncertain about the whole enterprise. His men were simply not ready, he argued. Many of his soldiers had been in the army less than a month, had only the most basic training in such skills as marching and shooting, and were in such poor physical shape that they were likely to wilt in the blazing summer heat and humidity of northern Virginia. For all his inexperience with command, McDowell recognized that no one on either side had ever managed such large numbers of men in a single body, not even the legendary Winfield Scott. This was a new kind of war: troops would move by train; orders would move by telegraph wire; and tens of thousands of soldiers would have to be moved to, from, and around battlefields. Simply inserting so many regiments into a battle was beyond the ken of even the West Pointers. "I had no opportunity to test my machinery," McDowell complained later, "to move it around and see whether it would work smoothly or not. There was not a man there who had ever manoeuvred troops in large bodies. There was not a man in the army. I wanted very much a little time; all of us wanted it. We did not have a bit of it. The answer [from Lincoln] was: You are green, it is true, but they are green also; you are all green alike."[9]

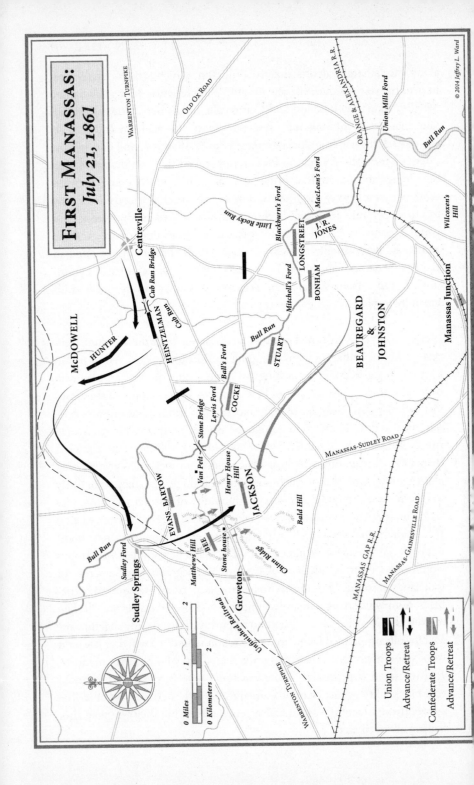

FIRST MANASSAS:
July 21, 1861

© 2014 Jeffrey L. Ward

If he had been uneasy on the subject of troop management before the middle of July, McDowell was horrified by what happened when, after seemingly endless delay that had held him up more than a week, his men finally marched out of their camps on July 16 toward Centreville and Manassas. The war's first great troop movement had started splendidly, fifty regiments of infantry and ten batteries of field artillery wheeling about in the hot dust, regimental colors flying, bayonets flashing, and band music rising on the wind. They had marched before the president. There were so many fancy carriages, members of Congress, senators, and fashionable ladies that it seemed more like the return of a triumphant army than the dispatching of a green and untried one toward an uncertain fate. Still, the army was superbly equipped and commanded by experienced soldiers: the four division commanders and eight of the eleven brigade commanders had been regular army men. The first day's march went rather well.

The second, on July 17, was a full-scale disaster. It began with the fact that officers, who did not yet know that the rebel army had withdrawn from its forward positions, were terrified of ambush. They saw nonexistent breastworks and shadow batteries in the woods. Stray shots at phantom pickets would prompt the "long roll" of drums, signaling an enemy attack.[10] That meant frequent stops, and the men quickly learned what frequent stops did to marching columns totaling thirty-five thousand men. The main effect was an accordion-like action, on a giant scale, that alternately froze men in place, in the heat and dust of a miles-long traffic jam, or caused them literally to have to run to catch up, sweating profusely while their equipment clanked around them. In the prodigious delays, the men hooted at passing officers, stopped at every creek to fill their canteens, and undertook excursions that involved everything from berry picking to chasing pigs and chickens.[11] They often discarded their packs, and even left their cartridge boxes behind. This was a volunteer army, after all—there was as yet no draft—and the men still cherished the illusion that they were individuals with individual rights and privileges.

When the Union forces reached Fairfax Courthouse and saw that the Confederates had abandoned it, they indulged in a celebration so wild one might have thought the war was over. Bands played, stores were looted, and soldiers were rampant in the streets. "Our dirty fingers were plunged into their jam pots," wrote one soldier from Rhode Island, "and we drank their whiskey, tea and coffee and ate their sardines and pickles with gusto."[12] It had taken the Federals a full two and a half days to travel twenty-two miles—a delay that allowed Johnston to steal his march on Patterson and join his troops with Beauregard's. When they finally arrived at camp near Centreville, officers discovered that the rank and file were out of food. The next day was spent correcting this problem. Saturday was consumed by reconnaissance, the reading of local maps, and efforts to scout a ford over the creek on the far rebel left. All of this was weirdly leavened by the presence of senators, congressmen, and cabinet officers, who hovered about McDowell's headquarters, passing out cigars and delivering opinions on the outcome of the battle. By Saturday evening, after seemingly endless delays for the most astounding variety of reasons had stalled his advance nearly two weeks, McDowell's Union army was out of excuses. They would have to fight.

That night—the last night—was lovely, soft and bright and experienced to the fullest degree by thousands of soldiers on both sides who could not sleep. "This is one of the most beautiful nights that imagination can conceive," wrote one Union soldier from his camp. "The sky is perfectly clear, the moon is full and bright, and the air is as still as if it were not within a few hours to be disturbed by the roar of cannon." In the Union camps regimental bands played, and the men sang "The Star-Spangled Banner." One newspaper correspondent, riding through the camp, called the scene "the picture of enchantment."[13]

That enchantment was cruelly brief. The first of the bugles began sounding reveille at two o'clock the next morning.

CHAPTER EIGHT

THE BULLET'S SONG

◆◆◆

"The first of all maxims for the conduct of a campaign," wrote Edward Porter Alexander, who would later become a Confederate general and who, this day, as a young captain of engineers serving in the Signal Corps, would play a critical role in the battle, "is to oppose fractions of the enemy's army with the whole unit of your own. In other words, compel the enemy to divide while you unite and strike him divided. Or, as our General [Nathan Bedford] Forrest put it in plain Confederate vernacular: 'Git thar first with the most men.'"[1]

The outcome of the Battle of Manassas—or as Northerners, who liked to name battles after watercourses, had it, Bull Run—turned on this very same tactic, in this case a secret and stunningly successful Federal march around the left wing of the Confederate army. The movement followed the military maxim, bringing a large mass of Union troops to confront a small rebel force. By the late morning of July 21, the Union tactic had created a mismatch so extreme that it should have resulted in the wholesale rout of the Confederate army and the triumphant arrival that day of the Union army at Manassas Junction. Richmond, ninety miles away, ought to have been trembling in mortal terror.

That the Federals failed to accomplish any of these things—in fact, failed so completely and miserably that almost the exact reverse happened—is the story of the first great battle of the Civil War. It is a story that features, as one of its prominent heroes, an unknown brigadier general named Thomas J. Jackson.

• • •

All battles take on a logic of their own. In this case that logic was supplied by the Union forces, since it was their plan that determined where and how most of the fighting took place during the nine-and-a-half-hour battle. General Irvin McDowell's scheme was simple in theory, difficult in execution. He had four divisions that totaled 35,000 men a few miles from Bull Run in Centreville, Virginia. His idea was to bring just enough force against a few sections of Beauregard's eight-mile-long, 32,000-man defensive line along the creek to occupy its attention and make it think an advance was in the offing, while the main Union column made a sweeping march to the north and west, unseen, under cover of woodland and dale. In other words, so far around the end of the Confederate line at the Stone Bridge, so far upstream on Bull Run that the rebels would not detect it until it was too late.

To create his diversion, McDowell planned to send two brigades (a Civil War brigade usually consisted of 2,000 to 2,500 men—though this could vary widely) to Mitchell's and Blackburn's Fords, where they would feign attack, and three brigades under Brigadier General Daniel Tyler to the Stone Bridge, the terminus of the Confederate left, where they would likewise lob shells and fire muskets, and otherwise pretend that they intended to mount a full-scale assault. Meanwhile, two full divisions under Brigadier Generals David Hunter and Samuel Heintzelman, some 18,000 men and thirty guns, would leave at 2:00 a.m., cross Bull Run at Sudley and Poplar Fords at about 7:00 a.m., then drive southward. Thus flanked, the Confederates would be forced out of their defensive position at the Stone Bridge, allowing Tyler's division to move west down the Warrenton Pike and into the fight, delivering the final blow that would send the Confederate army staggering in retreat toward Manassas Junction and Richmond beyond. On paper, the plan was perfectly sound. Its principal weakness could have been predicted from the logistical horrors of July 17: these green soldiers and officers did not yet know how to march, and certainly not over unknown roads in darkness.

Beauregard, remarkably, wanted to do the same thing to his adversary, only in reverse. His mirror-image plan was to unleash the forces on the right side of his line to turn the Union's left flank. This was in spite of the curious fact that Beauregard fully expected that his West Point classmate Irvin McDowell was going to hit the Confederate left.[2] But instead of strengthening his forces there in expectation of a defensive fight, the Creole general's answer to the expected Union advance was to beat McDowell to the punch, and do it so effectively that the rest of McDowell's army would have no choice but to break off its own attack. Beauregard had already concentrated the bulk of his force in his center and on his right. Now he would swing them into action and, in his words, "by a rapid and vigorous attack on McDowell's left flank and rear at Centreville, rout him and cut off his retreat on Washington."[3] It was an audacious plan, forsaking defense for an aggressive offense. At 4:30 a.m. Beauregard handed his final combat order for approval to Johnston, the ranking officer in the field, who had not yet had time to learn the local terrain. Johnston signed it. All that remained was to give the order to advance.

Or so it must have seemed to Beauregard, peering into the cottony darkness across Bull Run in the early-morning hours. The scheme, as it unfurled, was a disaster. No advance was ever made, and the promised tactical movements never came close to happening. The entire elaborate pantomime is noteworthy mainly because it failed to provide any deterrent to McDowell's own maneuver, and because it is such a perfect example of the almost comical incompetence of Beauregard and his staff.

His problems began with the combat order itself, a muddled, contradictory, and occasionally nonsensical document, later famous as the single most confusing order of the war. It had set no time for the attack, confused brigades with divisions, invented two-brigade divisions where none existed, and implied that the army would be split into two corps, consisting of those nonexistent multibrigade divisions, each with its own corps commander. (The Confederate army had neither corps nor divisions, and would not have a two-corps structure until fourteen months later.) One of those mythical corps was to be commanded by General T. H. Holmes, though Holmes himself had not been informed of this assignment. There was also the problem of language. Many of the orders were blatantly contradictory. One dispatch to General D. R. Jones, for example, consisted of such atrocious grammar that, strictly interpreted, it actually instructed Jones *to attack his Confederate colleague Richard Ewell*. All of this was very bad warfare, but no one had done anything like it before and there was nothing to measure it against. The generals and their staffs simply blundered ahead, unchecked by anyone who might know better.[4]

Soon the reality of Union plans and Union guns collided with this somewhat dreamy world of things as Beauregard wished them to be. At 5:00 a.m. the Federals opened fire—nothing in earnest, mostly rolling volleys of musketry aimed at the far bank. But the attack rattled Beauregard, who now began issuing a new stream of orders to answer it. One of these went to Brigadier General Richard Ewell, on the far right of the line, who had originally been ordered to lead off the Confederate advance across Bull Run. Now Beauregard gave him an entirely new order, directing Ewell to prepare to "make a diversion against the enemy's intended attack on Mitchell's Ford and, probably, Stone Bridge."[5] This, of course, superseded the earlier orders for the attack on Centreville. For some reason—neglect or sheer staff incompetence—other generals were not told about those changes.

Beauregard was clearly losing his grip, and Johnston, a recent arrival who had been forced to defer to the Creole's knowledge of the troops and terrain, could do nothing about it. Bory began shifting his brigades to his left, creating even more confusion as couriers rode forth from headquarters with a stream of ever-changing orders. Jackson was one of the principal victims of this, receiving instructions to move in behind three different brigades.[6] At 8:00 a.m., while thunder from the Federal guns still rolled down the line, and musket fire rattled in the wooded areas at the Stone Bridge and at Mitchell's Ford, the indomitable Creole had one final inspiration: having strengthened his own left, he now decided that he would go ahead and mount his cherished offensive against Centreville and the Union left anyway. He got approval from Johnston, who must have had some sense of how crazy and chaotic the battle plan was becoming, then issued yet another string of orders directing brigades under Generals Ewell, D. R. Jones, Longstreet, and Milledge L. Bonham to move forward across Bull Run. It was in keeping with everything else that happened that morning that Richard Ewell, who was to lead the advance, never received this order. Longstreet, who had never received the second set of orders issued at 5:30, had crossed Bull Run in obedience of the original battle order, and sat there wondering what to do with himself.

Beauregard, meanwhile, waited for his decisive, Napoleonic counterstroke to commence. He was waiting, and watching, at about 9:00 a.m., listening nervously to the firing upstream of his position, when a courier arrived with a remarkable piece of news.

Edward Porter Alexander was a young man when the war started, but he had already had an exceptional career in the army. Born into a distinguished Georgia family, he had excelled at West Point, graduating third in his class in 1857, and in the late 1850s had helped develop a new signal system for the US Army. The system—sometimes called "wigwag"—consisted of flagmen waving flags or torches back and forth to create codes that represented letters of the alphabet.[7] Corpsmen would use field glasses to read the signals, write them down, and deliver them to officers in the field. When the Civil War started, Alexander resigned his commission in the US Army to fight for the Confederacy, and by this means both armies came to use the same signal system.

Alexander had been directed by General Beauregard to build a signal system that would improve communication within Confederate lines. The slender, bearded Alexander had thus built four stations, a task he had finished less than two weeks before the battle. The main one was erected a mile east of Manassas at Wilcoxen's Hill. Others were situated in Centreville, on a hill on Van Pelt's farm east of the Stone Bridge, and at Confederate headquarters at McLean House, behind the center-right part of the Bull Run line. On this still Sunday morning, Alexander's system was going to receive its first combat test.

For him it would be a day of extraordinary luck. That good fortune began in the early dawn. Of his four signal stations, Alexander preferred the vantage point of the station at Van Pelt's, where he had pitched his tent, so he was upset when Beauregard ordered him back to the station at Wilcoxen's Hill, miles in the rear. Unbeknownst to Alexander, as he packed his haversack with the day's rations and prepared to leave, a gargantuan Federal cannon with a greater range than any other Federal artillery piece that fired thirty-pound conical, rifled shells was being wheeled, by herculean effort, into place east of the Stone Bridge on the Warrenton Pike, where the Union was about to begin the demonstration that would cover its flank march. At about 6:00 a.m. the gun was loaded with a percussion shell (which would explode upon impact) and, to the great glee of the Federal cannoneers, who believed it was likely to scare the Confederates to death, trained on the most visible target, which happened to be the Van Pelt house, a mile and a half away on the other side of Bull Run. Seconds later, a lieutenant yelled, "Fire!" and the historic First Shot of the Battle of Manassas went whistling through the still dawn air, over the heads of the rebel troops defending the Stone Bridge, and scored a direct hit. This was so much fun that the Union gunners fired two more shots at the house, each coming to earth in the same vicinity, each with the same satisfying blast. One of those shells hit Alexander's tent, and would probably have killed him if he had not left just a few minutes before, in disgust, to obey the order he did not want to obey.[8]

The second piece of luck came several hours later, and was equally extraordinary. After arriving at the station at Wilcoxen's Hill, Alexander began to scan the other signal stations. He soon saw the flags wigwagging from the Van Pelt station, and focused his field glasses to receive the message. But as he did so something strange happened. Somewhere off in the lush, green distance several miles northwest of the Van Pelt house, he saw a "little flash of light . . . a faint gleam, indescribably quick."[9] Though the flash was gone in an instant, he knew immediately that he had seen something very specific, as he put it, "the reflection of the morning sun from a brass field piece." He had no doubt about what he had seen. But what could a cannon possibly be doing there? Curious, he ignored the wigwags from the Van Pelt house and focused his glass on the spot, fully eight miles away, where the glint of light had originated. Now he could see, in the gaps of the trees, not only cannons but "the glitter of bayonets," too. There were large numbers of soldiers moving up there, miles from where they were supposed to be. He realized that he was looking at a massive Federal flanking march, far beyond the end of the Confederate line at Stone Bridge, which was commanded by a hard-drinking colonel named Nathan "Shanks" Evans and his small force.

It was 8:45 a.m. Alexander immediately signaled to Evans via the Van Pelt house, saying simply, "Look out for your left. You are turned." He then wrote out a longer note for Beauregard, because the general was not near a signal station at the time. "I see a body of troops crossing Bull Run about two miles above the Stone Bridge," wrote young Alexander, deliberately containing his wild excitement.[10] "The head of the column is in the woods on this side. The rear of the column is in the woods on the other side. About half a mile of its length is visible in the open ground in between. I can see both infantry and artillery."[11]

It would seem impossible to conclude from this description—of a column so large that a half-mile-wide gap in the woods revealed only part of it—that an enormous Federal turning operation was *not* under way. Amazingly, both Johnston and Beauregard did just that. They decided that, though this flanking march was both surprising and worrisome, it was nothing that a few brigades, shifted upstream to the Stone Bridge, could not handle. They continued to wait hopefully near Mitchell's Ford for the rolls of gunfire from their downstream brigades that would signal the beginning of Beauregard's grand, war-ending advance on the Union left.

●   ●   ●

Brigadier General Thomas J. Jackson, camped with his brigade on a gentle slope about half a mile behind Mitchell's Ford, rose hours before sunrise on the morning of the battle, knelt in his tent, and prayed. He prayed every morning. But on this day, the Sabbath, a day when he normally refused to have anything to do with secular matters, even refusing to write or post mail, he had much to pray for. There was his wife, Anna, whose thirtieth birthday it was that very day, for whom God's blessing and protections were sought, as always. There were the many benedictions of Jackson's own life, which he never failed to give thanks for, most recently his promotion, which he believed had come from "our kind Heavenly Father" and would allow him, as he had written to Anna, "[the opportunity] of serving my country more efficiently."[12] Jackson, deep inside himself, was an ambitious man and he knew it; part of the purpose of prayer was to restrain such vanity.[13]

And then there was the looming fight. Though we do not know what Jackson said to God in his prayers that morning, his correspondence around that date reveals his frame of mind. It was clear, first of all, that he believed that the outcome of the battle rested entirely in the hands of the Almighty. Mortal men were merely His instruments, vehicles through which His will manifested itself in the world. Jackson believed, without the slightest doubt, that in his fight against an unholy invader whose object was the "degradation" of his homeland, God was with him and with the righteous Confederate cause.[14] In this belief he was not unlike many other generals in the world, before and after him. Jackson's God, moreover, was like the protective, paternal God of the 118th Psalm, the sixth and seventh verses of which read, "The Lord is on my side; I will not fear. What can man do unto me? The Lord is on my side as my helper; I shall look in triumph on those who hate me."[15] God and God alone would choose the hour of his death. Since his life was in God's hands, there was no reason to be afraid.

Jackson's brigade awoke at about 3:00 a.m., ate a hasty breakfast, and then fell into ranks in the warm, windless early-morning darkness. The soldiers had no idea what they were about to do, where they were to go, or what role they might have in someone's battle plan. The rank and file never did. Those problems were left to Old Jack and the high command. For five hours they did nothing but shuttle back and forth behind Bull Run, according to Beauregard's inexplicable impulses. They were impatient. They were hoping that they would be lucky enough to do some fighting before the war was over. Jackson, too, waited. A young artilleryman who had been assigned to his brigade found the general wearing a shabby gray coat and a cap pulled over his eyes, "half sitting and half lying against the trunk of a small pine tree. . . . He did not move as we approached. When we reported, only his lips moved with this brief and characteristic order. 'When the infantry moves, follow.' We had not long to wait."[16] At 9:30 they were ordered to march northwest to the Stone Bridge.

They would never get there. En route, Jackson learned from a courier that Confederate troops under a general from South Carolina named Barnard Bee were "hard-pressed" in a fight well to the west of the Stone Bridge. Jackson's men could already hear the noise of battle, which meant that, whatever else may have been happening, the true Confederate left was miles from where it was supposed to be. Acting without orders—there was no one around to issue any, and fighting west of the Stone Bridge was in no one's battle plans anyway—Jackson set the men on a brutally fast march. One artilleryman recalled that they were "running that distance like panting dogs with flopping tongues, with our mouths and throats full of the impalpable red dust of that red clay country, thirsting for water almost unto death."[17] As they approached the battlefield on a narrow woodland road, with the sounds of musket fire and artillery fire ringing in their ears, they beheld a sight that was both shocking and bewildering: large numbers of Confederate soldiers moving in the opposite direction, broken, bloody, and in full retreat. Their commands were all cut to pieces, the men told the wide-eyed Virginians. The day was lost.[18]

Soon the beleaguered General Bee appeared, and rode to meet Jackson at the head of the column. "General, they are driving us!" he said. The two men knew each other. They had attended West Point at the same time and had fought side by side in the Mexican-American War. Though it is impossible from this distance to know the tone of Jackson's reply or the expression on his face as he delivered it, his words would seem to speak for themselves. "Sir," he said to Bee, "we will give them the bayonet."

The men Jackson saw retreating through the woods were the end product of McDowell's massive flank march, a maneuver that had seemed for hours like a disaster in the making but had instead turned out to be a brilliant success. The marching itself had been horrific: more than eighteen thousand men, along with horses, wagons, caissons, and artillery, had hit the road at 2:00 a.m. and had marched ten miles in seven hours, much of it in darkness. Men who had had an hour of sleep or had not slept at all stumbled over logs and roots and into brambles and were stabbed by branches of trees they could not see. As on the seventeenth, the weird accordion-like action happened again, alternately forcing the men to run with full packs to catch up or to stand stock still breathing the hot dust, waiting for who knew what logjam in the road three miles ahead to be cleared up. In the lulls, some soldiers picked blackberries and even took naps. Heintzelman's whole division, which was supposed to cross at Poplar Ford, had gotten lost, and had ended up merely trailing behind Hunter, lengthening the line and worsening the stops and starts. There was rising heat and great thirst. "We scrambled along through the dense woods and thickets, the darkness so intense that, literally, you could not see your hand in front of your face," wrote one of the men who made the march. They were supposed to arrive in full force at Sudley Ford at 7:00 a.m. but actually arrived at 9:30 a.m., bone weary and so thirsty that when they arrived many fell on their faces in the muck of Bull Run, sucking in the filthy water.

McDowell had been greatly worried about the pace of his march. He knew, too, that when his troops arrived at Sudley Ford rebel columns were already moving toward him. But because his maneuver had not been detected until Porter Alexander saw the gleam of a Union cannon at 8:45, McDowell's men now faced only a small Confederate force, a few brigades under "Shanks" Evans and Barnard Bee, who, acting on Alexander's tip, had hustled, without orders, west from the banks of Bull Run. McDowell's tactic had worked splendidly: he had gotten there first with the most men. Now those men turned south, out onto the open ground of Matthews Hill, where they found South Carolina colonel Nathan "Shanks" Evans and nine hundred Confederates waiting for them.

Even among an officer corps conspicuous for its striking, flamboyant, and eccentric characters, Evans stood out. He got the nickname Shanks at West Point for having extremely skinny legs, though that name might have been the only thing that suggested any relationship with that elite educational institution. Evans, an odd-looking man with a high, wide forehead and penetrating light blue eyes, was crude, gruff, insubordinate, and profane. He was a braggart, too, especially when he was drinking, which was nearly all the time, an activity made possible by a Prussian orderly who followed him about, carrying a gallon jug of whiskey that Evans called his "barrelita."[19]

But Evans was also a fearless fighter. He had positioned his small force directly in front of the Federal advance, and soon the battle exploded along a quarter-mile front. For an hour he and his nine hundred Louisianans and South Carolinians battled numerically superior Federal forces to a standstill—an astonishing display of prowess for men who had never seen anything like this before, and had never before heard the sickening thuds produced when .58-caliber bullets slammed into human flesh and human bone. Guns blazed from both lines as deafening noise and banks of dirty white smoke filled the air. Men fell, screaming. Some tried to take cover behind rocks or trees, but there was little cover anywhere. It was mostly an open fight. Two full Union brigades—under Ambrose Burnside and Andrew Porter—were brought against Evans, and still Evans repulsed them, even ordering a charge against a weak point in the Federal line by his first Louisiana battalion, one of the more remarkable assemblages of soldiers in either army. They were an assortment of dockworkers, stevedores, wharf rats, "the lowest scum of the lower Mississippi," who wore red fezzes and blue striped pantaloons and, under the command of soldier of fortune Roberdeau Wheat, were some of the toughest fighters in the Confederacy. In the heat of the battle, some of Wheat's Tigers, as they were known, dropped their guns and charged with bowie knives. Burnside was convinced that he was facing six regiments of infantry instead of the barely two he was fighting.

But Evans could not hold his position much longer. Just as his men were falling back, a collection of Alabama, Georgia, and Mississippi regiments under the command of General Bee and Colonel Francis Bartow had arrived to reinforce him. Bee was the beau ideal of the Southern officer. Tall, strikingly handsome, and well dressed, he had been a mediocre and mischievous but highly popular cadet at West Point, and had compiled a glittering record in the Mexican-American and Seminole Wars. Bartow was a criminal lawyer from Savannah, Georgia, who had studied law at Yale. Like Evans, Bee and Bartow had moved to the fighting without orders, and now they brought 2,800 fresh troops to help Evans in his desperate fight on Matthews Hill, giving the rebels about 3,700 men north of the Warrenton Pike. Still, that was less than half of the forces immediately ranged against them. Amid what one of his men called "a perfect storm of shot and shell," Bee now threw his men against the long blue line in front of him. Withering fire erupted from both sides, and the Federals raked the thin rebel lines with their artillery. At one point, seeking to flank the enemy, the 7th and 8th Georgia Regiments occupied a thicket, which instead of offering cover soon became a "whirlwind of bullets," or, as one of them called it, "a place of slaughter." One company alone (usually 100 men) suffered 30 killed and wounded. The 8th Georgia suffered 200 casualties.

It was soon apparent that the scanty Southern lines could not hold. At about 11:30, Bee, Bartow, and Evans, taking staggering casualties, and surrounded by the enemy on three sides, retreated under heavy fire. As they were falling back "in great disorder and confusion as they had no field officers left to rally them,"[20] said one of them, a third small Confederate force arrived on the scene. This time it was a collection of six hundred South Carolinians known as Hampton's Legion, outfitted and commanded by Wade Hampton, yet another exotic: a handsome man with flowing mustaches and long hair and one of the wealthiest planters in the South, who had personally paid to outfit his men. Like Jackson, and Bee and Bartow before him, Hampton had been ordered to help Evans on the left, found that that particular "left" did not exist anymore, and had made a three-hour march to the sound of the fighting.[21] The legion, which alone battled the Federal advance for nearly an hour, finally had to retreat, too.

By noon the Federals had chased the last of the bleeding Confederates from Matthews Hill. The battle, which had lasted two hours, had been entirely the result of the initiative of a few rebel officers. The Confederate army's top commanders had had nothing to do with it. They had not ordered the troop movements, they had not understood that the battle was going to take place on Matthews Hill and nearby Henry Hill and not where they had thought it would take place. All responsibility had passed to the brigadiers and colonels. They had seized the battle, they had fought with astounding ferocity and courage, and they had not broken in spite of great odds but were ultimately forced to retreat. On the top of Matthews Hill now stood an enormous mass of Federal troops, guns glittering in the midday sun. If McDowell had desired a final payoff for his plan, this was it. The flank march had worked; the rebels were in headlong retreat down Matthews Hill and up again toward the farmhouses on Henry Hill. His plan to have Tyler's forces from the Stone Bridge join the attack had worked, too. The arrival of their vanguard, under their bright, aggressive commander, William Tecumseh Sherman, had helped put Bee, Bartow, and Evans to flight. McDowell needed only to throw a portion of his eighteen-thousand-man force forward, and the battle would soon be won. There was nothing to stop him. There was nothing of any military significance, in fact, between him and Manassas Junction. If he had thought hard about that, it meant that there was nothing much between his army and Richmond, either.

CHAPTER NINE

SCREAM OF THE FURIES

❧

What Jackson and his brigade saw, when they emerged from the woods onto the top of Henry Hill—an open, gently swelling patch of land containing two homesteads, some fruit trees, and a small cornfield—was nothing less than a full-blown military disaster. There was absolutely no doubt about that, as there often was in the confusion of a battle, no room for misinterpretation, no sign of Confederate troops rallying or Yankees withdrawing, no dressing of gray-clad ranks, no pockets of stubborn resistance, no rebel field artillery moving resolutely forward to blast the Federals from the opposite hill. General Bee had not been exaggerating when he told Jackson that the enemy was "driving" his men. The scene stretching out in front of them was one of complete, bloody chaos.

There was, moreover, no sign of any of the upper command anywhere, no evidence of Beauregard or Johnston or any of their staffs. There were just these few brave little brigades and pieces of brigades—Bee's, Bartow's, Evans's, Hampton's—that had broken off from Beauregard's line and without orders had taken on the advancing Union army. They had fought hard and even heroically, and had held off repeated, equally courageous Union assaults. But they had been greatly outnumbered and outgunned. "The wounded commenced passing us," recalled one of Jackson's soldiers, "some with blood streaming down their faces, some with legs broken and hobbling along assisted by a comrade, and some seriously wounded and borne on stretchers."[1] Jackson's former VMI student Charles Copland White wrote, "As we approach the battleground we meet men straggling off. . . . They tell us that the enemy is in overwhelming numbers and that our men are in full retreat. . . . Now the shells pass over us with their strange hissing sound . . . exploding in the thickets and cutting the limbs off trees."[2]

The scene was shocking, too, in its stark simplicity. In their immediate front, Jackson's men could see what was left of the Confederate forces, either streaming toward the rear or wandering forlornly, often officerless, around the two farmhouses atop Henry Hill. At the same time, the Virginians could look a mere mile across open fields to Matthews Hill and Dogan's Ridge to see the heart-stopping reason why: an enormous blue mass of soldiers, "thick as wheat in the field," their bayonets flashing like silver in the noonday sun, their splendid batteries throwing flame and firing round after thunderous round—which were weirdly visible to the naked eye—at the retreating men.[3] Having driven their enemies from the hill, the Federals now appeared to be massing for another assault that would drive them clear back to Manassas Junction.[4] There was nothing to stop them. That would have been the assumption of anyone who saw the field of battle at noon. That is why what happened next was so remarkable.

Jackson's reaction to the alarm in Bee's voice said everything about his approach to the crisis. If McDowell's splendidly equipped legions were cutting everyone and everything in their path to pieces, Jackson would simply *give them the bayonet*. The notion was quaintly old-fashioned—Napoleonic, in fact—though the point of it was clear: a bayonet was an intimate and intensely personal way to kill someone. Jackson meant business. His first concern was not whether he should retreat along with the others, or how he could get Johnston or Beauregard to send him reinforcements, or how 2,600 men with a few cannons were going to stop the Federal juggernaut that had just driven more than 4,000 men from the field. His reaction was instinctive: Fight. Fight now. Hold the line.

Jackson, riding at the head of his column, which extended, four abreast, into the woods behind him, now met another distressed Confederate officer. This was John D. Imboden, a lawyer from Staunton, Virginia, who, from his position on the slope in front of Henry Hill, had waged a remarkably brave, one-battery duel with four small six-pounder guns against the assembled Federal artillery. But his three remaining guns were almost out of ammunition and many of his horses had been killed, so he, too, was retreating. Imboden, less scared than furious at General Bee for having left him alone for so long on Henry Hill, gave Jackson a bitter, invective-laced account of what had just happened. (Bee had actually ordered him to withdraw forty-five minutes before, but the messenger had died en route to him.[5]) Jackson seemed, oddly, more distressed by Imboden's choice of vocabulary than by the Federal shells crashing around him. Imboden recalled, "I expressed myself with some profanity, which I could see was displeasing to Jackson." Jackson then told him, "Unlimber right here. I'll support your battery."[6] (A "limber" was a two-wheeled, horse-drawn wagon to which a cannon was attached for transport, and also carried ammunition. "Unlimbering" meant detaching the cannon for action; a Civil War battery was a large operation, usually consisting of four to six cannons, each of which was drawn by six horses, and accompanied by as many as six ammunition wagons—"caissons"—also drawn by six horses each, plus several other supply wagons. A single battery might thus include a hundred men and seventy-two or more horses.) Imboden protested that he had only three rounds left and suggested that he move to the rear to resupply. But Jackson, anticipating the swarm of bluecoats that was likely to be coming at him, and having no artillery yet in front, wanted at least the appearance of firepower. "No, not now," he told Imboden. "Wait til the other guns get here, and then you can withdraw your battery."[7]

Jackson now selected his defensive position. What he chose, quickly and under heavy artillery fire, was deeply unorthodox. Almost any other general would have made the textbook move forward to the northern edge of Henry Hill, the nominal "high ground" from which his guns and infantry would have looked down the slope to the Warrenton Pike, across which the Union soldiers would have to come. But Jackson instead chose the far southeastern edge of the plateau—the *reverse* slope—to place his infantry and artillery. As would soon become apparent, it was a brilliant tactical ploy. First, though the top of Henry Hill was largely an open field, this side of it was thick with pine trees. Jackson's men could set up there, unseen by the Federals with their deadly rifled guns on Matthews Hill. There were also trees to give the Virginians at least some protection from artillery fire. Even better, Jackson's own cannons would be able to roll forward over the lip of the hill, fire, then be carried back to safety by the recoil onto the downward slope, making them hard to see, too. Finally, this position offered Jackson a wide and largely unobstructed field of fire. Union troops cresting the northern side of Henry Hill would now have to cross three hundred murderous yards of open ground to get to him.

With his plan in mind, Jackson now went to work. Roving back and forth on horseback while enemy shells filled the air around him with lead and iron, he brought his artillery forward and carefully packed the woods in his center and on both flanks with his five regiments: the 2nd, 4th, 5th, 27th, and 33rd of Virginia. As he was doing this, Beauregard and Johnston—having at length concluded that the battle was not where they thought it was going to be, and that Ewell was never going to advance— finally arrived at the scene of the real fight. They took charge immediately. (Johnston would soon agree to Beauregard's request to give him command of the battlefield, while Johnston assumed overall command from a farmhouse in the rear of Henry Hill.) They immediately saw the logic of Jackson's unusual position, and moved to reinforce him.[8] Jackson's brigade was suddenly the center of the entire Confederate army, the very heart of the battle. Beauregard would build his new strategy around Jackson. One of the first things he did was give Jackson more guns. Now there were at least thirteen guns at the edge of the woods, all under his command. The fight for Henry Hill—and the hopes of the Confederacy—would pivot for the next few hours around Jackson's 1st Virginia Brigade.

By about 1:00 p.m. the new line was in place, stretching for a quarter of a mile across the top of Henry Hill, fronted by those guns. Most of the men were on their bellies in the woods, lying "flat as flounders," recalled the 4th Virginia's John Lyle, as the Federal guns continued to boom from the far hill.[9] Jackson, presenting a large and inviting target on horseback, seemed relaxed, unworried, almost unnaturally calm. "General Jackson rides several times along where we are lying and often goes over to the artillery," wrote one of his men. "He seems to be very quiet, so we think that all is right, and that this is like battles generally."[10] Beauregard and Johnston went to work trying to patch together the scattered, disorganized, and demoralized Confederate brigades that sagged four hundred or more yards behind Jackson's right. It was difficult work. "Every segment of line we succeeded in forming was again dissolved, while another was being formed," wrote Beauregard, who for a change was making himself useful. "More than two thousand men were each shouting some suggestion to his neighbor."[11]

Where was Union commanding general Irvin McDowell while the Confederates, outnumbered and threatened with destruction, were feverishly trying to patch up their lines? The answer was that he was making his first big mistake of the war. He didn't see it that way. He was, at that moment, quite pleased with his situation, which looked to him very much like imminent victory. Though his flanking scheme had started badly, he had

surprised and then routed the enemy. Burnside's brigade had been bloodied, but McDowell still had the better part of eighteen thousand men on
the hill. Before him he saw a rebel army in chaos, confusion, and retreat.
Whatever force might be up there on Henry Hill—there was none that he
could see—would be no match for the sort of firepower and infantry he
had in place. But now, for some unknown reason, perhaps because he was
momentarily stunned by his own success, or because he believed that, with
such an astounding advantage in men and matériel, speed was no longer of
the essence, McDowell paused. For two full hours, no orders came from his
headquarters. It was as though, suddenly, there was no particular plan of
battle, and no one running the army, which suddenly found itself standing
about, awaiting orders.

McDowell's strange entr'acte had been a miraculous gift to the beleaguered Confederates, and they had used it well. But it would not last. At
2:30, the Union army finally started moving. Like the old Napoleonic
armies, it came with its field artillery out in front. Their attack began when
two batteries with eleven guns crested the northwestern side of Henry Hill,
a mere three hundred yards from Jackson's line, unlimbered, and opened
fire. In artillery terms, three hundred yards is virtually point-blank range.
Jackson's guns now roared to life, too, and thus began a furious hour-
long duel between Jackson, who at VMI had been one of the first to test
and recommend for adoption the rifled Parrott guns now aimed at him,
and the Union batteries commanded by Captains James B. Ricketts and
Charles Griffin. For Jackson's men, who had already had shells lobbed at
them for more than an hour by the more distant guns, it was a harrowing
experience. A storm of ordnance now flew at them, not just solid shot but
also antipersonnel projectiles such as "shell," which exploded into shrapnel, and "spherical case," which was hollow and loaded with smaller balls
that sprayed in all directions. Tedford Barclay of the 4th Virginia Regiment described what happened to his regimental mates: "William Patterson shot . . . with a cannonball through his breast killing him instantly. Ben
Brady, struck on the right hip with a piece of bomb shell, he lived for five
or six minutes. Charlie Bell was killed with a piece of the same bomb, lived
about two hours, his whole right shoulder was torn off."[12]

Jackson continued to ride up and down his line on Little Sorrel, who
was as unperturbed by gunfire as he was, repeating, "Steady, men, steady.
All is well." He moved, according to one admiring soldier, "in a shower of
death as calmly as a farmer about his farm when the seasons are good." He

seemed to be a different man in the heat of battle; his eyes blazed, his whole being seemed to glow with the ardor of the fight. One soldier in the 33rd Virginia recalled that former VMI cadets, observing the cool confidence of their commander, now "saw the warrior and forgot the eccentric man."[13] At one point, as shells exploded in fragments that embedded themselves in trees, men, and horses, Jackson, speaking with Imboden, had thrust his left hand into the air—a characteristic gesture that seemed to accompany prayer. According to Imboden, "as he spoke, he jerked down his hand, and I saw that blood was streaming from it. I exclaimed, 'General, you are wounded.' 'Only a scratch, a mere scratch,' Jackson replied, and binding it hastily with a handkerchief, he galloped away along his line."[14]

Though Jackson was clearly getting the better of the Union in his artillery duel—at short range the Federals' technologically superior rifled cannons lost their advantage over the old-fashioned Confederate smoothbores—he was worried about his flanks. At 12:30 he had repulsed a brief attack on his right by a Union brigade that had come upon the field by way of the Stone Bridge. Now he split Jeb Stuart's 300 cavalry and deployed them to his right and left, looking for advancing Union columns. They did not have to wait long. A courier from Stuart told Jackson of Union infantry moving on his left, to which Jackson, his eyes lighting up, replied, "Good! Good!" As he had intended, the enemy had not seen his men in the woods. The Federals heard the crack of rebel muskets, and soon a sharp fight was raging on his left between his 33rd Virginia Regiment and two Union regiments. (The Federals had initially mistaken Confederates for their own, which made this somewhat worse for them.) The Virginians loosed successive volleys and drove the Federals back. As they were reeling down the hill toward the Sudley Road, Jeb Stuart and 150 horsemen, who had been itching for a fight all day, now slammed into them, driving them from the field with heavy casualties. One of Stuart's horsemen described the killing of a Union soldier, a brutal act unimaginable the day before but already commonplace on this battlefield. "I leaned down in the saddle," he wrote, "rammed the muzzle of [my] carbine into the stomach of my man and pulled the trigger. I could not help feeling a little sorry for the fellow as he lifted his handsome face to mine while he tried to get his bayonet up to meet me; but he was too slow, for the carbine blew a hole as big as my arm clear through him."[15]

But the Federals weren't finished. They advanced again on the 33rd Virginia, this time with two howitzers they placed less than two hundred yards from the Confederate line. Alarmed by the Federal guns that were almost on top of his soldiers, regimental commander Colonel A. C. Cummings ordered a volley that cut down men and horses. Then his Virginians charged across the open ground. Before anyone knew quite what had happened, the whooping rebels had seized the Union battery. It was the first Confederate victory of the day. Cheers went up as the members of the 33rd, many of them merely boys just a month or two from the plow handle and mechanic's shop, exulted. They would not be able to hold this position long. But what they had done would become, in fact, the turning point of the battle, the instant when that great and apparently irresistible blue-clad wave finally hit an immovable wall. Jackson had thus repulsed attacks on his right and left, and his artillery had been devastating against the larger, rifled Union guns. And most of his men had yet to fight; they were still in the woods, invisible, flat on their bellies, impatient and a bit shell-shocked, waiting to attack.

It was at about this time that Barnard Bee, who had been busy since his retreat trying to locate what remained of his brigade, finally came upon the 4th Alabama, wounded, exhausted from their morning fight, and resting in the woods five hundred yards behind the storm of artillery and musket fire along Jackson's line. He did not recognize them at first. He rode up and asked, "What regiment is this?" Informed that the men were his own, he replied, "This is all of my brigade that I can find. Will you follow me back to where the fighting is going on?" The men—one hundred of them—responded with a resounding yes. Now Bee pointed to his left, up the slope toward the pine woods on the edge of Henry Hill. "Yonder stands Jackson like a stone wall," he said. "Let's go to his assistance."[16]

At the time, his statement, overheard by four witnesses, probably sounded like an inspiring bit of metaphorical language, something to help spur the men into the fight. But Bee's words would become one of the most famous utterances of the war, noteworthy both because they gave birth to a name and a legend, and because they were among the last words ever spoken by the dashing warrior from South Carolina, one of the battle's greatest heroes, who at that moment had less than an hour to live.

Now the battle changed. Up to this point it had been largely an artillery duel, but the charge by Jackson's Virginians and their seizure of Griffin's guns marked the start of a more personal struggle. This time it would be infantry against infantry, regiment against regiment, man against man. It began when the 14th New York, a regiment from Brooklyn wearing red trousers and red kepis, trained a murderous fire on Cummings's 33rd Virginia, which retreated from its captured guns under fire, losing an astonishing third of its men. Suddenly, after their great success, the troops on Jackson's left were collapsing. The emboldened New Yorkers, scenting victory, now came straight on against the Confederate's center—the 4th and 27th Regiments—who had been on their bellies in the woods for several hours. The usually reserved Jackson was all animation now, eyes alight, face glowing with the heat of battle, moving along his line, telling his men, "Reserve your fire until they come within 50 yards, then fire and give them the bayonet, and when you charge, yell like Furies."

The New Yorkers moved forward, and Jackson's men did what they were told, waiting, then opening on the enemy with a furious volley of canister and bullets. (Canister consisted of tin cylinders filled with iron shot that, when fired from a cannon, created the effect of a sawed-off shotgun and was extremely destructive to human beings at up to 250 yards.[17]) The Federals were driven back; they regrouped, came on again, and were repulsed yet again by rolling volleys of canister and lead. Undeterred, and acting more like veterans than the green troops they were, they attacked a third time, many of them this time coming within a few yards of Jackson's line in a loud and savagely close fight. They paid for it. At such short range, the Virginians cut them to pieces. The Yankee battle line faltered, stood as though frozen for a moment in the swirling eddies of smoke, and then broke.

Now Jackson prepared to charge. He ordered his artillery from the field—to clear the way for the infantry—then rode over to the commander of the 4th Virginia Regiment, Colonel James Preston. "Order the men to stand up," he said. "We'll charge them now and drive them to Washington!" Obeying their orders and screaming like whatever they conceived the Furies to be, Jackson's Virginians swept straight out of the woods, toward the retreating enemy, and toward those lethal Federal batteries on the far edge of Henry Hill. The peculiar, piercingly loud noise the advancing men made was something neither rebel nor Union troops had heard before, and whose exact inspiration is unknown. It was the implausible result of each man giving a sequence of three sounds that registered somewhere between the screech of a bird and the bark of a fox: a short, high-pitched yelp, followed by a short, lower-pitched bark, followed by a long, high-pitched yelp. Collectively, the noise sounded feral, unearthly, and inhuman, like an ululation from the pit of hell. It would become the stuff of Union nightmares throughout the war. As one Federal soldier put it: "There is nothing like it on this side of the infernal region. The peculiar corkscrew sensation that it sends down your backbone . . . can never be told."[18] The practice would spread through the entire Confederate army and it would soon have a name: the *rebel yell*.[19]

On came Jackson's Confederates across Henry Hill, toward Henry House and the two Federal batteries, where the remaining Union men maneuvered around dead and dying horses and fired canister that tore through the Confederate ranks. Still, Jackson's men came on, bravely crossing three hundred yards of open ground with all that flying death in the air around them. There had been nothing in their lives before to prepare these young men for this, for the astounding sense of pure vulnerability of so much soft human flesh in the presence of so much buzzing lead and iron. Some were scared and expected to die; others, like gunner William Thomas Poague, described a strangely calm feeling that might have been something like what Jackson himself experienced in battle. "This was a most novel sensation," he wrote later, "hard to describe, a sort of warm, pleasing glow enveloping the chest and head with an effect something like entrancing music in a dream. [But] my observing, thinking, and reasoning faculties were normal."[20] The time was about 3:30.

Jackson's two regiments drove forward, "piercing the enemy's center," in Beauregard's words, and capturing the Federal guns. "The charge of Jackson's men was terrific," wrote Private John Casler of the 33rd Virginia. "The enemy were swept before them like chaff before a whirlwind. . . . The men seemed to have caught the dauntless spirit and determined will of their heroic commander."[21] More Confederate troops were now on the field, having been ordered forward by Beauregard, and suddenly, as he observed, "the whole of the open surface of the plateau was swept clear of federals."[22]

But nothing was settled. As dramatic as it had been, Jackson's charge was only the beginning of a bitter fight for possession of those two Federal batteries, which would change hands at least three times as the battle surged forward and backward across the top of the hill. For whatever reason, these new troops on both sides fought fearlessly and stubbornly and went down in staggering numbers. Colonel Francis Bartow, one of the heroes of the morning, was shot dead. Barnard Bee was mortally wounded. Jackson, on a horse that was limping due to a leg wound, was holding his wounded hand aloft, his military tunic torn at the edges by several bullet holes. His five regiments were at the battle's white-hot center for the next hour and took by far the heaviest casualties of any brigade.

At the end of the third successful Federal surge forward—their battle line just at that moment was "gigantic in proportions, crescent-like in form," wrote one observer—it seemed that the Union boys had finally cleared the plateau and had won the battle.[23] McDowell certainly thought so. He wired Washington to that effect. "It was supposed by us that the repulse was final," McDowell wrote later in his official report of the battle, "for [the enemy] was driven entirely from the hill, so far beyond it as to be not in sight, and all were certain the day was ours. . . . The enemy was evidently disheartened and broken."[24]

He was desperately wrong. Though he did not know it, he was about to pay one final time for his earlier, two-hour delay. Suddenly it was McDowell's army—which had started the day with a brutal march and was now exhausted, thirsty, and out of ranks in large numbers—that was in trouble. His midday lapse—plus the heroism and hard-nosed fighting of brigades such as Evans's, Bee's, and Jackson's—had bought Johnston and Beauregard time, and time had brought them reinforcements both from their old Bull Run line and from Johnston's arriving Army of the Shenandoah. New, fresh Virginia regiments now collided with the Federals at the Henry House, driving several surprised New York regiments off the hill. Suddenly the Union boys, who had exulted in their victory a few moments before, were in full retreat. After two hours of brutal fighting, the Confederates held the precious hill again. The scene was horrific: the ground was thick with dead and dying men and horses, the wreckages of wagons and cannons and of the house where old Mrs. Henry had been killed that day by an artillery shell. But the hill was theirs.

Now, with astounding speed, Federal elation gave way to despair. McDowell, understanding that Henry Hill was lost, launched a final attack from a long rise just to the west called Chinn Ridge, trying yet again to turn the Confederate left flank. But as he was preparing his attack two more fresh brigades from Johnston's army, commanded by Jubal Early and Arnold Elzey, crashed into the Federal right, surprising those troops and sending them staggering backward. Union commanders tried to rally them but soon saw that it was hopeless. McDowell ordered them to withdraw. The retreat began in an orderly fashion. But a retreat, as it turned out, required as much skill and precision as an attack. And because these men had no experience of what it was like to retire before a victorious enemy, the retreat soon became a rout, and the rout a full-scale panic. Soldiers by the thousands now merged into an unruly, terrified, disorganized mob several hundred yards wide and several miles long whose single thought was to flee to the safety of Washington, DC. They reeled across the same

Bull Run fords they had crossed earlier in the day. They left behind them their provisions, overcoats, knapsacks, blankets, muskets, canteens, and cartridge boxes.

There was a slightly surreal cast to this chaos. Many civilians from Washington, including socialites and politicians and people who wanted to see the rebels receive a good whipping, had ridden out with picnic baskets and blankets to see the battle. They were now subsumed into—or trampled by—the wild, panicked mob. Some of the onlookers tried to get the fleeing soldiers to change their minds. "We called to [the soldiers]," recalled one US congressman, "tried to tell them there was no danger, called them to stop, implored them to stand. We called them cowards, denounced them in the most offensive terms, put out our heavy revolvers, and threatened to shoot them, but all in vain; a cruel, crazy, mad, hopeless panic possessed them."[25]

Jackson, meanwhile, had gone to a field station to have his wounded hand dressed. The first surgeon to see it told Jackson that the finger would have to be amputated. But Jackson received a second opinion from his young medical officer Hunter McGuire, who thought it could be saved. While McGuire was dressing the wound in a tent full of wounded men, President Jefferson Davis rode up, his face stern and deeply unhappy and pale as death. He had just arrived on the battlefield, and had been told by Confederate stragglers far in the rear of the terrible Southern defeat. He had believed every word of it, and was now a knot of despair, disappointment, and rage. According to McGuire, "he stood up in his stirrups . . . and cried to the crowd of soldiers: 'I am President Davis! Follow me back to the field!'" Jackson had not heard him say this, but when McGuire told him, he stood up, took off his cap, and said loudly, omitting all honorifics, "We have whipped them. They ran like sheep. Give me 10,000 men and I will take Washington tomorrow!"[26]

The magnitude of the victory soon became apparent to everyone, including Davis, who reluctantly allowed the men to wrap him in Confederate flags. Cheers rang through miles of Confederate soldiers, all the way back to Longstreet's troops at Blackburn's Ford, who had missed the entire show. The men were wild with excitement. As one wrote, it "passed all bounds, it approached madness. Every man of the thousands assembled threw their caps in the air, officers and all." Some of them even believed, as they stood amid the wreckage on Henry Hill, that this was the end of the war.

PART TWO

THE MAN
WITHIN THE MAN

CHAPTER TEN

GLORY AND DARKNESS

❦

The people of the Confederacy had fully expected a splendid victory. They had been quite certain that a Southern boy could whip several times his weight in cowardly Yankees, and they had been proven right. They had believed that, faced with Confederate resolve and Confederate gumption, the Federals would turn and run like scalded dogs, and the Northern boys had given them the truly immense satisfaction of doing precisely that. The Southern press was exultant. "The breakdown of the Yankee race, their unfitness for empire," gloated the *Richmond Whig*, "forces dominion on the South. We are compelled to take the sceptre of power." The editor of the *Louisville Courier-Journal* was more contemptuous still. The Northern war effort would not last much longer, he said, because the Yankees, who were "dastards in fight, and incapable of self-government," would "inevitably fall under the control of a superior race. A few more Bull Run thrashings will bring them under the yoke."[1] Political leader Thomas Cobb of Georgia deemed Manassas "one of the decisive battles of the world" and insisted that "it has secured our independence."[2] The triumph at Manassas seemed, quite literally, to be a dream come true.

Except that it really wasn't at all. Those dreams of glory had not allowed for the bloodiest day in American history, in which green troops, Federals included, fought and stood fire with an unexpected fury; they had not counted on the sheer destructive power of the weapons and the hideous, disfiguring things they did to young men, the cruel agonies of death they inflicted. Confederates lost 400 killed and 1,600 wounded, of whom 225 would later die of their wounds. Union losses were 625 killed and mortally wounded, 950 nonmortally wounded, and more than 1,200 captured.[3]

Jackson's brigade had taken the worst losses of all: 119 killed and 442 wounded. What had taken place was, by any previous reckoning in American history, a slaughter. And in spite of the crowing in the press, the South seemed to grasp that its triumph was also a tragedy. Though crowds massed in the streets of Richmond, there were no wild celebrations, no bonfires, no cannonades, and bells were silent in the steeples until the next day, when they summoned worshippers to prayer. In Savannah, Georgia, the gatherings had a similarly melancholy cast. "Our city is filled with mingled exultation and sorrow at the news of the recent triumph," wrote one resident. "Colonel Bartow and some of our best young men have fallen, and our city is filled with mourning."[4] Victory was also tempered by stark military reality: the exhausted, disorganized Confederate army was in no position after the battle to pursue its quarry into Washington to deliver a final blow.

In the North, reactions ranged from despair to visions of the Apocalypse descending. "Today will be known as Black Monday," wrote one New Yorker. "We are utterly and disgracefully routed, beaten, whipped." Horace Greeley, editor of the *New York Tribune* and one of the biggest boosters of an early invasion of the South, could scarcely conceal his gloom. "On every brow sits sullen, scorching, black despair," he wrote to Lincoln, in a suddenly defeatist mood. "If it is best for the country and for mankind that we make peace with the rebels, and on their own terms, do not shrink even from that."[5]

The disaster had seemed worse because of the fatuous overconfidence that preceded it. McDowell had been convinced at noon that he had the battle won, and he believed it again at about 3:30, when his men had seemingly cleared Henry Hill of Confederates. Back in Washington, Winfield Scott had spoken buoyantly of success, and had gone to church at eleven. When Lincoln in midafternoon received a wire saying that the Union seemed to be losing, he went to see Scott and found him asleep. Roused, Scott explained to the president that the fog of battle was often misleading and that he shouldn't worry. When the picture brightened, with wires from McDowell's headquarters saying he had "driven the enemy before him," Lincoln went for a ride. At 6:00 p.m. an ashen William Seward finally delivered the news. "The battle is lost," he said. "The telegraph says that McDowell is in full retreat, and calls on General Scott to save the capital." Presumably Scott was fully awake by that time.

Northern newspapers had been brimful of that same arrogance and presumption, often—and bizarrely—sticking with it into the following days. On July 22, readers of the *New York Times* were presented with a breathless and, in retrospect, comically inaccurate story of the Union victory. "After a battle of unparalleled severity," read the editorial, solemn and gloating, "in which our soldiers fought against great odds . . . they have come off more than conquerors—not only driving the enemy from their formidable positions, but seizing all their guns and equipments. . . . The glorious flag that flew at Sumter is now fully avenged."[6] What had taken place was not just a victory, according to the *Times*; it was also a total devastation of the Southern army. One can only wonder how many Northern hearts leaped when they read it.

But the North's agonies of despair were not really what they seemed, either. The first lesson of Bull Run was that, bad as it was, it was not the foretold Armageddon. There was no final settling of accounts. The Union army was battered and demoralized, but it still existed, and until the moment panic seized them, most of its soldiers had fought hard and well. Northern advantages in wealth, population, and industrial capacity were all just as they were. Washington was safe. And it soon became clear that the battle's ultimate effect would be to strengthen Northern resolve, not weaken it, as the initial shock and distress shifted quickly into a grim new determination. The day after the battle, President Lincoln signed a bill for the enlistment of 500,000 three-year volunteers, and three days later signed another for 500,000 more. The public response in the North was immediate and enthusiastic; new recruits jammed Union recruiting offices. Even more important, for the future of the war, Lincoln had found someone to lead these new men. At 2:00 a.m. on the morning after the battle, he sent a telegram to the dynamic thirty-four-year-old Major General George Brinton McClellan, fresh from his victories in western Virginia, ordering him to take command of the new volunteers, who would soon be gathered into an entity called the Army of the Potomac. McClellan happened to be Jackson's classmate at West Point and his opposite in almost every conceivable way. He was coming to Washington, as he and many other people in the North saw it, as the savior of the Union.

For the South, the unquestioned Confederate heroes of the Battle of Manassas were Pierre G. T. Beauregard and Joseph E. Johnston, in that order. Bory, hero of Sumter, got most of the credit. He really deserved very little of it. It is true that, once he had figured out that his great advance on Centreville was not going to take place, and once he had understood, at length, what young Porter Alexander had instantly realized from seeing the flash of a distant gun barrel, he moved expeditiously to the scene of the battle. And it is true that he did a reasonably good job of helping establish the Confederate line around Jackson's Virginia regiments, playing the role of dime-store general, riding up and down the lines, exhorting the men, leading a charge here and there, and generally offering a good example to green troops. But he had very little tactical effect on the battle itself.

None of that seemed to matter. For now the main story, and the one the press was running with, was that he had stayed at the front in the heat of battle and rallied the troops and had ordered charges at the right time. As the hero of the war's first engagement, at Fort Sumter, enormous expectations had been loaded onto him and he had, almost miraculously, lived up to them. No one knew anything yet of his astounding errors of command that morning, or of the wildly impractical if not outright crazy battle plans he had proposed in the preceding week. No one suspected that his victory rested substantially on the shoulders of subordinates acting without orders. Those annoying facts would surface soon enough. For the moment he was, again, the confirmed hero of the South.

Joe Johnston, meanwhile, actually deserved some of the laurels he received. He had gracefully agreed to retire to the rear, behind the lines and away from the fight, but from there exercised a large and telling influence on what eventually happened, calling up regiments and brigades, organizing them, and hustling them to the front. It was those replacements, inserted into Henry Hill and Chinn Ridge, that had finally made the difference. The other great public heroes of the battle were the martyred Barnard Bee and Francis Bartow. That week their bodies lay in state in Richmond with an honor guard, while lines of mourners filed by.[7]

Then there was Jackson. Though he had contributed as much or more to the Southern victory as Bee, Bartow, Evans, Hampton, or Early—and arguably had done more than either Beauregard or Johnston—recognition in the general public of what he had done came slowly. This was not due to neglect by his commanding officers. Johnston had forthrightly praised his "high, soldierly qualities" and his "admirable conduct" and given him large credit for reestablishing order on Henry Hill. Beauregard, in his official report, lauded the astuteness of the defensive position Jackson had chosen, praised his brigade's charge across the plateau, and said, "The conduct of General Jackson also requires mention as eminently that of an able, fearless soldier and sagacious commander, one fit to lead his efficient brigade. His prompt, timely arrival before the plateau of Henry House, and his judicious disposition of his troops, contributed much to the success of the day."[8] This was solid, if not rapturous, praise, and took its place in Beauregard's lengthy report detailing much praiseworthy officer conduct.[9] Still, such a commendation tended to stay where it was—inside the official army reports of the battle.

Jackson, meanwhile, ever modest and self-effacing in public, had experienced the battle from its blazing center and knew precisely what he and his brigade had done. In a letter to his old friend Jonathan Bennett, he wrote that "my brigade passed our retreating forces, met the thus far victorious enemy, held him in check until reinforcements arrived, and finally pierced his centre, and thus gave a fatal blow," and compared them to Napoléon's Imperial Guard. God gets credit, as usual, but pride, ambition, and a desire for recognition permeate his words, up to and including the exaggerated idea that his men delivered the fatal blow. They did not.

This tension—describing his personal achievement in a desperate fight while simultaneously denying that he had anything to do with it—persists in a letter Jackson wrote to his wife, Anna, the day after the battle:

> *My Precious Pet—Yesterday we fought a great battle and gained a great victory, for which all the glory is due to God alone. Although under a heavy fire for several continuous hours, I received only one wound, the breaking of the longest finger of my left hand. . . . My horse was wounded, but not killed. Your coat got an ugly wound near the hip, but my servant, who is very handy, has so far repaired it that it doesn't show very much. . . . The battle was the hardest I have ever been in, but not near so hot in its fire. I commanded in the centre more particularly, though one of my regiments extended to the right for some distance. There were other commanders on my right and left. Whilst great credit is due to other parts of our gallant army, God made my brigade more instrumental than any other in repulsing the main attack. This is for your information only— say nothing about it. Let others speak praise, not myself.*[10]

The problem was there were no others, just at that time, speaking any praise. Almost all commendations in Southern newspapers went to Beauregard, Bee, Bartow, and various South Carolina, Alabama, and Louisiana regiments. The Richmond papers—enormously influential in molding Southern opinion since their articles were reprinted everywhere—did not mention Jackson's role in the battle for an entire week. Then it was to report that he had had his finger blown off (untrue) and a horse shot from under him (untrue) but had remained "cool as a cucumber." So complete was the silence that, by the first week in August, Anna was upset over what appeared to be the total neglect of her husband's accomplishment. On August 5, Jackson, who was transparently sensitive to all this, wrote to calm her down: "And so you think the papers ought to say more about your husband! My brigade is not a brigade of newspaper correspondents. . . . It is not to be expected that I should receive the credit that Generals Beauregard and Johnston would, because I was under them; but I am thankful to my ever-kind Heavenly Father that He makes me content to await His own good time and pleasure for commendation."[11] Meaning, presumably, that he fully expected that "commendation" to come.

Unbeknownst to Jackson or Anna, however, his fame, or the first intimation of his fame, was already quietly spreading throughout the South. Within three days of the battle, the story of Bee exhorting his troops was already being told privately in Richmond among relatives and friends of soldiers. Confederate diarist Mary Chestnut, a bellwether of sentiment in Richmond and a private clearinghouse of information, wrote in her entry of July 24 that her husband "took the orders to Colonel Jackson, whose regiment stood so stock still under fire that they were called a 'stone wall.'"[12] This suggested that the story, too, was making its way through the army, where in many quarters there was already a clear sense of what Jackson and his men had done. Then, on July 25, the *Charleston Mercury*, another highly influential wartime newspaper from South Carolina, published its version of the Bee/Jackson exchange, rendering it as follows:

> He rode up to General Jackson and said, "General, they are beating us back."
>
> The reply was, "Sir, we'll give them the bayonet."
>
> General Bee immediately rallied the remnant of his brigade, and his last words to them were: "There is Jackson standing like a stone wall. Let us determine to die here, and we will conquer. Follow me."
>
> His men obeyed the call; and, at the head of his column, the very moment when the battle was turning in our favor he fell, mortally wounded.[13]

Though the sequence of events was completely wrong, as was the case in all early accounts and most later histories—Bee's warning to Jackson that he was being driven was uttered *at least three hours* before his "stone wall" comment—no one knew that or cared to know it, because the moment, as presented, was so perfectly dramatic. The star of the story, of course, was Bee, the hometown hero, the man who had stood against the Federal hordes on Matthews Hill. But it had the side effect of placing Jackson's name, in an equally heroic context, before large numbers of newspaper readers in the South. On July 29 the *Richmond Dispatch* published the story; on August 15 the *Lexington Gazette* in Jackson's hometown ran it. With these notices, public curiosity about Jackson started to grow. It is noteworthy that as the nickname began to attach itself to him, it also attached itself to his brigade. Soon enough, Thomas J. Jackson would be Stonewall to everyone in the South and eventually the North as well. But his five Virginia regiments that had fought so bravely and been so badly bloodied got the name, too. For the rest of the war and into the annals of American history, they would be called the Stonewall Brigade, the most famous fighting unit of the Confederacy.

Jackson gave a rare explanation of his performance under fire to John Imboden, who had asked him, in frank astonishment, "How is it that you can keep so cool, and appear so utterly insensible to danger in such a storm of shell and bullets as rained about you when your hand was hit?" Jackson gazed at the young officer of artillery and replied, "Captain, my religious belief teaches me to feel as safe in battle as in bed. God has fixed the time for my death. I do not concern myself about that, but to be always ready, no matter when it may overtake me. That is the way all men should live, and then all would be equally brave."[14]

As the story of Jackson's exploits on Henry Hill seeped forth into a nation that had never heard of him before, there were others, in both the United and the Confederate States, who very definitely *had* heard of him. These were men who had fought in the war with Mexico fourteen years earlier, most of whom were still alive and now fighting for one side or the other in the new war. The Mexican-American War was, at bottom, a political landgrab on an enormous scale. As Ulysses S. Grant phrased it in his memoirs, it was "one of the most unjust [wars] ever waged by a stronger against a weaker nation."[15] Yet from a soldier's point of view it was a sort of glorious aberration, a grand adventure to conquer a foreign land that had resulted in a series of military victories, some of them spectacular, all of them exotic and without precedent. There was nothing in the regular army to compare it to. No service in the Indian wars could possibly match the romance and grandeur of it, and none of the men who marched triumphantly into Mexico City or Monterrey among the drawn sabers and fluttering regimental flags and bands playing "Yankee Doodle" ever forgot those moments. In the face of overwhelming numbers, they had conquered *a nation*. The Mexican-American War had produced many heroes, most prominent among them Zachary Taylor, who would soon become president, and Winfield Scott, who would soon run for president. But it also featured, among its lesser lights, a slim, soft-spoken subaltern from western Virginia who had done something so extraordinary that his fellow soldiers and officers would not soon forget that, either.

The US Congress had declared war on Mexico on July 22, 1846. What followed was essentially a war of territorial expansion, though the nominal reason for it was the 1845 US annexation of Texas, which Mexico still considered one of its northern provinces. Americans wanted to keep Texas, and, under the expansionist banner of Manifest Destiny, also had designs on Mexico's other territories in the West, including California. Jackson had graduated from the US Military Academy at West Point on June 30, just in time for the war. He was twenty-two years old, and ranked a respectable seventeenth out of fifty-nine cadets in his class. He had received his marching orders in July, then traveled to Mexico with an artillery company in the late summer and early fall, an arduous, country-girding journey, mostly by riverboat.

In late November 1846 he arrived in the northern city of Monterrey, having just missed its conquest by the dashing General Zachary Taylor. Jackson found, to his disappointment, that there was little to do there. But he soon received new orders to join General Winfield Scott's 10,000-man expedition by sea to the coastal city of Vera Cruz, where he would launch an invasion aimed at Mexico City, 260 miles inland. It was an extraordinary operation, not least for the cast of officers who were present, many of whom would later gain fame in the Civil War. They included the following future generals: Ulysses S. Grant, Robert E. Lee, James Longstreet, George McClellan, Ambrose Burnside, Pierre G. T. Beauregard, Joseph E. Johnston, Braxton Bragg, George Meade, Joseph Hooker, Fitz John Porter, Albert Sidney Johnston, D. H. Hill, and John Pope.

Jackson had been thrilled by the prospect of combat. On the way to Vera Cruz he met a friendly if somewhat sharp-tongued young lieutenant named Daniel Harvey Hill, who had already seen fighting at Monterrey. Jackson had been recommended to Hill by a mutual friend, George Taylor, who had told Hill that Jackson "will make his mark in this war. I taught him at West Point. He came there badly prepared, but was rising all the time, and if the course had been four years longer, he would have been graduated at the head of his class. He never gave up on anything."[16] The two young men were introduced—they had been four years apart at West Point—and Hill was surprised to meet, instead of a rising star who seemed destined for greatness, a very "reserved and reticent" young man. In spite of his shyness, he was desperate to know what Hill's battle experiences had been like. As the two walked along the beach, Jackson asked him questions about commanding troops under fire. "I really envy you men who have been in action," the youthful Jackson told him. "We who have just arrived look upon you as veterans. *I should like to be in one battle*" [Hill's italics].[17] Hill later recalled that when Jackson spoke those words "his face lighted up, and his eyes sparkled as he spoke, and the shy, hesitating manner gave way to the frank enthusiasm of the soldier."[18] (Harvey Hill was destined to loom large in Jackson's life: as the man who got him his job at VMI, as his brother-in-law, and as a hard-fighting Confederate general who fought with Jackson in many battles.)

Jackson, who commanded a unit of artillery, saw his first action during the US Army's siege of Vera Cruz. He performed exceptionally well under fire. One of his West Point classmates even observed that "Old Jack" was "as calm in the midst of a hurricane of bullets as though he were on dress parade at West Point."[19] He was cited for "gallant and meritorious conduct," and received a promotion to brevet first lieutenant—by no means a routine upgrade.[20] He marched west with the army in April 1847, played a minor role in the American victory at the Battle of Cerro Gordo, and arrived near Mexico City in mid-August, now assigned to one of four light artillery companies under the command of the flamboyant and theatrical Captain John Bankhead Magruder. Magruder was a strange fellow. He was a drinker, a braggart, and a social climber. He was also a mean-tempered and often harsh disciplinarian who, for his own personal advancement, exposed his men to extreme danger. For this reason young officers did not like to serve under him. According to one observer, he despised Jackson, who was in most ways his opposite and, in any case, was not from an F.F.V. (First Family of Virginia) and so not worth Magruder's time. But for Jackson this was an unrivaled opportunity, and he had eagerly applied for the transfer. He wanted to be where the battle was hottest, and Magruder's presence as a commander virtually guaranteed that.

Jackson got his wish. At the Battle of Contreras, some ten miles south of Mexico City, he found himself in a three-hour duel against vastly superior Mexican artillery. In spite of the heavy enemy fire, Jackson refused to back down. He "stayed there without a thought of withdrawing," recalled a fellow soldier. "He had been ordered there, and his conception of duty as a lieutenant required him to stay. His men were falling all around him, and he too, with the last, would have fallen."[21] When the other section commander in his battery fell, mortally wounded, Jackson advanced into the smoke and confusion and continued to fire his guns. The Americans won the battle, but it was a hard fight, and Jackson had distinguished himself again. Whatever Magruder may have thought of him initially, he now dispensed high praise, saying that Jackson's conduct was "conspicuous throughout the day." General David Twiggs included Jackson on a short list of officers distinguished for their "coolness and determination . . . whilst under fire."

Jackson was beginning to stand out. His bravery under fire at Contreras—he was one of those soldiers who seemed completely at ease with death flying all around them—won him both a regular promotion to first lieutenant and a brevet promotion to captain. When asked later how he had reacted to being in a full-scale battle for the first time, he replied, in a rare moment of immodesty, that he had only been "afraid that the fire would not be hot enough for me to distinguish myself."[22] Though he later cited his faith in God as the reason not to fear death on the battlefield, at this point in his life he was not yet a deeply religious man. Long before he placed his life in the hands of God, even a casual observer could see that the young man wasn't afraid of bullets or cannon fire.

Still, he was not immune to the horrors of war, which he was fast learning. He wrote to his sister, Laura, "I have since my entry into this land seen sights that would melt the heart of the most inhuman of beings: my friends dying around me and my brave soldiers breathing their last on the bloody fields of battle, deprived of every human comfort, and even now I can hardly open my eyes after entering a hospital, the atmosphere of which is generally so vitiated as to make the healthy sick. . . . To die on the battlefield is relief compared to the death in a contaminated hospital."[23]

Jackson had fought well at Vera Cruz and Contreras, but those battles were not what Mexican-American War veterans remembered him for. What they would recall, in later years, was what he did in the final, decisive fight for Mexico City. As Winfield Scott's army moved ponderously forward, the last obstacle to the country's capital was a large castle atop a two-hundred-foot hill southeast of the city known as Chapultepec. As the army advanced, Jackson's artillery unit, which consisted of two six-pounder cannons and was attached to an infantry regiment, found itself on a narrow causeway beneath the castle's battlements, engulfed by enemy fire. Jackson later described his situation as being fully exposed "in a road which was swept with grape and canister, and at the same time thousands of muskets from the Castle itself pouring down like hail."[24] The Americans were trapped there, unable either to retreat or advance.

Jackson faced eight Mexican cannons with his two, at very short range. He immediately lost all twelve of his horses, which went down in bloody heaps and lay there, wounded or dying, in harness. Undeterred, he and his small squad unlimbered, rolled the guns forward, and started shooting back. One of the guns was hit and became immovable. The artillerymen, meanwhile, facing what seemed to be certain death, fled to the safety of a nearby ditch and bushes. But Jackson refused to leave the road. Pacing back and forth alone while shells filled the air around him, including a cannonball that rocketed between his legs, he yelled to his men, "There is no danger! See? I am not hit!" (He said later this was the first and only lie he ever told.) At first he got no takers; then, finally, an old sergeant walked up and together they dragged the remaining cannon across a ditch and up onto the road. They began firing again. As they did so, another member of the gun crew made his way forward. Instead of accepting his help, Jackson shouted, "Go back yonder! Tell Colonel Trousdale to send men forward! . . . Tell him with fifty men we can overrun the battery ahead!"

Jackson and his sergeant now stood with a single gun on the road amid a storm of ball, solid shot, shell canister, and musket fire so severe that no one else dared raise his head above the roadside ditch. His own crew had abandoned him; the entire infantry regiment to which he had been attached had disappeared, except for a small escort. What division commander General William J. Worth saw, when he finally rode up close enough to see what was going on, was young Jackson, now in advance of the entire American army, still aiming and firing his cannon, in a virtual single-handed duel with a significant part of the Mexican army. When Worth ordered Jackson to retire, Jackson refused to obey the order, saying that it was more hazardous to retreat than to stay put.

Magruder now arrived at the perilous scene. He immediately had his horse shot out from under him as he reached Jackson's six-pounder, then dragged himself up and pitched in with a few others from the gun crews to salvage the second gun. Soon Jackson had both guns working again, plying sponge and handspike, and firing furiously at the Mexicans. And now things began to change. A brigade that General Worth had brought up began to make itself felt, pushing forward. On the hill above them, the defenses of Chapultepec Castle began to crumble, and the long American lines began to surge forward and upward. Chapultepec soon fell.

But Jackson's work was not finished. A few miles down the road, at the gates of Mexico City, Mexican general Santa Anna rallied his remaining troops. General Scott ordered another attack. Jackson, still eager to fight, quickly found wagon limbers to which he could attach his two guns, and started out at a fast pace toward the city's San Cosme Gate. He was moving so fast, in fact, that he soon found himself well in advance of the rest of the army. In that precarious position—a mile ahead of Scott's infantry—he encountered two other young officers who had made the same mistake: his new friend Harvey Hill and another lieutenant from South Carolina named Barnard Bee, a man Jackson knew from West Point, a year ahead of him, and who had been brevetted for gallantry at Cerro Gordo. Hill and Bee had about forty men between them, but no guns, and were talking about going back when Jackson, dragging his two guns behind ammunition caissons, rolled up and cheerfully volunteered to give them artillery cover. The three of them were discussing this when Magruder arrived and ordered them to stand down. They pleaded with him to relent. He did, and the little group took off down the road in pursuit of Mexicans.

Half a mile down the road they came upon some 1,500 Mexican cavalry, who turned and charged at them down the narrow causeway, offering Jackson a tantalizing target. He opened fire, ripping huge bloody holes in the column. "Whenever they got a little too far," Jackson said later, "we limbered up and pursued at full gallop until the bullets of their rear guns began to fall near the leaders, then we would unlimber and pour it into them—then limber up and pursue. We kept this up for about half a mile."[25] Thus did Jackson find himself again in the position of fighting a very large force with a very small one.

By nightfall, the shooting had ceased; the city was not yet overrun and had not surrendered. The following morning, Jackson had his guns on high ground, trained on the San Cosme Gate. Residents had been warned that if they did not surrender by a certain hour the shelling would start again. When Mexican authorities ignored this, Jackson received an order to open fire on the main thoroughfare, filled with panicked civilians. He did so immediately; he later said that he could trace the visible line of death his guns had made. When asked many years later if he had any compunctions about killing those people, he answered, "None whatever. What business had I with results? My duty was to obey orders."[26] Later that day Winfield Scott marched into the city in triumph—the last, dramatic piece of a brilliant, bloody campaign.

News of Jackson's exploits, meanwhile, moved quickly through the army. There was no doubt at all about what he had done. It had been witnessed not only by his immediate superior but also by a division commander. And there was no question that the actions of this brave brevet captain had affected the course of the battle. He was singled out for lavish praise from Generals Worth and Pillow, and his name was even mentioned in the commanding general's report—an extreme rarity for a subaltern in charge of two field artillery pieces. But the highest praise came from Scott himself. After the army had occupied Mexico City, Scott hosted a reception for army officers to which Jackson was invited. He waited in the receiving line, heard his name read out, and finally came into the presence of the massive three-hundred-pound commander. Scott regarded him, clasped his hands behind his back, raised his chin in the air, and said in a booming voice so that everyone could hear, "I don't know if I will shake hands with Mr. Jackson!" Jackson blushed to the tips of his whiskers, and stared at the floor of the now silent hall. Scott now continued, "If you can forgive yourself for the way in which you slaughtered those poor Mexicans with your guns, I am not sure that I can!" With that, Scott held out his hand and smiled as the crowd applauded. Jackson shook it. He was thrilled. He could have received no higher form of praise. He had been on active duty for only fifteen months, and he had been promoted to first lieutenant and then to brevet major. No one in his class from West Point—indeed, no one in the entire army in Mexico—had been promoted faster. He was twenty-three years old, and in the small, tightly circumscribed world of the US Army, he was famous.

CHAPTER ELEVEN

A Very Small,
Very Bitter Fight

In the summer of 1861, as citizens in the North and South tried to sort out what had happened on Henry Hill and Chinn Ridge, they began to discuss a new topic: their generals. A few months before, no one had cared particularly about generals, who they were, what they looked like, or what they might have done in the Mexican-American War or in some dusty Indian outpost in the West. But all that had changed. Suddenly the world was awash in these folks, with their sashes, side-whiskers, and idiosyncrasies, and because the fate of the country and the lives of thousands of young men rested in their hands, they were the objects of keen, often obsessive interest. They were the new celebrities. Names of formerly obscure, regular army types such as David Hunter and Joe Johnston now populated the pages of the newspapers and soldiers' letters home, and the more often they appeared the more the names began to take on emblematic status. Beauregard was the dashing spirit of Southern victory, McDowell the symbol of unsettling, inexplicable Union defeat; Bee represented the notion of tragic glory, of the sacrifices that would have to be made. McClellan, remote and magnificent in Ohio and western Virginia, was the hope of the despondent North.

Jackson was not yet among those prominent names. To the extent that anyone knew him at all, he embodied the nickname Barnard Bee had given him. He was steadfast and immovable, an iron-hard fighter who would stand on the soil of Virginia, eyes ablaze and chin tilted toward the heavens, and defy the Yankee invaders. If this seemed two-dimensional, the man his soldiers saw was scarcely more defined. Their experience of him was strictly military, all protocol and logistics and army business. He did not make small talk, he rarely socialized, and he revealed little of himself to subordinates. He was usually polite, but the soft-spoken politeness itself— like his regular daily prayers, offered alone in his quarters—was a form of aloofness. Brigadier General Jackson seemed indeed like a wall: it was impossible to penetrate him.

But Jackson was, in a larger sense, anything but opaque. After the Mexican-American War he had spent five years in the regular army, in postings that included Pennsylvania, New York, and Florida, long enough to be well known to his peers and commanders. For a full decade, from 1851 to 1861, he had lived a very visible life in Lexington, a small college town of two thousand souls where everybody knew everybody else's business. He was deeply involved in the very small and very transparent world of VMI, where he was one of a handful of professors. He was a deacon at his church. He had married twice, owned a redbrick house in town and a modest farm outside of town, sat on the board of a local bank, and was active in the local debating society. He had several close friends. To them, and to many others in Lexington, Jackson was considerably more than this implacable, God-obsessed mystery whom people were starting to talk about. He was just Major Jackson, a shy and socially awkward man who was perhaps not a very good teacher but who had nonetheless built for himself a tidy, middle-class life—a very American story of hard work and self-betterment and modest success.

That story begins in 1851, not in Lexington but in the months just before he arrived there—in a swampy backwater in Florida, where young Brevet Major Thomas Jackson had finished his regular army career by doing something truly extraordinary: he had single-handedly transformed a small, sleepy garrison into a nightmare of recrimination, political infighting, and moral accusation.

Jackson's return from the Mexican campaign was, inevitably, less than glorious. After a brief posting to a barracks in Carlisle, Pennsylvania, he landed at Fort Hamilton, on the coast of Long Island, about ten miles from New York City. Compared with the swashbuckling and high adventure of Mexico, this new life was commonplace. It gave him his first real taste of the often dreary, routinized life of the peacetime army, where promotion was slow, action rare, and political backbiting the order of the day. Though he was quartermaster and commissary of his unit, he spent much of his time on court-martial duty, traveling to upstate New York and Pennsylvania to sit on military juries, ruling on desertions and insubordination and drunkenness and other army sins. On the brighter side, the new life offered him free time. He attended an Episcopal church, where he was baptized, read the Bible, and began what would become a full-blown obsession with his health and diet, eating stale bread and plain meat to ease his chronically upset stomach, taking water cures, and doing "leaping" and "swinging" exercises that caused much curiosity at the fort.[1] There he passed his twenty-fifth and twenty-sixth birthdays. In December 1850 he was reassigned to Company K of the 1st Artillery, and to a post that would soon make Fort Hamilton seem like a dream of happiness.

This was Fort Meade, Florida, a three-day march to nowhere through swamp and pine forest from Tampa, itself a forlorn outpost of two hundred souls in the flat, humid, lake-pocked terrain of central Florida. (The entire state of Florida had only eighty-five thousand inhabitants, half of them slaves.) Fort Meade's ostensible purpose was to protect white people from marauding bands of Seminoles—more specifically, those Seminoles who had not accepted the treaties under which they would be forced onto Indian territories in what is now Oklahoma. That there were hardly any of these Indians out there did not seem to matter. There had been much blood shed and money spent fighting them since 1817, and forts had been built and they all had to be staffed with armed men. Company K consisted of a commanding officer, fifty-two enlisted men, and four officers. They were the only human beings, as far as anyone knew, within ten miles of the fort. Jackson arrived there, with the rest of the company, on December 18, 1850.

His posting started well enough. His job was again quartermaster and commissary, in charge of property, supplies, and food. His commanding officer was a portly, balding Baltimorean with a protuberant mustache named William H. French, who had graduated from West Point nine years ahead of him. The two men had known each other for three years, and, if they weren't exactly friends, they seem to have been pleasant enough acquaintances. French invited Jackson to dinner several times in his first months there, where Jackson enjoyed the company of his wife, the lively Caroline Read French. Like Jackson, French was a stickler for duty and detail, and like Jackson he had won brevet promotions for valor in the Mexican-American War, and though he held the actual rank of captain (Jackson was a first lieutenant, one notch down), they were both brevet majors. They resembled each other in less benign ways, too: neither had an engaging personality, and both were ambitious for promotion and advancement. Unlike Jackson, French could be rude and abrasive.

He was also more than just a perfectionist; he was a meddler as well. He insisted on involving himself with the smallest details of barracks life, and often found fault with those details. He wanted a formal report, for example, on why a musket belonging to one of the enlisted men had been damaged. When Jackson, presiding over a case of drunkenness and unsoldierly conduct, found the corporal guilty and recommended punishment, French rejected it as too lenient.

Jackson came in for criticism in other ways, too. French dispatched him twice to find Indians. On both occasions, after marching long distances through jungles and swamps, Jackson failed to do so.[2] French was furious, and fired off a note to army headquarters accompanying the report of Jackson's second expedition with a vow "to go myself and endeavor to turn the Southern and eastern point of the lake," rather than "throw it on my subalterns should Indians be on the other side at this season which is 'corn planting time.'"[3] Jackson chafed under all this. He was unhappy. His health declined, notably his eyes, which were most likely afflicted by a condition known today as uveitis, an inflammation of the iris and pupil that causes eye aches, bloodshot eyes, sensitivity to light, blurred vision, and floaters. He may have suffered from dyspepsia as well. In February he tried and failed to transfer to another post.

Relations between the two men continued to deteriorate. As company quartermaster, it was Jackson's responsibility to supervise the construction of several buildings at the fort. He considered this an important part of his job. Now French began to assert control over the process, overriding Jackson's orders and making his own changes. Jackson's unhappiness soon gave way to anger. Whenever he encountered French at the fort, Jackson averted his eyes, an old military practice known as "cutting." French did the same, though in Jackson's case the behavior bordered on insubordination.[4] They spoke to each other only about official matters, and only when necessary.

Finally, Jackson could take it no longer. He wrote a formal protest to the commanding officer in Tampa saying that French was interfering with his rights as quartermaster. French, angered by Jackson's righteous nitpicking, blasted back in his own note to Tampa.[5] Jackson, in fact, was way out of bounds. He was, in effect, asserting that he was entitled to an independent command within a company of fifty-two men and four officers occupying a small fort. He was insisting that he should not be subject to the normal command structures of the army. Six days later he received a categorical rebuke from Colonel Thomas Childs in Tampa, who stated pointedly that "the Gen'l Comdg. knows no state of military affairs where the Comdg. Officer can divide responsibility with a junior." He also lectured Jackson: "A difference of opinion amongst Officers may honestly occur on points of duty. It ought never to degenerate into personalities, or be considered a just cause for withholding the common courtesies of life so essential in an Officer & to the happiness & quiet of garrison life."[6]

Still, Jackson was not finished with French. This dispute had been about rank and authority. The next one, which exploded over two weeks in mid-April, was about morality. It began with gossip, specifically a scandalous story about Captain French that made the rounds of the garrison in early April. The thirty-five-year-old French lived at the fort with his wife, two small children, and a household servant named Julia. In the account Jackson heard, French had been seen walking alone with Julia in late afternoon and early evening on several occasions, both on the post and in the woods. The suggestion, delivered with a wink and a nudge, was that French and Julia were lovers. Jackson had also heard that several of Julia's potential beaus among the enlisted men had understood that they were supposed to stay away from her because Captain French had "taken her for himself." In a small, remote garrison, such a rumor would have spread quickly.

And it might have remained a rumor had Jackson not decided to intervene. His reaction to the gossip was in some ways predictable. Adultery was a crime, both in the military and in civil society. It was also a sin against the laws of God—prohibited by the Sixth Commandment. So Jackson decided, without authorization, to conduct his own investigation—an extraordinary and risky move by a young first lieutenant against his commanding officer. If Jackson was fearless, he was also shockingly insensitive to what his action inevitably looked like: the opportunistic and even malevolent work of a disgruntled subaltern engaged in a highly visible power struggle with his commanding officer.

On April 12, unbeknownst to French, Jackson summoned and interrogated a dozen enlisted men in his office. He promised the interviewees that nothing would happen to them, then proceeded to ask them detailed questions about what they had seen. Where had French and Julia been observed walking together? At what hour? Had anyone seen or heard of any immoral conduct? Had one of them witnessed, through an open window, the two of them together on the captain's bed? Jackson's questions could be quite specific, too. When one enlisted man denied having seen the two on a bed together, and said he had only seen "a foot" in the room, Jackson wanted to know if the legs were "bare or covered" or belonged to a man or a woman. Thus it went, the young first lieutenant grilling the reluctant, deeply uncomfortable men. As a criminal investigation, it was a notable failure. A few of the men had seen French walking with the girl, that was all.

Sensing the peril of their position, the men immediately told their ser-geant what had happened, and the sergeant, sensing the peril of his posi-tion, immediately told French. And French exploded. The next morning he placed Jackson under arrest for conduct unbecoming an officer and a gentleman. He then called in the men who had spoken with Jackson, asked them in detail what had been said, and, for good measure, called in another eight to ask them if they had heard any such assaults on his character. This, too, turned up little of note. Some of the men acknowledged seeing the two together, though they had observed nothing improper. Several of the men acknowledged hearing the story that the "major had taken her for himself" but had treated it as a joke. In any case, no one had seen anything.

Jackson, meanwhile, had concluded that French was at least guilty of unbecoming conduct and proceeded to draw up charges. While he was working on them, he was visited by company surgeon Jonathan Letterman (later to become the medical director of the Army of the Potomac), who begged him to withdraw his accusations because of the pain they would cause French's popular and likable wife. Jackson listened to him, and his eyes filled with tears. "Inflicting pain on her was agony to him," wrote his brother-in-law D. H. Hill. "But his conscience compelled him to prose-cute the case."[7] In other words, his strong sense of the righteousness of his actions overrode the fact that he was potentially destroying French's mar-riage and his career at the same time.

On Sunday, April 13, Jackson sent a letter to Tampa asking for release from arrest and calling for a "Court of Inquiry" on French's behavior.[8] The next day, Jackson filed formal papers. His charge carried four "spec-ifications," roughly: (1) that French and Julia had had intimate relations; (2) that they had taken improper walks together; (3) that they had taken a walk together outside the fort; and (4) that it was common knowledge among Julia's prospective suitors that he had "cut them out." The language Jackson used showed his evident contempt for French, whom he portrayed as a harsh and dishonest man who was "not to be believed as speaking the truth, when his interest in his opinion requires him to speak falsely." French retaliated by firing off a letter that same day, defending himself from "so malicious a slander and falsehood," pointing out the innocence of his actions, and asserting that none of the men in the garrison had witnessed anything improper. French wanted Jackson court-martialed. He reminded his superiors that Jackson, feeling wronged, had "adopted the system of non-intercourse, vulgarly styled 'cutting' on the ground that he was deprived of his rights," and cast doubt on Jackson's motives. French wrote:

> *Foiled thus in his attempts to have my official conduct reprehended, he altered his course, and descending into the purloins of the camp he has changed his attacks to a charge upon me and my family, but so blindly and upon ground so absolutely untenable that finding himself without a support in proof, he wished to escape from the consequences of his act and be allowed to retire unscathed upon a plea of "a sense of duty."*[9]

What happened next was odd, since it was Jackson, not French, who had the weaker case. French started to unravel. He began to see conspiracies where none existed, and began a hunt for informants. On April 16 he accused Second Lieutenant Absalom Baird of conspiring with Jackson to undermine French's authority, and he placed Baird under arrest. (He would eventually file charges against all of his officers.) He filed eight court-martial charges against Jackson. "When Major Jackson is brought to trial for his outrageous conduct," he wrote, "the evidence which I will bring before the court will cover him with the infamy he deserves."

Even odder, all this hysteria and supposed moral calumny at Fort Meade received an ice-cold welcome in Tampa. The new commander there, General David Twiggs, who had been forced to read through many pages of charges and countercharges, found it all preposterous and a waste of his time. He told the two officers to stop what they were doing, to forget the issue, and to resume normal business. He had no intention of dealing with any of it. Jackson immediately accepted Twiggs's order and sent no further grievances to Tampa.

French, meanwhile, could scarcely believe that he was not going to be allowed to refute the charges against him. Unhappy with Twiggs's ruling, he applied to General Winfield Scott himself, citing "this most extraordinary case of outrage." Again, he was turned down flat. French, even more convinced of a large conspiracy, brought charges against surgeon Jonathan Letterman and Lieutenant Amos Beckwith for improper conduct, and court-martial charges against a noncommissioned officer for his role in Jackson's investigation. Twiggs, in Tampa, considered French now so far out of control that, on October 1, he relieved him of command and transferred him to Fort Myers. But the mortally offended French was not finished. In March of the following year, still trying to rescue his reputation from what Jackson had done to it, he appealed for redress directly to the secretary of war. This finally exhausted the patience of General Twiggs, who relieved French of command at Fort Myers. He also wrote a career-damaging reaction to French's behavior. French, he said, "has preferred charges successively against all the officers serving under his orders, and has shown himself incapable of conducting the service harmoniously at a detached post."[10]

Jackson, meanwhile, seemed not only unscathed by what had happened—he doesn't even mention it in his correspondence—but was also, quite happily, on his way to a new life. While French was drowning in anger and shame and frustration, Jackson, immune from regret, was busy making other plans. On February 4, before the disputes with French began, he had received an unsolicited letter from Colonel Francis H. Smith, superintendent of the Virginia Military Institute, asking for permission to place his name in nomination for the job of professor of natural and experimental philosophy and instructor of artillery.

Jackson's name had come up in the unlikeliest of ways. Smith, who had been having trouble hiring a new professor, had consulted his friend D. H. "Harvey" Hill, a professor at nearby Washington College in Lexington. Smith, desperate for a new candidate, had handed Hill a copy of the *Army Register* and asked him to recommend someone. Hill perused it, then came to the name of the young officer he had met in Mexico, Tom Jackson. Hill recalled how Captain Taylor had described Jackson as a man who would "make his mark," and how Jackson's heroism at Contreras and Chapultepec had confirmed precisely what he had said. Hill pointed to the name, at the top of page 278.[11] As luck would have it, one of Jackson's relatives was a member of the school's board.

Jackson, who had agreed enthusiastically to put his name in nomination, was offered the job at VMI in the first week in April and decided immediately to accept it. The timing is interesting, because by the time he brought his charges against French, he had the job offer in hand. He had only to keep his mouth shut, depart on his furlough, then resign and take the job. Instead, by bringing charges, he put that job, and his future happiness, at considerable risk. Either a lengthy court of inquiry or his own court-martial trial might well have prevented Jackson from taking the job, which required his presence in Lexington on July 1. And French did, in fact, suspend the April 14 orders granting Jackson his requested leave—which was for now his only way out.

All of this would suggest that Jackson, as a soldier and a Christian, truly believed that he had no choice but to do what he did. His tears when explaining his position to Letterman were authentic, as was the sympathy he later expressed to the officer to whom he was denying leave to be with his ill and dying family members. Jackson always possessed an absolute sense of what he was required to do—a personal code that was not always convenient for those around him.

Jackson departed Fort Meade, and Florida, forever on May 21, 1851, after forty-three days under arrest. He left behind him a dysfunctional garrison still seething with anger and suspicion. There is no record that he ever gave it a second thought. He later explained, according to his friend Robert Dabney, that "while campaigning was extremely congenial to his tastes, the life of a military post in times of peace was just as repulsive; that he perceived the officers of the army usually neglected self-improvement and rusted, in trivial amusements, at these fortresses."[12] To his sister he wrote cheerfully, "Good news. I have been elected Professor of Natural and Experimental Philosophy in the Virginia Military Institute, and you may expect me home in the latter part of June."

CHAPTER TWELVE

A HIGHLY UNUSUAL MAN

⚜

When Major Thomas J. Jackson, known to most of his friends as Tom, reported for duty at VMI on August 13, 1851, he was twenty-seven years old. By most accounts and photographic evidence he was, if not exactly handsome, a reasonably good-looking young man. He was tall. At just under six feet, he was nearly five inches taller than the average American male of the era. He weighed about 170 pounds. He wore his medium-brown hair short, in the military style of the day, and sported side-whiskers that extended nearly to the bottom of his chin—another army affectation. He had a wide forehead; a sharply defined, aquiline nose; a small, firm mouth; and strikingly transparent gray-blue eyes. When he walked onto the campus of VMI to watch a cadet parade and drill, he wore his very best outfit: a double-breasted blue frock coat, tapered white pantaloons, immaculate white gloves, a new kepi cap, and artillery boots—all in all, the very picture of a young West Point graduate and Mexican-American War hero about to assume an important professorship.

Except that none of it quite worked. The kepi, for one thing, was oddly positioned, pushed a bit too far forward, so that instead of looking jaunty, or stylish, it seemed somehow awkward. And even casual observers could not miss Jackson's newly blacked boots. Worn outside his pantaloons, they were both enormous and highly visible. One could only speculate—and many did—on the size of the feet they must have housed. When he walked, in those unnaturally long strides that reminded one of his friends of "a dismounted horseman," the gigantic boots were even more noticeable.[1] Even among the large crowd that had assembled to watch the cadets, Jackson stood out. There was something about him, then and later, whether in full prewar dress or in his later customary dishevelment, that was inescapably conspicuous. His welcome to the Virginia Military Institute, before anyone knew who he was or even that he had officially arrived, came in the form of a taunt, shouted by one of the cadets, aimed directly at him, and heard by everyone on the parade ground: "Come out of them boots!" the cadet yelled. "They are not allowed in this camp."[2] As it happened, that ill-mannered shout was an appropriate beginning to the most important and character-defining decade in Jackson's life. It signaled the trials that this terribly earnest and very different young man was going to face, both at VMI and with the wider public.

The Lexington he encountered in 1851 was a handsome, mountain-bracketed town of sturdy brick and clapboard homes and soaring church steeples built on an elevated ridge at the southern end of the Shenandoah Valley. It was a place of high, sculpted hills and miniature valleys within valleys, picturesque farms, clear rivers, and mountains that loomed up on either side of the town and were capped with snow in the winter: the Blue Ridge to the east, the Alleghenies to the west. The valley, which ran in a southwest-to-northeast line from Roanoke to the Maryland border, had been settled in the 1700s by Scots-Irish and German settlers who had migrated from Pennsylvania and pushed southward along the forks and tributaries of the Shenandoah River. They had built a world that was utterly different from the land east of the Blue Ridge Mountains. That was old-line, tidewater Virginia country, very English, very Episcopal, with roots going back to the earliest days of American settlement. In the valley people spoke with a different accent, worshipped differently, and put on, as they viewed it, fewer airs. They were mostly middle-class farmers and merchants, exemplary, upwardly mobile Americans of the era: hardheaded, hardworking, practical, devout, and not at all fancy. Their beliefs tended toward the dissenting Protestantism of Luther and Calvin. And they valued education almost as highly as they did their religion. It was said that the Scots-Irish settlements in the valley, in the words of one resident, "were noted for three things: churches, academies of learning, and distilleries."[3] (The latter provided the valley's surfeit of pastors with material for many temperance sermons.) Unlike tidewater Virginia, there were few large plantations and very little conspicuous wealth, though there was hardly any poverty, either.

Lexington, staunchly Presbyterian, Scots-Irish, and dominated by Washington College and the Virginia Military Institute, was very much of that valley. It was also, like most towns in that area, built on a very small scale.

The 1850 census revealed 1,743 souls; of these 1,105 were white, 552 were slaves, and 86 were free blacks.[4] Even Lexington's leading institutions were small: VMI had only 5 professors and 117 students when Jackson arrived. Washington College, virtually across the street, had only five professors and a few hundred students.[5] The colleges were the center of the town's social world, and Jackson, VMI's new professor of natural and experimental philosophy and a highly eligible bachelor whose Mexican-American War exploits had preceded him into the town (his Florida exploits, fortunately, had not), was in the midst of it, whether he liked it or not. Lexington was an intensely social place, where its residents, in all seasons, constantly paid social calls on one another and liked throwing parties. And it was in this small, narrowly circumscribed world—so profoundly different from West Point or the regular army, where he had spent the previous eight years— that Jackson's unusual personality came into full view.[6]

To people who met him socially, his most striking trait was his silence. Where others might expect a minimum of social chatter, a casual comment, a piece of common small talk about the weather, or a small de rigueur politeness, he was often determinedly quiet. When he did speak, he could be maddeningly literal. A visiting Englishman, discussing history, once said to him, using a typically British prefix, "You remember, Major, that at this point Lord Burleigh was Queen Elizabeth's great counselor," Jackson immediately interrupted him, saying, "No, I don't remember, for I did not know it."[7] When later asked whether he understood that the man's saying "you remember" was just a figure of speech, Jackson said, "I am quite aware that he did not intend to gauge my knowledge of history. But nothing would have induced me to make the impression on him that I knew what I did not."[8] Similarly, when someone used the term "you know" in casual conversation, again, as a mere figure of speech, Jackson would frequently interrupt to say that he did not know.

He refused to go along with the most routine conventions of everyday conversation. He would not say that he wished that any circumstance was different than it was, meaning he could not bring himself to wish that it were warmer, or less windy, or even that some accident had not happened. If someone said, "Don't you wish it might stop raining?," he would reply with a quiet smile, "Yes, if the Maker of the weather thinks it best,"[9] thus instantly killing the conversation. He would not acknowledge that he envied anyone, for any reason. He would not engage in flattery of any kind, even to give an idle compliment to a host. He absolutely refused to judge people or to say anything derogatory about them, even when bad-gered to do so. One such conversation, rendered later by a close friend, went like this:

"Hasn't your old army friend Captain C— some right objectionable habits?" he was asked.

"C— ? Oh, C— has some fine points of character," said Jackson.

"But it seems to me that he is wanting in fixed principles."

"Indeed? It would give me pain to think so."

"Come now, Major, I know that you understand Captain C— thoroughly, and I am sure you must disapprove of him."[10]

But Jackson never gave in.

Much of this behavior grew out of his faith, his desire to be uncompro-misingly truthful at all times, and his very particular sense of Christian courtesy. He explained his refusal to voice disapproval of others by saying, "It is quite contrary to my nature to keep silence where I cannot but dis-approve. Indeed I may as well confess that it would often give me *real sat-isfaction* to express just what I feel, but this would be to disobey the divine precept [judge not lest ye be judged], and I dare not do it."[11] One of his favorite books was George Winifred Hervey's *The Principles of Courtesy*, which laid down specific behavioral rules under such rubrics as "humil-ity," "gravity," "salutations," "gentleness," "deportment in the street," and "deportment at church."[12] Always intent on improving himself, Jackson had compiled, while a student at West Point, a lengthy list of sayings, aph-orisms, and proverbs under three categories: rules for conversation, choice of friends, and general principles. The following small sample explains at least some of his behavior:

—*Endeavor to be at peace with all men. Never speak disrespectfully of anyone without a cause.*
—*Never try to appear more wise or learned than the rest of the company.*
—*Use no hurtful deceit: think innocently and justly, and if you speak, speak accordingly.*
—*If you speak in company, speak late.*
—*Avoid triumphing over an antagonist.*
—*Say as little of yourself & friends as possible.*[13]

Though much of his social behavior had its roots in this strict personal code, Jackson was also deeply shy by nature, evidence of which was his terrible discomfort in any situation that required him to speak publicly. This, too, was on display in his first years in Lexington for all to see. He had joined the local debating society in the interests of self-improvement, and it periodically fell to Jackson to stand up and say something on some public issue of the day. His early efforts were excruciating to watch and embarrassing for both the flustered, red-faced Jackson and his listeners. When his turn came, he would stand and begin to speak, seem to lose himself in confusion, then stop abruptly. After a pause, he would resume speaking, continue haltingly for a while, then finally stop altogether, sometimes in midsentence. He would then sit down, staring straight in front of him. The debate would resume without him. Even more remarkable than this public mortification, though, was Jackson's refusal to accept defeat. He would often rise a second or even a third time *on the same evening*, undoubtedly to a good deal of wincing in the hall. Often these repeated efforts ended exactly as the first one had: abruptly, and with no resolution.[14] Once his performance was so inept that he even made the town newspaper, which referred to the "*nervous* speech of Major Jackson," making a point—cruelly, thought Jackson's friend Harvey Hill—of putting the word in italics.[15]

His shortcomings as a speaker were apparent in church, too. When his pastor, the Reverend William S. White, urged more parishioners to lead prayers in weekly meetings, Jackson went to see him. He told the minister that he wanted to comply but was afraid that he might not make a favorable impression on the congregation. "But you are my pastor and the spiritual guide of the church," he continued, "and if *you* think it my duty, then I shall waive my reluctance and make the effort to lead in prayer, however painful it might be."[16] White did call on him at the next meeting, and Jackson led the prayer in his faltering, agonizing, cringe-inducing way. The prayer was indeed just as painful for the audience as he said it might be. But here, too, Jackson refused to quit. When White, out of respect for Jackson's feelings, did not call on him for the next few weeks, Jackson protested. "My comfort or discomfort is not the question," he said. "If it is my duty to lead in prayer, then I must persevere in it until I learn to do it aright, and I wish you to discard all consideration for my feelings."[17] Though he was never eloquent, Jackson eventually learned to stand and speak or lead prayers competently, and without humiliation.

There were other idiosyncrasies, too—so many that they were difficult to keep track of. Though he was devoutly religious, and dutifully went to church several times a week, he was also famous for falling asleep during the service. He did this at almost every service, usually during the sermon. Because he insisted on sitting perfectly erect in his pew, the moment that sleep overtook him was a dramatic one, as he suddenly tilted to one side. This caused much mirth among the VMI cadets in the gallery, who watched and waited for it.[18] Jackson was fully aware of his problem, and it was typical of his stubbornness that he refused to do anything about it. When asked by female friends why he did not just lean back in his pew, so as to be less conspicuous—and less of a bad example to the cadets— Jackson replied, "I will do nothing to superinduce sleep by putting myself at ease, or making myself more comfortable; if, however, in spite of my resistance I yield to my infirmity, then I deserve to be laughed at, and accept as punishment the mortification I feel."[19] So he *was* humiliated by what happened to him. But he stuck to his principles, which held that yielding to sleep while trying to sit rigidly upright was a weakness that somehow deserved punishment. Indeed, Jackson always sat bolt upright, no matter where he was. He never crossed his legs. He never allowed his back to touch a chair. And church was not the only place he took public naps. He sometimes fell asleep, too, in the midst of conversations with friends.[20] These were the same friends who had to endure him standing up during his visits to them because he said it helped his alimentary canal stay straight. No matter what was happening or what interesting or momentous conversation was under way, Major Jackson would rise and leave, without fail, at 9:00 p.m.

To many of Jackson's acquaintances, the oddest thing of all about him was his obsession with his health. Though some who knew him considered him a hypochondriac, he was plagued by several very real, chronic illnesses.[21] When he arrived at VMI in the summer of 1851, the uveitis that he had first experienced in 1849 had become so acute that he felt pain just trying to focus his eyes on objects. He saw spots—floaters—and was at times so extremely sensitive to light that he feared he might go blind. He would never read at night, which led to what many considered his most eccentric behavior: sitting alone in the dark with his eyes closed, mentally preparing his lesson for the next day. He answered all letters from memory, so as not to have to read them twice. There was little else he could do to alleviate the symptoms. When he was suffering the worst pain, he would fill a basin with cold water, put his face underwater, and hold his eyes open as long as he could hold his breath. He would do that six times a day, using water drawn from a well or a river.[22] To persons without an understanding of such an affliction, that might seem very odd behavior indeed.

Though his eye problems occurred intermittently during his adult life, his dyspepsia seems to have been a more or less permanent condition. In the mid-nineteenth century the term was a catchall, incorporating everything from simple indigestion or sour stomach to gastritis, acid reflux, peptic ulcer, parasites, and even stomach cancer. It is not clear exactly what Jackson suffered from. But it caused him so much discomfort that, according to one of his staff officers in the war, "When I expressed my surprise that a man in Richmond had committed suicide, driven to it by dyspepsia, [Jackson] said that he could understand that and thought that if a man could be driven to suicide by any cause, it might be from dyspepsia."[23] He suffered, too, from sinus and ear infections. One in particular, in 1858, was so severe that it left him almost completely deaf in his right ear.[24]

He sought water cures, or hydrotherapy, from Massachusetts to western Virginia, usually at mineral springs, where he would spend weeks at a time, taking cold-water baths and drinking the waters. He visited such establishments fourteen times during the course of his life, and invariably claimed that they had given him relief. As part of the "water cure" he sometimes wore wet shirts next to his body. He also strictly regulated his diet, sometimes adhering to a regimen of stale bread and cold water, eating meat less than once a month.[25] He once spent a summer eating mostly fresh buttermilk and cornbread. As with everything else, he did not change his private behavior in public: from his days in postwar Mexico City onward he would bring his own food to dinner parties. "It is probable," he wrote his sister, Laura, in 1850, "that I am more particular in my rules [about diet and health] than any person of your acquaintance."[26]

Jackson was obsessive about anything that involved his health. In addition to his eyes and digestive system, he worried variously about his hearing, throat, liver, kidneys, nervous system, musculature, and the circulation of his blood. He read books on health, and was a diligent follower of the latest fads, including the inhalation of glycerin and nitrate of silver, and the swallowing of ammonia. He was a prodigious walker, traveling five miles a day, but he also engaged in the sort of strange-looking leaping exercises that his army colleagues at Fort Hamilton had noted. Then there were the stories that had passed into legend, many of which were recalled long after the war and may be apocryphal. During his early military service, according to a man who was in his class at West Point, Jackson "became convinced that one of his legs was bigger than the other, and that one of his arms was likewise unduly heavy. He had acquired the habit of raising the heavy arm straight up, so that, as he said, "the blood would run back into his body and lighten it."[27] Other stories were harder to verify, but circulated in Lexington nonetheless. According to one, the major believed that one side of him was smaller than the other, and to correct this he would exercise the smaller side more frequently, to "make it catch up with the other." It was also reported that he had requested that his landlady not use pepper in his meals because, according to a cadet at the time, "whenever he got any pepper on his tongue, it always took away the use of his right leg."[28] When it came to the unusual Major Jackson, no story seemed too outlandish to believe.

In all of these stories—amusing and otherwise—there is Jackson's terrible earnestness, his profound seriousness of purpose, and his unashamed, unflagging persistence in fulfilling that purpose. Though Jackson was in no sense naive, there is a simplicity and a purity about him—almost a *sweetness*, seen from the perspective of 160 years—that belies portrayals of him as nothing but an oddball and a crank, and a dour one at that. His behavior was never mean-spirited, never sullen or gloomy, and he rarely indulged a bad mood. Though he was stern, he was always polite, and almost always pleasant to those around him. People who did not know him well could not guess that his reticence in social situations grew from deeply held Christian principles. They could not understand that his often pathetic yet ultimately successful attempts at public speaking rose from personal principle and a conviction that he could overcome obstacles by sheer force of will. Thus he remained, for most people in Lexington in his early years there, a man imprisoned in the elaborate, codified, and highly idiosyncratic personality he had created for himself.

CHAPTER THIRTEEN

THE EMBATTLED PROFESSOR

◆⟨⟩◆

The course Jackson taught at VMI, "Natural and Experimental Philosophy," was brutally difficult. It had been brutally difficult when he took it in 1845 at West Point, where it was loathed and feared by most of the cadet corps, which included some of the brightest math and engineering students in the country. Jackson's VMI course used exactly the same texts, some of them written by William H. C. Bartlett, his old professor. The subjects included a dizzying array of the most difficult scientific and mathematical concepts of the day: electricity, magnetics (including electromagnetism and electrodynamics), acoustics, optics (reflection and refraction of light, microscopes and telescopes), analytical mechanics, the motion of celestial bodies, and astronomy. Unlike most of his fellow West Point cadets, Jackson actually *liked* the course and had done well in it, placing eleventh of sixty-two in his class. This was despite the fact that his previous schooling in rural western Virginia had given him little preparation for such advanced work, and had placed him at a huge disadvantage against classmates such as Philadelphia-raised George McClellan, the future Union general, who had spent two years at the University of Pennsylvania before he even arrived at West Point. Jackson was an exceptional math and science student; the dreaded Bartlett was one of his favorite professors.

The other subject he taught at VMI was something he knew a great deal about, too: artillery. Each day between 2:00 p.m. and 4:00 p.m. he would drill cadets in the transportation, deployment, and firing of mobile field artillery consisting of four six-pounder smoothbores and two twelve-pounder howitzers. In place of horses, underclassmen would pull the field pieces around the drill ground. Most of this was straight mechanical drill.

The "tactical" side of artillery—its use on a battlefield—was something Jackson was not called upon to explain.[1]

He was the most peculiar of teachers. According to the many accounts left by his former students, he did not really teach at all. Instead, he would assign what were considered to be extremely difficult lessons, and then listen to "recitations" of those lessons by cadets at the blackboard, correcting them as they went along. "At the appointed time [Jackson] 'heard' them, and this was about all of it," recalled one former cadet. "Discussions in the class-room were unknown, and even explanations were infrequent. . . . The text was the one great thing which he came to 'hear,' and we came to 'say,' if we could, and most of us commonly couldn't, when the said text was Bartlett's Course of Natural Philosophy, in three of the toughest volumes this scribe ever attacked—'Mechanics,' 'Optics and Acoustics,' and 'Spherical Astronomy.'"[2]

Jackson's behavior in the classroom seemed as peculiar as it did everywhere else. "When questioning the cadets," wrote future Confederate general James H. Lane, one of his students, "he had a peculiar way of grasping his lead pencil, with his thumb on the end towards the cadets, and when a mistake was made, he would say 'rather the reverse' and flip his thumb back on the pencil."[3] When befuddled cadets asked him to explain some point, Jackson's answer—devoid of imagination or technique—was simply to recite back to them the exact words of the text, which he had committed to memory and then rehearsed for several hours in darkness. Though this did nothing to help impart knowledge to his charges, some were impressed anyway by his command of the subject. "In the section room he would sit perfectly erect and motionless," recalled cadet James McCabe, "listening with grave attention and exhibiting the great powers of his wonderful memory, which was, I think, the most remarkable that ever came under my observation."[4] But Jackson's power of recall offered little help to students who had trouble understanding his course. When one cadet insisted, after hearing Jackson explain a problem twice in exactly the same way, that he still did not understand it, Jackson ordered him to leave the section room.[5] The result was that, while the brightest students managed to master the course, those in the middle and at the bottom were often left on their own to flounder, and sometimes to fail.

To make matters worse, Jackson placed great value on regurgitating every last detail of the assigned texts. When, in response to Jackson's question "What are the three simple machines?" a cadet answered, "The inclined plane, the lever, and the wheel," Jackson replied, "No, sir. The lever, the wheel, and the inclined plane." That was exactly as they were listed in the textbook, and that was how Jackson wanted it.[6] No amount of student outrage or protest could dislodge him from this position. His course managed to be both dreadfully dull and appallingly difficult, with few light moments. When the students begged him to give them a separate session to help them review for a test, Jackson met them in his classroom *in the dark*, where, according to one cadet, he "sat in front of us on his platform, and with closed eyes questioned us over many pages of a complicated study."[7] Whenever Jackson did manage to make what one student termed "an ironical remark," he would hasten to qualify his expression by adding, "Not meaning exactly what I say," even though the meaning was plain to everyone. The expression soon became a byword around the barracks.[8] Such remarks made Jackson seem to be what he was not: stupid, or uncomprehending. Cadets would call him Old Tom Jackson while pointing, significantly, to their heads and saying that "he was not quite right *there*."[9]

In the cloistered world of VMI, most of which was contained within a single building, the shortcomings of the man cadets called Old Jack, Tom Fool, Old Hickory, and Square Box (in reference to his large feet) were on intimate display. By the end of his first year it had become common knowledge that the grave, taciturn major was, if not completely inept, at the very least the worst teacher at the institute. If there was anyone who thought otherwise, he left no historical record. Even Colonel Francis H. Smith, VMI's superintendent and the man who both hired Jackson and kept him in his job, acknowledged his failure. "As a Professor of Natural and Experimental Philosophy, Major Jackson was not a success," Smith wrote later, after his most illustrious faculty member's rise to world fame. "He had not the qualifications needed for so important a chair. He was no *teacher*, and he lacked the tact required in getting along with his classes. He was a brave man, a conscientious man, and a good man, but he was no professor."[10]

But mere inability to impart knowledge was only the beginning of Jackson's problems as a professor. One might expect that such a stern pedagogue would rule his classroom with an iron fist. But the reverse was true. Jackson was a poor disciplinarian whose classroom often seemed on the edge of complete chaos. While he sat, gimlet-eyed, watching one of the cadets recite, the other students, arrayed in a horseshoe curve behind Jackson, would often be in a full-scale battle, pelting one another with spitballs and other paper projectiles. Others cheated by taking crib sheets to the blackboard with them, concealing them from Jackson but not from the other students. Former cadet Lane said he only saw Jackson attempt to catch one of them. "As he approached the guilty party," wrote Lane, "his heavy, creaking boots betrayed him; the cadet slipped the paper up his sleeve. . . . When Jackson reached him, he asked sharply 'What is that in your hand, Sir?' The Cadet turned suddenly with a surprised look, opened his hand and said 'a piece of chalk,' at the same time displaying it. 'Yes, a piece of chalk,' responded Jackson, and there was a general laugh at 'Old Jack' as he returned, foiled, to his rostrum."[11]

Sometimes the cadets would truss a first-year student in a chair and balance the chair against the classroom door so that it would tip over when Jackson entered. Cadets would walk behind him, mimicking his step, as he walked with his long strides through campus, head down, looking straight ahead. According to one student, "from behind buildings and around corners he was saluted with cries and catcalls."[12] Almost invariably, one of them would draw a picture of outsized feet on the blackboard in Jackson's section room.[13] Sometimes there would be caricatures in which his body was swallowed up by his boots. Over a decade, his teaching often took place in an atmosphere of what one cadet called "wanton disrespect."[14]

Through all of this, Jackson never lost his temper or his dignity; rather, he took it all with a strange, almost distracted, imperturbability, as though he were too thick to understand what was really happening. "They played tricks on him, they made sport of him," wrote D. H. Hill, a math professor at Lexington's Washington College at the time. "They teased him, they persecuted him. All in vain. He turned neither to the right nor to the left, but went straight on in his own ways."[15] It should be noted that Jackson was not a complete pushover: he put many students on report, and placed some of them in arrest. Though he made fewer charges than the other teachers, he usually made them stick. Nor was Jackson universally despised. Though almost everyone agreed that he was a bad teacher, several of his students later wrote that they admired him for his record in the Mexican-American War, his strong sense of duty, and his Christian ethics. Indeed, in 1858, Jackson's seventh year at VMI, a cadet named Leigh Wilber Reid wrote a strikingly prescient poem about Jackson, saying that he saw "The stamp of genius on his brow, and he / With his wild glance and keen but quiet eye / Draws forth from secret sources, where they lie." Reid had written poems about three other professors, all of them critical and derogatory.[16]

Jackson fared better as an instructor of artillery, a subject he was far better at explaining. As one of his students later wrote, a change would come over him at the sound of the guns. "The grasp on the sabre would tighten; the quiet eyes would flash."[17] In fact, he taught the most intensive artillery course in the South and very likely the equal of courses at West Point.[18] Over a decade he managed to impart considerable knowledge to several hundred students that would have a telling effect in the coming war. Scores of them would actually serve as artillerists under Jackson himself.

But here, too, he had trouble controlling his charges, who had far more freedom on the drill ground than in the section room to play pranks and otherwise disrupt the class. Cadets mimicked his commands, which he issued in drawn-out syllables in his high-pitched, mountain-inflected voice. They removed the linchpins so that the cannon wheels would fall away, sending the various pieces of the gun tumbling down the hill. Sometimes he caught them, and put them in arrest; often he did not. The trick, in any case, was repeated semester after semester. It became a sort of tradition. Another common prank was to spin the cannon in the direction of the major, causing him to leap out of the way.

Some of the tricks were not so harmless. Once a cadet dropped a brick from a third-story barracks window that barely missed Jackson. Jackson, striding forward as he always did and looking neither left nor right, took no notice of it, though as D. H. Hill said, "his escape was almost miraculous." The perpetrator was never caught. When asked later why he did not try to find out who had done it, Jackson replied, "The truth is, I do not want to know that we have such a coward in the corps of cadets."[19] His comment is a small revelation. Though his reaction might seem to be that of someone with strange physical habits who lacked connection with the real world about him, in fact he saw the act for what it was, and had a distinct, deliberate, and intelligent response to it. Jackson might seem opaque, out of touch, or just bizarrely insensitive to pranks or disrespect, but everything we know about him suggests that none of that was true. As his later wartime record would show, Jackson was extremely competent in the many skills required of a commanding general. He was highly perceptive and exquisitely sensitive to everything around him. His correspondence, much of which survives, is that of an incisive and articulate observer. Appearances and nicknames notwithstanding, he was nobody's fool. Unfortunately, he never wrote to his sister or to friends to tell them the stories of his struggles at VMI. We can only assume that he was, as you would expect him to be, mortified by his own inability to keep his charges under control.

His sensitivity to this problem came out in his first sharp disagreement with his boss, VMI superintendent Francis H. Smith. In the spring of 1852, Smith happened to be walking across the parade ground when he saw one of the cannons lose its wheels and scatter in several directions—the result of the linchpin-pulling trick. He walked over to Jackson and ordered him to report the cadet officers responsible for allowing this to happen. Stung by what he perceived to be sharp criticism—though it hardly sounds like that—Jackson immediately went back to his room in the barracks and wrote Smith a note requesting that he "put his severe reprimand in writing."[20] After that, Jackson's treatment of Smith became noticeably cooler. He did not, as far as we know, "cut" him as he had done Major French at Fort Meade, but for a time he would have nothing to do with him on anything except official business, and on that he was curt and deliberately abrupt.[21] As with French, Jackson, the normally duty-bound, strictly-by-the-book military man, had some obvious problems with officers of elevated rank, and with authority in general, especially when they said anything critical of him. This rogue character trait—nothing in his past quite accounts for it, and it would seem to violate both his military and Christian sense of duty—would come into play significantly during the Civil War, in ways that would have a profound effect on his military career.

Jackson had several notable confrontations with cadets who were unhappy with him or who felt he had been unjust. The most famous of these took place in April 1852. It involved a cadet named James A. Walker. Walker, a highly ranked student, had challenged Jackson in trigonometry class over an answer to a problem that Walker had written on the blackboard, insisting that he was right and telling Jackson that he had not made himself clear. Jackson told the cadet that he was out of line, whereupon Walker protested angrily. When Jackson told him to be quiet, he refused, and Jackson put him under arrest. After a court-martial, in which sixty-two pages of testimony were recorded, Walker was found guilty on all charges and dismissed from the institute.[22] His response was to challenge Jackson to a duel, and to write him a note saying that if he did not receive satisfaction he would kill Jackson on sight.

What happened next is not quite clear, though many versions exist. The most commonly cited is that told by D. H. Hill, who later said that Jackson had asked him for advice on whether to seek a restraining order. Hill advised him not to, saying that if he did so, the cadets would regard him as a coward. But Jackson disregarded him and went straight to the magistrate.

Hill saw this as the quintessential demonstration of Jackson's personality: he would do his Christian duty to avoid a fight, and he would accept the social consequences. "I have thought that no incident in the life of Jackson was more truly sublime than this," wrote Hill. "He was ambitious, covetous of distinction, desirous to rise in the world, sensitive to ridicule, tenacious of honor—yet, from a high sense of Christian duty, he sacrificed the good opinion of his associates." In Hill's version, Jackson at the same time let it be known that he would defend himself if attacked, and Walker never dared attack him. In any case, there was nothing in Jackson's behavior that suggested cowardice to anyone. The cadet was expelled, and that was the end of it.

We do know with great precision what happened to the expelled student. He entered the war with the 4th Virginia Regiment. He fought with distinction under Jackson as part of the Stonewall Brigade, rising steadily by Jackson's promotions and making colonel in March 1862. In May 1863 he was promoted to brigadier general and became, by Jackson's direct command on his deathbed ("I do not know a braver officer"), the Stonewall Brigade's last commanding officer.[23] Thirty-nine years after his expulsion from VMI, he acted as chief marshal at the unveiling of the Stonewall Jackson monument in Lexington. His nickname, given to him at the Battle of Gettysburg and which he kept for the rest of his life, was Stonewall Jim. He would later write of Jackson that "the cadets came to understand him and to appreciate his character for courage and justice, and to respect and love him for his kindly heart and noble soul."[24]

Walker was not the only one who complained publicly about Jackson. Superintendent Smith, in fact, had fielded a steady stream of complaints about him that never resulted in any direct action. But in the spring of 1856 he finally faced a full-scale protest. Acting on the basis of a number of complaints, the Society of the Alumni appointed a VMI graduate to investigate and prepare a report for the school's governing body, the Board of Visitors. In July, the alumni presented a resolution condemning the mismanagement of the Department of Natural and Experimental Philosophy, and saying that Jackson lacked "capacity adequate to the duties of the chair."[25] Though this might easily have been grounds for dismissal or reassignment, nothing of the sort happened. The board decided simply to table the resolution, and there the matter rested. When Jackson found out about this campaign against him a year later, he made a formal request that every charge be investigated. But the board—like General David Twiggs in

Tampa, who fielded a similar request—would have nothing to do with it. The members tabled Jackson's request as well.

It is noteworthy, considering how difficult it must have been for him to engage year after year in a difficult job for which he had no aptitude, that he even stuck it out. (His one attempt to leave was a failure, too: he applied for a job teaching math at the University of Virginia in 1854, but did not get the job.) One explanation comes from his second wife, Anna, who said that Jackson had once been asked by a friend if it wasn't presumptuous of him to take the teaching job at VMI when his eye illness made him incapable of doing it properly. "Not in the least," Jackson said. "The appointment came unsought, and was therefore providential; and I knew that if Providence set me a task, he would give me the power to perform it. So I resolved to get well."[26] He persisted because he believed God wanted him to.

CHAPTER FOURTEEN

DELIBERATELY AND INGENIOUSLY CLOAKED

Lexington knew the caricature Jackson, the health crank, the unbending, automaton-like professor, the social bore with high Christian principles. This was the strangely two-dimensional face he presented to the world, and he wore it for a decade, like armor. Because he seemed a decent enough man, a polite and conscientious man with no apparent malice in his heart, the town adopted him. If he could never adjust his habits and ways to those of Lexington society, no matter: Lexington would adapt itself to him. It got used to Major Jackson and in its own way came to appreciate him. He was a curiosity, a sort of minor civic institution.

But he was not what he seemed. Concealed behind this carefully constructed social front was a layered, highly complex, passionate, deeply sensitive man who loved deeply and grieved deeply. He had a poetic heart, and a nineteenth-century romantic's embrace of beauty and nature. He loved Shakespeare and European architecture. He was self-taught and completely fluent in Spanish; he was a devoted and talented gardener; and he read widely in world history and military history and reveled in travel. He had an ecstatic, almost mystical sense of God. He loved walking in the country around Lexington, gloried in sunsets and mountain views and in the blooming Shenandoah spring. He was a man who could laugh uproariously, and roll around on the floor in play with a child, speaking Spanish baby talk, a man who kept close track of news and gossip inside his large, extended family. He was a doting, affectionate, and passionate husband who, behind closed doors, had an expansive and often joyous personality.

135

Almost no one in Lexington—or anywhere else, for that matter—knew or suspected any of this. His students and fellow parishioners would have been astounded to learn it. Many would not have believed it. The real Thomas J. Jackson was almost entirely private. He was deliberately and ingeniously cloaked. The more fully realized part of him was revealed only to a very small group of people, all of them female, and all of them close to his heart. All came to full prominence in his life during his time in Lexington.

The first was his sister, Laura, who pervades Jackson's life. She was the focus of much of his love and all of his brotherly concern. She was his faithful correspondent, and though her letters to her brother have been lost, a large number of his letters to her have survived. They show her only in reflection, of course. But taken as a group they provide a sweeping twenty-year portrait of Jackson himself. The letters can be simply chatty, passionately religious, or elaborately rhetorical, but they cover almost all aspects of his life, from his marriages, to religion, to his health and his obsession with it, to grief, financial matters, relations with his extended family, his travels in Europe and the United States, and even to his fondness for peaches.

Laura was special for a number of reasons, but mainly because she was the only other surviving remnant of a family struck by repeated calamities. Thomas and Laura were born in very modest circumstances in Clarksburg, Virginia, a river junction town in the mountains and narrow valleys of far northwestern Virginia, not far from Ohio and Pennsylvania. (The area is now part of West Virginia.) Their father, Jonathan Jackson, was a failed country lawyer, a poor business manager, and a compulsive gambler whose main talent seemed to be running up large debts. Their mother, Julia Neale, from nearby Parkersburg on the Ohio River, seems to have been a much better sort, described by contemporaries as "very intelligent" and having a "comely and engaging countenance" and "a graceful and commanding presence."[1]

Jonathan and Julia married in 1817, and set up housekeeping in Clarksburg. They had three children: Elizabeth in 1819, Warren in 1821, and Thomas in 1824. They struggled financially. While Julia was pregnant with her fourth child, typhoid fever killed six-year-old Elizabeth. Less than a month later, her husband, Jonathan, died from the same illness. The day after his death Julia gave birth to a daughter, Laura. Julia was now, at twenty-eight, a widow with two small children and an infant.[2]

She was also destitute, and soon accepted the charity of the local Masonic order, which offered her the use of a tiny, twelve-foot-square, one-room house. She sewed, taught school, and somehow managed to feed her children. Her situation did not improve. Her children were pitiable sights in town, wearing ragged clothes and sometimes accepting the charity of local merchants and tradesmen. In 1830, when Tom was six, Julia met and married a man fifteen years her senior named Blake Woodson, another hard-luck country lawyer, but this time with eight children of his own scattered in various places. Desperate to save her family, she had made another marital mistake, worse than the first one: Woodson not only made little money but was harsh and verbally abusive to the family. The family moved far from Clarksburg, to the tiny hamlet of New Haven (now Ansted), southeast of Charleston, so that Blake could take a government job. He and Julia struggled and fell deeper into debt. She was soon pregnant again.

By the fall of 1831 there was so little money left that Julia decided, reluctantly but with no real choice, to send her children away. Warren would live with Neale relatives in Parkersburg. Seven-year-old Tom, as he was known, and five-year-old Laura would travel north to live with a collection of Jackson relatives at a place called Jackson's Mill, eighteen miles south of Clarksburg near the town of Weston. Little Tom begged not to be sent away, and when an uncle and his slave arrived to fetch them, he hid in the woods. When he left home, on the back of a horse, his mother wept uncontrollably. A month later, she gave birth to a boy, William Wirt Woodson. Three months later Tom and Laura were back in the same place, watching their mother die. She had fallen ill and had summoned her children to say good-bye. On December 4, 1831, she passed away. Tom and Laura, now orphaned, went back to the mill. The new baby—Jackson's half brother—ended up with one of the Neale relatives in Parkersburg.[3] (Blake Woodson remarried and died penniless a year and a half later.)

In spite of their apparently disastrous fortunes, there were compensations in this new life. The Jacksons of Jackson's Mill—six bachelor uncles, ranging in age from twenty-nine to ten, a step-grandmother, and her two adult daughters—were a proud, boisterous, occasionally rowdy, and very successful bunch. By the standards of Lewis County, they were rich. They owned lands up and down the river valley, and their splendid main residence was one of the finest houses in the region. They owned the largest sawmill in the area, as well as a grain mill, carpenter and blacksmith shops, housing for a dozen slaves, and a general store. There were sheep, cattle, chickens, and orchards on the property. The man in charge of all this was Jackson's father's brother, twenty-nine-year-old Cummins Jackson. Uncle Cummins, as Jackson called him, was a big, strapping fellow with an outsized personality, a shrewd businessman who dominated local commerce and had a fondness for suing neighbors, competitors, and anyone who annoyed him. He was later found to be dishonest, too, and was caught counterfeiting silver coins, an offense for which he would be indicted by a grand jury.

But to Tom and Laura their uncle Cummins was kind and solicitous, as were their maiden aunts, uncles, and step-grandmother. The evidence suggests that the children were loved and looked after. Except for the absence of their parents, and the inevitable loneliness Tom and Laura felt, Jackson's Mill was a wonderful place to grow up. There was the splendid, rushing West Fork River that ran by the mill; there were orchards and meadows and woodlands to play in. Young Tom drove oxen, tended cattle and sheep, chopped wood, rode and raced horses, and helped with the harvest. He made maple syrup. He was quiet, shy, serious, and hardworking. He was not exceptional in any particular way and was considered by his uncle Cummins to be the least bright of the three Jackson children. He read whatever books he could lay his hands on and learned slowly. He seemed to have a flair for math—what little he had access to. Though he grew up surrounded by large numbers of cousins, uncles, and aunts on both sides of the family, his great confidante and friend was Laura. Together they ranged over the large property. One summer a slave named Uncle Robinson helped them build a raft, and Tom rowed his sister across the river, where they played in a shady stand of poplars and maples. Sometimes Tom crossed the river by himself, and rested there alone beneath the spreading trees.

In spite of the relative comforts of Jackson's Mill, there was one more dislocating trauma the children would have to face. Four years after they arrived there—they were now eleven and nine years old—their step-grandmother Elizabeth Jackson died, an event with life-changing consequences for the children. Because the two maiden aunts had married and left the mill, Elizabeth had been the sole remaining female on the compound, which meant that the only people left to care for Tom and Laura were bachelor uncles and the slaves. To Neales and Jacksons alike, this was unacceptable. So Tom and Laura were sent away again. Laura went to Parkersburg with a Neale aunt; Tom went to a farm near Clarksburg owned by his father's sister Polly and her husband, Isaac Brake. Though Laura found a warm new home, Tom found nothing but a troublesome relationship with his uncle Isaac, who disparaged him, treated him like an outsider, and gave him at least one hard whipping.

A year later, Tom could endure it no longer. He ran away. In Clarksburg he told relatives that he was not going back. When a cousin begged him to return to the Brakes, he said simply, yet for a twelve-year-old boy quite stubbornly, "Maybe I ought to, ma'am, but I am not going to." The next day he walked eighteen miles to Jackson's Mill, where Cummins Jackson happily welcomed him back. He spent the rest of his childhood in that sturdy masculine environment, attending several small, rural schools and working alternately for Cummins and at a variety of jobs that included surveying, teaching school, and serving warrants and collecting delinquent accounts as constable for Lewis County. His childhood was, in that regard, not altogether exceptional for someone from that rural county in Virginia in the 1830s. Young men were expected to grow up quickly, and worked at whatever jobs were available.[4] Probably the most exceptional part was twelve-year-old Tom's adventure with his sixteen-year-old brother Warren down the Ohio and Mississippi Rivers, where they spent a summer and part of a fall cutting and selling wood to passing steamers. The work was hard, the money poor. Both boys got malaria and came home much the worse for what started out as a spirited adventure.

Nor was Jackson's orphanhood—for all that has been made of it—terribly unusual. Outbreaks of typhoid, yellow fever, and smallpox were common at the time, destroying families and leaving children bereft of parents. (The early 1800s were the heyday of orphanage-building in America.) Tom Jackson undoubtedly missed the love of a mother and father, but he was also busy, industrious, and part of a large, prosperous, and well-connected family that loved him. He lived in the home of a man of whom he would later write, affectionately, "Uncle was like a father to me." He had no choice but to endure his separation from Laura and Warren. They were thrilled to see each other periodically. They corresponded and remained close. When Warren died of tuberculosis when Tom was seventeen—he had never quite recovered from their ill-fated river trip—Tom and Laura were all that remained of the original Jackson family.

We know in some detail the circumstances of Laura's life: where she lived, whom she married, what her family's finances were like, and who her children were. But she herself is harder to see. In the few surviving photos of her, she looks a good deal like her brother, which is not entirely fortunate. She was plain and a bit masculine, with Jackson's thin lips, strong chin, prominent brow, and wide-set eyes. She suffered from at least some of the same ailments he did, especially uveitis. She was highly sensitive, particularly to perceived neglect by her brother, and her feelings could be easily hurt.[5] She married well. Her husband, Jonathan Arnold, was a prosperous landowner, lawyer, and cattle dealer from Beverly, Virginia. He was twenty-four years her senior, and she was his third wife. They had four children, the oldest of whom was named after her brother Tom, who loved them all dearly and played the part of the doting, indulgent uncle while spending significant parts of five summers with the family during his decade in Lexington.

In his letters to Laura, Jackson was unguarded in a way he never was at VMI or around most of his Lexington acquaintances. A letter in early 1853 was typical for its candor and its range. He describes his own passionate embrace of God—evoking a soaring vision of divinity that was not even hinted at in his solemn demeanor around town. "I hope," he wrote,

> that ere this spring your health has improved and that the returning spring will reanimate your feelings and suggest the idea that it is but the symbol of the endless beauties and enjoyments of the world to come. The passage of Scripture from which I have derived sufficient support, whenever applied, is in the following words: "Acknowledge God in all thy ways, and He shall direct thy paths." What a comfort is this! My dear sister, it is useless for men to tell me that there is no God, and that His benign influence is not to be experienced in prayer, when it is offered in conformity to the Bible. For some time past not a single day has passed without my feeling His hallowing presence whilst at my morning prayers.[6]

He then shifted, as he commonly did in his correspondence with his sister, from the divine to the quotidian: he spoke of the cold weather, of the news and activities of their many relatives, how people had filled their icehouses, and how he despaired of getting dried peaches, which he loved. As always, there was his health—complaining of "nervousness" and "cold feet"—and his diet:

> My dishes are very plain; in general brown bread is the principal article for breakfast and tea; and sometimes I probably do not taste meat for more than a month; and I have not to my recollection used any other drink than cold water since my return home.

Permeating most of his letters to her is a profound, unflagging optimism that even tragedy in his life could not undermine. It was linked to his relationship to God and his belief in the afterlife. But he was also a fundamentally cheerful man who insisted on looking at the brighter side of life. In a letter written a month later, while he was enduring his usual struggles keeping his cadets in check and having the same tired pranks pulled on him, he invoked the sunny optimism of his religion. "Our lives," he wrote,

> have been checkered in a most marked manner, and we are still, notwithstanding all the ill omens of our youth, living even beyond the usual period of human life, and I trust that before us are the brightest of our days. In taking a retrospective view of my own life, each year has opened, as I consider, with increased promise. And with my present views, the future is holding richer stores in reserves. . . . I too have crosses, and am at times deeply afflicted, but however sore may be the trials, they lose their poignancy, and instead of producing injury, I feel that I am but improved by the ordeal. But how is this accomplished? By throwing myself on the protection of Him whose law book is the wonderful Bible. My dear sister I would not part with this book for countless universes. I feel ready to make every sacrifice to carry out the will of Him who so loved us as to give His only begotten son to die for me.[7]

On April 15, 1853, he wrote Laura a letter whose playful tone would have flabbergasted his students at VMI:

> My Dear Sister: Our spring is opening beautifully, though it is said to be late. I wish that I could be with you this evening, Ah! Not this evening only, but many evenings. I am invited to a large party to-night, and among the scramble, expect to come in for my share of fun.[8]

The notion of Jackson scrambling for his "share of fun" at an evening party would have seemed implausible and possibly ridiculous to anyone who knew him. What accounted for this sudden exuberance was a significant change in the young major's life: he was in love, though he wasn't yet ready to tell Laura. He was in fact *engaged*, though no one else knew that, either. The courtship had happened rather quickly. After moving to Lexington, Jackson had met one of the town's gray eminences: the Reverend Dr. George Junkin, the president of Washington College, which was founded in 1749 and endowed by George Washington himself.[9] Junkin was a force in early American higher education. An ordained Presbyterian minister and a professor of classics, he had been the first president both of Lafayette College in Pennsylvania and Miami University in Ohio. He had taken the job at Washington College in 1848. While fulfilling his academic duties he also conducted regular services at the Washington College chapel and in a nearby town.[10]

Austere, imposing, intellectual, and deeply religious, Junkin was the sort of older man who had been missing in Jackson's life, and Jackson immediately liked him. He was soon a regular visitor to the Junkins' parlor in the large brick mansion with a white portico that was the Washington College president's residence. Junkin liked Jackson, too. According to Junkin's brother and biographer D. X. Junkin, who knew Jackson well, relations between the two "were those of a fond father and an affectionate son."[11] They spent hours discussing theological issues and Presbyterian doctrine. The Pennsylvania-born Dr. Junkin was also outspoken on the subject of slavery, which he regarded as a moral and an economic evil.[12] It is likely that the two men discussed this as well. (After secession, Junkin would leave for the North, condemning slavery as he left—a painful event in Jackson's life.)

But there was another reason Jackson was interested in the Junkin family. One of the reverend doctor's eight children was the spirited, devout, and cheerfully irreverent Elinor, known as Ellie, a year younger than Jackson and still resident in the Junkin home. He had met her on an early visit and had become more intimate with her when they both began teaching Sunday school at the Presbyterian church in February 1852. Soon he was falling in love with her, though it apparently took a bit of time before he understood what was happening to him. Harvey Hill describes a visit from Jackson during which, no matter what Hill said, Jackson would manage to maneuver the conversation back to Ellie. Jackson finally confessed, "I don't know what has changed me. I used to think her plain, but her face now seems to me all sweetness." Hill started to laugh and then replied, "You are in love. That's what is the matter!" According to Hill, Jackson then "blushed up to the eyes, and said that he had never been in love in his life, but he certainly felt differently toward this lady from what he had ever felt before."[13] By January 1853, the major was calling on her regularly.[14]

The chestnut-haired Ellie shook Jackson's life to its foundations. She was in most ways his opposite. She had a vibrant, outgoing personality, a finely tuned sense of humor, and was not at all shy about teasing the stern Major Jackson about his unusual behavior. She was, according to her niece, "one of the sunniest, happiest of beings."[15] Just as important, she was deeply religious, more so even than Jackson himself. Soon it was apparent to everyone who knew them that Jackson was seeking Ellie's hand in matrimony. Though Dr. Junkin and his wife, Julia, admired Jackson's piety and seriousness, they were surprised that such a solemn and socially ungraceful man should want to marry their spritely, extroverted daughter.[16] And Jackson had done so little self-promotion that for months the Junkins were not aware of his exploits in the Mexican-American War. But they soon got used to the idea, and encouraged it. Sometime in early 1853, the two were engaged.

There was just one problem. Ellie's older, unmarried sister, Margaret "Maggie" Junkin, was bitterly jealous of Jackson and entirely unreconciled to the idea that Ellie would marry him and thus leave her, at age thirty-two, to a dreary life at home, possibly as an old maid. But there was more to her opposition than simple fear of abandonment. Though she and Ellie were five years apart, they were inseparable friends. They dressed alike, shared the same room, and took walks and rode horses together. They shared each other's most intimate secrets. The two sisters were, moreover, complementary personalities: Ellie was intensely social; Maggie was shy, a bit withdrawn, more sensitive and emotional, and less comfortable in society.

Nor was Maggie somehow the weaker, less talented, or less attractive of the two. From the few photographs we have of her, if she was not precisely pretty and had less pretensions to fashion than her younger sister, she was certainly good-looking. She was petite, with fair skin, intelligent eyes, and a headful of auburn curls. She was also something of a prodigy, a rising literary star who had published stories, poems, and essays in some of the leading periodicals of the day. (She went on to achieve renown as the "Poetess of the South," publishing widely read and well-reviewed works on the war and other subjects; in her later life she corresponded extensively with literary friends Robert Browning, Lord Tennyson, Henry Wadsworth Longfellow, and Christina Rossetti.[17])

And now she had set her considerable talents against Major Jackson. Not only was he a competitor for Ellie's affections, but he was also the sober-sided, wholly prosaic soldier and science professor from the mountains of western Virginia seemed to collide with everything Maggie, with her literary training and romantic and poetic soul and as the daughter of a classicist, valued. She undoubtedly had also heard the stories about his peculiarities that circulated at VMI, which was only a five-minute walk from her home. It is not clear exactly what she said to her sister, but she evidently intervened. "Elinor is in love with a Major Jackson, a professor at the University [sic], and Margaret won't let him come to the house," wrote one of their cousins.[18] The result of Maggie's campaign was that, soon after the engagement was made, Ellie abruptly broke it off, and she and Jackson stopped seeing each other. Jackson, helpless against Maggie's influence, was miserable. "I don't think I ever saw anyone suffer as much as he did during the two or three months of estrangement," wrote Hill. "He . . . said to me one day: 'I think it probable that I shall become a missionary and die in a foreign land.'"[19]

And so he might have, had Maggie not decided to relent. Her recantation came in the form of a sentimental poem, addressed to Ellie, that admitted her deep jealousy but vowed to accept her sister's choice:

> Tis but the common work of Time
> To mar our household so
> And I must learn to choke the sob
> And smile to see them go. . . .
> Forgive these saddened strains, Ellie
> Forgive these eyes so dim!
> I must—*must* love whom *you have* loved
> So I will turn to him—
> And clasping with a silent—touch
> Whose tenderness endears
> *Your hand and his between my own*
> I bless them with my tears.[20]

The poem was followed by an equally penitent letter:

> *I will try to fling from me the intensely painful idea that anything shall ever divide me from you. I have been very wrong to let this idea gain so deep a seat in my mind, but it was because I sincerely believed it. Now it shall not be. However I may be of the opinion that you will not need me so much, if you become a wife, I will not abate one jot of my need for you and my clinging to you. I will endeavor to keep in check my selfishness, and I find a pure pleasure in yr. new happiness and prospects, and instead of not liking the major because he does the same thing I do, i.e. believes you necessary to his happiness, I will try to make that a very reason for liking him better.[21]*

With Maggie's reluctant reconciliation, the engagement was back on, though this time secretly, and the two were married at sundown on August 4, 1853, by Dr. Junkin in a modest ceremony in the parlor of the president's mansion at Washington College. By the time the rest of the town found out—to its amazement—that Major Jackson was married, he was already off on his honeymoon. But that was not the only piece of interesting news. Acquaintances also learned that Ellie and the major were not alone: Maggie Junkin, who was still not happy about losing her sister—she had told a friend that "the word marriage *jars my ears* to hear it"—had accompanied them on the trip. The three of them, together, journeyed north on a tour to Philadelphia, where they went sightseeing; West Point, where he proudly showed them the lovely campus of his alma mater; and Niagara Falls, which he had visited before and which he found endlessly entertaining. The last stop was Québec Province, in Canada, where they visited Montréal and Québec City, and where Jackson insisted on visiting the site of the famous Battle of the Plains of Abraham, where British general James Wolfe, in a daring assault, had died while defeating French forces under the Marquis de Montcalm in 1759. "I shall never forget," Maggie wrote later, "the dilating enthusiasm that seemed to take possession of the whole man; he stood a-tiptoe, his tall figure appearing much taller than usual, under the overpowering feeling of the moment . . . he swept his arm with a passionate movement around the plain and exclaimed, quoting Wolfe's dying words—'I die content! To die as he died, who would not die content!' "[22]

It was in Canada, too, that Jackson insisted on watching a Highlander regiment drill on Sunday evening, which his new wife felt violated the sanctity of the Sabbath. Jackson went anyway, stating that if Sunday was the only time he could see it, then it was not wrong to do so. Ellie disagreed and let him know it, saying in her direct way that what he was doing was "a very sophistical way of secularizing sacred time." Jackson thought it over and later agreed. For the rest of his life he took great pains to keep the Sabbath holy.[23]

On their return to Lexington in August, the couple set up housekeeping in a wing of the splendid Junkin residence—putting them in ever-closer proximity to Maggie, who, along with the senior Junkins, was the only occupant of the large house. If Maggie was still somewhat icy around him, Jackson, as always, got along very well with Dr. Junkin, who referred to him as "my dear young son."[24] We do not know much about the marriage itself, or what they were like behind closed doors. We do know that Jackson was happier than he had ever been and that he loved his wife dearly. "My wife is a great source of happiness to me," he wrote Laura on October 15, 1853. His evenings were no longer lonely. She made jokes, she teased him. He loosened up. Jackson proudly escorted her to church on Sunday—though she had no better luck than anyone else in keeping him awake—and both resumed teaching Sunday school. She almost certainly persuaded him to apply for the job as mathematics teacher at the University of Virginia— perhaps having concluded, as he should have, that his job at VMI was a dead end. The two went out frequently together into Lexington society, and were in modest demand as a couple. In the summer of 1854, Ellie and Tom traveled 130 miles to Beverly, where they spent the summer with Laura and her husband, Jonathan. Laura and Ellie got along well. As was the custom of the day, they exchanged locks of hair.

But friends agreed that Ellie's most telling effect on Jackson had to do with his religion, and his marriage to her coincided with a conspicuous deepening of his faith. "Elinor Junkin had more to do with the extraordinary piety which was afterward so conspicuous in 'Stonewall Jackson,' than has ever been told," wrote Maggie's stepdaughter Elizabeth Preston Allan. "Major Jackson found in [her] not only the sweetest woman he had ever known, and the most charming and engaging companion, but the highest type of Christian as well. Hers was the stanch, conscientious, God-fearing faith of the old Covenanters."[25] They both believed in the reality of heaven and eternal life with God. Indeed, when Ellie's mother passed away, Jackson wrote to Laura that "her death was no leaping into the dark. She died in the bright hope of an unending immortality of happiness."[26] With Ellie his belief seems to have evolved into its ultimate form, a constant, quasi-mystical union with the divine, in which God was alive in every part of his life, no matter how minute. As one friend later put it, "God was in all his thoughts . . . God, God Himself, the living, personal and present God . . . possessed his whole being."[27] Jackson himself summed it up in this extraordinary statement, in response to a friend's asking how he obeyed the biblical command to "pray without ceasing." He replied,

I can give you my idea of it by illustration, if you will allow it, and will not think that I am setting myself up as a model for others. I have so fixed the habit in my own mind that I never raise a glass of water to my lips without lifting my heart to God in thanks and prayer for the water of

life. Then, when we take our meals, there is the grace. Whenever I drop a
letter in the post-office, I send a petition along with it for God's blessing
upon its mission and the person to whom it is sent. When I break the seal
of a letter just received, I stop to ask God to prepare me for its contents,
and make it a messenger of good. When I go to my classroom and await
the arrangement of the cadets in their places, that is my time to intercede
with God for them. And so in every act of the day I have made the prac-
tice habitual.

When the friend asked if he sometimes forgot to do this, he responded,

I can hardly say that I do; the habit has become almost as fixed as to
breathe.[28]

Tom and Ellie's visit to the Arnold family in the summer of 1854 was
happy for other reasons as well. Ellie was pregnant. Though the long,
bumpy journey back to Lexington from Beverly must have been difficult
for her, she had no problems with her pregnancy and did not expect to
have any; her mother had given birth successfully nine times in ten preg-
nancies. Ellie spent the early fall making preparations for the baby's arrival.
On Sunday, October 22, 1854, she went into labor. A local doctor was in
attendance, as were her sisters, Maggie and Julia.

It is not clear exactly what went wrong, but Ellie was very quickly in
very deep trouble. It began when she gave birth to a stillborn son—a tragedy for the Jacksons, though not necessarily a threat to her own life. The
following is Jackson's own description of the events that followed. "The
Doctor said that all was well," he wrote. "The womb closed apparently
healthfully, though the child (a son) was dead. The Doctor left the house
for a few minutes, and I was admitted into the room and upon observing
her agonizing pain I desired the Doctor to return. He soon after entered,
but a sudden change had taken place: the womb had relaxed, and in a short
time her spirit took its flight."[29] What had happened after the delivery of
the dead baby was a massive and excruciatingly painful hemorrhage that
the doctor could not stop. Ellie bled to death.

Jackson was shattered. When his friend and VMI colleague Raleigh
Colston arrived to offer sympathy, Jackson led him "to the chamber of
death, and with unfaltering hand, removed the veil which covered the dead
infant resting upon its dead mother's breast. Then as quietly [he] replaced it.

There were no tears, no quivering of the lips, only a few whispered words."[30] As he sank into grief, Jackson struggled to reconcile his religious views— that God had taken Ellie deliberately for His own purposes and that she now dwelt in paradise—with his own deep sense of loss. His letter to his sister, Laura, written a day later, shows evidence of this war within him:

> *The Lord giveth and the Lord taketh away, blessed be the name of the Lord. It is his will that my Dearest wife & child should no longer abide with me, and as it is His holy will, I am perfectly reconciled to the sad bereavement, though I deeply mourn my loss. My Dearest Ellie breathed her last on Sunday evening, the same day on which the child was born dead. Oh! The consolations of religion! I can willingly submit to anything if God strengthens me. Oh! My sister would that you could have him for your own God! Though all nature to me is eclipsed, yet I have joy in knowing that God withholds no good things from them that love and keep his commandments.*[31]

At the funeral, held in Lexington the following day, VMI cadets marched in procession down Main Street to the cemetery, where a single casket containing mother and son was laid in the earth. When the mourners had all left, a pale, devastated Jackson continued to stand at the open grave, holding his cap in his hand while snow flurries swirled around him. Eventually his pastor came and led him slowly away. In spite of his fatalistic refusal to wish that she had not died—that would defy God's will—it would take him years to recover from her death. Though he went back to his section room at the end of the week and betrayed none of his misery to his students, he visited her grave daily, and friends began to fear that he was losing his mind. He wrote that God had "left me to mourn in human desolation" and was heard to say, when sick with a cold, "If only I could go up to God now!"[32] He told Harvey Hill that "he felt an almost irresistible desire to dig up the body and once more be near the ashes of one he had loved so well."[33] More than anything, he told Laura, he wanted to join Ellie in heaven. Fully eight months after her death, he wrote to Laura that his fondest wish on earth was still "that I might join her before the close of another day."[34] He did not want to wait.

In December of the year Ellie died, Jackson received a remarkable letter. It was from Maggie Junkin, his old adversary, who had never quite accepted him into the family and had never been completely cordial to him. Maggie, who had been so overcome by Ellie's death that she had not even been able to follow the coffin to the cemetery, and who had fled to Philadelphia, now told him frankly that she had felt "an irresistible desire to write to you" to find relief from her crushing sadness. She told him that the previous night she had suddenly been overcome by the sense that Ellie was "*forever gone . . .* I seemed for the first time to comprehend that Ellie was *dead.*" She asked Jackson to write to her, but said she would understand if he did not. Though he did not respond to her immediately, she was clearly in his thoughts, as evidenced by a letter he wrote to her brother in early February. "Dear Maggie!" he wrote. "How can I ever make an adequate return for her deep solicitude? My heart yearns to see her; and yet it may be best for her that we should not meet so soon; for my tears have not ceased to flow, my heart to bleed."[35] A week later Jackson finally replied to her with a deeply affectionate letter, saying that "you and I were certainly the dearest objects which she left on earth" and that "I have thought of you much, and prayed for you much, and your best interests are at my heart. I am very anxious to see you."[36] He later wrote that, though he still longed to join Ellie in death, Maggie's "kindness to me and affection for me has [sic] no little influence in lightening up the gloom which for months has so much envelopped [sic] me. . . . To sum up all dear Maggie I want to see you again."[37]

It was the beginning of a warm, complex, and unusual friendship. By the end of the summer of 1855 the two were back together at the Junkin house, where the family had insisted that Jackson stay. Once a busy, joyous place, the deaths of both Ellie and her mother within a few months of each other now made the elegant old house seem empty and sad. It was in this gloomy atmosphere that Maggie and the major got to know each other. Each evening at precisely nine o'clock, after Jackson had finished his class preparations, Maggie would visit him in his study. If she entered the room even a minute before nine, she later wrote, "I would find him standing before his shaded light, with his eyes shut, as silent and dumb as the sphinx." A moment later he would "fling aside his shade, wheel round his easy chair, and give himself up to the most delightful nonchalance."[38] They would then spend the next two hours in conversation.

They talked about everything. Jackson told her all about his childhood, the death of his parents and his years at Jackson's Mill, his life at West Point, and his military service in Mexico and in Florida. She heard stories of nighttime raids on Mexican gardens with fellow officers and of dances at the homes of Mexican nobility in the days after the war. He opened up to her completely, as he had with Ellie. He would also tell her funny stories, Maggie wrote later, "and be so carried away by them as almost to roll from his chair in laughter. More contagious and hearty laughter I have never heard."[39] She spoke of him as "sportive and rollicking, and full of quips and pranks . . . his cheerfulness and abandon were beautiful to see. . . . He was exceedingly fond of little children, and he would play them all manner of tricks, and amuse them endlessly with his Spanish baby-talk." She was not only able to overlook the oddities in his behavior but also astonished her family by declaring her new friend to be "the very stuff out of which to make a stirring hero"—a remarkable bit of prescience, uttered five years before the war started.[40] Maggie opened up, too, telling about her struggles as a writer and the difficulties of being taken seriously as a woman in the literary world. They studied Spanish together. He wrote a letter to her in that language, calling her "my dearly beloved sister" and signing it "Your very loving brother, Thomas."[41]

By the summer of 1856, Maggie and the major were almost certainly in love and thus faced a very serious problem. The constitution of the Presbyterian Church prohibited a man from marrying his dead wife's sister. In the eyes of the Church Maggie and Thomas were, by virtue of his marriage, forever brother and sister. They were both, moreover, living in the house of a prominent Presbyterian minister who happened to be her father. However reconciled they may have been to their fate, there were also signs that their feelings for each other sometimes caused an uncomfortable—if not unbearable—emotional strain. Maggie left abruptly on trips at least twice. In the spring of 1856, after spending a full winter in the same house with Jackson, she left on short notice to spend time with relatives, while Jackson, a few months later, departed for the relative safety of Europe. Whatever else might happen, Maggie Junkin and Thomas Jackson were never going to be together.

CHAPTER FIFTEEN

AN UPRIGHT CITIZEN

❧❦❧

Jackson's trip to Europe in the summer of 1856 probably had as much to do with his continued grief over Ellie's death as with putting distance between himself and the brilliant, engaging Maggie Junkin. Whatever the reason, he wanted to get away, and get away he did.[1] He secured a leave of absence from VMI and, embarking from New York City on July 9, made a solitary, three-month tour of the Continent; there, his intensity, thoroughness, academic rigor, and seriousness of purpose were perfectly characteristic of the man. Pushing himself sixteen hours a day, he covered an astonishing amount of ground, visiting London, York, Liverpool, Chester, Glasgow, Stirling, Edinburgh, Antwerp, Brussels, Waterloo, Naples, Rome, Genoa, Milan, Venice, Mantua, Modena, Florence, Leghorn, Pisa, Marseilles, Lyon, Paris, Calais, Bonn, Cologne, Frankfurt, Heidelberg, Baden-Baden, Strasbourg, Aix-la-Chapelle, Basel, Brienz, Thun, and Geneva. He rose early, and walked miles to see every sight he could squeeze in. He kept travel diaries. He hiked in the mountains. He later wrote in rapturous terms of "the romantic lakes and mountains of Scotland, the imposing abbeys and cathedrals of England; the Rhine, with its palisaded banks and luxuriant vineyards; the sublime scenery of Switzerland . . . the sculpture and painting of Italy."[2] It is noteworthy that Jackson, who had read extensively in military history and had studied Napoléon's battles closely, visited only one battlefield: Waterloo, in Belgium. The future general was apparently more interested in Renaissance art and Gothic architecture than in troop movements on a battlefield.

If Jackson's plan was to finally put his grief behind him, it succeeded. When he returned to teaching at VMI in October, the crippling sadness he'd felt was gone. He was ready to look for someone new. Maggie, more-over, was being courted that fall by Jackson's friend John T. L. Preston, a founder of VMI and one of Lexington's most prominent businessmen, who had lost his own wife earlier that year and had seven children. How Jackson felt about the relations between his close friends will never be known. In any case, Maggie was out of reach. In December 1856 Jackson traveled to Charlotte, North Carolina, to call on Miss Mary Anna Morrison, with whom he had spent time in Lexington several years before when she was visiting her sister Isabella, who had married his old friend Harvey Hill.

Anna, as she was known, was twenty-five, seven years younger than Jackson. In photographs of the period she was slender, brunette, and attractive. She was also intelligent, sensible, suitably pious, and came with all the refinements of a woman of her social standing. She was the daughter of Dr. Robert Hall Morrison, who had founded Davidson College in 1837 and now served as pastor to three country churches. Like George Junkin—in fact, almost exactly like George Junkin—Morrison was a Presbyterian minister, professor, and college president. Anna's mother, Mary Graham Morrison, belonged to one of the leading Carolina families: her father had been a prominent general in the War of 1812; her brother had been a governor, US senator, and secretary of the navy, and had been General Winfield Scott's vice presidential running mate in the 1852 presidential election. While Anna had pleasant memories of Jackson from their meetings in Lexington—he was engaged at the time, and she was with her younger sister—she was amazed to receive a letter from him talking about "blissful memories" of the time "we had been together in Lexington." She wrote later that "I can truthfully say that my fate was as much a surprise to me as it would have been to anyone else."[3]

But she was quite pleased with Jackson, as was her family, whom he impressed with his ardent Christianity, his ability to hold a job, and his war record. Dr. Morrison and Jackson also shared a profession: they were both college science teachers. The courtship lasted only a day: Jackson returned to Lexington an engaged man. From there the relationship was carried on through the mails. Jackson, meanwhile, moved out of the Junkin house (and away from Maggie) and took rooms in a hotel. On July 16, 1857, Anna and the major were married at her home in North Carolina. It was perhaps not entirely coincidental that Maggie Junkin and John Preston were married—after a brief rupture in the engagement that was smoothed over by none other than their mutual friend Major Jackson—only two weeks later.[4] Maggie, in turn, bought Jackson's wedding presents for Anna while on a trip to Philadelphia.

Jackson quickly settled into a happy, domestic life with Anna, marred only by the death of a daughter in infancy in May of the following year. Though the two grieved for the child—the second such heartbreaking loss for Jackson—there is no evidence that her death affected their happiness with each other. In the second year of their marriage, Thomas and Anna, who had been living in the Lexington Hotel, bought a house, which immediately became the center of their lives. Jackson, the transplanted orphan, had always longed for such simple domesticity—his own family, in his own home—and finally, at age thirty-five, he had what he wanted. The house was a simple, solid, dignified, two-story brick structure, just off Main Street in downtown Lexington. The Presbyterian church was a block away; VMI was a ten-minute walk.

Jackson's daily routine—adhered to rigorously—began at 6:00 a.m. with prayers and a cold bath, even in freezing weather. He taught class from 8:00 a.m. to 11:00 a.m., then returned home and studied the Bible and his class lessons until 1:00 p.m., when it was time for the midday meal, followed by thirty minutes or more of leisure time that Anna remembers as one of the "brightest periods in the home life."[5] Her description of him behind closed doors mirrors Maggie's:

> Those who knew General Jackson only as they saw him in public would have found it hard to believe that there could be such a transformation as he exhibited in his domestic life. He luxuriated in the freedom and liberty of his home, and his buoyancy and joyousness of nature often ran into a playfulness and *abandon* that would have been incredible to those who saw him only when he put on his official dignity. . . . He would often hide himself behind a door at the sound of the approaching footstep of his wife, and spring out to greet her with a startling caress.[6]

In the afternoon he would work in his garden, or ride with Anna out to a twenty-acre farm he had purchased outside of town. (From his days at Jackson's Mill, Jackson had acquired a love of growing food, and he was good at it; he was fond of canning tomatoes, propagating flowers with cuttings, and burying cabbages for winter use.[7]) Then came supper, a brief period of relaxation, and his traditional hour spent alone, eyes closed, reviewing his lessons in half-light. After that, he and Anna would sit together in their parlor and Anna would read to him, sometimes from Shakespeare, which he loved, or from history books. He was deeply in love with her, and when they were separated he missed her greatly. "Your husband has a sad heart," he wrote during one absence. "Our house looks so deserted without my *esposa*. Home is not home without my little dove. I love to talk to you, little one, as though you were here, and tell you how much I love you."[8] (Such endearments were not typical of most of the great Civil War generals. "Of the major figures in the Civil War whose letters survive," wrote Jackson biographer James I. Robertson Jr., "the stern VMI professor sent the most intimate, emotional, and sentimental messages."[9])

Though his life and work at VMI never really changed—he was always the austere and strangely inept professor—in the life of the town Jackson began to look more and more like the prosperous, upstanding middle-class citizen he had worked hard to be. In 1857 he became a deacon in his church, responsible for soliciting donations—which meant going door to door, asking for them—and distributing charity to the needy. He was considered the First Presbyterian's best deacon, discharging his duties and "reporting" his results to Pastor William White with an almost amusing military precision. As part of a board of five deacons, White later wrote, "he was the animating and guiding spirit of that body."[10]

He was also starting to accumulate wealth. In spite of a yearly salary of $1,350 from VMI, of which he tithed $180, and generous donations to other charities, he had both real estate and financial assets. He had purchased a substantial home and a working farm. He had also made a number of shrewd investments. He had purchased shares in the Lexington Savings Institution, the oldest bank in Rockbridge County. By the end of the decade he had not only made a good return on that investment but had also become a director of the bank, sitting on its board alongside some of the more prominent citizens of the town. He invested in the Lexington Building Fund Association, a purchase that by 1863 would net him a handsome profit of $1,644.[11] In partnership with Maggie's husband, John T. L. Preston, and VMI professor William Gilham, he invested in real estate. In 1860 he made his last big investment with them and another man, buying a leather tannery.[12] (He would make a large profit, quickly, on the tannery.[13])

Part of Jackson's new prosperity and social status was the human property he owned: six slaves, three of whom he had personally acquired, and three who were given to him as a wedding present by Anna's father. Though he had grown up in northwestern Virginia—a place with relatively few slaves that ultimately refused to secede from the Union with the rest of the state—Jackson had been around them all his life. His uncle Cummins owned as many as a dozen. One of those, Uncle Robinson, seems to have been a close friend to Tom and Laura when they were growing up. Jackson's relationship with his own slaves illustrates the relative complexity of a system that was often seen by Northerners in the stark terms portrayed in Harriet Beecher Stowe's 1852 book *Uncle Tom's Cabin*. He acquired his first slave, Albert, when Albert came to him and asked Jackson to buy him so that he would be allowed to buy his freedom by paying back the purchase price. Jackson agreed, although he was living as a bachelor and had no need of Albert's services. He initially rented Albert out as a waiter to VMI for $120 a year. When Albert came down with a protracted illness and could not earn money, Jackson took him in and cared for him. War came before Albert had fully paid Jackson.

The next slave who came into his possession was an older woman named Amy, who was about to be sold to pay off debt. She, too, begged Jackson to buy her, as Anna put it, as "deliverance from her troubles."[14] He had no immediate use for her, either, and found her a place with another family until Anna arrived. Amy turned out to be a wonderful cook, and Anna came to regard her as "a treasure." After the war started, Amy became sick, and Jackson secured a home for her and paid her board, medical expenses, and finally her funeral bill. A Lexington friend of Jackson's, impressed by his charity toward Amy, wrote to him, saying, "The cup of cold water you have ministered to this poor disciple may avail more in the Master's eye than all the brilliant deeds with which you may glorify your country's battlefields."[15] In response to the pleas of an elderly lady in town who could no longer care for a four-year-old slave named Emma, Jackson bought the little girl with the idea that she could be helpful to Anna later on. Emma had some sort of learning disability, but Jackson tried to teach the child catechism anyway. Then there was strong-minded, independent Hetty, who had been Anna's nurse since birth, and her two rambunctious teenage boys, whom Anna taught to read, and who later drove Jackson's carriage. From Anna's later account, Jackson was a kind, if stern, master. Though we have no record of how he regarded his slaves, Anna had a fairly traditional Southern view. In her memoirs, she referred to their slaves as among "other animate possessions of the family," lumping them together with the family's horse, milk cows, and chickens.[16]

But Jackson's dealings with his own slaves were just a small part of his relations with the larger African-American community in Lexington. In the fall of 1855, he started, with Pastor William White's approval, a Sunday school for blacks at the Presbyterian church. Though several earlier attempts had failed, Jackson believed strongly in his mission. In White's description, "he threw himself into this work with all of his characteristic energy and wisdom."[17] According to Anna, Jackson's motivation was simple enough: "His interest in that race was simply because they had souls to save." It was a formidable task. Most blacks were uninterested in attending, and some of the town's whites actively opposed the idea, partly because of the Old South notion that educated blacks were potentially dangerous. The example at hand was Nat Turner, a Virginia slave who had been taught to read and educated by his masters, and who had led a bloody slave rebellion in 1831 that killed sixty whites.

Jackson proceeded anyway, and soon had eighty to one hundred slaves in attendance at the Lexington Colored Sabbath School. The school was entirely his creation: he conceived it, financed it, organized it, promoted it, and recruited students as well as a dozen teaching assistants. His services began with prayer, which he gave, followed by the singing of "Amazing Grace," which he would lead also, in spite of being unable to carry a tune. There were Bible readings and oral examinations. Bibles were awarded to the best students. Jackson even delivered, in person, reports to owners of their slaves' participation and progress.[18] His personal influence in the school is evidenced by attendance figures, which dropped during his summer absence to fewer than fifty. From what evidence we have Jackson was well liked by blacks in town. In the words of William White, "He was emphatically the black man's friend."

Still, not all Lexington residents liked the idea of the school, not least because state law in Virginia prohibited whites from teaching blacks to read and write. On May 1, 1858, Jackson happened to encounter three lawyers he knew on the street in front of the county courthouse. One of them, Colonel S. M. Reid, clerk of the courts, said to him, "Major, I have examined the statute and conferred with the commonwealth's attorney. Your Sunday school is an 'unlawful assembly.'" The other two lawyers expressed agreement with Reid, and one of them, J. D. Davidson, said, further, that "probably the grand jury will take it up and test it." Jackson, normally the most civil of men, responded angrily, "Sir, if you were, as you should be, a Christian man, you would not think it or say so." Jackson then turned on his heel and strode away. Though Jackson went to Davidson's office later to apologize, the larger point was made: he would fight any interference with his school.[19] The school, in fact, continued in operation for thirty years.[20]

It is noteworthy that Jackson's Sunday school also offered him the opportunity to play pastor, a profession he might have preferred above all others but one for which he understood he had neither the personality nor the gift of public speech. "The subject of becoming a herald of the cross has often seriously engaged my attention," he once wrote an aunt, "and I regard it as the most noble of all professions. . . . I would not be surprised if I were to die on a foreign field, clad in ministerial armor, fighting under the banner of Jesus."[21] His choice of words is interesting, considering that he had, in effect, failed as a peacetime soldier and had certainly failed to become a minister of God.

Yet there he was, on the eve of the great Civil War, a man who through sheer determination had forged a prosperous life for himself, lacking only children to complete the picture. (That would change, too.) Reverend William S. White, who knew him as well as anyone outside his family, called him the happiest man he ever knew, a sentiment heartily endorsed by Anna Jackson.

PART THREE

VALLEY
OF THE SHADOW
OF DEATH

CHAPTER SIXTEEN

WHERE IS THE THUNDER OF WAR?

There had been army reviews before, but nothing like this one. The sheer scale of the Grand Review, as it was styled, dwarfed anything that had come before it in North America, and even rivaled the European pageants of Frederick the Great, Wellington, and Napoléon.[1] On the chilly, wind-swept morning of November 20, 1861, four months after the Battle of Manassas, on a treeless plain eight miles west of Washington, DC, George Brinton McClellan, the thirty-four-year-old general in chief of all Union armies, staged an exhibition that featured a veritable sea of blue-uniformed men: seventy thousand of them, ranged in glittering lines that stretched in a semicircle two and a half miles wide.[2] Thirty thousand spectators watched in wonder from fields, trees, housetops, and barns as the massive body wheeled before them, bayonets flashing and regimental flags flying, and led by saber-wielding officers.[3] In attendance were most of the people who mattered in Washington, including President Abraham Lincoln, Secretary of War Simon Cameron, Secretary of State William Seward, scores of senators and congressmen, and foreign diplomats. They had all come out from the city in carriages to this place, known as Bailey's Crossroads, in the cold weather to watch.

In spite of the presence of so many notables, this was McClellan's show. He was, by his own careful design, its featured attraction, and his stage management was, as usual, flawless. He arrived on a large, muscular black horse, a compact man who yet managed to inspire such descriptions as "broad-shouldered, strong-chested, strong-necked and strong-jawed." His hand was cocked jauntily on his hip. He was flanked by his immaculate, gold-lace-trimmed staff, a cohort of 1,800 prancing cavalry, and even a mounted cavalry band.[4] As smoke from a ninety-gun salute drifted across the assembly, "Little Mac" joined the president, Cameron, and Seward and together they rode down the long line of troops as a band played "Hail to the Chief" and the cheers of the soldiers rolled across the snow-streaked plain.[5] It was all, as the *Philadelphia Press* put it, "indescribably grand,"[6] so much so that it helped inspire a Washington woman named Julia Ward Howe to begin writing, the next day, new lyrics for the popular tune "John Brown's Body." The song would become famous as "The Battle Hymn of the Republic."

It was possible, in fact, to watch this military pageant and forget, momentarily, that it was this same army—or rather an earlier version of it—that had fled in full panic from a smaller rebel force at Manassas, climbing up one another's backs and over flabbergasted civilians to reach the safety of the capital. It was even possible to ignore for the moment the rather stark fact— it was becoming starker with each passing week—that only a few miles away from this throat-tightening spectacle, camped that very same Confederate army with precisely the same commanding generals—Johnston and Beauregard—and it was almost exactly where the fleeing Federals had left it in July. Since then no Union forces had advanced against it, no artillery had been fired in its direction other than a few rounds lobbed by a Federal reconnaissance party.[7] Indeed, the Confederate forces had been allowed to conduct their own reviews, unmolested, a mere dozen miles away—to Confederate general Joe Johnston's amazement.

What made such proximity so remarkable was that, whereas in July the Union had outnumbered its rivals 35,000 to 32,000, there were now 150,000 Federal troops in the field against 40,000 rebels, a mismatch so absurd that many politicians and pundits in the North were beginning to wonder why they were watching reviews at all instead of reading about military victories.[8] This was the grand irony of McClellan's Grand Review. The troops who were turned out for this parade alone—seventy-six regiments, seventeen batteries, and seven regiments of cavalry, roughly half of the Army of the Potomac—were greater in number than *all of the Confederate forces in Virginia*, and far better equipped. Though not everyone would have agreed with those troop appraisals—as we will see, that was part of the problem—there was plenty of reliable intelligence in the hands of Union generals and Northern politicians to suggest that it was true, or at least approximately true, and with numbers like that, rough estimates were all that was needed.[9]

The reason for such bristling passivity was not hard to find, even in a war that was unfolding in a rat's nest of political and military intrigue. It was the immaculately dressed man on the big black horse: George B. McClellan, the general who, possessed of an enormous, gleaming weapon, mysteriously refused to use it. He was one of the most remarkable public figures the United States of America has ever produced. The list of his personal attributes was as striking then as it is now. He was an extremely efficient and even gifted administrator. He was good at the business side of running an army. He was also egocentric to a nearly unimaginable degree, harshly judgmental of others, vainglorious, mean-spirited, dissembling, almost pathologically risk-averse, haughty, insincere, back-stabbing, callously dismissive of his peers, and, though he was not a coward in any conventional sense, he was certainly very troubled by the idea of sending large numbers of men into battle. To give edge to all of this, he believed himself to be God's chosen instrument on earth for the salvation of the Union. He was so convinced of this that, later in the war, he was able to justify jeopardizing an entire Union army to advance his own interests.[10] Part of McClellan's brilliance was that, to his bosses in Washington and to the nation at large, he did not *seem* to be any of those things—at least not at first. His true personality was as thoroughly cloaked, in its own way, as his classmate Tom Jackson's. He appeared, in the spring and summer of 1861, as the savior of the Union, a bright, briskly efficient, refreshingly straightforward, confident, and confidence-inspiring man who could right the terrible wrongs of Manassas and make "On to Richmond!" something other than the empty battle cry it had become.

McClellan had always seemed destined for greatness. Precociously smart, he had gone off to the University of Pennsylvania at fourteen, then matriculated at West Point at sixteen, two years under the minimum age, where he graduated second in the same class—1846—in which Jackson ranked seventeenth. Unlike the socially awkward Jackson, McClellan was immensely popular with his classmates. He served with distinction as an engineer in the Mexican-American War and was subsequently assigned by the US Army as an observer in the Crimean War. He resigned from the army at age thirty to become vice president and chief engineer of the Illinois Central Railroad. Two years later he became president of the Ohio and Mississippi Railroad. He did well at both jobs. "There is an indefinable air of success about him and something of the 'man of destiny,'" wrote a contemporary.[11] In late July 1861, following the Union disaster at Manassas, he had been given command of the Army of the Potomac, reporting to Winfield Scott. Brimming with confidence and buoyed up by a fawning press, McClellan gave a speech soon after he arrived in which he promised that the war he was going to wage would be short, sharp, and final. Indeed, he seemed to harken strangely back to the very early, romantic days of the war, when people believed that one big, glorious fight would settle the issue. "I expect to fight a terrible battle," he wrote to a friend. "When I am ready I shall move without regard to season or weather. . . . But of one thing you may rest assured—when the blow is struck it will be heavy, rapid, and decisive."[12]

He became instantly famous, and it went instantly to his head. "I find myself in a strange position here—President, Cabinet, Genl. Scott all deferring to me—by some strange operation of magic I seem to have become *the* power of the land," he wrote to his young wife, Nelly. "I almost think that were I to win some small success now I could become Dictator or anything else that might please me—but nothing of that kind would please me—therefore I *won't* be Dictator. Admirable self denial!"[13] In another letter to her he wrote, "Who would have thought, when we were married, that I should so soon be called on to save my country?"[14] As though he needed more of this sort of encouragement, the press insisted on comparing him to a young Napoléon.

But it turned out that Little Mac was very good at one thing, and it was not a small thing: training an army. Starting in August, he transformed the Army of the Potomac from the ragged corps that had lost its first battle and almost all its confidence into something that looked as if it could win a war. Working long hours, he tightened discipline, pulled in shirkers and wanderers, made everything from transport to the commissary work more efficiently, and drilled the men endlessly. He built fifty forts and redoubts around Washington, DC, with parapets twelve feet thick, armed with three hundred guns, and fronted by abatis (barricades of fallen trees). In a very real sense, McClellan rescued the Union in those early days from despondency and fear: someone had to rebuild the army and show the country that there was great hope for the future. He did it with chin up and cap bill down, and none of the men who cheered as he rode by them had any notion that he was anything less than the great commanding officer he seemed to be.

He was also showing just how deeply ambitious he was. He moved almost immediately against his boss, the debilitated Winfield Scott, who suffered from dropsy, vertigo, and paralysis and had trouble staying awake. McClellan largely ignored him, violating military protocol by dealing directly with the president and cabinet, and complaining loudly to all of them that Scott was holding things up, interfering with McClellan's grand plan for a fast and decisive end to the war. Scott complained bitterly about McClellan's maneuvering, but to no avail. On November 1, Scott retired, leaving McClellan as general in chief as well as commander of the Army of the Potomac. Little Mac had wanted it all, and, with astonishing speed, he had gotten it.

Meanwhile, he was behaving more and more as though he were, in fact, the power of the land. He rented a splendid house very near the White House, where he and Nelly threw lavish dinner parties. He went everywhere with a large entourage of aides and staff officers. His vainglory had an edge to it, too. The more entrenched he became, the more contempt he felt for his peers and rivals. He wrote to his wife, "I can't tell you how disgusted I am with these wretched politicians—they are a most despicable set of men. . . . I am becoming daily more disgusted with this imbecile administration." He thought Lincoln's cabinet contained "some of the greatest geese I have ever seen. . . . Seward is the meanest of them all—a meddlesome, officious, incompetent little puppy. . . . [Secretary of the Navy Gideon] Welles is a garrulous old woman. . . . [Attorney General Edward] Bates is an old fool. . . . The presdt. is nothing more than a well meaning baboon . . . 'the original gorilla.' . . . It is sickening in the extreme [to] see the weakness and unfitness of the poor beings who control the destinies of this great country."[15] McClellan's self-infatuation reached its apogee one evening in November, when Lincoln and Seward came to call on him at his home. They were told he was at a dinner party. They waited. An hour later McClellan arrived and was told about his visitors. He ignored them, walked upstairs, and retired for the evening. An hour and a half after they arrived, a servant informed Lincoln and Seward that McClellan had gone to bed. (It would not be the last time that he stood Lincoln up or publicly ignored him.)

The problem with McClellan—and by late autumn it was a large and growing problem—was that, for all his talk of ending the war quickly with a single decisive blow, and in spite of the army of half a million men he now commanded, he refused to advance against the enemy, or even to come up with a coherent plan of attack. This was in spite of continuous prodding from Lincoln, the cabinet, Republicans in Congress, and newspaper editors such as the *New York Tribune*'s Horace Greeley. It was, indeed, their criticism of him—"meddling" with army affairs, as he saw it—that made him so contemptuous of them. He had blamed the delays on Scott. But after November 1 Scott was no longer in command, and still no plans for an advance materialized, in spite of a warm, dry autumn that was favorable to the movement of large armies.

McClellan's reasons for refusing to march were constantly shifting. His position was first that the men were not ready, which was in many ways accurate. Then, as months rolled by and soldiers were trained and dazzling public reviews were staged, he retooled his arguments, now insisting that he was woefully undermanned and outgunned by Confederate forces. This was to be his plaint for the rest of his war career: he was being forced to send vastly outnumbered troops to their deaths because shortsighted politicians would not give him enough men or guns. This position also had the effect of shifting blame for inaction from him to Lincoln and the War Department. In November, McClellan complained bitterly that "I cannot move without more means . . . I have been thwarted and deceived by these incapables at every turn. . . . It now begins to look like a winter of inactivity. If it is so, the fault will not be mine."[16]

It should be noted that whether McClellan is considered by history to be a morally admirable character or not—most historians have seen him as pompous, egotistical, and self-defeating, largely the result of his own self-indicting letters to his wife and others—in his caution, conservatism, and desire for perfect preparedness before making a move, he was absolutely in step with many other commanding generals early in the war, on both sides. The sort of headlong, man-wasting aggressiveness that generals such as Grant, Sherman, Lee, and Jackson later brought to the war was not yet seen as sound strategy. Who, after all, had won at Manassas, the defense-minded Johnston and Beauregard, or McDowell, with his elaborate and daring end run around the Confederate flank? McClellan, in fact, argues his biographer Ethan Rafuse, was squarely in a larger, post-Enlightenment military tradition that placed "an emphasis on logistics, sieges, and carefully executed maneuvers whose costs and risks could be rationally calculated."[17] That tradition saw its fullest flowering in the Army of the Potomac, just as it was being rendered almost completely obsolete.

Whatever the reason, in a country clamoring for war, the blame for inaction rested largely with McClellan. In November 1861 he had three times the troops and three times the artillery of the Confederates in his front. That he did not credit this was partly because he was receiving grossly inaccurate intelligence from Allan Pinkerton, a McClellan hire from Chicago whose private detective agency seemed to specialize in exaggerating its clients' peril. In October, Pinkerton's operatives estimated that there were 150,000 well-supplied Confederates near Manassas. The reality was that McClellan had 120,000 against 45,000, a numerical superiority so crushing that, had he advanced, rebel forces would have been forced to retire behind the Rappahannock, if not to Richmond itself. In November Pinkerton made the ridiculous assertion that Joe Johnston had been reinforced with *75,000 fresh troops* and was preparing to attack Washington.[18] But these absurd bits of intelligence were only half the problem; they required some extremely credulous person to believe them. That was McClellan, who was turning out to be one of the most timid military commanders in American history. He wanted to believe Pinkerton because Pinkerton reinforced his own instinctive caution. Manassas had shown McClellan and everyone else just how much was at risk in a single battle, and how serious, well-intentioned, sober men with military experience could be made to look like fools in a matter of hours.

A grisly reminder of this new phenomenon had taken place that fall near Leesburg, Virginia, about forty miles northwest of Washington on the Potomac River. In response to unusual Confederate troop movements, McClellan had ordered his local division commander, Brigadier General Charles P. Stone, to make a "slight demonstration" to feel the enemy out. Stone passed the order on to Colonel Edward "Ned" Baker, a close friend of Abraham Lincoln's and a US senator from Oregon. On October 21, 1861, Baker crossed the Potomac with most of a brigade to reinforce a small raiding party, collided with Confederate forces under Nathan "Shanks" Evans, of Manassas fame, and was badly beaten at the Battle of Ball's Bluff. Baker was killed, and his men were sent reeling back down the muddy, hundred-foot bluff and into the river, where they were shot in the back as they tried to swim away. For the size of the expedition, Union losses were staggering: 223 killed, 226 wounded, and 553 prisoners taken. Evans's forces suffered less than 200 casualties.[19] The disaster at Ball's Bluff resulted in the formation in the Federal Congress of the Joint Committee on the Conduct of the War to investigate it, and in the rapid destruction of the reputation and career of Brigadier Charles P. Stone, the committee's first victim. In addition to bearing responsibility for the defeat, Stone, as it turned out, had been a little too cooperative in returning escaped slaves to their owners, and this was thought to reflect on his patriotism; he was thrown in jail as a traitor. It was believed by many in the Union, and later by Stone himself, that to protect himself, General McClellan had thrown him to the wolves.

The risks of command were equally apparent that autumn in the Union West, where another romantic egotist, General John Frémont, in a job fully as large-scale and important as McClellan's, was presiding over a different sort of disaster. On August 10, in the first big fight in the western theater, a Union army in southwestern Missouri had been soundly defeated by Confederates at the Battle of Wilson's Creek, losing 2,500 killed and wounded. A month later, 3,500 Union soldiers surrendered at the town of Lexington, Missouri, after a brief siege. Frémont himself, famous as the "Pathfinder of the West" and the Republican candidate for president in 1856, turned out to be a miserable failure, from the ridiculous imperial pomp of his St. Louis headquarters, awash in corrupt army contracts, to his issuance, on August 30, of an unauthorized proclamation in which he declared martial law and assumed all powers of the state, announced the death penalty for all Confederate guerrillas caught behind Union lines, and freed the slaves and seized the property of all Confederate activists in Missouri. It was a breathtakingly stupid move. As Lincoln pointed out to him, shooting guerrillas would immediately prompt Confederates to retaliate by shooting Union prisoners, man for man. Lincoln also told him that freeing the slaves—which Union elected leaders had taken pains in the Crittenden-Johnson resolution of July 1861 to assure the country was not the goal of the war—could, among other things, cost the Union the support of Kentucky, one of the Union-friendly slaveholding "border states." The price of rebellion could not be the emancipation of slaves. Not yet. Frémont compounded his error by sending his wife, Jessie, daughter of Missouri senator Thomas Hart Benton, to inform Lincoln that her husband refused to withdraw his proclamation unless the president ordered him to, and to point out that, were the Northern electorate to choose between Frémont and Lincoln, it would certainly choose Frémont. Lincoln ordered Frémont to withdraw his proclamation. In October he relieved Frémont of command.

Between the legendary Pathfinder in St. Louis and the dashing Young Napoléon in Washington, by December 1861 Union morale had been brought to its lowest point since the days immediately after the defeat at

Bull Run. The international community, meanwhile, so crucial to the fate of the Confederacy, was beginning to sound more and more convinced of the South's viability as an independent nation. In the late fall, the correspondent for the *Times* of London in Washington made an astonishing diary entry that read, "All the diplomatists [foreign diplomats], with one exception, are of the opinion that the Union is broken forever, and the independence of the South virtually established."[20]

CHAPTER SEVENTEEN

A Preternatural Calm

❖⟣⟢❖

The South, meanwhile, sitting smugly on its various victories, was in no hurry to make war, either. In the long, dry, warm autumn of 1861, while McClellan painstakingly built the prodigious war machine he refused to engage, the Confederate army quaintly built breastworks around Centreville, did little to reinforce Johnston's army, basked in the sun of its own supposed invincibility, and waited for recognition or intervention from the European powers, which most Southerners supposed would surely come. Furloughs were freely granted. Officers and privates alike returned to tend the harvests at their farms and plantations.[1] If European and other foreign diplomats in Washington believed that the Union was irretrievably broken, why shouldn't the Confederates themselves? Though Jefferson Davis's top generals in the East—Beauregard, Johnston, and G. W. Smith—pleaded with him to reinforce the Army of Northern Virginia and order a northward advance, the Confederate president, like McClellan but for vastly different reasons, steadfastly refused. There would be no great offensive strikes. Instead, armies would be recruited and dispersed over a vast defensive perimeter—a theory of war, propounded by the famed military tactician and historian Antoine-Henri Jomini and studied closely at West Point, that favored the holding of cities and other real estate over the mass destruction of enemy armies.[2] That theory would soon be discredited.

Jackson, predictably, was horrified. Camped with his brigade just a few miles from the Manassas battlefield, the man who had advocated total war even before the first shot at Fort Sumter was fired waited with growing anxiety and frustration as the weeks and months passed and no advance was ordered. "It does not appear that he was at all elated by the early successes of the Confederacy," wrote Henry Kyd Douglas, who was on his staff. "Nor did he concur in the opinion which so extensively prevailed in the fall of 1861, that the war would be a short one and our independence easily gained."[3] On September 30, Jackson and three of his colonels paid a call on President Davis, who was visiting at General Beauregard's headquarters. It was not a casual call. Jackson was no longer a shy college professor with unusual ideas. He was a general in the Provisional Army of the Confederate States, and he had an agenda.

It was his second encounter with the Confederate president. The first, which the thin-skinned, grudge-holding Davis would certainly have remembered, occurred when he arrived moments after the rout of the Federal army at Manassas, pale with rage and under the mistaken impression that all was lost. Jackson had loudly and unceremoniously informed him that he was completely mistaken. That meeting set the tone for much of their prickly relationship. Surprisingly, the two men had many traits in common. Davis had attended West Point, graduating in 1828. He had been a hero of the Battle of Buena Vista in the Mexican-American War, advancing and fighting gallantly with a bootful of blood. He had spent time at various outposts in the regular army. Though as a senator from Mississippi he had emerged as one of the ideological leaders of the South, like Jackson he had been a moderate, opposing secession until his home state actually seceded. He was fair, paternalistic, and progressive in his relations with his slaves. He was like Jackson in other ways, too. He could be warm and kindhearted around friends and allies, but his public persona was often stiff, cold, and unemotional. He was known for refusing to compromise. Like Jackson, he was a chronic dyspeptic. And he was a stickler for detail, once challenging General Winfield Scott, to the latter's everlasting chagrin, over $300 in mileage expenses on his army report. Unlike Jackson, he was transparently ambitious. "He is not a cheap Judas," said Winfield Scott of Davis, who as secretary of war from 1853 to 1857 had been Scott's boss. "I do not think he would have sold the Savior for thirty shillings. But for the successor-ship to Pontius Pilate he would have betrayed Christ and the Apostles and the whole Christian Church." Sam Houston of Texas found Davis "ambitious as Lucifer and cold as a lizard." That fall Davis had been engaged in a public fight with Pierre Beauregard over the latter's self-aggrandizing and misleading battle report. Davis argued, with justification, that Beauregard had attempted "to portray himself as the sole designer and executant of the Manassas triumph."[4] (Beauregard would lose, and be shipped to the western theater in January.) Davis also fought with the hypersensitive Joe Johnston, who, outraged that he had been ranked fourth on the list to be promoted to full general, wrote Davis a long and shockingly intemperate letter.

Though we have no record of what Davis thought of his meeting with Jackson, the latter was deeply disappointed. "I called on him this morning at about half-past ten o'clock," Jackson wrote Anna. "He looks thin, but does not seem as feeble as yesterday. His voice and manners are very mild. I saw no exhibition of that fire which I had supposed him to possess."[5] Davis asked about the status of Jackson's homeland—the northwestern part of Virginia. Thus cued, Jackson made his case for a strong military campaign in the region. Though it had strong Union sympathies, he believed it could be saved for the Confederacy. But Davis demurred. According to Jackson, he "did not even so much as intimate that he designed sending me there."[6] Davis changed the subject, instead chatting about what a fine general Robert E. Lee was. If Jackson's reaction was disenchantment, Davis took away something else entirely. From these two meetings, he got the not altogether inaccurate idea that Jackson was an offense-crazed fanatic—a notion that would soon have unfortunate consequences for Jackson's career.[7]

By October, when the Confederate army retreated from a position nearer the Potomac, Jackson could no longer contain his anxiety. He took his concerns to his superior officer, Major General G. W. Smith. A Kentuckian by birth, Smith was a smart, literate, illness-prone West Pointer and a veteran of the Mexican-American War who, from 1858 to 1861, had served as streets commissioner in New York City. Jackson, who found Smith sick in his tent, sat down on the ground near the head of Smith's cot and began talking. He was concerned, he said, that by spring the huge numbers of new recruits streaming into the Union ranks would become "an organized army" and would "have greatly the advantage over us." His solution was to march north immediately. "We ought to invade their country now," he said, "and not wait for them to make the necessary preparations for them to invade ours." He believed strongly, he said, that "McClellan's raw recruits could not stand against us in the field."

But Jackson had come with more than just vague nostrums for an offensive war. He had been busy doing what newly minted brigadiers were not supposed to do: thinking in sweeping geopolitical, military, and economic terms. He proceeded to lay out for the amazed Smith a full-blown plan to lay waste to the North, its armies, its industries, and its cities that would see Philadelphia in flames and Confederate armies camped on the shores of the Great Lakes. "Crossing the Upper Potomac, occupying Baltimore, and taking possession of Maryland," he told Smith,

> we could cut off the communications of Washington, force the Federal government to abandon the capital, beat McClellan's army if it came out against us in the open country, destroy industrial establishments wherever we found them, break up the lines of interior commercial intercourse, close the coal mines, seize and, if necessary, destroy the manufactories and commerce of Philadelphia, and of other large cities within our reach; take and hold the narrow neck of country between Pittsburgh and Lake Erie; subsist mainly on the country we traverse, and making unrelenting war amidst their home, force the people of the North to understand what it will cost them to hold the South in the Union at the bayonet's point.[8]

The vision was as prescient as it was breathtaking: the last quoted sentence is a nearly perfect summary of the logic behind the brutally destructive, punitive late-war campaigns of Union generals William Tecumseh Sherman in Georgia and South Carolina, and Philip Sheridan in the Shenandoah Valley.[9] Jackson's proposal to have Southern armies operate without their supply lines deep in enemy territory was made fully eighteen months before Grant stunned the nation by doing that very thing—which he and Jackson had both learned from Winfield Scott in Mexico—on the way to his critical victory at Vicksburg in the summer of 1863. When he had finished, Jackson asked Smith to use his influence with Johnston and Beauregard to sell them on the idea. Smith said he didn't think that would work, whereupon Jackson launched into another lengthy discourse, pointing out again the advantages of his plan. Such impassioned advocacy would have been unimaginable from Jackson the VMI professor. The new rank was opening him up, giving him a new sense of his own abilities, of how far he could push things. He was flexing new muscles. At length he said, "General, you have not expressed any opinion in regard to the views I have laid before you. But I feel assured that you favour them, and I think you ought to do all in your power to have them carried into effect." Smith then told Jackson "a secret": a plan to advance north of the Potomac had been "laid before the Government" at a meeting in early October by Johnston, Beauregard, and himself, he said. That plan had been rejected.

"When I had finished," said Smith, "he rose from the ground on which he had been seated, shook my hand warmly, and said, 'I am very, very sorry.' Without another word he went slowly out to his horse . . . mounted very deliberately, and rode sadly away."[10] Friends later said that Jackson found the South's indolence in the days after Manassas to be "the darkest period of our struggle."[11]

Meanwhile, in Jackson's and other Confederate camps near Manassas, autumn slid by, with little to mark the days. Drills were conducted four or five times a day. The men lived mostly in huge, conical Sibley tents, eighteen feet wide and twelve feet tall, supported by a center pole and open at the top to allow smoke to escape. Designed to fit twelve men, they often held twenty, and they were afflicted with the usual run of camp pests. Their canvas roofs and walls were often covered with black flies and mosquitoes—"gallinippers," as some soldiers called them. There were blood-sucking buffalo gnats that dived into ears and nose, blowflies, chiggers, fleas and, worst of all, lice ("gray backs") that roamed freely over the body and took up residence in its more hirsute areas.[12] As always, there was disease. Diarrhea and dysentery were universal. Men who had never seen combat and never would see combat were already dying at a steady rate. If Jackson himself suffered from these afflictions, which he almost certainly did, he never mentioned it.

The highlight of Jackson's time in camp was a mid-September visit from Anna—one of the perquisites of his new rank. The journey from her parents' home in North Carolina, where she now lived, was difficult. Because her escort did not have a military "passport" to the front, she was forced to travel alone by rail from Richmond to Manassas—something Southern ladies in antebellum times did not often do—and because of a missed connection was compelled to spend the night in the train car at Fairfax station. She spent a few hours at a house that was being used as a hospital—a "place of horrors," as she called it—where she saw soldiers building coffins.[13]

Jackson was thrilled to have her with him. In just a few months, their lives had changed dramatically. Their home in Lexington was abandoned and closed up, their slaves placed with other families. Their happy domestic routines—Jackson's job, the church, the black Sunday school, the Franklin debating society, their visits to the local springs—had all vanished from their lives. Jackson's garden, and his little farm outside of town, lay untilled and untended. Their beloved Amy had died that fall, and both had grieved for her. For the moment they had only each other, and they made the most of their time together. Jackson secured them a room near his camp. They attended church in a small farmhouse, and ate together at a mess table under the trees, which Anna enjoyed immensely. She met General Johnston, was impressed by his "polished manners," and watched a Grand Review of his entire command, finding it "the most imposing military display I have ever witnessed." She received many social calls from officers and enlisted men of the Stonewall Brigade, all intensely curious to see what their general's wife was like. The highlight of the visit was a tour of the Manassas battlefield, conducted by Jackson and his artillery chief, W. N. Pendleton, the minister from Lexington. She found the geography itself surprisingly ordinary, writing that Bull Run was "a small, insignificant stream," and that there was "nothing remarkable" about the terrain of the battlefield. But she was fascinated to hear Jackson and Pendleton describe the movements of the two armies. They toured Henry House, now famous, half destroyed with shot and shell; they saw human bones and the carcasses of horses.[14]

And then Anna had to leave. If the machinery of war was moving slowly or not at all in the larger army, Jackson's own situation was much more fluid. On October 7 he was promoted to major general, thus completing a dizzying ascent from a disregarded major of engineers to high command in six months. He was in rarefied company, now one of four division commanders in Johnston's army (the others were James Longstreet, Earl Van Dorn, and G. W. Smith), and earning three and a half times his salary at VMI—$4,812 annually compared with $1,300.[15] The promotion was perhaps the final measure of how his performance on Henry Hill was seen in the Confederate army's high command. Jackson's skill and courage as a field commander were undeniable.

Still, there were doubters. Many—if not most—of the officers in the army, while they acknowledged his performance at Manassas, questioned his aptitude for higher command.[16] "I fear the Government is exchanging our best Brigade Commander for a second or third class Major General," said one of them.[17] In late October, in response to lobbying from Congressman Alexander Boteler and others, Jackson was given command of what was to be called the Valley District—the area between the Blue Ridge and the Allegheny Mountains that consisted mainly of the Shenandoah Valley. On the chilly afternoon of November 4, Jackson arrived in the northern valley town of Winchester to take command. It was, among other things, a heartbreakingly beautiful place to make war.

CHAPTER EIGHTEEN

A SEASON OF STORMS

Compared with the Washington-to-Richmond corridor, the Shenandoah Valley was a military backwater. It wasn't in the far northwestern part of the state Jackson had told Davis he wanted, and Winchester's gently rolling, open geography would be hard to defend. But Jackson was pleased anyway. Winchester, a pretty town of foursquare brick homes Jackson had fallen in love with during his brief time there with Johnston, had enormous strategic importance as the northernmost defensive post of the Confederacy. With a population of 4,400, it was a bustling commercial center, a crossroads where nine turnpikes and railroads converged. The town was also the northern gateway and military key to the fertile Shenandoah Valley—that slanting, 150-mile-long, 25-mile-wide alley between two muscular, smokeblue mountain ranges whose agricultural yields in wheat, rye, hay, barley, oats, corn, and potatoes were unrivaled in the South. There was little doubt, moreover, that a Union occupation of the valley would be an outright disaster for the Confederacy, shutting off a critical food source and opening a tailor-made corridor of invasion to Richmond complete with its own railroad line and supply base.[1] When Jackson wrote Alexander Boteler that "if the Valley is lost, Virginia is lost," he was simply stating what anyone with any knowledge of local geography would have known. His mission, at the extreme left of the Confederate line, 80 miles west of Joe Johnston's headquarters in Centreville, was to prevent that from happening. He would have his hands full: in October a Union army of 5,000 had swept local militia aside and seized nearby Romney, Virginia, in a parallel river valley only 35 miles west of Winchester; that force had since swelled to 7,000 men. Fifty miles to the north, across the Potomac River in Frederick, Maryland, waited 16,000 troops under General Nathaniel Banks. And scattered along the Potomac and into the western mountains were some 22,000 troops reporting to General William S. Rosecrans.[2]

Against 43,000 Union troops Jackson had only a meager force. By December he had about 5,000 men: 2,000-plus in the battle-tested Stonewall Brigade, another 2,500 militia he had inherited or recruited, and some 500 cavalry under the brilliant but erratic Colonel Turner Ashby. The recruits did not daunt him; he had learned from his experience at Harpers Ferry how to deal with them. Officers would be summarily broken of their militia ranks; the men would be drilled five times a day until they learned real army discipline. The guardhouse waited for those who clung to their old freedoms. The difference now was that Jackson, as major general, was already a much harder man than the novice colonel, less forgiving of error, less tolerant of anything like a challenge to his authority. He was never angry or emotional and, indeed, as he laid out his camps around Winchester he was all business: rules were rules, violations were violations; consequences must follow.

This new order was on display in mid-November, when bad weather prompted enlisted men in the Stonewall Brigade to seek shelter inside the town of Winchester in spite of Jackson's strict orders to stay in their camps. There had been incidents: men were drinking and making trouble. His solution was to expand the original restrictions to include officers, who reacted angrily at what they saw as an assault on their personal privileges. Nine colonels and majors, including the brigade's temporary commander, sent a joint communiqué to Jackson huffily asserting that his order was "an unwarranted assumption of authority" and "an improper inquiry into their private matters" and freedoms "accorded in every other department of the army." Jackson replied immediately, and sternly, that these officers were "in violation of Army regulations" and that, either out of "incompetency" or "neglect of duty," they had been responsible for the arrests of several of their enlisted men in town. The carefully chosen term "neglect of duty" carried its own threat of court-martial. He then laid down the law in flat, uninflected language: "If officers desire to have control over their commands," Jackson wrote, "they must remain habitually with them, and industriously attend to their instructions and comfort, and in battle lead them well, and in such manner as to command their admiration."[3] In case anyone wondered how serious he was, he moved immediately to replace the brigade's commander. Business was business.

Two weeks later, he again displayed what seemed to his men to be a new, strangely unyielding, unforgiving view of war. A soldier named James A. Miller, of Harpers Ferry, had gotten drunk and shot and wounded his captain. An army court-martial had found him guilty and sentenced him to death by firing squad. Because Jackson was in a position to commute the sentence, a number of pleas for leniency were made to him on Miller's behalf, including an impassioned one from Jackson's friend Reverend James Graham. Jackson refused. He upheld the court-martial, and Miller was shot to death by the 2nd Virginia in Winchester on November 6. (It was later learned that Jefferson Davis, more sympathetic than his major general, actually did commute Miller's sentence, but a messenger bearing his order got drunk and never delivered it.[4]) The men were learning quickly that, in Jackson's command, unlike most of the rest of the army, or the army they thought they knew, there would be no bending of the rules. Jackson may have had trouble enforcing discipline in his section room with mischievous, fresh-faced college boys, but he had no trouble doing so in a rough army camp.

What Jackson mainly wanted was to attack a Union army. He had been made to wait passively for months in the camps around Manassas. Now, with something approximating an independent command, he was eager to advance. He was aware that with such a numerical disadvantage his only chance was to keep the enemy off balance. The way to do that, it seemed to him, was with tactical strikes. Two weeks after his arrival he wrote to Confederate secretary of war Judah Benjamin in Richmond with a plan, endorsed by Johnston, for a winter campaign "to capture the Federal forces at Romney."[5] He would need more men, and he proposed that three brigades in the Allegheny Mountains south and west of Winchester, under the command of Brigadier General William W. Loring, be ordered to join him. Thus reinforced—he would have more than ten thousand men—he would seize Romney.

Once in possession of Romney, he proposed to cross a sizable chunk of the Allegheny Mountains in winter and strike deep into northwestern Virginia (now West Virginia). The latter proposal was interesting for two reasons. First, it reflected Jackson's persistent, terrier-like refusal to give up on the idea of attacking and occupying his Union-leaning homeland. Second, it was, as Jackson modestly noted, "an arduous undertaking" that would involve "the sacrifice of much comfort." This was a spectacular understatement. While his scheme did not quite come up to Hannibal's crossing of the Alps with his army in the year 218 BC, the Alleghenies were steep, forbidding mountains. They were often covered with snow in December. They were subject to bitter cold and ice storms. Romney would be difficult enough. Probing, as Jackson suggested, into the country of the Little Kanawha and Monongahela Rivers could, in bad weather, prove disastrous. Still, Jackson was persuasive; Benjamin and Johnston approved the plan, pending the arrival of Loring's brigades in Winchester. Without Loring's men, Jackson could not even dream of attacking at Romney and beyond.

On paper, the forty-three-year-old Loring was everything the Confederacy wanted in a brigadier general. At age fourteen he had enlisted in the Florida territorial militia to fight Seminole Indians. After a brief career as a lawyer and legislator, he enlisted in the US Army and fought with distinction in the Mexican-American War. He was breveted a colonel for bravery at the Battle of Chapultepec, then had his arm shattered by a bullet as he was running through one of the gates to Mexico City in the company of his fellow officer Ulysses S. Grant. Though Loring later had the arm amputated, he stayed on active duty, fighting Indians in the Northwest and on the Texas–New Mexico frontier. In 1857 he tracked and killed the notorious Apache war chief Cuchillo Negro. Loring's weaknesses, which would soon be on display, were a belligerent, self-righteous streak that led him into confrontations with fellow officers, and a McClellan-like tendency to exaggerate the difficulties he faced.[6]

Jackson had wanted Loring in Winchester in early December. But the last of Loring's troops would not arrive until Christmas. Jackson, impatient for action, had occupied himself by doing minor mischief: he managed to break a dam on the Chesapeake and Ohio Canal, one of the main transportation routes between Washington and the Cumberland—part of his larger strategic plan to shut off Washington's coal supply. (The Federals quickly repaired it.) Occasionally his frustration with Loring's tardiness flashed into anger. When Colonel John M. Patton of the 21st Virginia in Loring's command reported for duty, he complained to Jackson that his men had had a desperately hard march. "I feel it my duty to say to you that my men are so foot sore and weary that they could just crawl up barely," he said. "Jackson snapped back, 'Colonel, if that is the condition of your men, I will not send them on this expedition. Take them back and report to your brigadier.'" Patton quickly decided that his men were not quite as exhausted as he had suggested they were.

One of Loring's three brigade commanders, William B. Taliaferro (pronounced "Tolliver"), offered a classic example of how quickly the war had changed men's fortunes. Taliaferro was from an old-line, aristocratic Virginia family. He had attended Harvard and William and Mary, and had served in the Virginia legislature. He had also been president of VMI's governing Board of Visitors during Jackson's tenure there. That meant, of course, that he knew all about the eccentric professor and the complaints against him and had witnessed firsthand the attempt to get rid of him. Now Taliaferro was a mere colonel in Major General Jackson's army. After the war he wrote about how this shifting perspective had changed his opinion of the man. "Jackson disclosed to me a trait which had not struck me before," he wrote. "There is a real difference in looking at a brevet major and a full major general. At [VMI] he was more than ordinarily passive. The fire was there, but he was a soldier in grain, and he believed it to be his duty, in his subordinate place, to execute, not to suggest. I had not noticed the saliency of his character—I will not say restlessness, but the desire to do, to be moving, to make, to embrace opportunity."[7]

Jackson could do none of this until Loring arrived. So he waited impatiently, reported to Johnston by telegraph once a week, tried unsuccessfully to convince Virginia governor John Letcher to send him more troops, complained about Loring's lateness, and attempted to sidestep the rising number of people who wanted to look at Stonewall Jackson, the hero of Manassas.

But there were compensations. Anna arrived just before Christmas, and the couple found warm, welcoming quarters in the house of the Reverend James Graham. The man who could, in effect, order one of his own soldiers shot was as playful and affectionate as ever in private with his beloved *esposa*. The food was good, and Jackson's messmates, most of them from Lexington and all with personal ties to him, were lively company. They included Jackson's chief of staff, John T. L. Preston, who was not only Maggie's husband but also Jackson's business partner and VMI colleague; Ellie's cousin George Junkin; Jackson's own cousin Alfred Jackson; and Sandy Pendleton, the charming twenty-one-year-old son of Jackson's friend the Lexington minister and Rockbridge artillery chief W. N. Pendleton. Such nepotism was so obvious that when Jackson asked another cousin from western Virginia, Judge W. L. Jackson, to join his staff, he declined, saying that "to appoint another of your relatives will occasion dissatisfaction."[8] Jackson, as usual, was much less guarded among friends and family. "We have a merry table," wrote Preston to Maggie, "I as much a boy as any of them, and Jackson grave as a signpost, til something chances to overcome him, and then he breaks out into a laugh so awkward that it is manifest that he never laughed enough to learn how. He is a most simple-hearted man."[9]

Jackson's Romney Expedition, as it would be known to history, began on New Year's Day 1862 in unseasonably warm weather. His plan was to move north to seize the town of Bath, thereby covering his flank and rear, then swing west and south to attack Romney. The plan sounded simple enough. It turned out to be anything but. The temperature started dropping on the first day, falling below 32 degrees by evening. A biting wind made it feel even colder. Overcoats, blankets, tents, and food that had been left behind on supply wagons never made it to camp, which meant that most of the men spent the long, freezing night without cover of any kind. They resumed the march at dawn, still exposed and without food, but now in wind-driven snow. Temperatures fell into the 20s. When Loring ordered his brigades into bivouac short of Jackson's destination for the day, Jackson, furious, ordered them all to pack up and move forward, without dinner, in the freezing darkness. Loring, who had been complaining bitterly about the mismanagement of the supply train, and about Jackson's failure to tell him anything about his plans or military objectives, was appalled. "By God, sir," he cried in the presence of his troops, "this is the damnedest outrage ever perpetrated in the annals of history, keeping my men out here in the cold without food!"[10] The men themselves were nearly mutinous, blaming "Tom Fool" Jackson for their misery.

Conditions would get worse, much worse. The next day the temperature dropped to 18 degrees. Still, Jackson pushed them, upbraiding Stonewall Brigade commander Richard B. Garnett when he allowed his men, who had not eaten in thirty hours, to stop and cook rations for the day. (He had never liked Garnett anyway and had worked to block Garnett's appointment to command his beloved brigade.) At sunset on the third day, as the column approached Bath, one of Loring's brigades, under Jackson's VMI colleague Colonel William Gilham, clashed with Union skirmishers. As darkness fell, Gilham ordered the men to bivouac in the snow-covered field. Jackson immediately overruled him, sending John Preston with orders for him to advance into Bath. Loring, again astounded by Jackson's orders, immediately countermanded them. Jackson arrived, just as angry, and the two exchanged heated words. Jackson gave up the advance. The next day Gilham committed what was, for Jackson, an unforgivable sin. Though he had been given direct orders to advance into the town of Bath, he had failed to do so. His skirmishers had been fired on again by the rear guard of the retreating Union forces, and, out of fear or caution, he had simply stopped. Then he had compounded his error by neglecting to tell Jackson what he had done. Gilham's mistakes would mean the end of his brief war career. Jackson brought charges against him, specifying that he had neglected his duty by failing "to attack the federal forces after over-taking them near Sir John's Run Depot on Jan. 4, 1862," and that he "did fail to report either directly or indirectly . . . the cause of his having failed to attack."[11] (Gilham later wrote critically of Jackson, saying that it was Jack-son's fault—choosing poor roads and ordering militia to do regular army work—that they had not captured the Federals at Bath.[12]) There would be no court-martial for Gilham. Instead, Jackson would place him on indefi-nite furlough, and send him back to VMI to resume his duties there.

It is worth noting exactly who Jackson had just pushed so abruptly out of the army. During the years Jackson had taught at VMI, William Henry Gilham had been the institute's highly respected commandant. He was the academic star of the institution, its most brilliant professor, the man respon-sible for much of its curriculum. A graduate of West Point and a veteran of the Mexican-American War, he was smart, elegant, self-possessed, and enor-mously popular with cadets. He was considered a brilliant drillmaster. He was, in short, everything that Jackson was not. In 1859 he had commanded the VMI expedition, in which Jackson had taken part, to Charlestown to provide security for John Brown's execution. But Gilham was more than just Jackson's colleague. He was also Jackson's friend and business partner in several ventures. There are no records of what happened between the two men, or how Jackson told Gilham what was going to happen to him, or how Gilham reacted to the news, or whether he was grateful, on some level, that Jackson did not drag him through a court-martial. It was probably no consolation to Gilham, who came so far short of expectations, that Jackson would be much less kind with other officers who got in his way.

The misery continued, unabated. January 7 was, for many of the men, the most horrific noncombat experience of the war. In a fierce north wind, with temperatures hovering in the 10-to-20-degree range, the men, wagons, and horses moved across icy roads frozen hard as a rock and cov-ered with six inches of snow. "It was a desperate time," wrote acting chief quartermaster Michael Harman. "Sleet, snow, horses falling and braking [sic] their legs; wagons stalled and overturned, soldiers shrieking from painful, frozen wounds."[13] Other accounts described the same horrors. "Men were frozen to death," wrote John Worsham of the 21st Virginia (Gilham's regiment). "Others were frozen so badly they never recovered, and rheumatism contracted by many was never gotten rid of. Large numbers were barefooted, having burned their shoes while trying to warm their feet at fires."[14] Sometimes men waited, shivering in the storm, up to ten hours while the army's 160-wagon supply train labored past. Men, horses, wagons—everything was slipping, falling. "Limbs were broken as well as guns and swords when a dozen soldiers went down at the same time," wrote Henry Kyd Douglas. "Horses fell and were killed."[15] To add to such appalling misery, the men also became infested with lice.[16] The final march was brutal, too, as the ice thawed to a muddy slush and the men plodded forward in a sleeting rain. Many of them were encased in icicles. On January 14, Jackson and his soldiers marched into Romney after two harrowing weeks. They discovered that the seven thousand Union troops and artillery who had occupied the town, alerted to Jackson's advance, had evacuated and fled north.

Jackson showed no sympathy at all for his troops' suffering. Though he had shared every bit of this misery with his men—often walking beside them, sometimes dismounting to "put his shoulder to the wheel of a wagon to keep it from sliding back"—he kept on driving forward, stopping for a few days only when he had no choice but to put winter shoes on his horses, whose falls had created mayhem in the ranks.[17] He seemed to feel only frustration at the failure of his column to move faster. For that he held his officers responsible. Before he had even returned to Winchester, Jackson was writing to Secretary of War Judah Benjamin to request that Richard B. Garnett, the brigadier general commanding the Stonewall Brigade and a soldier with an excellent reputation in the army, be relieved of command. "General G. is not qualified to command a brigade . . . he is not able to meet emergencies even in the proper management of his brigade in camp and on the march." It did not matter to Jackson that Garnett was an experienced soldier and a popular Virginia aristocrat with deep connections in the political and military community. Those were the very reasons his request was denied. As the coming months would prove, Jackson was not finished dealing with Garnett.

Nor was he finished, having seized Romney at such enormous cost to his men, with his plan to push deeper into northwestern Virginia. He now proposed to add reinforcements and march west into even more mountainous country, to capture the Federal supply depot at Cumberland, which was garrisoned with eleven thousand Union soldiers. When Benjamin denied him the troops, he came up with yet another idea—to destroy railroad bridges seventeen miles west of Romney. But it could not be done. Morale had been shattered, especially in Loring's brigades. Officers were despondent, defeated. As Jackson informed Benjamin in a January 20 letter, "General Loring's leading brigade, commanded by Col. Taliaferro, was not in a condition to move, the enterprise had to be abandoned. Since leaving Winchester, the 1st instant, the troops have suffered greatly, and Gen. Loring has not a single brigade in a condition for active operations."[18]

The hard march had also reduced the size of his army. Even the Stonewall Brigade had less than two-thirds of what it started with. There were many desertions, and much sympathy for the deserters. Men cursed Jackson openly, even members of the Stonewall Brigade. "That Jackson was not popular with his officers and men, even of his old brigade, *at that time*, is undeniable," Taliaferro wrote later. "For the true secret of the power of the American soldier is his individuality—the natural result of American citizenship; and Jackson's men thought, and, thinking, did not think that the ends accomplished by the Romney campaign justified the sacrifices which were made."[19] Jackson might have helped his cause with men and officers if he had given them even the most rudimentary idea of what they were doing, or where they were going. He had told no one anything of his plans, not even his second in command.

And now he would pay for that neglect. When Jackson put his army to winter quarters, he ordered Loring and his three brigades to stay in Romney to make sure Union forces did not reoccupy it. The Stonewall Brigade would return to Winchester, while various militias were posted in other towns. Once the orders were given, Jackson rode forty-three miles on the astoundingly resilient Little Sorrel through the mountains to Winchester, changed out of his mud-covered uniform, and hastened to the Graham house, where, according to Anna, "he came bounding into the sitting-room as joyous and fresh as a schoolboy" and took her in his arms. It would have been obvious to anyone who saw him that he had no regrets about what he had just done. He was, in fact, very pleased with the results of the expedition.[20]

He was naive. Back in the muddy, icebound "hog pen" that was the tiny town of Romney, with snow, sleet, and rain falling, raw sewage running in the streets, and a courthouse full of rotten meat, Loring and his officers were ready to explode. They felt deeply wronged, not only because of the brutality of the march and Jackson's strange penchant for secrecy but also because he had left them perilously exposed, with fewer than five thousand soldiers in close proximity to vastly larger numbers of Federals. (They were not, as it turned out, completely wrong. Jackson's own engineer had pronounced Romney indefensible with the forces Loring had, and Union records would later show that Union general Frederick Lander was preparing to attack Romney on February 3, until his health prevented it.[21] Jackson, on the other hand, had accepted his huge numerical disadvantage as the *premise* of the entire campaign, and it had not changed. He had tried, repeatedly and unsuccessfully, to secure more troops.) They even accused Jackson of favoritism—allowing his "pet" Stonewall Brigade to return home to the relative comforts of Winchester. They pointed to the large numbers of sick men in their ranks, all presumably the result of Jackson's shocking neglect. In fact, according to Jackson's surgeon Hunter McGuire, many of the claims of sickness were false: "I organized a guard and guard-house, arrested hundreds of Loring's men who claimed to be sick, had them examined by the surgeons and returned to duty unless they were sick enough to stay in the hospital. In this way in a very few days I sent back to Loring's camp fully 1,000 men."[22]

Once they realized that Jackson was not going to change his mind, two of Loring's officers—Colonel Samuel Fulkerson and Colonel William Taliaferro—now opened a campaign against him, appealing directly to the political establishment in Richmond. Fulkerson was old-line Virginia and a district judge. Like Taliaferro, he was a veteran of the Mexican-American War and knew Jackson from having served on the governing board of VMI in the 1850s. (It was more than a little ironic that the two men behind this campaign were *both* subordinate to Jackson and *both* his former overseers at VMI. Perhaps they could not quite accept the idea of the eccentric science teacher's transformation.) Fulkerson, who was well connected in Richmond, wrote a letter bearing a note of endorsement from Taliaferro to Virginia congressmen Walter Preston and Walter R. Staples. He told them that he wanted their help in persuading Secretary of War Benjamin and President Davis to free Loring and his brigades from Jackson's command. Mostly, they were just desperate to get out of the frozen mud of Romney. Fulkerson said that Jackson had subjected his soldiers to great hardship in an unnecessary and fruitless winter campaign and that the exposure to the cold had "emaciated the force almost to a skeleton" and would discourage reenlistment. In his long postscript to Staples, Taliaferro wrote:

> *My Dear Staples: I take the liberty with an old friend, which I know you will pardon, to state that every word and every idea conveyed by Colonel F. in his letter to you is strictly and most unfortunately true. The best army I ever saw of its strength has been destroyed by bad marches and bad management. . . . It will be suicidal in the Government to keep this command here.*[23]

After these chummy appeals, next came a formal petition to Loring, drafted by Taliaferro and signed by Fulkerson, six regimental commanders, and Colonel Jesse Burks, who had replaced William Gilham, running through the same complaints and asking Loring to take the matter up with the War Department. Loring added a note to the petition saying he agreed completely with its charges, then sent one copy to Jackson, as military protocol required, and gave the other to Taliaferro, who used his furlough to hand-carry the note to Richmond. Once there, he called on old friends and associates in the capital and the legislature, and lobbied hard to have Loring's command recalled. Fulkerson and several other officers from Loring's brigades were in Richmond, on furlough, doing the same thing. According to Jackson ally Alexander Boteler, "several prominent officers of Loring's command took every opportunity while there to deprecate Jackson and manufacture public opinion against him. They said he was rash, foolhardy, and fanatical; that he had no common sense; was, unquestionably, crazy and entirely unfit to be at the head of an army."[24] Not everyone believed this Loring-sponsored campaign. When Representative Walter Preston was approached by one of the officers, he replied, so that others could hear, "It's a great pity, sir, that General Jackson has not bitten some of his subordinates on furlough and affected them with the same sort of craziness that he has himself."[25]

It was all very odd, informal if not underhanded, unmilitary, and in gross violation of army protocols. As such, the Confederate high command should never have tolerated it. Instead, it was in the presence of Vice President Alexander Stephens and President Jefferson Davis that Taliaferro found his most receptive audiences. Stephens, Taliaferro told Loring, "denounced the Romney expedition in the severest terms," while Davis "did not hesitate to say at once that Jackson had made a mistake." In the same "Private and Confidential" note to Loring, Taliaferro wrote, "When I told him of Jackson's having left us at Romney and having withdrawn his forces to Winchester, I never saw anyone so surprised. . . . I think from all

I can find out that the Presid't is disposed to do us justice. . . . Jackson's prestige is gone, public sentiment is against him. The leading men of the N.W. have asked me if he was not deficient in mind."[26]

Whether the latter was true or not no longer mattered. Davis, upset by what he had heard, and willing, perhaps because of his personal feelings about Jackson, to bypass the entire army command structure, proceeded to instruct Judah Benjamin to recall Loring's brigades from Romney. The Confederate secretary of war was a talented, complex, flawed political operative. The son of English Jews, he was raised in Louisiana and attended Yale. He became one of his home state's leading lawyers at a young age. At forty-two he was elected to the US Senate. He was short, rotund, well groomed, and socially adept. "He always looked as if he had just risen at the end of an enjoyed dinner to greet a friend with pleasant news," wrote historian Douglas Southall Freeman.[27] He was ambitious, opportunistic, persuasive, and self-confident to a fault, and so blindly loyal to Davis that he would never side with generals in the field against him.[28] He was also, for all his lack of army experience, meddlesome, which meant, as Joe Johnston wrote irritably in his memoirs, bypassing army command on a regular basis by "granting leaves of absence, furloughs, and discharges, accepting resignations . . . upon applications made directly to himself, without the knowledge of officers whose duty it was to look to the interests of the Government in such cases."[29] If it didn't bother Davis to ignore military protocol in overriding Jackson's orders, it certainly would not bother Benjamin.

Thus did Jackson receive, on the morning of January 31, a short, abruptly worded telegram from Richmond:

General T. J. Jackson, Winchester, VA:
  Our news indicates that a movement is being made to cut off General Loring's command. Order him back to Winchester immediately.
                                  J. P. Benjamin, Secretary of War

By his own description, Jackson was astonished by what he read. He had just cleared, with considerable pain and suffering, all Union armies from three large Virginia counties, destroyed a hundred miles of railroad track, and had suffered only thirty-five casualties doing it.[30] The tone of the message must have struck him as strange, too—as though addressing an underling who did not need to understand the order's ramifications, instead of a full major general commanding six thousand square miles of Virginia. Within the hour, he had decided what to do, probably with the help of prayer. He would comply with the order as given. And then he would resign. His reply to Benjamin was as follows:

> *Hon. J. P. Benjamin, Secretary of War*
> *Sir:*
>   *Your order requiring me to direct General Loring to return to his command to Winchester immediately has been received and promptly complied with.*
>   *With such interference in my command I cannot expect to be of much service in the field; and accordingly respectfully request to be ordered to report for duty to the Superintendent of the Virginia Military Institute at Lexington; as has been done in the case of other Professors. Should this application not be granted, I respectfully request that the President will accept my resignation from the Army.*
>   *I am, sir, very respectfully, your obedient servant, T. J. Jackson.*

Unlike Benjamin, Jackson was sticking to military rules and running his correspondence through proper channels. He sent the letter by courier to his immediate superior, Joe Johnston, in Centreville. Jackson also wrote letters to his friends Governor John Letcher and Congressman Alexander Boteler explaining his action. Their substance was, as he told Letcher, that "a sense of duty brought me into the field and has, thus far, kept me here. It now appears to be my duty to return to the institute. . . . I desire to say nothing against the Secretary of War. I take it for granted that he has done what he believes to be best, but I regard such a policy as ruinous."[31]

Because Johnston held Jackson's letter while he tried to persuade him to change his mind, Boteler ended up receiving his letter in Richmond before Benjamin had received Jackson's reply. Astounded, the bespectacled, bearded Boteler hurried to Benjamin's office.

"In consequence of your order, Jackson has sent in his resignation," he told Benjamin.

"What!" the secretary of war exclaimed, wheeling around in his chair. "Jackson resigned! Are you sure of your information?"

"As sure as I can be of anything," Boteler replied, "as I have it here directly from himself, under his own hand and seal."

Benjamin read the letter, his keen political instincts undoubtedly suggesting to him the magnitude of the mistake he and Davis had made. "You had better show that letter to the president," he said. Boteler then walked over to Jefferson Davis's office and told him of Jackson's resignation, to which Davis responded, "I'll not accept it, sir!"

"I'm very glad to hear you say so, sir," answered the courtly Boteler, "for I'm sure we cannot afford to lose him from the service. But you don't know General Jackson. When he takes a stand in accordance with his own ideas of duty, he's as firm as a rock."[32]

Boteler hustled down to tell Governor John Letcher, who was just as furious about it as he was. He soon went off to vent his anger at Benjamin and Davis and anyone else he could find in the War Department. Suddenly, indignant letters and telegrams were flying across the state, and within a few days, everyone from Lexington to Richmond seemed to know about Jackson's resignation. Many people wrote to him directly to express their outrage. Typical of these was a note from the Reverend Francis McFarland of Mint Spring, Virginia, to Jackson. "I declare to you sincerely, General, no single fact has come to my knowledge during the war that has so grieved me, as the news of your resignation, & all speak of it with deep regret," he wrote. "When one in high position in our army, *who fears God* (of whom we have, alas, so few), should feel compelled to leave it, I would regard it as evidence of the frown of God upon us."[33] Even a member of Davis's own staff wrote, "No heavier blow has befallen us or is likely to befall us."[34]

Jackson himself seemed strangely unperturbed by all the commotion. "He was the *only* calm and unexcited man among us," wrote his host, James Graham, in Winchester, who was, like many of the town's residents, indignant at the affront. "There was no severity of temper, no acrimony of language, no suspicion of anger." He seemed unusually happy, relaxed, and talkative, and told Anna how much he was looking forward to getting back to their old lives in Lexington. As he explained it to them, "The department has indeed made a serious mistake, but, no doubt, they made it with the best intentions. They have to consider the interests of the whole Confederacy."[35]

Which was exactly what politicians in Richmond were now frantically doing. The general sentiment in the capital was overwhelmingly pro-Jackson, and Davis and Benjamin and their allies had been made acutely aware of that. In Romney, according to Jackson's quartermaster, "Loring is like a scared turkey, and so is his command." There was no question that Jackson must not be allowed to resign, and now a campaign was mounted to get him back, one that specifically did not include the perpetrators. Johnston had already pleaded with him not to resign, pointing out correctly that the breach of protocol was as much an affront to him as it was to Jackson. Letcher wrote him a long, supplicatory letter, which was hand-carried to Winchester by Boteler, who made the case personally. Jackson was perfectly calm during most of it, except when Boteler made the indelicate suggestion that Jackson might not want to be "an exception" in a world where others were dedicating themselves to the cause and making sacrifices. Jackson, as Boteler later recalled, answered in an agitated voice, louder than usual:

> Sacrifices! Have I not made them? What is my life here but a daily sacrifice? War has no charms for me; I've seen too many of its horrors. . . . The hope of being serviceable as a soldier brought me here. I gave up the peaceful pursuits of a congenial occupation for the cares, discomforts, and responsibilities of the camp. I left a very happy home, Colonel, at the call of duty, and duty now not only permits but commands me to return to it.[36]

But as the evening wore on, Jackson's resistance weakened. When Boteler was leaving, he said, "Well, what message can I take back to our good friend, the Governor?" Jackson paused for a moment, then replied slowly, "Tell him that he'll have to do what he thinks is best for the state." Two days later, Jackson requested that Letcher withdraw his resignation.

It was typical of the man that, reinstated in full power, and now free from the interference of Davis and Benjamin, Jackson immediately preferred charges against Loring. There would be no forgiveness, no accounts that would go unsettled. Under the rubric of "neglect of duty" Jackson detailed Loring's sins, from failure to attack at Bath to permitting long delays in his column's march, allowing his command "to become so demoralized . . . that it was necessary to abandon an important expedition against the enemy." He did not leave out the petition, which he said violated military rules, or even Loring's harsh words—"This is the damnedest outrage . . ."—spoken about Jackson to Loring's own troops.[37] Johnston agreed with Jackson that Loring should be court-martialed for allowing his regiments to lapse into "a state of discontent little removed from insubordination." (With the political storm raging, Loring in fact withdrew from Romney on February 3.)

But Davis and Benjamin wanted no such thing. Jackson and Loring would be separated forever and life would go on. Loring was actually promoted, but also banished to southeastern Virginia, and his command was dispersed. He spent the rest of the war butting heads with his superiors, including Confederate general John C. Pemberton, who blamed him for the disastrous Southern defeat at Vicksburg in 1863. Jackson himself retained the lion's share of Loring's troops, including all of his Virginia regiments. As Jackson had predicted, Union troops reoccupied Romney after Loring had abandoned it. The damage to the tracks and to the C & O dam were repaired. On balance, Jackson's winter campaign was hardly a success, and certainly did not endear him to his bosses, though it did make them painfully aware of the consequences of interfering with him.

But in a very different sense, Romney was enormously telling. It was not about conquest as much as it was about *command*, and the exercise of it by a new general in a new war that was being invented minute by minute. The Romney Expedition witnessed the emergence of an extreme style of leadership that posed for the first time a question central to the outcome of the war: Just how far could you push both officers and common soldiers in pursuit of military goals? What the Confederates had done was no ordinary march. Jackson had forced his men to walk more than one hundred miles through a succession of brutal winter storms, high winds, ice, mud, and temperatures that stayed well below freezing. In spite of repeated protests from his officers, conditions that worsened as they marched, and troops with frozen, bleeding, bare feet, he held fast to his objective. He had imposed his will on an army of highly individualistic American volunteers and militiamen, who had freely given their allegiance to their country. They did not see themselves—indeed, could not imagine themselves—as blunt, unthinking instruments of death. The war they had enlisted in had begun as an exercise in glory and freedom. Under Jackson, it began to look more like grim servitude. Many of the men and officers in Loring's command thought Jackson was literally crazy. He was, in fact, just slightly ahead of the soldiers'—and the nation's—perception of what this pitiless war was all about, and just exactly how much raw suffering and death lay in the path of victory.

Jackson had also demonstrated that pure gall and audacity counted for something. Romney had been evacuated because Jackson's advance had scared George McClellan, who, a hundred miles away in Washington, was in no mood to engage with an aggressive rebel army of unknown size in midwinter.[38] Though Generals Nathaniel Banks and Frederick Lander had wanted to move against Jackson, McClellan would not allow it.[39]

After the Romney campaign Jackson wrote a note to one of his colonels, who had reported at one point that it was impossible for him to execute an order. "If your cavalry will not obey your orders," Jackson wrote, "you must *make them* do it, and if necessary go out with them yourself. . . . Arrest any man who leaves his post, and prefer charges and specifications against him, that he may be court-martialed. It will not do to say that your men cannot be induced to perform their duty—they *must be made to do it*." That was pure army, of course, but somehow, from Jackson's hand, it had an entirely new ring.

It is noteworthy that two weeks after the close of the Romney campaign, another unorthodox but fast-rising West Point graduate who was greatly underestimated by his peers also submitted his resignation. On February 16, 1862, in the western theater, Union commander Ulysses S. Grant had won a stunning victory at Fort Donelson in Tennessee, capturing twelve thousand Confederate soldiers. When asked by the opposing commander for terms, he had replied, "No terms except unconditional and immediate surrender." Thus did the moniker Unconditional Surrender Grant become famous, just as Stonewall had attached itself to Jackson after Manassas. Like Jackson, too, Grant's success had led to his promotion to major general. But following his victory at Donelson, Grant immediately ran afoul of his superior, Major General Henry Wager Halleck. Halleck, who thought him rash, overly aggressive, and far too independent, in effect stripped him of his army. On March 7, 1862, Grant wrote to Halleck:

> *I have done my very best to obey orders, and to carry out the interests of the service. If my course is not satisfactory, remove me at once. I do not wish to impede in any way the success of our arms. . . . I respectfully ask to be relieved from further duty in the Department.*[40]

Halleck realized immediately that he had greatly overplayed his hand, and refused to accept the resignation. Grant was reinstated and given back his army. It was yet another sign that the war was changing, and that it was favoring certain individuals who did not play the game by conventional rules.

CHAPTER NINETEEN

A LOOMING PERIL

In the Confederate eastern theater, this strange war that seemed to roll on, month after month, with no actual fighting, was about to end. Everyone could feel it, and in the Southern diaries and letters of the era there is a strong sense of gloom descending. The writers could not know that the year 1862 would see a chain of battles in the East—Seven Days, Second Manassas, Antietam, Fredericksburg—whose previously unimaginable numbers of killed and wounded would make the first Manassas seem like a small fight. But they seemed to understand, in some part of their brains, that the war was about to take a brutal turn. It was amazing, in fact, how quickly the peaceful, warm, hopeful days of autumn had given way to the hard, bitter disillusion of midwinter. There would be no more languorous breaks, when men could ponder the gigantic illogic of what they were doing and hope that more level heads in Britain and France might intervene to settle the matter peacefully.

The participants in the Bath/Romney expedition in January had felt the lash of the wind and had shivered in subzero weather. But its sequel was, in its own way, worse. February and March brought unrelenting sleet, snow, and freezing rain to Jackson's army in its camps around Winchester, turning the earth to a deep, glutinous mud that engulfed horses and wagons and found its way into tents, clothing, and food and made it difficult even walking to the "sink," as men called the latrine. As always, the camps wreaked destruction on nature: forests were cut down for firewood and breastworks, once-clear streams became clogged with filth, and the air was filled with the smell of woodsmoke and offal and feces and unwashed men—the pervading stink of armies. The dense gray clouds meant that there was no starlight or moonlight; nights were cloaked in an eerie, opaque darkness.[1] Desertions—a new and unsettling problem that challenged the most basic Confederate assumptions about why the war was being fought—were becoming more and more frequent. Many of these men were walking north toward enemy lines, carrying with them not only their betrayal but troves of military intelligence as well.[2] In an even more unsettling development, slaves, too, were starting to cross through enemy lines in ever-larger numbers.

Thus the hard, unhappy winter unfolded. When Loring's men returned to Winchester from Romney in February, they arrived cold and wet and miserable and fully loaded with bitterness and grudges held. They were openly critical of Jackson and often ended up in fistfights with the members of the Stonewall Brigade, many of whom were equally unhappy about the Romney expedition but reserved to themselves the right to criticize Old Jack. Then there were the sick, so many that Winchester itself had been turned into an enormous hospital: churches became medical wards, pews became beds. In January and early February there were some 3,200 sick in a town whose normal population was less than 5,000, with illnesses that ranged from dysentery and pneumonia to scarlet and typhoid fevers.[3]

The war was closing in on them in very specific ways, too. Since the beginning of the year the Union's bad luck had turned decisively in a string of victories. At Roanoke Island on the North Carolina coast, Union troops had landed, won a quick victory, and captured 2,500 prisoners. Confederates had been routed at Mill Springs, Kentucky. In Tennessee, Grant had won battles at Forts Henry and Donelson. At the latter he had swallowed an entire Confederate army whole. Nashville itself, the state capital, had surrendered. These defeats had immediate political consequences: President Jefferson Davis, hailed as a genius in the wake of Manassas, was now the target of sharp censure, as though in a matter of months he had somehow gone from being clever and adroit to being lamentably stupid. He had "lost the confidence of the country," said the *Richmond Whig*.[4] One congressman bemoaned his "incredible incompetency," while George Bagby, editor of the influential *Southern Literary Messenger*, stated flatly, "We have reached a very dark hour. . . . Cold, haughty, peevish, narrow-minded, pig-headed, *malignant*, he [Davis] is the cause. While he lives, there is no hope."[5]

And though McClellan's army remained in its camps around Washington, it had swelled to an enormous size: 155,000. Jackson's fear was now fully realized. The once-raw Union recruits were well trained, highly disciplined, and superbly equipped, and now constituted a far more lethal threat than the one the Confederate army had faced the previous summer. There was no missing these signs. "Darkness seems gathering over the Southern land," wrote a disconsolate Maggie Preston in her diary in March. "Disaster follows disaster; where is it all to end?"[6] Jackson's quartermaster, John Harman, wrote his brother in a similar mood after news of Henry and Donelson and the evacuation of Nashville. He wrote, "This is the severest blow of all. . . . I have no hope that England and France will interfere, so we will be reduced to great straights [sic]."[7]

Jackson, meanwhile, laboring at his desk in his Winchester headquarters, was in an exceedingly dangerous position. There was peril all around him, it was fast closing in upon him, and he faced it virtually completely alone, with little hope of reinforcement. He was greatly outnumbered. Though on paper the valley army had ten thousand to thirteen thousand men, his ranks had been badly depleted by sickness, absenteeism, and desertion. He had also lost men to "recruitment furloughs," the result of a December 1861 law that granted leaves and paid bounties to men who agreed to enlist for the rest of the war. (Original enlistment terms expired in April.) A number of officers were absent on trips to their hometowns to drum up new recruits.[8] The effect was to reduce Jackson's effective troops to fewer than four thousand men. Harman, who had to supply them, thought the number was more like three thousand.[9]

Against him were ranged three Union forces, all under the command of Major General Nathaniel Banks, that totaled thirty thousand men—a ten-to-one advantage if they were all brought to bear on Winchester, which was not just a theoretical possibility. By the end of February, two of these forces had already crossed the Potomac River and entered Virginia; another was camped at Harpers Ferry. Banks's main force, a day's march away in Charlestown, had twenty-three thousand men, enough to envelop Winchester and crush Jackson where he stood.[10] The Union advantage extended to weaponry, too. Many of Jackson's men were carrying "percussion smoothbores," outdated muskets with a range of maybe a hundred yards against a Union army that had mostly rifled weapons accurate at three times that distance.[11] But many others had no weapons at all. In a remarkable letter to Governor John Letcher in early March, Jackson made what Union commanders would have considered an astonishing request. "As you say we must, under Divine blessing, rely upon the bayonet when firearms cannot be furnished," he wrote, "let me have a substitute, so as to make the arm six inches longer than the musket with the bayonet on." In the event that it was unclear what he was requesting, Letcher appended a note at the bottom of the letter before forwarding it to the War Department: "Respectfully referred to General Lee for information, with the hope that 1,000 pikes may be furnished to Genl. Jackson."[12] *Pikes*. Jackson was planning to go into battle, outnumbered seven to one, with medieval weapons against rifled muskets. Not only that but Lee, who saw pikes as a way to solve a larger weaponry shortage, actually *approved* the request. Long, sharp sticks were better than nothing. (The governor of Georgia, equally desperate, ordered ten thousand of them,[13] but they were never used in battle in the Civil War.)

Neither side was under any illusion about the other's strength. Unlike in McClellan's Washington camps, where overestimation of enemy numbers was becoming a way of life, Banks's troop estimates, made with the help of deserters, escaped slaves, and a spy network of Union sympathizers in the Lower Shenandoah Valley, were extremely accurate. Both commanders were fully aware of the absurd mismatch.[14]

Jackson was only in trouble, of course, if he could not be reinforced. To remedy this he sent Davis an urgent request in late February, along with the warning that large numbers of Federal troops would soon be moving against Winchester and thus threatening the valley itself. "It is unnecessary to say that I have not the force to send," came Davis's gently chiding response to Jackson's superior Joseph Johnston, suggesting the utter futility, if not outright preposterousness, of Jackson's plea, "and have no other hope of his reinforcement than by the militia of the Valley." Recruit your own soldiers, in other words, even though we have no weapons to give them. Davis's only advice, considerably less than helpful, was to "avoid the sacrifice of the army."[15]

Jackson was thus quite alone: sixty miles from the nearest of Joe Johnston's forces across the Blue Ridge at Culpeper, thirty-five miles from his brother-in-law D. H. Hill's four regiments in Leesburg, which in any case were spoken for, and many days' march from Brigadier General Edward Johnson's small command between Staunton and Franklin in the southwestern mountains. (They were there to guard the mountainous back door into the Shenandoah Valley.) The math was irrefutable: Jackson was going to have to fall back, a process that his quartermaster, John Harman, had already started by the end of February, moving clothing and supplies twenty-one miles south to the town of Strasburg. But even the sturdy, usually optimistic Harman knew that Strasburg would not be far enough away to offer safety. "I do not think they will stop there if we have to leave Win-

chester," he wrote his brother on February 26. "Nobody is coming to reinforce us."[16] That meant flight—continuous, perilous flight—or destruction.

This looming danger seemed to have little or no effect on Jackson himself. Unlike another rising general, William T. Sherman, who as Union
commander in Kentucky in the fall of 1861 had driven himself to distraction with paranoid overestimates of enemy troop strength and the fear
of defeat—which led him to request that he be relieved of command—
Jackson seemed not to mind his isolation.[17] As always, he shared scant
information with his staff, and worked hard and mostly alone to keep his
army supplied with food, clothing, munitions, and such minutiae as regimental flags. He dispensed furloughs and dealt with the ever-stingy War
Department in Richmond. The horrors of the Romney expedition had not
touched him. Hardship, or the prospect of hardship, or fear of what was to
come, had absolutely no effect on his thinking and never would. Nor had
he changed in another important way: while he still showed the world the
face of the stiff, somber, inflexible, and duty-bound officer, behind closed
doors with his wife and close friends he was, as in Winchester, an entirely
different person. When Anna had arrived just before Christmas, he had
stalked her, pounced on her at the landing of their quarters, swung her
around in his arms, and, with "the captive's head thrown back," recalled
Anna, kissed her "again and again" while a group of officers standing on the
sidewalk watched in mute amazement.[18]

In their snug quarters with the Reverend James Graham; his wife, Fanny;
and their three children, Jackson was once again the warm, affectionate,
expansive polymath he had been in Lexington with Ellie, Maggie, and
Anna. Graham, six months older than Jackson and an intelligent, reliable
reporter, wrote the following description of his guest that men in Loring's
command, who had just been driven mercilessly through the ice and snow,
would scarcely have believed:

> For about two months he slept every night under my roof and sat every
> day at my table, and bowed with us every morning and evening at our
> family altar. . . . Those nearest to him could not fail to see underneath his
> grave earnestness the brighter and more attractive elements of his nature,
> which even his habitual gravity could not always restrain from breaking
> forth—sometimes, which the world would hardly suspect, in a keen sense
> of humor; but often in expressions of warm affection. . . . Instead of that
> reticence or bluntness with which he is charged, he had a pleasant word

for every acquaintance. He met at my table and fireside a great many people of different conditions and rank and of both sexes, and to all of them he was uniformly cordial, even exerting himself for their entertainment if circumstances seemed to require it.[19]

Anna's own descriptions of life inside the Graham house seem to recall those happy, unguarded moments in their house in Lexington, but this time with an expanded cast of characters. One dinner party seemed to typify the social atmosphere of the Graham house that winter. A young officer and Fanny Graham's mother—with whom Jackson had struck up a warm, admiring friendship—began an improvised artillery battle in the Grahams' living room. The matron, wielding a chair for a cannon, fired at the officer, and the officer, wielding his own chair, fired back. Soon all the guests were playing, firing at one another, yelling and laughing. The Reverend Graham and his mother-in-law were firing side by side. They were so loud that Jackson, who had been in his room upstairs, came down to see what the fuss was all about. The room became very still while he surveyed the scene. Then he pronounced, with affected solemnity, "Captain Marye, when the engagement is over, you will send in an official report," whereupon the room exploded in laughter so loud that it was heard "far out into the street."[20]

Jackson's good mood and high spirits were at least partly the result of his excellent health. Since June 1861, two months into the war, all of those old ailments—the uveitis, the stomach troubles, the nagging sinus infections and aches, and various organ complaints—had mysteriously vanished. This had happened, in Jackson's words, "since leaving home."[21] Thus one of Jackson's oldest, strongest, and most visible obsessions had vanished altogether—and would not reappear during his life in the war. It is hard, from a distance of 153 years, to fully make sense of this. Jackson had, as we know, some very real ailments. The pain in his eyes and the floaters he saw before him were not figments of his imagination, nor was his burning dyspepsia. But the sudden and complete absence of these afflictions suggests, at the very least, that his state of mind had something to do with them. A man who was, at the very core of his existence, a warrior, had been forced throughout his life into other pursuits and occupations. Even in his army years, he spent only a few weeks in actual combat. Now, finally, it seemed that he was fulfilling some old destiny. And he felt, for one of the few times in his adult life, perfectly fine. There was something else, too, that made him happy. In February Anna became pregnant.

• • •

Nathaniel Prentiss Banks was a splendid-looking man. Everyone said so. Trim, compact, and athletic, with luxuriant, artfully tousled brown hair and a splendid military-style mustache, in his sharply tailored uniform, yellow dress gloves, and gleaming saber, he looked the very model of the Civil War general. He looked, indeed, in body type and facial structure, a good deal like his immediate superior, George McClellan, and he had something of McClellan's erect, confident, dignified, patrician bearing. Banks had what a contemporary called "a genius for being looked at."[22] This was curious, because there was absolutely nothing of the aristocrat in him. He had grown up in the working-class neighborhoods of Waltham, Massachusetts, the son of the cotton-mill foreman, had himself gone to work in the mill at age fourteen for two dollars a week, and had married a Waltham factory girl.[23]

But he was bright, engaging, and intensely ambitious. He taught himself law, was admitted to the bar at twenty-three, and by sheer force of will dragged himself up and out of the drudgery and dead-end world of the textile mills.[24] He started out as a "bobbin boy," replacing empty bobbins of thread with full ones. He acquired the nickname Bobbin Boy Banks, which he carried for the rest of his life. His entry into politics in 1830 began a stunning rise to power and influence. He was elected to the US Congress in 1853, and became Speaker of the US House of Representatives in 1856. As a nationally prominent antislavery Republican, he played a key role in getting John Frémont that party's nomination for president in 1856. He was elected governor of Massachusetts in 1858, and ran for the 1860 Republican presidential nomination against Lincoln, whom he later supported and who seriously considered him for a cabinet post. Just prior to the war, Banks had succeeded George McClellan as director of the Illinois Central Railroad, whose principal attorney, before his 1860 election to the presidency, had been Abraham Lincoln. With his sparkling connections and his booming oratorical voice, Nathaniel Banks was a potent force in the North, and Lincoln owed him many political debts. It was partly for that reason that he appointed Banks, with no military experience, one of the first Union major generals of the war, an exalted rank that left many West Pointers and regular army men over whom he had been promoted seething with anger and jealousy. He was the fourth-ranking general in the Union, and its most prominent "political" general.

And now it had fallen to him to make the first Union thrust into Virginia. This was no idle task. The very idea of probing into the Confederacy itself was frightening. The terrain was unknown, exotic; most of it was unmapped or inaccurately mapped. There were hostile civilians, ubiquitous spies, constant threats to supply lines, who-knows-what rebel armies or guerrilla units lurking behind every mountain, and the ultimate horror of being encircled or cut off in enemy territory.

But even with so much uncertainty it must be said that Banks, in the first week of March, camped in the Virginia towns of Charlestown and Martinsburg, had almost everything going for him. That began with nearly perfect intelligence of his enemy's strength, position, and defensive works. He knew with rare precision exactly how many regiments Jackson had and even the names of his regimental commanders. He knew Jackson's overall strength and the strength of the average company—thirty, well down from the one hundred it should have been. He knew where trenches had been dug and where earthworks had been built. He knew, from a deserter from the 2nd Virginia Regiment, that many of Jackson's men were carrying smoothbore muskets with percussion caps.[25] His staff officer David Hunter Strother, a northern Virginian who before the war had written humorous travelogues for *Harper's Monthly* under the pseudonym Porte Crayon, knew the countryside intimately.

Knowing all this, Banks also knew, with nearly absolute certainty, just what a crushing advantage he held. And in early March he began to exercise it. Since there was an outside chance that Jackson might be reinforced by Johnston in Manassas, Banks moved slowly, but quite deliberately. On March 7, advance units of his army, conducting a reconnaissance in force, moved to within four miles of Winchester. There his cavalry encountered Jackson's cavalry chief, Turner Ashby, and his own mounted troops in a wood. A sharp skirmish followed, which Union troops won handily. This confirmed what Banks and his commanders had heard elsewhere: that the feeble rebel force was no match for them. They had heard, moreover, that Jackson's army was about to evacuate Winchester. By March 10, Banks had moved closer, spreading his army in a ninety-degree arc north of the town, and moving to control four roads leading into Winchester from the north and east.

Jackson, meanwhile, was indeed moving out. He had no choice. His supply wagons as well as his artillery were either already in Strasburg or on the road. On March 11, his men followed. (He had sent Anna away the first week in March.) Winchester residents, about to be abandoned to the clutches of an invading army and unaware of the hard logic that made it necessary, were dumbfounded. It did not seem possible that Jackson would retreat. As one of them, a Mrs. Cornelia McDonald, wrote, she spent the night "in violent fits of weeping at the thought of being left, and what might happen to that army before we should see it again."[26] By the evening of March 11, much of Jackson's army was either on the road or camped four miles south, near the hamlet of Kernstown.

But Jackson, as it turned out, had never had any intention of abandoning Winchester without a fight. It was characteristic of him that he had told neither his senior officers nor his quartermaster about this. In the alarmingly transparent world of border-state Virginia, where Nathaniel Banks could learn everything about Stonewall Jackson and his army, down to gossip and small details, it was perhaps not surprising that Jackson was learning to value secrecy. But, as with the Romney expedition, he would pay a price for it. On the evening of March 11, Jackson convened a council of war, where he astonished his officers by proposing a daring and unconventional night attack on a federal position north of Winchester. He had always intended this, he said. His troops, now camped four miles south of town, would simply turn around, march to the north side of town, and attack. Jackson was under no illusion that he could win a pitched battle with a six- or seven-to-one disadvantage. But he could strike the Federals anyway, perhaps make them think that he was stronger than he was, perhaps help cover his retreat.

It is noteworthy that Jackson's proposal came as other Confederate armies in Virginia were falling back. Johnston, anticipating a Federal offensive in the spring, had retired from Manassas on March 8, headed for camps below the Rappahannock. D. H. Hill, at Leesburg in northern Virginia, had also moved south. Jackson, moreover, had not been ordered to attack anyone. The deeply—and characteristically—hedged orders he had received from Johnston instructed him only "to endeavor to employ the invaders of the valley, but without exposing himself to the danger of defeat, by keeping so near the enemy as to prevent him from making any considerable detachment to reinforce McClellan, but not so near that he might be compelled to fight."[27] In other words, retreat, but do it as slowly as you can.

Jackson's officers unanimously rejected his proposal. He explained it in earnest once again, in more detail, and they rejected it again, for several reasons. First, the supply wagons that Jackson thought were three miles south of town were actually seven miles away. Second, the men themselves were still strung out on the road for miles; a ten-mile forced march at night with tired men was simply not possible, he was told. He reluctantly gave the order to evacuate the town. By morning the last of the Confederate army was moving out, as the townspeople watched in sullen disbelief. The war would be very hard on them. Their marvelous but unfortunately situated town would be the scene of three major battles and a dozen skirmishes. It would change hands seventy-two times during the war, and thirteen times in a single day. It would eventually be depopulated and, for all practical purposes, destroyed.

Jackson, having put his idea to a vote, and having accepted defeat, was bitterly disappointed. As dawn lit up the skies over the smoky Blue Ridge Mountains, he and his medical officer, Hunter McGuire, rode to a promontory overlooking the town of Winchester and watched the long line of men snake southward. Both were overwhelmed by emotion—McGuire with sadness because he was leaving his hometown; Jackson with anger because he had lost an opportunity. "I was utterly overcome by the fact that I was leaving all that I held dear on earth," said McGuire later, "but my emotion was arrested by one look at Jackson. His face was fairly blazing with the fire that was burning in him, and I felt awed before him. Presently he cried out with a manner almost savage: 'That is the last council of war I will ever hold!' And it was—his first and last."[28]

Jackson could not know that on that same day, eighty miles to the east, events were taking place that would change both the course of the war and his own destiny. Lincoln, frustrated with McClellan's refusal to advance in spite of considerable prodding, relieved McClellan of overall command of Union armies. While he was left in charge of the Army of the Potomac, Lincoln and Stanton would now assume authority over the other parts of that army. This included the newly constituted 5th Corps under Nathaniel Banks, who had previously reported directly to McClellan.

McClellan, meanwhile, had radically shifted his plan of attack. In response to an order from Lincoln—"Special War Order No. 1"—that he move against Manassas on or before February 22, which he refused to obey, he came up with a plan to move his huge army by boat to the mouth of the Rappahannock, about eighty miles southeast of Manassas. They would thus land behind Johnston and move against Richmond. Unfortunately, Johnston's retreat to the Rappahannock had ruined that scheme. It had also done something far worse: it had exposed McClellan's prodigiously inaccurate estimates of Confederate troop strength. McClellan had claimed, based on intelligence from Pinkerton, that he was facing a hundred thousand rebel troops. Newspaper correspondents, visiting abandoned camps, found evidence of no more than forty-five thousand. Not only that, but many of the big cannons supposedly aimed at Little Mac's army turned out to be "Quaker guns," logs painted black and made to look like weapons. The news was shocking, and the press made much of it. "Utterly dispirited, ashamed, and humiliated," wrote Bayard Taylor of the *New York Tribune*,

> I return from this visit to the Rebel stronghold. For seven months we have waited, organized a powerful army, until its drill and equipment should be so complete that we might safely advance against the "Gibraltar" of rebellion. And now . . . we see that our enemies, like the Chinese, have frightened us by the sound of gongs and the wearing of devil masks.[29]

Under intense pressure—Secretary of State William Seward, among others, was ranting about McClellan's "imbecility"—McClellan on March 13 came up with a new plan. It would still involve putting 120,000 men on boats, but this time he would take them clear to Fortress Monroe at the end of the York-James Peninsula. They would then march one hundred miles up the peninsula and attack Richmond. Lincoln, who was convinced that attacking armies and not places was the way to win, did not like the idea. He wrote McClellan, in scolding tones, that his plan would amount to "only shifting, and not surmounting, a difficulty—that we would find the same enemy and the same, or equal, intrenchments, at either place. The country will not fail to note—is now noting—that the present hesitation to move on the intrenched enemy, is but the story of Manassas repeated. . . . You must act."[30] McClellan, nonetheless, would have his way.

It is worth remembering this moment, in the middle part of the chilly, rainy month of March 1862, in the second year of the war. Joe Johnston and D. H. Hill are falling back to the Rappahannock; Confederate armies are being routed in the West; Confederate coastal defenses in North Carolina are crumbling; Jackson is on the run in the Shenandoah Valley; the once buoyant optimism of the South is giving way to fear and hopelessness. Jackson's opponent Nathaniel Banks holds such a crushing numerical advantage that he is less worried about Jackson's pathetic, slapdash army than about missing the real action east of the Blue Ridge. To Banks and his bosses in Washington, Jackson is merely an insignificant buzzing on the periphery of the real war, something to be swatted away. They would soon have occasion to change their minds.

CHAPTER TWENTY

THE REALM OF THE POSSIBLE

※

Late on the chilly, rain-lashed afternoon of March 21, 1862, an elderly former militia officer named Jonah Tavener was traveling on horseback from his home in Loudoun County, Virginia, to the Shenandoah Valley. He had just come through Snicker's Gap, one of the main passes through the Blue Ridge Mountains, when he saw something that, in that month and year of the war, was still extraordinary: a large body of blue-clad troops—two thousand to three thousand of them—winding their way eastward. *Eastward.* Tavener may have been too old for the army, but he was not too old to understand an important enemy troop movement when he saw it. Undetected by Union scouts, he swung south of the marching column, where he soon encountered Confederate riders under the command of Colonel Turner Ashby, who happened to be an old acquaintance. He was taken to Ashby, to whom he told his story. Ashby immediately grasped its importance. He dispatched Tavener, along with a special courier, to Jackson himself, where his story detonated like an eighteen-pound percussion shell.[1]

The news changed everything. It altered Jackson's strategy and set in motion events that changed the war in the Shenandoah Valley and the war in Virginia. It even changed the fate of the Union troops Tavener had seen. Though he did not understand it at the time, Tavener had spotted a piece of McClellan's master plan to destroy the Confederacy, a plan as yet unknown to the brain trust in the Confederate War Department in Richmond. Tavener's little discovery had another effect, too: it prompted the opening move in what would become known to history as Stonewall Jackson's valley campaign.

To understand what Tavener saw, we have to back up five days, to a somewhat simpler moment when it seemed that fortune was smiling on the Union and all its works and there was no possibility that a minor irritant like Thomas J. Jackson could ever cause any real trouble in Virginia. McClellan was preparing for his unprecedented gambit: the movement of his army from Washington to the York-James Peninsula. He was also bound, by previous agreement with President Lincoln, to leave enough men to keep Washington, DC, "entirely secure." Fearful, as usual, that the enemy had more soldiers than he did, McClellan was scrambling to bring in every able-bodied man he could find. Thus on March 16, four days after Jackson's retreat, McClellan sent an order to Major General Nathaniel Banks in Winchester, summoning his two divisions to the Washington area, where their presence would free up soldiers for the great expedition. "Post your command in the vicinity of Manassas," he told Banks, "intrench yourself strongly and throw cavalry pickets well out to the front." He also instructed Banks to leave "something like two regiments of cavalry . . . to occupy Winchester and thoroughly scour the country south of the railway and up the Shenandoah Valley."[2] For once Little Mac was not exaggerating Confederate troop strength. That was because it was manifestly against his self-interest to do so. It would have deprived him of men he desperately needed. The valley could be dealt with briefly and dismissively; it was a strategic afterthought, a sideshow.

Thus Banks began preparations for departure. He sent a division (more than nine thousand soldiers), under the command of Brigadier General James Shields, to chase Jackson. Shields was to destroy him if possible, but, in any case, to make sure he was indeed far away from Winchester when the Federal troops marched out. Shields was one of the more arresting personalities of the early war. Like his immediate superior, Nathaniel Banks, he was wealthy, politically powerful, and entirely self-made. Born and raised in Ireland, he sailed for America at age sixteen but was shipwrecked off the coast of Scotland. He stayed in that country, working as a tutor to a wealthy family. Four years later he finally made it to New York, where he discovered that a wealthy uncle who had promised to help him had died. He briefly went to sea with a merchantman and eventually fetched up in Illinois, where he studied law and was admitted to the bar in 1832. He was elected to the Illinois legislature as a Democrat in 1836, thus beginning a rapid political ascent that was marred only by a smear campaign conducted against him by his fellow Illinois politician Abraham Lincoln. The campaign led Shields to challenge Lincoln to a duel; Lincoln apologized, and the two men somehow ended up friends. Shields became a justice of the Illinois Supreme Court, commissioner of the General Land Office in Washington, and a US senator from Illinois. He was a brigadier general in the Mexican-American War, where he was wounded twice, and led the decisive charge in the Battle of Churubusco. He became wealthy in various businesses that included a silver mine in Mexico. Shields was slender, five feet eight inches tall, and immaculately dressed. He was urbane, sophisticated, confident, charming, funny, and courtly.[3] He was also, in the words of one of his artillery officers, "vainglorious to the last degree."[4] This unfortunate latter trait would destroy his Civil War career.

His vanity must have been enormously flattered by his troops' triumphant march up the valley pike, strutting like an army of occupation and opposed only by Turner Ashby's small cavalry unit that served as Jackson's rear guard. Shields was now deep into the mysterious, lethal, alien world of the Confederacy. Redbuds were in early bloom. The sullen, hostile citizenry stared balefully at the Union soldiers as they passed. One of his soldiers thought, uncharitably, that some of them had a "cowed and stupid look."[5] Though Ashby's cavaliers could not match Shields's numbers or his firepower, they could make trouble, and that is what they did, burning bridges, sniping at pickets, and lobbing shells from their three-gun horse artillery. As equestrians, the Union cavalry was simply no match for them; indeed, they were awestruck by the seemingly deerlike ability of Ashby's troopers to jump fences and cross rough terrain at high speed, and generally ride circles around them. At one point Shields concocted a plan to circle and entrap the Southern cavalry, which failed laughably. "A gull would stand as good a chance to catch a fox, as our force to catch Ashby," wrote one of Shields's staff.[6]

Thus did Ashby's gallant seven hundred harass and annoy Shields as he drove south in the shadow of the hulking Massanutten Mountain. They certainly slowed him down. But they changed no Union minds. Shields's division entered the valley town of Strasburg unopposed, then pursued Ashby another five miles south. At that point Ashby's guns opened again, but at such a "ridiculous distance," according to one Union officer, that the Irish general concluded that his work was done.[7] Jackson, by Shields's reckoning, was now at least forty miles south of Winchester. He was no longer a threat. Shields's infantry turned and marched back to Strasburg. The next day, March 20, they returned to Winchester—a hard march in wind, rain, and bone-chilling cold. They were in a hurry. The war was going to be over soon, the action was all going to be to the east, and no one, not least Banks and Shields, wanted to miss it.

Ashby, trailing Shields northward through the valley, soon concluded that the Union general had given up his pursuit. That was the first stunning piece of news Ashby gave Jackson on March 21. Until the moment he heard it, Jackson had been facing both the destruction of his army and the loss of the valley. Ashby's scouts and spies had reported that Shields would likely pursue him to Staunton, a large, prosperous town that was the southern valley's counterpart to Winchester in the north. Staunton was Jackson's supply base. It was also a strategic gem: whoever held it held the Upper Valley, and the Upper Valley was the back door to Richmond. If Union troops could move, unobstructed, east through Rockfish Gap in the Blue Ridge and aboard the Virginia Central Railroad, they could virtually guarantee the city's fall. Jackson, outnumbered three to one, could either fight it out where he stood—in the vicinity of Mount Jackson—or fight it out farther south. Either way the outlook, in the absence of reinforcements, was grim if not hopeless. Jackson, with little real choice, had been planning to turn and fight even before he heard Ashby's news, even though there was almost no way he could have won.[8]

The second piece of news, even more electrifying to Jackson, came in the person of Jonah Tavener. Shields's abandonment of his pursuit had suggested to Jackson that Banks was leaving the valley to reinforce McClellan. Tavener's story offered striking confirmation. It also suggested a course of action. Two days before, on March 19, Jackson had received a letter from Joe Johnston, now camped safely behind the Rappahannock, fifty miles south of Washington. Johnston had a very specific agenda. He wanted Jackson to do everything he could to keep Banks from reinforcing the Union army at Richmond. "It is important to keep that army in the Valley," he wrote, "and that it should not reinforce McClellan. Do try to prevent it by getting and keeping as near as prudence will permit." This was easy enough for Johnston to say. He was not alone in the valley, facing a much larger Union force. Jackson was clearly not supposed to give battle. At that moment, no one in Richmond was in the mood for another humiliating Confederate defeat. In Johnston's fantasy world, Jackson would be able to dance so tantalizingly near that the Federals would have no choice but to keep Banks's divisions in the valley.

But in fact Johnston's message was exactly what Jackson wanted to hear. He wasted no time and consulted no one. He would never again repeat the

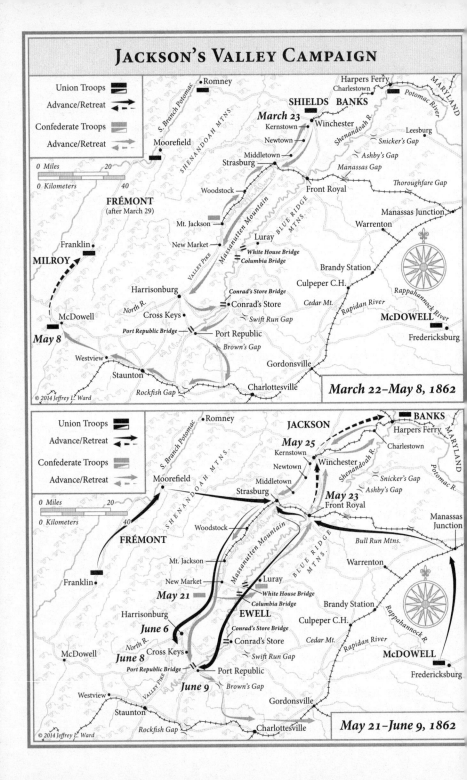

JACKSON'S VALLEY CAMPAIGN

March 22–May 8, 1862

Union Troops
Advance/Retreat
Confederate Troops
Advance/Retreat

0 Miles 20
0 Kilometers 40

MARYLAND
Harpers Ferry
Charlestown
Potomac River

SHIELDS BANKS

March 23
Kernstown Winchester
Newtown
Leesburg
Snicker's Gap
Middletown
Strasburg Ashby's Gap
Manassas Gap

FRÉMONT
(after March 29)

Woodstock Front Royal
Thoroughfare Gap
Manassas Junction
Mt. Jackson Warrenton

New Market
Luray
White House Bridge
Columbia Bridge
Brandy Station
Culpeper C.H.
Rappahannock River

Franklin
MILROY
Harrisonburg
Conrad's Store Bridge
North R.
Cross Keys
Conrad's Store
Cedar Mt.
Rapidan River
McDOWELL
McDowell
Swift Run Gap
May 8
Port Republic Bridge
Port Republic
Fredericksburg
Westview
Brown's Gap
Staunton
Gordonsville
Rockfish Gap
Charlottesville

March 22–May 8, 1862

© 2014 Jeffrey L. Ward

May 21–June 9, 1862

Union Troops
Advance/Retreat
Confederate Troops
Advance/Retreat

0 Miles 20
0 Kilometers 40

Romney
JACKSON **BANKS**
Harpers Ferry
MARYLAND
May 25
Kernstown Charlestown
Newtown Winchester
S. Branch Potomac
Moorefield
Middletown Snicker's Gap
Strasburg Ashby's Gap
May 23
Front Royal

FRÉMONT
Manassas Junction
Woodstock
Bull Run Mtns.
Mt. Jackson Warrenton
New Market
May 21
Luray
White House Bridge
Columbia Bridge
EWELL
Brandy Station
Harrisonburg Culpeper C.H.
June 6
Conrad's Store Bridge
North R.
McDowell *June 8*
Cross Keys
Conrad's Store
Cedar Mt.
Rapidan River
McDOWELL
Port Republic Bridge
Swift Run Gap
Port Republic
June 9
Westview Brown's Gap
Fredericksburg
Staunton Gordonsville
Rockfish Gap Charlottesville

May 21–June 9, 1862

© 2014 Jeffrey L. Ward

fiasco of his Winchester council of war. Armed with both Ashby's and Tavener's intelligence, he put his army on the road the next morning, March 22, heading straight back up the valley pike for Winchester. That day he conducted the first of many forced marches in the valley—twenty-three miles through mud and rain (twenty-seven miles for the rearmost units)—at a pace that caused scores of men to drop from exhaustion and wagons and supplies to fall miles behind the infantry. Men were hungry, footsore, and miserable, but they covered a large amount of ground quickly. They would soon be famous for it and earn another nickname for themselves: "Jackson's foot cavalry." Jackson's operating principles in combat were speed and deception. March 22, 1862, saw the first full-scale exercise of the former. Fast or not, though, it was an astoundingly risky move. The march placed Jackson ninety-five miles from his supply base, in a countryside abounding with Federal soldiers who were eager to destroy him. There were at least ten thousand Union troops at Winchester, perhaps far more. At that point Jackson had no way of knowing. Tavener had seen only a single brigade heading east. But from Jackson's point of view his mission was clear: keep Banks in the valley. He was accomplishing that the only way he knew. In his mind, too, was his beloved Winchester, whose residents he had abandoned without a fight eleven days before.

While Jackson was pushing his men furiously north, Ashby, well in advance, had plans of his own. At 2:00 p.m. he and a small force of riders hit Shields's supply train about four miles south of Winchester near the tiny hamlet of Kernstown, which consisted of a handful of businesses—butcher, wheelwright, blacksmith, cooperage, and tavern—and a stone church. He had unloaded enough shell and canister to get their attention, and nearly captured part of the supply train, when Shields summoned cavalry, artillery, and infantry and counterattacked. Ashby, greatly outnumbered, fell back six miles, to Newtown. Though he had done little damage to men or matériel, one of his shell fragments had managed to strike Brigadier General Shields in the chest and shoulder. He fainted several times and was carried from the field.

Turner Ashby embodied the immense cavalry advantages the South held early in the war. There were a number of reasons for this. The South had more people who used the horse as an integral part of their lives, and the landed Southern gentry was full of accomplished riders.[9] Northerners, meanwhile, were more likely to see horses as beasts of burden. Confederate cavalries also had superior animals, mainly because of the Southern fondness for racing, and because Southern cavalrymen supplied their own mounts. Most Southern towns had their own horse tracks. In the North, slow-moving draft horses were the preferred breeds.[10] Cavalry in the Civil War was rarely used to charge infantry; more often, it functioned as the army's eyes, tracking enemy movements, screening their own army's movements, using their high mobility to strike enemy communications and supply lines. To be effective required serious expertise, which necessitated far more training than the infantry received.[11] Even the greenest infantry could be more or less shoved into battle. Not so cavalrymen. In the North it was thought that it took fully two years to produce a seasoned trooper.

The dark-eyed, dark-skinned, heavily bearded thirty-three-year-old Ashby was, by all accounts, as brilliant a pure rider as anyone in Virginia had ever seen. In the remaining two months of his life his dashing, reckless, romantic bravery, riding in the service of Stonewall Jackson, would captivate the South. He came, in fact, to represent for many Southerners everything that was noble—and superior—about the Southern cause, in a world where Northerners tended to see shades of Simon Legree: he was said to be honorable, charitable, Christian, gentle except when in a fight, of pure character, and of course he could and did ride with reckless abandon through the ranks of his Yankee counterparts.[12] "Riding his black stallion, he looked like a knight of the olden time," wrote Henry Kyd Douglas, a member of Jackson's staff. "Galloping over the field on his favorite war horse, his white one, eager, watchful, he was fascinating, inspiring. Altogether he was the most picturesque horseman ever seen in the Shenandoah Valley."[13]

His background was less spectacular. He grew up on a modest family farm in Fauquier County that suffered considerable economic hardship. He never attended college, and instead went into the mercantile business, operating out of a shop near a railroad depot, at which he was not very successful. Nor was he exactly the beau ideal he seemed in articles such as the one in *Southern Illustrated News* that pictured him on a white charger and wearing a long coat and plumed hat, the very model of equestrian gallantry. He was in fact a fierce, driven, border-state partisan who specialized in a brutal and highly irregular form of warfare far from the eye of the public or the press. One example: In October 1861, after a fight with Union cavalry, Ashby and his troopers stripped four of the Union dead naked and spread one out in the form of the crucifixion, with holes cut through his palms.[14] It is hard to see the chivalry in such an act, which horrified Union soldiers. In 1861, too, he had avenged the wounding of some of his men in a skirmish by killing what he estimated in a letter to his sister was "twenty or thirty of them."[15]

Ashby was driven partly if not wholly by vengeance. In June 1861, he and his brother Richard had served in the 7th Virginia Cavalry, guarding the border counties of the lower (northernmost) Shenandoah Valley and hunting down Unionists. In one fight, Richard received a saber blow that took off part of his head and knocked him from his saddle. While he writhed on the ground, his attacker ran his sword through Richard's abdomen, stole his spurs and horse, and rode off. Turner later found his brother, blood bubbling from his mouth, begging for water. He suffered for a week, then died. "From that hour Turner Ashby was a changed man," wrote fellow Virginian Dabney Maury. "A stern sorrow his controlling motive, a deep purpose of vengeance possessed him, all his buoyancy and bright hopes of fame gave place to grief."[16] There is no doubt that Turner Ashby was a brilliant, dashing cavalier. He was almost unbelievably brave. He was also a stone-cold killer.

In spite of Ashby's strenuous efforts with his little force of 290 horsemen on the afternoon of March 22, neither Banks nor his division commander, Shields, had taken his presence seriously. They were convinced that Jackson was still forty or more miles away, and that Ashby, for whatever reason, was simply choosing to pester them, to no particular end. Jackson, meanwhile, rolling north at full speed, was now a half day's march away from Winchester and planning a full-scale assault. He, too, was very much in the dark about his enemy, but in a far more dangerous way. That evening Ashby reported to Jackson that only four Union regiments and one or two batteries remained in Winchester—a force so small that even Jackson's little army outnumbered it. But Ashby's normally reliable intelligence was dead wrong. Only one Union division had left the valley. Jonah Tavener had seen the first third of it on the afternoon of March 21. The other two brigades, under Brigadier General Alpheus Williams, had followed the next morning. But that left *a full division* under Shields, which outnumbered Jackson at least two to one.[17] Jackson was marching squarely, and unknowingly, into what amounted to a trap. It was indeed such an apparently perfect, elegant trap that James Shields would later falsely claim credit for having deliberately designed it to draw Jackson in.

CHAPTER TWENTY-ONE

A JAGGED LINE OF BLOOD

Generals Banks, Shields, and just about everyone else in command in the Union army in Winchester awoke on the overcast early morning of Sunday, March 23, with the same thought: that Turner Ashby, whatever odd mischief he had been up to the day before, was long gone. Two full Union divisions were going to march east across the mighty Blue Ridge Mountains to join McClellan in his grand enterprise and there was nothing to stop them. The war was going to be won, and soon, and they were going to be part of the army that would march triumphantly into Richmond before the summer's heats. And so it caused considerable surprise and consternation when a Federal reconnaissance patrol, sometime around 9:00 a.m., ran smack into Ashby's cavalry and horse artillery. He hadn't gone anywhere. Not only that, he had somehow been reinforced with four infantry regiments, and apparently intended not merely to harass but also to move aggressively forward up the eastern side of the valley turnpike. Ashby, believing his own faulty intelligence, and as always recklessly brave, was determined to sweep straight into Winchester and retake the town before Jackson arrived.

It was unfortunate for him that, while Banks and Shields, stationed in a house three miles north, in Winchester, persisted in believing that this small rebel force posed no threat, the wounded Shields's battlefield replacement, Colonel Nathan Kimball, very definitely did not. Kimball, a smart, sensible Indiana doctor and Mexican-American War veteran who would go on to a distinguished war career as a Union general, wasted no time in countering Ashby's attack. He threw troops forward and brought reinforcements up. Soon he had 3,000 men on the field facing Ashby's 450 north of the small village of Kernstown and east of the valley pike. (Kimball was not aware that Ashby's force was so small.) Ashby was repulsed just after 9:00 a.m., and then again at about 10:00 a.m. By 10:30 he had a pretty clear idea of what he was up against, and it was emphatically not the skeleton force he had told Jackson about, though he would compound his earlier mistake by mysteriously failing to tell Jackson of this potentially shattering development. Minié balls from Federal sharpshooters zipped through his ranks with their peculiar sibilant hiss, while the weirdly accurate, rifled Parrott guns of the Federal artillery began to find their range. One of Ashby's artillerists recalled what it was like to watch, for the first time, incoming artillery:

> I saw it flying in its graceful curve through the air, coming directly toward the spot where I was standing. I watched it until it struck the ground about fifteen feet in front of me. I was so interested in the skyball, in its harmless appearance, and surprised that a shell could be so plainly seen during its flight, that I forgot for a moment that danger lurked in the black speck that was descending to earth before me like a schoolboy's innocent plaything. It proved to have been a percussion shell, and when it struck the ground it exploded and scattered itself in every direction around me.[1]

Nathan Kimball, meanwhile, believing that he was still not seeing the rebels' full strength, and ignoring orders from his convalescent commander to attack, had made a wonderful discovery. Just north of Kernstown and west of the valley pike was an elevated promontory known as Pritchard's Hill, the sort of defensive position army commanders dream about. "The position commanded the plain or valley, and village in front," he later wrote. "No better position could be found to cover the approaches to Winchester with the forces I had." He proceeded to load the top of the hill with men and cannons until the place fairly bristled with firepower. By early afternoon Pritchard's Hill held 16 guns, 300 artillerists, and 6 full regiments—the better part of 3,500 men.

Banks and Shields continued to be certain, in spite of Ashby's peculiar behavior, that Jackson could not possibly be crazy or brave enough to, as Shields later put it, "hazard himself so far away from his main support."[2] To march on Winchester with such a small force would be suicidal, and it did not take a genius to see that. So secure was the Union command in this conviction that Banks left that afternoon by train for Harpers Ferry,

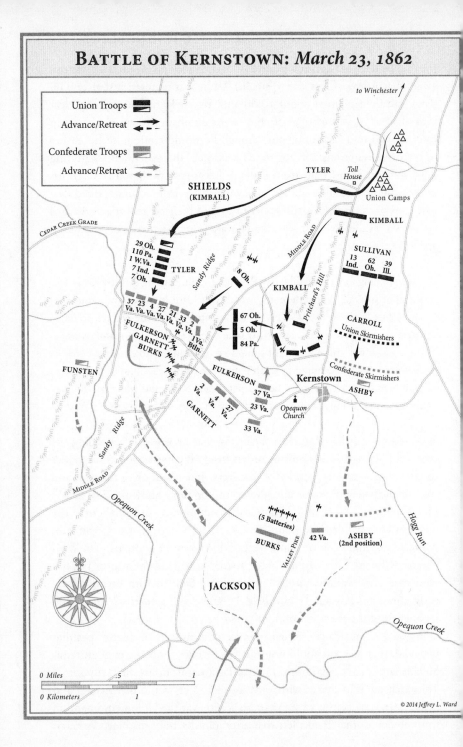

BATTLE OF KERNSTOWN: *March 23, 1862*

Union Troops

Advance/Retreat

Confederate Troops

Advance/Retreat

to Winchester

TYLER   Toll House

Union Camps

SHIELDS (KIMBALL)

KIMBALL

CEDAR CREEK GRADE

29 Oh.
110 Pa.
1 W.Va.
7 Ind.
7 Oh.

TYLER

Sandy Ridge

8 Oh.

MIDDLE ROAD

KIMBALL

SULLIVAN

13 Ind.   62 Oh.   39 Ill.

Pritchard's Hill

37 23 4 27 21 33 2
Va. Va. Va. Va. Va. Va. Va.

1Va. Btln.

67 Oh.
5 Oh.
84 Pa.

CARROLL

Union Skirmishers

**FULKERSON
GARNETT
BURKS**

FUNSTEN

FULKERSON

Kernstown

Confederate Skirmishers

Sandy Ridge

2 Va.
4 Va.
27 Va.

GARNETT

37 Va.

23 Va.

33 Va.

Opequon Church

ASHBY

MIDDLE ROAD

Opequon Creek

(5 Batteries)

BURKS

JACKSON

VALLEY PIKE

42 Va.

ASHBY (2nd position)

Hogg Run

Opequon Creek

0 Miles   .5   1

0 Kilometers   1

© 2014 Jeffrey L. Ward

en route to his new assignment in Manassas. He was quite pleased with it; he was trading an obscure sideshow for the main event. Shields, supremely confident and full of his usual bravado, told his subordinate Colonel Sullivan, in Sullivan's words, "that there was no danger of Jackson's fighting again; that he knew him, and Jackson was afraid of him."[3]

If that was true, Jackson had an odd way of showing it. At 7:00 a.m. he had put his men on the road again: 3 brigades, and 5 batteries of 24 cannons. All told, he had 3,500 infantry and artillerymen. "With the blessing of an ever-kind Providence," he wrote General Johnston before leaving, "I hope to be in the vicinity of Winchester this evening."[4] Out on the arrow-straight, macadamized valley pike, he drove his men brutally hard: fifty minutes of march; ten minutes of rest, sometimes less. After the grueling march of the day before, many fell out of the ranks. The phenomenon was known as straggling. It was the bane of Civil War armies, and it could embrace everything from nearly outright desertion to the inability of a soldier with a toe infection to keep up with the rest of his company. A man with severe diarrhea, for example—and there were many—would be forced to leave his marching column repeatedly. He would fall behind. Over many miles he would fall very far behind and would be literally hours behind his regiment, unattached and uncommanded. Some men straggled to pick blueberries or to drink from streams. Some were drunk, or suffering from hangovers. Many straggled because they did not want to fight. The practice was often so widespread that it was virtually impossible for commanders to court-martial all offenders even if they wanted to. Thus the disciplining of stragglers—arrest, court-martial, fines, confinement, and sometimes even the threat of the firing squad—was inconsistent at best, and depended on the mood of the commanding general. It was an enormous problem for both sides throughout the Civil War, and no commander ever solved it. Jackson, who drove his men harder and faster than any other commander in the war, inevitably faced the problem. On this march, which covered some thirty-seven miles in less than thirty hours, he lost several hundred that way.[5]

At noon on March 23, the vanguard of Jackson's army arrived five miles south of Winchester, and the rest of the men soon caught up. In the military terms of that era, this was blazing, unprecedented speed; seen from Washington, DC, it was a virtual blink of the eye. With Ashby's fleet and highly contentious cavalry in front as a screen, moreover, the army's march north had been completely undetected. Jackson immediately moved all of his troops off the exposed valley pike and into the woods just to the west. The day had brightened; the clouds had burned off, and the deep chill had gone out of the air. With two of his aides, Sandie Pendleton and George Junkin, Jackson rode out to reconnoiter. What they saw was a surprise: Kimball's artillery on Pritchard's Hill looked to be several times stronger than what Ashby had led them to expect. Though this seemed odd to them, they still had no reason to challenge their fundamental assumptions. Jackson now had a choice. He could rest his hungry, aching, foot-weary men and attack the next morning. That was the sensible thing to do. Staring up at the heights of Pritchard's Hill, however, Jackson realized how visible he was. If the Federals saw his full force, they might have time to bring up reinforcements, and Jackson would lose what he believed, incorrectly, was his advantage.

His reconnaissance had discovered something else, too. Roughly a mile to the west of Pritchard's Hill was a four-mile-long-by-three-quarter-mile-wide, elevated, intermittently wooded table of land the locals called Sandy Ridge. It was not only high ground; it was also higher than Pritchard's Hill and therefore ideal for artillery placement. In spite of the weariness of his men, Jackson decided he would attack immediately. He was worried only about doing so on the Sabbath, which he rigorously kept free of all secular activity. There could be nothing more secular than killing human beings with shells and bullets. "I was greatly concerned, too," he wrote Anna later, after she had told him she worried about fighting on Sunday. He had found it "very distasteful to my feelings . . . but I felt it my duty to do it, in consideration of the ruinous effects that might result from postponing the battle. . . . Necessity and mercy both called for battle."[6] He would move west through the small valley, scale Sandy Ridge, turn the Federal flank, then strike the valley pike in the Federal rear. There was nothing exceptional about the plan: it was standard West Point flanking tactics. But Jackson had seen in an instant something that Kimball had not: the critical tactical importance of Sandy Ridge. His assumptions of enemy troop strength, of course, were still those provided by Ashby the day before. He still believed he had more men and guns than the enemy had.

Back in Winchester, Shields, in pain from his shrapnel wounds, still refused to believe that he had anything to fear. At one thirty he ordered Kimball to "concentrate forces and fight the enemy on the plain." Kimball ignored him. Whatever happened at Kernstown was his problem now. He knew how well situated his troops were, suspected that the enemy was more numerous than he looked, and believed that Ashby's purpose was "to draw me from the strong position I held."[7] Determined to stay on the defensive, he could see Jackson's lead regiments under Colonel Samuel Fulkerson moving west through the woods below him. He opened fire, raining down shell (hollow iron spheres with timed fuses that exploded into fragments) and canister on the men below. Alarmed by the intensity of the fire, Jackson ordered Fulkerson to turn and try to flank the artillery on Pritchard's Hill. Fulkerson took one thousand men to within five hundred yards of the guns and was cut to pieces. Of the eighty-four men killed that day in his regiments, almost all died under Kimball's artillery fire.

Fulkerson's men fell back from the approaches to Pritchard's Hill—it was about two o'clock now—and with the main body of Jackson's troops continued hauling themselves west toward Sandy Ridge under the constant pounding of Kimball's guns. Fulkerson's ill-fated lunge had had the effect of a feint, and it was effective in screening the movement of the Confederate cannons. Jackson also had Ashby demonstrate beyond the valley pike, a true feint that also worked, convincing Kimball that there was still danger on the Union left, and causing him to draw off two regiments to deal with it.

While all this was happening, Jackson was pursuing his true purpose: a flank march up Sandy Ridge that would extend his line against a weaker force. In the words of John Lyle of the 4th Virginia, Jackson moved about on horseback with a pale countenance and a set jaw, furiously "stripping his front almost bare of troops to hurl the bulk of his small force on the right flank of the enemy."[8] What he really wanted to do, and what all his training as an artillerist told him to do, was to get his batteries up on top of Sandy Ridge as quickly as possible. They rolled on, unseen, while Jackson's infantry pushed forward over the marshy low ground, crossing that same no-man's-land of shot and shell, toward the heights of the ridge. "Their bravery was heroic and commanded the admiration and respect of all who witnessed it," wrote an Ohio infantryman who was looking down on the action from Pritchard's Hill.[9]

At 3:00 p.m.—ironically, almost the exact moment the dapper and placidly confident Nathaniel Banks was boarding a train for Harpers Ferry—Jackson's batteries thundered to life atop Sandy Ridge. It was also the moment Nathan Kimball realized the severity of his mistake in failing to secure his right flank. Jackson's guns were now 100 feet or more higher than his own, which were almost exactly a mile to the east. And now they began to find the range of Union infantry and batteries, while

Kimball's guns were forced into an artillerist's nightmare: shooting uphill at the enemy. Kimball's infantry were for the moment useless, motionless, flat on their bellies, and praying that the next shell fragment was not going to embed itself in their skulls. Though ranges of Civil War artillery varied, the most common gun of the war, the 12-pounder Napoleon smoothbore, could shoot 1,619 yards or just under 1 mile; rifled guns were accurate over larger distances: the 10-pounder Parrott had a range of 1,900 yards (1.08 miles), and the 3-inch rifles were fairly accurate at 2,000 yards (1.14 miles). Cannon shooting spherical case, or shrapnel, tended to operate at 500 to 1,500 yards, while the effectiveness of anything loaded with canister was limited to about 350 yards.[10]

Jackson, in his first real fight with an independent command, was quickly learning his trade. The last time any Americans had fought a war was fifteen years earlier, in a different country, with different weapons, and most of the men who were running this war had little or no experience of traditional battlefield command. (Indians had generally refused to fight pitched battles; fighting mounted Cheyennes or Comanches on the open plains or Seminoles in Florida swamps required an entirely different set of skills.) Civil War tactics were invented on the fly by men trying desperately to see through the sulfurous smoke and fog of battle, to understand terrain, troop movement, supply trains, the effects of artillery bombardment on infantry, and a hundred other things that were not covered in West Point's dry texts or in Napoléon's maxims. Jackson had made some very good moves—some calculated, some purely reactive. He had surprised the enemy with a fast and unexpected march so successfully cloaked that, to the dumbfounded Shields, who did not learn that Jackson himself was present on the battlefield until 3:30 p.m., he had appeared as if from nowhere. Such materializations from the ether would become a Jackson hallmark. He had grasped the tactical significance of Sandy Ridge before his opponent had. He had screened the movement of his artillery, had gotten it to the high ground first, and had used his advantage in elevation to devastating effect. He had, moreover, already understood and put into practice something that both Confederate and Union armies would be relatively slow to learn. Though it was common practice in military theory to attach batteries to brigades and have them support those brigades on the battlefield, Jackson had detached and massed his artillery on the hilltop, creating far more concentrated firepower.[11] He had, moreover, by the strength and surprise of his attack, forced Kimball—who had been led by Jackson's audacity to believe that the two sides had equal numbers of men—to play his tactical game.[12] With his numerical advantage, all Kimball had to do to win the battle was bring a large force against Jackson's right flank. He would have turned it quickly, and would just as quickly have captured the supply trains in the Confederate rear. If he had done so, he would have won a stunning victory. He would have been a hero. Instead, befuddled by the speed of Jackson's movement and the telling effect of his big guns, he swung heavily to his right, trading finesse for brute force.

But Jackson had made mistakes, too, and would make more this day. As in the Romney campaign, he had told none of his subordinates anything of his battle plan—not even Brigadier General Richard Garnett, a veteran soldier and the commander of the Stonewall Brigade as well as his second in command. This was shocking on its face—illogic from a supremely logical man. It had already resulted in confusion over whether one of Garnett's regiments was supposed to support Fulkerson's attempt to turn Kimball's artillery. That attempt itself had been a mistake; Jackson had allowed himself to be distracted by Kimball's guns from his main goal of gaining the ridge. The effect was to slow the movement westward of his regiments, which would now be fed into the battle in fragmentary fashion. Piecemeal attack—which ceded the advantage of massed firepower—was one of the cardinal sins committed by generals in the Civil War, even the best ones. Jackson was learning about that, too. But he would never learn to share information freely with subordinates; it was a glaring weakness, and it would haunt him here and throughout the war.

Sometime after 3:00 p.m., while Jackson was winning his artillery duel with Colonel Kimball, his young aide Sandie Pendleton climbed to one of the highest points on Sandy Ridge for a better view of Pritchard's Hill and the countryside around it. He was astonished by what he saw: at least ten thousand Union troops, with artillery to match, positioned squarely in front of Winchester. This was not the skeleton force of four regiments Ashby had reported. This was a *full division*. Not only that, Pendleton counted fully five regimental flags floating down one of the roads that led to Sandy Ridge, *coming directly toward him*. One of Kimball's brigade commanders, Colonel Erastus B. Tyler, a fur merchant from Ohio, was moving in force against the batteries that had been antagonizing him, and therefore toward the bulk of Jackson's army, which was still shifting leftward through the wooded low ground. Pendleton galloped back to Jackson to report the news. We have no record of Jackson's expression when he heard it, but we know what he told Pendleton. "Say nothing about it," he said. "We are in for it!" So Garnett and other commanders, who knew nothing about the battle plan, would know nothing about enemy troop strength, either. It is safe to say that no other general, on either side, would have chosen to proceed this way. Jackson, who had been planning a general assault, abandoned that plan. He would have to shift from offense to defense. Outnumbered again, he was suddenly in a desperate battle for survival.

The Battle of Kernstown, as this fight would be known, entered its second phase when Colonel Nathan Kimball, weary of the dominance of Jackson's cannons, sent Tyler's 2,300-man brigade to silence them. That was what Pendleton had seen coming at him. Tyler, deploying west along the Cedar Creek Grade Road, and then south along Sandy Ridge, ran headlong into the lead regiment of the Stonewall Brigade—the 27th Virginia— which itself was swinging west and north to defend the artillery. Badly outnumbered, these 200 men, under their intrepid commander, six-foot-four-inch, 260-pound Colonel John Echols, fell back behind a half-mile-long, shoulder-high stone wall that ran east to west and rose and fell with the broken landscape. At about four o'clock on Sunday afternoon, March 23, with only a few hours of daylight remaining, the battle, which had up to that point really been an artillery duel, became a desperate fight for control of that stone wall on Sandy Ridge.

Erastus Tyler's opening gambit, in this improvised war where commanding officers had to learn by trial and error, was a grievous mistake. To take his men more efficiently through the wood, he had formed them in what was known in military jargon as a close or massed "column by divisions." That meant that instead of long, linear, two-man-deep battle lines—the typical Civil War battlefield deployment—his men were configured in a large rectangular box that measured some seventy-five yards across its front and four hundred yards deep. Two companies made up the front line; behind them stretched the other forty-eight companies in twenty-four lines, set up front to back like dominoes. In that configuration they indeed moved easily through the woods on the northern part of Sandy Ridge. The weather had dramatically improved. On the second day of the Shenandoah spring, the sun was finally shining. "It was a beautiful day," wrote an infantryman in the 7th Ohio. "Birds sang in the trees and the warm sun brought out all the aromatic odors of the forest."[13]

Minutes later, the exhilaration of spring was gone. Tyler's lead companies found themselves at the edge of the leafless wood, looking 150 yards across open ground to the stone wall, from which poured volley after volley of musket fire, red jets of yellow flame piercing the billowing rolls of smoke, while their rebel opponents shouted "Bull Run!" as loudly as they could. Jackson's artillery opened up with canister on the Federal left, and Union soldiers, who were not trained to fight in a box formation, immediately found themselves in serious trouble. Once the firing started, it was almost impossible, because of the noise, smoke, and confusion, to shake themselves out into conventional battle lines by companies and regiments. The domino analogy is apt: the bluecoats offered a dense and easy target for Echols's riflemen at the wall. At the same time, they had temporarily lost the ability to use their huge numerical advantage to extend their lines. The fire was so hot that the 110th Pennsylvania fled backward through the ranks of the 29th Ohio, just behind them. Or, as an officer from the disgusted 29th saw it, "they broke and scampered like sheep at the first fire."

Thus did 200 Confederates, outnumbered 10 to 1, and aided by Tyler's tactical blunder, hold their own smartly against the oncoming brigade. Tyler's force had been virtually stopped in its tracks. But the battle was only five minutes old. From his position with the artillery on high ground, a quarter mile in the rear, Jackson saw that he needed more soldiers, and began to feed the fight. Under his orders, Lieutenant Colonel John Patton and the 21st Virginia, 270 men strong, advanced to the stone wall, where they poured a hot fire into the Union ranks. Still, the entire fight at this point was only two regiments against five. Tyler's first, unsuccessful assault had been on the eastern end of the stone wall. Now he noticed that the western end was undefended, and ordered an attack there. Colonel Sam Fulkerson, bringing his 23rd and 37th Virginia Regiments forward after being cannonaded for the better part of two hours, saw the same weakness, the same opening. What happened next was a deadly footrace. The 1st West Virginia rushed forward from the north, while the Virginia boys lunged from the south. The Confederates won, by seconds. They set up quickly behind the wall, 500 of them, opening up with their smoothbores loaded with "buck and ball" (a bullet attached to three pieces of buckshot that combined the characteristics of a musket and a shotgun) on the West Virginians, who were only fifty yards away. At point-blank range, the effect on the bluecoats was deadly.

Only ten minutes had elapsed since Tyler's first charge. He had been repulsed twice. Now the Confederates, realizing the size of the Federal force, began to bring additional regiments to the wall. Brigadier General Richard Garnett finally arrived, after his long march across the low ground with the rest of his Stonewall Brigade, and inserted the 33rd Virginia just to the right of the 21st Virginia. It is noteworthy that he not only had no knowledge of any battle plan; also, neither he nor his commander knew where the other was. By Jackson's orders, the 2nd Virginia came up, too, as did the Irish Battalion, to fill another gap in the wall. The Federals, meanwhile, had managed to untangle themselves into disorganized clots of men at the edge of the woods, 150 to 200 yards from the stone wall. They paid the price for their confusion, as many of their men in the front lines were dropped by their own friendly fire. At one point, the 1st West Virginia had unloaded several volleys into the backs of the 7th Indiana and the 7th Ohio. The Federals were nonetheless able, from behind trees and rocks and declivities, to deliver a constant stream of fire. Along the wall, the Confederate soldiers who fell almost invariably did so with horrible head wounds, many of them lethal, caused by huge .59-caliber minié balls that hummed like tuning forks in the sulfurous air and entered through the throat, mouth, eyes, forehead, and nose, blowing the men's brains out the sides and backs of their heads. Many soldiers later commented on the enormous sound of war: it was more of a giant, rolling roar than a succession of shots.

By 4:30 p.m., a little more than half an hour into the fight, Jackson's 1,200 men behind the wall had created a stalemate with the larger force, which was disorganized and strung out along a four-hundred-yard front that was fifty to five hundred yards from the stone wall. The fight went furiously on. There was little or no finesse here. It was a brutal, bloody, hard-nosed affair, rarely equaled in closeness of range and intensity of firing in the larger war that was to come, and no one, except the 110th Pennsylvania, was running away from it. Jackson himself told a friend five days later, "I do not recall ever having heard such a roar of musketry."[14] Wrote a soldier in the 7th Indiana, "The battle was on in all of its fury. The woods were soon enveloped in smoke. . . . The crashing of shells and shot and canister through the trees has left an impression on my mind that can never be effaced. . . . The regiments [were] mixed up through and through each other, but [we] never ceased to get rid of our sixty rounds of cartridges as fast as we could load and shoot."[15]

Jackson had thus far done remarkably well in spite of enormous disadvantages. He had less than half the troops his enemy had on the battlefield. His men were armed with smoothbores, while all but three Federal regiments had far more accurate rifled muskets.[16] He had only three rifled cannons against the Union's fourteen.[17] And his men had held the wall. He knew he could not hope to win. But he still had three regiments in reserve and less than two hours of daylight, and the odds had gone up considerably for a drawn battle—one that would accomplish everything he had been ordered by Johnston to do, and more. "I became satisfied that we could not expect to defeat the enemy," he later wrote, "and that our safety consisted in holding our position until night and drawing off under the cover of darkness."[18]

At almost the very same moment—around 4:30 p.m.—it occurred to Colonel Nathan Kimball, on his own high ridge a mile to the east, that he could lose. He had fully 3,600 men he had not used. Just as Jackson had earlier stripped his right of troops to seize Sandy Ridge, Kimball gathered up regiments on his unthreatened left and sent them double-quicking across the little meadowed valley between the two heights and into the fight at the eastern end of his battle line. Now came the final slugfest at the wall, the last hour of the fight. Most of the action had shifted east, where Kimball's fresh troops were shouldering into Jackson's bone-tired, battle-weary force. For Jackson it was a race to darkness. The fighting at the wall, brutal and constant for a full hour, now turned desperate. A measure of its intensity was the astounding tale of the regimental flag of the 2nd Virginia Regiment. The bearers of regimental colors were often targets of the enemy, both because they stood out as easy targets and because the flags were important in telling soldiers where the rest of their regiment was, and in which direction it was heading. The carnage began when the first standard-bearer, Sergeant Ephraim Crist, was shot in the head and killed instantly. Lieutenant J. B. Davis, who picked it up, was knocked out of action by a spent ball. Lieutenant Richard Lee then took up the flag and, with reckless bravery, jumped over the wall and brandished it at members of the 67th Ohio, who refused out of respect to shoot him, saying, "Don't shoot that man, he is too brave to die." They ordered him back over his wall, where he was soon wounded severely in the leg. A fourth, unknown man who grabbed the flag fell mortally wounded. Finally a full colonel, James W. Allen, leaned down from his horse, picked up the colors, and rode them to the wall, where his 250 surviving troops rallied around him. By the time the colors got there, they bore the marks of fourteen bullet holes, and the banner's flagstaff had been shot in two. The 5th Ohio had a similar experience. Five different standard-bearers were killed or wounded within a few minutes.[19]

Then something happened that no one, including Jackson, had counted on. At about five thirty, as the sun was setting over the battlements of the Alleghenies, and Jackson's goal of a drawn battle was in sight, the Confederate soldiers at the wall began to run out of ammunition. It began, predictably, with the courageous 27th Virginia, the men who had started the fight at the stone wall. They had carried only forty to sixty rounds in their cartridge boxes to begin with, and whatever ammunition the valley army had was sitting several miles away, back on the valley pike. Amazingly, in spite of this the Confederates, exhorted by Brigadier General Garnett, who stormed up and down the ranks, had managed to repulse three Ohio regiments that had assaulted the eastern wall. But the Federal numbers were beginning to tell. Fresh, well-armed Federal regiments were coming up to replace regiments that were themselves running out of bullets. And Kimball was beginning, at last, to use his numerical advantage to extend his line. Now, in the smoky blue twilight, came the hammer blow: two fresh Indiana regiments, the 13th and 14th, hit the eastern part of the wall, whose defenders had virtually no ammunition left. Fearing envelopment, Garnett, at about 6:00 p.m., called retreat. A few minutes later, Jackson, who had ordered up reserves from the valley pike, was astonished to see his men streaming to the rear. He found Garnett and furiously dressed him down for ordering the withdrawal. "He did not manifest any concern," Jackson later wrote of Garnett, "and was not using any efforts to rally his men. I rode up to him and asked him why he did not rally his men, or try to do so. He told me he had done so, till he was hoarse." Jackson, incredulous, then rode back and forth, as bullets whickered about him, loudly exhorting the men back into battle. He could not believe what was happening. He grabbed a young drummer next to him, and with his hand on the boy's shoulder, yelled, "Beat the rally! Beat the rally."

But he was too late, as were the reserve 5th and 42nd Virginia Regiments he had summoned, who arrived at about six thirty but could do no more than help cover the retreat. The rest was messy. Men fell back in disorder; regiments fell apart in the oncoming darkness; the army became formless. The Union cavalry for once showed some aggressiveness, riding around the disintegrating Confederate left flank and rounding up several hundred prisoners, who were later paraded through the streets of Winchester. "We all scattered, every fellow for himself, building fires out of fence rails and making ourselves as comfortable as possible after the fatigues of the day," wrote John Casler of the 5th Virginia.[20] Jackson ordered the bloodied army into bivouac about five miles south of the battlefield. He rode silently with them, and at one point stopped by a campfire. "General," said one of the men, "it looks like you cut off more tobacco today than you could chew." Jackson replied simply, "Oh, I think we did very well."[21] He had a small dinner of bread and meat—his first food of the day, gave thanks to God, and went to sleep on a bed of fence rails, without a blanket, next to his chief commissary, Wells Hawks. The next day Jackson's army headed south once again, pursued by the same army that had chased them less than a week before.

Jackson's men, battered, parched, and exhausted, agreed with his assessment of the battle. They knew that they had been badly outnumbered. They were equally aware that they had faced a Union foe that was just as brave and tough and resourceful as they were. (This was news to many of them.) They had marched twelve to fifteen miles in the morning, had been subjected to galling artillery fire, then had stood with astounding bravery at a stone wall for two hours under a barrage of Union lead. They had fought to their last bullet and were deeply proud of what they had done. "It was a terrific fight and all our men behaved like heroes," wrote Alexander Boteler Jr. of the Rockbridge Artillery, son of the congressman. "No one left his post unless ordered off the ground. . . . Our canister scattered them like scared sheep, and made them all run."[22] The almost universal feeling was that with ammunition they would have held. "The . . . little army had been heavily engaged, and although confronted by large odds, held its own, and only retired after shooting all its ammunition away," wrote John Worsham of the 21st Virginia Regiment. "It seems to me that the 21st Virginia would have held its line indefinitely if it had been supplied with ammunition. It was a regular stand-up fight with us, and as stated the men . . . fought as I never saw any fighting during the war."[23] Even Loring's old regiments seemed to find a new respect for their commander. And Confederate prisoners, to a man, expressed pride at what they had done.

Southern newspapers echoed the same sentiment. If their facts were slightly skewed, they fully understood that a very small force had stood toe to toe with a much larger one. "No battle has been fought during the war against such odds," said the *Richmond Dispatch*. "With a force not exceeding 3,500 men—men who had been on forced marches for weeks—we attack 20,000 fresh troops, repulse them again and again, until overpowered by numbers." The paper gave Jackson full credit: "A braver man God never made."[24] Amid all the recent bad news from the scattered Confederate armies, here, at least, was an example of pluck and courage. Here was hope. Jackson himself did not believe he had lost the fight. According to his map-maker, Jed Hotchkiss, he "never considered that he was beaten at Kerns-town."[25] To Anna he wrote, five days after the battle, "My little army is in excellent spirits. It feels that it inflicted a severe blow upon the enemy."[26]

The gruesome scene they left behind was witness to it—a pocked and devastated landscape full of pooled blood and bodies and pieces of limbs, clothing, hats, weapons, and a bewildering variety of personal items. Across the top of the wall, running its entire length, was a jagged line of blood, the residue of hundreds of Union minié balls hitting Confederate skulls.[27] A bloody, severed foot hung from a tree, testimony to the brute violence that had put it there. "The small bushes were cut to pieces, and every tree was filled with balls," wrote John C. Marsh of the 29th Ohio. "The dead lay thickly in those woods and behind the stone wall, some all torn to pieces with shell, some badly mangled with canister, but by far the larger portion were killed with rifle balls. It was curious to note the different expressions on the faces of the dead. Some seem to have died in the greatest agony; oth-ers wore a smile even in death."[28] Sandie Pendleton thought that, though smaller in scale, the Battle of Kernstown was "a harder fight than Manas-sas." In the end Union casualties exceeded Confederate casualties, perhaps predictably, considering that much of the battle amounted to an assault on a fortified position. The totals were: 118 Federals killed, 450 wounded, and 22 captured or missing; 80 Confederates killed, 375 wounded, and 263 captured.

Though he had expressed satisfaction with his performance, Jackson was frustrated that he had come, as he saw it, so agonizingly close to a draw against a superior foe. His unhappiness quickly manifested itself in his anger toward the unfortunate Garnett. Jackson believed that if Garnett had held on only a few minutes more, reserve troops would have arrived, there would have been no retreat, and darkness would have ended the fighting. Garnett, of course, had never been informed of that battle plan. Acting alone at the wall, he had behaved bravely and had ordered retreat only when, outnumbered and out of ammunition, and facing a possible envel-opment by a much larger force, he had no other choice, a decision that all of Jackson's regimental commanders later supported.

Jackson himself bore at least some of the responsibility for his defeat. This was his first fight as commanding general. He was learning. He was expanding his understanding of battle, which he had seen before only in pieces. He had done certain things very well. But seen from the front lines, the Battle of Kernstown was lost because Confederate soldiers ran out of ammunition, and that was Jackson's direct responsibility.[29] (Kimball made a similar though less costly mistake: he had failed to bring forward enough ordnance for his cannons.) Jackson had not anticipated an extended firefight and had not brought up reserve cartridges from his supply wagons. (Urging his men, as he did at the end, to charge with bayonets against rifles, was patently absurd, albeit a pure expression of Jackson's own combativeness.) He had also—somewhat mysteriously, considering his intimate control of his brigade's fight at Manassas—remained a quarter mile or so from the stone wall. Though there were good reasons for this—he could see the entire battlefield and the Union position more clearly from there—he was not available to redeploy his regiments where they were needed. (Kimball suffered from the same problem; he was even farther away from the action.) As twilight descended, Fulkerson's six hundred men at the western part of the wall were relatively unengaged. They could have been ordered to the eastern wall to great effect. They were fresher; they had ammunition to spare. Finally, Jackson had hampered Garnett's effectiveness by not telling him his battle plan; Garnett did not even know where Jackson was.

Perhaps the biggest lesson to be learned from Kernstown, however, involved not fighting but politics. Jackson's tactical defeat turned out to be one of the great strategic victories of the early war. It began with the sheer fierceness of his troops' resistance, suggesting to the Union command that he was stronger than he actually was. This impression was enhanced by Union-held prisoners, who crowed loudly that Jackson would soon be reinforced by thirty thousand troops. Banks, correctly suspicious of such tales, still could not quite bring himself to fully disbelieve them. This revised, more potent version of Jackson was further enhanced by James Shields. Puffing up his own accomplishment, Shields described for the Union War Department the desperate eight-hour battle he had fought against eleven thousand Confederate troops, five times what Jackson put on the field.[30] He told of how—far from being surprised by Jackson's attack—he had feigned weakness to deliberately lure and trap Jackson. Piling lies on top of lies, he claimed that he had closely managed the battle and even ordered Tyler's brigade to attack. "The havoc which has been made in the rank of the Rebels has struck a blow such as they have nowhere else endured since the commencement of the war," Shields told the War Department. "Jackson and his Stonewall Brigade and all the other brigades accompanying him will never meet this division again in battle."

But McClellan and the War Department in Washington drew the opposite conclusion. To them the battle meant that Jackson was far more dangerous than they had thought. The valley was not a sideshow; it was a full-blown theater of war. Thus McClellan, still in command of the valley and alerted to this new danger, made an uncharacteristically decisive move. The sensible thing might have been to leave Shields in the valley to fight Jackson. Instead, he canceled orders for *both* of Banks's divisions to leave the valley. He ordered the brigades that had already departed back to Winchester. And then he ordered a full-out pursuit of the small rebel army. "As soon as you are strong enough, push Jackson hard and drive him well beyond Strasburg," he wrote Banks. He still wanted Banks in Manassas, but now the terms were "the very moment the thorough defeat of Jackson will permit it." Thus were 19,000 sent out to destroy 3,500, and thus did two full divisions become useless to the Union army east of the Blue Ridge.[31]

Jackson's attack reverberated in other ways through the Union command. As McClellan began his epic move southward, Lincoln and Secretary of War Stanton discovered to their horror that he had not left the twenty-five-thousand-strong force he had promised to protect Washington. This role was to have been assumed by Nathaniel Banks's 5th Corps, which, of course, had been on its way to Manassas. Jackson's attack at Kernstown was the reason they never got there. McClellan, reluctant to give up any men from his expeditionary force, then proceeded to fudge the troop numbers. He included Banks's valley divisions in a "covering force" that was supposedly "in and about Washington."[32] It was actually eighty miles from Washington. Lincoln, furious and feeling betrayed, moved swiftly to correct the problem. He ordered troops back to Washington from the Rappahannock, thus killing any immediate idea of a pincer movement on Richmond. Next, he created two new independent commands, the Department of the Shenandoah under Banks, and the Department of the Rappahannock under Irvin McDowell. Both generals would report directly to Lincoln and Stanton. With Banks in supposedly headlong pursuit of Jackson in the valley, McClellan, stripped of a good deal of his power, was told sternly to focus on his single objective: Richmond.

CHAPTER TWENTY-TWO

THE SHOOTING WAR

❧

"At the distance of a few hundred yards, a man might fire at you all day without your finding it out."[1]

That's Ulysses S. Grant, making fun of the old .69-caliber, muzzle-loading, smoothbore musket the US Army used in the Mexican-American War. He was only slightly exaggerating. Though the weapon threw a frighteningly large projectile and could be fired quickly—up to four times a minute—using one was like shooting a marble from a shotgun. It was famously inaccurate at any range above a hundred yards, and often not much good beyond eighty yards. It was the standard infantry weapon of the 1840s and early 1850s, but had changed little since the invention of the muzzle-loading flintlock in France in 1610.[2] (The main change was a new detonator—a percussion cap instead of a flint.[3]) The smoothbore, which fired a round ball, or buck and ball, had defined warfare during Napoléon's military career (1793–1815). Lots of men stacked in close-order formations, concentrating their firepower on similarly stacked enemy troops, were necessary if anybody was going to hit anything. Battles took place, of necessity, at very close range.

But in the years following the Mexican-American War something happened to the old smoothbore that would change warfare forever and have horrific and far-reaching consequences in the American Civil War. This revolution came in the form of something very small: a conical lead bullet developed in 1849 by a French army officer named Claude-Étienne Minié. The minié ball, as it was known, permitted combat muskets to employ rifling—spiral grooves inside a gun barrel—which made them accurate up to four hundred yards and able to kill a man at a thousand yards. This in turn produced the deadliest small-arms fire in human history. Rifles were used by French and British troops in the Crimean War (1853–1856) to devastating effect, and were employed on a massive scale by both sides in the American Civil War. Though the correct pronunciation of the inventor's name was "Min-YAY," Americans insisted on pronouncing it without the acute accent—"Minnie"—which made this brutally destructive invention sound like a child's toy.

Minié had solved a very old problem. Gunsmiths had known for several centuries that rifling greatly improved both the range and accuracy of firearms. A bullet that fit the grooves tightly would prevent gases from escaping, thus improving the gun's range, and the rifling gave it spin that greatly improved accuracy. The highly accurate Kentucky long rifle, developed in the 1700s, was a good example of this technology. But such a weapon could be fired only a few times before the gunpowder fouled its grooves, requiring cleaning. A tight-fitting bullet was also harder to ram down the barrel, often jamming on the way. This meant that such rifles were impractical as infantry weapons. Though the smoothbore—which was loaded by ramming a loose-fitting round ball down an unrifled barrel—had far shorter range, it fouled far less frequently, was easy to load, and thus had the advantages of speed and rapidity of fire.

Minié's solution was elegant: a self-cleaning, cylindrical bullet with a hollow base that would expand when fired, thus fitting snugly into the barrel's rifling, and in the process clear the residue of the previous shot from the grooves. It could be loaded quickly—the bullet was in its unexpanded state—and many rounds could be fired before the barrel had to be cleaned. By the mid-1850s, rifled muskets using minié balls that had been simplified by Harpers Ferry armorer James Burton were being mass-produced in America, and in 1855 Secretary of War Jefferson Davis converted the entire US Army to the .58-caliber Springfield rifled musket. That, along with the British-made .577-caliber Enfield, which used the same bullets, would become the main infantry arms of the Civil War. That sort of ruinous power had never before been put into the hands of the common soldier.

What made the rifled musket even more lethal was that the battlefield tactics of the Civil War remained largely frozen in the Napoleonic era. A rifle that was reasonably accurate at three hundred yards should have dictated infantry formations that were spread out, more like skirmish lines. Instead, Civil War commanders stuck to the old close-order formations that Napoleon had used half a century before.[4] The typical battle line still consisted of men packed shoulder to shoulder—literally touching elbows—and stacked two deep. There were several reasons for this. First, while spreading soldiers out made them less vulnerable, it also took away their main tactical advantage: their ability to concentrate their firepower. A single individual with a musket was irrelevant; battles were won by hurling more lead, more accurately, at the enemy than the enemy hurled at you. Second, close tactical formations were the only way that officers could control and move men around a battlefield. In the noise and confusion of battle, a regiment of three hundred to six hundred men had to be able to hear the orders of its colonel and subordinate officers; those who could not actually hear had to be able to follow the movements of those who did.[5]

Imagine, then, a 2,500-man brigade, packed into tight battle lines, moving at "quick time," which meant they would cover eighty-five yards a minute, toward the enemy's defensive position. This was the orthodox Civil War "charge." Against smoothbores, the men had a very good chance of getting close to the enemy's position. Against rifled muskets fired from cover, the effect approximated pure slaughter. The war is full of examples of generals—one thinks of Ambrose Burnside at Fredericksburg, Robert E. Lee at Gettysburg, and Ulysses S. Grant at Cold Harbor—who continued to throw large bodies of men against entrenched defenders wielding rifled muskets, with catastrophic results. But even without massed frontal assaults, much of the war was fought at one hundred to two hundred yards, as it was at Kernstown—absolutely murderous range for the new weapons. This explains why the casualty rate was so much higher for the American Civil War than for preceding wars. Such accuracy makes it even harder to imagine a soldier standing erect in a field in a battle line, unprotected, biting off the paper end of a cartridge, pouring powder down the barrel, ramming a bullet down the barrel with his ramrod, inserting a percussion cap in the breech, then cocking the hammer—a process that took up to thirty seconds—while hundreds or thousands of men on the other side lined him and others like him up in the sights of their rifles. Ninety-four percent of all men killed and wounded in the war were hit by bullets. Jackson's love of the bayonet was an anachronism: less than half of 1 percent of wounds were inflicted by saber or bayonet.

That is not to say that the new muskets and their strangely whistling minié balls did not affect military strategy. They rendered cavalry, for example, nearly useless as an attacking body. Men on horses presented fat targets. Civil War commanders quickly learned how easy it was to empty saddles at long range. (They also learned how easy it was to kill mounted officers, and especially generals: 18 percent of Confederate generals were killed or mortally wounded, mostly by minié balls.) Cavalry, so important as an attacking unit in Napoléon's time, was thus consigned to support work: scouting and screening, raiding supply lines, or creating diversions—much as Ashby had done in the days preceding the Battle of Kernstown. The role of artillery changed, too. Napoléon had begun battles by moving his artillery up front, then firing canister to blow holes in enemy lines. Infantry charges would follow. Such tactics were used as late as in the Mexican-American War. They worked because the effective range of canister—250 yards or more—was greater than the 100-yard range of the smoothbores. But now the muskets outranged the cannons. Any general who opened a battle by moving artillery forward would soon see his artillerists and battery horses shot to pieces. (To some extent, this is what happened to McDowell in the early afternoon at Manassas.) Artillery thus moved back, and while canister was still used, much of the work of the guns was done against the other side's guns—known as "counterbattery work."[6]

The minié ball had other effects, too, most notably on the human anatomy and thus on the medical corps, surgeons, and generals who had to deal with it. The balls fired by smoothbores could, and often did, pass through the body intact, creating an exit wound about the same size as the entrance wound. They were also relatively easy to extract. But the soft, conical, hollow-bottomed minié balls flattened out, deformed, and often fragmented on impact. As these jagged pieces of lead tumbled through the body they caused extraordinary damage. If they managed to exit, they caused horrific, gaping wounds far larger than the entrance wound. The bullet's shattering, splintering, sometimes even powdering effects on bones were usually irreparable, and were the main reasons why surgeons often had no choice but to amputate, and why stacks of human arms and legs were a common sight outside field hospitals. And the soft, tumbling pieces of lead simply shredded whatever internal organs they encountered.[7] Because the injuries they caused were so often crippling or disfiguring, minié balls had a far more profound impact than round balls on the fighting ability of armies. An army reporting nine hundred wounded in battle, in a typical example, would lose seventy of those men to death, while the minié's effects meant that four hundred would be too crippled ever to fight again. The army thus suffered a permanent loss of nearly five hundred men.[8] Round balls were not nearly as destructive.

This great revolution, however, arrived unevenly on the battlefields of the American Civil War, a fact that had a large—but largely uncredited—impact on the early war campaigns of Stonewall Jackson. When the war began in 1861, a high percentage of the weapons in both armies were the old .69-caliber smoothbores. The Union quickly remedied that problem. In 1862 most Federal soldiers were equipped with either Springfield or Enfield rifled muskets. But the Confederacy lagged far behind. Jackson's valley army fought at Manassas and in the valley campaign with smoothbores, a condition that did not begin to change until he later captured so many Union arms that he was able to partially reoutfit his army.[9] According to a number of descriptions by ordinary soldiers, their equipment at the beginning of the war was badly outdated. John Worsham, an infantryman who served under Jackson, recalled an abundance of smoothbores, including old modified flintlocks, Mississippi rifles, pistols, and double-barreled shotguns. "Not a half dozen men in the company were armed alike," he wrote.[10] Unlike the Federals, the Confederate army as a whole was still using smoothbores well into mid-1863. "My recollection is that Gettysburg was our first battle in which we were at last entirely rid of smoothbore muskets," wrote Edward Porter Alexander.[11]

All of this suggests a rather extreme mismatch in firepower in the early part of the war. This inequality was apparent to soldiers on both sides. In one of Jackson's valley fights a Georgia regiment, equipped with .69-caliber smoothbores, stood fire for two and a half hours from Springfield-carrying Federals without being able to respond.[12] In many instances the Union troops, upon learning that their opponents were shooting outmoded muskets, exposed themselves and taunted their opponents. Many of them felt perfectly safe at a hundred yards.[13] It is true that, at close range, rifles lose some of their advantages over smoothbore muskets. But not all. Rifles are superior weapons, in accuracy and in the sheer destructiveness of their mushrooming, somersaulting bullets. Jackson was forced to deal with this disparity in firepower throughout his Civil War career.[14] In the early going, he had to deal defensively with the effects of this revolution in warfare. His opponents largely did not.

CHAPTER TWENTY-THREE

A FOOL'S PARADISE

The days after the Kernstown fight felt disconcertingly familiar: Jackson, mounted on Little Sorrel, chin thrown forward and cap settled on the bridge of his nose, was once again riding south at the head of his tiny, brigade-size army through the tentative Shenandoah spring with a much larger Union force in hot pursuit. He had faced an almost identical situation less than a week before, with no apparent options other than headlong retreat. Yet there he was. He was not only palpably *there*, marching up the valley pike with his men in columns of four, songs on the wind ("Listen to the Mockingbird"), and bullet-strafed regimental flags flying proudly, but also, in a few days, he had changed the war itself. With his ferocious little jab at Shields in Kernstown, he had single-handedly knocked McClellan's offensive off balance. By doing that, of course—and by bringing the attention of the world to the Shenandoah Valley—he had also had the effect of doubling the furies on his heels. Before, he had been chased by a single division—some nine thousand under James Shields—whose purpose was akin to swatting away an insect. Now came nineteen thousand men, under Nathaniel Banks himself, with a more resolute set of orders.[1] In the eyes of the War Department in Washington, Jackson had made himself a worthy foe. Now he would pay for his audacity.

Even a casual observer could have told you that Jackson was remarkably alone in the immense theater of transmountain Virginia. There were no Confederate armies standing by to rescue him; no such orders had been given. What that observer could not have told you was that the same description applied to Jackson's own life. Much of the world Jackson had known at the war's opening had either been wholly transfigured or had vanished altogether. That change had begun with exile from his homeland. The western part of Virginia where he had grown up—soon to be *West Virginia*—had since the early days of the war been in the curious process of seceding from a seceded state. It was already a Federal stronghold, crawling with bluecoats, and would formally join the Union within a year. The meaning must have been painfully clear to Jackson. If he tried to return to his native land—Clarksburg, Jackson's Mill, Beverly, or any of the old haunts where he still had deep family roots—he would be arrested and locked up. He was the enemy. In a very real sense, he could not go home.

Nor would he ever again embrace the love and friendship of his sister, Laura. The war famously divided brother from brother. Here it parted brother from sister. We don't know exactly how the break happened, but it happened precipitously, sometime after the beginning of the war in mid-April 1861. It was very likely the result of Laura's wartime politics.[2] She was as strong-willed as her brother, and she turned out to be an ardent, outspoken Unionist. Curiously, as late as April 6 there is no hint of friction between the two, who had been so close that they usually spent a full month together every summer. His letter to her of that date, a little more than a week before the outbreak of the war, is lengthy, thoughtful, and concerned, as he often was, with her relationship with God. He refers to her own "very kind letter" and tells her that if necessary he will pay the "whole salary" of a minister in her hometown of Beverly rather than see him leave. He goes on:

> *You speak of your temptations. God withdraws His sensible presence from us to try our faith. When a cloud comes between you and the sun, do you fear that the sun will never appear again? I am well satisfied that you are a child of God, and that you will be saved in heaven, there forever to dwell with the ransomed of the Lord. So you must not doubt. . . . Jesus says: "My yoke is easy and My burden light," and this is true, if we but follow Him in the prompt discharge of every duty . . . we should always seek by prayer to be taught our duty. If temptations are presented, you must not think that you are committing sin in consequence of having a sinful thought. Even the Saviour was presented with the thought of worshipping Satan. . . . Don't doubt His eternal love for you.*[3]

Comforting words, yet there the relationship ends, forever. Though Laura's husband, Jonathan Arnold, was a Confederate sympathizer—he would be arrested for it in 1863—and Beverly contained many people who agreed with him, she held fast to her convictions.[4] She nursed sick and wounded Federal soldiers in her own home. She even became something of an embarrassment to Jackson, accusing him publicly on several occasions of cheating on his West Point entrance exam, a charge for which no evidence has ever been found. Though Jackson sometimes queried travelers from western Virginia for news of her, he rarely spoke of her, and people around him avoided the subject.[5]

Much of Jackson's comfortable, familiar old world in Lexington had disappeared, too. Anna and his slaves were gone, the house vacant. She was in North Carolina with family members now. It would be nearly a year before he saw her again. VMI still functioned, but enlistments in the army had gutted its upper ranks. Most of his former students were already in the war. Many would serve with him, and many would die. His great friend John Lyle, the bookstore owner and debate society founder, was dead. Ellie and Maggie's father, Dr. George Junkin, whom he loved and revered as a surrogate father, pastor, mentor, and counselor, had left Lexington abruptly after Fort Sumter, dragging his heretical Unionist convictions back to Pennsylvania with him. He would never return. It was another crushing loss for Jackson. Maggie and her husband, John Preston, were Jackson's strongest surviving links to the town, but they, too, were enduring hardship. At the Battle of Kernstown Maggie's cousin and Jackson staffer Lieutenant George G. Junkin was taken prisoner. Junkin, who had lived with Jackson and Maggie at his uncle Dr. Junkin's house in Lexington for two years, and was close to Jackson, would spend the rest of the war in a Union prison camp. As the tide of war washed his past away, Jackson clung ever more resolutely to the twin pillars of his life: God and duty.

Both were in play as never before. Kernstown had been both intimate and brutal, a stark and bloody lesson in what it meant to fight an enemy who was as violent and determined as you were. There could be few illusions anymore about what war really meant, or about how much Jackson and his men risked. Back in war-shocked, Union-occupied Winchester, the courthouse was jammed with groaning, bleeding, disfigured men from both sides. One observer wrote, "A Confederate captain, Yancey Jones, was lying there with both eyes scooped out and the bridge of his nose carried away by a bullet. He was sometimes delirious and roared about forming his company and charging. An Ohio volunteer lay on his back, the brains oozing from a shot in the head, uttering at breathing intervals a sharp stertorous cry. He had been lying thus for 36 hours."[6]

With the Union occupation of Winchester and the valley's first real battle at Kernstown came bitterness and new contempt on both sides. "The
inhabitants believed that the army was a horde of Cossacks and Vandals,"
wrote David Hunter Strother, the Virginia-born writer who fought under
Banks,

> whose mission was to subjugate the land, to burn, pillage, and destroy.
> Hence they are received with distrust and terror, and their slightest disor-
> ders magnified by the imagination into monsters and menacing crimes.
> The [Union] soldiery, on the other hand, thought they were entering a
> country so embittered and infuriated that every man they met was a con-
> cealed enemy and an assassin, and every woman a spitfire.[7]

Strother was himself full of unalloyed contempt for these Virginians, a
feeling shared in one form or another by many people in the North. He
wrote:

> I have myself considered the Old Virginia people as a decadent race. They
> have certainly gone down in manners, morals, and mental capacity. There
> seems to be nothing left of their traditional greatness but a senseless pride
> and a certain mixture of dignity and suavity of manner, the intelligence
> of a once great and magnanimous people. It was high time that war had
> come to wipe out this effete race. . . . That will be the final result of the
> war, I do not doubt.[8]

It was inevitable, too, that a Union army marching conspicuously
through the valley would clash head-on with the institution of slavery. For
many slaves the opportunity for escape was just too obvious, and many
took that chance, crossing through army lines, seeking refuge and asy-
lum. In normal times—which these emphatically were not—the escaped
slaves would have been considered property and returned under the Fugitive Slave Act of 1850. Some Union commanders in the opening months
of the war did precisely that. But then an opportunistic Union general
named Ben Butler, who happened to be a lawyer, came up with a new way
of thinking about the problem. Confronted in 1861 with a demand for
the return of three escaped slaves in coastal Virginia, he decided that if he
took seriously Virginia's claim to being a foreign power, and if it was making war upon the United States, then he was under no obligation to return

any sort of property. Instead, he would hold the slaves as "contrabands of war." The concept, which Lincoln did not like, first because he thought it might destabilize border states, and second because he would not then or later accept the Confederacy's claim to sovereignty, quickly caught on anyway. (Congress would support Butler by passing the Confiscation Acts in 1861 and 1862, which allowed for the emancipation of slaves owned by masters in seceded states.) There was, in fact, little else the Union could do. Returning escaped slaves on a grand scale to the enemy was, in the long run, an absurd proposition. The "contrabands" were accepted, put to work, and paid for their services. Soon enough they would fight, too.

By the standards of the Deep South, the Shenandoah Valley had relatively few slaves, and almost nothing that resembled the brutal, impersonal culture that often existed on the giant plantations of South Carolina. Only one valley property owner had more than one hundred slaves. Most had far fewer than that. But because many of the slaves were rented out to non-slaveholding families for agricultural labor or housework, the institution was more pervasive than the numbers showed.[9] This phenomenon also provided at least one answer to a common question from Union troops: Why, if you do not own slaves, are you fighting for slavery? The answer was that ownership per se was only part of it; the institution pervaded the South on less apparent economic levels.

As Banks moved south, growing numbers of slaves began to enter Union lines. At Harpers Ferry, Federal troops faced what one soldier called "a flood" of escapees; in nearby Charlestown, a reporter wrote that "hundreds of contrabands are hourly seeking refuge within our lines."[10] They had different reasons for leaving. Some said they were tired of abuse and overwork. Many were treated well but just wanted freedom, or what they imagined it to be. A slave named George Washington, who had worked as a farmer and hotel waiter, said that his owner had never harmed him but that he simply preferred "freedom to slavery."[11]

Such defections produced a range of effects—all of them deeply unsettling—on valley residents. One farmer lost seven slaves within a few months—one-third of his workforce. Some escapees took what Virginians considered to be brazen advantage of the new Federal power. A slave named Shipley, accompanied by a Union escort of twenty-five soldiers, marched boldly to a farm in Newtown to reclaim his wife, Mary.[12] Even more unseemly to Southern sensibilities—hypocritically, in some cases—some of the Yankee soldiers enjoyed close relations, sexual and otherwise, with black women. One Confederate officer reported that three Union soldiers married black women while they were camped at Winchester.[13] Yet another sign of cultural transfiguration was the sight of a Union colonel lecturing a white slave owner for striking a female slave. Though most slaves stayed home, and many were not so unhappy with their lot that they would risk blind flight, it soon became apparent that, as Banks marched through the valley, he was not only pursuing Jackson. He was also tearing at the social and economic fabric of the Confederacy.

If one was forced to run for one's life, with a future that might be measured in days or hours instead of months or years, the Shenandoah Valley was a breathtakingly beautiful place in which to do so. Eleven months into the war, the place was still mostly unscarred, a graceful, mountain-walled land of clapboard farmhouses and steepled churches, rolling wheat and barley farms, valleys hidden within valleys, and land that rose and fell like gentle swells on the ocean. To outsiders the valley seemed, as it does today, a sort of idealized, postcard-perfect, Currier and Ives version of rural America. In the rain-drenched spring of 1862 it was a thoroughly sodden paradise, too. There was water everywhere, in cataracts that thundered out of the Alleghenies, in the swollen streams that ran along every road and path, and in the deep pools of the winding North Fork of the Shenandoah and its tributaries. Everywhere, too, were the valley's trademark fog and mist, thick and smoke-blue, swirling through valleys and gorges, making mountaintops vanish and the high ridges seem to float on the air like sleeping giants. Jackson loved the place. "This country is one of the loveliest I have ever seen," he wrote Anna, a sentiment he would express over and over again.[14]

It was also, at that moment, one of the most perilous. Though Jackson was directly engaged with two Union divisions, he had many more Union troops in the region to worry about. All threatened him. To his west, just over the Alleghenies in a parallel river valley, now camped Union general John Frémont, the old Pathfinder, disgraced in Missouri but somehow, through the magic of Republican politics, back in the field. He had 23,000 widely scattered men. Across the Blue Ridge Mountains in Fredericksburg, General Irvin McDowell of Manassas fame had 34,000 men. With Banks's 19,000, the Federals thus had some 76,000 troops in the area. (This did not include the Union troops at Harpers Ferry, which by May would number more than 7,000.)

Opposing them—in the broadest sense—were three small rebel forces.

In the Alleghenies just west of Staunton were 3,000 troops under General Edward Johnson. Just across the Blue Ridge, near Gordonsville, Major General Richard S. Ewell had 8,000.[15] Jackson himself would soon, with the new Confederate draft and the return of stragglers and men on furlough, have about 6,000 men. Together the Confederate forces totaled some 17,000.[16] Though the 76,000 would never face the 17,000 in a stand-up fight—Jackson would make dead certain of that—that was roughly the size of the troop disparity. They would all, Union and Confederate, figure in what happened in the valley theater in the coming months.

Jackson's immediate need, in the wake of Kernstown, was to forestall his own destruction. He moved south, quickly at first, marching twenty-five miles the first day straight down the valley pike to the town of Woodstock. Then, realizing that Banks was not exactly in hot pursuit, he slowed down, making a leisurely thirteen-mile march the next day to Mount Jackson. Jackson was in no hurry, "running" as slowly as he possibly could, using Ashby's rear guard to jab insolently at his pursuers. Banks followed, ever more sluggishly, then stopped altogether. Jackson, staying just out of reach behind Ashby's cavalry screen, stopped, too, seeing no point in running from someone who was not chasing him. Amazingly, considering the order McClellan had given Banks, Jackson and his army were able to remain in the immediate area of Mount Jackson *for the next twenty-three days*, unmolested and unpursued. It was a stall worthy of McClellan himself. Jackson moved only once during that time, shifting a few miles south to a more defensible piece of high ground east of the pike and just south of Mount Jackson called Rude's Hill.

With nowhere near enough men to attack Banks, but with free time suddenly on his hands, Jackson turned his attention to other things, such as reorganizing his army, which was still woefully short of supplies, weapons, and other equipment. While there he was confronted with a revolt of two hundred militiamen in Rockingham County, who had fortified themselves in the mountains and vowed to fight the new draft. Jackson put the mutiny down with characteristic grim efficiency. He sent seven regiments of infantry accompanied by cavalry and artillery—more than three thousand men—who shelled the mutineers into submission. They were all arrested, briefly jailed, then placed back in the ranks.[17] Jackson's dispassionate, businesslike approach to such problems made him even more formidable as a disciplinarian. The men knew that it would make little or no difference to him if he had to shoot them. Duty was duty.

Meanwhile, what was holding back this twenty-thousand-man Union army, fresh from its inspiring victory at Kernstown? The answer was, primarily, Nathaniel Prentiss Banks. Like McClellan, he was a deeply cautious man, and like McClellan he had to have his men and matériel precisely right before engaging the enemy. And everything was emphatically not right in the valley. There was, to begin with, the atrocious weather, constant driving rain, freezing winds, sleet, snow, and storms that encrusted men, horses, tents, and equipment in ice and caused tall trees to topple. Supply and artillery wagons churned the meadows into a deep, slippery ooze that mired horses and men and cannons and anything that fell into it. Sometimes the mud was so deep the men could not even drill, abiding in their frozen, muck-filled tents and trying vainly in the wind and rain to keep campfires alive.[18] There was the problem of supplies, too, or lack of them, Banks told the War Department. The Harpers Ferry-to-Winchester railroad was out of service; his men were on half rations. Some of them had no shoes. Banks complained bitterly, too, about the incompetence of his cavalry. Here he really did have an insurmountable problem. His men could not ride or shoot with Ashby's troopers, who bedeviled them at every turn. The Southern horsemen destroyed bridges and culverts, waited in ambush, and fired their light artillery at the invading Yankees from around blind corners.[19]

But Banks could not remain in place forever. On April 17, with clearing weather, his two divisions finally lumbered forward. At 7:00 a.m. his advance regiments triumphantly entered Mount Jackson, where they found nothing but the burning supplies and equipment the rebel army had left behind. Jackson had seen them coming. By midday the Union troops were pounding, under a hot sun, uphill through the muck toward Jackson's camp at Rude's Hill. Banks believed that if Jackson was going to stand and fight he would do it there, on this easily defended piece of high ground a mile to the east of the valley pike with a commanding view of the plain below. At last, Banks was ready to fight. With this in mind, he drew up his full corps in the wide river bottom just south of Mount Jackson, in what soldiers on both sides remember as one of the more striking military displays of the day.[20] His infantry formed battle lines, as though preparing for a frontal assault. By late afternoon, Banks's skirmishers were moving forward toward the crest of the hill.

But Jackson had anticipated this, too. Instead of an entrenched army, what the exhausted Federals found was an abandoned camp with the ashes of campfires. The only evidence of Confederates were the few stray shells tossed at them by Ashby's vanishing rear guard. Jackson had never had any intention of fighting at Rude's Hill. Indeed, he was happy to let Banks have Mount Jackson, and a lot more of the valley as well. An hour or two before, anticipating the Federal advance, he had put his army back on the turnpike heading south, once again staying just out of Banks's range. Jackson, who knew he could move faster than his enemy, did not seem especially worried. He sent everything he did not need on to Staunton, then bivouacked for the night about twelve miles north of Harrisonburg. The next day he moved off the valley pike and headed east under the shadow of the southern end of Massanutten Mountain, through the tiny towns of McGaheysville and Conrad's Store (now Elkton) and onward through the persistent mud to a smaller declivity within the Luray Valley known as Elk Run Valley.[21]

There, on April 19, his army made camp. None of his officers had even a vague idea of what he had in mind. Most of the men thought he was simply running away and that they would soon be driven ignominiously from the valley, where many of them lived. Such, they might have reasoned, were the mathematics of war. But somehow, in this bizarre, unwinnable endgame, Jackson had managed to find a superb little sanctuary. Elk Run Valley butted up against the towering Blue Ridge, which meant that Jackson's flanks were anchored in dense, steep, pathless forests. In his front was the swollen-to-bursting South Fork of the Shenandoah, a far more formidable river than the lazier North Fork.[22] And behind him he had a reliable escape hatch: a well-maintained road that led up and over the Blue Ridge and out of the valley at Swift Run Gap. Not only was Banks unlikely to attack him there with the force he had, but Jackson was poised, if Banks made a run at Staunton, to hit him from behind.

Now, again, something remarkable happened. Banks, his rickety supply lines lengthening, his worries mounting over the inadequacy of his cavalry, stopped pursuing Jackson. He remained at New Market for five days, then inched cautiously southward to the town of Harrisonburg, where he came to a full stop. This time he had a far more plausible reason for cutting off pursuit. On April 19 he had presented the War Department with the remarkable news that *Jackson had left the valley*. The Confederate general had disappeared, as though with a blinding flash of light, into the mist-shrouded ranges of the Blue Ridge. On April 20 Banks certified it. "The flight of Jackson from this valley, by way of the mountains, from Harrisonburg toward Stanardsville and Orange Court-house, on Gordonsville, is confirmed this morning by our scouts and prisoners." This was wholly untrue. Jackson was sitting in his pocket valley in the far eastern part of the larger Shenandoah Valley, less than twenty miles from the desk in Harrisonburg where Banks was writing his dispatches.

What accounted for Banks's blindness? It almost certainly had to do with the ineptness of his cavalry, which was not talented or brave enough to penetrate the brilliant Ashby's screens. It also had to do with Banks's desire to participate in the battle for Richmond, which was not going to happen if he was chasing Jackson's broken and pathetic little force in the valley. Banks *wanted* to believe that Jackson had gone. On April 22, as though to persuade himself that it was absolutely, incontrovertibly true, he repeated that "Jackson has abandoned the Valley of Virginia permanently." On April 24 he spoke of Jackson "at his present location near Stanardsville," which was east of the Blue Ridge in the Piedmont country.[23] Jackson, of course, hadn't moved. Leaving the valley permanently, in fact, was the last thing on his mind. While Banks was assuring Stanton that Jackson was nothing to worry about, Jackson was quietly concocting a plan to drive Banks himself from the valley.

To Banks and his officers the meaning of Jackson's departure was clear: their work was done. "There is nothing more to be done by us in the Valley," he wrote Secretary of War Stanton on April 30, using words that he would come to regret. "Nothing this side of Strasburg requires our presence." (North of Strasburg was the B & O Railroad, Washington's main supply channel to the West, which would always be a matter of strategic concern.[24]) He added that "Jackson's army is reduced, demoralized, on half rations."[25] Banks's cool, self-possessed tone convinced Washington that he was right. Lincoln and Stanton already believed that he had pushed perhaps a bit too deeply into Virginia, putting too much distance between him and other Union commands.[26] The result was that on May 1, Secretary of War Stanton ordered Banks to "fall back with the force under your immediate command to Strasburg."[27] More important, he also ordered Banks to detach Shields's division and send it to General McDowell in Fredericksburg. It seemed a curious finish to a curious campaign. Early in March, Banks had swaggered into Virginia with twenty thousand men and seized Winchester. One of his divisions had beaten Jackson at Kernstown, then driven him down the valley. But there had been no follow-through. In the thirty days after Kernstown his 5th Corps had covered a mere sixty-seven miles, during which time he had failed to catch, and then had lost altogether, a small Confederate army. And now, soon, he would be turning around, retracing his steps. The campaign was all strangely inconclusive.

At about this time something happened—quietly and without attracting notice—that would have a profound impact on the course of the war. Jackson, in his camp in Elk Run Valley, started to correspond for the first time in earnest with Robert E. Lee, and thus began an extraordinary partnership. Though Lee was officially President Davis's military adviser, the former had begun, with Davis's full approval, to function more like his chief of staff. And as more and more of Johnston's, Davis's, and the War Department's time was consumed dealing with McClellan's move up the peninsula, Lee began to exert more influence on the rest of Virginia. He was mostly trying to prevent McDowell, with his thirty-four thousand men at Fredericksburg, from advancing on Richmond and linking his forces with McClellan's. Jackson had already proven his ability to tie up Union troops in Virginia. Quietly, informally, and with Davis's approval, Lee had assumed de facto charge of the valley.

On April 21 Lee wrote a letter to Jackson that must have seemed a revelation to the younger man. Jackson's orders since March had always been, in effect, to protect himself and his supply lines, to venture near the enemy but not too near, to engage the enemy without taking undue risks. Now he heard a new voice, using an entirely new vocabulary. Lee opened by telling Jackson that he was worried about the concentration of Union troops near Fredericksburg. He then wrote, "If you can use General Ewell's division in an attack on General Banks, and to drive him back, it will prove a great relief to the pressure on Fredericksburg."[28] *Attack. Drive him back.* Lee had watched Jackson's bold, if imperfect, moves in the campaigns leading to Romney and Kernstown. Reading Jackson's correspondence from the valley, he was convinced that the two shared the same deeply aggressive instincts. It is worth noting that, at this moment, few in either the United States or the Confederate States yet had any idea of this rougher, more combative side of the courtly, soft-spoken Lee; Jackson was one of the first to see it and grasp it. Somehow, the two kindred spirits—whose personalities could not have been more different—had found each other.

And now Lee was offering Jackson precisely the opportunity he was looking for. On April 25 he went further. "I have hoped in the present divided condition of the enemy's forces," Lee wrote, "that a successful blow may be dealt them by a rapid combination of our troops. . . . The blow, wherever struck, must, to be successful, be sudden and heavy. . . . I cannot pretend at this distance to direct operations depending on circumstances unknown to me and requiring the exercise of discretion and judgment as to time and execution, but submit these suggestions for your consideration."[29] This was the music Jackson had been waiting to hear.

What Lee got back from Jackson on April 29 was exactly what he wanted—proposals for three different, equally daring offensive strikes at Union forces: one against Frémont's vanguard west of Staunton; another against one of Banks's detached forces near New Market; and still another against Front Royal and Winchester, in the northern part of the valley. Pleased, Lee left the choice to Jackson. That was just as well, because Jackson had already decided on the first—and probably the most audacious—of the three. By the time Jackson received Lee's response, his men were already marching.[30] Staunton, the prosperous commercial center of the southern valley, a critical base of food, clothing, arms, and other supplies, and the vital railhead of the Virginia Central Railroad, was the true key to military operations west of the Blue Ridge. Losing Staunton meant losing the valley and giving the Union the ideal staging ground for an eastward strike against Richmond. Staunton must be held. But the town was now threatened by two Union armies. On April 27 the vanguard of Frémont's western Virginia force, 3,000 men under General Robert H. Milroy, had seized the tiny, mountain-ringed town of McDowell, twenty-eight miles west and north of Staunton. Still farther north, at Franklin, was General Robert C. Schenck with another 3,000. Behind him, in the long valley of the South Fork of the Potomac, was Frémont himself, with roughly 10,000 more. Banks, meanwhile, had 19,000 at Harrisonburg, twenty-eight miles north and east of Staunton. That gave the Union some 35,000 troops within striking range of Staunton.[31] United, they would be able to seize the town and its critical railhead, thus completing the strategic conquest of the valley. That was the problem.

Jackson's solution was an extremely risky military operation. It would depend heavily on both speed and deception. He would move through the valley to Staunton, directly in front of Banks's encamped army at Harrisonburg and in full view of Banks's scouts and spies—there was no other way he could go—and join forces with General Edward Johnson. Together they would strike Milroy's Union force at McDowell before he could be reinforced by Frémont. Jackson would then turn, head back into the valley, and link with General Richard Ewell, who was currently camped with his division just on the other side of the Blue Ridge Mountains. Together they would attack Banks. If Lee had doubts—he must have, considering how many things could go wrong with such a plan, starting with the likelihood that Banks would attack Jackson at Staunton—he did not express them. Perhaps it was enough that, whatever Jackson did, he would cause headaches for the Union. Keeping to his Winchester vow to hold no war councils, Jackson told no one but Lee, and even Lee got only the barest of essentials. His generals, from Ewell to Johnson, were told only the parts of it that they absolutely had to know, which, of course, drove both of them to distraction.

Jackson's first step was to summon Ewell, who promptly crossed Swift Run Gap and entered the easternmost part of the valley on April 30 with eight thousand men. The idea was for him to take Jackson's place at Elk Run Valley while Jackson moved west, to Staunton. Ewell possibly understood that his purpose was to threaten Banks's flank. But he did not know what Jackson planned to do, or who or when he might be planning to attack. Ewell's men and officers, who were thrilled to be marching to the valley, were under the impression that they were going to join up with Jackson's army, and were excited at the prospect. But when they arrived they found, to their astonishment, that Jackson's army, whose distant campfires they had seen the previous evening, was nowhere in sight. "There was nothing, save the smoldering embers of the campfires of the night previous," wrote one soldier later. "Jackson had disappeared; whither no one seemed to know. Quietly, in the dead of night, he had arisen from his blanket, and calling his troops around him, with them had disappeared."[32] Ewell, who understood that he was being kept in the dark, was angry and frustrated, a reaction that was fully in keeping with his character.

Dick Ewell was one of that impressive array of volatile, difficult, and highly idiosyncratic personalities who populated the Confederate army's upper ranks. He was a slight five foot seven, with a broad, prominent dome of balding scalp above a fringe of brown hair, an angular nose, and a less than luxuriant beard and mustache. In the famous description of his fellow Confederate general Richard Taylor, Ewell, with his "bright, prominent eyes . . . and a nose like that of François of Valois," bore "a striking resemblance to a woodcock; and this was increased by his bird-like habit of putting his head on one side to utter quaint speeches."[33] He was also, wrote Taylor, a person "of singular modesty." Like Jackson, he suffered from dyspepsia. He would often dine only on a special preparation of wheat. He was an odd mixture of gentleness and brutal profanity. "He was a compound of anomalies," wrote John B. Gordon, later a general, who served in Ewell's brigade, "the oddest, most eccentric genius in the Confederate army. He was in truth as tender and sympathetic as a woman, but, even under slight provocation, he became externally as rough as a polar bear."[34] While what Lee later termed his "quick alternations from elation to despondency" and "his want of decision" made him ill suited for independent command, he was at bottom a smart, tough officer who liked to fight, could follow orders, and harbored no grand ambitions.[35] He had graduated thirteenth of forty-two cadets in the West Point Class of 1840 and served with distinction in Mexico and later in the American West. He was liked and respected by his men, who affectionately called him Old Bald Head. Standing in the mud below Swift Run Gap, staring at the picturesque fields, woodlands, and quaint gristmills of the valley below, he could not help but wonder what Jackson, about whose sanity he was already beginning to question, had in mind.[36] He stayed put, stewed about his predicament, kept his own counsel, and waited for orders.

Jackson, meanwhile, was on the move, pushing his force through a nightmare of mud and quicksand and moving water to Port Republic, heading for a pass through the Blue Ridge known as Brown's Gap. The sixteen-mile march was agonizingly slow. According to staff member Henry Kyd Douglas, it was conducted "over soft and bottomless roads into which horses and wagons and artillery sank, at times almost out of sight, dragged along by main force of horses and men, the General himself on foot, lifting and pushing amid the struggling mass."[37] Jackson often dismounted to help gather fence rails and stones to give the wagons more traction. Once, while he was doing that, he found himself behind a common soldier who was doing the same thing, and cursing Jackson for putting him through such travails. "It is for your own good, sir," came the voice, and the man turned and beheld the general himself.[38] Dead horses and busted wagons littered the sides of the road.

Weather was not the only worry. The men were exhausted. They were also eating a shockingly deficient diet. The basic Confederate fare in the war consisted of two principal items: salt pork and cornmeal. The former, sometimes called "bacon" or "sow belly," was what most Americans of the era would have considered nasty stuff: often blue-colored, cloyingly salty, fatty meat with hair, dirt, and skin left on. When the order was given to "cook three days' rations," soldiers would gather in small "messes" around a fire and a pot, and attempt to render their food into a form that could be carried in their grease-logged canvas haversacks. This process usually began by cooking the chunks of pork, then taking the grease and mixing it with the cornmeal. That mixture could be mixed with water, then fried to make easily transportable "corn dodgers" or other types of cooked cornbread patties. Either way, it was cornmeal and grease. Needless to say, such a diet was hard on the digestive tract. Sometimes their Commissary Departments did not even have sufficient supplies of salt pork, in which case soldiers would be given the dreaded, unpalatable "salt beef," a nauseating horror made of the lesser parts of the cow—organs, neck, head—that the soldiers called "salt horse." To dress it up, they would chop it, stew it in water, then crumble cornbread into it. The mixture was called "coosh," and it was not much of an improvement. The coffee was rarely authentic—more likely a substitute made from such things as chicory, roasted acorns, okra seeds, or wheat.[39]

Though this was the basic diet, it was not all Confederate soldiers ate. If they were lucky—or if they had captured Union supplies—they might get molasses, sugar, peanuts, dried peas, and even fresh vegetables. Their picket guards often traded with their Union counterparts, exchanging Southern tobacco for authentic Northern coffee. If they had time, they foraged for everything from corn to apples, peaches, cherries, spring onions, potatoes, eggs, and turnips. Best of all were the packages from home. But most of this was a matter of serendipity. Jackson's troops often subsisted on what might be considered starvation rations, which were virtually a guarantee of poor health.

On May 3, a warm, sunny spring day at last, Jackson and his army finally crested the heights of Brown's Gap, crossed through the Blue Ridge Mountains, and descended through the brilliantly green, rolling landscape of Albemarle County to a small depot on the Virginia Central Railroad known as Mechum's River Station. Word of his departure, which ricocheted through the southern valley, was greeted with shock and sadness in Staunton and other cities. "Suddenly the appalling news spread through the Valley that [Jackson] had fled to the east side of the Blue Ridge," wrote artillerist John Imboden. "Only Ashby remained behind with one thousand cavalry. Despair was fast settling on the minds of the people."[40] As it was among Jackson's own men, convinced now that they really were leaving for good. At Mechum's River Station, Jackson had—remarkably—managed to commandeer half a dozen trains with locomotives, which stood along the main tracks and sidings. His men boarded the cars sullenly. (A few regiments departed on foot.[41]) No one doubted, wrote Imboden, that the train "was to be taken to Richmond. . . . It was Sunday, and many of his sturdy soldiers were Valley men. With sad and gloomy hearts they boarded the trains. . . . When all were on, lo! They took a westward course!"[42] Loud cheers rang through the cars. They weren't running away after all. They were going back to the valley!

If Jackson's men did not know whom they were going to fight, at least they knew where they were and in which direction they were going, facts that continued to elude the Union command. Jackson's cat-and-mouse game in late April and early May was a work of considerable tactical brilliance, even if some of its effects were unintentional. Early Jackson historians gave him full credit for his deception; certain later chroniclers took some or all of that credit away. But a close reading of Union war dispatches shows that in a world full of spies, traitors, deserters, casual informants, and escaped slaves, where military secrets often migrated through enemy lines with amazing speed, Jackson managed to confuse almost everybody, and almost all of that confusion worked to his own advantage.

Banks was Jackson's principal victim. Almost from the moment he had been ordered by Stanton to withdraw and divide his forces, he had begun to have second thoughts, alternating between confusion and worry about his own well-being. Judging from his dispatches, he began to be afraid for his soon-to-be-split army's safety, a condition that would worsen in the coming weeks. On May 2, less than three days after reasserting the absolute truth of his claim that Jackson had left the valley, Banks wrote Frémont that Jackson "was seen today moving toward Port Republic. . . . His march is possibly a feint, possibly to join Johnson and attack Milroy near Staunton." Thus Banks had completely reversed himself. *Jackson was in the valley after all*, he now asserted. Jackson was not only there but was also in motion and dangerous. Banks happened to be right, for a change, and he was miraculously right again in his May 3 wire to Stanton, saying that Jackson had been reinforced in the valley by Ewell.

Now Banks began to rethink those sweepingly dismissive dispatches of just a few days before. "I do not think it possible to divide our force at this time with safety," he wrote Stanton that same day in a new, cautionary tone that must have mystified the secretary of war. (Shields was still with him and would not depart, with his ten thousand men, until May 12.)

The next day, Banks, now reconciled to Jackson's supposed presence in the valley, wired to say that "our officers are all confident that Jackson's force is near Port Republic." But, once again, he was completely wrong. This time the reason was, ironically, that Jackson had finally fulfilled Banks's own earlier claims and actually left the valley. (Just how befuddled the Union command was, as a whole, was evident in Irvin McDowell's note to James Shields on May 2, while Jackson was mired in the mud on the way to Brown's Gap, saying that he was well east of the Blue Ridge and that he had "pushed through Gordonsville" on his way to Richmond.)

At this point—May 4–5—Banks, Frémont, Milroy, and the entire Union command lost Jackson entirely. Their dispatches reflect this. They had seen him moving toward Port Republic, and then, suddenly, they did not see him at all. Jackson's railroad ploy was, in retrospect, brilliant. No one saw through it. By feinting east across the Blue Ridge, then making an about-face and moving his force by train from Mechum's River Station to Staunton, he had effectively made his army disappear. Banks, unaware of this movement, which placed his own army squarely in Jackson's rear—an enormous tactical advantage—asserted with placid confidence in a dispatch to Stanton on May 6 that Jackson's force, which he still believed was near Port Republic, was "greatly demoralized and broken." Union general Robert Milroy was just as badly deceived. On that same day he wrote his boss, John Frémont, saying that Jackson's movement from Port Republic toward Staunton or Waynesboro—which was a complete fantasy in the first place—was merely a feint in the direction of Confederate general Edward Johnson in the western mountains. And Milroy knew why it could not be anything but a feint: "[Jackson] cannot move from Port Republic toward my advanced position without leaving Banks in his rear . . . which he will not do."[43] That, of course, was exactly what Jackson was doing.

By midday the first train had arrived at Staunton, creating an uproar in the streets as the electric news of Jackson's arrival spread throughout Augusta County.[44] Jackson, worried that such a celebration would draw attention, ordered Ashby's men to seal off the town. No one was allowed in or out. Thus far his plan was working. Various Union commands did not know where he was; or, more accurately, Federal sources reported him at many locations, including Waynesboro, Port Republic, Gordonsville, Harrisonburg, Staunton, and en route to Richmond.[45] Even Richard Ewell did not know where he was. The other news Jackson received, to his undoubtedly pleasant surprise, was that Banks had withdrawn from Harrisonburg on May 4 and was moving back north again.[46] Exactly why, Jackson did not yet know.

By May 5 the trains had carried Jackson's entire army to Staunton, where they were joined by the command of General Edward "Allegheny" Johnson, a loud-voiced, bluff, popular old warhorse with a Mexican-American War eye injury that made one of his eyes wink continuously. He was a hard fighter, popular with his troops, and a man Jackson liked and admired. Jackson's army was also joined by two hundred cadets from VMI, whom he had summoned north from Lexington. Their role would be, as Jackson explained to VMI superintendent Francis H. Smith, limited to "care of the prisoners and baggage trains," which would allow "volunteers to go into battle who would otherwise be kept out."[47] Jackson met Johnson on May 6, wearing, for the first time, a full uniform of Confederate gray. Until then, he had worn only his old, mud-splattered blue major's uniform from VMI. He had gotten a haircut, too. At dawn on May 7, the commands of Jackson and of General Edward Johnson, some ten thousand men, marched west and north into the mountains for the town of McDowell.

What of Banks, who merely a week before had greatly outnumbered Jackson and threatened him with annihilation? That same day—May 7— he wrote Secretary of War Edwin Stanton from his camp at New Market to say, "Nothing important has occurred today." He noted blandly that Jackson's army, which he had characterized the day before as "broken and demoralized," had somehow occupied Harrisonburg. It had done no such thing. But something "important" was definitely occurring, more or less right under Banks's nose. Jackson was moving against Milroy, in such force that Milroy that same day sent an urgent plea for help. "Enemy is pressing us. . . . Must have aid," he wrote to his immediate superior, General Robert Schenck. "Cannot Blenker's force make a forced march, relieve you and myself? Cannot you join me? Ask Frémont to have Banks press in on the rear of Jackson."[48]

The Battle of McDowell, as it came to be known, was a small, fierce, bloody, four-hour firefight on a steep mountain slope that ended up being more equal—and far more lethal—than either side had expected it to be. It was fought because Jackson, moving invisibly and with remarkable speed, had succeeded in intercepting a smaller Union force under General Robert Milroy that had been preparing to advance against Staunton. Because Milroy's army was well in advance of the rest of Frémont's other divisions, which were scattered somewhere north of Franklin, Jackson, by arriving when he did, had achieved decisive numerical superiority. That was the idea—to strike at the enemy's weak points, prevent him from concentrating his forces. A similar plan at Kernstown had failed because of faulty intelligence. This time Jackson had taken better care to find out what he was up against.

In the late morning of May 8, having crossed several high, rugged mountain ridges, the bulk of Jackson's army, with General Johnson commanding the advance, ascended a long, flattened, ragged chunk of vertical land cut by steep hills and ravines known as Bull Pasture Mountain. From its crest the world seemed a simple place: below them to the west was a river, and behind the river was a small village, and spread out neatly on the valley floor, as in a giant amphitheater, were six regiments belonging to Milroy, and three to General Robert Schenck, a courtly four-term congressman from Ohio and former minister to Brazil who also happened to be one of the nation's most accomplished poker players and would later be known as the "father of British poker." He had just arrived that morning after a forced march triggered by Jackson's sudden appearance in Staunton. If Jackson had harbored any doubts about Union troop strength, the sight of the Federal camps allayed them. Combined, the Union had about four thousand men.[49] Johnson took his force off the main road and laid them out in long defensive lines on a steep, mile-wide spur of Bull Pasture Mountain known as Sitlington's Hill. Jackson's plan, already in play, was to use his superiority in numbers to move a large force of infantry and artillery by night on a flanking march around the Federal left. His engineers had already found a route that would allow them to strike the main road five miles west of McDowell. In that way he would block the Union army's retreat, envelop it, and destroy it.

But Milroy, as Jackson would soon learn, was no Nathaniel Banks. The gray-haired forty-six-year-old former lawyer and judge from Indiana was one of the more aggressive Union commanders in the East. He was fearless and even reckless. In the words of Robert Schenck, he was "undaunted and impetuous, though rather uncalculating."[50] He liked to fight, and wanted, more than anything else, to bring Old Testament–style retribution to the South for the sin of slavery. He wanted to attack Jackson with the full Union force but was overruled by Schenck, who nevertheless agreed to let him lead an attack that evening with a little over half their troops. They were not going for victory, just a temporary advantage. They would inflict a sharp, quick blow, and then, as Schenck put it, "retire from his front before he had recovered from the surprise of such a movement."[51] That was the idea, anyway.

The plan was daring in the extreme, bordering on foolhardy. Both Union commanders understood that Jackson and Johnson had joined forces. Both understood that they were outnumbered, camped in an indefensible valley, and facing an entrenched Confederate force on top of a high ridge. They knew that they would have to attack straight up the side of a mountain. The one advantage they had was surprise: an attack under those conditions, and with such a desperate disadvantage, was the last thing Generals Johnson and Jackson expected. While the troops under Johnson's command dug in on top of Sitlington's Hill, Jackson ordered his staff to his headquarters at a local hotel for a meal and some rest.[52] They were all eating, about a half mile away, when the Union attacked. (An interesting parallel occurred a month before, when, at Shiloh in Tennessee, Ulysses Grant was surprised by an early-morning Confederate assault while he was eating breakfast nine miles downriver. Like Jackson, he had not believed the enemy would attack.)

At about 4:30 p.m. Milroy, having received an erroneous report that Jackson was moving artillery to the summit of Sitlington's Hill—which would have been disastrous for the Union troops—gave the order to advance. Up the hill the Federals came, courageously and in good order, toward the waiting Confederates. What happened next, in textbook terms, should have been a disaster for the Union. But in the Switzerland-like topography around the small village of McDowell, there were good reasons why it was not. Mounting the hill, Milroy's regiments, mostly Ohioans, engaged with Johnson's battle line. At first the advantages seemed to be with the Confederates. They held the high ground, and could duck behind the crest of the hill to reload. The Federals, meanwhile, had to struggle upward over steep terrain that offered little cover. But these advantages soon vanished. Facing west, against a clear blue sky, the rebels presented neatly silhouetted targets, while the Union troops below were obscured in deepening shadow. Nor did the Confederates have artillery to take advantage of their high ground. As Jackson explained later, the terrain was too steep to drag the cannons up and, even if they managed to do that, the guns could not easily be removed and thus would be subject to capture. A final advantage was that the slope was so steep that the Confederate riflemen shot consistently high.

But the main disadvantage was the disparity in firepower: Union regiments were mostly equipped with Springfield rifled muskets. The Confederates all had smoothbores. Nowhere was this more apparent than in
the plight of the 540-man 12th Georgia Regiment, which had taken a
forward position in the center of the Confederate line. Facing them was
the 75th Ohio. Both sides quickly discovered the gap in firepower, which
meant that, along most of the 12th Georgia's line, soldiers had to hold their
fire, while Ohio riflemen loaded and fired at will. "The Yankee scoundrels
would not advance near enough," wrote a Georgia soldier.[53] The mismatch
was so severe that the right side of the Confederate line had to stand fire,
without returning it, for from one to two and a half hours. This problem
of firepower, plus an unfortunate choice of position—a V-shaped formation dictated by a jutting piece of land that left them exposed to fire from
two sides—meant that much of their regiment was simply shot to pieces.
To their credit, they did not back down; some of them, having run out of
ammunition, lay flat on the ground, ready to fight with bayonets. They suffered for such courage. Over the course of four hours, until darkness fell,
the Georgians sustained 182 casualties—fully 40 percent of the Confederate total.[54] "I felt quite small in that fight," wrote Captain S. G. Pryor of
the 12th in a letter to his wife after the battle,

> *when the musket balls and cannon balls was flying around me as thick as*
> *hail and my best friends falling on both sides dead and mortally wounded*
> *Oh dear it is impossible for me to express my feelings when the fight was*
> *over & I saw what was done the tears came then free oh that I never could*
> *behold such a sight again to think of it among civilized people killing one*
> *another like beasts one would think the supreme ruler would put a stop*
> *to it.*[55]

Pushing their unique advantages, Milroy's Federals struck Johnson's brigade along the hill's crest with unexpected fury. Suddenly it was a real
fight, and it was General Johnson's, because Jackson had, in his words,
"intrusted" him with "the management of the troops engaged."[56] Jackson's job was to command the reserves. While Johnson slugged it out with
Milroy's attacking regiments, Jackson ordered two Virginia regiments to
block the road that gave access to Sitlington's Hill from the main highway,
and, seeing how hot the fight had become, he quickly summoned reinforcements. "The engagement had now not only become general along

the entire line," wrote Jackson later, "but so intense that I ordered General Taliaferro to the support of General Johnson."[57] As one of Taliaferro's men observed, Jackson "was evidently in a bad humor."[58] Jackson also called up the Stonewall Brigade, camped several miles in the rear.

Thus did the Army of the Valley engage, as Taliaferro's Virginia regiments now advanced to the center of the line. (After Johnson was wounded in the ankle, Taliaferro took over command of the battlefield.) Though the 12th Georgia continued to sustain disproportionate casualties, sheer Confederate numbers began to take a toll. As night began to fall, Milroy's troops, exhausted and running out of ammunition, had no choice but to withdraw. Wrote Jackson, "Every attempt by front or flank movement to attain the crest of the hill, where our line was formed, was signally and effectually repulsed."

At 10:00 p.m., Milroy took his men off the hill. At 12:30 a.m., fully understanding how much danger they were in from the now united Confederates, Union forces silently began their full retreat, north, into the mountainous country beyond. Jackson set off the following day, May 9, in pursuit, leaving his two hundred VMI cadets in charge of prisoners and supplies and under the command of Maggie's husband, John T. L. Preston, and his former boss, Francis H. Smith. Jackson also took care to send a team of engineers to fell trees, roll boulders, burn bridges, and otherwise block the mountain passes in the Alleghenies that might have allowed Schenck to join with Banks. The Union forces, marching well into dark each day, managed to reach Franklin on May 11. Jackson arrived a day later, having been slowed down when Schenck's forces set the forest on fire. There he found Schenck's and Milroy's forces drawn up in a dominating position on a large hill. Jackson, for whom Banks, not Frémont, was the principal target, convinced of the "impracticability of capturing the defeated enemy, owing to the mountainous character of the country being favorable for a retreating army to make its escape," decided to withdraw.[59] On May 13, after the army had attended a Jackson-sponsored "divine service" to thank God for their victory, Jackson put his army back on the road to the valley. The goals: unite with Ewell and destroy Banks.

In conventional military terms, the Battle of McDowell was a tactical victory for the Union, though Milroy and Schenck had fought with superior weaponry and with odd and unpredictable advantages provided by the battlefield itself. They had inflicted disproportionately large losses on the enemy, while accomplishing their purpose of saving themselves by delaying Jackson's advance. Jackson lost 146 killed and 382 wounded, while the Federals lost 26 killed and 230 wounded. It was one of the rare examples in the war when the defending force suffered more than the attackers.

But in all other ways the field belonged to Jackson. He had won the battle, in fact, before it had ever been fought, by his valley-encompassing sleight of hand that had allowed him to evade a Union army and to place his own force in the field against a much smaller one. Jackson's great brilliance was *maneuver*—the chess-like movement of an army to the right place at just the right time—and McDowell was the most prominent early example of this. Union forces could surprise him, yes, and hit him, but they could never have held the town for more than a few hours. Milroy and Schenck were not only forced into a headlong retreat but had to flee fully forty miles up the valley of the South Fork of the Potomac, putting enormous distance between Union forces and Staunton and thus fulfilling Jackson's primary goal. Protecting Staunton had been his original idea. He had also put distance between the individual armies of Banks and Frémont. And by fooling Banks into thinking he had left the valley, he had gotten the additional benefit of Banks's ordered withdrawal from Harrisonburg. On May 1, Staunton and the precious Virginia Central Railroad had been threatened by two Union armies. Now, a week later, those threats were gone.

But the real value of McDowell was inspirational. Jackson's simple message on May 9, which he rewrote three times, shortening it from half a page to a single sentence—"God blessed our arms with victory at McDowell yesterday"—landed in Richmond with the force of a punch.[60] Nobody had ever heard of McDowell, and nobody could tell how decisive a win it was, or exactly what was at stake, but here, at last, was *a Confederate victory*. In a season that had seen disaster after disaster—including Forts Henry and Donelson, Roanoke Island, Port Royal, Shiloh, and New Orleans—and when the South was watching with growing despondency as McClellan's giant army began to crawl up the peninsula toward Richmond—this was worth something. The Southern press ran with it. "Who can doubt when Jackson speaks?" asked the *Lynchburg Virginian*. "Like a Christian hero, as he is, he ascribes the victory to the Lord of hosts. Long live Jackson!"

CHAPTER TWENTY-FOUR

HAZARDS OF COMMAND

A little more than a year after Jackson and his bright-eyed cadets marched picturesquely down the hill at VMI and off to war, this was what it had come to: a desperately hard world of death and dismemberment and terrible sickness that killed you as surely as bullets, and marches through hip-deep, ice-encrusted mud into camps that were nothing more than fetid pools of muck. The victory at McDowell had been purchased with much blood and sweat: Jackson's men had marched great distances and traversed two mountain ranges, all without the faintest idea of where they were going or why. They had fought a battle that left the corpses of their close friends strewn on a mountainside and had returned, with scarcely a break, to their interminable marches. War, in Stonewall Jackson's army, was never going to be anything but a hard and desperate thing. There was no stasis, no easy living, no resting on laurels—no rest at all, in fact. Oddly, his foot-sore army, amid its cursing and grumbling, was starting to embrace this idea. If Jackson was not exactly likable, he was certainly a man you could follow, and in spite of his delphic refusal to share information, he was at least predictable: you were going to march fast and far and then you were going to fight, and you were lucky if you got lunch.

This *hardness* and lack of ease carried into Jackson's own role as manager of his army as it campaigned from Kernstown to McDowell and beyond. Alone in the valley, nothing came easily. Command carried with it a thousand headaches, which included the constant wrangling with the War Department and with commissaries and quartermasters over supplies, the endless petty infighting among officers, and Jackson's constant battles with Richmond over officer promotions. He bore this burden silently. In camp he spent most of his time in his room, poring over maps and reports. "He is at times very chatty, but usually has but little to say," wrote his map-maker Jedediah Hotchkiss after Kernstown. "He stays to himself most of the time; eats very sparingly; does not drink tea or coffee and eats scarcely any meat."[1] And while he sometimes kept, Ahab-like, to his quarters, he pestered his staff at odd hours, too, with odd requests. Once, at midnight, came a quiet message from his office that he wanted to know the distance from Gordonsville to Orange Courthouse. Fifteen minutes later he requested the same information in writing. "For a while I was wont to wonder if the General ever slept," wrote Henry Kyd Douglas. "But I soon found out that he slept a great deal, often at odd times."[2] For a man who was all about action and movement, he was remarkably withdrawn from the common society of his fellows, though always furiously busy. When he did speak he was, as always, stingy with his opinions about anything at all, from the weather to his fellow officers and men. He held fast to his old Christian etiquette. "I never knew a man more guarded in his speech in reference to others," wrote Hotchkiss. "I do not remember to have ever heard him say ought in derogation of anyone, at any time."[3]

That did not mean that he did not have opinions, and strong ones, about his generals and senior officers and, in particular, about the man who commanded his prized Stonewall Brigade, Brigadier General Richard Brooke Garnett. Though Jackson had outwardly professed satisfaction with the results of the Battle of Kernstown—"Time has shown that while the field is in possession of the enemy," he had written Anna, "the most essential fruits of the battle are ours"—he remained quietly furious at Garnett for ordering the retreat. He was absolutely certain that if Garnett had not ordered the men back, the fight would have ended in darkness and stalemate.[4]

Though it is not precisely clear why, Jackson had never liked Garnett, a Tidewater aristocrat who had graduated five years before him at West Point. (A story circulated through the frontier army that Garnett had left behind a bastard son by his fifteen-year-old Sioux mistress; perhaps Jackson heard it.) Handsome, likable, and popular with his men, Garnett had spent twenty years in the army, mostly on the western frontier. Jackson had complained to Secretary of War Judah Benjamin as early as December 1861 that Garnett lacked discipline, and had reprimanded his brigadier for allowing his exhausted, chilblained brigade to fall out—in 18-degree weather—to eat a meal.[5] To Jackson, Garnett's actions at Kernstown merely fulfilled his own, long-held suspicions. Though Jackson's religious feelings were every bit as fervent in wartime as they had been in Lexington—he prayed many times daily; distributed religious tracts; diligently organized worship services and imported preachers to preside over them—there was not a shred of Christian forgiveness in what he did next.

On April 1, nine days after the battle, he relieved Garnett of his command, placed him under arrest, and charged him with neglect of duty. The charge was spelled out in a series of "specifications," the substance of which was that Garnett had been absent at several critical moments, had failed to "push his regiments into battle," and, most seriously, had given "the order to fall back, when he should have encouraged his command to hold its position."[6] This last carried more than a hint of an accusation of cowardice. Even more remarkable than the act itself of arresting a general—Lee, by contrast, never arrested any of his generals or subordinates—was that there was scarcely any substance to the charges, as Jackson's regimental colonels would all later testify. Garnett had performed well and even gallantly at Kernstown under extremely adverse conditions. To remain on the field would have meant the destruction or surrender of the valley army. Jackson's reserves simply did not get there in time to save it; his reserve ammunition was sitting on wagons miles back on the valley pike. Garnett's order to withdraw was what saved the army.

News of Garnett's arrest was received in the Stonewall Brigade with shock, anger, and sadness. According to Jackson's staffer Henry Kyd Douglas—an admiring and sympathetic chronicler of his commander—not a single officer at any level thought Jackson was right. Douglas wrote later that the brigade's "regret at the loss of General Garnett was so great and their anger at his removal so intense and universal that their conduct amounted to insubordination. [Garnett's successor] General [Charles S.] Winder was received in sulky and resentful silence, and for nearly three weeks General Jackson was permitted to ride past his old command without hearing a shout."[7]

Garnett himself was appalled, not just at the unfairness of the charges but at the threat they posed to his career and reputation. "The charge and specifications preferred against me by General Jackson . . . contain matters of the *gravest* import to me," he wrote a friend, "as they would, if established, blast my character both as a soldier and a man. You can readily appreciate my anxiety to have as speedy a trial as possible, for by *no other* means could I be fully vindicated."[8] As it happened, he never would be vindicated. Though both Jackson and Garnett spent weeks preparing for it, Garnett's military trial in the fall of 1862 was brief and inconclusive, interrupted forever by the war. No one who was familiar with the circumstances thought Jackson would have won.

How then to interpret what would seem, to almost any neutral observer, an unfair, unforgiving, and vindictive attack on an honorable man? There are no easy answers. Richard Ewell later offered the least charitable interpretation possible. "If Kernstown had been a victory," he wrote, "there would have been no charges against Garnett."[9] His meaning was unmistakable: Jackson was using Garnett as a scapegoat for their defeat. Whether that was true or not—his behavior during the war suggests that it was not—Jackson's quarrelsome streak certainly was more pronounced now that he had real power inside the army's command structure. He had a tendency to find fault with others, especially with people he did not like, and this found expression in a series of public feuds with other officers, always over what Jackson perceived as a failure to perform duty—moral, military, or otherwise. He, of course, never cared what people thought of him, which made all of this somewhat worse.

The prototype was his public fight with William H. French in Florida, where Jackson had shown a similar disregard for what his inflammatory, thinly supported charges could do to another man's life and reputation. There, too, it was difficult to imagine that somehow Jackson was doing this for his own advancement. In both cases he seemed honestly committed to punishing what he considered to be the other man's transgression. That most men would have let such things pass was irrelevant to him. At VMI he had feuded with Superintendent Francis H. Smith on several occasions. One disagreement was so serious that it led Jackson to resign as a director of the Rockbridge Bible Society. Smith, it must be noted, was an *ally*, and an active one, who had tolerated Jackson's idiosyncrasies and defended him against charges of incompetence as a teacher. In the Romney campaign, Jackson had charged William Gilham, his friend, former business partner, and VMI colleague, with neglect of duty. Gilham, mercifully, had left the army before Jackson could file the charges and specifications. Jackson had preferred charges against General William W. Loring for "neglect of duty" and "conduct subversive of good order and military discipline." Fortunately for all concerned, the War Department had shelved them.

Not all of this censure was undeserved. Gilham, brilliant and popular as a professor, was a minor disaster as a field officer. Loring had set out almost from the beginning to subvert Jackson's authority, and had encouraged his officers in what amounted to an orchestrated campaign of insubordination in Richmond. In any case, this pattern would continue throughout the war. But none of Jackson's officers would suffer as much, or as unfairly, as Garnett. There was, however, a highly pragmatic lesson in all of this for anyone who served as a brigade commander under Stonewall Jackson. If you retreated without specific orders to do so, you would be arrested and brought up on charges, with the attendant destructive effects on your career and reputation. It is impossible to measure the effect of Jackson's action on the battlefields where his army fought. On the other hand, it is impossible to imagine that such a thought would not cross the mind of a brigadier who was thinking about ordering retreat.

Garnett was not Jackson's only personnel problem. He had trouble, too, in his valley campaign with the man who, besides Garnett, constituted his chief headache: Turner Ashby. In his case, though, the command structure offered the subordinate officer protection that the unfortunate Garnett did not have. Ashby and his cavalry were technically an independent command, receiving orders directly from the Confederate War Department, an arrangement that went back to the earliest days of the war and the formation of cavalry regiments. He was not untouchable, but he was harder to get at. He was also something that Garnett was not: a legend in the making—one of the Confederacy's very first—a dashing, charismatic, and astoundingly brave man who had the unswerving allegiance of his men in a way that Jackson's other officers did not. Jackson was well aware of all that. He was also aware of how demonically effective Ashby could be in the lethal margins between armies, screening Jackson's men, causing minor havoc for the enemy, blinding him, slowing him down. Ashby's legend was such that some Federal prisoners said they believed he had magical powers. The evidence was that they had taken deadly aim at both horse and rider and their bullets simply would not hit them.[10]

While no one could deny Ashby's bravery and reckless élan, however, he had glaring weaknesses as a field commander. He was, to begin, a poor disciplinarian who often had little or no control over his men. For the buttoned-down, by-the-book Jackson, who insisted on unquestioning obedience to orders, Ashby was an administrative nightmare. On several occasions in April he failed spectacularly to follow orders. Once, after neglecting to post guards, sixty of his men were caught asleep in church and taken prisoner. Later, as his men retreated from Mount Jackson, they failed to destroy supplies and equipment, including a large supply of military stores as well as two locomotives—a cardinal sin in Jackson's eyes. Still later, ordered to destroy bridges, they were instead found drunk on apple-jack in an old foundry. When the Federal cavalry charged, they fled into the mountains.[11]

Sometimes Ashby's valor and incompetence merged. At Mount Jackson he had intended to burn a bridge over the Shenandoah River to slow the enemy's advance. But his mounted unit got there only a few steps ahead of the Federals. As Jackson's staffer Henry Kyd Douglas described it, "In a few minutes a heavy dust announced their approach; a regiment of cavalry in blue, with sabres glistening in the sun, came galloping in column of fours into view, led, apparently, by an officer on a milk-white horse. It was beautiful. Distance lent enchantment to it."[12] But soon the observers realized that the magnificent man on the white charger was really *Ashby*, who was actually being fired on by his pursuers. Ashby beat them to the bridge, where he tried to ignite a pile of "combustibles" that had been put there for that purpose. But he was too late. Federal cavalrymen were on him with drawn sabers. "One shot from a horseman at his side cut into his boot," Douglas wrote, "grazed his leg and buried itself in the side of his charger. The next moment, the avenging sword of the master came down upon the enemy and rolled him in the dust. To us, watching afar off, it was a moment of terrible anxiety. Not a word was spoken, not an exclamation. The bridge was not burned, but where was Ashby? Instantly he was seen to emerge from the bridge and follow his troops. Centaur-like, he and his horse came sweeping over the plain. They were soon with us." Moments later Ashby's horse sank to the ground, mortally wounded, as Ashby stroked his mane and gazed into his eyes. "Thus the most splendid horseman I ever knew lost the most beautiful war horse I ever saw," wrote Douglas.[13] In spite of his picturesque bravery, Ashby had failed to burn a strategically critical bridge.

Jackson had painfully mixed feelings about his brilliant, mercurial, unruly cavalry chief, a man he could not bend to his will. "Ashby never had his equal in a charge," Jackson later told his brother-in-law D. H. Hill in a moment of candor. "But he never had his men in hand, and some of his most brilliant exploits were performed by himself and a handful of followers. He was too kind-hearted to be a good disciplinarian."[14] While he acknowledged Ashby's abilities to inspire men, and his periodic effectiveness in repulsing disproportionate numbers of Union troops, he could not abide Ashby's lapses, some of which threatened the welfare of the larger army. The episode involving drunken troopers finally prompted him to act. On April 24 Jackson divided Ashby's force into two groups of ten and eleven companies and reassigned them to two infantry brigades, effectively stripping him of his command. Ashby would still be able to control the advance and rear guards, but would have to apply to the infantry brigades for men to do it. Some of Ashby's loyal officers were even sympathetic to Jackson's attempt to impose order on this large and unmanageable group. "There was still no regimental formation, and his large brigade with only two officers was an unwieldy body," said one of them. "It was more like a tribal band held together by the authority of a single chief. . . . Jackson saw the evil and tried to correct it."[15]

But Jackson had miscalculated. Ashby, furious, resigned, an act that shocked and depressed Jackson's entire command. "A great calamity has befallen us," wrote John Harman to his brother. To him it was further proof that "as sure as you and I live Jackson is a cracked man and the sequel will show it."[16] The drama that played out next was unique in Jackson's career. Jackson asked Ashby to withdraw his resignation, as Jackson himself had done two and a half months earlier. Ashby refused, and the two men exchanged angry words. Ashby came just short of threatening Jackson, asserting that "but for the fact that he had the highest respect for Jackson's ability as a soldier, and believed him essential to the cause of the South, he would hold him to personal account for the indignity he had put upon him." Instead of digging in, however, Jackson decided that, as imperfect as his cavalry commander was, Ashby's resignation would cause far more harm than his remaining in command. Jackson thus—remarkably—backed down. He revoked his order. "If I persisted in my attempt to improve the efficiency of the cavalry," Jackson wrote candidly to Robert E. Lee on May 5, "it would produce the contrary effect, as Colonel Ashby's influence, who is very popular with his men, would be thrown against me." Ashby, reinstated, made a few meaningless promises to tighten discipline, and that was that. Jackson, a man who did not give up so easily, continued to quietly urge that the War Department take some sort of decisive action.

Jackson's inflexible notions of duty also took a toll on his relationship with his talented, profane quartermaster, John Harman. While the army was at Rude's Hill, Jackson had granted Harman a forty-eight-hour furlough to return to his home in Staunton, where all five of his children were seriously ill with scarlet fever. When he arrived, two of them were already dead, and a third was in mortal danger. But when he asked Jackson to extend his leave, Jackson refused, and wrote him a letter explaining that duty trumped Harman's family's troubles.[17]

A few days later, the third child died, too, and Jackson refused Harman's request to attend the funeral. Harman was devastated, overcome with grief. (Harman would resign in mid-May, only to be talked out of it by Jackson, with promises of better treatment.[18]) Duty, in Jackson's army, was a hard master.

In spite of his evident toughness, there were still soldiers in Jackson's army who believed they could challenge his authority. As the army returned from Franklin to McDowell, Lieutenant Colonel Andrew Grigsby reported to Jackson that seventeen members of the 27th Virginia—part of the Stonewall Brigade—who had volunteered to serve for twelve months decided that, since a year had passed, they were no longer bound to stay in the army even though the recent Confederate conscription law had frozen them in place. They had stacked their muskets and demanded to be discharged. Jackson's response to the news, eyes flashing, was, "What is this but mutiny? Why does Colonel Grigsby refer them to me, to know what to do with a mutiny? He should shoot them where they stand." Jackson then issued orders to remedy the situation. The entire 27th Virginia Regiment, carrying loaded muskets, was assembled in a field. The seventeen insubordinate soldiers were then marched in front of them and given a choice: they could either return to duty or be shot to death on the spot. They all chose, meekly, to return. This was the last attempt at organized disobedience in Jackson's army.[19]

Not all of Jackson's relationships with subordinates during the valley campaign went badly. He had added the whip-smart, cocky Henry Kyd Douglas to his staff, after Douglas proved his mettle on a perilous all-night ride across the Blue Ridge Mountains to deliver a message to General Ewell.[20] In addition, he hired a new assistant adjutant general—another term for chief of staff—named Robert Lewis Dabney, a Presbyterian pastor who was also one of the leading Presbyterian scholars in the nation. Dabney also happened to be married to one of Anna's cousins. As a chief of staff, he was dismissed by the rest of the staff as only marginally competent, an impression he did not improve by shading himself with an umbrella while on horseback, which elicited jeers from the troops.[21] But Jackson liked and respected him, and especially liked his sermons, and, anyway, his young aide Sandie Pendleton ended up doing most of the routine adjutant work. After Kernstown, Jackson had also added to his staff the remarkable Jedediah Hotchkiss, a man who would play a large role in Jackson's success. Hotchkiss, thirty-three, was from Staunton. He was one of Virginia's leading geologists and an accomplished amateur cartographer. He was devoutly religious, and neither drank alcohol nor smoked. Jackson summoned him, asked him about the topographical work he had done in Virginia, and then gave him his first order: "I want you to make me a map of the Valley, from Harper's Ferry to Lexington, showing all points of offence and defence in those places. Mr. Pendleton will give you orders for whatever outfit you want. Good morning, sir."[22] At a time when many commanders were forced to use store-bought maps of atrocious quality, Hotchkiss was an extraordinary asset. Jackson had already used his talents in crossing the Blue Ridge and in the mountainous country around McDowell. His ability to understand and employ terrain would have everything to do with Jackson's next enterprise: the destruction of Nathaniel Prentiss Banks.

CHAPTER TWENTY-FIVE

HUNTER AS PREY

Major General Richard S. Ewell, the man they called Old Bald Head, was in a blazing rage. He was so angry, stalking back and forth in his quarters with his spurs on and his cap drawn low on his hairless pate, that his staff, at whom he had blown up several times that day, was studiously avoiding him. The date was May 13, 1862, five days after the Battle of McDowell. The object of his fury was none other than his fellow general Thomas J. Jackson, who had abandoned him precipitously at this muddy camp in the Elk Run Valley near Swift Run Gap ten days before. Jackson had told him almost nothing of his plans, and had left him to languish in what Ewell considered a godforsaken hole ever since. Ewell had learned of the victory at McDowell, only to be informed that Jackson was embarking on what Ewell considered the deeply misguided pursuit of Schenck and Milroy up the mountain-walled South Branch of the Potomac River. Ewell, meanwhile, had been left to stew in his own sour air, to fend off constant, annoying wires from Richmond asking him questions he could not answer, and to rage at Jackson.

"Did it ever occur to you that General Jackson is crazy?" he asked the unfortunate Colonel James A. Walker, who had tried to avoid such an interrogation. This was the same James A. Walker who, as a cadet at VMI, had challenged Jackson in his classroom, threatened him, and later been expelled.

"I don't know, General," Walker replied. "We used to call him Tom Fool Jackson at the Institute, but I don't suppose he is really crazy."

"I tell you, sir, he is as crazy as a March hare!" stormed Ewell. "He has left me here with some instructions to stay until he returns, but Banks's whole army is advancing on me and I haven't the remotest idea where to communicate with General Jackson. I tell you, sir, he is crazy."[1]

The source of Ewell's anger was news that Union general James Shields had detached his force from Banks and was marching with a full division through New Market Gap, across the Massanutten Mountain, northward up the Luray Valley, and over the Blue Ridge on his way to join McDowell at Fredericksburg. Shields, in other words, was passing directly under Ewell's nose, and there was nothing Ewell could do about it, and he simply couldn't stand it. Powerless to attack, he did the only thing he could: he dispatched part of the 6th Virginia Cavalry and several pieces of horse artillery under VMI graduate Tom Munford "to impede Shields's movement in every possible way."[2]

When Munford stopped by Ewell's quarters at midnight to check in before leaving, the latter was still so agitated that he leaped out of bed and, wearing only his nightshirt, went down on his knees on the raw floor and spread out a map under the light of a lard-burning lamp. "His bones fairly rattled," Munford recalled. "His bald head and long beard made him look more like a witch than a Major General. He became much excited, pointed out Jackson's position, General Shields's and General Banks's. . . . Then, with an ugly oath, he said: 'This great wagon hunter is after a Dutchman, an old fool!'" He was referring to General Robert Schenck's Dutch ancestry and to Jackson's keen interest in capturing Federal supplies. "Why, I could crush Shields before night if I could move from here," he went on. "This man Jackson is certainly a crazy fool, an idiot." And with that, Ewell showed Munford the brief, tersely worded wire he had received from Jackson: "Your dispatch received. Hold your position—don't move. I have driven General Milroy from McDowell; through God's assistance, have captured most of his wagon train."[3] Ewell jumped to his feet, utterly exasperated, and asked incredulously, "What has Providence to do with Milroy's wagon train?!"[4]

While Ewell fumed in his quarters, Jackson was already pushing his army hard, southward, back down the road they had taken from Staunton to Franklin. He was headed back to the valley, as fast as he could go. He would not keep Ewell in the dark long. Ewell was the key to everything. Without his eight thousand men Jackson could not even think about attacking Banks. That same day—May 13—Jackson sent Ewell a wire telling him he was coming back, and ordering him to follow Banks if he moved farther north. (Ewell would not get this until the next day, hence his rage at being neglected.) On May 15, six days after the battle, Jackson's troops had passed over the last high ridges of the Alleghenies and descended back into the valley, which in their absence had finally burst into glorious spring. "The old valley looked like paradise," recalled an artillerist. "Cherry and peach trees were loaded with blooms, the fields covered with rank clover."[5]

Two days later Jackson turned off the McDowell–Staunton road. His army wheeled and headed north toward Harrisonburg and Banks's camps in the heart of the valley. Jackson was now fully aware of Shields's departure, which meant that Banks was suddenly, and unquestionably, vulnerable. Jackson had been more than willing to move against Banks's two divisions with his own two smaller divisions. Now the numbers had swung wildly in his favor. The effect was like placing raw meat in front of a wolf. Two days before, Jackson had received a wire from Lee's adjutant, advising him of Lee's steadfast belief that "if you can form a junction with General Ewell with your combined forces you would be able to drive Banks from the Valley."[6] The phrase had a nice feel to it. It meant that the hated invaders would be thrown back clear across the Potomac. With Lee's blessing, Jackson now thought only of striking Banks. For the moment, nothing else mattered.

What he had in mind was not going to be easy. His main problem lay not in the valley proper but in the eastern suburbs of Richmond. McClellan's enormous army, advance units of which now camped six miles from the city, was the Confederacy's main concern. Shields's reinforcement of McDowell would give the latter some forty thousand troops, who Jefferson Davis and his War Department brain trust assumed were headed toward Richmond. (They were right. Unbeknownst to them, the order to "move upon Richmond" had been received by Irvin McDowell on May 17.[7]) The valley, in other words, looked again like the minor sideshow it was. Ewell was more urgently needed east of the Blue Ridge. So, probably, was Jackson. In spite of Lee's standing orders, Jackson might be pulled from the valley at any moment.

While Jackson was on the road north, approaching Harrisonburg, Ewell received orders, written several days earlier, from Joe Johnston that seemed to defeat all of Jackson's plans. "Should [Banks] cross the Blue Ridge to join General McDowell at Fredericksburg," Johnston wrote, "General Jackson and yourself should move eastward rapidly to join either the army at Fredericksburg, commanded by Brigadier General J. R. Anderson, or this one."[8] Half of Banks's army had *already* crossed the Blue Ridge.

Johnston's wire put Ewell, who wanted as much as Jackson to attack Banks, in a mild panic. Seeing no other way to solve his dilemma, and impatient with couriers, Ewell mounted his horse and rode fifty miles, crossing the Luray Valley, the swollen South Fork of the Shenandoah, and the Massanutten Mountain at New Market Gap. He rode all night, reaching Jackson's camp near Harrisonburg at daybreak on May 18. When he arrived, he refused breakfast and sat down in an old clapboard mill to discuss business with Jackson, a man whose sanity he had recently wondered about. The two men found much common ground and soon came upon an elegantly deceptive solution, one that used Joe Johnston's somewhat paranoid insistence on using couriers alone—instead of couriers plus telegraph—against him.

Ewell, again, was the key. In spite of his quick temper, he was ordinarily the model of a good soldier, following orders and rarely challenging authority. But in this case he asserted himself. He would stay with Jackson in the valley and continue the campaign against Banks. As long as Jackson took responsibility for what happened, he would agree to join their forces. He would, in effect, defy Johnston's orders. But the two conspirators needed some sort of official cover. So they decided to make up their own. The day before, Jackson had sent a message to Johnston asking for new orders—based on Banks's shift to Strasburg and Shields's transit eastward—that would allow him to attack Banks. Because of Johnston's insistence on using couriers, Jackson would not get his answer for three days. In the meantime, he and Ewell needed a reason for not obeying Johnston's order.[9] Sitting in the old mill, Ewell wrote a note to Jackson bearing a false dateline from Columbia Bridge in the Luray Valley—as though he had never made his midnight ride. He blandly described his predicament, told of the news of Shields's departure, and updated Jackson on the status of his army. Jackson then wrote out an equally flat response purporting to remind Ewell that "as you are in the Valley District you constitute part of my command" and requesting that "should you receive orders different from those sent from these headquarters, please advise me of the same at as early a period as practicable."[10] They were covered, at least for a while.

They then made a simple plan. Ewell's army would cross at New Market Gap three days later, and together they would drive north along the valley pike and assault Banks head-on at Strasburg. Their business concluded, Jackson and Ewell breakfasted amiably together, and the two attended Sunday services at the camp of the 12th Georgia Regiment, where the new chief of staff, the theologian and minister Robert L. Dabney, gave the sermon. Then Old Bald Head, who had not slept in twenty-four hours, mounted up and rode away. Jackson and Ewell both put their armies on the road early the next morning, heading for their rendezvous in New Market. Everything was going as planned.

Unfortunately, they were not yet free of interference. On May 20, just as Ewell and his eight thousand men were cresting the top of New Market Gap, heading down toward the valley pike, came the worst possible news. In a dispatch written three days earlier, Johnston had ordered Ewell outright, without any contingencies or allowance for discretion, to cross the Blue Ridge and join General Richard Anderson's division. There was no wiggle room this time. "If Banks is fortifying near Strasburg," wrote Johnston, "the attack would be too hazardous." Ewell, shaken by the news, again rode to Jackson's camp, a far shorter distance this time.

"General Ewell, I am glad to see you," said Jackson warmly as Ewell rode up.

"You will not be so glad, when I tell you what has brought me."

"What, are the Yankees after you?"

"Worse than that," Ewell replied, "I am ordered to join General Johnston."[11]

Considering what a stickler he was for regulations and army protocols, what Jackson did next was extraordinary. His clear duty was to release Ewell. But with Banks finally in his sights, he could not bring himself to do it. Bypassing Johnston and the normal chain of command, Jackson now appealed by telegraph directly to his new ally, Robert E. Lee. "I am of the opinion that an attack should be made to defeat Banks," he wrote, "but under instructions just received from General Johnston I do not feel at liberty to make an attack. Please answer by telegraph."[12] He dispatched a courier, who galloped off to Staunton, forty miles away, from which point the telegram would be sent to Richmond. Now Jackson committed what amounted to an open act of insubordination.[13] On Johnston's order to Ewell he scribbled his own counterorder, directing Ewell to "suspend the execution of the order for returning to the east until I receive an answer to my telegram." It was the sort of act for which Jackson would automatically have court-martialed one of his own officers. Ewell, who was still gamely playing along, had to wonder what might come of such a breach of the chain of command. But he stood firm.

Fortunately, the crisis resolved itself quickly. That evening a courier delivered a two-day-old message from Johnston, telling Ewell that he and Jackson were at liberty to attack Banks "supposing your strength sufficient." Johnston was not taking a hard line after all. A subsequent message reminded them that their goal was "the prevention of the junction of General Banks's troops with those of General McDowell." Lee, too, soon added his approval. Though they left no record of it, the two major generals, who had flirted with insubordination and had suddenly become close collaborators, must have been thrilled. They immediately concocted a daring variation on their original plan. Instead of marching due north up the valley pike, Jackson would throw out a cavalry screen north of New Market, then turn eastward and, along with Ewell, pass through the Massanutten to the Luray Valley. Their armies would march north together, concealed by the looming mountain, seize the town of Front Royal with its small Union garrison, then fall on Banks's flank, either destroying him or forcing him to withdraw toward the Potomac to protect his lines of supply and communication. Success depended once again on speed and deception, qualities that residents of the Shenandoah Valley were beginning to associate with Thomas Jackson.

In many ways Nathaniel Banks was not a bad general, certainly nowhere near the outright disaster that many of the purely political generals on both sides turned out to be. Though he had no army experience, the former Massachusetts governor and Speaker of the US House of Representatives had learned military ways quickly. He had paid attention. He had a marked talent for administration. He was good at handling the physical army, competent at supply and logistics, and did not lack nerve. His men liked and admired him. Where he fell woefully short was in strategic maneuver. Though he managed to get the details right, somehow, almost inevitably, he got the big picture wrong.

Banks had dragged his army back, reluctantly and disconsolately, to Strasburg. He and his senior officers felt only bitterness that they had allowed Jackson to escape, only to defeat Milroy and Schenck, and that they were executing a retrograde march after such an inspiring entrée into the valley. Most of all, having been stripped of Shields's division, and stuck in a lonely outpost in a theater of war that contained the mystically elusive Stonewall Jackson, they were suddenly, unaccountably vulnerable. "Here we are with a greatly reduced force, either used as a decoy for the Rebel forces or for some unaccountable purpose known only to the War Department," Alpheus Williams, the commander of the only infantry division remaining to Banks, wrote on May 17. "The worst part is that we have put ourselves in a most critical position and exposed the whole of this important valley to be retaken and its immense property of railroads and stores to be destroyed."[14] Williams was right: with five thousand men at Strasburg and a thousand at Front Royal, Banks was in peril from any number of directions. As he put it, their orders from Stanton obliged him, unreasonably, "to hold the debauches of two valleys twelve miles apart."[15] On May 22, Banks issued what amounted to a cry for help. "The return of the rebel forces of General Jackson after his forced march against Generals Milroy and Schenck, increases my anxiety for the safety of the position I occupy," he wrote Stanton. "I am compelled to believe that he meditates attack here."[16]

In his bitterness Banks had somehow forgotten the reason for his predicament: his own multiple messages to the War Department trumpeting the departure of Jackson's "pathetic and broken" forces from the valley, never to return. Banks had sold the idea too well. He had succeeded, now that he could finally see it clearly, only in isolating himself with an aggressive enemy in a theater of war that the enemy knew better than he did. All Banks could do was blame someone else, which is exactly what he did. His woes were the fault of General Irvin McDowell, he concluded, who in his greed, cowardice, and jealousy had managed to amass forty thousand men who did nothing more than sit idly about their camps in Fredericksburg, protecting Washington from phantom armies.[17]

It had taken Banks some time to see the big picture clearly. But now it was in sharp focus. He believed that Jackson and Ewell were going to attack him. He was absolutely right. But whatever Secretary of War Stanton may have thought of Banks's urgent wire, it was too late to do anything about it. With full, enthusiastic approval from Richmond, Jackson now began his move against Banks. His men left in the early morning, having deposited "all unnecessary equipment," which included knapsacks and tents, at the Rockingham County courthouse. At the same moment Banks was issuing his dire warning, Jackson and Ewell, who had crossed from the Shenandoah into the Luray Valley the day before, were fulfilling his worst nightmare.

He could not see them, of course. He had, in fact, no idea that Jackson was as close as he was, or that he was even in the valley at all. Though his information was hazy at best, Banks assumed Jackson was still in the vicinity of Franklin or McDowell and that Ewell had remained at Swift Run Gap, waiting for Jackson. Part of this was the sheer speed of Jackson's march, which defied all of the Union command's seemingly rational assumptions about what an army could do, or how fast and far it could move. From May 3, the day Jackson crossed the Blue Ridge on his detour to Staunton, to May 22, his army, with all its equipment and ponderous supply trains, had marched more than two hundred miles, through what were mostly abysmal conditions, often with short rations, inadequate supplies, and without such amenities as tents or shoes, crossing mountain ranges, roaring streams, and sodden valleys. One of Jackson's artillerymen wrote his mother that he had "been marching twenty-three days straight, with only three days of rest."[18] And now, exhausted and used up as they were, he was marching them again.

Part of Jackson's invisibility was a result of Ashby's devastatingly effective cavalry screen, which kept the entire Union command in the dark about Jackson's movements. Jackson had thrown it out to help cover his move across Banks's front at Staunton. When Banks retreated to Strasburg, Ashby followed, fanning out his troopers in a wide arc extending to Banks's pickets, who were posted as far south as Woodstock. Jackson explained this in a later report: "To conceal my movements as far as possible from the enemy, Brig.-Gen. Ashby . . . who had remained in front of Banks during the march against Milroy, was directed to continue to hold that position until the following day [May 21], when he was to join the main body, leaving, however, a covering force sufficient to prevent information of our movements crossing our lines."[19] While Banks sat nervously in Strasburg, utterly blind and figuring that whatever was coming at him would be both visible and headed north along the valley pike, Jackson was actually marching up the Luray Valley, behind a screen that was a combination of Ashby's hyperaggressive troopers and the impenetrable wall of the Massanutten, toward the Union garrison at Front Royal.

CHAPTER TWENTY-SIX

THE PROFESSOR'S TIME/SPEED/ DISTANCE EQUATION

◆══╣╠══◆

In the lazy, late afternoon of May 23, 1862, in the Strasburg camps of General Nathaniel Prentiss Banks, it seemed as though the world had gone to sleep. The air was still and hot; the canvas tents were stifling. There was little movement anywhere, and whatever moved did so very slowly. For many of these Union soldiers there was a feeling that the war was about to end without them, that they had missed out on whatever glory they might have secured for themselves with McClellan at Richmond. Now they seemed destined to finish their service in this lovely, irrelevant place.[1] Though some were disappointed, most had gotten more than their fill of soldiering, with its rotten salt pork, weevily hardtack, and muddy bivouacs. They were relaxed, and ready for the fighting to stop. "A general languor was manifested in the drowsy way in which the sentinels dawdled along their posts," recalled Banks's subordinate Colonel George H. Gordon, "or in the aimless sleepy air in which the troops addressed themselves to such amusements as were suggested by time and place." Colonel Gordon himself was doing nothing in particular.[2]

Just after 4:00 p.m., the stillness was broken by the sound of galloping hooves followed by the appearance of Corporal Charles H. Greenleaf of Company D, 5th New York Cavalry, at Banks's headquarters. He was exhausted. He had just ridden seventeen miles in less than an hour from Front Royal to Strasburg in the simmering heat, taking a detour to dodge rebel horsemen. He had come to report that a Confederate force of indeterminate size had attacked the Union troops there under Colonel John R.

Kenly. Greenleaf had been sent on an urgent mission to request reinforcements for the Union regiment stationed in Front Royal. General Banks
listened. He was not terribly upset by what he heard. After all, cavalry and
horse-artillery attacks by Ashby's ubiquitous troopers had become commonplace.

But as afternoon faded into evening, other reports began to pile up
at Banks's headquarters, each one adding more—and more alarming—
detail about these inexplicable events in Front Royal. Shortly after dark, an
escaped slave reported that Colonel Kenly was in full retreat. Later came a
note from a captain of the 1st Maryland Cavalry, saying that Kenly's regiment had been destroyed, that he had been killed and all his field officers
and surgeons captured, and that Stonewall Jackson was marching on Winchester with twenty thousand men.[3] Another cavalry officer reported that
he had been "attacked by three or four hundred cavalry and some infantry."

Even these accounts did not upset General Banks terribly. They all
seemed a bit hysterical, delivered by scared men who had likely fled whatever fighting was taking place. "Owing to what was deemed an extrava-
gant statement of the enemy's strength," Banks wrote, as though yawning
while he wrote the words, "these reports were received with some distrust."[4]
His aide David Hunter Strother put it more bluntly. After hearing the
apparently tall tale of Jackson and twenty thousand men, he remarked to
Banks "that this fellow was some coward who had ingloriously fled the field
and covered his ignominy by monstrous lying."[5] In spite of his skepticism,
Banks dispatched a regiment of infantry along with some cavalry to Front
Royal.

But the news kept rolling in. Throughout the evening telegrams arrived
from Winchester, relaying information from various refugees—soldiers,
teamsters, sutlers, and cavalrymen—that Front Royal had fallen to a
force of Confederates, variously estimated at 15,000 to 20,000.[6] At about
midnight, yet another officer reported that his unit had been destroyed
and that he had seen a rebel force of 5,000 or 6,000 "fall back on Front
Royal." By this point it was clear that *something* had happened out on the
foggy perimeters, and that it had involved more than just a few companies of men.

Amazingly, it was not until 10:00 p.m. that Banks took any of this seriously, and it was midnight—ten hours after the initial attack—before he
fully acknowledged that something disastrous had occurred on his flank,
a mere twelve miles away. By the time he went to bed, sometime after

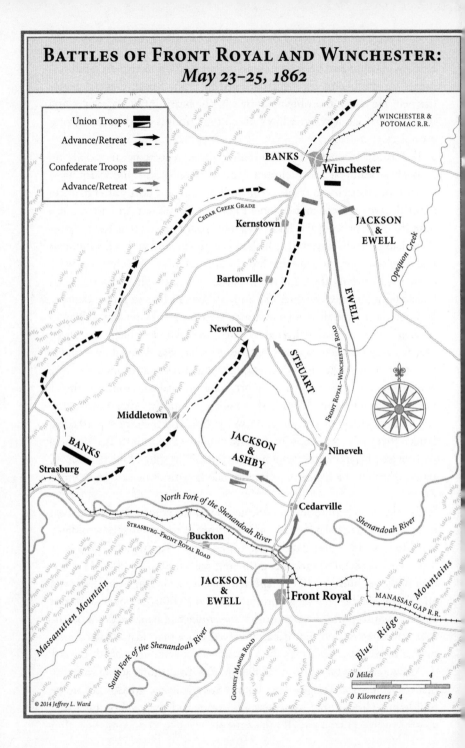

BATTLES OF FRONT ROYAL AND WINCHESTER:
May 23–25, 1862

Union Troops
Advance/Retreat

Confederate Troops
Advance/Retreat

WINCHESTER &
POTOMAC R.R.

BANKS

Winchester

CEDAR CREEK GRADE

Kernstown

JACKSON
&
EWELL

Bartonville

EWELL

Opequon Creek

Newton

STEUART

FRONT ROYAL–WINCHESTER ROAD

Middletown

JACKSON
&
ASHBY

Nineveh

BANKS

Strasburg

Cedarville

Shenandoah River

NORTH FORK OF THE SHENANDOAH RIVER

STRASBURG–FRONT ROYAL ROAD

Buckton

JACKSON
&
EWELL

Front Royal

MANASSAS GAP R.R.

Massanutten Mountain

GOONEY MANOR ROAD

SOUTH FORK OF THE SHENANDOAH RIVER

Blue Ridge Mountains

0 Miles 4

0 Kilometers 4 8

© 2014 Jeffrey L. Ward

1:00 a.m., he had come to accept, finally, that his worst fears had been realized, and much faster than he had ever dreamed possible. He and his staff now agreed—conceded might be a better word—that Ewell was at Front Royal and that the shadowy Jackson was very likely moving northward toward them along the turnpike. "The extraordinary force of the enemy could no longer be doubted," wrote Banks later. "It was apparent also that they had a more extended purpose than the capture of the brave little band at Front Royal. This purpose could be nothing less than the defeat of my own command."[7] He was used to being the hunter. He now understood that he was being hunted. He did not yet understand—and would have been far more upset had he realized—that the principal hunter, Jackson, in person and accompanied by the veteran army that had defeated Schenck and Milroy at McDowell, was also on his doorstep at Front Royal. Anticipating the worst, Banks got his wagon trains rolling late that night toward Winchester, which also happened to be in the direction of Maryland, safety, and home.

At seven o'clock in the morning that very same day—May 23—under the same hot sun and fair skies, some seventy-five miles to the east, President Abraham Lincoln and Secretary of War Edwin Stanton stepped from a steamboat onto a dock on the Potomac River. The place was Aquia Landing, a Federal logistical and supply depot less than ten miles by rail from the town of Fredericksburg. The two men had traveled all night from Washington to get there. It was a happy occasion. They had come to meet personally with General Irvin McDowell and to review his Army of the Rappahannock, all in anticipation of the big assault on Richmond.

In spite of McClellan's dithering, Union prospects had never been sunnier, and Lincoln knew it. The Union victory at Shiloh and the seizure of New Orleans were fresh memories, as were the even more recent victories by McClellan at Yorktown (May 3) and Williamsburg (May 6). In the last two months McClellan had managed to haul his sprawling army up the soggy, brush-choked peninsula to the gates of Richmond. Confederates had evacuated Norfolk and its shipyards on May 9, and were forced to scuttle their prize ironclad warship *Virginia* (formerly the *Merrimack*) on May 11. Admiral David Farragut's warships were steaming north toward Vicksburg, Mississippi, after capturing New Orleans, in a strategic thrust that would likely secure Northern control over the entire Mississippi River. And Union forces under John Pope and Andrew H. Foote had cleared the upper Mississippi nearly to Memphis with the capture of Island No. 10.

With the arrival of General James Shields's division from the valley, McDowell's army, which he paraded grandly that day before Lincoln and Stanton, was now 40,000 men and 86 cannons strong. It was almost as big as the entire Confederate force that had opposed McClellan on the peninsula. Three days hence, under Lincoln's orders, McDowell was to advance toward Richmond.[8] There was no one in the Union camp that day, or in the War Department in Washington, who believed that, with 150,000 to 160,000 men attacking the Confederate capital from two directions, they could fail to take the city. All the big logistical questions had been settled. What could possibly go wrong?

While Lincoln and Stanton were making plans with McDowell at Fredericksburg, and Banks's men were idling in the languid sunshine at Strasburg, Jackson and Ewell were pushing their soldiers as fast as they could down the Luray Valley toward Front Royal and the small Union garrison there. Their column stretched for twelve miles. They had started at dawn, marching four abreast down the river road, following the course of the South Fork of the Shenandoah in the shadow of the long, humped ridges of Massanutten Mountain on the west and the soaring Blue Ridge on the east. The Luray Valley was a miniature of the Shenandoah, and just as lovely. Jackson and Ewell rode with the vanguard. Jackson's division was the old valley army: all Virginians, most of them local. It held three brigades under Brigadier Generals Charles S. Winder and William B. Taliaferro, and Colonel John A. Campbell. Ewell's division was a much more representative unit of the Confederacy, containing regiments from Maryland, Georgia, North Carolina, Virginia, Mississippi, Louisiana, and Alabama. They were organized into four brigades under Brigadier Generals Arnold Elzey, Isaac Trimble, and Richard Taylor, and Colonel William C. Scott. The army's cavalries were commanded by Virginians: Brigadier General Turner Ashby and Lieutenant Colonel Thomas Flournoy. Colonel Stapleton Crutchfield, a former Jackson student at VMI, was in charge of artillery.

Just how many men Jackson actually had in his command as he marched on Front Royal is harder to say. Civil War troop strength is a notoriously muddy statistic, and the paper "returns" of an army often bore no resemblance to the size of the force a commander could deploy on a battlefield. Jackson, in the valley, offers a classic example. On May 3, he claimed 8,597 infantry. This number reflected huge growth since the Battle of Kernstown six weeks before, mostly in the form of new recruits who were anticipating being drafted. This probably seemed to the Confederate high command to be very good news. It wasn't, really. In the next three weeks the valley army suffered from what amounted to mass desertion and mass straggling—often it was hard to tell the difference between the two—much of it the direct result of the extreme hardship of Jackson's marches. Though the new recruits were most susceptible to this, forced marches with scant rations and minimal equipment in brutal weather conditions affected the veterans, too. On May 3 Jackson listed the Stonewall Brigade as containing 3,681 soldiers. Less than three weeks later, a mere 1,600 remained, *a loss of 57 percent of the force.* Such reductions were not limited to Jackson's favorite brigade. "We are all broken down with fatigue, loss of sleep, and irregularity in eating," wrote brigade commander Samuel V. Fulkerson to his sister on May 16. "Jackson is killing up all my men."[9] He estimated that his brigade had been reduced by half. As Jackson approached Front Royal, his division had less than 5,000 of the original 8,600 available for duty.[10] The result was that Jackson had far fewer troops than the Confederate command thought he did. So his actual strength was "closer to 12,000 effectives."[11] That was at least 4,000 fewer than anybody thought.

Whatever the true number, it served as no deterrent to Jackson's plans, which were now focused on cutting Banks off from his lines of supply and communication and destroying him. Jackson had made a good start. Once again, he had made an army disappear, only to reappear where the Union command did not expect to see it, and far sooner than Banks or anyone in the War Department in Washington would have believed physically possible. Though the existence of the single pass through the Massanutten connecting the Shenandoah and Luray Valleys was a mystery to no one—Shields had just passed through it on his march to Fredericksburg—Jackson had used it just as effectively, in combination with Ashby's lethal cavalry screens, as he had used the Virginia Central Railroad in his advance on McDowell.

It was as though Jackson had warped time itself: neither Banks nor Frémont nor any other Union commanders had ever moved with such sustained, deliberate, and determined speed over such large distances. They did not yet understand a general who virtually jettisoned his regimental supply trains, ordered his men to march without knapsacks or tents and with only light haversacks and a few days' cooked rations, who was happy to have his men sleep on the ground in the rain or snow and get up before dawn and march all day. Day after day. Though Milroy and Schenck had certainly learned how fast their army could move when fleeing, in mortal peril, from Jackson, no commander in the war had yet done anything like what Jackson had done on a sustained basis. Union commanders did not think to look for Jackson in the Luray Valley, because they did not think he could possibly have marched his men that quickly from Franklin, a distance of ninety miles in bad weather over mostly substandard roads that included mountainous terrain. They were looking for him, once again, where he wasn't.

At about 2:00 p.m. on May 23, while Ashby sliced west to cut telegraph lines, Jackson's Maryland and Louisiana regiments, emerging from the shadows of the Luray Valley, drove in the Union pickets and swept away the provost guard in the small village of Front Royal. Then they smashed into Colonel Kenly and his roughly one thousand men in camp just north of town. Like Banks, Kenly was taken completely by surprise. Like Banks, he had no idea that Confederate infantry was even in the general area. And because Banks for some reason had allotted him no cavalry, he had possessed no way to see what was coming at him. What followed was a surprisingly spirited fight, considering the lopsided Confederate advantage. Kenly, who had no idea how big a force he was facing, gamely withdrew to a promontory called Richardson's Hill and there, with a couple of rifled, ten-pounder Parrott guns, he held off the Confederates for two hours.

He was actually quite lucky that he wasn't simply blasted off the hillside, as he should have been. His luck came in the form of a critical mistake by Jackson's artillery chief, Stapleton Crutchfield, who had graduated first in the VMI Class of 1855 but had not yet fully learned his craft. He had ordered shorter-range smoothbores to locations appropriate only for longer-range rifled guns. This meant that they did not have the range even to suppress Kenly's own tiny battery, which, in the absence of counterbattery fire, was devastatingly effective.[12]

But Kenly did not have the numbers to last. At four thirty, as his Union regiment was slowly being surrounded, he fell back across the two forks of the Shenandoah that met just north of Front Royal, and found another piece of high ground, where he made another valiant stand, using his cannons to maximum advantage. Jackson, impatiently watching the action, and lamenting the unforgivable absence of cannon fire—"Oh, what an opportunity for artillery!" he complained later in the battle—ordered Flournoy's cavalry to seize the Parrott guns.

At 6:00 p.m., finding himself again in the closing jaws of a trap, Kenly, who still did not comprehend that he faced a twenty-to-one disadvantage, fell back northward again to the hamlet of Cedarville, to make a final stand. As Flournoy's four companies of cavalry closed in on what was left of his force, Union riflemen delivered one last devastating volley. Then, as they tried to reload, the Confederate horsemen were upon them. What followed was a rare, rollicking, often hand-to-hand fight between cavalry and infantry, featuring flashing sabers cleaving skulls, arms, and hands, clubbed muskets thudding against wheeling horsemen, the crack of pistol fire, and the screams of men and horses.[13] Colonel Kenly's head was split open by a saber. He would survive, but the battle was soon over. The Union soldiers who fled were quickly rounded up and captured.

Though Kenly and his men had fought bravely, the battle was a thorough defeat for the Union. Once again, Jackson's brilliance in strategic maneuver had made the fight itself almost an afterthought. At a cost of only 36 killed or wounded, Jackson had killed or wounded 83 and captured 691 Union soldiers. He had secured large quantities of commissary, quartermaster, and sutlers' supplies and had captured two splendid rifled cannons. After the battle Jackson remained on the field for several hours, overseeing the roundup of the prisoners and making sure his precious captured supplies were properly collected and inventoried. The day had been a rousing success. Not the least of it was General Ewell's personal epiphany. His courage in standing by Jackson had paid off, and his opinion of the man had changed. "The decided results at Front Royal," wrote Ewell, taking no credit for himself, "were the fruits of General Jackson's personal superintendence and planning."[14] It seemed that the "crazy" general actually knew what he was doing.

CHAPTER TWENTY-SEVEN

A LETHAL FOOTRACE

❦

Banks decided to run, as fast as he could, back to Winchester, eighteen miles north of his Strasburg camps. As he saw it, there was nothing else he could do. If he fled with his army over the mountains to the west, he would have to abandon his enormous cache of food, medicine, and equipment. To stand and fight, with rebel armies in his front and rear (as he thought), was suicidal. If he marched north, he at least had a chance of beating Jackson in a footrace, which was exactly how he saw it. "It was therefore determined," Banks wrote later in his official report, "to enter the lists with the enemy in a race or a battle, as he should choose, for the possession of Winchester, the key of the Valley, and for us the position of safety."[1] He did not need to add that the ultimate safety was Winchester's proximity to the Potomac and the North. (Union-occupied Harpers Ferry was thirty miles northeast.) The day ahead was thus all about *maneuver*, pitting Banks against Jackson in the very thing Jackson was best at.

At about nine o'clock on the cool, drizzly morning of May 24, Banks's troops moved out. They were not quite aware yet that they were running for their lives, though this was exactly what they were doing. Ahead of them, already strung out for more than fifteen miles along the valley pike, was their enormous train of five hundred army wagons plus another two hundred civilian wagons of one sort or another. Some of the wagons that had left before dawn were already rolling into Winchester as Banks's infantry started marching. With them, too, were large numbers of escaped slaves they had collected in their travels. Banks no longer commanded just an army but a vast assemblage of refugees and whatever assets they had managed to drag along with them. Many believed that Stonewall Jackson would kill them outright. All were terrified of being sent back to their masters. As one Con-necticut soldier saw it, there were "half as many negroes as soldiers."[2] They, too, traveled with wagons, some of them almost comically overloaded with human cargo. All were headed to Winchester by a single road: the hard mac-adam of the valley pike. It was a curious exodus, a sort of dark, fearful version of the same army's confident, triumphal march south in March and April.

Banks himself was deeply pessimistic. The way north was crossed in two places by main roads where his army and train could be intercepted. He had received reports that a Confederate army was already on its way to Winchester. His army could be sliced in half. Or he could arrive in Win-chester only to find the town occupied by rebels. Either way, all or part of his army would be cut off. And of course he still believed that the main body of the Confederate army—the strange, aggressive Jackson himself—was very likely closing in on him from *behind*. Though he did not betray his emotions to his officers, Banks believed that he might not survive the day. An hour before he departed, filled with longing for his family and fear-ful that he might never see them again, he wrote his wife the sort of letter many Civil War soldiers wrote before going into battle. He told her about Colonel Kenly's defeat at Front Royal, complaining bitterly that "our govt. separates its forces into little powerless squads without power to crush the foe—anywhere." In his anger at his bosses he had forgotten that his pre-dicament was largely his own fault. Or maybe that explains his excessive bitterness. Then he as good as bid her farewell:

> *Kiss the dear children for me. I love them and their mother greatly. Dear Birney—how I should love to hug her once more. And Fremont and Maud. Darling children. How I love them . . . I want our dear children to be just, to be truthful. That embraces everything . . . I have been very for-tunate in having so good a friend in my wife and I can never say how dear she is to me. Take care of our dear children. They are very fine creatures. It would be a pleasure to live if only to watch them; but life is not worth much. Remember me affectionately to my mother, my brothers and sisters. I need not write any more. I am in good health and good spirits—the best. Have perfect confidence in getting through our difficulties. Good-bye.*[3]

His wife may not have believed his feeble assurances at the letter's end, particularly since they were followed by the resoundingly final sign-off of a man who, apparently, fully expected to die.

Whether he lived or died, Banks's path, at least, was clear to him. Jackson, his larger force bristling on the Union flank, had no such advantage. Ahead of Jackson that day was a chess-like game of contingencies, multiplying options, and psychological puzzles. In spite of advances in weapons and mechanization, communications in the Civil War sometimes seemed to exist on the same medieval level as sanitation and personal hygiene. Just as it seemed incredible that it had taken Banks eight or more hours to figure out what had been happening twelve miles from him, it would seem to defy logic that Jackson, a man with an uncanny sense of terrain and troop movement, could not get a fix on the location of a 6,500-man army with a fifteen-mile-long wagon train. Yet that, strangely, is what happened on the day after the Battle of Front Royal.

Jackson had put the advance units of his army on the road at 6:00 a.m. Two hours later they had reached the tiny hamlet of Nineveh, about eight miles north of Front Royal. The assumption of such a march, of course, was that Banks was withdrawing along his supply lines to Winchester. But that was only a guess: Jackson had received no confirmation that Banks was actually doing that. What little intelligence he had gotten, in fact, from an engineer who had climbed the northern end of Massanutten Mountain to surveil the enemy, was dead wrong. His engineer had told him that Banks had two divisions totaling twelve thousand men, instead of the single division he actually had. At three to one—the real odds—a frontal assault would likely win the day. At three to two or one to one, Jackson's approach had to be much more measured.

Jackson, meanwhile, was keenly aware that Banks had other options besides Winchester, a destination the former Massachusetts governor might avoid precisely because, with his men and trains strung out along the valley pike, he would be so completely vulnerable to attack. If Jackson and Ewell lunged toward Winchester, Banks could easily slip behind them, march east through Front Royal, out of the valley, and back to the safety of Washington. Banks could also just stay put at Strasburg, perhaps awaiting reinforcements from Frémont to the west—a logical and extremely plausible option—which created its own complex set of contingencies.

And so, at 8:00 a.m., Jackson brought his entire army to an abrupt halt. He waited more than two hours for some intelligence of Banks's movements. Earlier that morning, he had dispatched his cavalry commander George H. Steuart with three hundred horsemen in the 2nd and 6th Virginia cavalry regiments north and west to the village of Newtown to see what, if anything, was moving down the pike. At 10:00 a.m. Steuart's riders collided with Banks's enormous line of wagons—the part carrying Federal sick and wounded—where they caused a great deal of havoc before being driven back by artillery. Black teamsters, especially, had panicked and fled at the sight of Confederate cavalry, leaving several dozen wagons in the ditch. At 11:15 Steuart's courier caught up with Jackson with news of what they had seen. Banks was indeed marching north, wagon train and all. But just where was his main force? Determined to find out, Jackson split his army, leaving Ewell in place north of Nineveh—merely ten miles from Winchester—and backtracking with his own division through Cedarville and then onward to the valley pike at Middletown. Jackson's patience, already wearing thin, was further tested by a feisty, stubborn force of Federal cavalry who, fighting to buy time for the main army, held him up for another two hours on the road to Middletown.

After a long and frustrating wait, the forward units of Jackson's force soon discovered what they were looking for. At 3:30 p.m. at Middletown, they crashed with murderous ferocity into Banks's army, which here consisted of massed groups of cavalry mixed with supply wagons. What followed, as Jackson's troops opened from the Union flank with muskets and cannons, was a scene of such horror that even some of the Confederate participants had trouble watching it. Men and horses fell screaming. Solid shot from the artillery cut massive, bloody chunks out of Union formations. As one Union soldier put it, lying beside his dead horse, there was a "mass of living and dying men piled up in a heap on the road."[4] Jackson, rarely bothered by slaughter in battle, later wrote, "In a few moments the turnpike, which had just before teemed with life, presented a most appalling spectacle of carnage and destruction. The road was literally obstructed with the mingled and confused mass of struggling and dying horses and riders."[5] He had shown less sympathy on the battlefield itself. When Henry Kyd Douglas, standing next to him, told him that he thought their attack amounted to murder, Jackson replied simply, "Let them alone." Meaning, let his soldiers do their awful work. Chief of Staff Robert Dabney saw the scene in biblical terms. "Behold the righteous judgment of God," he wrote, surveying the bloody wreck of a once-proud Vermont cavalry regiment, "for these are the miscreants who have been most forward to plunder, insult, and oppress us!"[6] Perhaps Jackson saw it that way, too. The clash was over in a few minutes. Jackson's men took two hundred prisoners.

But the victory was short-lived. Though Jackson had severed Banks's column and destroyed or run off several regiments of cavalry, this had not given him any clearer picture of the location of the main body of Banks's infantry. Had he hit the head, midsection, or tail of the snake? Unknown to him, Banks, upon hearing about Steuart's attack that morning, had ordered his infantry to leap-frog the long wagon train. Much of his army was thus well down the road to Winchester when Jackson arrived in Middletown. Banks himself arrived in Winchester at about 7:00 p.m., about two hours after his advance units. Jackson had in fact struck the rear guard—the snake's tail.

Still, he did not *know* that. He wanted to destroy Banks's entire army, not just a piece of it. And in the service of that idea he now made what would turn out to be an extremely costly mistake. Hearing the musket fire of a minor skirmish between stranded Union troops and the 9th Louisiana, he now guessed, incorrectly, that a significant portion of the Union army still remained cut off on the other side of Newtown. So he turned his army south. It took him another full hour and a half—until five forty-five—before he finally understood that he faced only a small and insignificant Union force. He immediately sent a rider to Ewell, who was stewing yet again about sitting and doing nothing all day, with a message saying, "Major-General Jackson requests that you will at once move with all your force on Winchester." Nearly twelve hours after his first units started out toward Winchester, Jackson finally launched the all-out pursuit of Nathaniel Banks.

Little daylight remained. The distance between Middletown, where Jackson started his final push, and Winchester was about twelve miles. Some of Banks's infantry and supply wagons were still on the valley pike, en route to Winchester. But they were no longer vulnerable to the sort of attack that would have destroyed them outright a few hours before. Darkness fell, and with it came a series of Union rearguard actions starting at Newtown—ambushes, really—that slowed Jackson's march to a crawl. Nor could Ewell, leaving as late as he did, and arriving near Winchester sometime after 10:00 p.m., have hoped to catch many Union troops. In darkness they had had to pick their way up the valley pike, which was cluttered with abandoned wagons, blankets, guns, oil cloths, sutlers' stores, and other equipment—while the 2nd Massachusetts Regiment and other pieces of Banks's army laid ambushes for them and contested their advance, setting up behind stone walls and opening up with brilliant muzzle flashes that lit up the night. Near Newtown, Ashby's troopers, who had been leading the way, fell out of rank altogether and abandoned themselves to the looting of the Union supply train, stealing anything they could get their hands on, including horses. They were lost to the army.[7] With all the stops and starts, and the stress of Federal bullets whirring by them in the darkness, it was another severe march by men who had already marched astounding distances since early March. Soldiers slept as they walked. Each time the army stopped, dozens simply collapsed.

Jackson's objective had been a high ridge just southwest of Winchester. At 3:00 a.m. the army paused just north of Kernstown, the site of a battle that already seemed to have taken place a long time ago, in a very different world. Jackson fully intended to drive his army those last few miles. With his men dropping out by the hundreds—often facedown, asleep—Colonel Samuel Fulkerson summoned up his old authority as a Virginia state judge, approached Jackson, and told him that enough was enough. He had to stop and rest his army or he would not have an army to fight with in the morning. "My men are falling by the roadside," he said. "Unless they are rested, I shall be able to present but a thin line tomorrow." Jackson listened patiently, then said, "Colonel, I do not believe you can feel for your men more than I do. This is very hard on them, but by this night march I hope to save many valuable lives. I want to get possession of the hills of Winchester before daylight." Jackson thought for a moment, then said, "Colonel, you may rest your command for two hours. I will go on with my own brigade."[8] But he soon relented. Though he hated giving up the high ground, and would not have ordered a halt on his own, he realized that he had pushed his army to the limits of its endurance. It had been a strange, unsatisfying day, with an inconclusive finish. What was undebatable was that, because of his own prudence and caution, however justifiable, Jackson had missed one of the great opportunities of the young war: to swallow an enemy army whole. Ulysses S. Grant had done it at Fort Donelson in Tennessee three months before, the only general to do so in the first year of the war.[9] He was famous for it.

President Abraham Lincoln and Secretary of War Edwin Stanton, pleased with the success of their military mission to Irvin McDowell's army, arrived in Washington shortly after sunrise on May 24, having steamed through the night up the Potomac River. They bid a hearty good morning to their colleague Salmon P. Chase, secretary of the Treasury, who wrote in his diary that the two men were "highly gratified by the condition of the troops and anticipating an imposing and successful advance [against Richmond] on Monday the following." The trip had, in fact, been one of the high points of Lincoln's brief career as commander in chief.

His buoyant mood ended abruptly the moment he and Stanton walked into the War Department and saw the grim, crestfallen faces of their staff, who had just received word of Jackson's rout of Kenly at Front Royal. Throughout the morning the news got worse as dispatches streamed in from the valley. Some were accurate, some wildly wrong. Banks was fleeing down the valley. Banks was cut off from Winchester. Six thousand to ten thousand rebels were on the road to Winchester. All this was made worse by the doomsday dispatches from the headquarters of Brigadier General John Geary, who commanded an infantry regiment and some cavalry on the eastern side of the Blue Ridge whose main purpose was to guard the Manassas Gap Railroad. Trusting unreliable sources, a nearly hysterical Geary reported that some twenty thousand rebel troops were closing in on him from the west and south, meaning that at least one of those armies was headed in the general direction of Washington, DC. None of these phantom rebel armies existed. But with the panic Jackson had created ricocheting around Washington, no one in the corridors of power could yet be sure of that. From Harpers Ferry came a deeply disturbing telegraph, saying, "The rebels have cut the wires between Strasburg and Winchester," and that there was "fighting within 8 miles of Winchester."

By midafternoon, while Banks moved north and Jackson was still trying to figure out where his adversary was, Lincoln and Stanton, now in their own thick fog of war, had concluded that General Banks had likely been cut off at Middletown and was therefore stranded midway between Strasburg and Winchester without his supply lines. Wherever he was, the reports all indicated that he was in grave danger. If Banks was in trouble, of course, so potentially were the garrison at Harpers Ferry and the B & O Railroad, Washington's lifeline to the West. No one had to remind the War Department that, in Confederate hands—specifically, *Jackson's* hands—the Shenandoah Valley also constituted a loaded shotgun pointed directly at Washington. Most Union forces in Virginia were either at Fredericksburg or in front of Richmond. What, exactly, was there to stop Jackson from marching on Washington? He had a habit of popping up in inconvenient places, and there was no telling where he might appear next.

Lincoln acted calmly and resolutely, considering how badly he had just been whipsawed, and in spite of whatever regret he may have felt in having stripped away troops from the valley to feed McClellan's ego. In response to this news he sent three telegrams: one to John Frémont, one to Irvin McDowell, and one to George McClellan. Frémont was immediately dispatched to save Banks. "The exposed condition of General Banks makes his immediate relief of paramount importance," Lincoln said. "You are therefore directed by the president to move against Jackson at Harrisonburg and operate against the enemy in such a way as to relieve Banks." To McDowell he delivered the harsh news that he was chopping his prodigious command in half and sending half of it to save Banks: "You are instructed to lay aside for the present the movement to Richmond and to put twenty thousand men in motion at once for the Shenandoah." To McClellan, who still believed he was facing a rebel army well in excess of a hundred thousand men, he gave the worst news of all: McDowell's entire force would now be withheld from him. It was McClellan's oldest and worst nightmare: to be deprived of troops by cynical politicians and left to face a numerically superior enemy.

Judging from the reactions of Frémont and McDowell, one would have thought that traveling to the Shenandoah to fight Stonewall Jackson was a cruel fate indeed. "This is a crushing blow to us," replied McDowell, whose main argument was that he could never get there in time to help Banks, needing at least ten days to get twenty thousand men into the valley. He later added, with undisguised bitterness, as though his job really did not consist of doing what his commander in chief asked him to do, "I shall gain nothing for you there, and shall lose much for you here. It is therefore not only on personal grounds that I have a heavy heart in the matter, but that I feel it throws us all back, and from Richmond north we shall have our large masses paralyzed and shall have to repeat what we have just accomplished." He closed by asking Lincoln if he wanted McDowell to personally command such an expedition. The answer, to his chagrin, was yes.[10] To make doubly certain that McDowell would comply, Lincoln immediately dispatched Salmon Chase to explain the orders to him in person.

Frémont, while nominally agreeing to obey the order, also tried mightily to beg off. The last thing he wanted was to be sent to rescue Banks. The enemy was everywhere around him, he told Stanton. He had few supplies. As usual, rain had bogged down the mountain roads. And so on. He found no sympathy. From Lincoln he received an irritated reminder that "this movement must be made immediately." Of the three recipients of Lincoln's missives, only McClellan, uncharacteristically, appeared to take the news well, replying stoically that "I will make my calculations accordingly." (The next day, however, he was writing his wife with more indignation than usual, saying that the president "is terribly scared about Washington" and that "it is perfectly sickening to deal with such people. . . . I get more sick of them every day—for every day brings with it only additional proofs of their hypocrisy, knavery & folly."[11])

Thus did Jackson, who had not yet even engaged with the main body of Banks's troops, rearrange, on a single afternoon, the carefully laid Union plans to join together two armies at Richmond and thus bring crushing numbers to bear against Joseph Johnston. By the night of May 24 more than thirty-five thousand troops were under orders, quite specifically, to stop Stonewall Jackson.

CHAPTER TWENTY-EIGHT

THE TAKING OF WINCHESTER

The evening after his army's miraculous escape from a more powerful enemy, Nathaniel Banks wired Lincoln to tell him that he had arrived safely in Winchester. Considering what had just happened to him, his dispatch was remarkably self-possessed. "I concluded," he wrote the president, "that the safest course for my command was to anticipate the enemy in the occupation of Winchester. My advance guard entered this town at 5 this evening with all our trains in safety."[1] Put in those unembellished terms, Banks's situation didn't sound so dire after all, though in the past thirty hours he had actually lost more than 25 percent of his supplies and more than a hundred of his men had been killed or wounded and another thousand taken as prisoners. But he had somehow outrun Jackson and Ewell. And against all odds he had arrived with most of his division intact in the sanctuary of Union-occupied Winchester, though his escape had been more the result of the Confederate confusion than of his own tactical acumen. Lincoln's worst fear—that Banks had been cut off—had not been realized.

Whatever comfort this may have offered the president or his War Department in Washington, however, was pure illusion. The stark truth was that as of dawn on Sunday, May 25, Banks and his entire army were in immediate danger of annihilation. Though Jackson had not caught his adversaries on the road, he had actually won the battle of maneuver by pushing his troops so relentlessly the night before, closing hard on his enemies, and precluding any possibility of reinforcement or unmolested retreat. He had thus left Banks only one option other than surrender. To protect his supply trains and whatever retreat he could muster, Banks *had to fight*. The alternative—instant, headlong flight before Jackson and his preternaturally aggressive cavalry—was unthinkable. At the same time, the raw Confederate numerical advantage meant that Banks was going to lose the fight. And though the dapper New Englander, as he gamely put it, was "determined to test the substance and strength of the enemy by actual collision," the only real question was how badly, and how quickly, he was going down. Whatever his faults may have been, Banks did not lack courage. His practical-minded division commander General Alpheus Williams had already concluded privately that he and his men were going to be prisoners of war. For Union troops, the dreary Sabbath dawn heralded approaching death, destruction, and imprisonment. They would fight hard anyway.

The Battle of Winchester began on the foggy morning of May 25 at 4:30 a.m. with the sharp crack of Jackson's muskets and the rolling thunder of his artillery. He and his division were drawn up just south of town, on the western side of valley pike. Ewell, with smaller numbers—some two thousand troops—was on the right, east of the pike. Union regiments were in place on the high ground in front of them. The battle lines stretched east to west for a mile and a half. For three hours, the two sides engaged. Eight Union rifled Parrott guns and sixteen mostly smoothbore Confederate cannons issued forth sheets of flame and smoke, shook the earth, and rattled windows in Winchester, while pulses of crackling musket fire swept across the fields south of town. Soldiers who were there that morning described a strange and terrible beauty on the battlefields, an effect of swirling fog and bright sunshine, dew sparkling on wheatfields, and shells bursting over the town in perfect white spirals, with jets of white flame piercing billows of white smoke.[2]

Some of the fighting was desperate. At 5:30 a.m. Ewell sent the 21st North Carolina Regiment forward into what amounted to a perfect trap sprung by the 5th Connecticut. In less than two minutes, the rebels sustained seventy-five casualties; in twenty minutes they lost eighteen dead and seventy-eight wounded.[3] As the barrage continued, Jackson seemed to be everywhere, roaming on horseback among his various batteries, urging the men on, barking specific orders at regimental commanders. At one point he approached Colonel John Neff of the 33rd Virginia. Gesturing toward an unoccupied spot on the high ground of Bower's Hill, he shouted, "I expect the enemy to bring artillery to occupy that hill, and they must not do it! Do you understand me, sir? Keep a good lookout, and your men well in hand, and if they attempt to come, charge them with bayonet and seize their guns! Clamp them, sir, on the spot!"[4]

At 7:30 a.m., after three hours of inconclusive fighting and while Banks's supply wagons rolled quietly north toward safety, two important things happened. First, fog descended like a stage curtain east of the valley pike, silencing what had been a brisk fight between Ewell and his Union counterpart, Colonel Dudley Donnelly. Second, while church bells tolled from the nearby streets of Winchester, Banks's brigade commander Colonel George H. Gordon decided to make a bold tactical move: he ordered the feisty, battle-tested 2nd Massachusetts—which had harassed Jackson's vanguard the night before—to extend his battle line on the Union right, the logical prelude to an attempt to turn the Confederate flank. Confederate brigadier general Charles S. Winder, in command at the front, saw the movement and immediately countered it, throwing three regiments out to his left. Unfortunately for Gordon, a flanking game was not one he could win. He did not have the manpower. Winder saw that, too. Just then Jackson came forward to ask him for a report on the progress of the battle. Winder told him that he thought the Union right could be taken. Jackson surveyed the battlefield and replied simply, "Very well, I will send you Taylor's brigade."

He meant thirty-six-year-old Brigadier General Richard Taylor, a Yale graduate and successful sugar planter but most conspicuously the son of Mexican-American War hero and US president Zachary Taylor. Though he was widely read in history and fluent in French, and a Southern gentleman from a long line of planters, Taylor also had the common touch and could swear like a stevedore. His men liked him. He was chosen because he was a hard fighter with a disciplined unit (the exceptions were the unruly Louisiana Tigers) and also because he happened to command the largest Confederate brigade on the field, with 2,500 officers and men. What happened next was a classic example of a successful Civil War flanking maneuver, using the advantage of numbers to extend a battle line farther than the enemy could extend his, then turning the enemy's flank and making him face fire from two directions. When Taylor came up, Jackson pointed to the ridge and the right wing of the Union army and said, "You must take it."

Taylor and his brigade now moved forward. Jackson, who liked being in the bullet-shredded air of the front lines, rode with them. They soon emerged from the base of the hill that had screened them and into full view of the enemy on the higher ground. Taylor told Jackson sternly that "this was not the place for the commander of the army." Jackson ignored him. A few minutes later, Federal muskets and Federal artillery loosed a howling volley. Many of Taylor's men fell. Others, hearing the whistle of shot and shell about them, began ducking their heads. This angered Taylor, who saw much more difficult work ahead of them. "What the hell are you dodging for?" he shouted at them. "If there is any more of it, you will be halted under this fire for an hour." Chastened, the men straightened up and moved forward. Taylor was struck, though, by the look of reproach on Jackson's face. Jackson put a hand on Taylor's shoulder and said, amid the storm of lead and steel, "I am afraid you are a wicked fellow." Then he turned and rode away.[5] Jackson was referring to Taylor's choice of language, which certainly was not what he admitted to in his memoir. (Most of our current profanities were then in use.) Whatever he said, Jackson had believed it was worth a mild reproof, even in the heat of battle.

As Taylor's brigade shook itself out into battle formation—an immaculate gray line a thousand yards across—in full view of both armies, there was a strange pause. The fire slackened momentarily, as though in anticipation of what was quite obviously going to happen next. The Louisianans advanced. Up the hill they came, in perfect order, Taylor in front with sword in hand, closing about half the distance between them and the Union troops. From behind a stone wall came a crackling volley, slicing through Taylor's ranks. But the Louisianans held their tight formation and continued to advance. On Taylor's command they charged. As he later wrote, "with cadenced step and eyes on the foe, [the men] swept grandly over copse and ledge and fence, to crown the heights from which the enemy had melted away."[6] Within minutes they had routed the enemy without firing a shot. And now, in a cascading sequence of companies and regiments, the entire Union line broke. Watching them run, Taylor's Confederates now opened fire. "The air seemed to be full of whizzing bullets," recalled Union general Williams, "which stirred up currents of wind as if the atmosphere had suddenly been filled with some invisible cooling process."[7] East of the pike, where the fog had finally lifted, Union soldiers were also falling back into Winchester. Ewell, able to see the foe at last, unleashed a brigade under Brigadier General Isaac Trimble, which swept east of the town to cut Union colonel Dudley Donnelly on the Martinsburg road north of town.

Jackson watched all of this, seated on Little Sorrel, his hand held high in what everyone by now believed was prayer. Then, according to cartographer Jedediah Hotchkiss, "as the enemy wavered & then broke & fled, he swung his old gray cap and shouted 'Now let's holler!' "[8] His staff began to cheer, and then the whole advancing line took it up, and the rebel yell rose to what Henry Kyd Douglas remembered was a "deafening roar, which borne on the wind over Winchester told her imprisoned people that deliverance was at hand."[9] It was between eight thirty and nine in the morning. The battle had lasted four hours. Jackson's soldiers were back on the streets of Winchester.

The Union retreat was, at first, a relatively measured affair. Somehow, Banks's infantry managed to stay with their companies and regiments. But such discipline could not last. The citizens of Winchester, particularly the women, shot at them with muskets and pistols from windows and doorways and shops as they passed through the streets. They threw glass bottles at the Federals, poured scalding water on them, and screamed insults. At least one woman shot a soldier dead with a pistol at point-blank range. Another woman, who fired on a colonel, was shot dead, a bright red spurt of blood erupting from her breast before she fell.[10] Jackson's troops were shooting at the flying Federals, too, many of whom laid down their arms and surrendered. "The enemy rose on the rise on the northern end of Winchester and poured a sharp fire of musketry into our confused rear," remembered Banks's aide David Hunter Strother. "Presently cannon boomed and shot whistled and shells hurtled over our heads. . . . At every report, the living mass started and quickened its motion as if by electricity. Overcoats and knapsacks strewed the fields."[11]

Soon the army was in full, chaotic flight north on the road to Martinsburg and the Potomac beyond. Union soldiers were running for their lives now, and they knew it; more than a thousand of them had already been taken prisoner in the streets of the town. For the rest, it was their excellent luck that Jackson's army was in no position to pursue them. Many of the Confederates, having slept less than two hours the night before, were so exhausted that they simply sat or lay down. Then, too, there was the utter pandemonium inside the town, now cluttered with discarded equipment, discarded wagons, burning wagons, and burning buildings, plus large numbers of blacks—part of Banks's enormous mule train—many of whom were escaped slaves, who had to be rounded up. All of this was complicated by a populace that was wildly ecstatic at its liberation. They rushed out of their houses, many dressed in their Sunday clothes, laughing, screaming, embracing the rebel soldiers, and giving cheer after cheer for Stonewall Jackson and Jeff Davis. Some, wrote Robert Dabney, stood "on their doorsteps, with their solemn faces bathed in tears, and spreading forth their hands to heaven in adoration."[12] They welcomed the troops with hugs and kisses and pails of milk and water and baskets of food. Jackson was dumbfounded at the reception he received. He wrote Anna the next day that it was like nothing he had ever experienced:

> *My precious darling, an ever kind Providence blest us with success at Front Royal on Friday, between Strasburg and Winchester on Saturday, and here with a successful engagement yesterday. I do not remember having ever seen such rejoicing as was manifested by the people of Winchester as our army yesterday passed through the town in pursuit of the enemy. The people seemed nearly frantic with joy; indeed, it would be almost impossible to describe their manifestations of rejoicing and gratitude. Our entry into Winchester was one of the most stirring scenes of my life. . . . Time forbids a longer letter, but it does not forbid my loving my* esposita.[13]

He got the same treatment from his own troops. "As he came the men pressed in shoals to the roadside and waved their hats enthusiastically," wrote one of Ewell's artillerymen. "It was deafening . . . I never saw a more thrilling scene. . . . General Jackson himself seemed much affected as he rode uncovered, bowing constantly."[14]

Luckiest of all for Banks's hapless forces, Jackson's cavalry support, inconsistent at best, now failed him completely. Because of their inherent speed, and the intimidating presence of horses, mounted troops could be devastating in pursuit of a fleeing enemy. But Ashby mysteriously disappeared the previous night. Brigadier General George Steuart, whose troopers were lounging several miles east of town while their horses grazed, refused to obey Jackson's order as delivered by Sandie Pendleton, standing on protocol and saying that he would only obey an order from Ewell. Ewell was then found, with some difficulty, and the order given. By that time it was too late for Steuart to do much more than annoy the Union rearguard. Jackson halted the pursuit after five miles. Without cavalry, and with many of the soldiers in his command at the margins of consciousness, he had little choice. His troops then did the unthinkable: they bivouacked at noon. The day was over. Jackson himself, bone-weary and suffused with victory, rode back to Winchester, entered the Taylor Hotel, refused all offers of food, then threw himself on his bed, facedown, with his boots and spurs on, and fell asleep. He had not even bothered to wire Richmond about his victory. He had not communicated with his bosses since May 21. Another day would not matter.[15] Later that night his wagons finally caught up with his army, and the men were issued their first rations in forty-eight hours.[16]

Banks's men got no such break. That day they lugged themselves thirty-five miles north toward the sanctuary of Maryland, after having marched eighteen miles from Strasburg to Winchester the day before, all under extreme duress and the threat of death or imprisonment. (Jackson's legendary "foot calvary" never made such a march after fighting a battle.) In two days they had eaten a single meal. They were at the limits of their endurance, marching on fear and adrenaline. To their credit, they conducted a mostly orderly, if utterly demoralized, march. Banks, who had never conducted a retreat before, managed it surprisingly well. He was at his best, buoyant and undaunted, riding among the men and encouraging them, lending a hand with stuck wagons, forcing stragglers back into line. But they were a beaten army. All the way north they were acutely aware, as General Williams put it, "of the probabilities that we should be followed to the river and attacked . . . before a tithe of our men could be crossed and while all our immense train was parked ready to deepen the awful confusion that must follow."[17]

The sense of panic and dread increased on the southern bank of the Potomac that night, where a thousand campfires burned in the darkness. Teams and wagons, guns and caissons were jammed together and an exhausted army had to figure out how to cross a three-hundred-foot-wide river that was four to five feet deep and moving fast.[18] They spent all night crossing. Men and horses drowned. But by the next morning the army was on the north side of the river. Though Banks's report to Stanton was deeply inaccurate in many areas—from his estimate of rebel strength (25,000 to 30,000) to his assessment of Confederate killed and wounded (triple his own, he said, which was wildly inaccurate) and the number of wagons lost (55 instead of 106 or more)—he could say with reasonable honesty that "my command had not suffered an attack and rout, but had accomplished a premeditated march of near 60 miles in the face of the enemy, defeating his plans, and giving him battle wherever he was found."[19] In two long days of retreats, following a surprise attack by a superior force, Banks had managed to keep most of his army and wagon train intact. Most Confederates would have said that he was lucky to escape with his skin. That was true, too.

But Jackson had won a staggering victory. It was striking on both tactical and strategic levels. He had marched his men 177 miles since his victory at McDowell 17 days before, and in less than 48 hours had driven Banks 53 miles, from Strasburg and literally into the Potomac River and across the Maryland state line. He had done this even though his artillery had failed him miserably at Front Royal, as his cavalry had at Newtown and

Winchester. Jackson's force had suffered fewer than 400 casualties. Banks had lost more than 3,500 men, 3,000 of whom were now prisoners of war. Jackson had already knocked the Union war in Virginia off balance; his victory at Winchester would soon shift the attention of the world from what seemed certain defeat in front of Richmond to the strange, shimmering new possibilities that were rising from the mists of the Shenandoah Valley.

Even more important for the Confederate war effort, Jackson's men had captured an enormous stockpile of matériel. It contained $125,185 of high-quality quartermaster supplies; 34,000 pounds of commissary supplies, including bacon, hardtack, salt pork, and sugar—so much of it that Jackson's men began calling their opposing general by a new name, Commissary Banks; 500,000 rounds of ammunition; rifled cannons; 103 head of cattle; and 9,345 stands of small arms. (A "stand" consisted of a rifled musket, bayonet, cartridge belt, and ammunition box.) There was also an astonishing trove of medicine and medical supplies, which Jackson's aide Sandie Pendleton thought was probably larger than those in the rest of the Confederacy combined. There were two well-stocked military hospitals with a capacity of 700 patients that came equipped with their own staff and Union doctors. Jackson, who could have sent those doctors off to a Confederate prison, instead set a Civil War precedent by giving them immunity to continue their work with wounded Federal soldiers, after which he allowed them to return to the Union army. In a world grown suddenly very hard and cold for Federal soldiers in the Shenandoah Valley, it was a small bit of Christian charity.

Something else had taken place, too, at Winchester, something less tangible though quite as real as the battle itself. The moment of victory also marked the birth of the legend of Stonewall Jackson, of the idea of the man as warrior and hero that would soon loom much larger than the man himself. What the Confederacy had desperately needed, in a war it was obviously losing, was a myth of invincibility, proof that their notions of the glorious, godly, embattled, chivalric Southern character were not just romantic dreams. Proof that with inferior resources it could still win the war. Jackson, in his brilliant, underdog valley campaign, had finally given it to them. His personal eccentricities, his often brutal treatment of his own men and officers, his devout and zealous Christianity—all would from now on be seen as the attributes of genius. His dazzling stand at First Manassas would be seen in this new light. No one on either side of the Civil War would ever look at him the same way again.

CHAPTER TWENTY-NINE

LINCOLN'S PERFECT TRAP

News of Jackson's victory at Winchester rocked the political and military establishments in Washington. What he had done did not seem quite plausible. He had twice eluded Union forces that had been sent to destroy him. He had moved farther and faster and more secretly than anyone in the Union high command had believed possible and had defeated Union forces more than one hundred miles apart. He had then pursued his helpless quarries for thirty and thirty-five miles, respectively. He had driven Banks clean out of the South. None of this could be explained by conventional notions of warfare, certainly not by warfare as it was being practiced by any Union commanders of the period. There was something *lethal* about this Confederate general, something grim and unyielding and inexplicable and alarmingly single-minded. Whatever dark magic Jackson possessed now made faint hearts in the nation's capital uneasy. Where would he appear next? Rumors multiplied, abetted by Banks's wildly inaccurate estimates of Jackson's strength and the shrill bleats of alarm from General John Geary, just east of the valley, who reported that fully *three* Confederate armies were closing in on him, one of which was pointed at Leesburg, which meant that it was also pointed directly at Washington. This was pure hysteria. But the Federal War Department did not know that yet.

In the midst of all this speculative frenzy, Edwin Stanton seemed to come completely unhinged. That afternoon the bearded, bespectacled secretary of war sent what amounted to an SOS to the governors of thirteen Northern states asking for their help in saving the nation's capital from Jackson's ravening army. "Intelligence from various quarters," he wrote, "leaves no doubt that the enemy in great force are marching on Washington. You will please organize and forward immediately all the militia and volunteer forces in your state." To the governors of Rhode Island, Massachusetts, and Pennsylvania, he issued an even more urgent appeal: "Send all the troops forward that you can immediately. Banks is completely routed." He also ordered the War Department to take immediate "military possession" of Northern railroads. Treasury Secretary Salmon Chase soon joined the paranoid chorus, saying that Jackson's army had "endangered Harper's Ferry & even Washington."[1] Even US senators were spreading the word that "Banks was flying—that Washington was menaced."

Lincoln, too, was upset by the news from the valley, but whatever unease he felt soon faded. There is little evidence that he panicked, as many historians have suggested, or that he truly believed that Jackson posed a direct threat to Washington.[2] But he was not above using Jackson's attack to prod the eternally irresolute McClellan into action. In a wire to McClellan on the day of the battle, Lincoln told him that the enemy was driving Banks and threatening Leesburg. "I think [Jackson's] movement is a general and concerted one," he continued, "such as could not be if he was acting upon the purpose of a very desperate defence of Richmond." Then he closed: "I think the time is near when you must either attack Richmond or give up the job and come to the defence of Washington. Let me hear from you instantly." McClellan responded within a few hours, reassuring Lincoln yet again that "the time is very near when I shall attack Richmond" but also pointing out, with his characteristic, finely tuned sense of self-preservation, that Jackson's attacks were designed "probably to prevent reinforcements being sent to me."[3]

Lincoln's main objective, however, in the wake of Jackson's victory, was not to fortify Washington but to destroy Jackson where he stood. It was obvious that, isolated in the northern end of the valley, the rebel general was vulnerable—almost absurdly so, given how many Union troops were now converging upon him. Under Lincoln's orders, Frémont was marching posthaste with his 15,000 men from Franklin to the valley, with the aim of cutting both Jackson's escape route and his supply line. McDowell, with 21,000 men, was hurrying west across the Blue Ridge. All told, 36,000 Union troops were presumably on the march, well more than twice Jackson's force. That did not include Banks's 7,000 men just north of the Potomac, bloodied but operational, or another 7,000 at Harpers Ferry, and Geary's 4,000 just over the mountains—bringing the total to 54,000—all of whom might be mobilized.[4] When Lincoln and Stanton heard that Jackson had marched *north* three days after the battle, it seemed to them that, in addition to rattling the walls of Washington's parlors and salons, he had also made a fatal error.

Jackson did not see it that way. Flight from Winchester after his victory had never crossed his mind, and anyway his old "unconditional friend," Confederate congressman Alexander Boteler, had shown up in Winchester on May 27 bearing orders that restated what Lee had told Jackson on May 16: to "demonstrate" against Harpers Ferry to seem to threaten points east. Lee and Jackson thought alike anyway. After the accidental success of Kernstown, it had been Jefferson Davis's idea to use Jackson deliberately to draw off Federal forces. Now he and Lee wanted to push this strategy as far as they could, forcing the Union high command to strip troops from its Richmond and Fredericksburg lines. They did not yet know that they had already succeeded. Neither did Jackson have any inkling of the fear he had inspired in the Northern capital. But he fully grasped that there was nothing quite like a victorious Confederate army marching unfettered and unopposed in the Virginia borderlands to get Washington's attention.

After letting his exhausted army rest for two days, Jackson set it on a northeastward march on May 28. His men, lifted by their stunning victory, were in a buoyant mood. The trials of the past month, the lack of sleep and incessant hard marching in rain and mud, the rancid food and lack of such amenities as real coffee, all seemed to drop away. They had cursed their commander for keeping them in the dark about where they were going and why, but with hindsight they could now see clearly how extraordinary their achievement was. They understood exactly how far they had marched. They could see how their speed, endurance, and hard fighting had won the day, and they now spent hours before campfires reconstructing the campaign and writing proud letters home about how they had done it, from Kernstown to McDowell to Winchester. Many now had a completely different view of Jackson. This group included his crusty, pragmatic quartermaster, John Harman, who on May 9, the day of the McDowell battle, furious at Jackson on a dozen counts, had written his brother to say that "we have been worsted by mismanagement. I am more than ever satisfied of Jackson's incompetency." Two and a half weeks later, following the Battle of Winchester, he was writing his brother breathlessly: "We have not only astonished the Yankees, but moved the world. I cannot believe that such a movement was ever made under the circumstances."[5] One of Jackson's privates wrote home, "This is one of the most brilliant moves of the war and Old Jack will be a greater man than ever."[6] Jackson's burgeoning legend grew in part from his own soldiers' accounts of him.

There were also the glowing accounts in the Confederate press, which quickly made their way into the ranks. "The name of 'Old Stonewall' seems likely to become as famous as that of 'Old Hickory,'" wrote the influential *Richmond Dispatch*. "His last victory appears to have been a crusher. . . . In all the transactions this year, Jackson has proved himself to be a man of high military genius."[7] Wrote the *Southern Literary Messenger*, "Jackson has proved himself the captain we have all been seeking."[8] And if that were not enough to make the men happy, there was the cornucopia of war delicacies that had been delivered to them at Winchester, which included figs, lemons, oranges, ham, bread, various exotic canned goods, and authentic coffee.

On May 28, the army arrived at Charlestown, the town where Jackson and his cadets had provided security for the hanging of John Brown in December 1859, an event that now seemed a lifetime away. The Stonewall Brigade under Brigadier General Charles S. Winder fought a brief engagement with 1,500 Union troops, whom they quickly drove away. By the morning of May 29 the main body of Jackson's army was camped three miles from Union-occupied Harpers Ferry. There he sat, unchallenged for the moment, a mere sixty miles upstream of Washington, on the Maryland border. That a Confederate army could do this at all, a year into the war, was the point of the exercise. Jackson had no illusions about what was going to happen to him. That same day he learned that Irvin McDowell was marching on Front Royal. The next day he learned that Frémont was closing in on him, too, from the west.

For once, most of his men also understood exactly what was happening. This was not just another retreat southward along the pike. Jackson's move north had placed his army in grave and immediate danger of isolation and destruction. According to Jackson's aide Henry Kyd Douglas, "everyone else thought it very imprudent to go [to Harpers Ferry] in the first place."[9] But there Jackson stood, and he seemed in no great hurry to leave. Indeed, on May 30, as Union armies closed in, Jackson seemed to operate at an oddly leisured pace. He met a delegation of local ladies in the morning, then in early afternoon rode out to the front to speak with General Winder and observe a minor artillery duel.[10] While the shells shrieked and buzzed, he dismounted, seated himself at the foot of a large tree, then stretched out and fell asleep, where his sometime staffer Alexander Boteler—a talented artist—sketched him, as he put it, "with his arms folded over his breast, his feet crossed like those of a crusader's effigy."[11] In Boteler's account,

> [I] was busily engaged with my pencil when, on looking up, I met his eyes full upon me. Extending his hand for the drawing, he said with a smile: "Let me see what you have been doing there," and on my handing him the sketch he remarked: "My hardest tasks at West Point were the drawing lessons, and I never could do anything in that line to satisfy myself—or, indeed," he added laughingly, "anybody else."[12]

Such lighthearted moments with Jackson never lasted; in the next instant he was telling Boteler he had important work for him to do. He wanted the congressman to travel to Richmond to try to secure more troops. Such reinforcements could not help him out of his present predicament; it was far too late for that. But Jackson had larger plans. What he told Boteler, in this extraordinary moment of peril, is revealing of how his mind worked in a crisis. He began by enumerating, with remarkable accuracy, the forces being mobilized against him. Then, in Boteler's account, Jackson said:

> McDowell and Frémont are probably aiming to effect a junction at Strasburg, so as to head us off from the upper valley, and are both nearer to it now than we are; consequently, no time is to be lost. You can say to them in Richmond that I'll send on the prisoners, secure most, if not all of the captured property, and with God's blessing will be able to baffle the enemy's plans here with my present force, but that will have to be increased as soon thereafter as possible. You may tell them, too, that if my command can be gotten up to 40,000 men a movement may be made beyond the Potomac, which will soon raise the siege of Richmond and transfer this campaign from the banks of the James to those of the Susquehanna.[13]

He was still contemplating a scorched-earth invasion of Pennsylvania. But his more immediate problem was saving himself. He gave orders for the main body of his army to return to Winchester the next day. (Winder and the Stonewall Brigade would collect the 2nd Virginia from its mountaintop camp across from Harpers Ferry and follow later.) Jackson and Boteler, meanwhile, took a one-car train down the almost comically degraded tracks of the Winchester and Potomac Railroad, for Winchester. Jackson fell asleep en route. While he was napping his mapmaker Jed Hotchkiss galloped up to Jackson's car and drew rein at the window. He carried the worst news possible. He told Jackson and Boteler that Colonel Z. T. Conner's 12th Georgia Regiment—which Jackson had left at Front Royal to hold the town and guard captured supplies—had been routed by Union forces. This meant that General Irvin McDowell, or at least his advance unit, *was already there*. Front Royal was twelve miles east of Strasburg. Jackson's army, meanwhile, was *more than forty miles north of it*. The implications were excruciatingly clear. While Hotchkiss waited expectantly for orders—there were none—Jackson read Conner's dispatch. He then tore it into pieces, threw the pieces on the floor, told the conductor, "Go on, sir, if you please," and went back to sleep.[14] The message, in Conner's urgent, messy scrawl and sent from Winchester, read as follows: "General: Just arrived. Enemy in full pursuit. Unless immediately succored, all is lost."

Conner would soon pay for such melodrama. When Jackson arrived in Winchester, he immediately summoned the colonel to his headquarters and asked him for an explanation. Conner gave him a detailed account of how the Confederates had been overwhelmed by superior Union numbers.

"Colonel Conner, how many men did you have killed?" asked Jackson.

"None," he replied.

"How many wounded?"

"None, sir."

"Colonel Conner, do you call that much of a fight?" snapped Jackson, and then dismissed him. As he left the room Conner remarked to Jackson's commissary Wells Hawks, "Major, I believe General Jackson is crazy."

A few moments later, Jackson's aide Sandie Pendleton emerged from the general's office. "Colonel Conner," he announced, "you are to consider yourself under arrest."

Amazed, Conner said, "Now I *know* he is crazy!"[15]

With that encounter Conner's military career was over. Jackson cashiered him for dereliction of duty. In this case—as opposed to that of the hapless Richard Garnett—Jackson had every reason to do what he did. Conner was not the only one to feel Jackson's wrath; his second in command, Major Willis Hawkins, was arrested for cowardice. For the 12th Georgia, which had fought so courageously and suffered so many casualties at McDowell, it was a calamity of a different sort.

If news of his impending doom bothered Jackson, he did not show it. He sent no urgent dispatches to Richmond; he asked no counsel of any of his officers. He wrote no dramatic letters home, as Banks had, bidding a sentimental farewell to his wife as his own death loomed. Jackson seemed, in fact, at the center of this building storm, to be completely calm. Hotchkiss remarked that the general was "in fine spirits." That same evening he had even enjoyed the diversion of Alexander Boteler's company. Boteler later related that he had taken the liberty of ordering two whiskey toddies to be sent up to their hotel room in Winchester, even though he knew Jackson did not drink. When he offered one to Jackson, the general replied, "No, no, Colonel, you must excuse me; I never drink intoxicating liquors."

"I know that, General," Boteler insisted, "but though you habitually abstain . . . there are occasions, and this is one of them, when a stimulant would do us both good."

Jackson shook his head, but nevertheless picked up the tumbler and drank part of it. "Colonel, do you know why I habitually abstain from intoxicating drinks?" Jackson asked. "Why, sir, because I like the taste of them, and when I discovered that to be the case I made up my mind at once to do without them altogether."[16]

The presence of McDowell's troops in Front Royal was only one of Jackson's worries. The larger potential threat to him—and the key to his defeat, in Lincoln's mind—was not McDowell but Frémont. The president had studied the map of Virginia and had noticed not only that there was a road from Franklin, where Frémont was camped, to Harrisonburg but also that the distance was a mere forty miles. Harrisonburg, in the middle of the valley, lay north of Jackson's supply base in Staunton. As Lincoln saw it, there was no way Jackson could beat Frémont to Harrisonburg, which meant that Jackson would have Union armies to the north and south of him. He would be isolated, his supply lines cut. Even Jackson could not escape from such a trap. "Move against Jackson at Harrisonburg . . . immediately," Lincoln had ordered Frémont. "Put the utmost speed to it. Do not lose a minute."

But General John Frémont, the formerly magnificent but now greatly diminished Pathfinder, who had failed in the western theater and had thus far been a model of inactivity in the mountains, saw an entirely different world. Frémont had two problems: First, he was a man who insisted on seeing obstacles where none existed. Second, in this case there actually *were* obstacles, which made everything doubly bad. Mired in constant rains in the valley of the South Branch of the Potomac, sixty miles from his supply base, Frémont's army had suffered. Many commissary wagons had never gotten through. The men were on less than half rations, prompting Frémont's chief of staff to complain that "our people were next to starving."[17]

Frémont's more serious problem was that the apparently convenient route on Lincoln's map was actually a horrendously steep, twisting, unsurfaced country road that crossed two mountain ranges. More significantly, during the McDowell campaign Jackson had anticipated such a crossing and had sent Jed Hotchkiss with a crew of engineers to destroy that and other mountain passes to the Shenandoah Valley. They had done admirable work. Hotchkiss recorded in his diary on May 11 that he had procured axes and crowbars and by "sending details far up into the gorges . . . and cutting down trees and rolling large rocks into the road made a very effectual blockade especially of the road leading from Franklin to Harrisonburg."[18] It meant that Frémont—as he saw it, anyway—could not follow Lincoln's orders.

This changed everything. Frémont was now taking the long way around, north along his supply lines and then east, pushing his army up the South Branch valley to Moorefield, where he would take a right turn and head to Strasburg to cut Jackson off. Lincoln, understanding nothing of Frémont's problems, was furious when he found out. "I see that you are at Moorefield," he wired Frémont angrily. "You were expressly ordered to march to Harrisonburg. What does this mean?" But there was nothing he could do. Lincoln ordered Frémont and his army to occupy Strasburg by the evening of May 30, which would put his 15,000 men there well ahead of Jackson. But here, once again, fate took a hand. Because of heavy rains and bad roads, and Frémont's rather obvious inability to move an army as Stonewall Jackson could, Frémont had to camp that night twenty miles west of Strasburg, at Wardensville. He would not be able to reach Strasburg until the thirty-first. Union brigadier general James Shields, meanwhile, back in the valley now and looking for payback, though not quite so blustery as before, also was poised to reach Strasburg on that same day. Meaning that, in spite of the delays, the jaws of Lincoln's marvelous trap were finally in position to snap closed, and just in time, too. It was also that very same day—*May 31*—that Jackson, with his main column, infantry, artillery, wagons, and 2,300 Union prisoners, dragged themselves out of their camps north of Winchester in a heavy downpour. They had more than twenty miles to go. An objective observer would have said they had no chance.

All of this set up one of the most stirring footraces in military history, a perilous gauntlet run that few believed Jackson could possibly win. Citizens of Winchester gazed with fading hope upon their shabbily dressed, somber-faced general as he rode out of town and tried to convince themselves that things were not as bad as they seemed. "We left our friends in Winchester trembling for our fate & more than we trembled ourselves," wrote Kyd Douglas. "Everybody felt the great danger, but everybody looked at Old Jack & seeing him calm & cool as if nothing was the matter, they came to the conclusion that their destruction could not be as inevitable as they supposed."[19]

Jackson pushed his "foot cavalry" hard that day, though perhaps for once they did not need to be pushed. Every man understood the peril he was in and knew that speed was his only hope. They knew, too, that, strung out in a ponderous, fifteen-mile-long column on the valley pike, they were exceptionally vulnerable to flank attacks from the two Union armies that had been sent to destroy them. Rumors swept through the ranks that Union forces had already occupied Strasburg, that they were already cut off, that Banks and Brigadier General Rufus Sexton were marching in their rear with a combined force as large as their own. The army itself, in its entirety, was at risk. One need only exchange Union for Confederate commanders to see what might have happened to it. Jackson would have cut such an army to pieces on the road.

Nothing of the sort happened. That afternoon the entire unwieldy train made it safely—to many of the men, miraculously—into bivouac just north of Strasburg. They had run the gauntlet unharmed; Jackson had won the critical leg of the race. There were no Union troops in sight. In Boteler's description, Jackson was "standing there like a hunted stag at bay defying his pursuers."[20] Though his own soldiers did not yet understand why, or to what magic they owed their deliverance, they gratefully made their camps in the rain. But now, ironically, it was Jackson who was really worried. That was because the Stonewall Brigade under Charles S. Winder and the 1st Maryland Regiment (Confederate), which had trailed the main army from Harpers Ferry, had not quite reached Strasburg. It was not for want of trying. They had marched thirty-five miles or more that day without food. They had finally collapsed late in the evening at Newtown, ten miles north of Strasburg, where many of them simply fell down and slept in the muddy fields. Jackson now knew that he had not only to hold his own position the next day against the two Union armies. He also had to hold the valley pike open for Winder and his cherished brigade. He would need another miracle.

But how, exactly, had he escaped? The answer had more to do with the character and sensibility of his opponents than with strictly military strategy. The one who had the clearest shot at him was James Shields, the Irish-born politician who had been promoted to major general after the Battle of Kernstown, who had once bragged that Jackson was afraid of him, and who only days before had vowed confidently that he would "soon clear out the Shenandoah Valley."[21] Shields's main problem now was, in fact, fear: his own, of Jackson's growing legend, which was beginning to disconcert otherwise rational men. It was dressed up in different ways and rationalized in different ways, but it came down to the same thing.

The fear began with basic assumptions about Jackson's army. Though Jackson still had merely 15,000 men at his disposal, and the Union War Department believed this, in the eyes of its field generals Jackson's strength had grown enormously. A close reading of Union dispatches shows various Union scouts estimating Jackson's strength the day before at 30,000 to 60,000. That same day General Geary put the number at 25,000 to 30,000; McDowell himself accepted the 30,000 figure. On the day Jackson slid through, Shields himself was reporting Jackson at Winchester with as many as 40,000 troops.[22] Shields believed the higher numbers because he wanted to and, believing them, found his own 11,000, unreinforced as yet by the other 9,000 of McDowell's troops, to be inadequate. Then, too, he saw phantoms: he got the ridiculous idea that Confederate James Longstreet was moving up the Luray Valley with an army—ridiculous, because that would have left virtually no Confederate troops to defend Richmond.[23] He also became convinced that Turner Ashby's small cavalry, which Jackson had deployed on the road near Front Royal, was actually a large and formidable force. He did not have, moreover, specific orders from McDowell to attack, even though he knew as well as anyone that the whole idea, and the thing Lincoln wanted more than anything in the world, was to cut off Jackson's retreat.

So Shields, tying himself in mental knots at his camp in Front Royal, did nothing at all. It was not until early evening that he finally got up the small amount of courage required to test the enemy's strength by sending a regiment against Ashby. The rebels were almost instantly routed; he had been afraid of nothing. But by now Jackson's army was in Strasburg and it was too late to do anything about it. Shields, meanwhile, saved his most creative excuse for last. Two days later he wired the War Department to say that his decision to stay put had been quite deliberate and calculated. "We would have occupied Strasburg," he wrote, "but dare not interfere with what was designed for Frémont. His failure has saved Jackson."[24] Having shifted the blame to Frémont, he added, breathtakingly, that he was off to chase Jackson, and "*I have no fears of their numbers, which have been ridiculously exaggerated by fear.*"[25]

Was Frémont really to blame? He was to blame in the larger sense that in spite of constant goading from Washington he had failed to bring up his army in time to cut Jackson off. He had arrived late on the afternoon of May 31 in camps about five miles east of Strasburg. He had been in no mood to push his men farther. Like Shields, he could list any number of excuses and reasons for his lateness: the men were exhausted from brutal marches in bone-drenching rains and knee-deep muck; they were sick, disabled, broken-down, hungry from want of rations. Straggling had reduced the size of his army. They were indeed demoralized, and had been since their muddy camps in Franklin. There was something of the loser about Frémont, something that suggested only bleakness and indecision and hardship and misery and none of the glory and clarity that soldiers craved. They reacted by giving him glum half efforts, by straggling and complaining. Jackson had faced the same conditions, the same scanty supplies, the same numbers of barefoot, sick, waterlogged troops; his desertion rates were far worse. Considering Lincoln's sharp, almost scolding tone in his dispatches to Frémont—and his constant exhortations to move faster—it is astonishing that the Pathfinder elected to give his men a full day of rest on May 29, a mere twenty miles from Strasburg.[26] Shields was wrong: both he and Frémont had failed together, and thus, together, they had "saved" Jackson.

The next day was, if anything, more dramatic than the last. A snapshot of troop deployments on the morning of June 1 would have found Jackson camped just north of Strasburg; Shields twelve miles east in Front Royal; Frémont five miles to the west; and Winder, ten miles north on the valley pike. The latter was soon barreling south toward safety, fearful that he was too late. Jackson had decided that he would wait for Winder and his roughly two thousand men. He had erred in allowing his command to become so badly separated. Now he would fight, if necessary, to reunite it. He would fight both armies if he had to.

His instincts—which would prove correct—told him that he would not. In a sign of extreme disrespect for Shields, he sent no infantry at all in his direction but once again merely fanned Ashby's cavalry out on the road from Front Royal to Winchester. Ashby's pickets would tell him if Shields made a move to cut off Winder. Jackson, meanwhile, threw the hard-fighting Ewell and his division out to the west, where they formed a line of battle and waited for Frémont, fully ready to fight. Just before 10:00 a.m., Frémont's big guns thundered, Ewell's replied, and an artillery duel sent booming echoes through the hills. North of town, the men of the Stonewall Brigade, hurtling southward, took it as a bad omen: they were already too late.

But Frémont, as it turned out, was making only the most cursory of probes. When Ewell sent skirmishers bristling forth, and the crack of muskets rolled through the valley, Union troops withdrew to their lines. The artillery still thundered, but to no particular effect. To Ewell's surprise, there was no push. While Ewell held Frémont at bay, the first of Winder's units hove into view. It was an emotional moment. "We could plainly see the smoke of the discharges of the guns we had heard . . . and we knew that Jackson was holding back Frémont til we got by," wrote McHenry Howard of the 1st Maryland (Confederate) in a later memoir. "To our relief, everything continued quiet on the Front Royal side where we looked for trouble from an advance by Shields or McDowell."[27]

At noon the Stonewall Brigade arrived in Strasburg, a bit shaken by the stress of the morning march and by having walked forty-five miles in two days with no food—an astonishing feat of marching that shamed Frémont's army and seemed to confirm what at least one Federal officer believed: that "Stonewall Jackson's men will follow him to the devil and he knows it."[28] The men were ecstatic to be reunited with the army, though they were not yet out of harm's way. It had been a harrowing last few miles. "How different our feelings then!" wrote Private Randolph H. McKim of the 1st Maryland (Confederate). "Our spirits rose and we forgot our fatigue and were ready to sing 'Baltimore, ain't we happy!' What the men said to each other then was of a different complexion—'Old Jack knows what he's about! He'll take care of us, you bet!' From that hour we never doubted him."[29] Frémont, who had his command ready for battle by late morning, was simply frozen by uncertainty and fear: that Jackson outnumbered him, that he would have to fight Jackson without McDowell's help. With an army about the size of Jackson's, he was cowed into inaction even though his friends in Washington had told him in no uncertain terms that "he must find Jackson and fight him, or his chances thereafter for further preferment or reputation were as naught."[30] Apparently that wasn't motivation enough.

With his army now reunited, Jackson pulled out of Strasburg and once again—this was starting to look bizarrely familiar—headed south on the valley pike. This time he had two armies to worry about. But anyone with a memory for recent history would also have known that Stonewall Jackson in "flight" up the Shenandoah Valley was a prelude to large, unanticipated, war-changing events.

CHAPTER THIRTY

A STRANGE FONDNESS
FOR TRAPS

By early June, it could be fairly said that Jackson had done everything Jefferson Davis and Robert E. Lee had asked him to do, and more. For two and a half months he and his small, highly mobile force had occupied the attention of ever-larger Union armies. He had managed, by the sheer weight of his daring and audacity—and a growing reputation for both—to create a diversion that had temporarily stalled the Union campaign in front of Richmond. He had even thrown the Northern capital into a brief fit of panic. Now, having narrowly slipped through Lincoln's pincers, the last thing anyone expected him to do was to turn and fight. He did not need to. His escape over the Blue Ridge to the safety of Robert E. Lee's army was guaranteed. But escape had never figured in his plans. On June 5 Jackson, having sent his trains of captured supplies and sick and wounded men south to Staunton, turned off the valley pike at Harrisonburg, marched a few miles south and east on a narrow, rutted clay road, and under the looming 2,900-foot southern tip of the Massanutten Mountain bivouacked his army in rolling farmland near an obscure river-junction hamlet called Port Republic, and spun around to face his pursuers.

This time they were coming at him from two different directions. To understand the nature of the threat, we have to back up several days to a time when Jackson was still retreating southward. After Shields had failed to intercept Jackson at Strasburg, the pugnacious Irishman had conceived what seemed to him a brilliant idea. While Frémont pursued Jackson in the now familiar way—straight down the valley pike—Shields would reverse

Jackson's stunning juke-step march against Front Royal. The Union general would start from his camps in that town, then slide southward along the South Fork of the Shenandoah, cross the Massanutten at New Market, and block Jackson's southward retreat. Though he began his march down the boggy roads on the east side of the massive mountain in yet another of the seemingly eternal rainstorms that swept Virginia that spring, he was more confident than ever that this time he would "bag" the rebel Jackson. If the previous engagements with Jackson were about speed and maneuver, this one, featuring three armies instead of two, would be more like an intricate game of martial chess, played out among the roaring rivers, ravines, spurs, and ridges of the Luray and Shenandoah Valleys.

The game this time was mostly about bridges—four of them—strung out over roughly forty miles in the Luray Valley between the towns of Luray and Port Republic. They were important because the South Fork of the Shenandoah—a navigable river in normal times that carried flatboats downstream to Harpers Ferry—was in flood stage, swift, swollen, and unfordable. Shields realized that he desperately needed the northernmost of those bridges, named White House and Columbia, to cross the river, cut through New Market Gap, and intercept Jackson in the Shenandoah Valley. On June 1, while Jackson was still passing through the jaws of Lincoln's trap, Shields had dispatched one of his best officers, Colonel Samuel S. Carroll, to travel ahead of the army to seize and hold those bridges. He had other work for Carroll, too. Ten miles south was another bridge at the hamlet of Conrad's Store, over which Jackson and his army had passed when retreating from Banks in April. It was the most direct escape route from the midvalley to the Blue Ridge Mountains. Shields, convinced that Jackson was indeed trying to escape, ordered Carroll to burn the Conrad's Store bridge. "Everything depends on speed," Shields told him. "Jackson must be overtaken." And then, underscoring how vastly important this assignment was, he promised the young officer a brigadier generalship if he succeeded. "You will earn your star," he said, "if you do all this."[1]

It was a good idea. Unfortunately for Shields, Jackson had beaten him to it. Jackson had noticed that Shields had not joined Frémont in pursuit of him, and had guessed correctly that the Union general was taking the back way through the Luray Valley to cut him off. Jackson had immediately dispatched Samuel Coyner of Ashby's cavalry, who rode down the valley pike, crossed the mountain at New Market, and at dawn on June 2, after struggling through deep mud, a driving thunderstorm, and "the roughest road,"

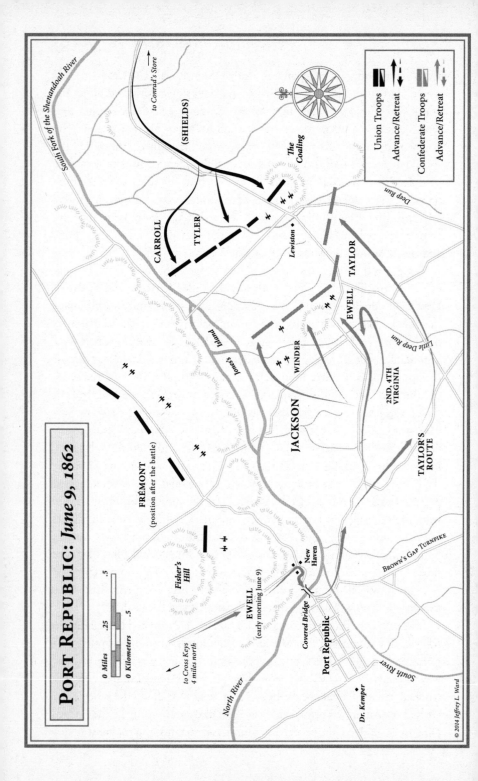

PORT REPUBLIC: *June 9, 1862*

to Conrad's Store

South Fork of the Shenandoah River

(SHIELDS)

The Coaling

CARROLL

TYLER

Lewiston

TAYLOR

EWELL

WINDER

JACKSON

Jones's Island

2ND, 4TH VIRGINIA

TAYLOR'S ROUTE

Deep Run

Little Deep Run

FRÉMONT
(position after the battle)

Fisher's Hill

to Cross Keys
4 miles north

EWELL
(early morning june 9)

New Haven

Covered Bridge

Port Republic

North River

South River

BROWN'S GAP TURNPIKE

Dr. Kemper

| Union Troops | Advance/Retreat | Confederate Troops | Advance/Retreat |

0 Miles .25 .5
0 Kilometers .5

© 2014 Jeffrey L. Ward

managed to burn both the Columbia and White House bridges. Carroll's men, on foot and saddled with four pieces of artillery Shields had ordered them to carry, were two days behind them.[2]

Curiously, Coyner and his Confederates had exactly the same orders Carroll did for the bridge at Conrad's Store: destroy it. Coyner of course beat Carroll again, and burned it the next day. But how could it be in both generals' interests to burn the same bridge? Because, once again, Shields had grossly misread his opponent. Instead of fleeing to Stanardsville on the eastern side of the Blue Ridge, Jackson was doing the thing Shields least expected him to do, which was to stand and fight. And because he had chosen to stay put, the very last thing he wanted was for the two Union armies to be able to easily unite against him. Burning the Conrad's Store bridge and the two bridges near New Market Gap meant that would never happen. Jackson had decisively won the opening gambit. As the badly bogged-down Shields would soon discover, he could neither cut off Jackson's retreat, nor unite easily with Frémont.

Thus, three of the bridges. The fourth, and most critical to Jackson's strategy, was in the town of Port Republic, a small cluster of buildings in the delta formed by the North River and the South River just before they flowed together to form the South Fork of the Shenandoah. Shields, increasingly lost in his own private fog of war, would misunderstand its importance, too. Jackson had chosen Port Republic over every other place he could have gone—and by now he and his brilliant cartographer, Jed Hotchkiss, knew all of them—because of its peculiar location at the junction of the three rivers. His army, on the morning of Sunday, June 8, was camped in the rolling wheatfields north of the town, facing attack from Frémont's army from the direction of Harrisonburg and from Shields coming down the Luray Valley. The Union armies were so close that they posed a classic problem of military strategy: Jackson could not afford to throw his entire army at one or the other; he could not take them in succession, or "in detail." He would somehow have to deal with *both at once*. It was yet another reason for him to march for Brown's Gap as fast as he could, depart the valley, and join the Confederate forces at Richmond. It is hard to think of another general, on either side, who at this point in the war would not have done so.

But Port Republic, like so many of Jackson's choices of positions in the war, then and later, was actually a terrific tactical play.[3] Its beauty lay in the fact that it offered both the protection of a roaring river and an escape hatch if things went wrong. Its best feature, tactically speaking, was a sturdy covered bridge over the rampaging North River. This was the fourth bridge. In the absence of the others, it was the only way for either army to cross the river. If Frémont beat him on the battlefield, he could easily retreat over the North River and burn the bridge. East of town there was the South River, breast-high and moving like a millrace but still fordable or bridgeable with pontoons or wagons. It separated him from Shields's oncoming army. If he lost that fight, he could recross the lesser stream and head to Brown's Gap a few miles away on a good road that ran south out of town.

On the morning of June 8 Jackson's army looked like this: Its headquarters was in the small village of Port Republic. Seven thousand men under his direct command were camped outside of town just north of the North River, while Ewell's five-thousand-man force was camped about four miles north at a hamlet known as Cross Keys. Jackson's numbers were down because his brutal marches had once again taken a fearsome toll on his army, which now had at least three thousand absentees.[4] It was the price paid for his extraordinary maneuvers. "We have been on a retreat for five days and an awful time it has been," wrote one artillerist. "I never saw so many men with their feet all swollen and bleeding."[5] Facing Ewell across gently swelling farmland covered by wheat, clover, patches of timber, and the occasional picturesque farmhouse were twelve thousand bluecoats under Frémont in full battle lines and ready for a fight. To the east, bogged down in muck and mire downstream near Conrad's Store, lurked Shields's brigades.

For all of his cleverness in isolating his enemies and in devising a place where he might fight both of them, Jackson now made several critical errors in judgment. Having chosen this river straddle as his main tactical play, he proceeded to neglect the key to it all: the North River bridge. Though that bridge needed no protection from north of Port Republic, where most of Jackson's army was bivouacked, it was deeply vulnerable from the south and east. But Jackson had placed only a very light guard on the two river fords across the South River, over which the threat from the east would come. There were no guards on the bridge itself. He made an even more serious mistake by ordering Quartermaster John Harman's enormous wagon train with most of the army's supplies to park in the fields behind headquarters, both highly visible and highly vulnerable to any attack from the east. (An advance unit from Shields had only to cross the fordable South River to get at them.) Worse still, loss of the North Bridge would mean that Jackson's army and its supplies were on opposite sides of the unfordable river. Indeed, Jackson himself might have been separated from his own army.

What had happened to cloud Jackson's mind? His staff was convinced that he was a victim of complete physical exhaustion. He was at least as tired as his men, many of whom had simply dropped by the roadside. He was often up at what he euphemistically called "early dawn"—what we would call the middle of the night—working on the endless details of command, many of which he insisted on keeping track of himself. Colonel Samuel Fulkerson wrote that his commander "is remarkable for his energy and industry . . . and sleeps very little. Often while near the enemy, and while everybody except the guards are asleep, he is on his horse and gone, nobody knows where."[6]

He thus took the fate of the entire army on his shoulders, its life and death, its hard marches and whatever food and clothing he could secure to keep it going. All of this cost him rest. There is little evidence that he had had a single full night's sleep since the valley campaign began. On many nights the wet weather precluded sleep at all. On June 4, Jackson's tent was the victim of a small flash flood in the middle of the night that carried away his hat and boots. He tried to sleep anyway, even though the tent was still full of water. The next morning, according to Douglas, it was still full of "various small articles of apparel and furniture . . . floating about like little boats."[7] Such was life on the march that spring. Jackson was so weary that he sometimes fell asleep fully clothed, even wearing his sword and boots. Sandie Pendleton, who was probably closer to his commander than any of his aides, thought that in the first week of June "General Jackson was completely broken down."[8]

The consequences of Jackson's strange lassitude were not long in coming. At about 8:30 a.m. on the dry, mild morning of June 8, approximately 150 cavalry with four guns under the command of Colonel Samuel Carroll forded the South River, galloped into Port Republic, and created an astounding amount of havoc in a short time, capturing three staff officers and nearly taking Jackson himself, who escaped only by a mad gallop the length of the main street and over the North River bridge.[9] The immediate result of the assault was that Carroll's raiders suddenly found themselves in possession of that bridge. It was Jackson's worst nightmare. Carroll had only to burn the bridge and Jackson and his army would be cut off from his supply trains and his escape routes. Frémont would have him cornered against the rampaging North River.

And then something miraculous happened. Carroll, who might have changed the war and made himself a hero by burning the bridge, was actually *determined to hold it*. That was because his superior, Major General James Shields, had explicitly ordered him, in writing, to do so.[10] It was one of the campaign's greatest tactical mistakes, and it still is not clear how Shields could have been so foolish. In keeping with his character—he was a chronic liar—Shields later blamed it all on Carroll, who by "some unaccountable misapprehension" had failed to burn the bridge. Shields, in reality, had not been able to make up his mind and had given at least one set of conflicting orders, though his final order was clear enough: "Hold it at all hazards."[11] Carroll did, until he and the rest of his little group—plus some infantry that had remained in the rear—were chased off by a determined Jackson backed by two regiments and artillery.

Still, why would Shields have ordered Carroll to, as Union general Nathan Kimball later put it, "hold the only bridge over which Jackson could possibly escape from Frémont"?[12] The real reason may have been petty jealousy, which would also have been in keeping with Shields's deeply deficient character. According to an Ohio soldier, on the previous day Shields had said in a voice "loud and rather sarcastic, 'Frémont thinks he is going to raise hell up there, and I'll show him.'" The idea was that Frémont wanted the bridge burned to trap Jackson; Shields wanted to deny Frémont that glory. Kimball, generally a reliable source, later made the same accusation.[13]

As for Jackson's own tactical lapses, there was another reason for his sudden blindness that morning: Turner Ashby, his brilliant, erratic cavalry chief, was dead, killed in a skirmish with Union cavalry on June 6. (His death underscored how dangerous life was for Civil War officers, who had a 50 percent greater chance of being killed than privates.[14]) Though he had failed to execute Jackson's orders at half a dozen key moments—most egregiously at Winchester—Ashby had closed out his life with a rush of redemptive glory.[15] During Jackson's retreat south in June, he had been his old brilliant self, launching daring attacks that slowed Frémont's army, at one point even rallying straggling infantry to make a successful counterattack. For all his flaws, he was supremely brave, capable of feats of endurance in the saddle that amazed his contemporaries, and uncannily aware of where the enemy was. Such devotion to duty had taken its toll on him, as it had on Jackson. At the time of his death he was, in the description of a contemporary, so thin he looked emaciated. With his dark skin; long, dark beard; and long hair he presented a wild sight. "He told me that he had been under fire for sixty consecutive days, but he found no inconvenience from it," wrote the soldier. In place of meals, Ashby said, "I eat a few apples, drink some spring water, and draw up my swordbelt a hole or two tighter, and I'm all right. It's just as good as eating.' "[16] He had the blind loyalty of his men, but in his absence the cavalry quickly lost whatever meager discipline it had, and bore at least some of the blame for Carroll's freakish success that morning at Port Republic. Still, in his official report, Jackson praised Ashby as he had never praised anyone else:

> The close relation which General Ashby bore to my command for most of the previous twelve months will justify me in saying that as a partisan officer I never knew his superior; his daring was proverbial; his powers of endurance almost incredible; his tone of character heroic, and his sagacity almost intuitive in divining the purposes and movements of the enemy.[17]

But on the morning of Sunday, June 8, there was no time to mourn the fallen hero. From the north came the distant roll of artillery: Frémont's big guns were opening up on Ewell. The Battle of Cross Keys had begun.

Frémont should have won the battle quickly. He had a two-to-one numerical advantage, and better than that in artillery. If he had thrown his entire force directly at Ewell's line, which was set up on a long ridge, he would very likely have broken it. But with Frémont nothing was ever that simple. He was facing not just Stonewall Jackson now but also the myth of Stonewall Jackson, and the myth told him and his officers that they were facing twenty thousand battle-hardened Confederate troops instead of the five-thousand-plus effectives in front of them. At Frémont's council of war he and his brigade commanders worried about this terrible numerical disadvantage and bemoaned the poor condition of their ragged, starved-out, exhausted army. A hundred and fifty years later, you can almost hear the defeatism. One thinks of the astonishing moral distance between their outlook and that of the dead Ashby, a man who slept little, often went hungry, and fought bravely and almost continuously without complaint.

After some inconclusive skirmishing, the main battle began, as most of these battles seemed to, with long-range artillery. And while cannons were very satisfying to shoot, watch, and listen to, they often did little significant tactical damage. For a cautious warrior such as Frémont, this probably seemed like a good way to fight without getting his hands dirty. (George

McClellan, another hesitant fighter, loved nothing better than the idea of bringing up his big guns in front of Richmond and pounding the city into submission from afar.) The cannonade began at Cross Keys at 10:30 a.m., roared for six full hours, and consisted mostly of shooting at other batteries. An enormous amount of ordnance was used up in the process. A single Union battery shot six hundred rounds that day, meaning one round per cannon every three minutes. In spite of this, there is little evidence that much damage was done. Another Union battery stood on the front lines for four hours of this shelling and lost only one man killed, one wounded.[18]

The battle on the ground, on the other hand, clearly belonged to the Confederates. It was conducted entirely by Richard Ewell, barking his profane orders in his squawky voice from his headquarters, which, unlike that of Frémont, was up on the field of battle near his artillery. Jackson, wary of the arrival of the rest of Shields's army, remained four miles south, in Port Republic. Rebel soldiers under Brigadier General Isaac Trimble tore into the Union left, driving three brigades back a full mile. In the center, Brigadier General Robert Milroy, who had fought Jackson so well at McDowell and who was impatient with Frémont's passive battle management, launched a two-thousand-man assault in midafternoon on his own initiative, only to see his men cut to pieces by Virginians in the woods. There was plenty of hardnosed fighting on both sides, too, men standing in the open and loading and firing and stepping or inching forward or backward depending on the flow of the battle.

Why a particular regiment of soldiers advanced or retreated at this and other battles in the Civil War is still something of a mystery. At bottom, fighting was about the ability to hurl enough lead at a concentrated group of soldiers so that, seeing enough of their friends go down, they became convinced that they had to withdraw. Often it was just that simple. At other times the effects of musket fire were almost imperceptible, as much the result of a soldier's belief in his chances of survival as of the actual danger he faced. Belief counted for a lot—in one's general, in the captain in front of you brandishing his gleaming sword, in the bravery of one's fellow soldiers, in the idea of winning itself. A rout might start with men taking small steps backward while reloading, then taking slightly larger steps backward while their enemy, two hundred or three hundred yards away, began to move very slightly forward. Soon the retreating line would begin to lose individual soldiers, then groups of them, and finally the entire line would turn and run—all without ever experiencing a single definitive moment when the battle turned.[19] Sometimes regimental and brigade commanders simply became lost in the thick clouds of gunpowder smoke. Blinded and feeling isolated, and with the whoops and shouts of the enemy newly magnified in their ears, they might also be inclined to retreat. Though it is impossible to measure the effect of Jackson's growing reputation as a winner on his men, it was undoubtedly strong.

By early evening, when Frémont ordered his troops to withdraw from their advance positions under cover of his artillery, it was clear that Ewell had gotten the better of him. He now occupied the ground from which Frémont had launched his first attack. The final tally of casualties—288 for the Confederates and 684 for the Federals—suggests the level of Confederate dominance. Still, Frémont's force was bloodied but not beaten; he would be able to fight the next day.

Jackson, meanwhile, spent most of the day in Port Republic, fully expecting Shields to follow up on Carroll's attack. Jackson spent time placing artillery on the bluffs that overlooked the village—enough to be sure that he could stop Shields if he tried another attack across the South River. When one of his officers pointed out this possibility to him, he replied, waving his hand toward his commanding artillery positions, "No, sir! No! He cannot do it! I should tear him to pieces!"[20]

The news of Ewell's victory at Cross Keys thrilled Jackson's men. They had been attacked by Frémont's full army, had struck a hard blow in return, and had driven him back. More important, as far as Jackson's staff was concerned, was the meaning of the victory. With Frémont checked and Shields not yet in evidence, they all believed that Jackson would now do the supremely logical thing: slip out under cover of darkness, take his exhausted army on the road for Brown's Gap, and call an end to the long campaign. They had underestimated their commander once again. That evening he amazed them all by ordering his quartermaster, John Harman, to bring up the supply wagons, roll them across the North River bridge, and give the troops rations to cook. They were going to stay and fight. Among his staff members there was a good deal of eye-rolling and looks exchanged. "The General seemed to like traps," wrote Henry Kyd Douglas, "and, at any rate, was not yet satisfied with the risks he had run and the blows he had inflicted. . . . We were getting used to this kind of aberration, but this did seem rather an extra piece of temerity."[21] And so the huge supply train rumbled forward; campfires were lit; and, likely to the astonishment of Shields and Frémont, no Confederates showed any signs of leaving Port Republic.

CHAPTER THIRTY-ONE

SLAUGHTER IN A SMALL PLACE

A ny Union officer who was surprised by the idea that Jackson was not slipping quietly away in darkness would have been shocked to learn of his
actual plans. He had been thinking about what he would do as he paced
the high ground around Port Republic and listened to the thud of artillery
from Cross Keys. He had concluded that, as he put it later, "as no movement was made by General Shields to renew the action that day, I determined to take the initiative and attack him the following morning."[1] And
that was only the first phase of an extraordinary plan—some might have
called it purely crazy—to destroy both Federal armies. It may or may not
have been the scheme of a man who was in the middle of a physical breakdown. It was certainly, as Douglas had observed, a lot of risk even for Jackson to take, which was saying something. The idea was to move the main
body of his army, including Ewell, by night to Port Republic, cross the
South River, and attack and defeat Shields's two brigades in the early morning. Then—having left a reinforced brigade under Brigadier General Isaac
Trimble to hold off Frémont—Jackson would recross both the South River
and the North River, march to Cross Keys, and defeat that Union army as
well, this time once and for all. All before early afternoon.[2] If anything went
wrong, the cavalry was to hold the road to Brown's Gap open for escape.

The plan was Beauregard-like in its wild optimism. Indeed, Jackson's
staff officers were all amazed at their commander's lack of anxiety. The
combative Ewell, who bridled at the timetable for marching from Cross
Keys to Port Republic with his tired infantry, was nonetheless by now a
full believer in his eccentric commander. Late that night he was sitting in
front of his tent in conversation with new cavalry chief Tom Munford—

the ranking cadet at VMI when Jackson first arrived and one of Jackson's first acquaintances there—when the bald-pated Ewell said, in his fidgety, nervous way, "Look here, Munford, do you remember my conversation with you at Conrad's Store when I called this old man an old woman? Well, I take it all back! I will never prejudge another man. Jackson's no fool; he knows how to keep his own counsel and does curious things, but he has a method to his madness."[3]

That method was sorely tested on the morning of June 9. What was supposed to be a relatively simple task—getting the army across the South River—turned out to be a logistical nightmare. Engineers had worked through the night to build a makeshift bridge by placing wagons in the riverbed and then laying wooden planks on top of them. But the bridge was made poorly; there were gaps in the planks, and the wagons were of different heights. Soldiers began crossing in single file, and many fell off into the fast-moving, chest-high water. Many more had to wade the river in thick fog, stumbling and floating off downstream in the process. Jackson had lost his advantage almost before he started.

But he was so fatigued and impatient that instead of waiting for his five full brigades—some eight thousand men in total—he marched boldly up the small river valley with only four of the Stonewall Brigade's five regiments (the Stonewall) and two batteries under the command of Charles S. Winder. Facing him were two Federal brigades under Brigadier General Erastus B. Tyler, a wealthy Ohio fur merchant and one of the tougher Union fighters in the valley, and Colonel Samuel Carroll, who had made the daring raid that almost netted Jackson. Shields, who should have been with them, was stuck in Luray, forty miles north, preparing to fight yet another ghostly apparition of General James Longstreet. Though he repeatedly assured Tyler and Carroll that "I will be with you soon," he would never show up.

But his subordinates' defensive position was superb. Their right flank was anchored on the rampaging South Fork. Their left, a mile away across open wheatfields, was anchored on a lovely, elevated, mountain-laurel-covered shoulder that jutted out from the foothills of the Blue Ridge. On that shoulder was a flat piece of ground where charcoal had been made, known as the Coaling. The cannons that Tyler had placed there commanded the entire river plain below.

By attacking with such a small force, Jackson had made a mistake. Perhaps he was still bone-weary and not thinking clearly. He had risen at 3:00 a.m. that day after another cruelly short night. But by failing to wait for his main force—including most of Ewell's army—he was feeding his troops into slaughter. It was not long in coming. The worst of it was at the hands of the Federal gunners on the Coaling, spraying canister at rebel troops in the shelterless fields and at the base of the shoulder. The Confederates had their hands full with the Union infantry, too, which outnumbered them. Winder's men fought hard, but the replacements they desperately needed were mired for the moment in a thick tangle of wagons, men, and horses back at the South River. At about 8:30 a.m. Winder and three regiments mounted a heroic charge against twice their number, surging forward through the flat farmlands. They were soon under murderous fire. One of those regiments, the 7th Louisiana (the lead unit of Brigadier General Richard Taylor's brigade), would lose half its men.

While the battle raged and the Confederate line shuddered along its length, Jackson, who now understood that just about everything was going wrong, made two critical moves. He sent orders to Isaac Trimble to abandon Cross Keys as quickly as possible, cross the North River bridge, burn it down, and join the rest of the army east of Port Republic. Frémont, stuck on the other side of the river, would be unable to follow. Jackson, his light eyes blazing with the glow of battle—the men were beginning to call him "Old Blue Light"—also grabbed his mapmaker, Jed Hotchkiss, and ordered him to gather the rest of Taylor's 1,700 Louisianans, who had just appeared on the field, and, in his words, "take that battery."[4] By that he meant those Federal guns on the Coaling that were tearing his men apart.

Thus began the final drama of Stonewall Jackson's valley campaign. Could Winder and the bloodied Stonewall Brigade hold until Taylor took out the Federal guns on the Coaling? Could he take them out at all? The question was eventually settled by some of the bloodiest, most intimate fighting that these veteran soldiers had ever seen. Ewell, arriving on the main battlefield, was able to reinforce Winder enough to slow the Federal advance. But the carnage in the wheatfield was awful. The 31st Virginia lost 97 of its 226 officers and men.[5] Now everything depended on Taylor's Louisianans. For them the battle began when, upon their arrival on top of the Coaling—just as loud cheers went up from the battlefield below as the Union troops broke Winder's line, forcing it backward—Federal guns unleashed a storm canister "full in the faces of the Louisiana infantry . . . tearing great gaps in their ranks, strewing the [slope] behind them with the wounded and dying."[6]

The fighting soon centered on those Federal batteries and their cannons, limbers, caissons, horses, artillerists, and supporting infantry. Much of the combat was brutally personal, bayonet against bayonet, clubbed musket against clubbed musket, men killing men and being covered in the blood of their enemies. Artillerymen swung their rammers—normally used to load cannons—in the absence of anything better.[7] Horses were bayoneted and shot to keep the Union from removing its guns, and their screams joined those of the men. "It was a sickening sight," recalled one of the Louisianans, "men in gray and blue piled up in front of and around the guns and with the horses dying and the blood of men and beasts flowing almost in a stream."[8] Said Taylor, "I have never seen so many dead and wounded in the same limited space."[9] Three times the Federal batteries were seized and then lost, and soon the entire focus of the battle had shifted from the wheatfield to the Coaling. The great Federal counterstroke against Winder stalled.

At about 10:00 a.m., with a final, mighty surge, Taylor, reinforced now by two regiments under Ewell, finally took the last gun, while Winder, on the plain below him, with pieces of various regiments, swept forward. The Union line staggered, then broke, and the bluecoats turned and headed hastily back up the road they had come in on. Jackson took a moment to pray, with his head bowed and his right hand in the air, as was his custom. And then he unleashed his artillery—deadly, bone-and-sinew-shredding canister from the equivalent of giant shotguns—on the receding blue column. A four-mile chase netted 450 prisoners, 800 muskets, and a field gun. But the land soon became too thickly wooded for further pursuit. The battle was over.

Somehow it was perfectly in keeping with Frémont's character that he should arrive, bayonets bristling, on the ground across the South Fork of the Shenandoah, where he could only watch helplessly as the Confederates marched their prisoners to the rear. It had escaped his notice, some hours before, that an entire Confederate division had left his front. At about ten o'clock he finally got up the courage to form his army in battle line and move forward, only to find that there was not a single enemy picket in sight. All he found was a church full of dead and dying men, with the now familiar pile of stacked arms and legs outside. Undaunted, Frémont marched crisply to the North River, where he discovered that the bridge had been burned. In the absence of any other obvious course of action, he mustered his impressive force on the riverbank opposite the battlefield. "In the afternoon he had advanced into the open ground near the river," recalled Confederate chaplain J. William Jones, "and as I gazed on his long line of battle, his bright muskets gleaming in the rays of the sun, his battle-flags rippling in the breeze, I thought it the finest military display I had ever seen."[10]

It was also entirely pointless. Frémont decided to open fire with his artillery anyway, which sent Jackson into a fury because many of the shells fell among the casualties. Frémont, he wrote later, "opened his artillery upon our ambulances and parties engaged in the humane labors of attending to our dead and wounded and the dead and wounded of the enemy." Jackson wrote a personal note to Union major general Irvin McDowell to complain about it. In the battle he had suffered 800 casualties to Tyler's 1,018—disproportionately high considering he had outnumbered his opponent. Even his staunchest supporters on his staff thought his tactics that day were too impetuous.

In any case, the Battle of Port Republic was over, and he had won it decisively. Usually, in the oddball logic of Stonewall Jackson's valley campaign, victory meant that some form of hunt and chase would begin anew. Not this time. On June 8, ironically just as Ewell was being attacked by Frémont at Cross Keys, Lincoln and Stanton had finally decided that they had had enough of this rogue rebel general marching and countermarching in the valley and twisting their war policies into knots. Lincoln had concluded, possibly correctly, that with Jackson's skills and daring he could probably distract Union authorities indefinitely from the real business at hand: the assault on Richmond, the end of the war. "It is the object of the enemy to create alarms every where else and thereby divert as much of our force from that point as possible," wrote Lincoln to Stanton. "On the contrary, we should stand on the defensive every where else, and direct as much force as possible to Richmond."[11] And so that day new orders went out recalling both Frémont and Shields, though they were not received until the next day. Shields was to join McClellan as soon as possible. Frémont was to withdraw to Harrisonburg and assume a defensive position. He was so scared that Jackson might pursue him that he went an additional twenty-five miles, to Mount Jackson. He did not have much of a future. Less than a month later, when he was placed under the command of a former subordinate—John Pope—Frémont angrily resigned. Shields, who continued to try to blame his defeat at Port Republic on Samuel Carroll—to the increasing disgust of Shields's peers—was put on the shelf and quickly disappeared from public view.

Jackson, meanwhile, was master of all he surveyed. Two Union forces were withdrawing from his front. There was a certain beautiful symmetry to it. The campaign, which started with a single enemy army pursuing Jackson southward through the valley, would end with two beaten Union armies withdrawing from him in a *northerly* direction. A week later, Jackson, in one of his most famous utterances, advised his mapmaker, Hotchkiss, to "never take counsel of your fears."[12] A person who followed such advice, of course, would be doomed to a short life. But at Port Republic Jackson had indeed disregarded the fears that any sane person would have had and produced a stunning victory in a manner that left military men in Richmond and Washington, as well as in the Shenandoah Valley, shaking their heads. His short, unadorned message to Richmond was all the more powerful for its brevity. "Through God's blessing," he wrote, "the Enemy near Port Republic was this day routed with the loss of six (6) pieces of his artillery." Period. He was even briefer with Anna, someone he had been neglecting of late. "God greatly blessed our arms near Port Republic yesterday and today," he wrote. Though he was aware that the Union had changed its mind about fighting in the valley, he did not yet know that Lee and Davis had come almost simultaneously to the same conclusion. The game was in Richmond now. Richmond must be saved.

PART FOUR

STIRRINGS
OF A LEGEND

CHAPTER THIRTY-TWO

ACCLAIM, AND
A NEW MISSION

Jackson was suddenly famous. In spite of his heroics at Manassas, he had until late May 1862 been little more than a catchy nickname operating in the back alleys of Virginia. His troubled winter march on Romney was not much of a credential, nor was his defeat at Kernstown, in spite of its grand political and military repercussions.[1] McDowell was a small-scale dustup on a mountain in a part of the country few had ever heard of. Jackson's victory at Winchester changed all that. His back-to-back victories over two Union armies two weeks later confirmed—if anyone needed more proof—that he hadn't just been lucky. Now, a little more than a month after his first win at McDowell, his name was pulsing through the nation's arteries as the great new military genius of the South. The agents of this transformation were largely the Virginia newspapers, whose stories were circulated and reprinted all over the Confederacy and who, desperate for good tidings in that hopeless spring, loudly trumpeted the news: with less than 17,000 troops (and sometimes far less), Jackson had taken on and routed 52,000 troops in three Union armies. He had inflicted 4,600 casualties (killed, wounded, or captured), seized 9,000 small arms and a vast trove of Union supplies, and had kept more than 40,000 Federal troops from joining McClellan in front of Richmond. In five battles and many smaller engagements from March 23 to June 9, he had marched his men 646 miles, knocked the entire Union war plan in the eastern theater off balance, and had done it all at a cost of 2,750 men. In the late spring of that year he was very likely the most famous soldier in the world.

The Southern press spared no adjectives in relating Jackson's victories. The *Richmond Dispatch* insisted that in "striking blow after blow . . . in stunning succession" Jackson's victories in the valley rivaled Napoléon's legendary Italian campaign.[2] In the flush of victory after Cross Keys and Port Republic, the *Richmond Whig* exulted:

> These two battles are among the most brilliant, if not the most brilliant, of the war. They are the crowning glory of Jackson and his associates. . . . Jackson and his army, in one month, have routed Milroy—annihilated Banks—discomfited Frémont, and overthrown Shields! Was there ever such a series of victories won by an inferior force by dauntless courage and consummate generalship?[3]

While the Confederate press strutted and crowed, Northern newspapers were feasting as usual on spoon-fed misinformation about supposed Union victories over the upstart rebel general. After Cross Keys, a Washington abolitionist paper bragged, ridiculously, that "a battle between Jackson and McDowell" had resulted in "the loss of Gen. Jackson's entire command. . . . Nine thousand prisoners fell into Gen. McDowell's hands."[4] But even in these deeply biased accounts there was a sense that Jackson was something different, a new nemesis to worry about and pay attention to. In the days after the humiliating Union defeat at Winchester, the *New York Times* had persistently painted Nathaniel Banks as "one of the ablest and most useful of our chieftains" because he had *kept Stonewall Jackson from crossing the Maryland border.*[5] Those papers began covering their tracks soon enough, unable to avoid the stark truths of Jackson's victories. Either way, the odd, provocative name "Stonewall Jackson" was finding its way into the culture of the North. Several months later a Northern magazine—the *American Phrenological Journal and Life Illustrated*—even featured an advertisement for Pyles O.K. Soap claiming that Jackson himself used their product and liked it. "Stonewall Jackson nabs it, and sighs for more," read the copy.[6]

His fame spread just as quickly through soldiers' letters, both Union and Confederate, that were often read aloud on family hearths. In the South, these were overwhelmingly adulatory. "I wish we had a whole army filled with Jacksons, and the Yankees would soon be shipped from our soil," wrote a soldier of the 11th Virginia regiment. Wrote another from the 6th Louisiana, "Jackson is perfectly idolized by this army." Northern soldiers sent home their own praise, too, calling him "a man of decided genius," and "this great leader" who had "outgeneralled all our commanders." One Union quartermaster was even court-martialed for pointing out that "Stonewall Jackson had whipped the US in every battle."[7] Porter Alexander, at the time Johnston's chief of ordnance, wrote that Jackson's valley exploits were "unsurpassed in all military history for brilliancy and daring."[8]

Exactly who this new celebrity was, was harder to say. Though his men cheered him loudly when he rode by and boasted of his genius in letters home, they were also painfully aware of how hard they had been used, and how many of their comrades—nearly a third of his force—had simply fallen away, unable or unwilling to follow.[9] And yet this seemingly pitiless man with so little apparent sympathy for human suffering was also a devout Christian. He prayed in his tent and in the woods at 3:00 a.m. He prayed on his horse and prayed in the midst of battle. He encouraged his men to attend religious services, distributed Christian pamphlets, and arranged for preachers to give sermons in the regimental camps. Christians especially took note that he insisted on giving God credit for his victories and even refused to read newspapers that proclaimed his own renown. This was not mere convention or pro forma humility. He genuinely feared that pride and excessive ambition would anger God and destroy the Confederacy. "The manner in which the press, the army, and the people seem to lean upon certain persons is positively frightful," he told his brother-in-law D. H. Hill, referring to himself. "They are forgetting God in the instruments He has chosen. It fills me with alarm."[10] He wrote his Lexington pastor, the Reverend William S. White, asking him to warn his congregation that "if we fail to trust in God & give him all the glory, our cause is ruined."[11] In all this, he seemed to many to be the epitome of the selfless leader, a commodity in short supply in both armies. "No thought of personal advancement, of ambition or applause," wrote Robert Lewis Dabney, his chief of staff at the time, "ever for one instant divided the homage of his heart with his great cause."[12]

Perhaps no commander in the war was quite as isolated from common humanity as Jackson was. Command is lonely anyway; Jackson's policy of sharing little or no important information with his officer corps made it doubly so. He held no councils of war, consulted no one about strategy or tactics. Unlike most generals in the war, he did not even ask for casual advice from peers or subordinates. This isolation was almost certainly made worse by the absence of any emotional leavening in his life: there was no Laura, Ellie, Maggie, or Anna to whom he could spill out his heart behind the safety of closed doors. The loving, affectionate, domestic side of his dual personality had temporarily disappeared. Though he never admitted it—even in letters to Anna—he must have been terribly lonely.

The most human part of him—and the most surprising to his men— was his exceptional kindness, something that everyone who knew him well, from West Point forward, inevitably commented on. It was perhaps the least understandable of all of his unusual personality traits. It did not seem to fit with the rest of him. In spite of the crushing demands of his job, he sat for hours with his surgeon Hunter McGuire to comfort him after a family tragedy, which prompted McGuire to write later of "his great kindness, his tenderness to those in trouble or affliction."[13] Brigadier General William B. Taliaferro, one of the leaders of the revolt against Jackson after Romney, and a man Jackson disliked, who was recuperating from an illness in the valley, wrote that Jackson "insisted that I should rest myself upon his bed; and as he assured me that he had no immediate expectation of collision with the enemy, I consented, and he carefully, with his own hands, threw his blanket over me. I mention this incident to show the genuine kindness of his nature."[14] All of this was part of his growing notoriety, too—a notoriety that, as it lodged itself in the thinking of the Union command, would have everything to do with what happened next in the Virginia theater of the Civil War.

While people in the North and South sought to calibrate the man, and to discover what he was made of, the fundamental truth of him was still his string of stunning victories in the valley campaign. It was so transformative that it naturally inspired jealousy—both then and later—the gist of which was, as Longstreet was the first to say publicly after the war, that Jackson's accomplishment had come against less than excellent Union generals. No one would argue the central point: Banks, Shields, and Frémont were in many ways typical of the early war generals on both sides who did not fight especially well and were soon weeded out. Jackson took what they gave him and ruthlessly exploited their weaknesses. The same could be said for the wartime career of Ulysses S. Grant, who in the first two years of the war operated in a similarly chaotic environment against inferior opponents. At Fort Donelson, where he insisted on "unconditional surrender," which made him famous, he was up against Gideon J. Pillow, one of the worst generals in the war. Lesser generals were the rule, not the exception, in the early part of the war, and the great generals made their names against inferior opposition because that was the only opposition that existed. Such arguments, moreover, miss the fact that Jackson and Grant were both among the great early innovators of the war, for whom the quality of the opposing commanders was merely one of many problems they faced and solved. Both were doing things without precedent in military history, executing marches and military maneuvers and transporting troops and building supply lines in ways that were quite new.

While Jackson was leading his army through the last phase of the valley campaign, an event of singular and momentous importance had taken place in Richmond. That event was not, as one might have expected, the wounding on June 1 of Major General Joseph E. Johnston at the Battle of Seven Pines, a bloody eleven-thousand-casualty stalemate fought after Johnston had attacked McClellan's left wing east of Richmond. Though that might have been a crippling blow to a Confederacy already short of competent generals, it turned out to be a wonderful piece of good fortune. The transformative event was an order, issued by Confederate president Jefferson Davis at 1:30 p.m. on June 1, appointing Robert E. Lee to replace Johnston as commander of the Army of Northern Virginia. This was by no means an obvious move. Lee, while widely respected, had not performed well in his only prior field command in western Virginia in 1861, and had spent the war in a desk job as Davis's military adviser. Many generals in that army did not believe he was equal to the work. A bit too fussy, was the feeling. Now Davis was entrusting him with the fate of Richmond and, by extension, the South. Though no one suspected it at the time, Davis had made what was probably the single most important decision of the war, on either side.

But from the moment he took the job Lee was in an unsustainable position. He had quite possibly taken the worst job in the world. He was outnumbered by McClellan almost two to one. In a pitched battle in front of Richmond, he would stand little chance of surviving. In a siege—favored by Little Mac—he stood no chance at all. A Federal assault, meanwhile, could happen at any moment. This meant that he needed every soldier he could get his hands on, which meant that he needed Jackson, and he needed him now. One of Lee's first moves was to send his valley subordinate three brigades of eight thousand troops so that he could crush whatever remained of Federal resistance in the valley and then join the army in front of Richmond. But Lee soon thought better of it and summoned his newly reinforced valley commander directly to Richmond. Jackson would have preferred to take forty thousand men and burn Philadelphia and Baltimore to the ground, thereby forcing McClellan from Richmond. While Lee would soon come around to his way of thinking, it was too late for that now.

Jackson threw out a wide cavalry screen to "block all awareness of Confederate preparations and movements," then launched 18,500 men and their supply trains over and through the Blue Ridge Mountains. Since he could only lay hands on two hundred train cars, his wagons, cavalry, and artillery all went by roads, while the infantry marched and rode the rails by turns in a hopscotching system of Jackson's own design. It was this large-scale, highly secret troop movement east to join Lee that Confederate congressman Alexander Boteler had observed on that railroad platform in Charlottesville on June 19. Jackson, with his fame ringing through the South and his legend in full ascent, was going east to join Lee and save Richmond. With that city's fate hanging in the balance, Jackson's turn from the valley was one of the most thrilling moments of the war. "We are on the eve of stirring times," wrote Jackson's quartermaster, John Harman, a feeling shared by many of the men in that army.

For Jackson an entirely new war began at an hour past midnight on June 23. That was when he left Fredericks Hall, near Charlottesville, on horseback, bound for a meeting of generals at Lee's headquarters east of Richmond. Jackson traveled as an ordinary subaltern. He carried only a pass for "one officer" and was accompanied by two soldiers and a guide. Using relays of commandeered horses, he rode fifty-two miles in fourteen hours. When he arrived at a large, two-story mansion a few miles northeast of the Richmond city limits, he was told that Lee was working. Unwilling to disturb the senior officer, Jackson walked back into the yard to wait. A few minutes later, Major General D. H. Hill rode up and was startled to discover his brother-in-law Tom, dusty and tired-looking, leaning against a fence. In spite of his frail physique and sometimes sarcastic tongue, Hill was a first-class fighter. He was almost as religious as Jackson. The two men were greeting each other warmly when Lee's aide beckoned them.

Inside the house they found Lee and two other major generals: James Longstreet and Ambrose Powell "A.P." Hill. Longstreet was a strapping six foot two with broad shoulders, a broad face, and a heavy beard. Everything about him was broad and blunt. He had graduated from West Point three years before Jackson. He was bright, self-important, and opinionated. He was also fearless, imperturbable on the battlefield, a dependable if unspectacular fighter who had burnished his reputation at the Battle of Seven Pines. He favored defensive fighting, a position that put him considerably in advance of the thinking of most military men of the moment. Lee trusted him. He had been born in South Carolina but grew up mostly in Georgia. He had spent his military career in a string of dusty outposts, mostly as paymaster. The loss of three children in an epidemic was said to have robbed him of his humor. Jackson knew him from Manassas. "Little Powell" Hill had been in Jackson's West Point class where, along with other members of the Virginia aristocracy, he had made fun of the orphan from the western mountains. He was proud, sensitive, and thin-skinned, and had a hair-trigger temper; he would prove to be one of the South's best fighters. His graduation from West Point had been delayed because of the venereal disease he had contracted—a sickness that helped spoil his chances to marry the lovely Ellen Marcy, who instead chose Powell's close friend George B. McClellan. All four Confederate generals had been at West Point at the same time.

Then there was Lee himself, the soldier's soldier with three decades of spotless military service. He had been born in 1807, the son of Henry "Lighthorse Harry" Lee, a hero of the Revolutionary War. He had graduated second in his class at West Point and distinguished himself in the Mexican-American War, where his daring exploits as a scout and engineer were crucial in enabling Winfield Scott to break enemy defenses in three major American victories. He was the quintessential Virginia aristocrat. He lived in a Greek Revival mansion that was one of the largest homes in antebellum Virginia, and was married to the daughter of George Washington's step-grandson, whom George and Martha Washington had raised as a son. Tall, handsome, and a bit heavyset, with a full gray beard and a head of gray hair, Lee was so gentle and polite, calm and stately that it was difficult to see the fighter in him, though in fact he had a far more pure strain of military character than even Jackson himself. Jackson's interests ranged to literature, poetry; Lee devoted no time to literature and did almost no general reading; his interests beyond his family and his religion were few, and even though he was quite devout, even here he lacked Jackson's taste for more complex theology. The Bible was sufficient. Unlike Jackson, he had by hard study and a career in the service made himself highly proficient in tactics, logistics, and engineering; those military sciences he knew as well as anyone.[15] Just at that moment, Jackson was by far the more famous of the two. Since Lee had not yet proven himself, there were many in the Confederate army, including Jeb Stuart and Gustavus Smith (to whom Jackson pleaded his case for an invasion of the North in August 1861), who did not feel he should have been given the job. His King of Spades nickname originated in his orders to dig fortifications around Richmond, which suggested to his soldiers that he was afraid to go out and fight.

At Lee's field headquarters Stonewall Jackson, who refused food but accepted a glass of milk, now found himself the object of considerable interest.[16] In his "rusty gray dress and still rustier gray forage cap" he stood out "from the spruce young officers under him," according to one of Lee's staff.[17] Jackson was at that moment the most celebrated field commander in the war, and, in fact, in the Western Hemisphere. No one, North or South, had yet done anything like what he had done. Lee as a line general was a largely unknown quantity; he had only just taken command of an army. Though the Manassas victory had brought fame to Beauregard and Johnston, the former was in sharp decline, and Johnston, now wounded, had accomplished nothing since then. In the North there was only Grant in the western theater, though his performance at Shiloh had tarnished him. As Jackson stood there before his peers that afternoon, he was a bit of a wonder. He was also what he was to everyone else: a stubborn mystery.

Lee explained his plan, which had its origins in Jeb Stuart's daring hundred-mile ride with 1,200 cavaliers around McClellan's entire army between June 12 and June 15. Stuart had discovered, among other things, that McClellan's right flank was vulnerable. Not only did it contain far fewer soldiers than the force south of the Chickahominy, but also the flank itself was "in the air"—not anchored by any natural formation or obstacle. And it was that flank that Lee proposed to turn. He described the Union army's position astride the Chickahominy River, a sluggish, swampy creek that ran roughly northwest to southeast, on the east side of Richmond. It roughly bisected the peninsula that was defined by the York and Pamunkey Rivers on the north and the James River on the South. The problem Lee faced was that he did not believe he could carry a frontal assault against the 30,000 troops in the Federal 5th Corps under Major General Fitz John Porter who were dug in behind the Chickahominy.

His solution was to send Jackson's army on a march to the north of Porter's army. He would march clear around the Union right, flank, then turn and strike to the south, threatening the main Union supply line. If the plan worked, Porter, facing envelopment, would be forced to abandon his position. As that happened, the Confederate army would commence a gigantic wheeling motion, sending sixty thousand soldiers *en echelon* against the collapsing Federal right. Forced from its defensive redoubts and falling back to protect its supply base on the York River, McClellan's army would have to come out into the open and fight, giving away all of its present defensive advantages. Just as important, the Union army would have to abandon its positions in front of Richmond.

The key, in any case, was Jackson. It had to be. His very name might be enough to turn the Union right. The generals agreed, with Lee's endorsement, that Jackson's army was to be in place on the night of June 25 and that he would begin his flank march in the early-morning hours of June 26. The four-hour conference broke up at about 7:00 p.m. on June 23. In the next forty-eight hours, Jackson had to ride back to his camp at night in the rain, and then march his army more than thirty miles into the brushy, swampy tangles of the York-James Peninsula and get it ready to fight. His legend said he had the fastest-moving army in history. That notion would now be severely tested.

CHAPTER THIRTY-THREE

THE HILLJACK
AND THE SOCIETY BOY

In the fourteenth month of the Civil War, its two most celebrated generals, east or west, were George McClellan and Stonewall Jackson.[1] They were both in the Virginia theater, so it was inevitable that they would fight. The two men were famous for such different reasons. Jackson owed his instant celebrity to his victories in the valley. McClellan's fame was barely rooted in conquest at all. Though he had won a small fight in the western theater and a minor battle at Williamsburg on his way up the peninsula, Little Mac was mainly known as the man who had rescued the army—and the United States itself—from its deep despair after the Battle of Manassas. In personality and physical build the two men were virtual antipodes. McClellan was as compact, hearty, and outgoing as Jackson was gaunt, reserved, severe, and silent. Jackson was the equivalent of an attack dog who had to be restrained from marching on Philadelphia and Baltimore, while McClellan had had to be cajoled, coaxed, and sometimes lugged by Lincoln and Stanton every step of the way to Richmond, where he still had not managed to mount an attack. Jackson often camped with his men; McClellan never did. Mac was constantly telling his men how good they were and how proud he was of them; Jackson did this only rarely. McClellan never visited battlefields, and had an instinctive horror of the bloody front; Jackson took Anna on a tour of Manassas.

In spite of these differences, the two generals shared one very large and important attribute: they had both been members of the Class of 1846 at the US Military Academy, a class that eventually produced more generals—

twenty-two, twelve Union and ten Confederate, including two lieutenant generals and fourteen major generals—than any West Point class to that point in history. But even as part of this tiny, cloistered world where the graduating class numbered only fifty-nine, their experiences at West Point were as different as the men themselves.

It was remarkable that Jackson had been allowed into the place at all. His education, like that of many rural Americans of his era, fell somewhere between inadequate and incomplete. His uncle Cummins, who raised him, had never liked the idea of book learning much anyway and considered Tom the least smart of his brother's three children. Thus whatever instruction Jackson got was spotty at best: winter months at a rural elementary school (the children were needed for summer and fall for harvests); a brief time at a school that he persuaded Cummins to start at Jackson's Mill; and a few years at slightly more sophisticated schools in the nearby town of Weston. He did like learning, and read whatever he got his hands on, which wasn't much. By the time he was fifteen, he was accomplished enough—by Virginia mountain standards, anyway—to receive a county appointment to teach eleven- and twelve-year-olds in a log cabin.

In spite of his educational shortcomings, in the spring of 1842 Jackson had made application to his local congressman, Samuel L. Hays, for an appointment to West Point. Jackson and three others took a set of informal examinations, the most important of which was mathematics, a discipline in which Jackson had little formal training. Unfortunately, he was not quite as good in that subject as his friend Gibson Butcher, who got the appointment instead. Jackson was deeply disappointed. He had seen the academy, with its free education and promise of a military career, as a chance to escape the rural life at Jackson's Mill.

Then something happened to offer new hope. It took Butcher exactly one day to bust out of West Point. He quickly realized that he hated the whole idea of the place, returned home immediately, and told his friend Tom Jackson what he had done. Jackson, sensing opportunity, decided to reapply. He used his family connections to marshal recommendations from local officials, took crash courses in math and grammar from family friends, then traveled by stagecoach and train to Washington, DC, where he unloaded the whole scheme—Butcher's resignation plus his own hastily solicited endorsements and renewed application—on a surprised Congressman Hays, who happened to be a neighbor of his uncle Cummins. Jackson got the appointment.

But mere appointment was only the first step in a West Point candidacy. In those days applicants had to travel to the academy in June to undergo the ordeal of formal entrance tests. In the examination room, Jackson was required to stand at a blackboard and solve problems presented to him by the examining board. Nothing in his own academic background had prepared him for such a trial, and he found the examination excruciatingly difficult. As he labored through his problems, sweat streamed off his face. He wiped it off first with one cuff and then the other. Somehow he also became covered with chalk. His classmates found the process painful to watch. Several days later, the board posted the results of the examination: of 122 candidates, 30 had failed, leaving only 92 students who would enter the first-year class. Jackson's name was the very last on the list. It was thought by some that he had not passed at all, but somehow the sheer, wretched, sweat-stained doggedness of his effort had convinced the board to let him in.

When the new admit arrived at his barracks, wearing his plain gray homespun clothing, a coarse felt hat, and oversized leather brogans and carrying a pair of weather-stained saddlebags, he looked very much like what he was: a semieducated bumpkin from the Allegheny Mountains.[2] He seemed quite out of place. He was visibly uncomfortable. When a fellow cadet from Virginia named Dabney Maury came to his room to say hello, Jackson, in Maury's words, "received my courteous advances in a manner so chilling that it caused me to regret having made them, and I rejoined my companions with criticisms brief and emphatic as to his intellectual endowments."[3] Those companions included future Confederate generals George Pickett and A. P. Hill.

George Brinton McClellan's entrance into West Point could not have been more different. While Jackson's father was a failed lawyer, compulsive gambler, and alcoholic who died when Jackson was two and left the family destitute, McClellan's Yale-educated father built a thriving surgical practice in Philadelphia, founded a medical college, edited an influential journal, and owned a stable of trotting horses. He had married Elizabeth Steinmetz Brinton, from one of Philadelphia's leading families. Together they moved in the upper stratum of that city's society, counted Daniel Webster among their friends, and gave their son George an education fully appropriate to his social rank.[4] He was sent first to an elite private elementary school, and then to a private tutor with whom he learned to read the classics and to converse in both Latin and French. He was a brilliant student, a prodigy in both language and mathematics. He was also charming, engaging, and anything but a grind. He was, said his sister, "the brightest, merriest, most unselfish of boys."[5] He briefly attended a preparatory academy and then, at age thirteen, enrolled in the University of Pennsylvania. Two years later he had, according to his father, "nearly completed his classical education at the university," and he enrolled at West Point at age fifteen and a half.[6] Most of the other admits were at least eighteen, and some were twenty or older. While the miserable Jackson toiled and sweated at the blackboard, the magnificently prepared McClellan breezed into the academy. According to one classmate, "he went at once to the head of the class, and remained there until the end."[7]

What he and Jackson encountered there, when classes began in the fall, was one of the nation's toughest and most demanding academic programs. As the nation's top engineering school, West Point was math-heavy and math-driven. The academy was, moreover, a true university, requiring students to pass courses in ten different fields of study.[8] Examinations were held twice a year, in January and June, and each one was an academic watershed: if you failed, you went home, never to return. When Jackson went on the school's only vacation—a single furlough in the middle of a four-year course of study—he told his nephew Thomas Arnold that at one point he was allowed only three weeks to "learn the English grammar" and that if he failed he would have been sent home immediately. "Oh, I tell you I had to work hard," he said.[9] The daily regimen itself was tough, too: cadets awoke at 5:00 a.m., and the day that followed included ten hours of homework in addition to classes and drills. The barracks were primitive and chilly in winter; food was often "bull-beef" and boiled potatoes. Strangely—in retrospect—the only part of the curriculum specifically related to the operations of an army was Professor Dennis Hart Mahan's fourth-year course on engineering, fortifications, and military tactics. Mahan, moreover, devoted a mere nine hours of class time to army organization and battlefield tactics. The brevity of the course, plus the fact that many of its dogmas were frozen in Napoleonic times, would limit the effect of Mahan's teachings on the Mexican-American and Civil Wars. (Grant later dismissed the effect almost entirely;[10] Jackson did take two of Mahan's principles to heart: "celerity" and "boldness."[11])

Jackson struggled. He stayed up late at night, piling anthracite coal on his metal grate while "boning" his lessons for the next day. As he would do later at VMI, he spent hours staring at a blank wall while rehearsing his homework in his mind. "No one I have ever known," said one of his barracks mates, "could so perfectly withdraw his mind from surrounding objects or influence, and so thoroughly involve his whole being in the subject under consideration."[12] And though he developed a few friends, he remained for the most part a social misfit. He walked around campus with his head down, looking neither right nor left.[13] He was modest and shy to a fault. He blushed when spoken to. When he did speak, according to schoolmate John C. Tidball, "his voice was thin and feminine—almost squeaky—while his utterances were quick, jerky, and sententious," and did not encourage further conversation.[14] He did not participate in extracurricular activities such as group swims in the Hudson, summer dances, or bull sessions. He was always too busy studying.[15] Then, too, he had a stomach ailment—presumably dyspepsia—that caused him to stand or sit in a bizarrely stiff posture. According to one of his classmates, he was afraid that he might otherwise compress some of his internal organs and make the condition worse.[16] All of this foreshadowed his health obsessions as an adult. Other cadets found such practices bizarre, to say the least.[17]

One of the better-known anecdotes of Jacksonian behavior came from the same cadet, Dabney Maury, who had tried unsuccessfully to befriend him on the first day. During summer, when they lived in tents, Maury and two of his Virginia friends, A. P. Hill and Birkett Fry (also a future Confederate general), were "lolling upon our camp bedding" when Jackson happened by on evening "police duty," which involved cleaning up trash. In Maury's account, he "lifted the tent wall, and addressed [Jackson] with an air of authority and mock sternness, ordering him to be more attentive to his duty, to remove those cigar stumps, and otherwise mind his business." Jackson responded with such a "stern and angry" look that Maury later went to his tent to apologize. "Mr. Jackson," he said, "I find I made a mistake just now in speaking to you in a playful manner not justified by our slight acquaintance. I regret that I did so." Jackson leveled a stony gaze at him and said, "That is perfectly satisfactory, sir." Maury then returned to his friends, telling them flatly, "Cadet Jackson, from Virginia, is an ass."[18] That was the last meaningful social interaction the three aristocratic Virginians had with him at West Point.

On one occasion—and only one—Jackson provided a glimpse of the unbending moral absolutism that was to characterize his later dealings with William French in Florida. During one inspection, a cadet had stolen Jackson's scrupulously clean musket and replaced it with his own dirty one. Jackson reported the loss. The cadet was soon found with Jackson's weapon and then lied about how he had gotten it. For once Jackson's shyness left him: he was furious. He demanded that the cadet be court-martialed and expelled. It was only after much persuasion by his peers and officers that he was convinced not to press charges.[19]

McClellan had none of these problems. His main worry was whether he would lead his class, or have to settle for second or third place. He was so smart that he could coast through courses others found difficult. He wrote his brother that he was doing "not much, I confess" in the way of studying. In French he did hardly anything at all, and still ranked eighth in the class.[20] McClellan was not only obviously brilliant, but he had a sparkling, gregarious personality that made him one of the most popular cadets in his class. Even his academic rival Charles Stewart found him to be a generous and honorable man who had "not a mean thought in him." Nor was McClellan a narrow or prudish conformist. On New Year's Eve during his first year he and several friends risked punishment to procure a late-night feast of oyster pies from a well-known, off-limits local tavern.[21] Teachers liked him, too. Erasmus Keyes, his artillery instructor—who would later command the 4th Corps of the Army of the Potomac under McClellan in the peninsula campaign—wrote that "a pleasanter pupil was never called to the blackboard."[22] McClellan made many close friends, including his roommate A. P. Hill. Those friends tended to be from the South, and from the upper echelons of society. McClellan would always carry a deep, abiding sympathy for that part of the country. (That feeling would become more and more apparent as the war progressed.) It is not known how much interaction he and his classmate Jackson had, though in such a small group of young men they certainly came into frequent contact with each other. (After the Mexican-American War, Jackson made a point of visiting McClellan and Dabney Maury when he was on court-martial duty at West Point, where both were on the faculty.[23]) In any case, there would seem to have been an uncrossable social and academic gulf separating the two cadets, one that very little could possibly change.

Then something interesting happened. Into this rather predictable narrative of the casually successful Philadelphia blue blood and the struggling Appalachian orphan came a new story line entirely: Jackson, who had started his West Point career dead last in the weakest section, known as the Immortals, began a steady rise in the class ranks. It is hard to imagine the sort of pressure he was under that first semester as the worst student in a class that was undoubtedly going to shrink substantially, as West Point classes did. The fear of washing out, and returning home a failure, must have been harrowing. He barely made it through the January exams, which weeded out another 16 students. His 62nd in math saved him. After the June exams at the end of the first year, only 72 of the original 122 students remained. Someone paying close attention that spring might have noticed the remarkable progress of cadet Thomas J. Jackson, who suddenly ranked 51st in the class.

Against all expectations he was rising fast, finally catching up to all that secondary education he had never had. In his second year he encountered the guts of the academy's math program, much dreaded by cadets: analytical geometry and calculus. He was, as it happened, very good at both. In the January 1844 exams he rose to 21st—a stunning achievement, considering where he had started out. He did well in other subjects, too. Only in drawing was he still mired with the other Immortals. (Drawing was entirely related to military uses, sketching fortifications and so forth.) He was by now so confident that he wrote his sister, Laura, that "unless fortune frowns on me more than it has yet, I shall graduate in the upper half of my class."[24] By the end of junior year—when he roomed with future Union cavalry general George Stoneman, almost as taciturn as he—he had placed 11th in natural philosophy (the subject he later taught), one of the academy's toughest courses, and 30th in general merit. By the time he graduated he ranked 17th in a class of 59, a feat driven partly by his number 4 ranking in logic, which many cadets considered "a bugbear"—a course even harder than natural philosophy. One cadet compared Jackson to "a meteor."[25]

There were other changes in Jackson's life, too. Though he was still stiff, formal, and shy, he had found his place in the class. He had clearly earned his classmates' respect. He actually loved the place. "It grieves me," he wrote Laura in his last year, "that in a short time, I must be separated from amiable and meritorious friends whom an acquaintance of years has endeared to me by many ties." In spite of his oddities, his schoolmates noticed that he did have a "sweet smile of recognition" for people he knew.[26] Perhaps his best trait was his kindness, which was noted by more than one of his classmates. Future Confederate general William Gardner noticed it when Jackson, unsolicited, came to console him while he was under arrest and confined to quarters. Sickness and grief in his fellows seemed to always elicit sympathy from Jackson.[27] One of Jackson's roommates, Tennessean Parmenas Turnley, wrote later, "While there were many who seemed to surpass him in intellect, in geniality, and in good-fellowship, there was no one of our class who more absolutely possessed the respect and confidence of all."[28]

Except possibly George McClellan, of course, the nineteen-year-old undisputed star of the class. He finished second. As president of the Dialectic Society—which held the intellectual elite of West Point's senior class— he delivered the valedictory address at graduation. He was as much of a grand success walking out of the academy's doors as he had been entering through them four years before. But if his classmates thought he was perfect, his correspondence showed that he was perhaps not quite. There were flashes, in his letters home, of the petulance, self-pity, and vainglory that would later damage his career. He bridled for much of his West Point life, for example, that he was not number one in the class, which he attributed to unfairness. "Toiling uphill is not what it is cracked up to be," he complained to his mother. "I do not get marked as well for a good (or better) recitation, as the man above me."[29] When he found out he would graduate number two instead of number one, he wrote his family, "I must confess that I have enough malice in me to want to show them that if I did not graduate at the head of my class, I can nevertheless do something." And always there was his almost melancholy sense of the burden of his own talent. "I know not what fate has in store for me," he wrote his sister, "I only know that I must expect the hardest of trials a proud spirit can bear before I can effect anything." He might have been writing in the spring of 1862, as his old classmate Tom Jackson was bearing down on his Army of the Potomac, unseen, from the high, rain-swept battlements of the Blue Ridge Mountains.

CHAPTER THIRTY-FOUR

THE DEFENSE OF RICHMOND

⊷⊰⊱⊶

The news of Stonewall Jackson's arrival in front of Richmond ran through the Army of Northern Virginia like an electric current, and it spread from mouth to mouth until suddenly, according to one soldier, "a deafening shout burst from our men; thousands of throats took it up and rent the very air; it died away only to be repeated with greater emphasis and volume. . . . Stonewall Jackson here! The genius of our Southern cause— its very soul. What could he know of failure? Every soldier in the ranks felt safe; the magic of that name, the prestige of his corps, was such that the most doubting Thomas had no longer any fears."[1]

They had prayed that Jackson would come, and now, in their hour of greatest peril, he and his army had marched in, fresh from their brilliant valley campaign, ready to save the day, the city, the Confederacy. The moment was purely theatrical: one of the South's few authentic heroes had arrived at the very time and place where he was needed most—the gloom-ridden, despondent city of Richmond, in whose eastern approaches stood McClellan's restless Army of the Potomac—to redeem the Southern cause. Until his arrival, there had been little to hope for. The bloody stalemate at the Battle of Seven Pines on May 31–June 1 had accomplished nothing more than to fill the city's hospitals with wounded men. And now came the very real prospect that the city might fall. Plenty of Northerners believed that it would; newspapers in New York and Boston were boasting of the inevitable victory. Expecting the worst, many Richmond residents had already fled. President Davis and other politicians had dispatched their families southward. Trains loaded with Confederate gold and government documents were ready to roll out of the city at a moment's notice. Major

348

General Joseph E. Johnston, recuperating from his recent wounds, was so certain that McClellan would capture Richmond that he arranged for a special train to take him out of the city.[2] While Union soldiers drilled in their camps, gnawed on hard biscuits, and complained about the heat, Richmond prepared for battle, siege, and more death.

How could one dusty, disheveled major general and 18,500 ragged troops possibly live up to such outlandish expectations? That is one of the most intriguing questions of the war. Because Jackson, against all odds, *did*. He fulfilled all of his countrymen's most wildly optimistic and absurdly unrealistic expectations of him, and he did it before summer's end. It is a matter of record that, mainly on the strength of Lee's daring and Jackson's astounding maneuvers, within two months the capital being threatened was no longer Richmond but *Washington, DC*, a city into which the defeated Union army beat a humiliating retreat—the greatest military disaster of the war to date.

Just how that happened is one of the great stories of the war. It did not happen right away. First the rebel generals had to deal with the immense army in front of them.

The counteroffensive began as an idea in the mind of Robert E. Lee. In late June 1862 the problem he faced was obvious enough: how to force a very large Union army away from Richmond. Even though with Jackson's troops and other reinforcements he would soon have eighty-five thousand to ninety thousand men at his disposal, he did not believe he could succeed in a frontal assault against the entrenched Federals. He was absolutely certain that he could not win a purely defensive battle.

What he could do, however, was use the enormous size of the Union army against itself.[3]

That army, camped deep inside enemy territory, was dependent on its lines of supply to deliver the six hundred tons of food, clothing, weaponry, ammunition, fodder, tents, and multitudinous other sundries it needed every day to survive. It was far too big to live off the land. Without those supplies it would turn very quickly from a fighting force into an assemblage of starving men and horses. The lines that fed it were long and sinuous: they had their origins in New York, Philadelphia, Baltimore, and other Northern cities. The matériel came by wagon, train, and eventually by boat down the Chesapeake Bay and then up the York and Pamunkey Rivers to a place called White House Landing, about twenty airline miles

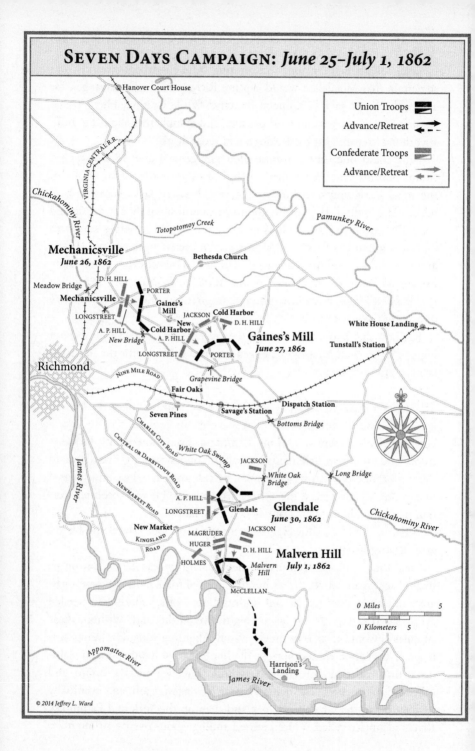

SEVEN DAYS CAMPAIGN: *June 25–July 1, 1862*

Hanover Court House

Union Troops

Advance/Retreat

Confederate Troops

Advance/Retreat

Chickahominy River

VIRGINIA CENTRAL R.R.

Totopotomoy Creek

Pamunkey River

Mechanicsville
June 26, 1862

Bethesda Church

Meadow Bridge

D. H. HILL

PORTER

Mechanicsville

Gaines's
Mill

JACKSON

Cold Harbor

LONGSTREET

New
Cold Harbor

D. H. HILL

White House Landing

A. P. HILL

A. P. HILL

Gaines's Mill
June 27, 1862

Tunstall's Station

New Bridge

LONGSTREET

PORTER

Richmond

NINE MILE ROAD

Grapevine Bridge

Fair Oaks

Savage's Station

Dispatch Station

Seven Pines

Bottoms Bridge

CHARLES CITY ROAD

White Oak Swamp

JACKSON

James River

CENTRAL OR DARBYTOWN ROAD

White Oak Bridge

Long Bridge

NEWMARKET ROAD

A. P. HILL

LONGSTREET

Glendale

Glendale
June 30, 1862

Chickahominy River

New Market

MAGRUDER

JACKSON

KINGSLAND ROAD

HUGER

D. H. HILL

Malvern Hill
July 1, 1862

HOLMES

Malvern Hill

McCLELLAN

0 Miles 5

0 Kilometers 5

Appomattox River

Harrison's
Landing

James River

© 2014 Jeffrey L. Ward

due east of Richmond. Lee knew it well. The White House plantation had been the home of his wife, Mary's, great-grandmother Martha Custis at the time she married George Washington. It had later been inherited by Lee's son Rooney. When Federal troops took possession of the mansion and converted it to Little Mac's headquarters, it was Mary's principal residence. McClellan, always attentive to proper protocol, saw to it that Mrs. R. E. Lee was escorted through the lines.[4]

In the late spring of 1862, this pier on the Pamunkey had become the lifeline of McClellan's epic move against Richmond. In the river were boats of every sort, steam-powered and sail-powered and man-powered, stacked and gammed in rows that spread out into the lazy current and that were tethered ultimately to a succession of floating wharves where goods were unloaded. There were floating hospitals, too, sutlers' stores selling every-thing from toothbrushes to potted lobster, roads jammed with wagons, quartermaster officers, sailors, African-American laborers, and other con-trabands, mules, and horses.[5] Here, too, was the terminus of the telegraph wire from Washington, strung along a circuitous, two-hundred-mile path from the War Department to Wilmington, down the Eastern Shore of Maryland, and up the York-James Peninsula. With its electrical current, electromagnets, and pulses of Morse code, it was one of the technological wonders of the age. Through it ran all of Lincoln's chiding and coaxing, as well as McClellan's dilatory, self-protective replies. From White House Landing the supplies were loaded onto train cars on the Richmond and York River Railroad and hauled westward to the Union camps in front of the Confederate capital.

Thus everything the Union army needed to survive—all that tonnage produced by McClellan's vast logistical machine and transported from points hundreds of miles away—ultimately ran down a single, vulnerable railroad track. To threaten it was to threaten the army itself. Lee under-stood this. As he considered the scene in front of Richmond, he saw some-thing else, too. The Chickahominy River, which ran parallel to the James and roughly bisected the peninsula, was swollen and unfordable: the bogs and marshes of its timbered bottomlands were up to a mile wide in places, making it impossible for cavalry or artillery to cross. At high water—which there was plenty of that spring—it was too swampy even for light infantry.[6] Crossing was possible only by bridge, and there were only half a dozen of them spread along fifteen river miles in front of Richmond; some of them were washed out.

To protect the railroad line on both sides of the Chickahominy, McClellan had been forced to split his army. Jeb Stuart's swashbuckling ride had shown Lee precisely how he had done it. McClellan had deployed eighty thousand men in front of the city, south of the river. But north of the river, on his right flank, he had placed only a single army corps of thirty thousand men under General Fitz John Porter, an army lifer and McClellan crony who had graduated a year ahead of Jackson at West Point and had later been a cavalry and artillery instructor there.[7] (The rest of the Union right was camped on the south side of the river.) Because of the difficulty of moving an army across the Chickahominy, Porter could not be easily or quickly reinforced. In this Lee saw a compounding of Union weaknesses. He saw opportunity. A successful attack north of the Chickahominy against the numerically inferior Porter would in turn threaten the Union's railroad and supply depot, which would then compel McClellan's main force to fall back from its advanced positions in front of the city.

There were two problems with Lee's idea. The first was that Porter occupied one of the war's best defensive positions, one that Confederate engineers themselves had scouted earlier and determined would be almost impregnable.[8] Lee's answer to this, in the plan he outlined at the generals' meeting on Nine Mile Road, was to avoid attacking Porter directly. Instead, he would send Jackson and his army to march around Porter's flank and head straight for the railroad in his rear. With Jackson behind him—specifically Jackson, his name ablaze with its new celebrity—Porter would have no choice but to pull out of his breastworks and rifle pits and move rearward. He would then be out in the open, where Lee could unleash his wheeling attack. Of course, all this required precision in both timing and movement. The maneuvers were to be executed by an inexperienced staff under a novice commanding officer and subordinate officers who were unused to cooperating with each other.

The second, and far more serious, problem was that by placing sixty-five thousand Confederate troops—six of his ten divisions—north of the Chickahominy, Lee had at most twenty-five thousand troops under Generals John Magruder and Benjamin Huger to defend the city. He was not only leaving a token force to defend the Confederate capital—an almost crazy risk all by itself—he was also planning to deploy the bulk of his army on the far side of a swollen river, from which point it would be difficult or impossible to come to Richmond's aid. It was the inverse of the tactical dilemma Lee intended to inflict on McClellan. To say that Lee's plan was fraught with danger is to understate the point: he was risking everything—his army, his capital city, perhaps the survival of the Confederacy itself. If McClellan and his generals understood for a moment what Lee was doing, and acted on it, they would have little trouble smashing Richmond's defenses. As Lee saw it, he did not have much choice. Waiting in Richmond for McClellan to haul up his big siege guns and blow the rebels out of their trenches did not seem to him a reasonable option.

It was thus to Lee's considerable dismay that, at about 8:30 a.m. on June 25, the day before his planned offensive, and after most of his troops had been moved into place for the next day's advances, brigades of McClellan's army attacked the Confederate army in front of Richmond. Several miles north, Lee listened to the sounds of the battle, and worried. Had McClellan learned of his plans? Was this the beginning of the final assault that had been so long in the making? It must have taken an enormous effort of will not to modify his plans. But he did not. He believed he knew McClellan, and he did not think McClellan was going to hazard his infantry against Richmond's trenches. Lee would soon be proven right. In reality what he was hearing was a halfhearted advance by a general who had been prodded into it and still wasn't certain he wanted to do it. McClellan wrote to Stanton that same day with his now familiar complaint that he was badly outnumbered: "The rebel force is stated at two hundred thousand, including Jackson and Beauregard," he wrote.[9] If he truly believed this, his actions defied logic. Why would he willingly attack a force twice his size? Why did he, at the same moment, seem so confident that he himself was not going to be attacked? These questions have never been answered, though divining Confederate numbers and deployments was not exactly a dark art. One of McClellan's brigade commanders, Brigadier General George G. Meade, figured out that the Confederate front at Richmond was thin and vulnerable; even the correspondent for the *Philadelphia Inquirer* got Lee's troop strength roughly right.[10] But something inside McClellan wanted it that way. In the same letter there was an undertone of tragic vainglory, almost martyr-like, that hinted at his state of mind: "I regret my great inferiority in numbers but feel I am in no way responsible for it," he went on. "I will do all that a General can with the splendid Army I have the honor to command & if it is destroyed by overwhelming numbers can at least die with it & share its fate."[11] It was a kind of miracle, in fact, that McClellan was finally sending the men forward at all.

He would not send them very far. Though the initial Union attacks gained ground, the Union commanders soon began to worry that they were facing some version of the 180,000-to-200,000-man Confederate army of Pinkerton's fictions and McClellan's nightmares. General Joseph Hooker, commanding a division, somehow concluded that he was outnumbered three to one, a bit of utterly unjustified paranoia that made its way quickly back to its most receptive audience, George McClellan. The fear was enough to send the Union brigades, under Little Mac's orders, scurrying back to their entrenchments. McClellan, who had been managing the battle from three miles in the rear by the technological innovation of the battlefield telegraph, then rode to the front. Climbing a tree as bullets zipped by him—he never seemed personally afraid of gunfire—and seeing no overwhelming enemy presence, he sent his troops forward again. They proceeded to retake the six hundred yards of ground they had lost in the morning. Then night fell. The fight that day pitted approximately seventeen thousand Federals against roughly seven thousand rebels.[12] If the attack seemed tepid, it was because McClellan had never had any intention of sending his army in a full assault on the city. He was clinging to his old idea: the way to take Richmond was to get close enough to move one hundred big siege guns up and pound the place into rubble. His plan that day was to take just enough real estate to allow that to happen. For whatever reason, he could not shake a genuine distaste for sending his brave, adoring soldiers into a bloody fight. "Every poor fellow that is killed or wounded almost haunts me!" he had written his wife, Nell, on June 23 from White House. "My only consolation is that I have done my best to save as many lives as possible."[13] Lee would turn out to have no such scruples.

While the 1,067-casualty Battle of Oak Grove, as it came to be known, was being fought in front of Richmond, Jackson and his army were moving toward their appointed destination above the Union right, from which they would launch their flanking movement the following morning. Their march was a small disaster, the first of many disasters, small and large, that would occur in the week of battles that came to be known as the Seven Days. Jackson's columns started late, in the rain, and proceeded in airless, suffocating heat. The streams were all running high. Commissary wagons were bogged down in deep mud. Bridges were out—having been washed away or destroyed by Union cavalry. Maps were abysmal and often completely wrong. Lee's directions were impossibly complicated. ("If a second column continued on the Ash Cake Road to J. Overton, & thence on the road to Pole Green Church, it would strike the road from Shady Grove Church to Old Raleigh, a mile & three quarters east of the Shady Grove Church," and so on.[14]) This was not the open, gently rolling, mountain-bracketed land of the Shenandoah Valley. Here you could not see anything. Here an army division could be half a mile from you and you would not know it. Making everything worse was the fumbling presence of Robert L. Dabney, a leading Presbyterian theologian and friend of Jackson's but a desperately poor choice for chief of staff. In this new wilderness he was completely overmatched; a severe case of diarrhea combined with Jackson's reluctance to share information with him made him almost useless. Equally distressing in this soggy labyrinth was the absence of mapmaker Jedediah Hotchkiss, whom Jackson to his regret had dispatched on other business back to Staunton. Then, too, whatever secrecy Lee had hoped for had been blown sky high, as evidenced by the persistent Federal cavalry attacks: the Union high command was well aware of Jackson's approach. At the end of the day the exhausted army was forced to stop six miles short of its destination. They had covered twenty-five miles. Still, considering that Jackson was to launch an offensive in the morning, six miles was a long way. The single bright note was the arrival of Jeb Stuart with two thousand cavalry, whom Lee had sent to cover Jackson's left during the following day's march.

That night offered a rare window into Jackson's preparations for war. At about midnight, Generals Chase Whiting and Richard Ewell called on him at his farmhouse headquarters to suggest a route of march for the next day. Jackson listened, and told them he would consider it. As the two generals left, Ewell remarked to Whiting, "Don't you know why Old Jack would not decide at once? He is going to pray over it first!"[15] When Ewell discovered he had left his sword in Jackson's room and returned for it, he indeed found Jackson on his knees, deep in prayer. According to Robert Dabney, the general had spent the evening pacing his chamber, receiving visits from officers, and "wrestling with God." After Ewell and Whiting left, he spent the rest of that night in prayer and preparation for the great operation that was now before him.[16]

He would have done better to sleep. Jackson, in fact, was once again in an advanced state of exhaustion. He was likely also in the early phases of some sort of severe cold or sickness—"fever and debility," as he described it to his wife later in the week.[17] Including that night, he had spent three sleepless nights in a row. He had had no more than seven hours' sleep in the preceding four days. During that time he had ridden more than ninety miles without rest to and from Lee's meeting, then added another twenty-five miles on June 25 with his army. The day ahead was to be momentous. Jackson must have been a physical wreck. It was amazing that he could even stay awake in his saddle. Somehow he went on.

The march the next day—June 26—was as bad as the last. Jackson's men were in a new world now. Nothing went right. Directions were almost impossible to follow. Jackson had ordered his troops to move at 2:30 a.m. but because of balky supply trains and lack of fresh water, they did not move until 8:00 a.m. Jackson's refusal to share information with his officers hurt even more here in tangled thickets where delegation of authority was a necessity. When his column did move, it was struck repeatedly by Union cavalry, which fought small, sharp engagements, burned bridges, and felled trees that acted as barricades. Jackson's troops, swelled now to nearly twenty-four thousand, were forced to march at a dead-slow pace, feeling their way through the wooded thickets "with skirmishers deployed." By 9:00 a.m., as Confederate divisions under D. H. Hill, A. P. Hill, and James Longstreet waited near the Chickahominy, and troops under General John Magruder marched and countermarched and shouted orders to nonexistent regiments and generally carried on an elaborate charade in front of Richmond to deceive the enemy, Jackson's army was already six hours behind schedule. If nerves were beginning to fray, there was good reason. Richmond itself was at stake. Everyone knew that. Everyone knew that McClellan could move forward again at any time, and they wondered: Where is Jackson?

McClellan, meanwhile, was behaving exactly as Lee had believed he would. As the morning of the twenty-sixth passed, he issued no orders to follow up his attack of the previous day. That was because, at least in part, he had concluded that he himself was about to be attacked. He had waited too long, and his procrastination and delays had finally caught up with him. It was a consequence he had not really counted on, because he had wildly underestimated Robert E. Lee. Now, with one of the most remarkable opportunities of the war before him, his fears got the better of him. There was his usual willingness to believe the exaggerated Confederate troop numbers. But added to that was a new variable: fear of Jackson's reputation. McClellan knew for certain now that Jackson was bearing down on his right; in a letter to Stanton on June 25 he predicted that "Jackson will soon attack our right & rear" and pleaded again for more troops, but this time saying, "If I had another good Division I could laugh at Jackson."[18] But he did not, and the effect was paralyzing. He neither attacked Magruder nor sent troops to reinforce Porter. He waited for whatever fate God had in store for him—an odd attitude for the nation's commanding general in a war where he held enormous inherent advantages.

But Lee could not know this. Nor could he know why his grand plan to evict Fitz John Porter from his works, which relied on Jackson to make the first move, was failing, and failing miserably. Jackson was nowhere to be found. At 3:00 p.m. Jackson's West Point classmate A. P. Hill, the sensitive, slender young aristocrat who wrote poetic letters to his sister and lady friends but who in wartime was a hard-bitten, unsentimental killer, decided that enough was enough: on his own initiative, he ordered his division to cross the Chickahominy. Soon Little Powell and his men were advancing through the shell-swept village of Mechanicsville toward Porter's thirty thousand, who were dug in along a mile-long line in the sixty-to-seventy-foot-high banks behind a small tributary of the Chickahominy called Beaver Dam Creek. Lee, who had come to the same conclusion that Hill had—in Lee's words he was "obliged to do something" to distract the larger Union force in front of the city—declined to call off the attack. Hill believed in any case that Jackson was on his way and that his critical flanking movement was still in progress. They were saving Richmond, after all, even if they were doing exactly what Lee's plan had tried to avoid: a frontal attack on Union defenses.[19]

The result was what Lee himself might have predicted: more of a slaughter than a fight. The Battle of Mechanicsville (also known as the Battle of Beaver Dam Creek) offered yet more evidence of what was becoming increasingly apparent to most of the war's participants: men with rifled muskets shooting from good cover had enormous advantages over their attackers. The cover in this case was splendid. Wrote Porter Alexander, "They had fortified it with infantry breastworks & pits for guns & by cutting down all timber in range to give unobstructed fire."[20] They had also constructed an extended abatis—an obstacle made of sharpened logs and branches. The open fields west of the creek also offered clear fields of fire for the Union artillery, expertly positioned on the high ground behind the infantry, which laid down a devastating barrage from the moment the rebel soldiers appeared, with horrific effects. One soldier in A. P. Hill's division said that everyone would duck when a shell passed, then look behind to see where it had landed. "The body of a stalwart young fellow suddenly disappeared, and on the ground where he had stood was a confused mass of quivering limbs which presently lay still," he wrote. "The same shell, as I learned afterward, carried away the top of a man's head in our own regiment."[21] It was this brutal, raking artillery fire that led Hill to advance toward the Union position, where he thought there would be better cover.

But the fire was just as lethal near the swamp. As the rebel soldiers approached, they could see from a thousand feet away what lay ahead of them: first the cannons ranged on the top of the creekbank, then the rifle pits, and below those the wide swamp, abatis, and other felled trees. Most who made it to the water were cut down. In a five-hour firefight the Confederates lost 1,500 of the 10,000 men who were engaged, many of them on a final, suicidal assault at a place called Ellerson's Mill. "A more hopeless charge was never entered upon," later wrote Porter Alexander. The 44th Georgia Regiment, which made it to the creek where its men were lacerated by musket fire and ran out of ammunition, suffered 361 casualties of 514 men who entered the fight. In one soldier's description, the dead in the swamp looked like "flies in a bowl of sugar."[22] The 1st North Carolina Regiment lost 133 killed and wounded, including its colonel, lieutenant colonel, major, 6 captains, and 10 lieutenants. Of the 14,000 Union soldiers engaged in the fighting, only 361 were lost.[23] It was a lopsided victory for the defense. The Confederate assaults against the Union 5th Corps' fortress-like positions never had any hope of success. McClellan, meanwhile, wired Stanton triumphantly that evening, "Victory today complete and against great odds. I almost begin to think we are invincible."[24]

But where was Jackson? The question has haunted histories of the war ever since. And what, by extension, had become of Lee's elaborate plan? The answer lies partly in a document known as "General Orders No. 75," dated June 24, 1862, in which Lee gave detailed instructions to his generals. The document is as confusing today as it was then, an attempt to both arrange and predict a sequence of movements involving more than sixty thousand men in a swamp-ridden, densely wooded country they did not know and did not even have accurate maps for, and generals who had no experience working together under a commander who had never wielded an army. Jackson's difficulties were all rooted in some way in General Orders No. 75. Its vague language and wishful thinking constituted Lee's first big mistake of the war.

Jackson's location, as the first of A. P. Hill's troops advanced on Beaver Dam Creek, was roughly an hour short of the place he was supposed to reach in the early morning. His problem that day, as it was the day before, was that he could not make his army march fast enough to meet the time-table established by those orders. Though he was frustrated and impatient, he could do nothing about it; the obstacles were too great. At 9:00 a.m., fully aware of how far behind he was, Jackson sent a courier to General Lawrence Branch, who was to be the second chess piece to move in Lee's plan, telling him that he was already six hours behind Lee's schedule. For reasons unknown to history, Branch decided not to pass that message on. A. P. Hill had based his attack at least in part on the idea that Jackson would soon arrive. No one had told him otherwise. Nor, for that matter, had Hill tried to contact either Jackson or Branch.

But the worst confusion came from the orders themselves. Lee had instructed Jackson to advance to an old Revolutionary War–era meeting-house called Polegreen Church, let the other generals know that, then lead a movement down the north bank of the Chickahominy toward Cold Harbor. The assumption was that Jackson's arrival at Polegreen Church would take him so close to Porter's force that the Federals would have no choice but to pull out. But Lee's maps were wrong. Though they showed the church virtually on top of the position Porter's men occupied on Beaver Dam Creek, in fact it was more than three miles away. When Jackson and his army pulled up just past Polegreen Church at a place called Hundley's Corner at about 5:00 p.m., where they reunited with Ewell's division, they thus found themselves in the middle of nowhere. Strangely, they could hear the sound of distant gunfire from the south.

It was a confusing moment. Jackson's orders said nothing about making an attack, or riding to the sound of battle. Indeed, attacking Porter was exactly what Lee did not want to do. He wanted to *maneuver* the Union general out of his position. The orders stated explicitly that Jackson was to bear to the east of the creek, toward the Union supply line. What, then, were these guns? Was the plan already under way? Were Confederate troops crossing the Chickahominy? Had he somehow turned the Federal flank? Jackson, whose face, according to an aide, was "anxious and perplexed," had no way of knowing. He would have assumed that Lee knew how late he was. He might also have assumed that if Lee had different plans for him, Lee would have contacted him. But Lee did no such thing. He did not even try. So Jackson, attempting to follow his orders, which told him to advance to the church and to avoid Beaver Dam Creek, stayed put. There may have been a further misunderstanding: in Lee's battle report he says he expected Jackson to flank Porter; Jackson's report indicates that he thought his goal was a crossroads at Cold Harbor much farther in the Union rear.

Jackson has been criticized through the years by generals on both sides and by historians for failing to arrive on time at Mechanicsville and then, when he got there, for failing to attack, even to the point of blaming him for the Confederate defeat. Most of this is unfair; he was in a subordinate position, doing what he believed Lee wanted him to do, and that did not include attacking any Union position. He was indeed late, but he assumed Lee knew that, and in any case his lateness had more to do with Lee's timetable than with his own failure to move his army as quickly as possible. (Jackson himself had suggested at the generals' meeting on June 23 that the advance should take place on June 25; but the ultimate responsibility for the decision lies with Lee.) Though he failed to reach his appointed destination on June 25, Jackson still had managed a twenty-five-mile march under horrendous conditions in terrain that no one, Lee included, understood. "The Confederate commanders knew no more about the topography of the country than they did about Central Africa," wrote General Richard Taylor. "Here was a limited district, the whole of it within a day's march of the city of Richmond . . . and yet we were profoundly ignorant of the country, were without maps, sketches, or proper guides."[25]

Though Jackson cannot be held responsible for the shortcomings of General Orders No. 75, and certainly not for the loss at Mechanicsville, his actions that afternoon still seem both strange and out of character for one of the most aggressive military commanders America has ever produced. Like his fellow generals A. P. Hill and Lawrence Branch, he seems to have assumed that the job of communication belonged to someone else, perhaps to Lee's staff. Thus he arrived at Hundley's Corner, just down the road from the church, and did not dispatch a courier to Lee or to anyone else—an odd and uncharacteristic passivity that could be explained by lack of sleep and sickness. Then, too, he was unused to playing the role of subordinate. We will never know. Jackson does not offer any reasons in his official report and indeed seems to find it scarcely worth mentioning. During that day the only message he sent to anyone was the brief note to Branch saying he was late. Nor did he avail himself of the services of Jeb Stuart, the only Confederate officer who actually knew something about the local terrain. Lee scrupulously avoided placing blame on any of his generals, including Jackson, for the bloody disaster of June 26.[26]

Behind all of the blunders and miscommunications, staff failures and misunderstandings that swirled around the Confederate defeat at Mechanicsville, however, lay a single, very large truth: *Lee's plan actually worked.* It did not work precisely when it was supposed to, and it did not work exactly as he had imagined, with his legions executing a perfectly sequenced rightward turn behind Jackson's army, driving McClellan's army south along the Chickahominy. But Lee's calculation—that the presence of Jackson's twenty-four thousand men along with his outsized reputation on the Union right flank would scare the Federals out of their entrenchments on both sides of the river—was correct. While McClellan's wires to Washington after his army's victory at Mechanicsville were jaunty and optimistic, claiming his near invincibility, as the evening progressed he began to feel weak and vulnerable. Any doubts in his mind that Jackson was there in force were now gone. He knew, moreover, that Jackson's veteran army had not engaged at Beaver Dam Creek and was therefore the equivalent of a very large gun pointed at the rear of the 5th Corps and, beyond, at the railroad and Union supply base.

McClellan was not wrong. Jackson's presence there made Porter's position behind the creek instantly indefensible, precisely as Lee had envisioned it would. Perhaps a more courageous or resourceful general would have brought up reinforcements and fought the massed Confederate divisions north of the river while launching the main attack to the south. This was Porter's suggestion. Other generals suggested variants of this plan. They all believed Richmond was vulnerable. They all thought the solution was to attack. McClellan disagreed. More convinced than ever that he was facing a two-hundred-thousand-man force, he began, in the wake of his victory, to think only of how he was going to save his army. Lee, after his defeat, was thinking only of how he was going to corner and destroy his adversary.

At about 1:00 a.m. on June 27, after the Battle of Mechanicsville, George McClellan made the breathtaking decision that he would abandon both his supply line and his grand plan to capture Richmond. He decided to retreat. He did not think of it this way, and did not describe it this way to his superiors. His own choice of words to describe the course he set for the Army of the Potomac was "change of base." By this he meant that he was forsaking White House Landing and the railroad as conduits for his daily ration of supplies, and shifting those operations to a new supply base, at Harrison's Landing on the James River, eighteen airline miles due south across the peninsula. Cutting the supply line meant that his army could no longer stay where it was. All of those men would march to the banks of the deeper James, where they could shelter under the massive guns of the US Navy's ships.

McClellan ordered Fitz John Porter to fall back during the night, though he would not have enough time to move his entire corps across the Chickahominy. He would instead move a few miles south and set up along another swamp to protect the bridges, which were his only avenue of escape. As Porter remembered later, McClellan impressed upon him "the absolute necessity of holding the ground, until arrangements over the river can be completed."[27] Porter saw this as a sort of code. He believed McClellan was telling him that the 5th Corps was going to be sacrificed so the rest of the army could assault and take Richmond. Porter, always the good soldier, replied, "I shall hold it to the last extremity."[28] What he was really doing, though he did not yet know it, was covering a retreat. The rest of the army would have to move soon, and quickly. For the moment it was frozen in front of Richmond in contemplation of another Confederate attack.

CHAPTER THIRTY-FIVE

VICTORY BY ANY OTHER NAME

Thus began the chase across the York-James Peninsula that became the centerpiece of the Seven Days battles. Because of McClellan's choice of strategy, the question was not whether the Union army would be defeated but how badly it would be defeated. It was in many ways the oddest sequence of the war: a large army retreating from a smaller one, as though it could not possibly, with the resources of an industrializing nation behind it, just stand and fight. Mechanicsville and its aftermath established the model for the campaign: the Union army would wage a defensive battle by day, always on the ground of its choosing, and then retreat south toward the new base on the James River under cover of darkness. As at Mechanicsville, the rebel advance was marked by incompetence, shoddy staff work, inefficiency, miscommunication, and an almost shocking failure to take advantage of the openings McClellan gave them. In spite of this, the Seven Days was a thrilling, war-changing Confederate triumph. Lee's, Jackson's, and everyone else's mistakes were debated and hashed over ad infinitum in the years following the war. But the indisputable fact was that the Army of Northern Virginia, under its brilliant new commander, had driven off the invader. It had saved Richmond. That was all anyone in the South needed to know. The Seven Days made Robert E. Lee famous. His generals, who did well enough, basked in borrowed light.

But the details were ugly. They got uglier as the two armies plunged southward, locked in their bloody embrace. Confusion reigned in the Confederate camps on the morning after Mechanicsville. Though McClellan had decided to shift his base of operations the night before, Lee did not know that yet. He would not know it for certain for several days. The immense Army of the Potomac was out there, amorphous and moving through a densely wooded landscape, and because of its very immensity its contours and destination were hard to fathom. Lee's assumption was that the Union would try to protect its supplies and would move large numbers of troops north across the Chickahominy toward White House Landing to do that. He was therefore surprised to find that Porter's victorious 5th Corps had vanished from its camps, and had quietly fallen back three miles to a new defensive position along Boatswain's Swamp, about half a mile from Chickahominy and two miles above the bridges they would have to use to cross the river.

While Lee remained ignorant of McClellan's intention to change his base, he knew that he still had a Union corps in front of him and he knew that he wanted to destroy it. And he believed, incorrectly, that the railroad was still the larger army's Achilles' heel. Lee thought that Porter had moved eastward behind a small stream called Powhite Creek, three and a half miles east of Beaver Dam Creek, and was waiting in a north-to-south line for him there. His plan for the next day was thus in many ways like the first. Jackson and D. H. Hill would be sent on a flanking march around the Union left to the village of Old Cold Harbor, thus forcing them from their breastworks. If all went according to plan, divisions under generals A. P. Hill and James Longstreet would then drive the Yankees eastward into Jackson's and D. H. Hill's clutches. Jackson would also be just a few miles from the railroad— still Lee's main target. It was a sound, if unimaginative plan. The trouble was that it bore no resemblance to the reality on the ground. And Jackson, once again in the role of the instant legend who was supposed to save the day, would be the principal victim of the confusion.

At 9:30 a.m. on June 27 Lee and Jackson sat on a tree stump while Lee described Jackson's flanking march to Old Cold Harbor. By 11:00 a.m. Jackson had his command moving. This time he had orders directly from the mouth of Lee himself. Lee then sent A. P. Hill and Longstreet forward, expecting to clash with Union forces at about noon. But the Federals were not at all where Lee thought they were. What happened next amounted to blind groping in a tangled wilderness: one army searching for another. It wasn't until Confederate general Maxcy Gregg stumbled into the center of the Union line that Lee understood what had happened. Porter's 5th Corps army was strung out in a big, convex arc for a mile and three-quarters along the steep banks of a sluggish body of water known as Boatswain's Swamp, facing north and west.[1] The troops were ranged along a high bluff in three stacked lines of breastworks, with cannons behind them, all fronted by a swamp of varying widths. Like Beaver Dam Creek, it was a formidable defensive position, one of the strongest of the war. Sometime after 2:00 p.m. Lee sent A. P. Hill's men forward in a series of bloody assaults that accomplished nothing. Lee was committing the same old tactical sin that everybody else committed: piecemeal attacks against a strong position. The Battle of Gaines's Mill had begun.

Where, again, was Jackson? This time on a wild-goose chase into the peninsula's knotty backcountry that had no purpose at all. He was turning a nonexistent flank, headed for a nonexistent supply line, following a Confederate battle plan that was no longer relevant. But Jackson knew none of this. So he marched. He also suffered, as all the commanders did, from the lack of accurate maps and place names. Anticipating this problem (and without his great terrain-and-map man, Hotchkiss), he had engaged the services of a twenty-five-year-old private, John Henry Timberlake, whose family farm was nearby. Jackson told Timberlake he wanted to go to Cold Harbor, and Timberlake took him on the shortest and fastest route in that direction. Suddenly the sound of gunfire was heard—and as on the previous day, gunfire was something Jackson was supposed to bear away from.

"Where is that firing?" Jackson asked, astonished, standing up in his saddle.

"From over at Gaines's Mill," replied Timberlake.

"Does this road lead there?"

"Yes," Timberlake replied, "it passes the mill en route to Cold Harbor."

"But I do not wish to go to Gaines's Mill," replied Jackson impatiently. "I wish to go to Cold Harbor, leaving that place on the right."

"Then the left hand road was the one you should have taken. Had you let me know what you desired, I could have directed you in the right direction at first."[2]

Part of the confusion was that Jackson did not know there were *two* towns named Cold Harbor, old and new, more than a mile apart. He wanted *Old* Cold Harbor. Now he had to backtrack to the north and resume his eastward march. It would cost him at least ninety minutes. When one of his officers asked him if the delay would ruin the day's plan, Jackson replied, "No, let us trust that the providence of our God will so overrule it, that no mischief shall result."[3] His entire march was already irrelevant. But no one had told him that.

As the Confederate assaults on the Union lines behind Boatswain's

Swamp were repulsed, one after another, Lee concluded that the only way to break them was to launch a massive, concerted assault across the nearly two-mile front. He spent the afternoon working furiously to make that happen. He finally sent a messenger to order Jackson into the fight. In the meantime he marshalled the trailing divisions of Jackson's command under Generals Richard Ewell and Chase Whiting, and inserted them on the center and right of his line. He ordered Longstreet, on the far left, forward. By 5:00 p.m. Lee's effort was starting to coalesce—so much so that General Porter, who had sent an optimistic message to McClellan at 4:00 p.m. saying "our men have behaved nobly and driven the enemy back many times," now sent an urgent call for help, saying that he was being pressed hard and that without reinforcements, "I am afraid I shall be driven from my position."[4]

McClellan was alarmed by Porter's SOS but did nothing more than send a few brigades that would arrive too late to be of much use. (One was commanded by Jackson's old nemesis from his army days in Florida, Brigadier General William H. French.) McClellan had remained far from both fronts and seemed convinced that he was going to be attacked that day at all points. He had sent an 8,500-man division to Porter earlier that day and seemed to think that was enough. The only help Porter got later came in the form of patronizing encouragement. "If the enemy are retiring, and you are a *chasseur*, pitch in," McClellan told him.[5] Later, still clueless about what was happening, he urged Porter, "Try to drive the rascals and take some prisoners and guns." McClellan, closeted at headquarters and out of touch with both fronts, had apparently lost the will to command. He would no longer consider launching an attack of any sort. He simply awaited whatever Lee had in store for him and dreamed only of getting his army safely to Harrison's Landing.

At about 5:00 p.m. Lee caught up with Jackson, who was dutifully following Lee's morning instructions and who in obeying his orders to move to Old Cold Harbor—supposedly well behind the Union lines—had in fact landed not far from the Union right. Lee, who must have understood that Jackson's pointless march was a result of his own mistake, nonetheless seemed impatient. Jackson was commanding more than half of his army. Lee needed all of that army in the fight, and he needed it right away. The two generals met on Telegraph Road, less than a mile from the fight at Boatswain's Swamp. Jackson, as usual, looked nothing like a general. According to one of Jeb Stuart's soldiers who saw Jackson a bit earlier in the afternoon, his coat "was positively scorched by the sun. . . . The cap of the general matched the coat. . . . The sun had turned it quite yellow indeed, and it tilted over the wearer's forehead, so far as to make it necessary for him to raise his chin, in looking at you. He rode in his peculiar forward-leaning fashion, his old rawboned sorrel, gaunt and grim. Moving about slowly, and sucking a lemon [one of the few recorded instances of this] . . . he had rather the air of a spectator."[6] Lee greeted Jackson warmly, while soldiers around them erupted into loud cheers and rebel yells and then offered what has sounded to many historians like a mild rebuke.

"Ah, General, I am glad to see you! I had hoped to be with you before."

Jackson mumbled something in reply that bystanders could not hear. Lee then turned for a moment toward the sounds of the battle.

"That fire is very heavy," he said. "Do you think your men can stand it?"

"They can stand almost anything," Jackson replied. "They can stand that." Lee gave him new orders. Jackson then saluted and galloped away, his eyes alight with the prospect of battle after so much dreary marching. Jackson, who had seemed bleary-eyed and lethargic all day, was now full of fire and resolve. Robert Dabney commented that he had only seen this sort of "tempest of passion" on his face three times in his Civil War career. He issued orders to his commander to press the attack. Finally he was engaged.

With Jackson in hand, Lee was now ready to launch the massive attack he had been working on all afternoon, during which time the fighting had raged on and he had taken heavy losses. It was very likely his largest single attack of the war.[7] There was nothing piecemeal about it this time. He had managed to bring roughly thirty-two thousand men forward along a curving, two-mile front against Porter's entrenched thirty-four thousand. At 7:00 p.m. Lee sent them forward. What followed was some of the roughest fighting of the war, as long rolls of musket fire and billows of white smoke swept across the long bluff, and Union cannon pounded canister into the graybacks as they came forward. The butchery was shocking, even for men who were getting used to it. "Never before did I see so many dead men," wrote one soldier, "such a scene of carnage, men with no arms, some without legs, others with part of their heads off, some with their bowels out."[8] The smell of blood mingled with the smell of black powder.

Just before dark Porter's lines, exhausted after repelling attacks for eight hours, broke in two places. Perhaps the most spectacular drive was that of a thirty-two-year-old Kentuckian and former Indian fighter named John Bell Hood, commanding the 4th Texas Brigade (containing Georgians and some South Carolinians) in Chase Whiting's division under Jackson's command. Just before the final attack, Lee rode up to Hood and asked, "Can you break this line?" Hood said he would try. "May God be with you!" Lee shouted, lifting his hat as he rode away. Hood's men then moved forward at the quickstep, without pausing to fire, through what Confederate colonel Evander Law called "a withering storm of lead and iron." They passed through and over dead and wounded men, mangled horses, and busted wagons. They fell by the score, victims of canister and enfilading fire from most of the left side of the Union lines. Hood took a thousand casualties. At one hundred yards they broke into a run, erupting into the full, high-pitched, whirring scream of the rebel yell, which sounded to Longstreet's men like the noise made by "forty-thousand wildcats."[9] Across the swamp they came, and up the rise, and suddenly they had broken through to the artillery. Just as suddenly the Union defenses, which had held solidly through attack after attack, began to break. Though Hood became the battle's most visible hero, it would turn out later that brigades from James Longstreet's divisions had broken through at about the same time. But that didn't matter anymore. The Union retreat had begun.

The battle was soon over. In seven hours' fighting over possession of a swamp and the bluff that rose above it, the Union sustained six thousand casualties and the Confederates nine thousand. On an hourly basis, Gaines's Mill was one of the war's costliest battles. The ratio was predictable for a force attacking such a strong defensive position. The very capable Fitz John Porter, with a single corps plus a division, had held off most of Lee's army for seven hours. But in the end it had been Lee's battle, his first great victory, against a worthy opponent on the opponent's chosen field of combat. He, and he alone, had managed the victory. Jackson, in a subordinate position, was just another battlefield commander. He performed adequately: he followed orders. He had no special role in the final attack and in fact it was Lee, not Jackson, who had ordered the latter's divisions into place. That night Jackson went to the tent of his new friend Jeb Stuart, woke him, and the two men sat on blankets and talked of the next day's work. Jackson observed that Gaines's Mill "was the most terrific fire of musketry I ever heard."[10] During that night came the results of that musket fire: the screams and moans of the wounded and dying rising from the swamps, woods, and fields.

McClellan took the defeat at Gaines's Mill hard. The invincibility he thought he had glimpsed had vanished in the white smoke of its musket fire, as had whatever confidence he had left, and in its place came only heartache and bitterness that his outnumbered men had been so wantonly sacrificed. Even though he himself had been miles from the battlefield, sequestered in his headquarters office, here at last was a real, palpable, verifiable threat, a rampaging Confederate army of untold numbers with Stonewall Jackson in its midst, a reason to run as fast as he could to his new base. He called a meeting of his commanders that evening, told them about his plan for retreat, and got their support for the plan by selling them on the magnitude of the Confederate threat.

Not all of his generals agreed. Division commanders Joseph Hooker and Phil Kearny were indignant when they learned of the decision. They had been watching, ever more skeptically, the amateur theatrics of General Magruder in front of Richmond and were fully convinced that rebel strength there was a sham. They knew how vulnerable Richmond was. They were so upset that they pressured their corps commander, Samuel Heintzelman, into taking them, at a late hour, to McClellan, where they made their case for an immediate attack on the city. Heintzelman supported them. McClellan was unmoved. The change of base, the euphemism he insisted on, would take place. Kearny, known for his hair-trigger temper, exploded at McClellan, denouncing him, according to a staff officer who was there, "in language so strong that all who heard it expected he would be placed under arrest until a general court-martial could be held, or at least he would be relieved of his command."[11] Actually, the retreat was already under way: Mac had ordered Erasmus Keyes and his 4th Corps to begin retreating through White Oak Swamp toward Harrison's Landing. The rest of the army—100,000 men, 300 pieces of artillery, 4,000 wagons, tens of thousands of horses, and 2,500 cattle—would soon be in motion.[12]

McClellan did something else that night, too: shortly after midnight, feeling bitter and despondent and abandoned by his government, which had once again failed to send him the troops he needed, he sent one of the war's most infamous telegrams to Secretary of War Stanton. He told Stanton of the desperate battle he had not witnessed, and its outcome, then wrote:

> *I have lost this battle because my force was too small. I again repeat that I am not responsible for this & I say it with the earnestness of a General who feels in his heart the loss of every brave man who has been needlessly sacrificed today. . . .*

I know that a few thousand men more would have changed this battle from a defeat to a victory—as it is the Govt must not & cannot hold me responsible for the result.

I feel too earnestly tonight—I have seen too many dead & wounded comrades to feel otherwise than that the Govt has not sustained this Army. If you do not do so now the game is lost.

If I save this Army now I tell you plainly that I owe no thanks to you or any other persons in Washington—you have done your best to sacrifice this Army.[13]

With those words, accusing the secretary of war of treason, or something very like it, McClellan must have surely known he was committing career suicide. Or maybe he was so absorbed in his own pathos that he could not see what he was doing. In any case, an enterprising man named Edward S. Sanford, who was head of the War Department's telegraphic office, took it upon himself to remove the final nine words before delivering the telegraph, thus saving McClellan from himself. Instead of an abrupt dismissal, McClellan received a reasonably sympathetic response from Lincoln in reply: "Save your army at all events. Will send reinforcements as fast as we can."

Once again Porter's army fled by night from Lee, managing to get all of the roughly twenty-nine thousand men he had left across the Chickahominy. Once again the Confederates awoke to a deserted battlefield and deserted enemy camps, strewn with abandoned supplies. That day—June 28—would see the vaunted Army of the Potomac in full flight southward across the peninsula toward Harrison's Landing. In military terms McClellan was taking a very large risk. A one-hundred-thousand-man army, strung out over fifteen miles of road, was an exquisitely vulnerable target, all the more so since an entire army would be jammed onto a single road across a single bridge through a swamp, with constant jarring stops and starts. It was McClellan's good fortune that Lee faced a version of the same problem Jackson had faced at Winchester: Lee knew the enemy was retreating, but where was it going? On June 28 his army was virtually frozen in place while he tried to figure it out.

As Lee saw it, McClellan had three options: he could move his army east and cross the Chickahominy to protect his supplies; he could retreat back down the peninsula the way he had come; or he could move to the James River. The first thing Lee did was to send Richard Ewell's division and Jeb

Jackson's boyhood home: Orphaned at the age of seven, Jackson was sent to live with six bachelor uncles, a step-grandmother, and two aunts at prosperous Jackson's Mill in mountainous western Virginia (now West Virginia). The main residence (left) was one of the finest houses in the region.

Jackson's sister, Laura Jackson Arnold: They were orphans and extremely close friends growing up. After the war started Laura became an ardent supporter of the Union cause and cut all ties to her brother. They never reconciled.

Jackson in the Mexican-American War, 1847: Just out of West Point, the shy young man traveled south to fight in Mexico, where he showed almost reckless bravery in the battles that led to the fall of Mexico City. He was rapidly promoted.

The Virginia Military Institute as it looked on the eve of the Civil War, in mountain-ringed Lexington, Virginia. The castellated barracks on the right contained Jackson's classroom and also his bachelor quarters. On April 21, 1861, Jackson and 176 young cadets marched from those barracks for Richmond to join the Confederate army. Many of them, including Jackson, would never see Lexington or VMI again.

3

Main Street in Lexington as it looked in the Civil War era. A block away, Jackson founded and ran a successful Sunday school for slaves. Here he made his life before the war as a college professor, investor, farmer, homeowner, husband, and church deacon.

Jackson's home in Lexington: Behind its doors he was a complex, passionate, highly sensitive man who loved deeply and had a nineteenth-century romantic's view of beauty and nature. He loved Shakespeare, European architecture, and gardening. He taught himself to be fluent in Spanish.

Jackson's first wife, Ellie: The vibrant and irreverent daughter of a college president was his first love. She died tragically while giving birth to their stillborn son. Jackson was so grief-stricken that friends began to worry that he was losing his mind.

The woman he loved but could not marry: Maggie Junkin was the brilliant, engaging sister of Jackson's first wife, Ellie, destined to become a famous poet. Though they clearly loved each other, rules of the Presbyterian Church forbid a marriage.

9

Jackson as college professor in 1857: He was the most peculiar of teachers: a humorless, puritanical, gimlet-eyed stickler for detail. He taught the toughest course at the Virginia Military Institute.

Second wife, Anna, and daughter, Julia: Married in 1857, Thomas and Anna were blissfully happy in Lexington, where they bought a house and a farm and owned six slaves. This photo, taken three to four years after his death, shows his daughter, Julia, whom he knew only briefly.

Confederate president Jefferson Davis: He disliked and distrusted Jackson at the start of the war. His political meddling in Jackson's command led to Jackson's controversial resignation in 1862.

Henry Kyd Douglas: The handsome young Douglas was a member of Jackson's staff and one of the general's favorites. His memoir is one of the most important records of Jackson's wartime career.

Wartime Harpers Ferry: This is what the town and its approaches looked like when Jackson seized it in September 1862. His victory resulted in the largest surrender of Federal troops in the war, larger in numbers than the surrender of Generals Cornwallis or Burgoyne in the Revolutionary War.

Robert E. Lee: He and Jackson formed an extraordinary partnership that changed the course of the war. In their stunning victories at Second Manassas and Chancellorsville they demonstrated a high-command teamwork not previously witnessed on either side.

Confederate general Richard S. Ewell: "Old Baldy" was one of Jackson's toughest and most reliable generals. But it took him a while to get over his conviction that Jackson was "crazy as a March hare."

Confederate general Daniel Harvey "D. H." Hill: He was Jackson's brother-in-law and one of the Confederacy's leading generals. Of the Battle of Malvern Hill, where he fought alongside Jackson, he said, "It was not war, it was murder."

Ambrose Powell "A. P." Hill: Jackson's great weakness was his inability to get along with his fellow generals, especially the hardnosed "Little Powell" Hill. Jackson put him in arrest after Cedar Mountain, and the two feuded continuously after that.

The brilliant, erratic Turner Ashby embodied the immense cavalry advantages the South held early in the war. His dashing, reckless exploits as Jackson's cavalry chief became the stuff of legend. This photograph was taken after his death.

19

Jedediah Hotchkiss: The maps he made were a critical part of Jackson's astounding maneuvers in his Shenandoah Valley Campaign. In an era where maps were few and unreliable, Jackson had a sure grasp of terrain and how to use it.

White Oak Swamp: This Civil War photo of White Oak Swamp tells you everything you need to know about the condition of much of the terrain during the Seven Days battles. It was here that Jackson and his corps stalled and missed an opportunity to destroy the Union army.

Confederate general Joseph Johnston: One of the top rebel commanders early in the war, he was among the first to spot Jackson's talent and to recommend his promotion.

James Longstreet: He and Jackson were Robert E. Lee's top lieutenants. He was a solid fighter whom Lee called his "old warhorse." While he inspired respect from the enemy, his rival Jackson inspired fear and awe.

James Ewell Brown "Jeb" Stuart: The stiff, reserved Jackson and the ebullient, outgoing Stuart were completely different personalities but the best of friends. Stuart and his cavalry were Jackson's eyes and ears on his most famous marches.

Hunter Holmes McGuire: Considered by many to be one of the best surgeons in the war, he was Jackson's medical officer and one of his most important staff members. After the war he became president of the American Medical Association.

24

Destruction at the Dunker church: Jackson's fight on the Confederate left at the Battle of Antietam was the single bloodiest phase of the single bloodiest day in American history. He successfully repulsed repeated attacks by the Union army.

Union general Nathaniel Banks: The former governor of Massachusetts and speaker of the House of Representatives was one of Jackson's main opponents in his legendary Shenandoah Valley Campaign. Jackson's victory over Banks at Winchester catapulted the rebel general to international fame.

Union general Joseph Hooker: "Fighting Joe," or, as Lee contemptuously called him, "Mr. F. J. Hooker," won a reputation as an aggressive fighter. But his caution led to his humiliation by Lee and Jackson at the Battle of Chancellorsville.

Union general George McClellan: A gifted administrator and motivator, he was also vainglorious, mean-spirited, dissembling, haughty, backstabbing, and callously dismissive of peers. He called his boss Lincoln "the original gorilla."

Fredericksburg, Virginia, as it looked before the battle, a charming, prosperous river town of five thousand souls where George Washington spent his boyhood and James Monroe once practiced law. For reasons that would become painfully clear to the Union army, Lee decided to stand and fight on the high bluffs behind the town.

The destruction caused by Federal artillery at the Battle of Fredericksburg, December 11, 1862. Witnesses on both sides were stunned by the barbarity of this attack on a civilian target. A disgusted Robert E. Lee observed, "These people delight to destroy the weak and those who can make no defense."

Union general Irvin McDowell: He had victory in his hands at First Manassas, but his delays opened the way for Jackson's brilliant defensive stand and subsequent counterattack.

Union secretary of war Edwin Stanton: Jackson's military victories repeatedly thwarted Stanton's war plans. After Jackson's spectacular victory at Winchester, Stanton seemed to come completely unhinged, sending an SOS to northern governors to send troops to save Washington, DC, from Jackson's army.

The wartime general: In November 1862, following the Battle of Antietam, Jackson was photographed in Winchester. Note the wrinkled and weather-beaten condition of his uniform.

Moss Neck Manor, one of Virginia's great estates, on the grounds of which Jackson and his staff spent the winter of 1862–63. It was a time of religious revivals and snowball fights and band concerts and social visits and book reading and the sort of leisure soldiers rarely got. Here Jackson befriended a golden-haired five-year-old named Janie Corbin, who would die tragically of scarlet fever.

Union general John Pope: As Lincoln's carefully chosen spearhead of the new campaign to toughen the war, Pope was full of bluster and big talk. But Jackson's spectacular flank march and the Battle of Second Manassas drove Pope's army back into Washington, DC.

The last photograph: Taken less than two weeks before his mortal wounding at Chancellorsville, it shows a man physically transformed from his years in Lexington. His wife thought he was "much more handsome."

36

The house at Guiney's Station where Stonewall Jackson died. He was taken here after being accidentally shot by his own men. Though his arm was amputated, he seemed to be recovering but contracted pneumonia and died a few days later. His last words were "Let us cross over the river and rest under the shade of the trees."

Jackson's death mask: It was made on May 11, 1863, after Jackson's body had been taken by train to Richmond. His gaunt, emaciated face shows the effects of the pneumonia.

Stuart's cavalry to White House Landing to find out. They found the railroad unguarded and part of it destroyed; they found tons of supplies in flames. McClellan's old headquarters mansion—the Lee place—was burning, too. (The Union had already loaded three thousand fugitive slaves onto canal boats for evacuation.) Though this was the first clear evidence of a general retreat, Lee would not be completely sure until early the next morning that the Union army was headed for the James River.

What he did know for certain was that his original plan had worked. By threatening their supply lines he had levered the Federals out of their trenches and forced them to abandon their planned siege of Richmond. It was his first great stroke of tactical brilliance. But that was only the first step. He now had in his hands—he could see it with startling clarity—the opportunity to capture or destroy a large part of the Union's largest army. He had the chance—perhaps the only time he would ever be given it—to end the war right here. This was not just conjecture; McClellan himself believed it, too. An army strung out for fifteen miles with its full supply train was a case study in vulnerability. *Time*, of course, was the critical element. Lee had to catch the snake in midflight.

The plan he concocted for Sunday, June 29, had two main elements: first, Major General John B. Magruder, he of the recent theatrics, would advance east from Richmond and engage the Union rear guard, fixing it in place, making it fight, and thus slowing the pace of the retreat. Jackson would rebuild the destroyed bridges on the Chickahominy, then cross the river with his divisions under Chase Whiting, Richard Ewell, D. H. Hill, and himself, and join the fight. Meanwhile, divisions under James Longstreet, A. P. Hill, and Benjamin Huger would swing south and east in an arc whose terminus was at a crossroads called Glendale. If all went according to plan, the following day, the thirtieth, the Confederate army would hit McClellan from three directions—Jackson's twenty-four thousand coming down from the north, through the White Oak Swamp—and with luck they would catch enough of it out in the open to deal it a crippling blow. It was, in a sense, a race to Glendale.

Like almost every other grand plan Lee made during the Seven Days, the one for June 29 did not work as he had anticipated. Once again, Jackson, with fourteen of Lee's thirty-five brigades, was the main victim of the confusion, and, as with the fiasco at Mechanicsville, he has come under sharp criticism over the years for the supposed missteps that resulted from it. Once again, the criticism, focused on his failure to show up at the Battle of Savage's Station that day, was unfair. Jackson, again, was following Lee's orders. When Jackson met with Lee that morning, he had been given straightforward orders: repair the Grapevine and Alexander's Bridges on the Chickahominy, which Porter's men had destroyed, then cross the river and come to the aid of Magruder in his attack on the Union rear. Jackson proceeded with the first task, completing repairs of the Grapevine Bridge quickly; unfortunately he had assigned the other bridge to the incompetent Dabney, who failed and was quickly replaced. (Jackson would need both bridges for his corps and ponderous supply train.) While he was repairing them, Magruder had launched a lukewarm attack on the Union force near a railroad depot called Savage's Station, but soon became fearful that he was facing a larger force and asked Lee for reinforcements. Jackson, meanwhile, sent a courier to Magruder to tell him that his troops would begin crossing the Chickahominy at about 2:00 p.m.[14]

He was preparing to cross several brigades when, at about 3:00 p.m., he received new orders in the form of a communiqué from Lee's adjutant, Colonel R. H. Chilton. The message was addressed to Jeb Stuart, who was still at White House Landing, and read as follows:

> *The Gen'l Comd'g. requests that you will watch the Chicahominy* [sic] *as far as Forge Bridge, ascertain if any attempt will be made in that direction by the enemy, advising Genl. Jackson, who will resist their passage until reinforced.*[15]

Stuart had sent it on to Jackson, who added the following reply—"Gen'l Ewell will remain near Dispatch Station & myself near my present position"—and sent it by horseman right back to him. Both the note and Jackson's understanding of it are perfectly clear: he was to guard the lower bridges on the Chickahominy and prevent the enemy from crossing. Why? Because Lee was still not absolutely certain that McClellan would not try to recross the Chickahominy. With the power at his disposal—if he only believed in it—McClellan could still do whatever he wanted, and Lee knew it.

But by midafternoon both Lee and Magruder were wondering, *Where was Jackson?* His lateness was getting to be a daily occurrence. Magruder sent a courier to Jackson to find out what was wrong, and Jackson made the problem worse with his clipped, uninformative reply, saying that he could not help Magruder because he had "other important duties to perform." By this he meant guarding the crossings, as Lee had ordered him to do. But the note's almost insolent brevity enraged Magruder, who could not imagine what could be more important than coming to his assistance. Though Lee insisted to Magruder that he had ordered Jackson to cross and fight, blame for the misunderstanding must rest squarely on either Lee or his adjutant, Chilton: Lee if he wrote the order, and Chilton if he sent something to Stuart other than what Lee had told him to. Once again, Jackson and his 24,000 men were prevented from engaging in combat. Magruder managed to mount a tepid attack in late afternoon, bringing 14,000 of his men against 16,000 Union troops under Major General Edwin Sumner. The advance soon burned itself out. The threat he had posed was so slight at Savage's Station that an entire Union corps under Samuel Heintzelman had slipped away—precisely what Lee had been trying to prevent. Still, the net result in military terms was a Confederate victory. After the battle, Sumner fled south, and what he left behind suggested an army in panicked retreat: 1,000 men who became prisoners—stragglers from the retreating army—and 2,500 sick and wounded.[16] In their haste they had also left tons of supplies, some only partially destroyed. In Dabney's description, they found "all the apparatus of a vast and lavish host":

> The whole country was full of deserted plunder, army wagons, and pontoon trains partially burned or crippled; mounds of grain and rice and hillocks of mess beef smoldering; tens of thousands of axes, picks, and shovels . . . medicine chests with their drugs stirred into a foul medley . . . overcoats torn from the waist up. For weeks afterward the agents of our army were busy gathering in the spoils.[17]

In one railroad ditch the discarded molasses ran knee deep, a symbol, just at that moment, of the helplessness of the most extravagantly equipped army in history.[18] Jackson's letter home to Anna was that of a victorious general in pursuit of a fleeing enemy. "An ever-kind Providence has greatly blessed our efforts and given us great reason for thankfulness in having defended Richmond. Today the enemy is retreating down the Chickahominy towards the James River. Many prisoners are falling into our hands."[19] McClellan's "change of base" had meanwhile appeared in the newspapers and had quickly become a Confederate joke. It was a "catch word among our fun loving troops," wrote one soldier in his memoirs, "to signify discomfiture or defeat; if two dogs fought and one ran, the men cheered and shouted, 'Look at him changing his base' "[20]

In spite of the crossed signals, on the morning of Monday, June 30, Lee still had a clear opportunity to destroy a large part of McClellan's army. The latter had, once again, marched all night; its lead columns under Erasmus Keyes were already camped on the James River. The rest of the army had just made it across White Oak Swamp and onto the gently swelling plains and woodlands around Glendale where seven of McClellan's eleven divisions were now camped, eight to nine miles from their destination at Harrison's Landing. Lee's scheme to reach Glendale ahead of some of the Union army had failed. But his basic idea of attack would be the same: nine divisions would converge in a concentric assault on the retreating Federals. McClellan himself, unaccountably, had chosen this moment to withdraw to the gunboats on the James River, where the head of his army was camped, thus leaving his rear guard to confront the full fury of Lee's army, which he knew was coming. His behavior is difficult, or perhaps impossible, to justify, the more so since later that day he boarded the warship *Galena*, where he enjoyed dinner with wine with the captain while a major battle was under way. In doing so he left units from five different corps to work out tactical details among themselves.[21] It was as though the exhausted, anxiety-ridden general had again, as he had at Gaines's Mill, temporarily lost the resolve to exercise command. His behavior would be the basis for many later accusations of cowardice and dereliction of duty. "The Corps Commanders fought their troops according to their own ideas," General Samuel Heintzelman testified later of the fighting that day at Glendale. "We helped each other. If anybody asked for reinforcements, I sent them. If I wanted reinforcements, I sent to others. He [McClellan] was the most extraordinary man I ever saw. I do not see how any man could leave so much to others, and be so confident that everything would go just right."[22]

Lee, on the other hand, was quite in the middle of things. It was a momentous day. The future of the war and the nation itself was conceivably riding on what his army did, and he was keenly aware of it. He met with Jackson at Savage's Station just after dawn. Jackson had ridden up on Little Sorrel at the head of a large mounted escort, looking as dusty and nondescript as ever. "He sat stark and stiff in the saddle," wrote an observer later. "Horse and rider appeared worn down to the lowest point of flesh consistent with effective service. His hair, skin, eyes, and clothes were all one neutral dust tint. . . . The 'mangy little cadet cap' was pulled so low in front that the visor just cut the glint of his eyeballs."[23] Lee arrived a few moments later, handsome, smartly dressed, and as usual the picture of perfection on horseback. The two generals exchanged a warm greeting, then began to talk animatedly in tones that were just out of the hearing of several curious observers. Then one of the two generals—the observers did not agree on which one it was—began to mark off a diagram in the dirt with his boot, talking earnestly all the while. When it was finished, the draftsman—Lee or Jackson, but most probably Lee—in the words of one of the observers, raised his foot and stamped it down and said, this time loud enough to hear, "We've *got* him."[24] Jackson then mounted his horse and rode away. Lee looked after him for a moment, then rode off, too.[25] They did not "have him" in the sense that McClellan's forces, like Banks's before Winchester, were deployed in a long line of march. McClellan was too smart for that, marching by night and setting up carefully chosen defensive positions during the day. Lee most likely saw the likelihood—or virtual certainty— that he would be able to fall on a piece of the army with his larger force. He was right: while he and Jackson had their meeting, 70,000 Confederates were advancing on 55,000 Federals at Glendale.

What happened over the next few hours was one of the great missed chances of the war. Lee's plan—even more complex than his scheme for Mechanicsville—required the orchestrated movements of 12,000 men under Benjamin Huger, 20,000 under A. P. Hill and James Longstreet, 13,500 under John Magruder, and 24,000 under Stonewall Jackson. Jackson, with the largest force, would take the same road the Union army had taken, across White Oak Swamp. The others would come in from the west and attack the Union flank. Under Lee's orders, they were all moving that morning.

Jackson's day had started with a miserable night of rain that had soaked him in his bed. He very likely did not sleep at all. Though he was sick and exhausted, he put his army on the march at 3:30 a.m., crossing the Chickahominy River and passing through Savage's Station and its litter of supplies, some of them burning. The march once again was slow, this time in part because his men could not resist loading themselves up with Union discards: coffee, ammunition, clothing, shoes. It took his men seven hours to cover five miles to the bridge at White Oak Swamp, where they arrived at about noon to find the single bridge destroyed. At approximately 2:00 p.m. Jackson opened an artillery barrage against the Union forces on the high ground south of the swamp, and sent his cavalry chief, Thomas Munford, across the deep water to scout the crossing. Munford came under murderous fire and returned. He reported that there would be no possibility of reconstructing the bridge with William Franklin's 6th Corps and its nineteen thousand men and artillery sitting atop the bluff on the other side.

And there, at the ruins of the White Oak Swamp Bridge, Jackson stalled, never to move again that day. It was the first failure in a string of failures. Jackson was not the only one who failed to advance: Huger's division would be stymied by felled trees on the road; Magruder would spend the day in futile marching and countermarching. Thus Lee could muster only a little more than twenty thousand men under Longstreet and A. P. Hill when he finally mounted his attack at 4:00 p.m. Though the fighting was hard and bloody, and the Confederates breached Union lines once, the Battle of Glendale ended in a stalemate. Following the pattern of the Seven Days, the Union force retreated once again by night, this time to a strong position at Malvern Hill, a few miles toward the James River. "Never, before or after," wrote Porter Alexander, "did the fates put such a prize in our reach."[26]

Where was Jackson this time? The answer, broadly speaking, was that he was having what appears to be a temporary, though fairly complete, mental and physical breakdown. The description of him as "worn down to the lowest point of flesh consistent with effective service" conforms to almost all accounts of him that week. He was not himself. He was sick with fever, debilitated, possibly dehydrated. He had had an absurdly small amount of sleep since June 23. Jackson wrote Anna that he had been in a "wet bed" the night before in a torrential storm and had gotten up at midnight.[27] By the time he arrived at White Oak Swamp he had probably been in the saddle for ten hours.

Indeed, the old Jackson seemed to disappear altogether that week. Anecdotes about him seem oddly substanceless; he wasn't even indulging in his usual diversion of badgering his own generals. He seemed emotionally drained, too, strangely empty. In a letter to Anna, all he could muster was a formal, colorless, almost pro forma wish: "I do trust that our God will soon bless us with an honorable peace, and permit us to be together at home again in the enjoyment of domestic happiness."[28]

Faced with the sharp Union artillery fire, Jackson decided immediately that he would not try to force his way across the swamp. This seemed completely out of character. Though he would have sustained large losses attempting it, he had never been shy about expending blood. He then looked for another way out of the swamp. Tom Munford continued his search downstream and found an undefended crossing. He sent word of this back to Jackson, adding that the Union flank on the other side of this swamp crossing also appeared to be undefended. He heard nothing back, and Jackson never followed up. Though this was only a "cowpath," as Munford described it, and would present great difficulties for a full army corps to cross, Munford later wrote that "I had seen [Jackson's] infantry cross far worse places, and I expected that he would attempt it."[29] Jackson's subordinate Wade Hampton, the wealthy South Carolina plantation owner whose "Hampton legion" had fought bravely at Manassas, found yet another crossing, only a quarter mile from the destroyed bridge. Hampton returned and told Jackson that he could quickly build a log bridge for infantry but not artillery. Jackson ordered him to do it. Several hours later a serviceable bridge existed that could have put whoever crossed it 150 yards from the unsuspecting Yankees. When Hampton returned to tell Jackson, he found the general seated on a log, quite motionless, with his eyes closed. His cap, as usual, was pulled down to his nose. Hampton gave Jackson his report and volunteered to lead an advance over his new bridge. To Hampton's complete amazement, the general did not speak, nor did he even move. He "sat in silence for some time, then rose and walked off in silence." Jackson later was found prostrate and asleep underneath a tree, in spite of the daylong artillery battle that was screaming overhead. He seemed almost perfectly passive. When Longstreet sent an aide to him asking for his help, Jackson replied that he could do nothing. He later fell into such a deep sleep that his aides had trouble waking him. He fell asleep at dinner with a biscuit between his teeth. When he was awakened, he suddenly seemed to come to his senses, saying, "Now, gentlemen, let us at once to bed, and rise with the dawn, and see if tomorrow we cannot do *something*."[30]

That was little consolation for Lee. Jackson commanded his largest force, and he had failed not only to cross the swamp but even to distract the Union army into keeping units in place to watch him. In midday the threat from Jackson seemed so slight that Union major general William B. Franklin was able to release two brigades—nearly ten thousand men—to help fight Longstreet and Hill. Franklin himself was later critical of his adversary, saying "it must be evident to any military reader that Jackson ought to have known about Brackett's Ford, only one mile above White Oak Bridge, and ought to have discovered the weakness of our defense at that point."[31] Nor had Jackson bothered to contact Lee about this, who was a mere forty-five minutes away by courier. Jackson acknowledged none of this in his official report, saying only that the relatively deep swamp, the destruction of the bridge, and the strength of the enemy position prevented crossing. He did, however, react when, two weeks later, he overheard surgeon Hunter McGuire, aide Sandie Pendleton, and artillery chief Stapleton Crutchfield talking about the campaign. When one brought up the subject of why Jackson had not gone to the aid of Longstreet and Hill, Jackson interrupted, "If General Lee had wanted me, he could have sent for me." His statement managed to be both cryptic and accurate. Lee had never once communicated with Jackson during the day, not to request that he cross the swamp, nor to find out why he had not crossed the swamp.

Lee was appalled at the results of the day. "We of Gen. Lee's staff knew at the time that he was deeply, bitterly disappointed," wrote Porter Alexander, "but he made no official report of it & glossed over as much as possible in his own reports."[32] Lee had not yet learned how to wield the full power of his army, how to make it move in concert, how to deal with its sometimes balky or independent commanders. Then again, for all appearances he had just won another stunning victory, once again driving the Union forces before him. Whatever contretemps there were remained between Confederate generals and their staffs. Few of the rank and file had any idea of who was supposed to be where and doing what, and what opportunities might have been missed. To them and to the rest of the South it was all pure rebel glory, vindication of the idea—as Manassas had been—that Yankees were no match for the Confederate fighters. The morning after the battle Jackson, on horseback, happened upon a group of troops from Magruder's command, most of whom were seeing him for the first time. "Such cheering I had never heard before," wrote one Georgia soldier, of the man he called "our most famous general. The soldiers went wild as they tossed their caps in the air."[33] As the Army of Northern Virginia pushed the hated Yankees inexorably toward the river, Jackson was a bigger hero than ever.

Glendale was not the end of the Seven Days, though it should have been. In his disappointment and frustration, mixed with fatigue and sickness that sounded a bit like what Jackson was experiencing, Lee decided he wanted to strike one last time at his enemy before it took shelter under its navy's guns. He believed the Army of the Potomac was badly demoralized: evidence of it was everywhere on their marches, thousands of rifles, knapsacks, blankets, and other supplies strewn randomly on the ground. He would fight yet again on ground of the Union's choosing, and once again it was excellent defensive ground: a mile and a half long, half a mile wide, gently sloping, amphitheater-like meadow bordered by thick woods, the swamps and ravines on the margins. It was called Malvern Hill.

The place was more like a killing field, a defensive position that Fitz John Porter, architect of the fearsome works at Mechanicsville and Gaines's Mill, considered to be the strongest of the campaign by far. The Union advantage started with its artillery: 268 cannons, many of them rifled, plus 26 giant siege guns that McClellan had been preparing to use against Richmond. The guns were everywhere: stacked on the brow of the hill, bristling on the army's flanks, and even ranged in front of the infantry, where their flesh-shredding canister loads would enjoy a clear field of fire. Around them, stacked to the top of the rise, were the blue masses of infantry, fifty-four thousand of them. The borders of the amphitheater were unassailable: ravines, swamps, streams, and thick woods meant that the Union troops could not be flanked. Which meant that the Confederate attack would be funneled into a narrow front with no cover. The rebel infantry would have to attack the Union position by coming up the rise, straight into the teeth of the strongest artillery emplacement of the war. It sounded like suicide, and Jackson and his brother-in-law D. H. Hill, who formed the Confederate left at the base of the slope, and along with Huger's and Magruder's troops would do the fighting this day, understood this at once. Hill thought it was "hopeless" and had warned Lee not to try to fight there.[34] Jackson, who saw no chance for a successful assault, wrote in his battle report:

> The enemy in large force were found strongly posted on a commanding hill, all the approaches to which in the direction of my position could be swept by his artillery and were guarded by infantry. The nearest batteries could only be approached by traversing an open space of 300 or 400 yards, exposed to the murderous fire of artillery and infantry.[35]

The Confederate strategy began with an idea. James Longstreet, looking at the spectacle of raw force arrayed in front of him, had the notion to bring up artillery on the left and right, subject the Federals to a pounding cross-fire, and hope that this might have some effect on their apparently ironclad defenses. As a tactical plan it wasn't much good; in practice it was a disaster. Even though Jackson and others tried to bring up batteries quickly—at one point he personally helped haul a North Carolina gun forward—the Confederate guns came up piecemeal and to little effect.[36] They were losing, and losing badly. Soon after the artillery duel started, Jackson sat down on a stump to write a note to Jeb Stuart. While he was writing, a shell from a rifled Parrott gun exploded nearby. Half a dozen men were killed or wounded, and dust and dirt rained over Jackson and his letter. He calmly shook the dirt off the paper and finished his writing. He then stood up, gave directions for the dead and wounded to be carried off, mounted, and rode off. The last words of his letter were "I trust that God will give our army a glorious victory."[37] He could not have been more wrong. For the Union gunners, the battle was more like a large-scale turkey shoot. Whenever a Confederate battery would unlimber, the massed Union guns would open up on it, blowing it to pieces. When Jackson requested that his division commander Brigadier General Chase Whiting bring up his guns, Whiting protested, saying that he had only sixteen of the fifty he was supposed to have. Whiting further complained that his gunners would be cut to shreds. "They won't live in there five minutes!" said the man who had graduated first in the Class of 1845 at West Point and had been Jackson's tutor in the latter's plebe year. "Obey your orders, General Whiting, promptly and willingly." Whiting, now furious, replied, "I have always obeyed my orders promptly, but not willingly under such circumstances."[38] The guns were brought up. It took a moment for the Union batteries to register this. And then they blew the guns, wagons, men, horses, limbers, and caissons to bits. Jackson, meanwhile, continued giving orders, in one case while a battery was being destroyed before his eyes. "He sat erect on his horse in this hurricane of canister and grape," recalled one soldier, "his face was aflame with passion, his eyes flashing." Whiting thought he was aflame with something more like madness. "Great God!" he cried out to anyone listening. "Won't some ranking officer save us from this fool?"

Other Confederate gun crews were just as helpless before the massed counterbattery fire from the hill. After the war, McClellan's chief of artillery, Brigadier General William Barry, told Jackson's artillerist Tom Munford, chillingly, how easy it was to destroy the rebel guns. He said he had "fifty pieces massed at Malvern Hill, which he could concentrate on any battery that came out in the open and that they melted like wax under his rain of projectiles."[39]

Thus it went. By midafternoon Lee decided that Longstreet's misguided barrage plan was not going to work. There would be no attack that day. Thinking ahead to a battle the following day, Lee began to move some of his reserves. He shifted some of them to be in place for the following day and left the field of battle. And then something strange and tragic happened. Earlier in the day, Lee, through his adjutant, Chilton, had issued an order to all his commanders that was predicated on the idea that Longstreet's idea might work. The directive read as follows:

> *Batteries have been established to act upon the enemy's line. If it is broken, as is probable, [Brigadier General Lewis] Armistead, who can witness the effect of the fire, has been ordered to charge with a yell. Do the same.*

Lee's orders sounded simple enough. If Armistead saw Yankees retreating from the Confederate cannon fire, he was to charge and yell, which would signal a general assault on Union lines. But the order gave no time for the attack and no time limit; the decision to advance was left to a brigadier who had never led a brigade in battle (and was further distinguished for having been kicked out of West Point after an incident in which he broke a plate on Jubal Early's head); finally, amid the din of battle a "yell," even by a full brigade, would have been inaudible to most of the men on the Confederate lines. That Lee could have even issued such an order was inexplicable. Perhaps he was exhausted; later that day—as Jackson had the day before—he fell asleep on the field.

While Jackson and D. H. Hill had concluded that an advance would be foolhardy, sometime in late afternoon others suddenly had different ideas about what was going to happen. First Chase Whiting and then John Magruder sent notes to Lee saying that parts of the Union line were retreating. Magruder, moreover, reported that Lewis Armistead was driving a body of the Union forces. Neither report was true. McClellan was in no sense retreating, merely rearranging, and Armistead's minor advance had succeeded only in getting various rebel units pinned down.[40] Lee, who was no longer on the field, for some reason credited these optimistic reports and dictated the following message to Magruder: "General Lee expects you to advance rapidly. He says it is reported that the enemy is getting off. Press forward your whole line and follow up Armistead's success." Just before the late-arriving Magruder received those orders, he somehow received a copy of the earlier order from Chilton for a general advance. This was at about 5:00 p.m. Now his orders were perfectly clear: he had to attack, he had to follow Armistead. So he went forward with maybe seven thousand men against the war's greatest defensive concentration. Confederate guns boomed again, and again were immediately targeted for destruction.

Magruder's first attacks did nothing but sacrifice several thousand men to Federal artillery and musketry. But they had another unfortunate effect, too. They became the inadvertent signal—per the orders Chilton had delivered—for a general advance. At about five thirty, Jackson, who was commanding the D. H. Hill units, ordered those brigades forward, too. The result was pure slaughter, some of the worst of the war. To their credit, the Southern infantry did not give up. They pressed attack after attack and were badly shot up, a huge percentage of them by artillery. "It was not war, it was murder," said D. H. Hill later. Mass murder, actually. By sundown more than five thousand rebels had fallen, compared to three thousand Federals. They lay on the field, in one description, "woven into a carpet of cold or agonized flesh . . . enough of them were alive and moving to give the field a singular crawling effect." Later burial details would report exploding corpses and pigs eating pieces of flesh that once belonged to live human beings. In their doomed attack, Lee's men had performed with extraordinary bravery.

After the battle was over, Lee still did not seem to quite understand what had happened. He sought out Magruder. "General Magruder, why did you attack?" he asked. It was an odd question, considering the second, quite specific, order that he had issued. Magruder replied, "In obedience to your orders, twice repeated." That night, at about 1:00 a.m., a group of Jackson's generals and other officers, worried that McClellan might attack in the morning, went to Jackson's headquarters, where they found him in a deep sleep. As surgeon Hunter McGuire described it, they sat him up and shouted in his ear "something about the condition of our army, its inability to resist attack, etc." Jackson, barely awake, replied, "Please let me sleep. There will be no enemy there in the morning." His officers thought he was crazy. He was right.[41] As had become their habit, the Union forces again withdrew by night, again over the howls of McClellan's commanders, most notably Fitz John Porter and Phil Kearny, who thought he could still make a run at Richmond. "If an army can save this country," came Little Mac's canned reply, "it will be the Army of the Potomac, and it must be saved for that purpose."[42] By the next morning they were gone. Malvern Hill was a bloody, and pointless, end to the Seven Days, which had seen a total of 36,463 casualties, half again more than at the Battle of Shiloh, whose killed-and-wounded numbers had shocked the nation. The casualties in this single week, in fact, equaled those in all the battles of the western theater in the first half of the year 1862, including Shiloh. It was by far the bloodiest week in the nation's history.

CHAPTER THIRTY-SIX

IN WHICH
EVERYTHING CHANGES

—⊱⊰—

Though few people understood the Seven Days battles at the time, the resounding Confederate victory was a good deal more pyrrhic than it looked. There was no question that the campaign had, by its shocking implausibility, changed the war. Within a month of his appointment as commander of the Army of Northern Virginia, Robert E. Lee had turned national expectations upside down. He had driven the largest army the country had ever fielded to the banks of the James River, where it cowered and feared to come out from under Mother's skirts. He had given new life to the Confederate dream of permanent, peaceful independence.

But the irony here—and it was grand and tragic irony—was that Lee's counteroffensive actually marked the end of that brief, fragile period when the Union could still be preserved without making slavery the war's central issue—without, in other words, destroying the South. From the first days of the war, the stated goals of Lincoln and Congress had been to quell the rebellion and restore the Union. Congress had been quite explicit about this; the previous summer it had passed a resolution specifically disavowing any intent to end the institution of slavery. For a time this remained the essential position of moderate and conservative (i.e., nonradical) Republicans in the North, as well as both "war" and "peace" Democrats, neither of whom believed that freeing Southern slaves was worth spilling Union blood. Lincoln appeased the radicals in his own party and pursued his policy of fighting a war for limited ends.

But by the summer of 1862 that brittle political calculus was falling apart. Lee's victory coincided with a pronounced hardening of Northern attitudes. This shift was embodied in the rise of the radical Republicans, whose beliefs included three fundamental truths: that slaves should be freed, that freeing them could only be accomplished by war, and that the nation's fate could no longer be separated from the issue of slavery.[1] While the nominal reason for fighting continued to be suppression of the rebellion, the political winds were shifting: In January of that year, House Republican leader Thaddeus Stevens had called for total war and the emancipation of slaves. In March, Congress had forbidden US Army officers from returning fugitive slaves; in April it had abolished slavery in the District of Columbia; in June it had prohibited slavery in the territories; and in July it had authorized the enlistment of black soldiers and allowed for court proceedings to liberate slaves of "convicted" rebels. By the time of the Seven Days, the ruling Republican Party itself had been radicalized. Antislavery bills were flooding the halls of Congress, and it was hard to find anyone in the party who still believed that simply putting the Union back together as it once existed should be the goal of the war.[2] Though the debate raged about how exactly emancipation should happen—from gradual, voluntary emancipation to compensated emancipation to outright confiscation of human "property"—a consensus was emerging: slavery must end.

More than any leader other than Lincoln himself, McClellan was buffeted by these shifting military and political winds. He was a moderate "war" Democrat who wanted to end the conflict quickly, and as gently as possible, with the South and its institutions fully intact. By conquering Richmond he believed he could convince hard-liners on both sides to retreat from their positions long enough to negotiate peace. If he had succeeded, it would have established him as the savior of the Union and probably would have made him president. He had of course failed miserably. But he held fast to his vision of a limited war. In a meeting with Lincoln on July 8, six days after the Battle of Malvern Hill, McClellan handed his superior an extraordinary letter. The war, he wrote,

should not be . . . looking to the subjugation of the people of any state. . . . It should not be, at all, a War upon population; but against armed forces and political organizations. Neither confiscation of property, political executions of persons, territorial organization of states or forcible abolition of slavery should be contemplated for a moment. . . . All private property and unarmed persons should be strictly protected. . . . Mili-

tary power should not be allowed to interfere with the relations of ser-
vitude. . . . A declaration of radical views, especially upon slavery, will
rapidly disintegrate our present Armies.[3]

The note was a superb summary of an opportunity that had already vanished by a man who had personally made it disappear. If McClellan had won at Richmond, there might well have been a negotiated peace; Robert E. Lee might never have become the hero of the South; the Union might have been put back together with a South whose economy and institutions were still intact. Lincoln might have been a one-term president. We will never know. Lincoln read the letter in McClellan's presence, amazed at the jarring impudence of this timid general who had just dragged his beaten, sick, and demoralized army into its James River camps. Lincoln made no comment. Four or five months earlier, he might have agreed with McClellan. But not now. Three weeks after the end of the Seven Days campaign, the president delivered to his cabinet the first draft of what would become known as the Emancipation Proclamation. Among other things, the document asserted that, on January 1, 1863, "all persons held as slaves within any state or states, wherein the constitutional authority shall not then be practically recognized, submitted to, and maintained shall then, thenceforward, and forever, be free." Lincoln was not yet ready to issue it publicly, not after McClellan's humiliation by Lee on the peninsula. But the draft was a sign of how fast the change was sweeping in.

It is interesting to note, too, that however patriotic the abolitionist radicals in the North may have been, the very last thing they wanted was for Little Mac to win the battle for Richmond. Winning might have meant the preservation of slavery and the Southern way of life.[4] With no national emergency to force the end of slavery, the abolitionists would lose their influence.[5] And so on, through a very long chain of hypothetical events. Because McClellan lost, the very thing he had wanted most was lost, too.

If all of this swirling change was hard to grasp, the Seven Days' immediate effects were not. The Army of the Potomac was, for the moment, useless and purposeless. Lincoln, who "was nearly as inconsolable as I could be, and live," after the Union humiliation of the Seven Days, was pilloried from near and far as an ineffectual leader. "Not a spark of genius he has," thundered Henry Ward Beecher from a Brooklyn pulpit, "not an element for leadership." Abolitionist Wendell Phillips in Boston wrote that "He may be honest—nobody cares whether the tortoise is honest or not. He has neither insight, nor prevision, nor decision."[6] The stock market fell precipitously. The price of gold rose. And of course the South, for the moment, saw only good coming from its victory: Britain and France, horrified by the casualty counts and impressed by Confederate military prowess, seemed more interested than ever in some sort of mediation.

But that remained a fond hope, and nothing more. A more likely future was suggested when, on July 2, the day after McClellan's army had slunk miserably away from its victory at Malvern Hill, Lincoln, with a grim determination to finish what he started, ordered up three hundred thousand new volunteers. He understood that the rise of Lee and Jackson meant this was going to be a long, hard, expensive fight. The war, the new war, the actual war, was to be all about conquest, subjugation, and destruction.

The immediate aftermath of Malvern Hill was pure horror, at least for the burial details that Jackson ordered out onto the killing ground. In a steady downpour and mist that hung like a shroud over the field, the men gathered and stacked the dead and pieces of the dead. Unlike most Civil War battles, in which artillery caused less than 5 percent of casualties, at Malvern Hill more than half of the Confederate killed and wounded had been victims of Federal solid shot, shell, spherical case, and canister. The results were ghastly. Body fragments lay everywhere. Many corpses were headless. Some were just mounds of decaying ooze that yesterday had been human beings. Jackson worked the detail, trotting up and down and hurrying the men along. When someone asked why he was in such a rush to clear the field he replied, "Why, I am going to attack here presently, as soon as the fog rises, and it won't do to march troops over their own dead, you know."[7] He seemed his old hyperaggressive self again—rested, impatient to attack.

He was in favor of hot and immediate pursuit. But for the moment that was a difficult idea: the field hospitals were jammed, the roads to Harrison's Landing had turned to muck, and no one had much of an idea exactly where McClellan was anyway. Jackson rode to Lee's headquarters, a bullet-strafed farmhouse, to petition him. The two men were studying maps before a fire when Confederate president Jefferson Davis, unexpected and unannounced, walked into the room with his brother, Colonel Joseph Davis. "President, I am delighted to see you," said a surprised Lee. While Lee and a staffer chatted with the guests, Jackson, who had been sitting near the fire on the other side of the room, had risen and was standing stiffly by his chair, as though waiting for someone to notice him. Jackson had not recognized Davis at first, according to Hunter McGuire, who was with him. But when McGuire whispered the man's identity Jackson "stood as if a corporal on guard, his head erect, his little fingers touching the seams of his pants, and looked at Davis."[8] Davis now noticed Jackson, too, and the two men stared silently at each other for a moment. Lee, realizing that Davis did not recognize Jackson, then broke in with one of the most famous introductions of the Civil War: "Why, President, don't you know Stonewall Jackson? This is our Stonewall Jackson." Then, according to McGuire, "Mr. Davis started to greet him, evidently as warmly as those he had just left, but the appearance of Jackson stopped him, and when he got about a yard away Mr. Davis halted and Jackson immediately brought his hand up to the side of his head in military salute. Mr. Davis bowed and went back to the other company in the room."[9]

Though Jackson left no record of his thoughts, he had already had three unpleasant run-ins with Davis, and his behavior almost certainly reflected this. The first had happened at Manassas, after Davis had arrived at the battlefield and breathlessly tried to rally the troops from what he thought was a terrible defeat. Jackson, flush with victory, had loudly dismissed the president's panicky apprehensions and had vowed to march on Washington. The second was their meeting near Manassas on September 30, 1861, from which Jackson had emerged disenchanted and Davis had decided that Jackson was an overly aggressive fanatic. The third contretemps happened after Romney, when Davis allowed Jackson's orders to General Loring to be superseded by Secretary of War Judah Benjamin—an unwarranted intrusion of politics into military operations—prompting Jackson's resignation. His troubles with authority figures, from VMI superintendent Francis Henney Smith to his Florida superior, William H. French, are well documented; Davis may have awakened some of the same uncharitable feelings in him.

In any case, Jackson soon got his wish; the bloodied Army of Northern Virginia trudged forward in the heat and humidity and mud toward the Union position. When they got there they found that it was nearly impregnable. McClellan's army was dug in on the heights overlooking the river; behind them were the redoubtable ship-mounted guns of the navy. Lee and Jackson agreed that there was no question of attacking. They had missed their chance to destroy the army. It was a depressing moment, made worse by the knowledge that malaria, dysentery, and typhoid were sweeping their ranks and that sickness, death, and straggling had reduced some regiments by half. The peninsula, which seemed to the soldiers to be no more than a tangled, humid, malarial swamp punctuated by an occasional farm field, was a miserable place to wage war.

Still, Jackson wanted more. A few days later, he summoned his faithful ally Alexander Boteler to his camp and once again outlined a plan—this was becoming quite familiar to Boteler by now—for an invasion of the North. He wanted Boteler to take his proposal to Richmond. In Jackson's view, the Confederacy was "repeating the blunder we made after the Battle of Manassas, in allowing the enemy leisure to recover from his defeat." Boteler protested that Davis would just send him back to Lee. Why didn't Jackson just speak to Lee himself?

"I have already done so," Jackson replied.

"Well, what does he say?"

"He says nothing," Jackson said, then quietly added, "Do not think I complain of his silence. He doubtless has good reasons for it."

"Then you don't think," Boteler persisted, "that General Lee is slow in making up his mind?"

"Slow!" Jackson said with sudden energy. "By no means, Colonel. On the contrary, his perceptions are as quick and unerring as his judgment is infallible. But with the vast responsibilities now resting on him, he is perfectly right in withholding a hasty expression of his opinions and purposes." He then paused for a moment. "So great is my confidence in General Lee that I am willing to follow him blindfolded. But I fear he is unable to give me a definitive answer now because of influences at Richmond." With that rare glimpse into Jackson's feelings about Lee, Boteler was once again dispatched.[10] Each time Jackson proposed this idea of taking the war to the North, he sounded a little less crazy, though what he and Boteler were doing amounted to gross insubordination.

In the weeks that followed the Seven Days, Jackson was perfectly Jackson: self-contained, serious, hardworking, engaged with the minute details of managing his army. "He seems to have no social life," observed one soldier. "He divides his time between military duties, prayer, sleep, and solitary thought. He holds converse with few."[11] Though his recent performance paled next to the brilliance of his valley campaign, the more momentous Confederate success before Richmond had elevated him even higher in the popular mind. He was cheered everywhere he went. Often the cheers grew into the weird, corkscrewing ululation of the rebel yell. He acknowledged the cheers by lifting his hat, then invariably spurred

Little Sorrel and galloped away from all that adulation, which he believed was rightly due God and not him. "He is of course a great military genius and has made such an impression on the men that 'Old Jack' is at once a rallying cry and a term of endearment," wrote cavalryman Charles Minor Blackford. "The army is full of stories about him and everybody, citizens and soldiers, is trying to get a glimpse of him."[12]

Those stories had begun to reverberate through the South. "The masses of his countrymen," wrote Allen C. Redwood, who fought with the 55th Virginia Regiment,

> found something peculiarly acceptable in the character of the man, apart from his services: his retiring modesty, his indifference to display, his simple trust in the Giver of all victory, were shining virtues in the eyes of a people who had only taken up arms in behalf of what they considered their dearest rights, and with no care for the pomp and circumstance of war. His very homeliness was a recommendation to the essentially practical-minded Southerner, regarding himself as the peer of any man, and constitutionally intolerant of the pretension symbolized by gold-lace and other fripperies of official rank.[13]

Jackson received all sorts of gifts from these new admirers, too, in the wake of the campaign. Baskets of food arrived daily, usually intercepted by his staff, who knew he had no use for them and were afraid they might be returned.

His renown was no longer limited to the South. If Lee's attacks had been poorly orchestrated and Jackson had been less than fearsome in some of them, those niceties were lost north of the Potomac. Indeed, one popular Northern explanation of what had happened credited the victory to the onslaught of the invincible Jackson on the Union flank, sweeping in from the west, where he had left a wreckage of Union armies. In a version of this, the *New York Times* said inaccurately that "Stonewall Jackson rushed from the Valley of the Shenandoah . . . and got in the rear of our whole army" by means of a "*coup de guerre*." *Harper's Weekly* marveled at his "suddenness" and described "the furious attacks of enormous Rebel armies." An editorial writer for the *New York Times* expressed the wish that a rumor of Jackson's death were true because "he has evinced more real genius . . . than anybody on either side."[14] Jackson was for many Northerners the embodiment of the "pitiless, fanatical, religiously-obsessed warrior."[15] But for others he was emerging not simply as a Cromwellian zealot in a cause they despised, but also as someone with qualities they otherwise might actually admire: competence, fearlessness, valor in the field, humility, and devotion to God. To his enemies he was the strangest, most intriguing, and most threatening of all the Confederate generals.

Those who had known Jackson before the war were amazed at the sheer speed of his transformation, which had raised him so far and so quickly above so many other powerful and influential people. One of the best examples involves Jackson and one of his brigadier generals, Robert Toombs. In the days just before the war began, Henry Kyd Douglas happened to see both men within days. First he had observed Jackson in Lexington, "pursuing the noiseless tenor of his way, instructing a class of mischievous cadets in natural philosophy and almost unknown beyond the limits of that town." A few days later, Douglas happened to be in Washington, DC, where he saw the US senator from Georgia Robert Toombs—later one of the founding fathers of the Confederacy and its first secretary of state—give a fiery speech on the Senate floor in favor of the acquisition of Cuba.[16] Roughly fifteen months later, Douglas and Jackson were riding through an area where the brigade commanded by Toombs was camped. Jackson noticed immediately that there were large gaps in Toombs's picket lines. He immediately rode to brigade headquarters, where he found the general lying down in the shade of a small fly tent. Jackson "routed him out" and according to Douglas "directed General Toombs with some sharpness to go at once, in person, and make the necessary connection."[17] Jackson then turned and rode away. This once-powerful national figure was now being given curt, peremptory commands by the eccentric former physics professor. "*Tempora mutantur, nos et mutamur in illis,*" Douglas commented. *Times change, and we change with them.*

On that same ride, Jackson and Douglas had discovered, to Jackson's great delight, a field that was full of blackberries, one of the general's most coveted fruits. The problem was that the field was in a sort of no-man's-land between Federal and rebel picket lines, and that day, wrote Douglas, "there was a deal of spiteful firing between them." Jackson went happily into the field anyway, calmly picking and eating the ripe fruit even though, as Douglas observed, "the bullets seemed to be as plentiful as blackberries." At one point he turned to his increasingly anxious aide and, with a large, juicy berry between his thumb and finger, asked Douglas casually "in what part of the body I preferred being shot." Douglas, nervously handing the general berries while minié balls whistled overhead and buried themselves in the trees around them, replied that while his first choice was to be hit in his clothing, he preferred anyplace other than his face or joints. Jackson said he had "the old-fashioned horror of being shot in the back and so great was his prejudice on the subject that he often found himself turning his face in the direction from which the bullets came." Just then a bullet thudded into a sapling near their heads, and Jackson, with a "vague remark about getting his horse killed," reluctantly left the feast.[18]

The strange, almost recreational mood of the blackberry field persisted after the Confederate army moved its camps to Richmond on July 8. Jackson's divisions were near Mechanicsville, about three miles from the city. The weather improved, food became better and more plentiful, and there was time to relax and write letters home. Best of all were the accolades: if Lee and Jackson were famous, so were the men who fought for them. They were aware that, however it had happened—in fact they had won one battle, lost two, and fought three draws—they had done a marvelous thing.[19] They were cheered by their compatriots. "These were the halcyon days of Jackson's troops," remembered a gunner with the Rockbridge Artillery. "Well-earned rest, good rations, abundant supplies from their valley homes, proximity to the capital with its varied attractions, the praises and admiration of its people for Stonewall and his followers all combined to make it most pleasantly remembered ever afterwards."[20] One infantryman remembered that Jackson gave his company permission to spend the day in Richmond. "That was a great day," he recalled. "We left Richmond a year ago in new uniforms, with the fair complexion of city men. . . . Now we returned as veterans ruddy and brown, with the health and hardness that outdoor living creates. Our welcome was an ovation, and it made us feel our standing in public esteem. The only thing we regretted as our time closed was that the day did not last forever."[21]

Jackson himself mostly stayed out of Richmond, attending to the mountain of administrative detail involved in running his divisions. He was a thorough and highly capable administrator but gets little credit for it. In one of his dispatches to Ewell, you can see his thoroughness: he wants to know the condition of all his batteries, the number and kinds of guns that still worked, the number of men and serviceable horses, which of their guns and caissons had been captured, which they had taken from the Yankees, which they had *exchanged* with the Yankees after the battle, and so on.[22]

But there was another reason why Jackson did not want to go to Richmond, and it was made manifest on his only visit to the city. On Sunday he decided to attend services in a real church for a change, and so he rode into the city with staff members McGuire, Pendleton, and Douglas. At first they went unnoticed, mainly because few people knew what Jackson looked like, and with his wrinkled uniform and general absence of pomp there was nothing to catch anyone's eye. They entered the Presbyterian church and were escorted to a pew. Jackson, as was his habit, fell asleep and slept through most of the service, which included the fiery preaching of the Reverend Moses Hoge. The service proceeded as usual until, just as the benediction was being given, "a gentle excitement and rising confusion indicated that [Jackson] had been discovered."[23] Though the church doors opened, most of the attendees rushed for Jackson's pew instead, some of them climbing over the backs of other pews to get to him.[24] He tried to escape but, as Douglas told it,

> For awhile [Jackson] was cut off and surrounded and could not cut his way out; there was no relief in sight. The staff were run over and squeezed into a corner and otherwise disregarded, and were very little stars on the solar splendor of our Chief. But in the end we came to his rescue and got him out. Pretty girls tried to be polite to us, but it was too late; we would have none of it![25]

While he was in Richmond Jackson also paid a few calls. He went to the governor's mansion and met with Lee and his old friend Governor John Letcher. The two generals then continued on to the Confederate "White House," a splendid gray neoclassical mansion, where they met with Davis and other Confederate generals. After a while the other generals departed, leaving Lee, Davis, and Jackson to meet together in private. When the three came out, Davis and Lee, according to an observer, lingered for a moment on the front steps, then "bade Jackson farewell in a manner that indicated they would not see him again."[26] Whatever ill will there had been between Jackson and Davis was no longer apparent, and would not resurface during the war.

The meeting had been called to discuss a new threat. While the two armies had been locked in combat east of Richmond, a new Union army had been formed in the western part of the state under the command of Major General John Pope, and it was on the move. On July 12, the day before the meeting, Lee had learned that advance elements of that army were already near Culpeper, a town only twenty-seven miles northeast of the key strategic town of Gordonsville, the junction of the Orange and Alexandria and Virginia Central Railroads. They seemed to be closing fast. Lee's response was to formally divide his army into two commands, under Jackson and Longstreet. In case anyone wondered what Lee thought of his generals after the Seven Days, this was clear evidence of his continued high opinion of Jackson. The generals who had not performed well in his view, John Magruder and Benjamin Huger, were quickly shipped off—Huger to duty as inspector of artillery and ordnance; Magruder, eventually, to command of the Confederate Trans-Mississippi, which included Texas, New Mexico, and Arizona.[27] Lee would now leave Longstreet between McClellan and Richmond, and dispatch Jackson to meet Pope. Jackson would march the next day. Because he did not know what McClellan might do, Lee could spare Jackson no more than fourteen thousand troops (two divisions) to face fifty thousand bluecoats in the Piedmont. The confrontation was another absurd mismatch. But it had a curiously familiar ring.

CHAPTER THIRTY-SEVEN

No Backing Out This Day

❧❦❧

The new Union threat Jackson faced in Virginia was really an old Union threat, but one that had been renamed and placed under new management. The Army of Virginia, as it would be known—a Yankee army with a Confederate name—had been stitched together from the three armies Jackson had beaten up in his valley campaign. Its 1st Corps was John C. Frémont's old unit, now under the command of the angular, Teutonic Franz Sigel, a general of modest abilities who had fought in mostly losing campaigns in the western theater and whose main credential was that he had commanded revolutionary troops in Germany in 1848.[1] The army's 2nd Corps was commanded by Nathaniel Banks, the former Massachusetts governor and Speaker of the House who was still licking his wounds from his defeat at Winchester. The 3rd Corps was under the ponderous gourmand Irvin McDowell, the goat of Manassas, who had recently been left to guard Washington while McClellan waged war in the peninsula. Together they directed more than fifty thousand soldiers. Even as an assemblage of failed, early-war Union generals, they were an odd grouping.

But they were no odder than the man who had been appointed to command them. John Pope was a swaggering narcissist who had distinguished himself at West Point (Class of 1842, top third) and in the Mexican-American War and who had spent time before the war as an army surveyor and topographical engineer mapping southern routes for the transcontinental railroad. (The routes were never used.) In March 1862 he had won considerable fame for his capture of the town of New Madrid, Missouri, and the neighboring rebel-held Island No. 10 in the Mississippi River along with 3,500 prisoners. Like McClellan a year before, the confident, distinguished-looking Pope was very much the man of the hour, very much the Great New Hope of the Union.

But as Lincoln's new appointee he was in all other ways designed to be as unlike McClellan as possible. He was a staunch Republican, outspoken against slavery. He was in favor of causing suffering and disruption to the civilians of the South. His objective, as he told the Joint Committee on the Conduct of the War, was "to defend Washington, not by keeping on the defensive, nor by fortifying in front of the enemy, but by placing myself on his flanks and attacking him day and night."[2] In the view of his many supporters in Washington, he was an aggressive fighter, an image he cultivated in one of his first orders to his troops, which became quickly infamous. Addressed to the "Officers and Soldiers of the Army of Virginia," it said:

> Let us understand each other. I have come to you from the West, where we have always seen the backs of our enemies; from an army whose business it has been to seek the adversary and beat him when he was found; whose policy has been attack and not defense. . . . I desire you to dismiss from your minds certain phrases, which I am sorry to find so much in vogue amongst you. I hear constantly of "taking strong positions" and holding them, of "lines of retreat," and of "bases of supply." Let us discard such ideas. . . . Success and glory are in the advance, disaster and shame lurk in the rear.[3]

The speech was quite obviously aimed at McClellan. But it also infuriated a large segment of the military. Pope might as well have called the Army of the Potomac cowards. Then, too, there was the indisputable fact that few people who knew him seemed to like him much. Confederate general Richard Taylor wrote memorably that Pope's character was marked by "effrontery while danger was remote equaled by helplessness while it was present and mendacity after it had passed."[4] Union major general Fitz John Porter, McClellan's most devoted subordinate, had a similarly low opinion of Pope. "I regret to see that General Pope has not improved since his youth," he wrote a friend, "and now has written himself down as what the military world has long known, as ass."[5] John Frémont, who disliked Pope, had resigned rather than serve under him. (Pope was also of a lesser rank.) A correspondent for a British magazine captured the confident general in the summer of 1862: "Tall, corpulent, and athletic, with keen dark eyes, and beard and hair black as midnight, Gen. Pope had the air of a commander. Vain, imprudent, and not proverbially truthful; but shrewd, active, and skilled in the rules of warfare. . . . He spoke much and rapidly, chiefly of himself."[6]

But Pope was just getting started. A few days later he issued a series of harsh new orders that were unprecedented in their hostility toward Southern civilians who were seen—correctly—as a major impediment to Union operations. Indeed, Pope was responding to the anger much of the army felt at what they took to be McClellan's "pussyfooting." "We are the most timid and scrupulous invaders in history," a Massachusetts colonel wrote at the time. "It must be delicious to the finer feelings of some people to watch our velvet-footed advance."[7] Thus Pope announced that in the future his troops "will subsist upon the country," which meant that they now had full license to take anything and everything from Southern farms, from corn in the fields to cattle, pigs, chickens, tobacco, ice, smokehouse meats, and fruit preserves. The order was seen immediately for what it was: permission to pillage. There was more. Houses where gunshots originated would be burned. When damage was done to Union property, all citizens within five miles would be rounded up to repair the damage and even pay for it. Suspected guerrillas would be arrested and made to take loyalty oaths. Those who violated the oaths could be shot; others would be sent south through the Confederate lines—in effect, deported from Yankee-controlled to rebel-held territory. News of Union depredations inspired by these orders roared through the South, along with wild rumors about the wholesale rape of the Virginia Piedmont.

Lee himself took deep, personal offense. Though normally reserved in his judgments of others, including his enemies, he was outspoken on the subject of Pope, whom he said was "a miscreant" who must be "suppressed." He even wrote a letter on behalf of President Davis to new Union army chief Henry Halleck, protesting that Pope and his men had taken on the roles of "robbers and murderers," and that if they were captured they would not be granted the normal privileges of prisoners. If any unarmed citizens were shot by Pope's men, Lee warned, he would execute an equivalent number of Union officers.[8] Halleck did not bother to respond, and Lee never made good on his threat. Jackson considered Pope's orders "cruel and utterly barbarous," according to his brother-in-law Rufus Barringer. This from a man who had once advocated a "black flag" war in the North.[9]

Most soldiers and civilians, North and South, held Pope solely responsible for his brash words. Indeed, many historians have suggested that he was acting alone. But whether he was seen as a bold new commander, an ass, or, as Lee believed, an evil to be eradicated, Pope was in reality the carefully chosen spearhead of Lincoln's new campaign to toughen the war. The new Republican strategy was to stop playing nice, stop pretending that noncombatants in the South were somehow innocent, stop trying to preserve or defend enemy property—or, as one Union soldier had it, stop being "compelled to mount guard over rebel commissary stores, while Jackson's crew were refreshing themselves with sleep."[10] Congress had been hardening its stance for months. Now the army would, too, in direct contravention of the lofty Democratic theory of war McClellan had put forward to Lincoln in his July 7 letter. The truth was that Secretary of War Edwin Stanton had personally vetted Pope's troop address, and Abraham Lincoln had approved it. Lincoln had also approved, in advance, Pope's equally notorious general orders. Lincoln was in effect using Pope as a mouthpiece, speaking through him to McClellan, Southern civilians, the Union army, and the nation at large.[11] Unfortunately for Pope—the blustery, overconfident front man— many of the things he said would come to haunt him for the rest of his life.

Pope had assumed command just as McClellan was retreating from Lee's army across the York-James Peninsula. His orders, as they evolved, were mainly to guard the approaches to Washington. He did that by deploying his army across the forty-mile-wide patch of rolling, river-cut Virginia foothills between the Potomac River and the Blue Ridge Mountains, roughly along the line of the Rappahannock River. Any rebel army marching north from Richmond would have to cross it. On his left flank, the Army of Virginia linked with Federal troops under Ambrose Burnside near Fredericksburg. The latter arrangement was crucial. In early August McClellan was ordered to abandon the peninsula and take his army north to join Pope. Much of that army would disembark at a landing on the Potomac River near Fredericksburg called Aquia Creek, where it would march west to fortify the existing Union line. (The rest would come ashore at Alexandria and march south.) McClellan protested the move bitterly, insisting that first, with an additional 20,000, then 50,000, then 55,000 troops—the number kept escalating—he could take Richmond from Lee's mythical 200,000.[12] But that moment had passed. A new savior had arrived. The strategy now was to unite the two forces. Together they would form a sort of superarmy, with more than 150,000 men, that would be able to move, north to south, upon Lee and his works at Richmond.

Until then, Pope was to hold the line. In spite of this he was thinking bold, aggressive thoughts, appropriate to a man who had only seen the backs of fleeing rebels. Not far south of his army's position was the Virginia Central Railroad, Richmond's critical link to the Shenandoah Valley. If Pope could advance just twenty-five miles or so, he could take the towns of Gordonsville and Charlottesville, and he could cut that line. That was what he planned to do. Arriving on July 31 from Washington to assume field command, he wired his new boss, Henry Halleck, "Unless Jackson is heavily reinforced from Richmond, I shall be in possession of Gordonsville and Charlottesville within ten days."[13]

Jackson's orders from Lee, of course, were to prevent that very thing from happening. He had arrived in Gordonsville on July 19 with a force of roughly fourteen thousand men. With no immediate threat in sight, and with too few men to attack Pope, he rested and drilled his army. Courts-martial for the cases of Richard Garnett (Kernstown) and Z. T. Conner (Front Royal) were convened. (The Garnett trial would be interrupted and never concluded.) He tried to fire his cavalry chief, Beverly Robertson, but Lee would not allow it. Jackson accommodated the request of his sickly and inept but well-meaning friend Robert Dabney to return to civilian life, and welcomed the brother of his wife, Anna, Joseph Morrison, as an aide. (Reverend Dabney resumed his career as one of Southern Presbyterianism's most influential theologians.)

Though Jackson seemed more like the Old Jack everyone was used to, the effects of sickness and fatigue from the valley campaign and the Seven Days were still quite apparent. Jed Hotchkiss thought he looked "weary," and "the worse for his Chickahominy trip."[14] Anna's cousin, a doctor, had seen Jackson in person, and had reported to her that her husband was "not looking well and very thin." She was so concerned that she wrote to Hunter McGuire about it, to ask him to convince Jackson to take a short leave. "I have urged him," she wrote, "to treat himself to a *rest* and cessation from labor for a few weeks. Sixteen months of uninterrupted mental & physical labor is enough to break down the strongest constitution, but he is so *self-sacrificing*, & is such a *martyr to duty*, that if he thinks he cannot be spared from the service, I'm afraid he would sacrifice his life before he would give up."[15] With large Union armies abroad in Virginia, Jackson, in fact, could never be spared.

In his debilitated state, he had been writing to Anna less than usual, too, and perhaps this had increased her sense of alarm. Shortly after his arrival in Gordonsville, he wrote,

> *My darling wife, I am just overburdened with work, and I hope you will not think hard at receiving only very short letters from your loving husband. A number of officers are with me, but people keep coming to my tent—though let me say no more. A Christian should never complain. The apostle Paul said, "I glory in tribulations!" What a bright example for others!*[16]

Though McClellan had not yet begun his withdrawal, by July 27 Lee felt confident enough in his opponent's essential timidity to send Jackson reinforcements in the form of Ambrose Powell Hill's "Light Division" and a brigade of Louisianans. Lee, keenly aware that he was sending this hot-tempered general to work with the secretive, hypercritical Jackson, sent the latter a little admonitory note. "A. P. Hill you will find I think a good officer with whom you can consult," Lee wrote, "and by advising with your division commanders as to movements much trouble will be saved you." What Lee did not know was that enmity between his two generals dated to their West Point days, and that Hill was still seething with anger at what he considered (unfairly) Jackson's failure to fight at Mechanicsville and Savage's Station and his lateness at Gaines's Mill.[17]

But A. P. Hill's arrival changed everything. With twenty-two thousand men, Jackson now had the means to attack. He dispatched scouts and cavalry, looking for some weakness in Pope's position that would allow him to advance. On August 7, he found it. Pope, in apparent ignorance of the habits and predilections of his adversary, had permitted a piece of his army, specifically its 2nd Corps, to dangle tantalizingly out beyond the rest of the force near the town of Culpeper. It was pure coincidence that the man who commanded this vulnerable, detached Union force was none other than Nathaniel Prentiss Banks. Jackson prepared to move immediately against him. When Jackson's men heard that "Commissary Banks" was in their front, they cheered and capered about. "Get your requisitions ready, boys! . . . Old Stonewall's quartermaster has come with a full supply for issue."[18]

But Banks was nothing if not an ambitious, enterprising man. And now he saw an opportunity to win back some lost grace. Though there is considerable dispute about what Pope's orders said—Banks later insisted that he was directed to attack the enemy if the enemy approached, and Pope's defenders insisted that Banks was supposed to avoid bringing on a general engagement until the rest of the army came up—there was enough wiggle room for Banks to conclude that he could advance against Jackson.[19] He thus moved south of Culpeper, where, on August 9, he encountered his old adversary at a place called Cedar Mountain. Though Banks hardly needed encouragement, Pope's inspector general Brigadier General Benjamin S. Roberts took care that morning to remind him of what was expected of him. As Banks recalled later: "General Roberts, when he indicated the position [of the Union troops], said to me, in a tone which it was hardly proper for one officer to use to another, 'There must be no backing out this day.' He said this to me from six to twelve times. I made no reply to him at all, but felt it keenly because I knew my command did not want to back out; we had backed out enough."[20]

Whether he was goaded into it or shamed into it, or whether he simply thought he was following Pope's orders, Banks should never have offered battle. He was up against a superior force commanded by a superior general, who would that day bring fifteen thousand men into battle against Banks's nine thousand.[21] Pope insisted to the end of his life that he had never intended Banks to take on Jackson's entire force alone. All logic would have been with him; against a commander like Jackson, notorious for beating large armies with small ones, it seemed a suicidal move. But Banks picked a fight anyway.

The battlefield at Cedar Mountain was simply laid out: Union and Confederate troops faced each other in battle lines that ran roughly north to south for about two miles. The opposing lines were on average about half a mile apart. Most of the terrain was open: cornfields, wheatfields, and pastureland. On the south a large, conical green hill loomed up over the open, gently swelling landscape. The northern extremities of both lines disappeared in patches of thick woods. At about 3:00 p.m. the now customary artillery fight started. For two hours the two sides pounded each other. Though the Union had superior weapons, Jackson the artillerist and former artillery instructor got the better of his adversary, carefully choosing his gun positions on the mountain itself and behind his lines to create a devastating converging fire.

As his artillery took its toll on men, horses, and enemy guns and caissons, Jackson roved over the field on horseback, his eyes wide and luminous with the light of battle, like a man who had been born to do this and only this. He cared nothing for his own safety. At one point he and a group of his staffers on horseback were numerous enough to attract the attention of Union batteries. Suddenly the air was full of projectiles that either exploded above or plowed up the soil around them. Jackson was unperturbed. "General Jackson had been sitting with his right leg thrown across the pommel of his saddle," wrote cavalryman John Blue, "as immovable apparently as a statue, with his field glasses watching the artillery duel." With the evident peril closing in on them he turned to his nervous companions and said, with a faint smile, that the Confederate guns "were making it pretty warm" for the Yankees. A moment later, a shell exploded very close to the group, wounding three horses. Jackson immediately led the group to the rear and told them they would be better off out of sight. "They will hardly aim at a single horseman," he assured them. His order was obeyed happily and without question, while Jackson returned to his observation point.[22] A moment later a rider arrived to tell Jackson that one of his key generals and a division commander, Charles S. Winder, had been mortally wounded by a shell fragment. Jackson raised his hand in silent prayer.

At 5:45 p.m. Banks's infantry attacked. Two brigades under Brigadier General Christopher Augur advanced two-deep through the cornrows and thickening heat toward the waiting Confederates. Soon long rolls of musket fire exploded along most of the line. Sheets of yellow flame pierced billowing clouds of white smoke, while volleys of sizzling minié balls filled the air like angry insects. It was a stand-up fight, with little cover. On the Confederate right, Brigadier General Jubal Early, a hard fighter who would make a name for himself at this battle, repulsed advance after advance. By some estimates there were *nine* of them.[23] From the base of Cedar Mountain, General Richard Ewell's batteries continued to fire, as Jackson, close to the front, watched contentedly through his field glasses. He was clearly transported by the sights and sounds of the battle, wrote Blue. He was "a different person altogether," who only by great exertion managed to stop himself from riding into combat.

But Blue noticed something else, too. Jackson was not only watching the action on the field, he was also looking "anxiously to the rear." Why? Because Jackson had once again gone into battle with only two of his three divisions. D. H. Hill's division—representing most of Jackson's numerical superiority—was due to arrive at any moment. But where was it? Jackson ordered a member of his staff to ride to General Early and "say to him, stand firm, Gen. Hill will be with him in a few moments."[24] Early was indeed holding his own as the battle raged on.

The real and immediate peril, however, lurked not in the open field but on Jackson's left, in the deep woods behind the wheatfield, where he could not see it. He had received a report from Jubal Early of Federal bayonets moving in and around those woods, and had sent word to brigade commander Thomas S. Garnett to "look well" to his left. (He had no relation to Richard B. Garnett.) Unfortunately, no one did; or if someone did, he did not look very hard. Garnett's superior, the mortally wounded Charles Winder, had been replaced by William B. Taliaferro, who was far more concerned with the battle in the center and right. The result was that Jackson's left wing was in considerable disarray: its soldiers were not where they should be. His old Stonewall Brigade, on the far Confederate left, which had been hanging back from the front, was supposed to be marching to a position even with the rest of the Confederate line, and closing up the gaps on the far left. The 10th Virginia Regiment, which had been ordered to help reinforce Garnett's left, had not yet arrived.

At this moment of unexpected vulnerability, less than twenty minutes into the battle and just a few minutes after Jackson had told Early to hold on, Nathaniel Banks decided to order an attack on the Confederate left. It seems to have been more a product of his annoyance with the Confederate artillery than a deliberate or calculated plan.[25] In any case, it shouldn't have worked. Just ten minutes later, when the Stonewall Brigade had come up and the 10th Virginia was moving into place, it could not possibly have worked. But Banks, unknowingly—as far as we can tell—had hit an invisible, 1,400-foot-wide seam, the weakest point in Jackson's line. Shortly after 6:00 p.m., three and a half regiments with 1,500 bluecoats under Brigadier General Samuel Crawford scrambled out of the woods and into the open field in a straight-ahead assault. In front of them, across the open wheatfield, stood Garnett's four regiments plus a battalion (a collection of companies and smaller than a regiment). The numbers, and the terrain, would all seem to have been in favor of Garnett. A body of men smaller than his own was advancing, unprotected, through a quarter-mile-wide wheatfield, while his own men enjoyed the cover of woods and brush. Crawford's men never should have reached the other side of the field. They should have been cut down.

They weren't. Whether it was the sheer audacity of the Federals, or the faintheartedness of the 21st Virginia, which quickly broke and ran, or the fact that the bluecoats crossed the field so quickly that the rebels had no time to reload—or some combination of these—within minutes Garnett's men were "broken, thrown back in masses from front to rear, and intermingled with their assailants," wrote Union brigadier general George H. Gordon.[26] Some of the fighting was close and brutal. "Guns, bayonets, swords, pistols, fence rails, rocks, etc., were used all along the line," recalled infantryman John Worsham. "I have heard of a 'hell spot' in some battles and this surely was one."[27]

Having shattered Garnett's brigade, Crawford's regiments, flush with victory, rolled on, swinging to the left, back out of the woods, and straight into the cornfield where the main battle was taking place. There they slammed into the flank of four regiments of Alabama and Virginia troops under Taliaferro, who had been battling Augur's Union line. It was still only six fifteen or so. The entire duration of Crawford's attack thus far was fifteen minutes. Since infantry will not stand flanking fire—seeing bullets coming at them from two sides—Taliaferro's men fell back, too, and suddenly the entire Confederate left was collapsing. "Field and woods were filled with clamor and horrid rout . . ." wrote Gordon, "until the left of Jackson's line was turned and its rear gained. . . . As Campbell [Garnett] had been overthrown, so next was Taliaferro; and then came the left of Early's brigade . . . until on both sides of the road vast irruption had been made, which involved the whole of the enemy's line."[28]

Jackson, meanwhile, had been observing Augur's unsuccessful attacks against his center and right across the cornfield when a sudden, loud roar of musketry came up from his left. He cocked his right ear (he was almost deaf in the left), listened for a few moments, and concluded, "That firing is very heavy." He wheeled, spurred his horse, and galloped off down the line, leaving his staff struggling to catch up. Suddenly the old professor was on fire. He galloped four hundred yards, leaped two fences, and plunged into the woods where Garnett's men were in wild, chaotic retreat. Jackson reined in, sat there for a moment taking in the scene before him, "calm as a statue" as shells exploded and rebels streamed past him, then turned and cantered toward the rear.[29] He needed A. P. Hill's division *now*. He finally found Hill—who had grown up in Culpeper, eight miles away—putting his men into line and attempting to slow the retreat. Jackson curtly informed him that he was late and ordered him to bring his regiments immediately forward. Jackson approached one of Hill's brigade commanders, Brigadier General Lawrence Branch, a famous orator in the antebellum House of

Representatives, saying, "Push forward, General! Push forward!" As Branch's men moved forward they chanted, "Stonewall Jackson! Stonewall Jackson!"[30]

Jackson wheeled again, and galloped back into the murderous heart of the battle—the place in the woods where Garnett's brigade had been driven back. Now, his blue eyes blazing and his face aglow as if possessed, the hatless major general rallied his troops. He reached for his saber but the scabbard was so rusted he could not draw it out. So he unsnapped the scabbard and, brandishing it, used the flat of it on the heads and shoulders of retreating troops, urging them to stop and turn around. A few moments later he took hold of a battle flag and raised it over his head, dropping the reins to do so, and continued his ride forward toward the front, holding both saber and flag aloft. As he did so he shouted to the men. There is some disagreement about exactly what he said, but it probably included "Rally, men! Forward! Jackson is with you! Your general will lead you! Follow me!"

The effect was immediate and electric. "Our men followed with a yell and drove everything before him," wrote Charles Minor Blackford, who was with him. "It was a wonderful scene—one which men do not often see. Jackson is usually an indifferent, slouchy looking man. But then, with the 'Light of Battle' shedding its radiance over him, his whole person changed. . . . The men would have followed him into the jaws of death itself; nothing could have stopped them and nothing did."[31] The whole scene, he might have added, could not have been more out of character for the stern, reserved general. He had done something like this only once—in the road at the Battle of Chapultepec in Mexico, while he stood in a rain of bullets and shell and tried to rally his battery—but he had not done it since and would never do it again. His ride through the disintegrated Confederate left was also extremely dangerous. Considering that he was on horseback, and waving a sword and flag amid that "tornado" of bullets, officers near him marveled that he wasn't hit. Taliaferro wrote later that his escape "from death was miraculous." Taliaferro also understood that Jackson could not stay where he was. As he described it, "[Jackson] was in the very thickest of the combat, at short range. I rode up to him and insisted that he should retire, painfully and emphatically telling him that it was no place for the commander of an army." Jackson looked surprised when his division commander said this, then said, "Good, good," and rode to the rear.[32] As he did, the rebel yell rose around him. He had certainly rallied the troops in his immediate vicinity—though his heroics would have had little effect on the other end of a two-mile battle line.

Several Union prisoners, captured on the battlefield, were also impressed by Jackson's performance. One young Federal soldier, in the custody of Captain Blackford, asked him, "What officer is that?" When Blackford told him, the young soldier "seemed carried away with admiration . . . he waved his broken sword and shouted 'Hurrah for General Jackson! Follow your general, boys!'" Blackford, touched by his response, quietly let his prisoner return to his lines.[33] Jed Hotchkiss, who was also with Jackson, recorded that other "Yankee prisoners cheered Gen. Jackson as he rode past them coming back after the fight."[34]

As Jackson was galloping heroically to the front, conditions were already changing in the Confederates' favor. Though Crawford's indomitable men had managed to rout Garnett's brigade, Taliaferro's brigade, and half of Early's brigade, they had finally shattered themselves against the 13th Virginia Infantry, commanded by Colonel James A. Walker, the VMI cadet who had challenged Jackson and been expelled. Their flanking movement, which had, implausibly, nearly forced Jackson's entire army to retreat, was spent. There were no reinforcements on the way, no attempt was being made to consolidate their gains; Banks had left them alone on the field to fend for themselves.

And now Hill's men came on, eight thousand of them, fresh and ready to fight, and soon it was the Union forces who were retreating. Jackson's superior numbers began to take their toll. As Brigadier General Crawford described it, his retreat through Confederate fire was horrific: "The reserves of the enemy were at once brought up and thrown upon the broken ranks. The field officers had all been killed, wounded, or taken prisoner, the support I looked for did not arrive, and my gallant men, decimated by that fearful fire . . . fell back again across that space leaving most of their number on the field."[35] Jackson's center was once again stable. General Ewell, on the right, who had been unable to advance because of Confederate artillery across his field, now launched a full assault on the Union left. Banks understood what was happening to him. With his right shattered and his left in imminent danger, he ordered his full line to retreat, leaving the dead and wounded on the field. As the light in the sky began to fade, Jackson's troops now swept forward as Confederate cheers and yells filled the air.

It had been yet another hard, pitiless fight, and the battlefield bore witness to it. Though the infantry battle had lasted less than ninety minutes, more than 3,000 soldiers had fallen. Jackson's troops had killed or wounded 1,786 Federals and taken 617 prisoner. Banks had killed or wounded 1,376 and taken only 42 prisoner.[36] As always, Jackson wanted to pursue the enemy, and ordered A. P. Hill, with his fresh troops, to follow them. As always, pursuit after a battle was almost impossible to execute. Hill's men got only half a mile before darkness came on. The army was worn out, used up. The temperature during the day had been in the 90s; by nightfall it was still 86 degrees. There would be no more pursuit that night.

The next day Jackson sent Jeb Stuart on a reconnaissance mission. Unhappy with his current cavalry chief, Beverly Robertson, he had summoned Stuart under the pretext of having him perform a "tour of inspection." The two friends had colluded (as Jackson and Ewell had) to subvert military protocol, and the straitlaced moralist Jackson had lied about it. He seemed to feel no particular remorse. Stuart was Ashby without the administrative shortcomings and the hair-trigger temperament. Jackson liked the very *idea* of Stuart. He and his horsemen soon demonstrated yet again why Jackson, Lee, and everyone else found him so necessary, riding behind enemy lines, and even capturing a signal station.[37] What he found was discouraging. Pope, stung by his defeat, was moving up troops to reinforce Banks. One of McDowell's divisions under General James Ricketts had arrived to cover Banks's retreat, and Franz Sigel's 1st Corps was on its way to the front. Jackson would soon be colossally outnumbered, and he knew it. On August 11, after burying Confederate and Union dead under flags of truce, he began withdrawing his force to Gordonsville. Meanwhile, something interesting was happening—or not happening—that was at odds with Pope's warlike bluster of the preceding week. The Union commander had vastly superior numbers at his disposal, he no longer seemed in any hurry to attack Stonewall Jackson.

Though Jackson had won a clear victory, Cedar Mountain had been no tactical gem. He had fought before his army was at full strength; he had failed to realize the weakness of his left (though the confusion following Winder's mortal wounding was to blame for this, too); his habitual secretiveness had prevented his commanders from understanding his battle plan, if he even had one. The Battle of Cedar Mountain seems to have been fought on both sides without clear schemes of attack. It was more of a stand-up slugfest punctuated by Samuel Crawford's brilliant but doomed dash across the Union flank. To his credit, Jackson had planned and executed a highly destructive artillery barrage, one that claimed many Union lives and much matériel and that clearly got the better of his adversary.

He had also, with his heroism on horseback in the heat of the battle, shown himself to be an inspiring field officer. There were many such brave men in the war on both sides; you can see them in old paintings on horseback and with sabers drawn, shrouded by white smoke and exhorting their men forward. But they were likely captains or majors or colonels, not corps commanders. Jackson's men had seen him and heard him and they had followed him forward, and in so doing had helped drive the Federals back. After the battle, there was no one in his corps who did not know what he had done. Jackson himself considered his victory at Cedar Mountain his greatest military achievement, and he was uncharacteristically proud of it. If his confidence had suffered at all from the Seven Days campaign, it had now been restored. "I congratulate you most heartily on the victory which God has granted you over our enemies at Cedar Run," Lee wrote to Jackson on August 12. "The country owes you and your brave officers and soldiers a deep debt of gratitude."[38] That same day Jackson wrote Anna, "On last Saturday our God again crowned our arms with victory. . . . I can hardly think of the fall of Brigadier-General C. S. Winder without tearful eyes." Then he veered into that somewhat abstracted, impersonal, divinity-infused style that he often used in his letters: "Let us all unite more earnestly in imploring God's aid in fighting our battles for us. . . . If God be for us, who can be against us? That He will make our nation that people whose God is the Lord, is my earnest and oft-repeated prayer."[39]

Most important, Cedar Mountain was another victory. It had his name on it, and now Jackson, seemingly invincible, was more famous than ever. The day after the battle, a Union prisoner who was being held near Jackson's tent was discovered standing behind Little Sorrel, systematically plucking hairs from the horse's tail. Noticing this, one of Jackson's staff ordered the man to stop it just as Jackson himself emerged from his tent. "My friend," Jackson asked in a soft voice, "why are you tearing the hair out of my horse's tail?" The prisoner, removing his hat, replied, "Ah, General, each one of these hairs is worth a dollar in New York."[40]

CHAPTER THIRTY-EIGHT

THE HUM OF A BEEHIVE

❧❧❧

While the Virginia yeomanry suffered under Pope's harsh new regime, which turned once-prosperous farmers into paupers overnight, Jackson's own soldiers also found themselves in a much harder and less forgiving world.[1] The most obvious signs of this were the new Confederate conscription laws, passed in April of that year, that extended terms of service for currently enrolled soldiers and made all males from eighteen to thirty-five subject to the new draft. The early war had been fought entirely with volunteers, many of whom believed that military regulations infringed on their basic rights to liberty and the pursuit of happiness. These were people, after all, who had revolted against a centralizing government, natural antistatists who did not want *anyone* in authority telling them what to do. During Jackson's valley campaign, he had lost thousands of men who simply went home. In June, Longstreet complained that soldiers were moving between the army and their homes "without the slightest regard for official policy." Many never came back. The ones who did were punished lightly or quietly forgiven. None was shot for desertion, though hundreds easily could have been.[2] In the first phase of the war, the army and the public at large would not tolerate mass shootings of deserters. Jackson, like other generals, had understood this.[3]

But by the summer of 1862 the national mood had changed. Southerners were tired of seeing stragglers and deserters—"dirty villains," as the *Richmond Examiner* called them—lounging about grogshops, boardinghouses, and hotels while brave men fought and died on the fields of war. As a result, those early days of tolerance and understanding were coming to an end.[4] Stragglers, once considered an inevitable if unfortunate part of war, were increasingly treated as what they often were: men who would not fight. On the march from Richmond to Gordonsville, Jackson's division commander Charles S. Winder had ordered thirty stragglers "bucked and gagged"—a painful form of punishment that consisted of tying the offender's hands together at the wrists and slipping them down over the knees, while running a stick under the knees and over the arms. The "gag" was a bayonet placed in the mouth and tied from behind with string. Men would be left in this trussed position from sunrise to sunset. Winder hated stragglers. Though Jackson ordered him to stop the practice, Winder persisted in his other favorite punishment, hanging stragglers and other disciplinary cases from trees by their thumbs so their toes barely touched the ground, and leaving them that way all day.[5]

The new severity brought far worse punishments. Before the Battle of Cedar Mountain, a court-martial established by Jackson had convicted three soldiers of desertion and sentenced them to death. Two of them were conscripts who were guilty of nothing more than missing their families and going home to see them, something many members of the Stonewall Brigade had done, often repeatedly, in the valley campaign. Jackson entertained two pleas for leniency. To the first, from a colonel in the 10th Virginia, from whose regiment two of the men came, he replied with icy fury, "Sir! Men who desert their comrades in war deserve to be shot! And officers who intercede for them deserve to be hung!" For Jackson, straggling and desertion were the ultimate violations of duty. Next came a chaplain with his own gentle plea. "General, consider your responsibilities to the Lord," he implored Jackson. "You are sending these men's souls to Hell!" Jackson replied, "That, sir, is my business. Do you do yours!" Jackson "then handled the chaplain rather roughly," according to Jed Hotchkiss, "taking him by the shoulders, whirling him around, and pushing him out of the tent."[6] Jackson hated deserters with a special passion. He had only restrained himself from shooting them before because public opinion wouldn't have tolerated it.

On August 19, the day of the executions, Brigadier General William Taliaferro's full division marched out in columns to a field beside the Mount Pisgah Baptist Church in Orange County, Virginia, while a regimental band played a funeral march. The prisoners were blindfolded and forced to kneel in front of their caskets. The firing squad formed at six paces and fired a volley into the prisoners. Two were killed instantly. The third, who was still alive and tried to stand, was shot again.[7]

The next day two Confederate soldiers who had deserted to the enemy were captured by Jeb Stuart's cavalry. Jackson ordered them hanged from the limb of a tree by the roadside and left there while the rest of the army passed by, just in case anyone hadn't gotten the message.[8]

The Battle of Cedar Mountain might have seemed at first like a version of Malvern Hill—a pointless slaughter brought on by a foolish attack that accomplished nothing in particular for either side. Jackson had withdrawn two days later to his previous position below the Rapidan River. The Union was no closer to its objective of taking the Virginia Central Railroad in Gordonsville. But a major change *had* taken place, and it had happened in the minds of Union war boss Henry Halleck and John Pope. Jackson's lunge at Culpeper, as it turned out, had scared them.[9] On July 31, Pope had vowed to Halleck that he would be "in possession of Gordonsville . . . within ten days." But at five forty-five in the morning after his defeat at Cedar Mountain—exactly ten days later—he sounded like a different man. Now he warned Halleck that he expected "a very severe engagement" to follow and that "I will do the best I can, and if forced to retire will so do by way of Rappahannock Crossing."[10] Though he continued to rattle his saber, advising Halleck on August 12 that "The enemy has retreated under cover of night. . . . Our cavalry and artillery are in pursuit," in fact he had little or no interest in advancing against Jackson. The wind had gone out of his sails.

Halleck, meanwhile, was even more worried than Pope about the danger that lurked south of the Rapidan: "Your main object should be to keep the enemy in check until we can get reinforcements to your army," he wired Pope on August 11. On August 13 he said flatly, "Do not advance across the Rapidan," and repeated that order on the sixteenth.[11] Pope's orders were to wait for McClellan's army to join him. Halleck, meanwhile, was badgering Little Mac into speeding up his massive troop transfer. McClellan, for personal and political reasons—not least because he thought that helping his detested colleague John Pope was contrary to his self-interest—was slow-walking the entire enterprise.

Lee's objective, conversely, was to strike Pope before McClellan got there. Lee had thus ordered Longstreet's corps to join Jackson near Gordonsville, leaving a mere three divisions to guard all of Richmond. By August 16 Lee had an army of 54,000 men—30,000 under Longstreet and 24,000 under Jackson—facing Pope's 50,000. Lee did not know how much of McClellan's army was on its way to reinforce the Army of Virginia. But he knew he was running out of time. Once McClellan joined Pope it would be impossible to force the Federals from central Virginia, or to head north, as Lee was planning. Lee would be forced to withdraw.

Lee, Jackson, and Longstreet spread maps in front of them and pondered their next move. Lee quickly saw that Pope had made a potentially fatal mistake. In his new, post–Cedar Mountain defensive posture, he had backed himself and his entire army into the delta formed by the junction of the Rapidan and Rappahannock Rivers. Though there were several fords across the Rappahannock, there was only one main bridge across which his army could escape. Burn it, Lee theorized, and he could cripple the Union retreat. Thus cornered, with his back to a great river, Pope's army might be destroyed. It was one of those moments of crystal-clear vision that rarely happen in war. Pope was exquisitely vulnerable. Lee ordered an immediate advance. Unfortunately, he once again could not make the cumbersome machinery of his army move fast enough. By the time he got it in motion, Pope, aided by an intercepted message, had discovered his error and had promptly moved his army behind the Rappahannock. A disappointed Robert E. Lee ordered the two wings of his army—Longstreet on the right and Jackson on the left—forward to the south bank of the Rappahannock. On August 20 the two armies were staring at each other across one of the most formidable natural obstacles in the region.

Now the game began in earnest, but with more pressure on Lee than ever. He knew that the Union armies might be only days from rendezvous, and he had left Richmond virtually undefended.[12] To engage Pope before that happened, Lee would have to cross the Rappahannock at one of its three bridges or half dozen fords. Pope, understanding this, vigorously defended the crossings. For three days, from August 21 to 23, in a series of artillery fights and skirmishes that included an ineffectual Jeb Stuart raid into the Union rear at Catlett's Station, Lee's army probed for weak points in the Union line. When he was repulsed, Lee simply slid his army crabwise upstream, north and west, Jackson's corps in the lead, looking for better opportunities and stretching Pope's already thin lines. Pope and his generals showed considerable defensive skill. They mimicked Lee's moves and parried his thrusts.[13] On August 22 one of Jackson's brigade commanders, Jubal Early, finally got beyond the Union right flank and managed to cross the river at Sulphur Springs. But he was isolated there by rains and a rising river, and suddenly found himself and his brigade trapped on the enemy's side of the river. He was rescued from fast-closing Union forces only after Jackson's engineers managed to build a makeshift bridge.

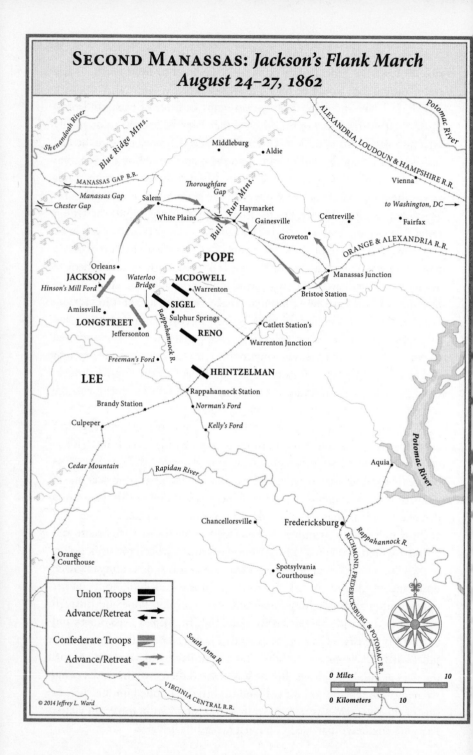

SECOND MANASSAS: *Jackson's Flank March*
August 24–27, 1862

© 2014 Jeffrey L. Ward

By August 24, Lee's army was once again in stalemate, facing Pope across the Rappahannock. This time they were farther upstream, but with no better chance of crossing than they had had four days before. Artillery continued to boom but was increasingly meaningless. Pope's defensive maneuvers had gotten him what he most needed: time. That day the first of his reinforcements began arriving. Many more were on their way, marching west from Fredericksburg or south from Alexandria. The Army of Virginia and the Army of the Potomac, it seemed, were on the verge of unification.

That Sunday afternoon, August 24, Lee summoned Jackson to his headquarters near the town of Jeffersonton, behind the Confederate left. Jackson was in a bad mood. His army's maneuvers had produced nothing. He had been forced to save Early from almost certain destruction. Nothing had been gained. Jackson arrived to find that "headquarters" was really a table that had been set up in an open field, away from any structures, human or natural. "There was not even a tree within hearing," recalled one officer. This was to be an *extremely* confidential meeting. Lee was seated at the table with a map laid out in front of him. James Longstreet was seated on his right, Jeb Stuart on his left. Jackson approached the table and stood, facing them.[14] While artillery grumbled in the distance, the four generals talked. Though staff officers loitering nearby listened as hard as they could, they could make out nothing. Hunter McGuire recalled many years later that at some point in the meeting "Jackson . . . was very much excited, drawing with the toe of his boot a map in the sand, and gesticulating in a much more earnest way than he was in the habit of doing. General Lee was simply listening, and after Jackson had got through, he nodded his head, as if acceding to some proposal."[15] The only record of what was said came from Douglas, who heard Jackson say, at the meeting's end, "I will be moving within an hour."[16]

Though we do not know what words were spoken, we know with great certainty what the meeting was all about. What had gotten Jackson's attention was one of the most profoundly daring plans of the war, one that violated both military theory and common sense in equal measure. To pry Pope out of his secure position behind the Rappahannock, Lee proposed that Jackson and his entire corps march in a sweeping arc around the Union right, climbing north across the foothills of the Blue Ridge, then turning east through the Bull Run Mountains, and landing on the plains deep behind Union lines. His mission was to cut the Orange and Alexandria Railroad, Pope's main supply line. In that sense, the plan was similar to what Lee had proposed in front of Richmond: to force a Union army to withdraw to protect its supplies. Except that now, any rebel force in Pope's rear would also be on Washington's doorstep. Once Pope discovered what had happened, he would have no choice but to leave his Rappahannock camps and move toward Washington. James Longstreet, meanwhile, would try to keep Pope's attention engaged as long as he could. When Pope fell back, Longstreet would follow Jackson's route north. Twenty-five mounted couriers from the vaunted Black Horse Troop would keep Lee and Jackson in touch.[17] If there was one lesson Lee had learned at the Seven Days, it was the importance of communication.

The risks inherent in Lee's plan were breathtaking. By dividing his army he left each half vulnerable to attack. If Pope learned that there were now two small rebel armies separated by fifty miles, he could attack and destroy Lee, then turn on Jackson. Then, too, there was the problem of McClellan's army, some of which might be landing at Washington (two entire army corps, in fact, under Franklin and Sumner). That would leave Jackson trapped between McClellan and Pope, with Lee unable to help. Whatever happened, Jackson would be alone in the Union rear with no supply line and no reinforcements within a two-day march. From the moment he left the Rappahannock, he would be in constant peril. The closer he got to Washington, the more hazardous his position would become. Jackson, who had proven his ability to operate alone and without support while engaging multiple Union armies in the valley, was the obvious choice for the job. As in the valley campaign, Lee left the details of Jackson's operation to him. Jackson was ecstatic: he was being ordered by Lee to strike deep in the heart of enemy territory, surrounded by unprecedented peril, with almost unimaginably high stakes.

He lost no time getting started. At 6:00 p.m. on the night of August 24, Longstreet's brigades quietly replaced Jackson's troops along the river. At 3:00 a.m. on the twenty-fifth, Jackson's bugles blew reveille, the men were rousted, and the army trooped off, tack creaking, wagon wheels rattling, shanks of bayonets clanking rhythmically against canteens. None of the men had the slightest idea where they were going. But that was nothing new. They joked that Jackson's piety expressed itself in the directive "Let not thy left hand know what thy right hand doeth."[18] But by now they knew Jackson well enough to know that they were headed for a fight.

The march was textbook Jackson: The corps he brought across the river at Hinson's Ford was light, lean, and stripped for action. The men carried only their muskets, cartridge belts with sixty rounds of ammunition, and haversacks with three days' cooked rations. All baggage, knapsacks, and bedrolls were left behind. Other than his eighty guns, with caissons and limbers, the only other rolling stock were ambulances. A herd of cattle trailed the column. By deliberate design, a twenty-four-thousand-man corps, with its immense human needs, was marching deep into enemy territory and into a country that had already been heavily foraged, with no supply train and no supply line.[19] It was the sort of enterprise that a general such as George McClellan, with his obsessive worry about supplies, could never have imagined.

There were new marching rules, too. This time there would be constant movement, no breaks, no more fifty minutes on and ten minutes off. There was to be no straggling, no removing of clothing or shoes when crossing streams. There was to be a minimum amount of noise, too. And there was even more than the usual secrecy. Those who knew the country knew they were marching north, but no more. Even Jackson's division chiefs were kept in the dark. According to William Taliaferro, their only instructions were to "march to a cross-road; a staff officer there will inform you which fork to take; and so to the next fork, where you will find a courier with a sealed direction pointing out the road."[20]

Though the terrain was broken and uneven—nothing like the often deadflat, macadamized valley pike, where Jackson's foot cavalry had won its reputation for marching—the men moved with extraordinary speed, leaving the column only to grab ears of green corn or half-ripe apples from roadside fields.[21] Even by Jackson's standards, his soldiers performed brilliantly. "They outmarched and broke down the artillery horses," wrote one soldier. "So enthused were both officers and men that I never heard a word of complaint."[22] Another soldier wrote, "The fine weather, magnificent country, the mysterious march through fields and byways . . . the possible collision at any moment with the enemy . . . all served to keep us intensely interested."[23]

They conducted of one the war's most remarkable marches: twenty-six miles in a single day, with full ordnance and artillery. The column moved with the same sort of sustained speed that had produced those odd, warping effects on enemy perception in Jackson's valley campaign. As events unfolded, it would not seem possible to anyone along the Rappahannock or in Washington that an army of that size could possibly have covered that much ground, secretly, in one day. Even the normally hard-to-impress Jackson admitted that it was "a severe day's march."[24] Near sunset, as Jackson's column approached the town of Salem, twelve miles north of Pope's right, he dismounted and climbed a large rock by the side of the road to review his troops. He presented a strange spectacle, standing hatless, high above the road, illuminated by the rays of the setting sun. When the men saw him they forgot their exhaustion and burst into cheers. But as the hurrahs rolled through the regiments Jackson, worried that the noise might alert the enemy, signaled gently to the men to stop. They did, and immediately passed the word through the ranks: "No cheering." Instead, as they passed the lone man on the rock they raised their caps in mute tribute to their strange, transcendent leader. Jackson, softened by this remarkable display, said to a member of his staff, "Who could not conquer with such troops as these?"[25] When Jackson's column finally halted, in darkness, the weary men "dropped beside their stacked muskets," recalled one of them, "and without so much as spreading a blanket were instantly asleep."[26]

Back on the Rappahannock, Longstreet's batteries were trying to keep Pope's mind on his front and not on his flank and rear. At 8:45 a.m., a Union colonel in Banks's command on Pope's far right saw an arresting sight: a column of rebel infantry and artillery marching in a northwesterly direction away from the village of Jeffersonton. At nine thirty he had an even more interesting report: four batteries and six to eight regiments had passed within the hour, "well closed up and with colors flying."[27] At eleven twenty-five Nathaniel Banks sent Pope a note with his own analysis. "It seems apparent," he wrote, "that the enemy is threatening or moving upon the Valley of the Shenandoah via Front Royal with designs upon the Potomac, possibly beyond."[28] Pope immediately wired Halleck with the perplexing news, telling him that he believed the rebel column contained twenty thousand men, and saying that he was ready to dispatch Irvin McDowell to pursue them.

But instead of actually doing anything about this mysterious rebel column, Pope spent the better part of the day shuffling the various parts of his army, and extending his line, for some unknown reason, to the left. While doing all that, he failed to order his cavalry to scout the enemy outside his own lines. Somehow, by the end of a day that saw Jackson's men in bivouac far to the north, Pope had come to agree with Banks that the mysterious Confederate column was headed toward the valley. Pope would always have trouble perceiving the obvious. That was lucky for Lee, whose plan was working perfectly.

On the second day Jackson was moving again in the pitch darkness of "early dawn." Soon his divisions under Ewell, Hill, and Taliaferro turned east, pushing ahead with the same resolve they had shown the previous day. The pace once again was an unforgiving three miles an hour. At midday the column crossed the narrow defile through the pretty, modest elevations of the Bull Run Mountains. By four o'clock on August 26, while James Longstreet's guns continued to fire across the Rappahannock, Jackson's men found themselves very far indeed behind Pope's lines—roughly twenty miles—in the small town of Gainesville. They had marched fifty miles in thirty-two hours. At about this time Jeb Stuart and two brigades of cavalry had caught up with Jackson.[29] They had been ordered there by Lee, who thought Jackson needed Stuart's scouting and screening abilities more than Longstreet did. From now on, Stuart would be Jackson's eyes, shadowing his every move. While Stuart's horsemen were fanning out, Longstreet was starting to pull away from his position on the Rappahannock. He and Lee had agreed that the best way to reunite the two armies would be for Longstreet to follow in Jackson's path, through Thoroughfare Gap in the Bull Run Mountains. Where they might meet was unknown: it would depend on how Pope responded to Jackson's incursion.

Jackson now moved to cut the railroad line. He knew there was a large Union supply depot at Manassas Junction, but he believed it might be heavily defended. So he decided to strike the smaller Bristoe Station. At 6:00 p.m. his cavalry swept aside the few surprised Federals who were there. Soon they heard the whistle of a train returning from delivering supplies to Pope's army at Warrenton. Though the Confederates tried frantically to derail it, they were too late: the train roared through, carrying word of the rebel presence eastward to Manassas and beyond. A few minutes later another train arrived. This time Jackson's men were ready, having placed obstacles along a quarter mile of track. He and his staff watched from a small rise by the tracks as the train came on. When shots were fired, the engineer throttled up, the train boomed through the station, and hit the obstructions. "Down the embankment rushed the engine," recalled an observer, "screaming and hissing, and down upon it rushed the cars, piling up on one another until the pile reached higher than the embankment."[30] Soon another train arrived, smashing into the wreckage of the first. A third train approached, but the engineer spotted trouble and turned back toward Warrenton, now carrying the news directly to Pope.

Having wrought considerable destruction on the rail line—the principal goal of his expedition—Jackson now turned his attention to the Union supply depot at Manassas Junction, five miles farther toward Washington on the Orange and Alexandria line. He sent Isaac Trimble, the stalwart Marylander who had performed well at Cross Keys, along with 500 infantry and some of Stuart's cavalry, to attack the Federal force there. Trimble made quick work of it. His regiments swarmed into the lightly defended depot, setting upon his adversaries before they had time to unlimber most of their cannons. Trimble's men took 300 prisoners, including the post commander, 175 horses, and 8 pieces of artillery, plus an enormous trove of Union supplies while sustaining only 4 casualties. It was sometime after midnight. Jackson, after marching more than 50 miles, had completely severed Pope's supply line.

At about the time Trimble was taking Manassas Junction, John Pope was sitting in his headquarters near Warrenton concluding that something was seriously wrong. He had been receiving ever more alarming reports all day and into the night: rebels under Jackson, Longstreet, Hill, and Stuart were seen approaching Thoroughfare Gap. At 8:00 p.m. he received a telegraph from Manassas telling of a Confederate attack on the railroad. By midnight, with his communications cut, Pope had decided that ten thousand to fifteen thousand Confederates were already east of Thoroughfare Gap and that Lee's army was somewhere behind them.[31] He now also understood that the daunting rebel force on the south side of the Rappahannock was no longer there.

Pope, however, was anything but disconsolate. Once he accepted that he had somehow been duped by fifty thousand Confederates, it occurred to him that his misfortune might actually be a brilliant opportunity. He knew now that Lee had either split his army or at the very least had strung it out along a fifty-mile arc. He also knew that only part of it had crossed through Thoroughfare Gap and that this advance guard was vulnerable. In the early morning of August 27, Pope gave orders for his full command to march back toward Washington and "crush the enemy." With the addition of Samuel Heintzelman's and Fitz John Porter's corps from McClellan's army, he now had sixty-six thousand men. The army would march along parallel tracks spread out over eight miles, with its left on the Warrenton Turnpike and its right tracking the Orange and Alexandria Railroad. Their goals were the towns of Gainesville and Manassas Junction. Whatever piece of Lee's army they found, they would overwhelm and destroy.[32]

Those weren't the only troops moving in Jackson's direction. Alarmed by the Confederate raid—though not certain that it was any more than small-scale cavalry mischief—Henry Halleck had dispatched four thousand men by train to the front to clear the area of rebel raiders. Halleck had also ordered General William B. Franklin's ten-thousand-man corps—which had traveled by boat from the James River to Alexandria—to march on Gainesville from the east. As of the morning of August 27, something approaching eighty thousand Union soldiers were moving against Stonewall Jackson.

Jackson, who was fully aware that he was going to be attacked, potentially from several directions and almost certainly by numerically superior forces, had no intention of sitting still. Leaving Ewell with three brigades at Bristoe Station to watch for the Union advance, early in the morning of August 27 he took divisions under Hill and Taliaferro to Manassas Junction to join Isaac Trimble. Their mission: to deal with and dispose of an almost unimaginably large cache of Union supplies housed in warehouses, boxcars, and wagons.

They would not be able to enjoy this Yankee largesse right away. They were attacked twice, in sequence, by small Union forces convinced they were flushing out a gang of rebel guerrillas instead of Stonewall Jackson himself with some of the toughest fighting men in the Confederate army. The first attack came from the 2nd New York heavy artillery, arriving for duty at Manassas Junction. They opened fire on some cavalry, and actually had some fun making the rebels jump and flushing them from a barn until the New Yorkers saw, to their horror, nine thousand infantry and twenty-eight artillery pieces arrayed in a semicircular arc against them. They beat a hasty retreat.

The second attack was a more serious affair. The force Halleck had urgently dispatched by train to deal with the railroad raiders consisted of a New Jersey brigade under Brigadier General George Taylor plus two Ohio regiments. At about 10:00 a.m. Jackson's men became aware of Taylor's men advancing in precise battle lines from the east. There were only 1,200 of them. Taylor, who had no idea what he was up against, had decided to move forward with the smaller force. Onward they came, into the waiting half-mile-long defensive arc that had been set up earlier to deal with the New Yorkers. Onward came the bluecoats, bayonets and rifle barrels luminous in the sun, into Jackson's waiting death trap. He let them come, ordering his men to hold their fire until Taylor's force was inside the arc of the Confederate line. Then rebel guns opened with murderous rounds of canister from the Union flank, tearing enormous holes in Taylor's line, while thousands of Confederate muskets exploded from the center. The

Union soldiers attempted a bayonet charge, but the line was shredded before it traveled fifty yards. When it became fully apparent that the Union troops would be slaughtered where they stood, Jackson did something out of character. He had admired the toughness of Taylor's men. After Union lines broke for a third time, Jackson ordered the cannon fire to stop, took out a white handkerchief, rode out in front of the Rockbridge artillery, and shouted, "Surrender! Throw down your arms, and surrender!"[33] The response was a bullet fired at Jackson's head. That soldier quite possibly regretted his arrogance, if he lived that long.

Taylor's men stood Jackson's fire courageously for ten minutes. Then, seeing that his retreat was about to be cut off by Stuart's horsemen, Taylor managed what started out to be a reasonably orderly retreat, though he himself fell with a mortal wound. But as the Confederates pursued, and continued firing canister, the retreat soon turned to panic and rout. The Federals lost 339 of 1,200 men, 201 of whom were taken prisoner. Many more would have died if the Ohio regiments, arriving late, had not been there to help cover their comrades' retreat. Jackson paid General Taylor a high compliment in his battle report, saying, "The advance was made with great spirit and determination and under a leader worthy of a better cause."[34]

Having driven the enemy away from Manassas Junction, Jackson's men turned to the prize at hand. The sheer tonnage of what they now possessed was beyond anything seen in the war. There was, moreover, no way they could possibly carry it all off with them, and they all immediately grasped that fact. The only question mark was their sobersided, regulation-bound general. Would he turn the men loose? He would. He did. What happened next was one of the great, extended revels of the Civil War. Before them, in a hundred boxcars and in many sheds and warehouses, was a cornucopia of Union industrial and agricultural production: pyramids of artillery ordnance, crates of new boots, shoes, underwear, and other clothing, Springfield muskets. There were also pickled oysters, canned fish, and whole hams, oranges, lemons, potted lobster, mustard, wheels of cheese, still-warm field ovens surrounded by baked goods, canned fruit, cigars, and candy. The men, lately deprived of rations and often wearing tattered shreds of rotting butternut homespun and sometimes without shoes, ran wild from boxcars to warehouses, stuffing their pockets and haversacks, taking whatever they could find. Some of their antics were comical. In addition to being a railway depot, Manassas Junction was a place of refuge for runaway slaves. Some of the men broke into their shanties and emerged "wearing colored women's wardrobes," according to one observer, especially hats. "When these half-starved men sang songs of merriment and danced around their campfires, eating lobster salad and drinking Rhine wine, the scene was ludicrous in the extreme."[35]

Jackson did take care to limit access to two precious commodities: he placed all medicines and medical supplies under guard, and he ordered a large cache of whiskey dumped on the ground. "Don't spare a drop, nor let any man taste it under any circumstances," Jackson ordered one of his captains. "I fear that liquor more than General Pope's army."[36] He didn't get all of it, of course, and many a canteen—particularly in Stuart's outfit—was happily filled with liquor.

While the bacchanalia proceeded—along with the gathering and loading of supplies Jackson's troops would actually be able to carry away with them, and preparing the rest for destruction—"Old Baldy" Ewell was conducting far more serious business. He had been left at Bristoe Station with three brigades to confront whatever force Pope sent to deal with the railroad raiders. At about 3:00 p.m. that force arrived in the form of five thousand soldiers under Major General Joseph Hooker, a handsome, intelligent West Point graduate who had fought aggressively in the peninsula campaign. True to form, Hooker deployed and attacked Ewell immediately, provoking a sharp fight that raged for an hour until the rest of Hooker's division began to arrive and Ewell realized he was facing a much larger force. Jackson's orders to Ewell were to fall back in the presence of a superior force and join the rest of Jackson's troops at Manassas Junction. At about 4:00 p.m. Ewell proceeded to do just that, conducting a textbook retreat, falling back while fighting, inflicting three hundred casualties on the enemy, and slowing the Union advance to a crawl. It was exactly what Jackson had wanted: Ewell had stung Hooker and temporarily stopped the movement of Pope's army toward Manassas Junction. He had bought the army a few hours.

Jackson was determined to use them well. That night his men packed up everything they could carry, which included 50,000 pounds of bacon, 1,000 barrels of corned beef, 2,000 barrels of salt pork, and 2,000 barrels of flour, plus tons of ammunition, weapons, and other quartermaster and commissary stores. Then they set fire to the rest, a magnificent, raging conflagration that reddened the sky for miles around.

But what to do now, in the fire-tinged darkness of the Manassas plain with eighty thousand Federals closing on him? The logical thing for Jackson to do was to head north and west to Thoroughfare Gap, toward safety, avoiding a fight with his three divisions against Pope's five corps or roughly fifteen divisions, for twenty-four hours. Lee and Longstreet were on their way, following in his footsteps. They would be there in twenty-four hours. He could unite with them, then turn and face Pope. He and his corps already had done extraordinary things. They had marched fifty-five miles, destroyed a Union railroad and telegraph, blunted a Union offensive at Bristoe Station, and captured or destroyed considerable tonnage of Federal supplies. More important, they had forced Pope from his secure defensive line on the Rappahannock. The stasis of August 24 had given way to the fluid chaos of August 27.

But Jackson was not, as virtually any other general would have been, thinking of escape. It was characteristic of the man that at such a moment of impending danger he was thinking only of how he could smash John Pope. He would be outnumbered, of course, possibly two or three to one. Thus he knew his only chance was to make sure the battle was fought on his terms and on his chosen ground.

But how to do that?

Before he left Manassas Junction Jackson had made up his mind. He knew the terrain well from the Battle of Manassas and he knew there was an unfinished railroad line several hundred yards north of the Warrenton Turnpike, west of the Sudley Road that had seen so much fighting in the First Manassas. The line, which ran for more than two miles, offered a superb defensive position, most of it in moderately thick woods. Jackson could bide his time there, near the tiny hamlet of Groveton, and wait for his opportunity to strike. Groveton, moreover, was less than ten miles east of Thoroughfare Gap, which meant that Jackson would be in a position to link with Longstreet's army when it arrived. In the event of total disaster he could retreat to the north. At midnight, Jackson and his three divisions marched out of Manassas Junction for their new bivouac. Though his divisions under A. P. Hill and Richard Ewell got lost in the dark, by the following morning Jackson had his entire twenty-four-thousand-man force "packed like herring in a barrel" in the woods in front of the railroad excavation. By Jackson's orders, the army was very quiet. Cooking was forbidden, along with music and shouting. Except for the periodic crash of Jeb Stuart's horse artillery as he routed Federal scouting parties, according to one soldier, "the woods sounded like the hum of a beehive on a warm summer day."[37]

CHAPTER THIRTY-NINE

AT BAY ON HIS
BAPTISMAL SOIL

※

For Major General John Pope, the world was a bright, promising place on the morning of Thursday, August 28, 1862, full of hope and possibility. He was certain that he had corralled the elusive Stonewall Jackson at Manassas Junction. All of his scouting reports told him that this was true. Jackson had finally gone too far. And now Pope would throw his full force against the trapped rebel commander. The night before, he had ordered a massive convergence on the junction, fifty thousand men advancing in a carefully spaced seven-mile-wide arc to prevent Jackson's escape. That movement was under way. Pope was so convinced of his impending victory that he told Irvin McDowell, commander of his 3rd Corps, "If you will march promptly and rapidly, we shall bag the whole crowd." Jackson had surprised the Union high command with his daring march. Now he would pay for it.

Or perhaps not. At noon a Union division under one-armed general Phil Kearny, whom Winfield Scott once called "the bravest man I ever saw," arrived at Manassas Junction to find nothing but smoldering desolation, charred skeletons of boxcars, and debris scattered everywhere. Beyond the wild destruction it had left behind, there was no sign of Jackson's column. Confederate stragglers insisted that the men had all marched off to Centreville, seven miles to the northeast. This turned out to be a wonderfully effective and entirely unintentional piece of misdirection. Though Jackson had ordered Ewell and Hill to march north to Groveton with the rest of the column, a series of misunderstandings and bad directions had led them to march eastward—*toward Centreville*—in the process losing themselves in the darkness. Though the stragglers were telling the truth—authentically selling their comrades out—they did not know that the rebel generals had soon corrected their mistakes and marched on to Groveton. Their divisions were now neatly tucked into the woods with the rest of Jackson's force.

Still, Pope chose to believe these honest shirkers. At 2:00 p.m. he issued orders for a *new* massive convergence, this time on the town of Centreville. Now, as the afternoon waned, the fatal weakness in Pope's character—his indecision under pressure—began to show itself. Soon after issuing those orders he received word that Longstreet's army had reached Thoroughfare Gap, where it had clashed with a small Union force. In his zeal to catch and destroy Jackson, Pope had somehow neglected the rest of the Confederate army. Consumed by an impulsive desire to correct that mistake, he abruptly changed his orders again, directing his army to turn and march west. He soon rescinded those orders, too.[1] Pope's waffling only grew worse.[2] At 5:00 p.m., swayed by persistent reports of Jackson's march eastward, and believing he could defeat Jackson, then wheel and fight Longstreet, Pope ordered his troops to turn yet again and resume their march to Centreville, much to the dismay of his generals—especially McDowell, who had been raising alarms about Longstreet's approach from the west. The fact remained: after a full day of probing with scouts and cavalry and entire divisions, and frenzied countermarching over an area familiar to many of them from the Battle of Manassas thirteen months before, Pope still had no idea where Jackson and his twenty-four thousand men were.

While Union soldiers, whipsawed by their commander's shifting orders, marched hither and yon over the rolling fields and timbered groves searching for him, Jackson was looking for an opportunity to strike. His concealment had only been a temporary ruse. He had been waiting all day for a large Union force to pass by on the Warrenton Pike, as a spider waits for a fly, though in this case the spider was less than half as big as the fly. He was impatient and running out of daylight. And he had not heard from Lee. Throughout the day he had been restlessly riding his lines, mostly alone. "When he was uneasy he was cross as a bear," wrote cavalryman W. W. Blackford, "and neither his generals nor his staff liked to come near if they could help it."[3] His demeanor changed temporarily when a courier arrived in late afternoon with the news that Lee and Longstreet were only twelve miles away and would likely arrive in the morning. Jackson's normally stern face, according to one observer, "beamed with pleasure" and relief. "Where is the man who brought

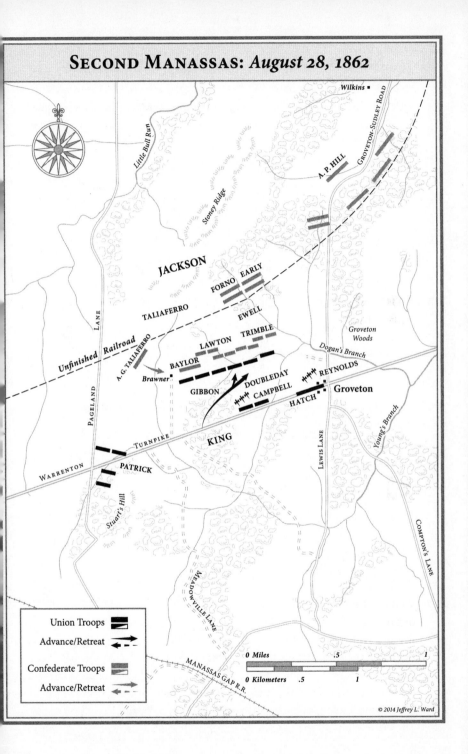

SECOND MANASSAS: *August 28, 1862*

Wilkins

Groveton-Sudley Road

A. P. HILL

Little Bull Run

Stoney Ridge

JACKSON

FORNO EARLY

TALIAFERRO

EWELL

Groveton
Woods

Unfinished Railroad

LAWTON TRIMBLE

Dogan's Branch

LANE

A. G. TALIAFERRO

BAYLOR

Brawner

GIBBON

DOUBLEDAY

CAMPBELL

REYNOLDS

Groveton

PAGELAND

HATCH

TURNPIKE

KING

LEWIS LANE

Young's Branch

WARRENTON

PATRICK

Stuart's Hill

COMPTON'S LANE

MEADOWVILLE LANE

Union Troops	
Advance/Retreat	
Confederate Troops	
Advance/Retreat	

0 Miles   .5   1

0 Kilometers   .5   1

MANASSAS GAP R.R.

© 2014 Jeffrey L. Ward

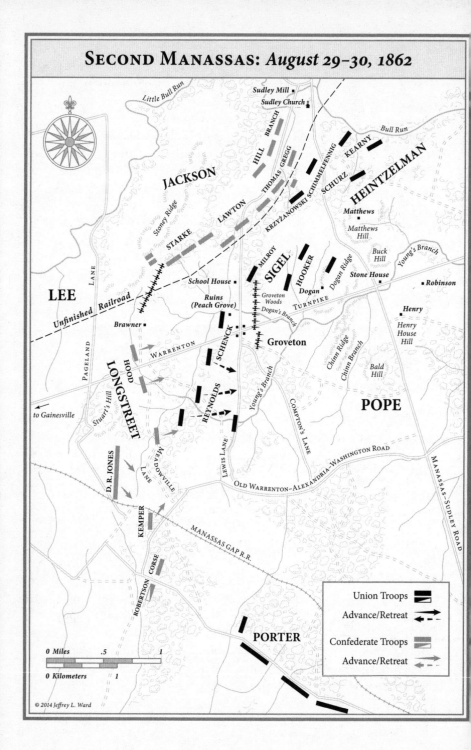

SECOND MANASSAS: *August 29–30, 1862*

Little Bull Run

Sudley Mill
Sudley Church

HILL BRANCH

Bull Run

KEARNY

SCHIMMELFENNIG

SCHURZ

THOMAS GREGG

HEINTZELMAN

JACKSON

KRZYZANOWSKI

Stoney Ridge

LAWTON

STARKE

Matthews

Matthews Hill

MILROY

SIGEL

HOOKER

Buck Hill

Young's Branch

School House

Dogan

Dogan Ridge

Stone House

Robinson

LEE

Ruins (Peach Grove)

Groveton Woods

Dogan's Branch

TURNPIKE

Henry

Unfinished Railroad

Brawner

SCHENCK

Dogan's Branch

Groveton

Henry House Hill

PAGELAND LANE

Warrenton

HOOD

LONGSTREET

Stuart's Hill

REYNOLDS

Young's Branch

Compton's Lane

Chinn Ridge

Chinn Branch

Bald Hill

POPE

to Gainesville

MEADOWVILLE LANE

LEWIS LANE

D. R. JONES

Old Warrenton–Alexandria–Washington Road

MANASSAS–SUDLEY ROAD

KEMPER

MANASSAS GAP R.R.

CORSE

ROBERTSON

PORTER

Union Troops

Advance/Retreat

Confederate Troops

Advance/Retreat

0 Miles   .5   1

0 Kilometers   1

© 2014 Jeffrey L. Ward

this dispatch?" he asked. "I must shake hands with him." The news gave him all the more reason to draw Pope into battle. But he needed the mechanism by which to do that.

At about 5:30 p.m., that mechanism came tramping eastward down the Warrenton Turnpike. When corps commander Irvin McDowell received Pope's 5:00 p.m. order to march on Centreville, he had put his army on the road. Its advance units were four brigades under the command of Brigadier General Rufus King, an epileptic who was still woozy from his last, quite recent seizure. Among them was an unusual group of Indiana and Wisconsin regiments under their commander, John Gibbon, who had taught artillery tactics at West Point and authored a popular textbook on the subject. They were distinguished both by their origin—they were one of a few western brigades fighting east of the Mississippi—and by their attire: dark blue frock coats, light blue pants, white leggings, and outsized black hats with plumes. Known as the "Black Hat Brigade," they looked somewhat pointlessly ornate, more like bandbox soldiers than a group of fighting men. Though this was their first fight, they would quickly distinguish themselves. They would go on to fame and legend as the "Iron Brigade," one of the hardest-fighting units of the war and the Northern equivalent of the Stonewall Brigade.[4]

King's men had just had a leisurely dinner and were proceeding at route step down the Warrenton Turnpike, strung out for a mile on the road. The men were relaxed, even a bit drowsy, "chatting, joking, and laughing in their usual manner," according to one of them, perhaps about the ridiculous cascade of ever-changing orders issuing from headquarters.[5] As they shuffled forward, a lone rider appeared in front of the woods on the north side of the road, maybe 150 yards off. He was obviously a rebel. He was within easy musket range, but no one seemed to be in the mood to shoot him. He didn't look like much. He wore a dusty, rumpled uniform and weather-beaten cap. He rode a substandard horse. He ranged back and forth over the broom sedge in full view of the Union column, surveying it as though attempting to understand its meaning. Then he turned abruptly and galloped away.

As he thundered back into the woods, where half of the Army of Northern Virginia lay concealed, one officer, watching him approach, said, "Here he comes, by God."

The inquisitive horseman was Jackson. And this was the opportunity he had been waiting for. After such an anxious morning and afternoon, he was pleased with the prospect of battle. According to one observer, he was suddenly "as calm as a May morning." He turned to his officers and said, in a soft voice, "Bring out your men, gentlemen." The soldiers had been waiting for this moment all day; now the looming action sent a wave of anticipation through their lines, like electricity. They understood that large numbers of men had been looking for them. "The hunt is up," one of them wrote later. "Jackson is at bay on his baptismal soil, with Pope in front and the whole North behind him."[6] Moments later, Jackson's artillery sounded, shells screamed into the Union lines, and several thousand men in blue coats dived for any cover they could find by the roadside. They quickly retreated to the woods south of the turnpike, unlimbered, and returned fire, and soon salvos from both sides were shattering the evening air.

But what sort of force were the Federals facing? Gibbon huddled with fellow brigade commander Abner Doubleday, another artillerist who had the great distinction of firing the first Federal shot from Fort Sumter.[7] Pope's communications throughout the day had assured them that Jackson's main force was at Centreville. There was no question about that. And all Gibbon had seen were a few enemy guns banging away in the distance—very likely some of Jeb Stuart's horse artillery, making its usual mischief. Gibbon and Doubleday decided that the best way to shoo this nuisance away would be to storm the battery. They sent skirmishers out, and the 2nd Wisconsin and 19th Indiana Regiments fell in behind them, and they all moved smartly toward the wooded area north of the turnpike.

But as they were nearing musket range of the rebel artillery, the guns suddenly stopped firing. There was an odd, momentary silence, as though in response to a change of orders; then a line of Confederate skirmishers rose from the grass in front of the guns, and the advancing bluecoats could see white smoke from their musket barrels and hear the abrupt, rattling staccato of their volleys. The presence of infantry was odd. And then suddenly the woods themselves seemed to come alive. A wave of gray-clad soldiers rose, en masse, and swept down the gentle slope in perfect battle lines, a quarter of a mile away and closing, red battle flags with starred blue crosses fluttering over the ranks. Soon they were within range and then terrible, long, rolling volleys swept the field. The air buzzed with .58-caliber pieces of lead, and men started falling in great numbers. This was not a regiment of Jeb Stuart's troopers with some light artillery. Gibbon and Doubleday had stumbled on old Stonewall himself.

What followed was an old-fashioned slugfest, a powder-scorched prize-fight in which the fighters—initially the Iron Brigade against the Stonewall Brigade—stood toe to toe, neither side seeking shelter or retreat. The two lines blasted away at each other, eighty yards apart along a half-mile front. They maneuvered for each other's flank. Though Jackson had the advantage of numbers, it took him an excruciatingly long time to bring his regiments up, and he never fully succeeded. Frustrated, he himself took command on the field, ignoring the chain of command and feeding men into the fight as fast as he could. "I met Gen'l Jackson near a gate trying to rally some stragglers," recalled one soldier, "more excited and indignant than I ever saw him, riding rapidly among them and threatening with his arm raised."[8]

Whether it was the ferocity of the Union fighters, or Jackson's inability to bring more of his force into the fight, an hour and a half after it started the battle between his right wing and the advance units of McDowell's corps was deadlocked. Neither side had given an inch. "It was a stand-up combat, clogged and unflinching, in a field almost bare," wrote General William B. Taliaferro, who was seriously wounded in the fight, as was General Ewell. "In the dying daylight they stood, and although they could not advance, they would not retire. There was some discipline in this, but there was much more of true valor."[9]

At such close range, the firing was accurate and murderous. One of every 3 men in the fight was hit by a bullet. The 2nd Wisconsin suffered 276 casualties out of 430 soldiers, while the Stonewall Brigade lost 340 out of 800.[10] Two Georgia regiments suffered 70 percent casualties, a percentage almost unheard of in the Civil War. More than a third of the Federal officers were left dead or wounded on the field.[11] Darkness ended the fight. Spectral lanterns soon bobbed and floated across the field as roving details brought the wounded in. "Here, under the trees, lay the sufferers, awaiting each his turn to receive the attention of the two or three surgeons in this part of the field," wrote one of Doubleday's staffers. "Lighted by torches or bits of candle, these surgeons were busily engaged in their melancholy labors."[12]

To Jackson, the meaning of the bloody shoot-out at Groveton was clear. He had deliberately picked a fight with a piece of Pope's army, thus revealing his hiding place, and he fully expected to be attacked by Pope's entire force the next day. That was what he wanted. Lee understood this, but no one in the Union army did, and the improbable idea that Jackson was not in retreat was a source of great confusion to his enemies over the next two days. His choice did not seem rational. A rational man would not choose to maintain his position in the woods, awaiting certain destruction by a much larger army. As Jackson saw it, he had a perfectly good chance to strike a blow at Pope before more of McClellan's reinforcements arrived. And he knew, moreover, that Lee was on his way.

To Gibbon, Doubleday, and their division commander, Rufus King, the meaning of the fight was far less clear. King at first insisted on following his orders, which meant continuing down the turnpike to Centreville to engage Stonewall Jackson. Gibbon argued that such a move was pointless, since all evidence, including testimony from captured Confederate prisoners, suggested they were in the presence of the legendary Stonewall himself. They would be better off beating a sensible retreat south toward Manassas Junction, with the hope of finding reinforcements.[13] Gibbon pushed the point, won the argument, and King's brigades fell back. They knew they could not possibly fight Jackson alone.

Pope had his own, inevitably personal interpretation of the evening's events. He and his staff had watched the battle's brilliant illuminations from a patch of high ground near Bull Run, eight miles to the east. By 9:30 p.m. he was convinced that King's brigades had struck Jackson's corps. Once again, Pope saw nothing but opportunity. He was an optimistic man. Jackson, he theorized, had been camped at Centreville and was now retreating westward to escape destruction, staggering beneath the weight of his stolen supplies. King's brigades had intercepted him in midflight. Pope's vision thus conformed to all of his own hopes and preconceived notions. Thrilled at this development, he wrenched his entire army once again from its appointed courses by ordering a dawn attack. "I stated to several of my staff officers that were present," he testified later, "that the game was in our hands, and that I did not see how it was possible for Jackson to escape without very heavy loss, if at all."[14] For all of his swagger, Pope, having been deceived three times by Jackson, this time took precautions. His army would spread out and march on Jackson's position from both the east and the west, placing Jackson in a box and leaving no room for error. Pope was unaware that, in his unshakable conviction that Jackson was fleeing and did not want to fight, he had actually been deceived a fourth time.

Even more impressive than these deceptions, Jackson had accomplished what he had really wanted all along: to goad Pope into attacking him, entirely on Jackson's own terms, before the Army of Virginia had been fully reinforced by McClellan. Adrift in visions of glory, Pope had been drawn into a battle he did not have to fight.[15] Jackson posed no offensive threat to an army three times his size, after all. He was certainly no threat to Washington. Time, moreover, was on Pope's side. The wiser, more conservative course would have been to fall back toward the capital, wait to unite the two armies, then move forward against Lee, Jackson, or anyone else who tried to stand in their way. The Union numerical superiority would be crushing. Instead, Pope was putting his army into needless combat against one Confederate corps while a second one, with none other than Robert E. Lee in tow, loomed up from the west. Instead of laying an elaborate trap for Jackson, Pope was actually walking into one, and both Lee and Jackson knew it. Jackson had no intention of using his three divisions as bait or sacrifice; he had come to understand the profound advantages that men firing from defensive cover had in this war. And he had carefully chosen a superb defensive position.

On the morning of August 29, expecting the full fury of the Union army to fall upon him—an expectation that would not be disappointed—Jackson shuffled his force east and north, placing his twenty-four thousand men in a gentle two-mile arc behind the unfinished railroad spur. To level the land for railroad tracks, engineers had dug trenches in some places ("cuts") and piled dirt in others ("fills"). The effect was that of a linear fort, dead-level in a few isolated places and occasionally a bit too deep, but largely continuous along a wooded ridge. Any infantry that hoped to carry it would pay dearly in blood.

That would be the story of the battle. At daylight artillery on both sides began their barrages, and soon Franz Sigel's Union skirmishers advanced into the woods north of the Warrenton Turnpike. They were probing, looking for the exact location of Jackson's men. Behind them came the lines of battle, broken into clusters and odd groupings by the thickets. A Union general described "the weird clatter of rebel bullets against leaves and tree-trunks and branches." And suddenly "the rattling fire of skirmishers changed into the crash of musketry, regular volleys, rapidly following each other. We [had] evidently struck Jackson's main position."[16]

What followed was the first of many savage fights that day that raged along Jackson's two-mile line, the opening of the battle that would come to be known as Second Manassas or, as Northerners called it, Second Bull Run. With nine thousand men in place, Franz Sigel fought the battle's first phase, mounting steady assaults on the center of Jackson's position. For four hours Sigel's troops came on, advancing in successive waves through the woods against the Confederates, who mostly fired from behind the cuts and fills of the railroad embankment. The Union attacks were repulsed, and many Union boys fell, but they were starting to take a fearful toll. The battle was just beginning.

Pope, who arrived on the field at noon and conducted a reconnaissance of the front, had a very clear idea about how to fight this battle. His plan was to keep Jackson occupied in his center and left, while Fitz John Porter's 5th Corps fell on the Confederate right. Porter would strike the crippling, turning blow; he would flank Jackson, cut off his retreat, while the rest of the army would drive straight ahead. Pope had given those orders to Porter in the morning—or so Pope thought—but as the day progressed there was still no sign of Porter's corps. In keeping with his scheme Pope unleashed another series of devastating attacks on Jackson's increasingly weary, depleted lines. At about 2:00 p.m. he sent Joe Hooker's division forward, and again the woods exploded in sheets of flame and smoke, minié balls thudded into trees and human flesh and bone, and again the Federals advanced through what one of them called "a hurricane of death."[17]

Now the hours of constant defensive battle against superior numbers began to tell on the beleaguered rebels. Men from Massachusetts and New Hampshire regiments finally broke Jackson's line and came pouring over the edge of the embankment. Suddenly they found themselves down in the cut with their enemies, exchanging fire at such close range that the muzzles of their weapons touched, and swinging their muskets by their barrel ends. It was brutal, destructive, highly personal warfare. In spite of their fierce, almost unbelievably brave charge, the Union soldiers, under their commander, Cuvier Grover, could not sustain their drive. The enemy position was too strong, and their assault had cost them a third of their force. Like all the other Union attackers that day, they faltered, broke, and fell back. As they did so, two Confederate brigades under Taliaferro's replacement, William E. Starke, counterattacked, routing Grover's and three other brigades in the process. Since Jackson was under strict orders from Lee to fight only a defensive battle, there was no question of further pursuit. That attack was followed by yet another thrust at Jackson's center, also repulsed.

The fight wasn't over yet. With Porter's ten thousand fresh troops still nowhere to be seen, shortly after 5:00 p.m. Pope ordered Kearny to move against A. P. Hill's division on Jackson's left. This assault was the most brutal yet, the brunt of it falling on Brigadier General Maxcy Gregg's five regiments of South Carolinians, who were dug in on a rocky knoll behind the embankment. Gregg, a brainy South Carolina lawyer whose side interests included botany, astronomy, and ornithology, rallied his men by shouting, "Let us die here, my men!" That they did, by the score. They had been fighting almost continuously for eight hours. They had lost a third of their brigade and were running out of ammunition.[18] Alarmed, A. P. Hill sent a message to Gregg asking if he could hold his position. Gregg replied that, even though he was almost out of bullets, he could "hold the position with the bayonet."[19] Hill relayed the news to Jackson, and Jackson sent his unadorned reply through his aide Henry Kyd Douglas: "Tell him if they attack again he must beat them." Jackson then thought better of it, and accompanied Douglas on horseback. They were met by a worried A. P. Hill, who was on his way to see Jackson. Jackson was sympathetic. But there was no question of retreat. "General, your men have done nobly," he told his West Point classmate. "If you are attacked again, you will beat the enemy back." History does not record Hill's reaction. But a moment later, as a new, rising sound of musket fire came from Gregg's front, Hill said, "Here it comes!" then turned and galloped away. Jackson called after him, "I'll expect you to beat them!"[20]

What happened next was as close as Jackson came to disaster that day. Kearny's ten regiments drove forward into the Confederate lines. They charged, broke, fell back, then charged again and again, line after line of bluecoats driving closer and closer to the embankment. There seemed no end to it. Kearny's men were on the verge of a shattering breakthrough— one that might also have closed off Jackson's only path of retreat—when 2,500 Confederates under General Jubal Early arrived on the field. In the battle's most brilliant counterattack, Early's fresh troops collided with the exhausted Federals, raking their depleted lines with fire, and almost immediately pushing them back. Soon they were in full retreat. Within ten minutes of Early's attack, Kearny's force was reeling out of the woods toward the turnpike as the rebel yell rose behind them and the Confederate lines rolled forward, stopping only when Hill reminded Early that his orders were not to advance beyond the embankment. That was the end of the fighting that day on Jackson's front.

When it was over Hill sent a staff officer with a message for Jackson: "General Hill presents his compliments and says the attack of the enemy was repulsed." Jackson smiled. "Tell him I knew he would do it," he said.[21] Jackson's army had withstood the best the Union could throw at it and had paid for it in unimaginable amounts of human blood. Jackson and his commanders had furiously plugged holes in their lines all day and had fought off the repeated assaults by an army that was just as determined as his own to win. Pope had helped them by attacking sectors of the line instead of making multiple simultaneous advances. Jackson had been able to shift reinforcements to meet each Union threat.[22] He ended the day in possession of virtually the same ground he had started with—ground that was now littered with dead and wounded men.

But that was by no means the full story of one of the most tactically complex and politically charged days of fighting in the war.

Jackson's first concern, on the clear, warm morning of August 29, before the successive waves of Union assaults began to crash and break against his lines, was the whereabouts of Longstreet's corps. He knew it had passed through Thoroughfare Gap and the village of Gainesville. He knew it was close. Now, above the line of trees to his west, he could see an enormous cloud of dust rising in the still summer air, heralding the imminent arrival of thirty thousand men and more than eighty pieces of field artillery. They had been sent to him from God and they had arrived in time and the question was where to put them. He had carefully selected a position on his right, almost perpendicular to his own line. Together the two Confederate wings would form a three-mile-long, slightly warped L—or, as some would describe it later, an open jaw with Jackson as the mandible—that put Longstreet immediately on the Union flank.

At 8:00 a.m. Jackson sent Jeb Stuart and his cavalry to Lee and Longstreet. Stuart's job would be to guide Longstreet's column in and install it in its new position. At 10:00 a.m., under Stuart's guidance, Robert E. Lee led John Bell Hood's Texas brigade east on the Warrenton Turnpike to the place designated by Stuart. As Lee did so he noticed that there were skirmishers everywhere, hundreds of them, fanned out and darting through the light and shadow in the woods. But he could not tell whose side they were on. He dispatched scouts to find out. After a couple of tense minutes, he got his answer: *they were Jackson's men.* This meant that the two armies, which had traveled a combined one hundred miles or more at an interval of two and a half days, had somehow managed to fit their fifty-four thousand soldiers and trains perfectly together deep in enemy territory and in the presence of a large Union army. And they had done it, for all practical purposes, in secret. Lee's plan had been more than daring. That it was working bordered on implausible. The three generals soon met and made plans, though there is no record of what was said. By noon, Longstreet's men were fully deployed, positioned invisibly in woods just as Jackson's men had been on August 28. East of them were open fields all the way to Bull Run.

Lee's most obvious move at this point—as Jackson was being hammered by Union assaults—would have been to throw Longstreet forward against the Union left, using the full power of his L formation to turn Pope's flank. But in one of the battle's odd twists, that did not happen. Longstreet stayed in the woods. Jackson was left on his own to absorb the terrible fury of the pounding, dawn-to-dusk Union attacks. As would become apparent during the day, Lee and Longstreet had good reasons for holding back.

The first of these had to do with the wayward column of Union general Fitz John Porter. That morning he and his 5th Corps found themselves about two miles due south of Jackson's right wing, listening to gunfire from the front, and waiting for orders. What he got from Pope was a masterpiece of self-contradiction and military nonsense. The rambling "Joint Order," written at 10:00 a.m. from Pope's headquarters near Henry Hill, seemed to direct him to simultaneously advance, stay put, and fall back. It was, in any case, not a clear order to advance against the enemy. Part of the order revealed Pope's own shocking ignorance of Longstreet's location: "The indications are that the whole force of the enemy is moving in this direction at a pace that will bring him here to-morrow night or the next day." Porter knew better. Every soldier on the Union left knew better. Irvin McDowell had been informed of Longstreet's arrival by his calvary chief at 9:30 but he inexplicably failed to tell Pope, a shocking lapse that would eventually severely damage McDowell's reputation. In the spirit of Pope's simultaneous and contradictory demands, Porter elected to stay where he was, assuming he would receive clarifying orders.

Pope, meanwhile, assumed that Porter would move against Jackson's right and spent the entire day waiting for it to happen. Porter's attack was to be the pivot of the entire battle. Porter, of course, did not have a clue that his superiors two miles to the east were waiting for him to do anything. (This issue—Porter's orders from Pope and how he carried them out—was the subject of the war's most famous court-martial. Porter was initially found guilty and removed from command. Not until long after the war were the charges overturned and Porter reinstated.[23]) At four thirty Pope, now furious and convinced that Porter's failure to move was related to his political alliances, finally sent an order for Porter to advance, but Porter did not receive it until 6:00—too late, he believed, to move such a distance and attack before dark. Pope later lashed out at Porter, writing,

"During these long hours General Porter still remained idle with his corps in column, and many of them lying on the ground, for ease of position probably, as they were not under fire. . . . It is not unreasonable to say that, if General Porter had attacked Longstreet . . . with ten or twelve thousand men . . . the effect would have been conclusive."[24]

Porter, frozen in place as he was, was to be the great strategic pawn of the battle. He was more than just the key to the failure of Pope's grand plan of attack. He was also the main reason why Longstreet's corps stayed out of the fight. During several scouting expeditions that day, Lee, Longstreet, and Stuart had discovered two truths, both of which were disappointing to Lee, who wanted very much to attack. First, there were several Union divisions right in front of them that covered more than half of their mile-plus-long front. It was not clear to Lee how numerous his enemies were or what the terrain would be like. His main worry, sitting just south of them on the Manassas-to-Gainesville Road—directly on their right flank—was Porter, whose intentions were unknown. For the Confederates to attack now, Longstreet reasoned—he was the voice of caution—meant shifting a large part of his own force to guard against a flank attack, thus weakening the whole operation. And he reminded Lee that they still did not know what sort of terrain lay in front of them. Three times that day Lee proposed to attack; each time Longstreet talked him out of it.

The day's fighting might thus have ended with Early's repulse of Kearny except for one final, strange twist. Lee decided, at the last minute, and with only a little daylight left, to send John Hood forward with his Texans, Georgians, and Carolinians along the Warrenton Turnpike in a reconnaissance in force. The idea was to discover what was in front of them, in preparation for Lee's planned advance the next day. Hood moved forward at about six thirty. By coincidence John Pope had also sent a force forward along the Warrenton Turnpike, but for such a bizarrely different reason that it requires explanation. Pope had seen Confederate wagons moving west down the Warrenton Turnpike and had come to the conclusion that the rebels, reeling from Kearny's brutal though ultimately unsuccessful assault, were retreating. Though Pope's chief of staff pointed out that the wagons were probably ambulances conveying wounded to the rear, Pope would not believe it. Instead, as a blazing sun streaked the sky over the Bull Run Mountains, he ordered an immediate pursuit. Soon Brigadier General John Hatch with three brigades was marching westward down the turnpike to strike a blow at the fleeing rebel army. As he left, his superior, Irvin

McDowell, who agreed with Pope, barked, "General Hatch, the enemy is in full retreat! Pursue him rapidly!" The Union command could not shake the idea that Jackson was scared and running away, though all of Jackson's behavior since August 26 argued against that idea. For some reason Pope was not thinking about the whereabouts of Longstreet.

Imagine, then, the surprise of General Hatch when, as his brigades crested a ridge overlooking Groveton, they suddenly faced a headlong frontal assault from several thousand of General Hood's eager, battle-tested fighters. As Hatch immediately understood, the Confederates were not retreating. They were not fighting a rearguard action. The rebels were in force, and looking for a fight. He sent a message to Irvin McDowell saying as much. When McDowell received it, he exploded, "What! Does General Hatch hesitate?! Tell him the enemy is in full retreat and to pursue them!" No amount of pleading was going to save Hatch from a fight. So he fought bravely on, into and beyond darkness, and his men were beaten and driven back and many ended up wandering lost in the dark. There had not been much point in the battle—Lee was able to gather very little battlefield intelligence from it—and there were only a few hundred casualties on both sides, testimony to the difficulty of trying to hit a moving target in the darkness. Soldiers who watched from miles around as the fight illuminated the night described its strange beauty. They were unused to seeing so many muskets fired after dark.

Thus the day's battle—one of the war's greatest and bloodiest combats—finally ended. Pope, who still did not understand that he had struck Longstreet, closed the day out with an early-morning dispatch to Halleck that suggested he had won a decisive victory. He wrote, "We fought a terrific battle here yesterday with the combined forces of the enemy. . . . The enemy was driven from the field which we now occupy. . . . The news just reaches me from the front that the enemy is retreating toward the mountains. I go forward at once to see."

Jackson, at his headquarters several miles away, would have been astonished to read that message. He was ending his day by patching up his lines and preparing for renewed attacks in the morning. Now that Robert E. Lee was present, he had assumed command of the battlefield. Jackson was following Lee's orders, which meant holding fast, defending his position. According to Hunter McGuire, Jackson ended his day around a campfire, where his black servant Jim made coffee for him and his staff. McGuire told Jackson that Maggie Junkin Preston's nineteen-year-old stepson, "Willy"

Preston, had been mortally wounded that day. The blue-eyed, beardless Preston, a former VMI cadet, had recently joined the Stonewall Brigade and had quickly become one of Jackson's favorites. When McGuire said this, Jim "rolled on the ground, groaning in his agony of grief." Then McGuire noticed Jackson's face.

> The muscles were twitching convulsively and his eyes were all aglow. He gripped me by the shoulder till it hurt me, and in a savage, threatening manner asked me why I had left the boy. In a few seconds he recovered himself, and turned and walked off into the woods alone. He soon came back, however, and I continued by the fire, drinking the coffee out of our tin cups, when I said: "We have won this battle by the hardest kind of fighting." And he answered me very gently and softly: "No, no; we have won it by the blessing of Almighty God."[25]

We will never know what passed through Jackson's mind when he heard about Willy. Perhaps it was a vision of that vanished old world of Lexington, a world inhabited by his dead wife, Ellie, and her spirited sister Maggie, Jackson's beloved surrogate father George Junkin and his great friend John Lyle, and by apple-cheeked young men in immaculate uniforms marching peacefully across the VMI parade ground. All of that was gone, vanished—more completely than he would ever know. It had lived in some way in Willy. Now Willy, too, was gone.

One of the most important players in the Battle of Second Manassas was a man who was never there: George B. McClellan. After moving his army north, he had assumed command of those parts of it that had not joined Pope's army, most significantly the corps of Edwin V. Sumner and William B. Franklin, containing fourteen thousand and eleven thousand men, respectively. Together they were larger than Jackson's entire force. As Lincoln and Stanton saw it, the logical thing was to move this impressive force to the battlefield as quickly as possible. But it never happened. From August 27 to August 30, in an effort that required considerable energy, McClellan kept these troops in or near Washington. In the peninsula campaign his endless dithering, pettifoggery, inflated enemy troop estimates, and stubborn refusal to advance suggested to many observers that McClellan was incompetent. At Second Manassas, his behavior started to look to his critics—including the Secretary of War—more like malfeasance or even treason.

There was no doubt that McClellan detested Pope and would have been happy to see him fail. His correspondence is full of the wish that his rival might be defeated and the hope that his own fortunes would thus be bolstered. His letters drip with contempt, jealousy, and naked ambition. On July 22 he wrote his wife, Ellen, "I see that the Pope bubble is likely to be suddenly collapsed—Stonewall Jackson is after him, & the paltry young man who wanted to teach me the art of war will in less than a week either be in full retreat or badly whipped. He will begin to learn the value of '*entrenchments, lines of communication & retreat.*'" On August 10: "I have a very strong idea that Pope will be thrashed during the coming week—& very badly whipped he will be and ought to be—such a villain as he is ought to bring defeat upon any cause that employs him. . . . I am inclined to believe that Pope will catch his Tartar [Jackson] within a couple of days and be disposed of.[26] On August 23: "I take it for granted that my orders will be as disagreeable as it is possible to make them—unless Pope is beaten, in which case they may want me to save Washn again."[27]

The question—argued over in detail by memoir writers and historians for the last one hundred fifty years—was whether he withheld reinforcements out of pure malice and self-interest or because he was simply being his old cautious, conservative self. Here the picture becomes murkier, mainly because of the cynical and cowardly machinations of his superior, General in Chief Henry W. Halleck. In the wake of Jackson's rout of the small force under Brigadier General George Taylor, McClellan's natural conservatism had asserted itself. In a long meeting with Halleck on the night of August 27 he insisted that, because there was obviously a large Confederate force between Pope and Washington, the capital itself was in danger, and thus General Edwin V. Sumner's 2nd Corps was needed to defend it. He also argued that the eleven thousand men in William B. Franklin's command should not move to Pope's aid until they had their full artillery with them. They might otherwise be beaten in detail. (Bringing up artillery would take at least several days.) Pope, moreover, already had sixty-seven thousand men, including elements of McClellan's army, to face fifty-five thousand Confederates. Such assertions were perfectly McClellan-like in their caution and aversion to risk, and he wrote to his wife to say that he was pleased that he and Halleck were in agreement. Halleck, moreover, had already seemingly abdicated his proper role as arbiter between the two rival generals, telling Little Mac in a letter earlier that day that he (Halleck) "had no time for details" and "you will therefore, as ranking general in the field, direct as you deem best." Halleck had not only agreed with McClellan's strategy; he was also trusting him to make his own decisions.

But Halleck was buffeted by stronger winds. Secretary of War Edwin Stanton—looking for information with which to discredit McClellan—had demanded pointedly of Halleck whether McClellan had promptly obeyed his orders to quit the James River, and, more tellingly, *if Franklin had been ordered to Pope's relief and whether those orders had been obeyed*. Halleck, afraid that his own neck was on the block, now wrote a long, untruthful reply saying that he had done everything possible to prod McClellan into action. Then, to McClellan's astonishment, at 12:40 p.m. on August 28—the day of Jackson's Groveton fight—Halleck bypassed Little Mac and personally ordered Franklin to march to Manassas Junction. He got back a plaintive note from McClellan saying, "The moment Franklin can get started with a reasonable amount of artillery he shall go." Halleck, now going all out to cover himself, wrote, "Not a moment must be lost in pushing as large a force as possible toward Manassas." McClellan, perhaps now realizing that there was considerable subtext to his correspondence with Halleck, replied flatly: "Your dispatch received. Neither Franklin nor Sumner's corps is now in condition to fight a battle. It would be a sacrifice to send them now."[28] This of course looked like McClellan was simply refusing, out of spite, to obey orders.

At 2:30 p.m. on August 29, while the battle raged in front of Jackson's railroad embankment and successive Union assaults were being repulsed and no reinforcements from McClellan's army were in sight, Lincoln sent McClellan an innocently hopeful wire: "What news from direction of Mannassas [sic] Junction?" McClellan replied that he believed the enemy to be in retreat and that "I am clear that one of two courses should be adopted: first, to concentrate all of our available forces to open communication with Pope; second, to leave Pope to get out of his own scrape, and at once use all our means to make the capital perfectly safe. No middle course will now answer. Tell me what you wish me to do, and I will do all in my power to accomplish it." Lincoln answered that he preferred the former, but in any case left the ultimate decision to Halleck. Halleck, in turn, sent his own deeply hedged reply to McClellan, saying that Sumner's column should remain to defend Washington and that Franklin should advance, but that he really need to go only far enough to reconnoiter the enemy's location and strength. "Perhaps he may get such information at Anandale as to prevent his going farther," Halleck wrote. He was most concerned about a strike on Washington, so Franklin should probably stay close to home. This hardly amounted to "prodding" McClellan to order an advance. Halleck was clearly trying to have it both ways.

Thus were large numbers of reinforcements kept from the Army of the Potomac. Though when taken out of context the phrase "leave Pope to get out of his own scrape" sounded faintly treasonous—and would haunt McClellan for a long time, especially in the 1864 presidential election—in fact McClellan was guilty only of infelicitous language. He was right: those *were* the two options. And Henry Halleck had been perfectly complicit in retaining Sumner's and Franklin's forces near Washington. In McClellan's mind, his orders were now clear. He ordered Franklin to move forward but to stop at Annandale, well short of the battlefield. Halleck, meanwhile, shifting once more to cover himself, wrote a note to McClellan at 7:50 p.m., saying, indignantly, "I have just been told that Franklin's corps stopped at Annandale . . . this is contrary to my orders; investigate and report the facts of this disobedience." But Halleck's dizzying duplicity had another consequence. Now Lincoln and Stanton became enraged at McClellan, believing that he was deliberately refusing to help Pope. "He has acted badly toward Pope," Lincoln told his secretary John Hay. "He really wanted him to fail." While the latter was almost certainly true, there is little hard evidence that McClellan, acting from pure enmity, actually wanted his country to fail, too.[29]

Pope had made several telling mistakes in the campaign, but the most harmful was to misinterpret—almost willfully, it seemed to his subordinates—the stream of intelligence he received about the presence of James Longstreet. Hatch had encountered a piece of his corps, as had Porter and Reynolds, and there was no shortage of reports of a large Confederate force crossing Thoroughfare Gap. Porter had even told Pope personally on the night of August 29 that there was a body of men sitting precariously on the Union left. Pope, who had become convinced that Porter, a McClellan protégé, was the head plotter in a McClellan-led cabal to thwart him, refused to believe it. Pope decided that Longstreet, instead of extending Jackson's existing line, had moved in behind Jackson in a position of support. No one knows quite why he thought this. Just as it is difficult to understand why, on the hot, still morning of August 30, Pope continued to believe that his enemy was retreating.

That conviction had put him in an expansive mood. He had once again persuaded himself that he was on the brink of victory. That morning he stood on a treeless knoll at his headquarters, smoking a cigar and exchanging jokes and pleasantries and congratulations with his generals. Just before noon he ordered another massive pursuit of the supposedly retreating rebel army. Porter would lead it, Hatch and Reynolds would follow; Hooker and Kearny would follow a parallel path to the north. The men were assembled, the artillery rolled up, and the chase after the retreating rebels began in earnest. Predictably, it lasted less than an hour, the time it took for skirmishers to discover that something big and massed and threatening was still sitting back in those woods by the railroad embankment. Jackson's men had not gone anywhere. That was the end of Pope's delusion.

Lee had decided against a morning offensive. He would wait for Pope to attack, then look for a weakness to exploit. If Pope did not attack, Lee had a backup plan: late that afternoon Longstreet would advance eastward across the open fields toward Chinn Ridge and engage Union forces, while Jackson pulled out from behind the embankment and marched around the Union right, striking deep in the Union rear, a miniature version of his march to Manassas Junction.

But Pope did attack. At 3:00 p.m. Porter's ten-thousand-man corps, which Pope had made sure was going to do the fighting this day, was sent forward, en masse, against Jackson's right. Men who saw it remembered it as one of those picture-book assaults: the Federal lines advancing in perfect order, bayonets and musket barrels flashing like heliographs in the slanting afternoon sun, battle flags streaming above the regiments. There was a strangeness to the movement, too, for those who could see it. They were hitting Jackson's *right*, literally under the noses of Longstreet's watchful thirty thousand. "Evidently Pope supposed I was gone," wrote Longstreet later, "as he was ignoring me entirely. His whole army seemed to surge up against Jackson as if to crush him with an overwhelming mass. I could plainly see the Federals as they rushed in heavy masses against the obstinate ranks of the Confederate[s]."[30]

What followed was desperate, furious combat, much of it conducted as before at close range. Rebels fired from cover behind the cuts and fills of the excavation; Federals used anything they could find—rocks, trees, dead horses, even dead comrades. Along one part of the line Confederates quickly ran out of ammunition and began to throw stones at the enemy. Some they threw hard and straight, others they lobbed over the edge of the embankment onto the Federals huddled below, severely injuring some of them. Some of the Union boys threw them back. The fighting became so intense at the

"Deep Cut" that Jackson was worried his lines might break. He later wrote, "As one line was repulsed, another took its place, and pressed forward, as if determined, by force of numbers and fury of assault, to drive us from our positions. So impetuous and well-sustained were these onsets as to induce me to send to the Commanding General for reinforcements."[31] Unlike the previous day, Jackson had no uncommitted reserves to bring forward.

Longstreet, upon receiving Jackson's request, realized two things at once: first, that his reinforcements would never reach Jackson in time, and second, that the battlefield presented his batteries with a clear opportunity for enfilading fire. He ordered more guns forward to supplement the batteries that were already blasting away. Their combined fire now tore into the second and third waves of the Union assault and pinned many attacking Federals against the unfinished railroad. The effect was immediate and devastating.[32] Three times Porter's forces rallied. Three waves of assault crashed and disintegrated against the insurmountable Confederate wall. They finally broke altogether. Some withdrew gracefully, others did not, as the Confederates piled out of their trenches in pursuit. In Jackson's words:

> Soon a general advance of my whole line was ordered. Eagerly and fiercely did each brigade press forward, exhibiting in parts of the field scenes of close encounter and murderous strife not witnessed often in the turmoil of battle. The Federals gave way before our troops, fell back in disorder, and fled precipitately, leaving their dead and wounded on the field. During their retreat the artillery opened with destructive power upon the fugitive masses.[33]

Many just ran rearward in a confused, chaotic mass, a retreat that bordered on panic and took Porter and other commanders time to quell— some of it at the points of bayonets. Eventually order was restored.[34] But not before Irvin McDowell managed to overreact to the danger. Sensing an impending First Manassas–style rout, he ordered Brigadier General John F. Reynolds forward with his 7,000 men from his position behind the Union lines, moving it north of the turnpike. This might have seemed sensible enough if there had been no danger on the Union left. But there was enormous, catastrophic danger on the Union left. Reynolds's advance meant that the Federal left was now virtually wide open and vulnerable. There were only 2,200 Union troops in place south of the turnpike, essentially an open field for Longstreet's advance.

Lee and Longstreet were not immediately aware of McDowell's mistake, but they understood that Porter's frontal assault had failed, that his ranks were shattered, and that the large force that had been on their right—Porter again—was no longer there. They decided, simultaneously and while the smoke was still rising from the last of Jackson's volleys, that the moment had come for Longstreet's corps to finally rise from the woods and move against Pope's left. It was not completely clear what was ahead of them, but Lee knew he was burning daylight, and he knew he had an opportunity, straight from classical military textbooks, to envelop and possibly destroy Pope's army. Longstreet, who had argued persuasively for a full day against an advance, was now ready. He was fully aware that he was in the pivot of one of the battle's—and the war's—great climactic moments. In his own words, "As [Porter's line] broke the third time, the charge was ordered," and then "twenty-five thousand braves moved in line as by a single impulse."[35]

And now the rebel wave rolled forward, to the astonishment of the Union command, especially John Pope. With Hood's Texans in the lead, it crushed everything in front of it, including a full brigade and battery. For thirty minutes Hood bulled straight ahead, unstoppable. The rebel goal was Henry Hill, the center of the fight at First Manassas. If the Confederates possessed it they could cut off a Union retreat down the Warrenton Turnpike. But first they had to cross Chinn Ridge, where hastily assembled Union forces put up a surprisingly tenacious defense, allowing time for Pope to place some seven thousand troops on Henry Hill, which lay only three hundred yards behind it. At about 6:00 p.m. Chinn Ridge finally fell. The Confederate victory there meant that Longstreet had finally demolished the Union left.

It was at about this time, too, that Pope as much as conceded defeat. Some Union regiments and brigades were already streaming eastward down the Warrenton Pike. At five fifty he gave orders to the rest of his army to retreat to the line of Henry Hill. He also ordered Nathaniel Banks to destroy all public property at Bristoe Station—completing Jackson's work—and retreat with his corps to Centreville. A brisk defense on Henry Hill—where Federals held off an advance of three thousand Georgians—spared the Union army the sort of headlong, panicked flight of the First Manassas. Jackson's troops might have made a difference there. But for some reason Lee never ordered Jackson's eight fresh brigades forward. Jackson had been told only to "look out for and protect [Longstreet's] flank," most likely because his brigades and divisions had been so badly wounded, scattered, shuffled, and commingled with each other while absorbing the repeated assaults over three days, that Lee believed he was in no shape to attack.[36]

Pope's army, in any case, was quite soundly beaten. (The casualties—10,000 Union and 8,300 Confederate—gave no indication of the thoroughness of the beating Pope took.) At 8:00 p.m. Pope ordered a full retreat of all his units to Centreville. By 11:00 p.m. most of his army had retreated across Bull Run. There was no panic this time, just heartbreak and humiliation. At Centreville, they encountered soldiers of General William B. Franklin's corps, who instead of cheering or sympathizing with their bloodied comrades, mocked them. Some said plainly they were happy that Pope had been beaten, echoing the sentiments of their leader. In doing so they were acting out the larger drama of the Union army, with, as one soldier put it, all of "the arrogance, jealousy, and hatred which then was the curse of Union armies in Virginia."[37] Soon Pope and his generals decided that staying at Centreville was a bad idea, too, since the rebels would simply march around them. For once he was not wrong. This was exactly what Jackson tried to do. On September 1 he slipped away and marched north and east around Pope's flank, hoping to cut off the Federal retreat. Anticipating this, two divisions under Pope clashed with Jackson in the Battle of Chantilly, a quick, violent, rain-drowned affair fought in a riotous thunderstorm that ended in stalemate and cost the life of the remarkable Major General Phil Kearny. He had mistakenly galloped into rebel lines, then, realizing his error, had turned and ridden away. One observer recalled that "as he galloped off lying prone on his horse's neck, [he] was killed. No trace of a wound was to be found, the bullet having entered the anus."[38]

There would be no more Confederate pursuit of the Union army. By this point it hardly mattered. Lee could not destroy the Union army, and he could hardly demoralize it any more than he already had. After the battle Pope's men resumed their retreat, slogging through the mud and rain to Alexandria. Those who participated in it remembered great disorder and confusion, vast snarls of wagons, ambulances, caissons, and wounded men—in the words of historian Bruce Catton, "the disorder inseparable from retreat."[39] The men walked with heads down, disheartened as much by the knowledge of how badly they had been mishandled by their own generals as from their shameful retreat from the field.

Though Chantilly had been largely a pointless afterthought—Jackson had not wanted to fight it—the idea of a victorious rebel army loose on the outskirts of Washington put yet another major scare into the capital. Stanton ordered the weapons and ammunition in the national arsenal transported to New York. He also ordered a steamer held in readiness to help the president escape, if necessary. Henry Halleck, the leader of the Union war effort, seemed on the verge of a breakdown, battered from his fight with McClellan, suffering from a painful case of hemorrhoids, and horrified by his army's precipitous retreat that he had been powerless to stop.[40]

Pope himself was deeply depressed. On September 2 he wrote a letter to Halleck that was alarming in its tone of meekness, gloom, and resignation. "As soon as the enemy brings up his forces again," he wrote, "I will give battle when I can, but you should come out and see the troops. They were badly demoralized when they joined me, both officers and men, and there is an intense idea among them that they must get behind the intrenchments. . . . You had best decide what should be done. The enemy is in very heavy force and must be stopped in some way."

Lee's message to Richmond, meanwhile, which was played and replayed in newspapers throughout the South, was a measure of the true size and sweep of this Confederate victory:

> The army achieved today on the plains of Manassas a signal victory over the combined forces of Genls McClellan and Pope. On the 28th and 29th each wing under Genls Longstreet and Jackson repulsed with valour attacks made on them separately. We mourn the loss of our gallant dead in every conflict yet our gratitude to almighty God for his mercies rises higher and higher each day, to him and the valour of our troops a nation's gratitude is due.

Perhaps the most astonishing thing of all to happen at the Battle of Second Manassas took place at the very end of the campaign. On the afternoon of September 2, the sun had finally come out and Generals Pope and McDowell were riding at the head of their retreating column, followed by their shuffling, silent, disconsolate men. In the road ahead they saw a small group of horsemen led by a small man riding a great black horse and wearing a jaunty yellow sash. It was George McClellan. As he approached he saluted crisply and proceeded to inform them—to their numb amazement—that by order of President Lincoln he was now back in full command of the armies of Virginia. A few moments later General John Hatch, who hated Pope and felt mistreated by him, addressed his infantry in a parade-ground voice that was heard by all, "Boys, McClellan is in charge of the army again! Three cheers!"[41] His men erupted, shouting and screaming "with wild delight."

CHAPTER FORTY

THE MONGREL,
BAREFOOTED CREW

—◆◆—

Robert E. Lee was going north. As he saw it, he did not have much choice. His army was beaten up, half starved, barefoot, threadbare, and minus nine thousand experienced fighters who had been killed or wounded in the previous three months. With such a force, there was little to be gained and much to lose by attacking Washington's fixed defenses, now bolstered by more than a hundred thousand men. Remaining where he was, in a country that had been stripped of its bounty by ravening armies—and poised precariously at the end of a rickety, vulnerable supply line—made no sense, either. Returning to Richmond would likely reset the clock for another massive Union assault.

Invading the North, on the other hand, had clear advantages, even with his tattered army. It would allow Lee to retain the initiative and replenish his depleted commissary. By threatening Washington and other Northern cities he would keep blue-clad troops clear of long-suffering Virginia. He had political motives, too: a Confederate army abroad in a nation already deeply divided over the conduct of the war, civil liberties, and the emancipation of slaves could help elect more "peace" Democrats in the fall elections in the North.[1] Lee, who was acutely aware of the advantages that would accrue to the North in a long war, was intent upon securing peace, and quickly. On September 8 he wrote to Jefferson Davis with an idea for a peace proposal that would deliberately be "made when it is in our power to inflict injury upon our adversary."[2]

So north it would be, across the Potomac and into Maryland and then on

to Harrisburg, Pennsylvania, cutting railroads and bridges and telegraphs—
Washington's connections to the West—as he went. If he could somehow
pull that off, as he told a "much astonished" General John G. Walker, "I
can turn my attention to Philadelphia, Baltimore, or Washington, as may
seem best for our interests."[3] This of course was exactly what Jackson had
suggested more than a year before to men in Richmond who thought he
was being unreasonably aggressive. So of course Jackson liked this idea very
much. (Longstreet, typically, was the voice of caution.) There was hardly
any delay in putting it into action. Jackson fought the Battle of Chantilly
on September 1. Lee then gave his army a single day of rest. At daybreak
on September 3 the Army of Northern Virginia marched for the enemy's
ground: the United States of America.

Jackson's new fame went with them. It is impossible to underestimate
the pride, wonder, and unalloyed happiness that surged through the Confederacy after Second Manassas. Victory had scarcely seemed possible.
Ruin had seemed inevitable. Yet there it was: a huge Union army slinking
back into Washington's defenses, while the ragged boys in butternut and
gray stood magnificent and bloody and triumphant on the field. Though
the name of James Longstreet was spoken reverently, the clear heroes of the
day were Lee and Jackson. Lee was the mastermind, the great solemn presence and genius of war whose strategies had driven not one but two Federal
armies from Virginia within two months. Jackson was Lee's iron fist, his
righteous tool of destruction. Southerners saw it that way. They also saw
the two generals, quite accurately, as a team. The two men thought alike
and acted in concert. Lee trusted Jackson, alone of his generals, to make
his own decisions. The nearly miraculous linking of the two armies near
Manassas on the morning of August 29 was not only the culmination of
one of the war's most brilliant tactical maneuvers, it also was the product
of a sort of high-command teamwork not previously witnessed on either
side.[4] The *Richmond Whig* put it this way:

> The central figure of the war is, beyond question, that of Robert E. Lee.
> His the calm, broad military intellect that reduced the chaos after Donel-
> son to form and order. But Jackson is the motive power that executes,
> with the rapidity of lightning, all that Lee can plan. Lee is the exponent of
> Southern power of command; Jackson, the expression of its faith in God
> and in itself, its terrible energy, its enthusiasm and daring, its unconquer-
> able will, its contempt of danger and fatigue.[5]

Meanwhile, the stories of Jackson's march around Pope were passing quickly into legend. Everywhere he went now, people wanted to see and touch him. Men wanted to shake his hand and speak to him. Children pressed as close as they dared when he passed. At Martinsburg, Virginia, he rode down the town's main street to tumultuous cheers, and women clustered around him and actually managed to cut off buttons from his coat. Some of them screamed for locks of his hair, to which the blushing general replied, "Really, ladies, this is the first time I was ever surrounded by the enemy!" When he sought refuge in a hotel, citizens surrounded the place, rattling the doors and windows, even as his poor horse, Little Sorrel, was being stripped of his hair by souvenir hunters.[6] Jackson, who disliked such adulation, escaped it only by setting up a secret headquarters outside of town.

In Frederick, Maryland, despite an otherwise chilly reception by the town's mostly non-slave-owning, pro-Union citizens, Jackson was ambushed in the street by two "bright Baltimore girls" who had concealed themselves in his carriage. One took his hand, while the other "threw her arms around him," according to Henry Kyd Douglas, "and talked with the wildest enthusiasm, until he seemed simply miserable." A few minutes later, the young ladies rode off, "leaving him there bowing, blushing, and speechless." Jackson, fearing another such encounter, did not venture out again until late in the evening.[7] That same day in Frederick, Jeb Stuart's chief of staff, Heros Von Borcke, experienced what it was like to be mistaken for the famous Stonewall Jackson. Von Borcke wrote later, "All remonstrances with the crowd were utterly useless. . . . I was very soon followed by a wild mob of people of all ages, from the old greybeard down to the smallest boy, all insisting that I was Jackson and venting their admiration in loud cheers and huzzas. Ladies rushed out of their houses with bouquets. . . . To escape these annoying ovations I dismounted at last at a hotel, but here I was little better off. It was like jumping in the mill pond to get out of the rain."[8]

Some of Jackson's enemies, too, were swept up in this wave of national adulation. A short time later, as he was riding by a large body of captive Union soldiers, "Almost the whole mass of prisoners broke over us, [and] rushed to the road," wrote one South Carolina soldier. "[They] threw up their hats, cheered, roared, bellowed, as even Jackson's troops had scarcely ever done. . . . The General gave a stiff acknowledgement of the compliment, pulled down his hat, drove spurs into his horse, and went clattering down the hill, away from the noise."[9] It is hard to know how his new celebrity struck him. Perhaps he really could not tolerate the idea that he, and not God, was getting credit for his victories. Perhaps, too, as his brother-in-law D. H. Hill theorized, what bothered him most was the temptation he felt, the warring of his own desires. Maybe some part of him *liked* being famous. Maybe that was what bothered him.

The notion of Lee and Jackson as invincible warriors had more practical effects. It gave new hope and inspiration to many Northern antiwar Democrats and Lincoln opponents whose vision of an endless, bloody, and unaffordable war was starting to look more and more real. European leaders had followed each turn of the Virginia campaigns with rapt interest, and the Confederate victories had convinced many of them that Lincoln would never be able to restore the Union by force of arms. With their triumph at Second Manassas, Lee and Jackson—who became overnight folk heroes in Europe—had made the case for de facto Confederate independence. All that remained now, many influential Europeans believed, was to formally acknowledge that state of affairs, either by an offer of mediation or outright diplomatic recognition or both. A majority in the House of Commons—saddled by a Union blockade with a "cotton famine" that had left three-fourths of British cotton millworkers unemployed or working part-time—clearly favored it, as did rising numbers of ordinary Britons. The British prime minister, Lord Palmerston, who had blocked a parliamentary resolution favoring mediation in June, now seemed ready to accept the idea. The Union had received "a complete smashing [at Second Manassas]," he wrote Lord John Russell, "and it seems not altogether unlikely that still greater disasters await them, and that even Washington or Baltimore might fall into the hands of the Confederates."[10]

The French seemed to be leaning Richmond's way, too. That summer Emperor Louis-Napoléon seriously considered a Southern alliance in exchange for cotton, and told his foreign secretary to "ask the English government if the moment has not come to recognize the South."[11] By September, according to the French foreign secretary, "not a reasonable statesman in Europe believed the North could win."[12] Confederate diplomat John Slidell, riding this wave of pro-Southern feeling, said, "I am more hopeful [of recognition] than I have been at any moment since my arrival." Even better, there was clear American historical precedent for all this. Colonial victory over Great Britain in the Second Battle of Saratoga in 1777 was a turning point in the Revolutionary War and led directly to French recognition of American independence and subsequent intervention on the American side. All this was in play as never before when Robert E. Lee, Stonewall Jackson, James Longstreet, and the Army of Northern Virginia tramped north.

The Confederate army that splashed across the Potomac River into Maryland on September 4 and 5, fresh from its victories in the Seven Days and at Cedar Mountain and Second Manassas, shocked the civilians who saw it. "They were the roughest set of creatures I ever saw," wrote a correspondent for the *Baltimore American*, "their features, hair, and clothing matted with dirt and filth; and the scratching they kept up gave warrant of vermin in abundance."[13] Many were without shoes, their uniforms so tattered they barely held together, their slouch hats so riddled with tears and holes that their greasy hair protruded from them at odd and comical angles. They stunk so badly—many had not even removed their clothing in weeks— that it was said that you could smell the vaunted Army of Northern Virginia long before you could see it.[14] The most striking thing about the men was their *gauntness*, the startling hollowness of eyes and cheeks and chests. Many were malnourished; most suffered from diarrhea brought on by everything from poor sanitation to bad water to a steady diet of roasted green corn and green apples. They were victims of the long and unreliable supply line that stretched all the way to Richmond, victims, too, of the Confederate military withdrawal from central Tennessee, where most of the South's pork was produced, and of the severe summer drought that had ruined the corn crop in several states.[15]

As always, Lee's men were poorly armed. By Union standards, what they carried across the river with them was just as unsettling as their beggarly appearance. Fully 30 percent of their muskets were still the antiquated .69-caliber smoothbores. There were also large numbers of .54-caliber muskets—three types, in fact—including some models that dated from 1841. Some were captured Springfield .58-calibers; and the balance— most—were imported, British-made .577-caliber Enfields. (A requisition from Jackson's command in the fall of 1862 listed twenty thousand .69-caliber cartridges and forty thousand .58-caliber cartridges.[16]) Their batteries were woefully inferior, too. Not only did they possess vastly fewer rifled guns than the Union, but also some 20 percent of their cannons were ancient Model 1841 six-pounders. The quality of their fuses was often atrocious: many shells either failed to burst or burst prematurely; a good number exploded while still in the guns.[17]

Lastly, for anyone who could see it, the army that marched up into Maryland was simply not the same one that had departed from the vicinity of Washington just a few days before. Lee approached the river with fifty thousand to fifty-five thousand men, a force that had been replenished by Richmond after Second Manassas. Twelve days later he had less than forty thousand.[18] The cause was straggling on an unprecedented scale. Some of the men fell away for lack of shoes, some because of illness or diarrhea or malnourishment. Many wanted nothing to do with an invasion of the North. They were fighting only to protect their homeland, as they saw it, only to repel the invader. But "straggling" didn't quite cover what was going on: a lot of this was outright desertion by men who had a bellyful of fighting and marching and suffering.[19] (The Union, too, was experiencing straggling at record levels: Union general in chief Henry Halleck was so frustrated by it that he wrote McClellan to suggest that "shooting them while in the act of straggling from their commands is the only effective remedy."[20] McClellan himself complained that "the states of the North are flooded with deserters and absentees."[21])

Strangest of all, perhaps, was that the undernourished, lice-infested troops who stayed with the army were remarkably *happy*. Morale was high. Hopes were high. They were fully conscious of their new fame. The name of the Army of Northern Virginia was now known to the whole world. They were the heroes of the Confederacy and they knew it. In spite of great disparities in troop strength and in the quality of weapons, ammunition, and supplies, from the start of the war to the present—First Manassas, Jackson's valley campaign, Seven Pines, Seven Days, Cedar Mountain, and Second Manassas—the Yankees had not beaten them. They had a sense, moreover, that one more big victory might change everything. When they crossed the river at White's Ford, near Leesburg, they did so, in the words of one of Jackson's soldiers, "with great enthusiasm—bands playing, men singing and cheering!"[22] The regimental band was playing "Maryland, My Maryland"—a pro-Southern song that portrayed Lincoln as a tyrant. ("The despot's heel is on thy shore, Maryland! / His torch is at thy temple door, Maryland!") Even Old Jack got caught up in the excitement, removing his hat while the band played, and, once on the other side, accepting gifts from Confederate sympathizers of a powerful gray mare and a prize melon.[23]

The mysterious new land they were entering—Maryland—was a slave state that had not seceded and thus remained divided in its loyalties. Just how divided no one knew for sure. It had been an article of faith among

Confederate officialdom that the state was ripe for conversion. They believed that their troops would be welcomed with open arms by a people who had felt the heavy hand of a Federal government that had occupied it militarily, arrested its citizens and legislators without warrants or charges, and suppressed its newspapers and rights of free speech. Lincoln had done all that, and more, while trying to keep Maryland in the Union.[24] But the Confederates were wrong, especially in the town of Frederick, where they arrived on September 6. Able-bodied men did not throng to their ranks. There was no uprising or movement to force Maryland to join the Confederacy. The majority of citizens treated them coldly and fearfully, having made sure to hide their money and valuables.

But that would not change Lee's plans. With the knowledge that McClellan's army was on its way to intercept him, he had an idea for yet another daring maneuver whose key player, once again, was Stonewall Jackson. As the rebel army moved north, Lee had worried about the two Union garrisons in his rear, one at Harpers Ferry with 10,400 men, and one at nearby Martinsburg with 2,500. Left alone, this force, the size of a full army corps, would menace both Lee's supply lines and his escape routes. As anyone who had ever been there knew, Harpers Ferry was extremely vulnerable, a custom-made trap wedged into the delta formed by the confluence of two great rivers, with mountains rising as high as a thousand feet on three sides. Harpers Ferry had been Jackson's first command. He knew its weaknesses better than anyone.

On September 9, Lee, camped at Frederick, Maryland, decided to divide his army and send part of it to capture Harpers Ferry. He had done so in consultation with Jackson, who was very much in favor of the plan, and had based it on the assumption that McClellan would move with his typical slowness. That would allow Jackson to reunite with Lee and Longstreet before McClellan caught up. Longstreet, who had opposed the idea, later recalled that he came upon Lee and Jackson together, eagerly plotting the destruction of the Union garrison. Seeing the enthusiasm of his colleagues, he yielded. "They had gone so far that it seemed useless for me to offer any further opposition," he wrote, "and I only suggested that Lee should use his entire army in the move."[25]

Lee's decision was embodied in a fateful, ten-paragraph directive dated September 9 and known as Special Orders 191. In it, he split his army into four pieces. Three of them, under Jackson—consisting of twenty-six of the army's forty brigades—were to march to Harpers Ferry, where they would surround and attack the garrison simultaneously from three directions. Because of the Ferry's peculiar terrain, the three would have to take entirely separate routes: General Lafayette McLaws's division (five thousand men) would secure Maryland Heights on the Maryland side; Brigadier General John Walker with his two-brigade division (less than four thousand men) would secure Loudoun Heights across the Shenandoah River in Virginia; and Jackson's three divisions (fourteen thousand men), with a long march around to the west, would seal off Harpers Ferry by seizing Bolivar Heights. Longstreet, with the rest of the army, would march west through the Blue Ridge (South Mountain) to the town of Boonsboro, using D. H. Hill as his rear guard against attack through the mountains. Special Orders 191's flaw was immediately obvious: for as long as it took for Jackson to seize the Union garrison at Harpers Ferry, the rest of Lee's army—merely sixteen thousand men—would be isolated and at the mercy of the entire Army of the Potomac. Thus Lee gave Jackson just three days to get the job done.

Once in the vicinity of Harpers Ferry, Jackson's forces deployed quickly. After a sharp fight, McLaws seized Maryland Heights from the 1,600 Federals whom Union commander Dixon Miles had stationed there on the morning of September 13. That afternoon, Walker took the undefended Loudoun Heights. Jackson, meanwhile, moved his forces in on the western flank of the town and began to set his artillery in position. Jackson, the old artillerist, with the immense advantages offered by the spectacular headlands around Harpers Ferry, was planning a big-gun assault from three directions on the roughly 13,000 Federals below. (The Martinsburg garrison had retreated before Jackson's advance and joined the other Union troops.) Though Jackson was a day behind schedule, and McClellan was already at Frederick, Lee did not yet see any reason to panic. McClellan was McClellan, after all.

Except, of course, when he was in possession of the greatest intelligence leak of the Civil War. That same day a corporal from Indiana named Barton Mitchell found an envelope containing a sheet of paper wrapped around three cigars. The cigars were of excellent quality, something enlisted men rarely got to sample. Before lighting up, Mitchell and another soldier decided to take a closer look at the document. It was addressed to D. H. Hill, contained the names of prominent Confederate generals, and closed with "By Command of R. E. Lee." It was signed by Lee's adjutant, R. H. Chilton. News of the find quickly climbed the chain of command. Soon

Major General Alpheus Williams, commanding the Union 12th Corps, was peering at "Special Orders 191," a document that appeared to provide, in elaborate detail, the movements, whereabouts, and precise strategy of the entire Army of Northern Virginia. The order was so detailed, precise, and comprehensive, in fact—rare in the war—that some of its original Confederate recipients had taken action to prevent just such a leak: Longstreet had put it in his mouth and chewed it up like a plug of tobacco; Walker had pinned it to the inside of his jacket; Jackson had meticulously burned it. It was a stroke of luck that General Williams's aide Colonel Samuel Pittman, who had known Chilton well in prewar army days, could confirm that it was Lee's chief of staff's handwriting.

McClellan understood immediately what he had. After reading it, he threw his hands in the air and exclaimed, "Now I know what to do!" Later that same day he was in his tent chatting with his old army friend Brigadier General John Gibbon and another officer when he pulled the folded orders from his pocket. "Here is a paper with which if I cannot whip 'Bobbie Lee,' I will be willing to go home," he told them. "It gives the movement of every division of Lee's army." He then vowed to "put Lee in a position he will find hard to get out of," and noted that "Castiglione will be nothing to it." His reference was to the Battle of Castiglione in Italy in 1796, in which Napoléon Bonaparte famously routed an Austrian army.[26] The message of 191 was perfectly clear: Lee had divided his army, and his separated units could thus be attacked and beaten in detail. It was probably the greatest single military opportunity of the war. McClellan wired Lincoln, saying, "I think Lee has made a gross mistake and that he will be severely punished for it. . . . I have all the plans of the Rebels and will catch them in their own trap if my men are equal to the emergency."

At about 5:00 p.m. that same day Jeb Stuart received a provocative piece of intelligence. A Confederate sympathizer happened to be standing near McClellan's tent when he had received the copy of Special Orders 191, and had described McClellan's reaction. Though the spy did not fully understand what had happened, it was clear that McClellan certainly knew *something*. Stuart immediately sent a courier to Lee with the news, then sent another dispatch at about midnight on the same subject. Since the message has been lost, it is impossible to say what Stuart told Lee, or what Lee suspected, though it is unlikely that Lee knew McClellan had a copy of the order itself.[27] But he would soon be very aware that McClellan was not behaving in his usual way.

That change was visible the very next day. Lee, who had told Brigadier General G. John Walker on September 6 that McClellan "would not be prepared for offensive operations for three weeks," now watched in amazement on September 14 as McClellan's army pushed its way forward through three passes in South Mountain, the elevated, elongated, north-to-south-running formation that marked the extension of the Blue Ridge Mountains into Maryland.[28] There were pitched battles that day at Turner's Gap and Fox's Gap, where D. H. Hill fought a fierce rear-guard action; and Crampton's Gap, where a vastly outnumbered Lafayette McLaws—who was also manning the guns on nearby Maryland Heights—tried to hold back William Franklin's 6th Corps, whose mission was to relieve Harpers Ferry. In all, some 28,000 Union troops faced some 18,000 rebels. The Confederate purpose was not to win, but to delay the Federal advance long enough for Jackson to come up from Harpers Ferry. They very definitely did not win. By the end of the day, they were blown out of all three passes, suffering 2,685 casualties to the Union's 2,385.

They did, however, buy Lee precious time. Even though the Union commanders knew with certainty that Lee's weakened and divided army lay before them, none pushed aggressively forward. Franklin, headed for the Ferry with 12,300 men, came to a complete standstill. McClellan, moving through the northern passes, and suspicious that Longstreet's main force lay just ahead, slowed to a crawl. Though Special Orders 191 had specified troop movements, the document had said nothing about *troop strength*, which meant that McClellan could indulge his usual wild fantasies. "The Battle of South Mountain was one of extraordinary illusions and delusions," wrote D. H. Hill. "The Federals were under the self-imposed illusion that there was a very large force opposed to them, whereas there was only one weak division until late afternoon [at Turner's and Fox's Gaps]. They might have brushed it aside almost without halting."[29] McClellan believed—and he had taught his more cautious generals to believe—that the greatest threat came from what they could not see, from those phantom army corps lying in wait in the next valley or wooded grove, warming themselves by ten thousand campfires and waiting to fall upon his outnumbered army.

For the moment he was triumphant, and he wasted no time in trumpeting his achievement to his bosses in Washington. "It has been a glorious victory," he telegraphed, and followed it the next morning with two more dispatches saying that the enemy was retreating "in a perfect panic, &

that Genl. Lee last night stated publicly that he must admit they had been shockingly whipped. . . . It is stated that Lee gives his loss at 15,000."[30] He did not mention the rumors that were sweeping his army: that Lee and Longstreet were dead. McClellan had the rebels on the run. He knew for certain that Jackson was still in Harpers Ferry. His great opportunity to destroy Lee had come at last.

Lee was not the only one who was surprised at the sudden—and suddenly aggressive—Union advance. That same day, on the west side of Harpers Ferry, Jackson still believed he had plenty of time to finish his mission. He had instructed both McLaws and Walker not to open fire "unless forced to." His plan was to ask for surrender, then wait twenty-four hours to see what Union commander colonel Dixon Miles would do. But as the day progressed, and the sounds of battle rose from the passes at South Mountain, it became clear to General Walker on Loudoun Heights—who could hear all this and even see some of it—that this plan would not hold. He had wigwagged a message to tell Jackson about the battle taking place at Crampton's Gap, which Jackson had dismissed as a minor cavalry fight. But Walker could hear the artillery that Jackson could not, "which left no doubt in my mind," he wrote, "of the advance of the whole federal army."[31]

Walker then contrived to be "forced" to open fire. He promptly placed two of his regiments on the treeless crest of the mountain, in full view of the Federal batteries on Bolivar Heights. "As I expected, they opened at once a heavy, but harmless fire," Walker wrote. "I directed my batteries to reply." Soon McLaws's batteries began banging away from across the river, and Jackson's followed. The Confederate cannonade kept up all afternoon, while the Federals quickly learned that you could not win an artillery fight with an opponent whose guns were positioned at much higher elevations. As one Federal soldier described it, "The *infernal screech owls* came hissing and singing, then bursting, plowing great holes in the earth, filling our eyes with dust, and tearing many giant trees to atoms."[32] It was a convincing display, both to Jackson's forces and to the men who were ducking the shellfire below. When Walker later admitted his ruse to Jackson, Jackson replied, "It was just as well. . . . But I could not believe that the fire you reported indicated the advance of McClellan in force. It seemed more likely to be merely a cavalry affair." Jackson was silent for a few moments, then added, "I thought I knew McClellan, but this movement puzzles me."[33]

Back in Hagerstown, an equally puzzled Lee was growing more and more despondent. His troops had been defeated and driven back at South

Mountain by an inexplicably energetic Union army, and still he had heard nothing from Jackson. By the evening of September 13 he had decided he could no longer stay where he was. He would have to retreat. At 8:00 p.m. he sent a courier to Lafayette McLaws—commanding by far the closest and most accessible of the three units assailing Harpers Ferry—saying, "The day has gone against us and this army [Longstreet's corps] will go to Sharpsburg to cross the river." He ordered McLaws to get back to Virginia as fast as he could. Then, just as all of Lee's plans seemed to be falling apart, he received a dispatch from Jackson. "Through God's blessing, the advance, which commenced this evening, has been successful thus far, and I look to Him for complete success to-morrow. The advance has been directed to be resumed at dawn."[34] Because Lee trusted Jackson's judgment—he believed him implicitly—this changed everything. New orders went out. McLaws and the rest of the army were now to coalesce at the little town of Sharpsburg, a mile or so north of the Potomac.

The next morning Jackson quickly made good on his promise. At dawn on September 15 he opened up with everything he had on the mist-shrouded town of Harpers Ferry. On Maryland and Loudoun Heights, fifty guns shattered the morning's calm and rained shell and shot while Jackson's own carefully placed guns blasted the Federal troops and batteries on Bolivar Heights from three sides. The Federal return fire sputtered on erratically for a while, then stopped altogether. At about 8:00 a.m., as Jackson was readying his 14,000 for an advance against Miles's roughly comparable force, a rider emerged from the Federal lines holding a white flag of surrender. Though 1,300 cavalry had managed to escape under cover of darkness before, Jackson soon had as his prisoners 12,415 Union soldiers, 13,000 small arms, 73 cannons, 200 wagons, 1,200 mules, and a trove of supplies. He had done it all at a cost of 39 Confederates killed and 247 wounded, mostly at the battle for Maryland Heights. Though little blood was spilled, Harpers Ferry was on paper the most comprehensive Confederate victory of the war.[35] It was the largest surrender of Federal troops, larger in numbers than the surrender of British Generals Cornwallis or Burgoyne in the Revolutionary War.[36] The defeat was so humiliating that when news of it was released in Washington, War Department censors cut the numbers of Union soldiers captured in half.[37] Jackson immediately sent a courier to Lee with the good news. "Through God's blessing," he wrote with the sort of understatement that was missing from his West Point classmate's self-congratulatory bombast, "Harper's Ferry and its garrison are to be surrendered." Lee was ecstatic. He ordered Jackson's note to be read to his army. Then he wired Davis in Richmond, saying, "This victory of the indomitable Jackson and his troops gives us renewed occasion for gratitude to Almighty God for His guidance and protection."

The Union surrender that followed provided one of the war's most theatrical spectacles. "The entire garrison of 13,000 [sic] men was drawn up in imposing lines," wrote Heros Von Borcke, "presenting, with their well-kept equipments, their new uniforms and beautiful banners, a striking contrast to Jackson's gaunt and ragged soldiers, who formed opposite to them, and whose tattered garments and weather-beaten features showed only too plainly the hardships they had undergone."[38] When the mythical Jackson himself rode into Harpers Ferry with his staff at about 11:00 a.m., Union soldiers and other observers were stunned by his shoddy appearance. "He was dressed in the coarsest kind of homespun, seedy and dirty at that," wrote a correspondent for the *New York Times*, with no attempt to conceal his withering contempt. "[He] wore an old hat which any Northern beggar would consider an insult to have offered him, and in general appearance was in no respect to be distinguished from the mongrel, barefooted crew who follow his fortunes . . . and yet they glory in their shame."[39] The contrast became even more marked when the ranking Union officer, Brigadier General Julius White, rode up with A. P. Hill and drew rein in front of Jackson. (Garrison commander Dixon Miles had been wounded in the leg by one of Jackson's shells and would die the next day.) In contrast to his rebel counterpart, White was handsomely uniformed and mounted on a splendid black horse. Jackson offered him no terms but unconditional surrender. But he also made generous concessions, partly dictated by necessity. Captured soldiers would be paroled, not imprisoned, which meant they could walk away, without their weapons. Enlisted men were allowed to keep their overcoats and blankets and were given two days' provisions. Officers would retain their sidearms and baggage.

While Jackson was gathering his spoils—and once again allowing the men free rein with the nonalcoholic supplies—a drama was unfolding five miles away in the valley below Crampton's Gap. Early that morning, Major General William Franklin and his twenty thousand bluecoats had streamed down out of the pass on South Mountain in pursuit of their objective, the relief of Harpers Ferry. Special Orders 191 had told McClellan exactly where Jackson was and what he would be doing, and Franklin was going to save Harpers Ferry. Together the garrison plus Franklin's corps would field some thirty-three thousand men, almost as many as in Lee's entire army. Facing Franklin were Lafayette McLaws's paltry five thousand. As McLaws's men prepared to be crushed by the obviously superior force, they could hear the roll of Jackson's artillery in the distance.

"Up in the valley we could see heavy masses of infantry bearing down on us," wrote Confederate cavalry officer W. W. Blackford, "their lines of skirmishers extending clear across from mountain to mountain as they came hastening down to the relief of their beleaguered garrison."[40] On they came, until those skirmishers arrived within musket range of the Confederate lines. But just as the inevitable clash was about to occur, the reverberating roar of Jackson's guns stopped. The Union soldiers stopped, too, seemingly intrigued by the sudden silence. Then, as everyone stood frozen, came a sound, distant at first, then louder and louder as it rolled up the valley and through the Confederate ranks. It was the sound of wild cheering. The rebels had finally understood the meaning of the silence: Harpers Ferry had surrendered. A short time later, a courier arrived on a foaming horse to confirm the news. As the rebel yell rang through the Confederate column, a Yankee skirmisher stood up on a stone wall and yelled, "What the hell are you fellows cheering for?" A rebel soldier shouted back, "Because Harper's Ferry is gone up, God damn you!" To which the Union soldier replied, "I thought that was it."[41]

Maybe it was those rolling rebel cheers. Maybe it was Jackson himself, or, once again, the *idea* of Jackson, unbeaten, mysteriously powerful, and fresh from another bloody meal of Union soldiery. But for some reason Franklin, in the middle of his McClellan-ordered advance on Harpers Ferry, simply gave up. At 11:00 a.m. he told McClellan, "They outnumber me two to one. It will of course not answer to pursue the enemy under these circumstances." Four hours later he made essentially the same report. Thus, for the rebel general McLaws, whose brigades had fought hard twice, once at Maryland Heights and once at Crampton's Gap, a moment of serendipity. In the afternoon he and his command marched down to the Potomac and across the pontoon bridge and into Harpers Ferry while his enemies looked on, helplessly now, from a distance.

CHAPTER FORTY-ONE

THE BLOOD-WASHED GROUND

◆═╣═╠═◆

For Robert E. Lee, the news that Jackson had seized Harpers Ferry changed almost everything. He could reunite his army. He could stand and fight. His lines of communication and path of retreat were secure. What it did not change was that, on the morning of September 15, the day of Jackson's victory, Lee was still isolated, alone, and more vulnerable than he had ever been. He therefore did the only thing he could possibly do, facing the bulk of McClellan's victorious army with a mere fifteen thousand men: he bluffed, and waited for Jackson.

After his retreat from South Mountain, Lee had chosen the best defensive position he could find on short notice, on the flanks of the twelve-block rural town of Sharpsburg, about eight rolling country miles west of Turner's Gap. He placed his men on a long, undulating ridge that ran from three miles north of the village to a mile and a half southeast of it. This was all high ground. Behind him, at a distance of roughly a mile at its nearest point, was the Potomac River. From the ridge the land sloped gently down and eastward in a swelling plateau of open pastures, cultivated fields, and woodlots to Antietam Creek, which ran generally about a mile west of the ridge. At its northernmost point, the line of ridges touched the Potomac; on the far south it met the westward-looping creek. Lee's position behind Antietam Creek was in most ways a risky proposition. Its main advantages were the natural elevation of the ridge and the limited creek crossings available to the Union troops—four arched stone bridges—which could be swept by Lee's batteries.

The disadvantages were striking, even to a casual observer. The most obvious weakness was that Lee had backed his army up against a major river, as Colonel Edward Porter Alexander of Lee's staff pointed out, "with no bridge & only one ford, & that the worst one on the whole river."[1] He had in effect done exactly what John Pope had done—before the latter realized the egregiousness of his mistake and corrected it—in placing his army between the Rapidan and the Rappahannock a month before, except that Pope at least had access to a bridge. There was, moreover, only one road to Boteler's Ford—the only nearby crossing—which ran along high bluffs for much of the two miles south from Sharpsburg and was so narrow at points that, as Alexander observed, "a horseman could not easily pass a wagon."[2] The ford itself was deep and rocky. "No army," Alexander said, only a bit hyperbolically, "could retreat over such a road as that under fire."[3] Lee, an astute student of terrain who would have understood this as well as anyone, had presumably decided, with considerable contempt for his opponent's abilities, that there was little chance that his army would be retreating across the Potomac under fire. Then there was the *length* of Lee's line itself—more than four miles. Even with his full army—or what was left of it—he did not have enough manpower to adequately defend all of the ground from the Potomac to the Antietam. He thus had a built-in weakness from the start: his lines were stretched thin in places and his left was not really anchored on the Potomac at all. It was "in the air," and in spite of the artillery Lee mounted on a northern hill, it would remain that way.[4]

For now the charade was all that mattered. Lee spread his paper-thin lines across a wide front and fired his guns at whatever Federals showed themselves on the other side of the creek, or at nothing in particular. He was openly and defiantly offering battle to McClellan, which, in view of McClellan's intimate knowledge of Confederate plans, must have puzzled him. Jackson, McLaws, and Walker couldn't possibly have arrived yet, could they? But a perplexed McClellan was a cautious and fearful McClellan, and that was precisely what Lee wanted. September 15 passed, and with it one of the truly spectacular military opportunities of the war. McClellan had told William Franklin earlier that he wanted to "cut the enemy in two and beat him in detail." Here was that opportunity, or half of it, anyway, and he passed on it. He was again the victim of his own inflated estimate of Lee's troop strength. He later testified that the rebels had about 100,000 men, instead of somewhat fewer than 40,000. His lieutenants were in rough agreement. His loyal friend and principal adviser Fitz John Porter pegged the number at 100,000 to 130,000, Edwin Sumner at 80,000.[5] McClellan's dithering wasn't entirely

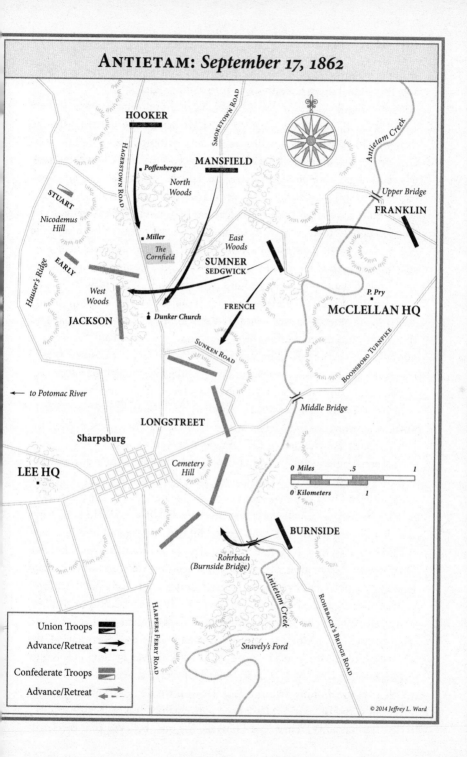

ANTIETAM: *September 17, 1862*

HOOKER

HAGERSTOWN ROAD

SMOKETOWN ROAD

Poffenberger

MANSFIELD

North
Woods

Antietam Creek

STUART

Nicodemus
Hill

Upper Bridge

FRANKLIN

Miller

The
Cornfield

East
Woods

EARLY

SUMNER
SEDGWICK

Hauser's Ridge

West
Woods

P. Pry

McCLELLAN HQ

JACKSON

Dunker Church

FRENCH

SUNKEN ROAD

to Potomac River

BOONSBORO TURNPIKE

Middle Bridge

LONGSTREET

Sharpsburg

Cemetery
Hill

0 Miles   .5   1

0 Kilometers   1

LEE HQ

BURNSIDE

Rohrbach
(Burnside Bridge)

HARPERS FERRY ROAD

Antietam Creek

ROHRBACH'S BRIDGE ROAD

Snavely's Ford

Union Troops

Advance/Retreat

Confederate Troops

Advance/Retreat

© 2014 Jeffrey L. Ward

without its advantages: it did give him more time to concentrate his available forces, including Franklin's 6th Corps, for an attack.[6]

September 16 came, and with it yet another opportunity to crush Lee, and still the Union forces stayed put. McClellan busied himself with the things he loved best: reconnaissance, placing batteries, assigning bivouacs, checking on his supplies of food and ordnance. The pause allowed Jackson, who had taken his men on a "severe" forced march overnight, to join Lee's battle line at midday, a mirror image of Lee's dramatic arrival near Manassas. It must have given both men pleasure, in a purely tactical sense, to be able to again unite their forces in such a dramatic way under the noses of the enemy. In spite of their rough seventeen-mile journey, Jackson's men were still flushed with victory when they arrived at Sharpsburg. For such a ragged, underfed lot, they were astoundingly cheerful. Bands played "Dixie," while thousands of Confederate soldiers sang its words. "Such inspiring, soul-stirring music I never heard as the volume of harmony rolled and thundered through that little vale in the forest," wrote William T. Poague, a gunner with Jackson's Rockbridge Artillery. "It seemed to put new life into both men and animals . . . as we followed 'Old Jack' through the village. . . . We felt ready for anything our beloved General might undertake."[7] One wonders what the Yankee pickets, who had been told that the Confederate army was reeling from its defeat at South Mountain, in a panic and on the run, its generals wounded or dead, made of such high spirits.

Jackson seemed to be in a good mood, too, though as usual that did not mean a sudden burst of warm feeling toward his colleagues in the upper ranks. He had been feuding again with his general officers. On September 4, after he had personally countermanded A. P. Hill's orders to his troops, which appeared to contradict his own, Hill had approached him in a fury, pulled his sword from its scabbard, turned the hilt toward Jackson, and said, "I submit my resignation, sir!" Jackson ignored the proffered sword and said quietly, "General Hill, consider yourself under arrest for disobedience of orders." For the next several days Hill repeatedly asked Jackson to give him a written copy of the charges against him. Jackson refused. He informed Hill through an aide that should his case come before a court-martial, the charges would be furnished to him. This made Hill even madder. It was only on September 10—six days later—that Hill received permission to return to the command of his division. Still, Jackson would not drop the charges. His fight with Hill may not have been entirely the result of Jackson's quirky style of command. Henry Kyd Douglas, for one, believed that the feisty, independent Hill, who hadn't liked Jackson since their earliest days at West Point, had it coming to him.[8] While in Frederick, Jackson placed another general, William E. Starke, in arrest for allowing his Louisiana troops to take goods from local shops without paying for them. When it turned out that the guilty parties were actually from the Stonewall Brigade, Jackson released Starke from arrest. But he never apologized or even noted his mistake.

In spite of his harsh treatment of his generals, Jackson could as usual be surprisingly kind, and even funny, in his own peculiar way, even under the immense pressure of the march from Harpers Ferry. When he arrived in Sharpsburg a local citizen invited him to breakfast. He declined, but the daughter of the house sent food to him anyway. Jackson, who was glad to get it, asked his aide Henry Kyd Douglas who the sender was.

"I dunno, General, but it was the fair one."

"Well, as she has sent me my breakfast to the field, I will call her Miss Fairfield."

Amused at this conceit, Jackson then took a pencil and wrote:

> *Sharpsburg, Sept. 16, 1862*
>
> *Miss Fairfield:*
> *I have received the nice breakfast, for which I am indebted to your kindness. Please accept my grateful appreciation of your hospitality.*
> *Very Sincerely Yours,*
> *T. J. Jackson*[9]

At 4:00 p.m. on the afternoon of September 16, McClellan finally made his first, very tentative, move. Major General Joseph Hooker crossed Antietam Creek with his three-division, fourteen-thousand-man 1st Corps, swept around to the north end of Lee's line, and advanced in what amounted to a reconnaissance in force. His batteries opened, and his infantry drove in the rebel skirmishers until the resistance stiffened, revealing the rough contours of the main Confederate line of resistance astride the north-to-south-running Hagerstown Pike. Hooker now knew more or less where the rebel line was, and there he stopped.[10] Less happily, from a tactical standpoint, he had also revealed to Lee the position and direction of the opening attack of the Battle of Antietam the next morning.

Joe Hooker was the sort of general Abraham Lincoln was looking for. He was tall, good-looking, clean-shaven in a sea of military beards, forthright, transparently ambitious, and conspicuously brave. Though there were rumors of hard drinking and womanizing, his personal habits did not seem to interfere with his martial talents. He liked to lead from the front and had thus earned the moniker Fighting Joe. He had indeed fought hard and well in the peninsula campaign, which had earned him promotion. He had chafed under McClellan's cautious leadership. At about dawn on September 17, mounted on a muscular, milk-white charger, he ordered the first attack of the Battle of Antietam. His objective: a slightly raised piece of open ground just east of the Hagerstown Pike, where, on the flank of a plain, foursquare German Baptist church—their habit of baptism by total immersion had led to their nickname, Dunkers—stood thick ranks of Confederate cannons. This was the heart of the Confederate left, the wing of Lee's army that was under the command of Stonewall Jackson.

Hooker attacked after daybreak. His troops came straight at Jackson's two divisions under Generals Alexander Lawton (taking the wounded Ewell's place) and John R. Jones in a north-to-south assault across a half-mile-wide front. One Union division under Abner Doubleday moved along the axis of the turnpike near the West Woods; another, under James Ricketts, moved from the East Woods across a prim thirty-acre cornfield. With Doubleday were "those damned black hat fellers," as the Stonewall Brigade called the men who would earn the name Iron Brigade on this battlefield.[11] On they came, as big Union twenty-pounders detonated east of Antietam Creek, and Hooker's guns fired first solid shot and exploding shell (shrapnel), then case (exploding spheres that shot a hundred bullets forward on detonation), and finally double-shotted canister from the front.[12] From Nicodemus Hill on the west near the Potomac, artillery under Jeb Stuart poured in destructive fire from the Union flank, ripping holes in the Iron Brigade and others. Jackson's battle line stood mostly on open ground, starting just north of the Dunker church and stretching half a mile from the West Woods through the southern part of the cornfield.

As the lines engaged, it seemed to the combatants as though the world had exploded into a storm of buzzing iron and lead. The bluecoats came ahead anyway with breathtaking resolve, striding forward in line, stopping, peering through the moving wall of white smoke, tearing cartridges with their teeth, loading, ramming, firing, and as often as not falling screaming to the ground. When the first of them emerged from the cornrows, a line of rebel infantry rose and dropped much of the line where it stood, as a scythe moves through wheat. A Confederate shell, landing in the midst of the 6th

Wisconsin Regiment, exploding as it struck, took out as many as thirty men.[13] The battle was as intimate as it was violent, fought at close range by men who could see each other clearly, a free-for-all in the choking fog and smoke and heat, with attacks and counterattacks coming from seemingly every direction. There was something fearless and primitive and elemental in the combat that morning, a kind of madness or possession, as soldiers left their humanity behind and became mere feral killing machines.

By 7:00 a.m., an hour into the fight, Jackson had fought Hooker to a horrific standstill. The losses sustained by both sides—measured as the percentage of a regiment that had fallen—were already unprecedented in the war. But the Confederates were starting to wobble. Division commander Lawton could feel it, and told Jackson as much. In response Jackson summoned John Bell Hood's 2,300-man division of troops from Texas, Mississippi, Georgia, and the Carolinas, generally considered the toughest fighters in Lee's army. They had been in a reserve position behind the lines, where they had just been given their first rations in three days and were sitting down to enjoy them. Infuriated at the interruption, they marched to the front, and with the predominantly Texas Brigade in the lead and the weirdly barking, yipping, whirring noise of the rebel yell echoing across the killing ground, smashed into the Federals and drove them sharply back. The effect of Hood's counterattack was stunning and immediate: the Federals reeled, turned, then split right and left for the cover of the woods, with Hood's men in hot pursuit.

The fight raged in the cornfield and along the turnpike. It spilled into the East Woods and the West Woods, where men faced fire from several directions and there was more of that wild, fierce, close-range combat between men who, obeying some instinct that transcended all reason, would not run away. But Hood could not beat the Union army by himself. As his men rolled triumphantly into the northern end of the cornfield, resistance stiffened, and once again they were in that tornado of canister and minié balls, hearing the sickening dull thuds of lead and iron hitting flesh. The entire field by this time was shrouded in opaque, greasy smoke, in places so thick that the only things visible were the waving battle flags. At one point a Pennsylvania regiment took aim at the oncoming 1st Texas, resting their muskets on the lower rails of a fence and shooting at the Texans' legs, which were all they could see.[14] The Texans soon broke and retreated through the incessant and deafening musket fire, leaving an appalling 80 percent of their comrades lying on the ground.

Thus the prototype of surge and countersurge that defined the fighting that morning. The advances would start strong, out of musket range, with the full support of their main artillery. But as the men moved forward into the fray, several factors came into play. There was the inevitable loss of men to enemy fire; at Antietam this could be upward of half of a fighting unit. The advancing companies and regiments also became disorganized as terrain separated men or they became disoriented in the swirling smoke or, even more critically, lost their field commanders. As they approached the enemy, of course, they moved farther and farther away from their own artillery—which at some point could no longer fire without hitting them—and closer to the enemy's shotgun-like canisters. And finally they actually hit the enemy's defensive line itself, often stocked with fresh reserves. And then the momentum changed, and the enemy came on.[15]

After an hour of frenzied fighting on a field now washed in blood, Hooker's and Jackson's corps seemed less coherent fighting units than assemblages of human wreckage. Half of the Confederates in Lawton's three brigades had been killed or wounded. Lawton himself had been wounded, one of his brigade commanders was dead, and eleven of fifteen regimental commanders were killed or wounded. A third of the men in Jackson's old division were lying on the field. Their commander, Brigadier General John R. Jones, was wounded, and his replacement, William E. Starke, was dead. Hood lost 60 percent of his men. When he was asked where his command was, he replied, "Dead on the field." On the Union side, Hooker's 1st Corps lost 2,600 men, or a third of its strength. Hooker himself was wounded. One of his division commanders, Brigadier General James Ricketts, who had 3,150 men at his disposal at the beginning of the fight, could muster only 300, a combined result of casualties, straggling, and battlefield dislocations.[16] Hooker's own description of the fighting in the corn captures the effects of its animal violence:

> In the time I am writing, every stalk of corn in the northern and greater part of the field was cut as closely as with a knife, and the slain lay in rows precisely as they had stood in their ranks a few minutes before. It was never my fortune to witness a more bloody, dismal battlefield.[17]

The 1st Corps was, for the moment, fought out. But the fight on the Confederate left was far from over. While Jackson had already used up his main reserve—Hood's division—McClellan still had enormous firepower waiting to enter the battle. Onto the field now marched Major General Joseph Mansfield's 12th Corps, which had been biding its time just north and east of the cornfield. Mansfield was a white-haired army lifer, an engineer by training who had never had a combat command and had lobbied incessantly for this one in the preceding months. He was commanding a corps that consisted mostly of the men who had fought with Nathaniel Banks in the valley. He should have been ordered to attack with Hooker; two full Federal corps might have turned the rebel left. But McClellan gave no such orders. This was to be the pattern of the day's Union attacks: piecemeal and without coordination, thus failing to capitalize on the enormous Federal advantage in numbers.

As Hood's attack lost steam, Mansfield's 12th Corps advanced, driving the bloodied, exhausted rebels back, 7,200 fresh troops sweeping south over the same ground that had been fought over all morning. This was at about 7:30 a.m., half an hour after Hood's slashing counterattack, and ninety minutes into the fighting. From his command post in the West Woods, Jackson worked furiously in the rising pandemonium to hold off disaster. He reformed scattered units, repositioned artillery, moved Stuart's guns nearer to his main force, sent batteries to the rear to be refurbished, and brought up new supplies of ammunition.[18] He replaced part of Lawton's broken division with a brigade borrowed from D. H. Hill in the Confederate center, and deployed it across the cornfield. He brought Jubal Early's brigade up from the flank and positioned it in the West Woods. He brought what was left of Hood's division and set it up as a reserve on his right.

But the momentum had already swung hard in the Union's favor. The 12th Corps seemed to move at will, driving not only the remnants of Jones, Lawton, and Hood, but also the borrowed brigades from D. H. Hill near the East Woods. Even worse, Jackson had no more troops to bring into the battle.[19] He had foreseen this when he had first sent Hood forward, and had asked Lee for reinforcements as early as 7:00 a.m. Lee had answered that he would send him the divisions of McLaws and Walker. Those reinforcements had not yet arrived. The 12th Corps was now in possession of the battlefield, and most of the ground from the East Woods to the West Woods. Disaster suddenly loomed on the Confederate left. All that remained, it seemed, was for Colonel Andrew Grigsby's Stonewall Brigade and Jubal Early's brigade—maybe 1,400 men—to mount the rebels' last stand. The only good news, had they been aware of it, was that both

Union corps commanders, Mansfield and Hooker, were wounded, Hooker severely in the foot, and Mansfield mortally in the chest.

But the situation was worse than Jackson had imagined. At about 9:00 a.m., as he waited for the 12th Corps to mount yet another attack, he saw something even more disturbing off in the distance. From the vicinity of the East Woods, across the mangled cornfield, suddenly appeared a massive, fast-moving column of blue. Though he could not identify it, this was the lead division of Major General Edwin Sumner's 2nd Corps, led by Sumner himself, whose objective was to smash the Confederate left once and for all.

Or at least that is what Sumner intended. His execution of this worthy plan, however, was nothing short of bizarre. Edwin Sumner was the very picture of the old warhorse. At sixty-five he was the oldest of the "old army" officers in McClellan's force. He was crusty and tough and old-school and famous for his booming voice, which had given him the nickname Bull. He was a stand-up fighter and unquestionably brave, the sort of man you would send to take a heavily defended hill. But he was not terribly smart, and the range of his thought was remarkably narrow. He was coming across the field now, at the head of the 5,500 men under division commander John Sedgwick.

It was at this moment that, while Early and Grigsby prepared to make the Confederate left's last stand in the West Woods, Jackson's long-awaited reinforcements began to arrive. Half an hour later he might have been overrun; but Lee, with his knack for inserting soldiers into battles at the right place and at the right time, had come through.[20]

Sumner, meanwhile, convinced that the rebel flank was vulnerable—and from his reconnaissance it did indeed look that way—proposed to move into and through the West Woods north of the Dunker church, then wheel to the left, and sweep down on the rebel lines from the north.[21] To do this he had formed Sedgwick's division into three classic, two-deep battle lines, each five hundred yards long and separated by thirty to fifty yards. Thus deployed, unsupported by other Union forces, and ignoring the scattered fighting units of the 1st and 12th Corps around them, they came rapidly on. Such a marching formation was appropriate to a parade ground or a military review. On this battlefield it amounted to suicide. "There was absolutely no preparation for facing to the right or left in case either of their exposed flanks should be attacked," wrote Francis W. Palfrey, then a lieutenant colonel with the 20th Massachusetts. "The total disregard of all ordinary military precaution in their swift and solitary advance was so manifest that it was observed and criticized as the devoted band moved on."[22]

Unfortunately for Sedgwick's men, Jackson had understood immediately how exposed they were. And now, thanks to Lee, he had the reinforcements to do something about it. He moved them quickly into place, both inside and to the west of the West Woods. He began by orchestrating some 4,400 men into both a frontal and a flank assault on the 125th Pennsylvania near the Dunker church. Soon the Pennsylvanians were reeling out of the woods, in full retreat. This was the first move in Jackson's counterstroke. To prevent Sumner from turning his left, he moved one of McLaws's brigades to the western side of the woods. He ordered the brigades fighting the 125th Pennsylvania to break off their attack and move north in the woods to intercept the east-to-west-advancing Sumner. Jackson had his battle line in place literally moments before Sumner's advancing battle lines appeared in the open lot that was inset west of the Hagerstown Road and north of the main woods.[23] The Union troops under Sedgwick and Sumner, marching forward in their three textbook battle lines, apparently did not see what was waiting for them in the woods. They kept moving.

And now the woods exploded. Suddenly there was a great roar and tumult of musketry and screaming men, and bullets were everywhere as the Confederate artillery, somehow positioned perfectly to smash the 2nd Corps, boomed from behind the woods. Confederate riflemen, firing from behind uneven ground and limestone ledges, swept the three sets of double Union lines with volley after volley. Rebel batteries opened from the west, adding shell and canister to the melee. Eventually Stuart's artillery also joined in. Barksdale's Mississippians and Early's Virginians emerged into the open space along the pike and slammed into Sumner's trailing brigades, and soon Sumner's entire force was engulfed in fire. Sumner, at the head of his troops, finally grasped just how close to annihilation he was. "Back, boys, for God's sake, move back! You are in a bad fix!"

But it was too late to save them. Union brigade commanders tried vainly to get their troops to change front, but all that ensued was a mass tangle of confused and panicked men as all regimental order vanished and the Federals nearest the woods simply broke and ran. The lines tended to compress, too, which offered a conspicuous mass of blue-clad human flesh for the rebels to shoot at. Things only got worse from there. Regiments collapsed like dominoes. Where the Federals had been hit first on their flank, now they faced fire from front, rear, and flank, trapped in the lethal three-sided box that Jackson had prepared for them. "A terrific fire of musketry opened in the woods in Sumner's front across the pike," wrote Black Hat Brigade commander John Gibbon. "Instantly, as it appeared to me, the whole open space between the 'east' and 'west' woods was filled with a disorganized mass of panic-stricken men going to the rear."[24] Twenty-three hundred Union soldiers fell in fifteen minutes in the fight that would soon be known as the West Woods Massacre. (That is five men every two seconds.) Union division commander John Sedgwick was wounded three times and carried from the field.

Though Jackson's men tried to follow their success with another attack across the cornfield against the East Woods, they soon found themselves being blasted by canister from fifty Union guns. They stopped and drifted back. A Union attempt to relieve Sumner faltered, too, this time met by troops from Walker's division, who had also arrived just at the right time to meet the Federal advance. The lone exception to Jackson's sweeping success was the stubborn 12th Corps brigade commanded by Brigadier General George Sears, which had captured the Dunker church and actually moved two hundred yards beyond it into the West Woods. He somehow managed to keep his precious foothold—it was the original objective of the Union attack that morning—all the while calling for reinforcements and utterly unaware that the Union 2nd Corps had been completely routed. He discovered this unpleasant fact at about noon, and shortly before Jackson's troops blasted him on both flanks, driving him back.[25] Though the guns and muskets continued to roar, the Federals seemed to be more concerned with self-preservation than breaking the rebel line.

At this point the battle had lasted for four hours. Jackson had been assaulted by two full Union corps and the lead division of another in successive waves that cost twelve thousand casualties on both sides. He had initially lost so much ground that he was in danger of being swallowed outright by advancing Federal forces. But by shrewd deployment of the reserves Lee sent him, at the end of the day "my troops held the ground which they had occupied in the morning," Jackson wrote in his battle report.[26] McClellan had not gained an inch of terrain. During all this Jackson, from behind the Dunker church, was a study in motion, watching the battlefield, directing the fire of his batteries, exhorting his men, issuing orders. John S. Mosby, a cavalryman who observed Jackson briefly, was amazed at how he seemed "transfigured with the joy of battle" as he issued orders "in a quiet way."[27] Jackson later told D. H. Hill that he never felt safer than in the firestorm at Antietam. He was convinced that "God would protect him & that no harm would befall him."[28]

Jackson's achievement was all the more remarkable because he had done it in spite of the absence of key generals—A. P. Hill (en route from Harpers Ferry), Richard Ewell (wounded at Second Manassas), Isaac Trimble (wounded at Second Manassas), and Charles S. Winder (killed at Cedar Mountain)—and the fact that eight of his fourteen brigades were commanded by colonels with little experience. Just as important, his performance at Antietam showed that he had clearly mastered the role of executive officer—subordinate to Lee on the field yet working closely with him, taking initiative when he needed to, cooperating with other generals, and deftly managing his side of the battlefield.[29] If this particular martial skill was sometimes lacking during the Seven Days, the fights at Antietam and Second Manassas proved that he had learned to operate *within* an army as well as in independent command. His personal presence on the battlefield had become a critical component of Confederate success. Thirty miles away, where Richard Ewell was recovering from the amputation of his leg after his wounding at Manassas, and hearing the distant sound of artillery at Sharpsburg, he became extremely agitated and finally confessed to his doctor that he could not listen to the battle without worrying that Jackson would be killed. The future of the Confederacy, he believed, depended in large part on his chief's survival.[30]

At noon, surgeon Hunter McGuire met Jackson at his command post behind the lines at the Dunker church. McGuire was eating one of the peaches a local woman had given him. Jackson's face brightened when he saw his favorite fruit. "Do you have any more?" he asked. McGuire gave Jackson several pieces, which he consumed immediately and with great relish. He apologized to McGuire for his gluttony, saying it was the first food he had eaten all day.

"Can our line hold against another attack?" asked McGuire, surveying a field littered with the dead and dying.

"I think they have done their worst," Jackson answered calmly. "There is now no danger of the line being broken."[31]

Jackson, who had a remarkable ability to read a battlefield through the smoke and thunder and chaos of a fight, turned out to be right. There would not be another attack. The battle on the Confederate left—and Jackson's part in the Battle of Antietam—was over. That afternoon he and Jeb Stuart would, under Lee's orders, gather troops for an advance against the 1st, 6th, and 12th Corps. But the two men would decide very quickly that they did not have nearly the numbers or firepower to pull it off.

Meanwhile, as the roar of musket and artillery fire to their right attested, the fight was just beginning for James Longstreet and the rest of Lee's army.

George McClellan was worried. After what had happened to him in the morning, he had good reason to be. He had sent three army corps to turn the rebel flank. They had been badly mauled, and at midday the defiant rebel left stood exactly where it had been when Hooker's first assault began. What had gone wrong? From the luxury of the rear, well behind the creek, surrounded by his reserves of more than thirty thousand men, it was hard to tell. McClellan's headquarters was in a large house on a commanding elevation, where the scene in and around it was as unlike Jackson's primitive, artillery-raked command post behind the Dunker church as it could possibly be. "Here was the immense cavalry escort waiting in the rear," wrote Captain George F. Noyes, a staffer with division commander Brigadier General Abner Doubleday, "staff horses picketed by dozens around the house, while the piazza was crowded with officers seeking to read with their field-glasses the history of the battle at the right."[32] At the center of all of this sat McClellan, almost preternaturally calm, conversing quietly with staff members, consulting Fitz John Porter as usual, sending and receiving messages, and gazing through a telescope to try to make sense of what was happening. But according to Noyes it was almost impossible to see anything, even from a vantage point several hundred yards closer to the front. "I could not distinguish a single battery," wrote Noyes, "nor discern the movements of a single brigade, nor see a single battalion of the men in gray. Smoke-clouds leaped in sudden fury from ridges crowned with cannon, or lay thick and dim upon the valleys, or rose lazily up over the trees; all else was concealed; only the volleyed thunder was eloquent."[33]

The fact was that, through those great shifting pools and shrouds of smoke, the battle was already spinning out of McClellan's control. He had not intended to break off his attack on the rebel left. But that attack had extinguished itself, partly because many Union commanders were wounded, partly through simple battlefield attrition, and partly because of the extreme havoc that had been wrought on regimental and brigade-level organization. Not only that, but one of Sumner's 2nd Corps divisions—under the stout, red-faced William H. French, Jackson's old Florida nemesis, who had earned the nickname Blinky for his habit of rapidly fluttering his eyes when he spoke—that was supposed to follow him onto the field, had lost sight of Sumner and instead moved obliquely south and west, driving into the Confederate center and touching off a battle there.[34] McClellan's purpose in attacking the rebel left had been to turn it if possible but in any case to force Lee to shift troops from the rest of his line, thus weakening his center and right. This was exactly what had happened. Lee had actually thrown *nearly three-fourths of his available force* into Jackson's fight.[35] Unfortunately McClellan's spyglass did not reveal this astonishing fact to him. What was more, in spite of his 9:00 a.m. orders to Major General Ambrose Burnside and his 9th Corps on his far left to cross the creek and move against Lee's right, Burnside still seemed frozen in place. To McClellan this was all very unsettling.

Antietam was really three battles, fought more or less sequentially on September 17 between dawn and dusk. The first of these was the four-hour Hooker–Jackson donnybrook in the north. The second, just as frenzied and recklessly violent, took place in the center. At about nine thirty, while Jackson was demolishing Sumner in the West Woods, French's 5,700 Union troops advanced against 2,500 rebels under D. H. Hill, who were deployed within the embankments of the Sunken Road, a small, dirt lane used by farmers that had been worn down over the years by rain and wagon wheels. From its first moment, Hill's Confederates opened fire at a range of 60 yards and took out 450 of the 1,400 men in French's lead brigade. The rebels held most of the advantages: they were firing from superb cover and they were closely supported by artillery. The Yankee troops had neither. They stood and delivered from 80 yards out, one brigade at a time, and went down by the hundreds. Though the men behind the embankment were shooting from cover, they, too, fell in heaps where they stood, mostly from ghastly head and neck wounds, back into their long trench. Most such firefights burn themselves out quickly. Incredibly, this "savage, continual thunder" went on for nearly two full hours.

By noon dead men lay in piles everywhere, and the Federal numbers were beginning to tell. Major General Israel Richardson, one of the Union's finest commanders, had joined French on the field with his three-brigade division of Sumner's 2nd Corps. At about 1:00 p.m. Richardson's Federals finally turned the rebels' right flank. There was chaos in the Sunken Road as they were struck from front, flank, and rear. Now French's men moved against their left, too, at which point the Sunken Road turned from a stout defensive position to a death trap, earning its historic name: Bloody Lane.

The Confederate line collapsed completely. Many men surrendered. Many more ran and many of them were shot as they ran. They retreated in disorder for half a mile, where they found Lee's "center" that had been stripped earlier of its manpower and now held nothing but some artillery and whatever infantry Longstreet had been able to cobble together. Clearly, the center would not hold. The rout thus presented yet another great opportunity: Richardson and French were now in a position to destroy Lee's main line of defense in front of Sharpsburg. There was little left to stop them. As Edward Porter Alexander put it gloomily, "Lee's army was ruined. The end of the Confederacy was in sight." Richardson saw it, and requested artillery from McClellan to finish the job. McClellan refused. Richardson was preparing to attack anyway when he was wounded in the leg by case shot and carried from the field. This temporarily stalled the Federal advance.

While all this action was taking place, the third battle in the sequence, utterly different from the other two, was being fought on the Confederate right. The fight had begun at about 10:00 a.m., when soldiers from Ambrose Burnside's thirteen-thousand-man 9th Corps attempted to cross the lower bridge over Antietam Creek. The Confederate defense across the river consisted only of a depleted force under Confederate brigadier general D. R. Jones. After Lee's leftward troop shifts of the morning, he had only four thousand men defending a mile of front south of Sharpsburg. It was yet another mismatch, if only Burnside could take advantage of it. Unable to find a suitable ford, Burnside focused on the twelve-foot-wide bridge—known to history as Burnside's Bridge—assaulting it several times in the morning, and each time being repulsed by seven hundred to eight hundred Confederates firing from the high, steep, wooded ground on the other side. At 1:00 p.m. Burnside's men, under an officer who had formerly run fashionable dance clubs in New York, finally broke through, using a rudimentary tactic: they ran like hell across the bridge, taking appalling casualties. Now his corps was crossing, moving up the slope toward Lee's thin defenses in front of the town. There was little to stop him.

For all of his caution and hands-off management, and the chaotic reversals of the day, McClellan found himself in midafternoon poised for a definitive, lethal strike at Lee. On the right, elements of the 1st and 12th Corps had rallied, and now were organized and strong enough to advance yet again on Jackson's lines. They were supported by Franklin's 6th Corps, which was deployed near the East Woods. In the center were French's and Richardson's troops of the 2nd Corps, victorious at the Sunken Road, rested and resupplied with ammunition. Just behind the creek waited Porter's entirely fresh 6th Corps. On the southern end of the line, Burnside was now over the bridge and ready to attack the Confederate right. McClellan had missed opportunities on September 14, 15, and 16 to smash Lee's divided army. Here was perhaps his best opportunity to destroy the entire rebel force in place.

Even better, McClellan had twelve thousand fresh troops under Major General William Franklin and four thousand more under Fitz John Porter to do the job. But here, once again, far from the fighting and lacking any feel for the battlefield, he fell prey to his own fears. Though Franklin was pleading to be allowed to attack, General Sumner, still in shock from what had happened to Sedgwick's division, made his own passionate case that the condition of the 1st and 12th Corps—"all cut up and demoralized," as he put it—made the Union right vulnerable to attack, and that Franklin's men must be kept as defensive reserves. Little Mac, unable to see clearly the situation on his right where he stood, agreed with Sumner, and opted for defense over offense. Franklin would not be unleashed. It is noteworthy that McClellan was not just seeing phantoms here: Lee *did* want to attack the Union right that afternoon, and was planning to until Jackson and Stuart talked him out of it, so there would be no advance again that day on the Union right. In the center, the delay following the retreat from the Sunken Road had allowed Longstreet to patch up his battle lines so that instead of virtually nothing at all, there now was something vaguely resembling resistance. The Union momentum—hurt as much by the absence of General Richardson as the long delay—had dissipated.[36]

This left the southernmost sector of the battle as McClellan's last big chance to strike at Robert E. Lee. By 3:00 p.m., Burnside finally had some momentum. He had dithered virtually all day in crossing the creek, which had allowed Lee to shift critical manpower from his right to his left. But now he advanced up the slope and engaged in a sharp fight with the outnumbered Confederates, and by 4:00 p.m. he was pushing the enemy steadily back. The 9th Corps had seized virtually all the high ground to the east and south of Sharpsburg. The town itself was in flames, its streets filled with beaten and demoralized rebel soldiers. There were no reserves left to save them. Burnside's men had only to drive 1,200 yards farther to cut off the rebels' line of retreat and flank the rest of Lee's line.[37]

Lee, who was watching all this with a sinking heart, suddenly saw something else in his field glasses. Two hours earlier, A. P. Hill had arrived at

Lee's headquarters to tell him that his troops, detailed by Jackson to handle the surrendered Union soldiers and equipment at Harpers Ferry, were on their way. Now, from behind the ridge Lee could see a great cloud of dust rising in the clear sunlight, and a column of troops came into view. It was Hill's Light Division, arriving without a moment to spare. Led by Hill in his trademark red battle shirt, they had left at 6:30 a.m. and covered seventeen miles in eight hours, and if they were tired they did not show it. Neither Burnside nor McClellan saw them coming. Deploying immediately on the field, at about 4:30 p.m. Hill's men drove hard into Burnside's flank and rolled it up. Soon the 9th Corps was retreating to its bridgehead, where the Confederates were happy to let it remain. The Union had suffered 2,350 casualties in Burnside's attack, while the Confederates lost just over 1,000.[38]

The day's battle was over. A snapshot of the field would have shown—in addition to the dead and wounded, broken weapons and busted caissons, dead horses, wrecked batteries, and discarded knapsacks and blanket rolls—that Lee's army was in very nearly the same position it occupied as the day began. Only now there were more than sixty thousand Union troops in close proximity to their lines—most of them only a few hundred yards away. Only Porter's 5th Corps was still behind the creek. With its four thousand men, McClellan could have used it to reinforce Burnside. But it wasn't in Little Mac's soul to commit his only reserves to a battle with an uncertain outcome.

A great flaming-red sun set on the battlefield, and soon the darkness came on and with it the weirdly beautiful sight of lanterns floating and dancing like fireflies over the killing fields while details searched for the wounded. The count of dead and wounded was ghastly: 22,717 men, 10,316 for the Confederacy and 12,401 for the Union. It remains the highest count for a single day in any American war. Jackson, in the cornfield and West Woods, had fought the single bloodiest part of it. This was in spite of the rather remarkable fact that McClellan had committed only 50,000 men to the fight. A third of his army never fired a shot.

The following morning Jeb Stuart's chief of staff, Heros Von Borcke, found Jackson leaning on a fence behind the Confederate lines. He was drinking a cup of rare, hot coffee that his servant Jim had prepared for him from the contents of a Federal knapsack. Jim was always with him, and devoted to him, tending to matters involving food, clothing, bedding or lodgment, baggage, the care and maintenance of Little Sorrel, or whatever else was needed. It is not clear where Jackson found him, though it is likely Jim was a slave whom Jackson hired from his owner, one William C. Lewis of Lexington.[39] He rode his own horse. He was an attractive, light-skinned, middle-aged black man with refined manners. Though he professed admiration for Jackson's temperance, he himself liked both liquor and playing cards.[40] Before them were deployed some unwounded 30,000 Confederates, still in their four-mile-long line. Nearly all of them had been in the fight. By contrast, McClellan had *33,000 fresh troops*, 13,000 in new reinforcements plus 20,000 who had been present but had not taken part in the battle. That was in addition to his main army. McClellan could not, or would not, see his advantage. In his mind Lee had more than 100,000 men, possibly more. Jackson, typically, had the reverse view: he believed it was still possible to mount a Confederate attack. According to his aide Douglas, he was "ready to fight at the drop of a hat."[41] Meanwhile Lee, Jackson, and Longstreet fully expected a renewal of the Federal attack.

But September 18 passed with only intermittent picket fire. No attack came. McClellan had had enough. "I concluded that the success of an attack on the 18th was not certain," he wrote later. "I should have had a narrow view of the condition of the country had I been willing to hazard another battle with less than absolute assurance of success."[42] But he also seemed perfectly content with what he had accomplished. "I feel some little pride," he wrote his wife, "in having, with a beaten and demoralized army, defeated Lee so utterly, & saved the North so completely."[43] He had of course not defeated Lee at all. He had made a series of uncoordinated, piecemeal assaults and had failed to do what he needed to do to win, which was to move simultaneously against Lee's center and right while attacking his left. He had actually achieved a drawn battle against a force half his size, a fact that would give the clear tactical victory to Lee.

But the purely *strategic* victory clearly belonged to Little Mac. The best evidence for this, on a strictly military level, was the withdrawal, starting after sundown on the night of September 18, of Lee's army. His soldiers left in a thunderstorm, then marched south to Boteler's Ford, where they crossed the knee-deep, three-hundred-yard-wide Potomac to Shepherdstown, Virginia. There they became entangled in a massive traffic jam that did not sort itself out until the following morning. The army had to fight a single rear-guard action when four Federal brigades managed to cross and threaten to seize some forty cannons. Jackson sent A. P. Hill and four regiments to remedy this, resulting in what Jackson called "an appalling scene of destruction of human life" as Hill's men first ran the Yankees into the river, then shot them as they tried to cross it.[44]

Though it was a small affair, with no more than six hundred men killed or wounded on both sides, and did not really constitute the pursuit of Lee by McClellan, Jackson's fierce and immediate counterstroke gained considerable fame as the Battle of Shepherdstown. Southerners saw it as a thumb in the eye of Federals who would dare to pursue Lee's army into Virginia, a clear victory after the hazy outcome at Sharpsburg. Though initially depressed by the battle's outcome and Lee's retreat, Southerners, too, came to see value in Lee's Maryland expedition: vastly outnumbered, he had fought McClellan to a draw; he had crossed the river unmolested and of his own free will; and Jackson's stunning capture of twelve thousand prisoners was a great victory. Asked the *Richmond Dispatch* in response to claims of a glorious victory in the Northern press, "If we have been thus badly beaten . . . why has McClellan not crossed the river and destroyed the army of Gen. Lee? . . . The truth is this: the victory, though not so decisive as that of Manassas, was certainly a Confederate victory."[45] That was a comforting thought, but not really true. It came to seem even better in the wake of two Confederate reverses in the West in October at Corinth, Mississippi, and at Perryville, Kentucky.

But all that was just white noise compared to the real significance of the Battle of Antietam, which was political and not military. For two months, Lincoln had been sitting on his draft of an Emancipation Proclamation. He had been waiting for a decisive victory so that issuing the document would not seem an act of desperation. McClellan and Pope had given him nothing but bitter, shattering defeats at Seven Days, Cedar Mountain, and Second Manassas. But now, with Lee's withdrawal from the field, Lincoln decided that the outcome at Antietam was good enough. The hour had come. "I wish it was a better time," he told his cabinet in a meeting on September 22, five days after the battle. "The action of the army against the rebels has not been quite what I should have best liked. But they have been driven out of Maryland." That same day he issued the proclamation, which warned the seceded states that unless they came back into the Union by January 1, 1863, their slaves "shall be then, thenceforward, and forever free." Lincoln was using his war powers to seize Confederate property; he had no constitutional authority to free slaves in the border states of Maryland, Missouri, Kentucky, and Delaware. But for the other states the proclamation would create, in effect, an army of liberation, assuming that army could defeat and occupy individual Confederate states. That, of course, was a gigantic assumption. It was not even clear, on September 22, that Union soldiers—including George McClellan—would fight a war that was now explicitly about freeing slaves.

The Battle of Antietam arrested the singular momentum of the Army of Northern Virginia. But the Emancipation Proclamation changed the very nature of the war. It would no longer be about putting the Union back together. It was now explicitly about ripping it apart—and with it the social fabric of the South itself—and building something entirely new. Wrote Ralph Waldo Emerson in the November 1862 *Atlantic*, "It is not a measure that admits of being taken back. Done, it cannot be undone by a new administration. . . . It makes a victory of our defeats."[46] As Halleck told Grant, "There is now no possible hope of reconciliation. We must conquer the rebels or be conquered by them."[47] After the Emancipation Proclamation, the only way the war was going to end was if one side won it by sheer force of arms—something the Confederacy would simply never be able to do. The proclamation also marked the beginning of the end of the South's long dalliance with the European powers. Soon enough, they would gently withdraw to permanent onlooker status, having decided that the Confederacy was unlikely to win. Britain, meanwhile, was fast coming to the conclusion that it wanted nothing to do with an ally who, in spite of its protests to the contrary, appeared now to be fighting for the cause of slavery.

CHAPTER FORTY-TWO

STONEWALL JACKSON'S WAY

꜒ꜗ꜖

Had the war changed Thomas J. Jackson? After eighteen months of brutal dislocation that had changed so many others, the question is worth asking. There was no simple answer. He could, and did, often seem completely opaque, even to his own staff. Between his administrative duties—managing equipment, supplies, munitions, medical matters, and food, dealing with Richmond, overseeing promotions and other personnel matters—and his basic responsibilities for marching and fighting, Jackson presents such a seamless blur of activity that it is easy to lose sight of the man behind the rank.[1] A rare exception was the two-month period that followed the Battle of Antietam. The Union army had offered no immediate pursuit. There was no fighting. There were no forced marches. Jackson spent almost all of that time in various camps near Bunker Hill, just north of his beloved—and dramatically changed—Winchester. And though he was still quite busy, in this period of extended rest the man himself became more visible.

He comes most sharply into focus through the eyes of a British army colonel named Garnet Wolseley, who visited Jackson's camp in the second week of October along with two English reporters. Wolseley was one of the brightest stars in his country's army. He would later become commander in chief of the British army and thus the most powerful military figure in the world. He had gone out of his way to meet the famous Confederate general, even though he had been told that the taciturn Jackson would be a difficult interview. But Jackson was not at all what he expected. With a newly shaven upper lip and chin and "only a very small allowance of whisker," Jackson cordially welcomed his visitors into his tent.[2] He began the conversation by speaking of his trip to England and the Continent in 1856, particularly of his fondness for English cathedrals, then asked his guests questions about various English subjects. In contrast to so many observers who found Jackson disappointing in person, Wolseley, an outsider who saw him unfiltered by the lens of the wartime army, was enormously impressed. (A later British visitor, a member of the House of Commons, said Jackson was the best-informed military man he met in America.[3]) This was not because Jackson's manner had changed—one of the reporters present recalled him as courteous but somewhat distant and reserved—but his *presence* clearly had.[4] Jackson was still Jackson, and dressed like Jackson. But Wolseley, the soldier's soldier, believed himself to be in the company of a brilliant and fully formed leader of men.

"Dressed in his gray uniform, he looks the hero that he is," Colonel Wolseley wrote in a British magazine a few months later,

> and his thin compressed lips and calm glance, which meets you so unflinchingly, give evidence of that firmness and decision of character for which he is so famous. . . . Though his conversation is perfectly free from all religious cant, it is evident that he is a person who never loses sight of the fact that there is an omnipresent Deity ever presiding over the minutest occurrences of life. . . .
>
> With such a leader men would go anywhere, and face any amount of difficulties; and for myself, I believe that, inspired by the presence of such a man, I should be perfectly insensible to fatigue, and reckon upon success as a moral certainty. . . . Jackson, like Napoleon, is idolized with the intense fervor which, consisting of mingled personal attachment and devoted loyalty, causes them to meet death for his sake and bless him while dying.[5]

Many of Jackson's men would have agreed with Wolseley. Whether his wild popularity was somehow rooted in his unusual personality, or, as his cynical brother-in-law D. H. Hill believed, solely in his ability to win on the battlefield—or some combination of the two—there was clearly more to him than the old science teacher with a few glorious victories under his belt. Almost everyone who had known him before noted this change. His old friend Mrs. Fanny Graham from Winchester saw the transformation in physical terms. "He is looking in such perfect health—far *handsomer* than I ever saw him," she wrote Anna after the general had stopped by for tea at her home in Winchester.[6] A few months later Anna, too, would remark on this improvement in his looks that is apparent today in his few portraits.[7] Gone is the almost petulant expression of the prewar photographs, replaced with the face—apparent in his famous "Winchester" portrait that his wife and friends all said was a true record of his appearance—of a man who indeed looked much more handsome, older, wiser, and more complete. It was perhaps no accident that someone whose many physical ills had virtually vanished—except for his unidentified sickness during the Seven Days—would seem physically transformed.[8] Though he was considerably thinner than he had been before the war, he was otherwise, for the first time in his adult life, completely healthy.

Part of his change, too, was the fame itself, which attached itself to him and would not let him alone. He was adored and idolized all over the South. One Alabama private wrote, "If Jesus Christ were to ride along the ranks on the foal of an ass, there would not be half the cheering and huzzahing" the general received.[9] When he walked to regimental church services, men would drop what they were doing, including their card games, follow him, and stand in rapt silence while he knelt and often prayed aloud for them. (They were just as likely to return to their cards when he had departed.[10]) His mere presence in camp often sparked the feral crescendos of the rebel yell. Henry Kyd Douglas described a night in camp when "there broke forth that wild and joyous yell for which the Stonewall Brigade was famous. Other brigades and divisions took it up and it sprang from camp to camp with increasing vigor, until the bright arch of Heaven seemed to resound with the thundering acclaim. . . . When it was at its height I saw the General come out, bareheaded, from his tent, walk to the fence and lean his elbow on the topmost rail. . . . When it was all over, he returned slowly to his tent, and said in soliloquy as he entered: 'That was the sweetest music I ever heard.'"[11]

One of the most telling signs of his renown—and his inability to escape it—was the song, written on the eve of Antietam, that was sweeping through Confederate ranks and that would become one of the more popular Confederate songs of the war. Set to a spirited, upbeat tune, "Stonewall Jackson's Way" was a faithful reflection of the way he was seen in the ranks in the fall of 1862. In its third verse, the song dares anyone to "scoff" at Jackson's habits of worship.

STONEWALL JACKSON'S WAY

Come, stack arms, men! Pile on the rails,
Stir up the camp-fire bright;
No matter if the canteen fails,
We'll make a roaring night.
Here Shenandoah brawls along,
There burly Blue Ridge echoes strong,
To swell the brigade's rousing song
Of "Stonewall Jackson's way."

We see him now, the old slouched hat
Cocked o'er his eye askew;
The shrewd, dry smile, the speech so pat,
So calm, so blunt, so true.
The "Blue-Light Elder" knows 'em well;
Says he, "That's Banks, he's fond of shell;
Lord save his soul! We'll give him hell,"
That's "Stonewall Jackson's way."

Silence! Ground arms! Kneel all! Caps off!
Old "Blue Light's" going to pray.
Strangle the fool that dares to scoff!
Attention! It's his way.
Appealing from his native sod,
"Hear us, hear us Almighty God,
Lay bare Thine arm; stretch forth Thy rod!"
That's "Stonewall Jackson's way."

He's in the saddle now. Fall in!
Steady! The whole brigade!
Hill's at the ford cut off. We'll win
His way out, ball and blade!
What matter if our shoes are worn?
What matter if our feet are torn?
"Quick-step! We're with him before morn!"
That's "Stonewall Jackson's way."

The sun's bright lances rout the mists
Of morning, and, by George!
Here's Longstreet struggling in the lists,
Hemmed in an ugly gorge.
Pope and his Yankees, whipped before,
"Bayonets and grape!" hear Stonewall roar;
"Charge, Stuart! Pay off Ashby's score!"
In "Stonewall Jackson's way."

Ah! Maiden, wait and watch and yearn
For news of Stonewall's band!
Ah! Widow, read, with eyes that burn,
That ring upon thy hand.
Ah! Wife, sew on, pray on, hope on;
Thy life shall not be all forlorn;
The foe had better ne'er been born
That gets in "Stonewall's way."

Jackson had a contentious relationship with his fame, which he battled with a combination of flight and prayer. Cheers from his men would usually prompt him to spur and gallop away. It was said that Little Sorrel understood his master's wishes and would speed up as soon as he heard shouting. Though Jackson had vowed not to read newspapers, he was aware that the press was full of his exploits, and he wrote Anna to caution her, in words that might have been drawn from his own prayers, to ignore them. "Don't trouble yourself about representations that are made of your husband," he wrote. "These things are earthly and transitory. There are real and glorious blessings, I trust, in reserve for us beyond this life. It is best for us to keep our eyes fixed upon the throne of God and the realities of a more glorious existence beyond the verge of time. *It is gratifying to be beloved and to have our conduct approved by our fellow-men*, but this is not worthy to be compared with the glory that is in reservation for us in the presence of our glorified Redeemer."[12] (Italics added.)

He often included the same sorts of caveats in his thank-you notes for the many gifts he received, which included everything from gilded spurs, gold braid, and dress swords to socks, scarves, and apple pies. "My Dear Mrs. Osburn," he wrote in one letter, "Your very kind note and beautiful and useful presents from your daughter have been received. Please give my thanks to her, and accept them for yourself. I know of none who rejoices more than myself at your release from that thralldom to which you refer [Federal occupation], but you must not overestimate me in the work. I have been but the unworthy instrument whom it has pleased *God* to use in accomplishing his purpose."[13]

But he did more than just redirect credit for his victories to the divinity. During this interlude, Jackson, who believed that godliness among his troops would help win the war—and by contrast blasphemies such as carrying mail on Sunday might doom the cause—began to play a more active role in his army's religious life. He had always done this, to some extent. But now, and for the next seven months, he went at it more systematically. Though he would consent, in the absence of a pastor, to lead prayers, he himself never proselytized, never preached, never criticized any soldier for failure to attend religious services. His work was entirely behind the scenes, ensuring that Christian pamphlets were distributed in camp, recruiting regimental chaplains, lobbying Richmond for more money to pay them, sometimes donating his own money, and arranging for popular preachers to give sermons. His efforts coincided with the wave of Christian revival meetings that pulsed through Jackson's camps that fall. They were partly the product of the eighteen months the soldiers had spent in close proximity to death and their concerns about their own spiritual salvation. They were partly due to the work of preachers who saw a ripe opportunity to save souls. Jackson loved all of it, and attended as many camp meetings and services as possible, especially those featuring the Reverend Joseph Stiles, whom he particularly liked. He was delighted when more than one hundred men from the Stonewall Brigade showed up for a meeting. "It appears that we may look for growing piety and many conversions in the army," Jackson wrote Reverend Dabney happily.[14]

Though a deacon's bench was the closest Jackson ever came to the ministry, people sometimes treated him as though he had pastoral, if not saintly, powers. On one occasion, in October at Bunker Hill, a young woman approached Jackson while he was on his horse, lifted up her eighteen-month-old son, and asked the general to bless him. "He turned to her with great earnestness," wrote an observer, "and with a pleasant expression on his stern face took the child in his arms, held it to his breast, closed his eyes and seemed to be, and I doubt not was, occupied for a minute or two with prayer, during which we took off our hats and the young mother leaned her head over the horse's shoulder as if uniting in prayer. . . . When he finished he handed the child back to its mother without a word, who thanked him with streaming eyes while he rode off back down the road."[15]

There were signs, too, that Jackson, though separated from Anna and thus from that more animated and emotional side of his personality, had not entirely lost his ability to relax. His unique relationship with Jeb Stuart deepened during this time. During the fall camp the two visited each other frequently, and soldiers marveled not only at how Stuart was allowed to kid Jackson, but also how Jackson seemed to save his few stillborn attempts at humor for his swashbuckling friend. One night Stuart arrived at a late hour at Jackson's headquarters to find the general asleep. Instead of returning to his own camp, he took off his saber and lay down next to Jackson to sleep, which touched off a nightlong struggle for the single blanket. The next morning Stuart awoke to find Jackson and some of his staff warming themselves by a campfire.

"Good morning!" said Stuart. "How are you?"

"General Stuart, I am always glad to see you here," Jackson replied. "You might select better hours sometime, but I am always glad to have you. But General," he said, rubbing his legs, "you must not get into my bed with your boots and spurs on and ride me around like a cavalry horse all night!"[16]

At about that time the dapper Stuart, tired of seeing Jackson in the same tattered coat, had commissioned a tailor in Richmond to make Jackson a new one of fine wool, with gilt buttons and lace. He sent his aide Heros Von Borcke to Jackson with the carefully wrapped gift. Jackson opened it, gazed at it for a moment in "modest confusion," then said, "Give General Stuart my best thanks, Major. The coat is much too handsome for me, but I shall take the best care of it, and shall prize it highly as a souvenir."[17] He folded it carefully and placed it in his portmanteau.

But Von Borcke was under orders from Stuart to press the issue, and insisted that Jackson try it on. He did, it fit perfectly, and he liked it so much that he wore it to dinner that night, to the slack-jawed amazement of Jim and his staff. Word of the general's new coat spread quickly through the camp, and soon soldiers were running to see it for themselves. Jackson was very pleased with his friend's gift, which he would eventually wear into battle—thus shocking the rest of the army, too. He wrote Stuart, "I am much obliged for the beautiful coat you have presented me. . . . When you come near don't forget to call & see me. Your much attached friend."[18]

Jackson proved that he could be unpredictable in other ways, too.

Shortly after the Battle of Antietam, a Virginia man had invited Jackson and his staff to dinner. Before the meal, the host appeared with a decanter of whiskey and asked if anyone would like an "appetizer." To the amazement of the group, Jackson, instead of politely declining, asked, "Have you got any white sugar?" The answer was yes. Jackson strode to the table, and, with "a skill and ease which seemed shocking in contrast to his reputation," mixed himself a toddy, drank it off, complimented the host on the flavor, then offered some to General D. H. Hill and Henry Kyd Douglas.[19]

"Mr. Douglas," Jackson said, "you will find it very nice."

Douglas demurred, saying he had a headache and that he did not like the taste of "spirituous liquors" anyway.

Jackson's reply surprised his listeners. "In that I differ with you and most men," he said. "I like the taste of all spirituous liquors. I can sip whiskey or brandy with a spoon with the same pleasure the most delicious coffee or cordial will give you. I am the fondest man of liquor in this army and if I had indulged my appetite I would have been a drunkard. But liquors are not good for me. I question whether they are much good to anyone. At any rate I rarely touch them."[20] Douglas recalled seeing Jackson take a glass of wine only a few times during the war. Liquor, like his own soaring ambition, was so seductive that it needed to be forcibly suppressed.

While Stonewall Jackson was resting and reorganizing his troops that fall—he and James Longstreet had both been promoted to lieutenant general on October 10, each commanding half of Lee's army—George Brinton McClellan, the erstwhile young Napoléon, was losing his moorings. Though he crowed about his "victory" over Lee, he had done nothing to follow it up, nothing to make it stick. In spite of warm, dry weather, custom-made for fighting a war—and with flooding rains and cold weather looming ahead—he refused to move. He cited the by now familiar litany of reasons why he could not: exhausted troops and horses, lack of clothing and shoes, lack of wagons, a river too deep to cross or not deep enough to protect Washington, Lee's superior numbers, etc. And this drove Lincoln, Halleck, the War Department, the Republican press, and much of Congress to distraction. Halleck noted that after urging McClellan to move during the first week of October, to no avail, he had "peremptorily ordered" him on October 6 "to cross the Potomac and give battle to the enemy."[21] This, too, produced no results. Lincoln followed with more gentle prodding. "You remember my speaking to you of your over-cautiousness," he wrote his general on October 13, as though lecturing a troublesome child. "Are you not over-cautious when you assume that you can not do what the enemy is constantly doing? Should you not claim to be at least his equal in prowess, and act upon that claim? . . . It is easy if our troops march as well as the enemy; and it is unmanly to say they can not do it."[22]

But McClellan was feeling powerful again. He had rejuvenated a discouraged army. He had saved the North from a Confederate invasion. He had the love of his men and plenty of political support from Democrats in a country whose fall elections were about to tilt in their direction. At the same time, he could see quite clearly that his tormentor, Lincoln, was facing bitter attacks from a wide spectrum of political interests. The president was denounced as a moral coward by Democrats who called the Emancipation Proclamation "another advance on the Robespierrian highway of tyranny and anarchy." His conservative supporters hated him for selling out to the radicals, and the radicals assailed him with "vehement and injurious demands for a more vigorous prosecution of the war."[23] McClellan's habitual criticism of his bosses in Washington now deteriorated into withering scorn. "The good of the country requires me to submit to all this from men whom I know to be greatly my inferiors socially, intellectually & morally!" he wrote his wife, Ellen. He called Lincoln a "gorilla," Stanton a "great villain," Halleck "a fool . . . with no brains whatever!"[24] Flushed with victory, he wanted nothing less than Stanton's head and Halleck's job.

On October 26, six weeks after Lee's withdrawal from Sharpsburg, and under considerable pressure from Washington, McClellan finally put his army on the road. And though this southward movement was accompanied by great fanfare in the Northern press and renewed cries of "On to Richmond!" the great march of the Army of the Potomac proved nothing but a slow, spiritless trudge. It took McClellan eight days to cross the Potomac and penetrate a mere twenty miles into Virginia, a task Jackson could have accomplished in a day with a barefoot army on half rations. In the meantime he had allowed Longstreet to slip between him and the Richmond defenses. He inched his way into the area around Warrenton, where on November 7 he encountered a howling snowstorm, proof positive that he had already waited too long to mount a major campaign.

But McClellan's brief, bright hour was over. That same day, while long lines formed in front of Mathew Brady's gallery in New York City to see gruesome photographs of dead soldiers at Antietam, his Civil War career ended. Lincoln, long-suffering and almost preternaturally patient with his problem child, had finally had enough. During the snowstorm, Lincoln's emissary, the picturesquely named Brigadier General Catharinus P. Buckingham, arrived to tell McClellan that he was relieved, effective immediately, and replaced by Major General Ambrose Burnside. And that was that. There would be no reinstatement this time, no glorious return with bugles blowing and soldiers hurrahing. Though McClellan took the news with surprising calm and dignity, he was bitterly disappointed. "I feel as if the Army of the Potomac belonged to me," he wrote two days later. "It is mine. I feel that its officers are my brothers, its soldiers my children. This separation is like a forcible divorce of husband and wife." Of Burnside he said accurately, "He is as sorry to assume command as I am to give it up."[25]

Burnside was a curious figure in the war. He truly did not believe he was up to the job of commanding the Army of the Potomac. He had been offered it twice before by Lincoln, once in July 1862, after the Seven Days fiasco, and once after Lee had embarked on his invasion of Maryland. Each time he had turned it down. He had tried to duck it this time, too, and had relented only when Buckingham informed him that refusing the job meant that his detested rival Joe Hooker would get it instead. That was Burnside in a nutshell: a decent, unambitious man who mistrusted his own abilities. Though he had not had much financial success in life prior to the war, he was not without intelligence and initiative. In 1853 he had left the military to attempt to manufacture and sell a single-shot, .54-caliber carbine of his own design. Though he went bankrupt, and the factory he had started passed from his ownership, the Union ended up purchasing fifty thousand of them. Known as the "Burnside carbine," it became the third most popular such weapon in the war after the Sharps and Spencer. Its success contributed to Burnside's wartime rise in the army. At the time the war started, Burnside was working as a cashier for the Illinois Central Railroad, run by George B. McClellan, who had graduated a class ahead of him at West Point. A strapping six-footer with luxuriant facial hair, Burnside was honestly humble and had a simple, frank, hearty manner that endeared him to his friends. He could also be stubborn to a fault. He had trouble sleeping.

He was certainly smart enough to understand that his job now was to move, and move very quickly, in a southerly direction. He did just that. His grand plan, approved by Lincoln, was to feint toward Longstreet's camps at Culpeper, then slide south and east toward Fredericksburg, cross the Rappahannock, and move directly on Richmond. The first part of the plan went well enough. Two advance corps arrived in the town of Falmouth, a mile upriver from Fredericksburg on the northern bank, on November 17, before Lee could shift his troops to block a crossing. But there they stopped: the pontoons Burnside needed to ferry his 110,000-man army across the river had not arrived. They would not arrive for a week, by which time Lee was dug in on the heights across the river.

Lee had never intended to fight at Fredericksburg, and, unaware of Burnside's pontoon problem, was wary of his enemy's intentions. Thus he summoned Jackson, whose newly created 2nd Corps marched out of Winchester on November 22. The weather was cold and getting colder. Sleet, snow, and icy winds whipped the marching columns. The men awoke in the morning with frost in their hair and their food frozen in their haversacks. Many were barefoot, and some of their frozen feet bled as they marched, leaving traces of blood on the ground.[26] Many were without blankets or tents.[27] They came at a steady pace, marching 175 miles in twelve days, cresting the magnificent heights of the Blue Ridge—as some of them had done on Jackson's dramatic backdoor march to Front Royal in his valley campaign—descending through the rolling, river-crossed Piedmont, and landing in full force in Fredericksburg on December 4.

While Jackson marched eastward, his thoughts were of his wife, Anna, who was nine months pregnant and due to give birth any day. He had reason to be concerned. He had lost his first wife, Ellie, and a son in childbirth in 1854. His daughter Mary Graham, to whom Anna had given birth in 1858, had lived only a month. Two days before his departure for Fredericksburg he had written Anna, saying, "Don't you wish you were here in Winchester? Our headquarters are about one hundred yards from Mr. Graham's, in a large white house back of his, and in full view of our last winter's quarters, where my *esposa* used to come up and talk with me. Wouldn't it be nice for you to be here again?"[28] In fact she would have been horrified to see the town, which had lately become a repository for the human debris of war. Makeshift hospitals overflowed with wounded from the Maryland campaign; a fire started by an exploding Union powder magazine had destroyed many of the town's buildings, and others had simply been pulled apart for other uses. There was not a single item for sale in any Winchester store.[29]

On November 28, while he was still camped near Gordonsville, Jackson received a note from his wife's sister saying that Anna had given birth to a healthy, eight-and-a-half-pound girl at the family home near Charlotte, North Carolina. The letter was written in the voice of the new baby, saying,

"My aunts both say I am a little beauty. My hair is dark and long, my eyes are blue, my nose straight just like papa's. . . . My mother is very comfortable this morning, and hopes you will write and give me a name."[30] Jackson was joyous, and wrote to Anna, "Oh! How thankful I am to our kind Heavenly Father for having spared my precious wife and given us a little daughter!"[31] He went on,

> *I cannot tell you . . . how much I wish I could be with you and see my two darlings. But while this pleasure is denied me, I am thankful it is accorded to you to have the little pet, and I hope it may be a great deal of company and comfort to its mother. Now don't exert yourself to write to me, for to know that you were taxing yourself to write would give me more pain than the letter would pleasure, so you must not do it. But you must love your esposo in the meantime.*[32]

Jackson told no one about the birth of his daughter, and even forbade Anna to put the news on the telegraph. He was experiencing "a joy with which a stranger could not intermeddle." Later, more in control of his emotions, he implored his wife not to "set your affections upon her, except as a gift from God. If she absorbs too much of our hearts, God may remove her from us."[33] He named the child for his cherished mother and his beloved but estranged sister: Julia Laura Jackson.

Jackson had no time to share these feelings with anyone anyway. Battle loomed. For reasons that would soon be painfully clear to the Union army, Lee had decided to stand and fight behind the Rappahannock. He actually could not believe that Burnside wanted to fight there. As one Confederate officer put it, "If the world had been searched by Burnside for a location in which his army could be best defeated and where an attack should *not* have been made he should have selected this very spot."[34] Fredericksburg was a charming, prosperous river town of five thousand souls where George Washington spent his boyhood and later bought a home for his mother. James Monroe once practiced law there.

More important militarily were its immediate surroundings. West of the Rappahannock was a broad plain that climbed in a gentle upward sweep to a long, slightly elevated range of wooded hills that ran behind the town, roughly parallel to the river. Though the slopes were not steep, the natural defensive positions on the ridge were superb. Union troops would have to advance across half a mile to a mile of open ground, where they would be at the mercy of Confederate artillery. As they closed on the ridgeline, they would then be faced with some seventy thousand Confederates and their artillery firing downhill at them from behind sturdy entrenchments that included a stone wall, a sunken road, and considerable wooded cover. The one Federal advantage beyond sheer numbers was a high ridge that rose on the left bank of the river known as Stafford Heights. Artillery posted there had complete command of the town and plains below. This meant that the Confederates could not stop the Union army from crossing the river, nor could they mount an effective counterattack. But those big guns would offer little or no help to the blue-clad men as they assaulted the heights west of the river.[35]

Lee took full advantage of the local geography, installing his army along the crest of the ridge, which offered both elevation and, in some places, superb natural fortifications. The most striking characteristic of his line was its unusual length: *seven miles*. He had neither attacked, nor defended, anything close to that scale thus far in the war. On the left was James Longstreet's 1st Corps, dug in mainly along Marye's Heights, which were fronted by a six-hundred-yard-long stone wall and sunken road. On the right, occupying a front of more than two miles, was Jackson's 2nd Corps, tucked into the woods in a deep formation reminiscent of Second Manassas. The main difference was that he and his guns now commanded the high ground.

The Battle of Fredericksburg began on December 11, when Burnside ordered his men to build pontoon bridges across the Rappahannock in preparation for crossing. As the engineers attempted to anchor the wooden pontoon boats in place across from the town and lay four-inch-wide planks across them, Brigadier General William Barksdale's brigade of 1,800 Mississippians opened fire on them from the buildings across the river, driving them back each time they emerged onto the boats. Frustrated and impatient with the delay, Burnside ordered his artillery chief to "bring all your guns to bear on the city and batter it down."[36] Soon soldiers on both sides were watching what Colonel Edward Porter Alexander, recently appointed Longstreet's chief of artillery, called "perhaps the most impressive exhibition of military force . . . I have ever witnessed."[37] For two hours the guns boomed; cannonballs whizzed, hummed, whistled, screeched, or whirred, depending on who was hearing them; buildings collapsed; trees were uprooted; fires raged all over town; and entire blocks lay in smoldering ruins. The barrage damaged almost every structure in the town.

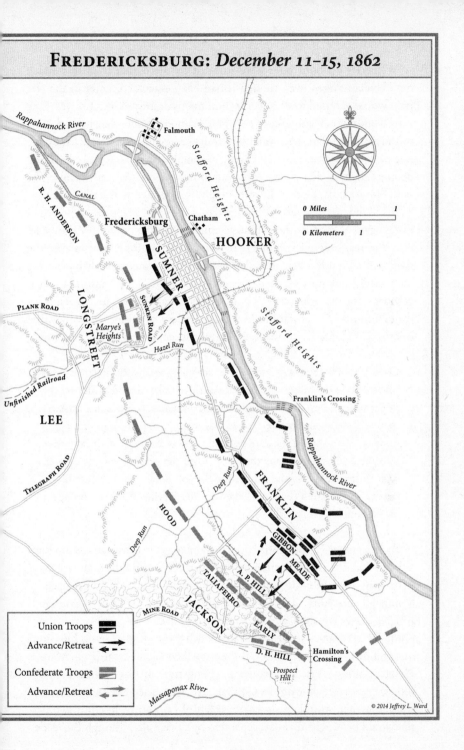

FREDERICKSBURG: *December 11–15, 1862*

Rappahannock River

Falmouth

Stafford Heights

R. H. ANDERSON

CANAL

Fredericksburg

Chatham

HOOKER

SUMNER

PLANK ROAD

LONGSTREET

Sunken Road

Marye's Heights

Hazel Run

Stafford Heights

Unfinished Railroad

LEE

Franklin's Crossing

Rappahannock River

TELEGRAPH ROAD

Deep Run

FRANKLIN

HOOD

Deep Run

GIBBON

MEADE

A. P. HILL

TALIAFERRO

MINE ROAD

JACKSON

EARLY

D. H. HILL

Hamilton's Crossing

Prospect Hill

Massaponax River

0 Miles 1

0 Kilometers 1

Union Troops

Advance/Retreat

Confederate Troops

Advance/Retreat

© 2014 Jeffrey L. Ward

Witnesses on both sides were stunned by the barbarity of this attack on a civilian target, even though it had been evacuated. Later in the war men would get used to seeing cities and towns destroyed. But not yet. One New York gunner wrote later that he felt guilty about what he had done to the helpless town. Lee, watching from the heights, was disgusted by the spectacle, made worse by the frenetic Federal looting that followed. "These people delight to destroy the weak and those who can make no defense," he said. "It just suits them."[38] In spite of all this apocalyptic thunder, the Federals still did not manage to dislodge Barksdale's Mississippians, who began firing again as soon as the engineers emerged on the pontoons. Burnside, now furious, ordered volunteers to *paddle* the pontoon boats across the river and establish a bridgehead. This was soon done, though Barksdale's men would put up a spirited street-to-street fight—the war's first urban combat—for the next twelve hours. Behind it all, above the left bank lay the enormous Federal war machine, fully packed, provisioned, and waiting to cross. As Confederate artillerist Porter Alexander described the scene,

> Over 100,000 infantry were visible, standing apparently in great solid squares upon the hilltops, for a space of three miles. Scattered all over the slopes were endless parks of ambulances, ordnance, commissary, quartermaster & regimental white-topped wagons. . . . Still more impressive to military eyes . . . were the dark-colored parks of batteries of artillery scattered here and there among them. . . . Over the whole scene there hung, high in the air, above the rear of the Federal lines, two immense black, captive [observation] balloons, like two great spirits of the air attendant on the coming struggle.[39]

By December 12, Burnside had managed to get his army across the Rappahannock. The next morning he launched his attack. His plan to assault Lee's long line had two components. The main attack was to be made by William B. Franklin's "Left Grand Division" against the Confederate right, roughly sixty-five thousand Federals against Jackson's thirty-seven thousand. The secondary strike was to be made by the "Right Grand Division" under Edwin Sumner against the entrenched Confederates on Marye's Heights. Sumner's assault would fix Longstreet in place while Franklin rolled up Jackson's line on the Confederate right. Then the two grand divisions, together, would crush what was left of Lee's army. In effect two battles would be fought that day, separated by three miles. Though Burnside's plan was somewhat simple and crude, relying on brute force for its effects, there was no reason—on paper, anyway—why it could not work. As Burnside would soon discover, the reality on the ground was quite different.

Jackson, waiting on Prospect Hill, was visibly happy that morning. In the words of an aide, he was "in his most serene and cheerful mood."[40] He was pleased with fatherhood, pleased with the high spirits of the men and guns he had carefully deployed. That morning he wore the new coat Stuart had given him along with a new blue-gray lieutenant general's hat with a band of gold lace that Anna had sent him, to the general bewilderment of his men, many of whom did not recognize him. He was unusually talkative, too. When Longstreet asked him if he was not "scared by that file of Yankees you have before you down there," he fired back, "Wait until they come a little nearer, and they shall either scare me or I'll scare them!" When Von Borcke asked him a version of the same question—Could he hold against such numbers?—he replied, "Major, my men sometimes fail *to take* a position, but *to defend one*, never! I am glad the Yankees are coming."[41]

Most of all, he knew that he had built a prodigiously strong defensive position, stronger even than at Second Manassas. His lines were stacked a mile deep, with so many reserves—three-fourths of his entire 2nd Corps— that he had roughly eleven men *per yard* of defensive ground. His first and second lines consisted of A. P. Hill's battle-tested veterans of the "Light Division," heroes at Cedar Mountain, Second Manassas, and Antietam. The two generals were still feuding but did not allow personal issues to interfere on the battlefield. Behind them were Taliaferro's division on the left and Early's division on the right. These were some of the best and most seasoned fighters in the Confederate army. Stuart's brigades with horse artillery were posted on the far southern end of his line.

The morning of December 13 broke cold, still, and foggy. From the top of Prospect Hill, the core of the Confederate defense, soldiers could see nothing but the dense mist that lay wet and heavy in the river valley. At about ten o'clock, in one of the war's most spectacular and theatrical moments, the fog suddenly lifted to reveal an open plain that was alive with moving dark lines of men, horses, and artillery. "On they came, in beautiful order," wrote an eyewitness,

> as if on parade, their bayonets glistening in the bright sunlight; on they
> came, waving their hundreds of regimental flags, which relieved with
> warm bits of colouring the dull blue of the columns and the russet tinge

of the wintry landscape, while their artillery beyond the river continued with unabated fury over their heads, and gave a background of white, fleecy smoke, like midsummer clouds, to the animated picture.[42]

The entire battle, in fact, unfolded in what one observer termed "a giant panorama," in which much of the fighting was visible to everyone on both sides.

In the battle's opening moments a young major named John Pelham, the commander of Jeb Stuart's horse artillery, did something absolutely extraordinary: he hauled two pieces of artillery to a forward position on the Union left. One was quickly disabled, leaving him with a single twelve-pounder Napoléon. For nearly an hour, while he somehow dodged the heavy barrage aimed directly at him, he managed to hold up the advance of Franklin's entire Grand Division. Only when he grudgingly withdrew under orders were the Federal batteries finally free to focus on Jackson's position. For a solid hour, from 11:00 a.m. to noon, from both sides of the Rappahannock, Franklin's guns pounded the Confederate lines. At noon the guns went silent, and then two infantry divisions, under Brigadier Generals John Gibbon on the right and the irascible, ambitious Major General George Gordon Meade on the left, marched forward up the gentle slope, dark antic lines moving against the frost-covered ground.

Jackson had, in fact, not been softened up at all. He had deliberately held his fire, saving his precious ammunition for use against the oncoming infantry. When Meade and Gibbon closed to about half a mile—amazed at the rebels' odd silence—Jackson's fifty-plus guns exploded in the wintry air, throwing out clouds of smoke pierced by long sheets of red flame, raking the advancing lines with shell, spherical case, and double-shotted canister. His guns tore great bloody holes in Federal regiments. Beaten back, the Union men regrouped and came on again, and were again rocked by this storm of lead and iron, which included a deadly crossfire from Pelham's guns. Still the Federals came forward, now into musket range, where they continued to be cut down by Confederate fire. Federal batteries in front of the river, meanwhile, began to find the range of those Confederate guns, knocking many of them out. In the noon hour the battle raged on.

At about 1:00 p.m. Meade, undeterred, renewed his attack and again came under the same galling fire. As the division advanced, soldiers in the brigade of twenty-four-year-old Colonel William Sinclair, desperate for cover of any kind, found their way into a wide tongue of tangled, thickly wooded terrain that jutted forward from the same woods that held the rebel infantry. They expected to find rebels there, but they found no one at all. Earlier that day A. P. Hill, commanding that section of Jackson's line, had apparently decided that the area was impenetrable and thus had left it unoccupied. He was wrong, almost disastrously so.[43] Though the grove was tangled and swampy, it was navigable and far safer than standing in the open and at the mercy of Jackson's canister, and the deeper the Federals penetrated, the more they understood that they had found a spectacular gap in their enemy's defenses. They struggled upward through the thickets and then suddenly the lead group of Meade's men—4,500 in total—were busting through a six-hundred-yard-wide gap in the Confederate line, rolling back the flanks of the two Confederate brigades under Brigadier Generals James H. Lane and James J. Archer that Hill had positioned on either side of this swampy gap. As the rebels fell back, the gap grew even wider. Meade's soldiers drove straight on to the crest of Prospect Hill, where they caught Brigadier General Maxcy Gregg's South Carolinians completely by surprise and routed them, too, mortally wounding Gregg in the process. By now they had penetrated so deeply that they were actually shooting at the rebels' backs, causing even more panic and pandemonium in the collapsing center of the Confederate line. Suddenly—only a few minutes since Sinclair's men first plunged into the woods—Meade's division seemed on the verge of slicing Jackson's carefully laid defenses in two.[44] Gibbon's division had moved forward and was engaged in a sharp firefight on the right side of the gap's tangled thickets, while another Union brigade, under Brigadier General Conrad Feger Jackson, was fighting on the left.

There were just two problems with this apparently stunning breakthrough. First, General Franklin, whose decision to send only two divisions forward was met with bitter protest by Meade, had no plans to follow up with additional troops. This was due both to his own innate timidity and to the bizarre and tentative orders he had received from Burnside that morning. If Burnside had wanted Prospect Hill carried at all costs, he had never said so. Second, and far more serious, what Meade had broken was merely the front ranks of the Confederate defense. The larger formation remained intact and dauntingly deep. Jackson, who learned of the breach from one of Gregg's panicked men, showed no particular concern. He knew exactly how deep his lines were, and he knew that an entire division waited just behind Gregg's broken brigade. His response was to tell a staffer, in a calm voice, to order Jubal Early forward.

As they had at Antietam, Early's men came on in a rush. With the sound of the rebel yell reverberating through the trees, his men scrambled forward and crashed into the wobbly Union lines, which had already suffered massive casualties. After more than an hour of fighting, the men were exhausted. No reinforcements were on the way. As Early came on, so did the Confederate brigades that had been surprised by Meade's attack. They now regrouped and moved forward, too, both against Meade and against Gibbon on his right. Not only was the gap sealed, but the Confederates now closed on the Union forces along their entire front. What remained of the contest was violent, bloody, and brief. Meade's men discovered, as they reeled in disorder from the woods, that when they emerged onto the open plain, momentarily safe from musket fire, they were now at the mercy of Jackson's artillery. Adding to the horror, the tall broom sage across which they were retreating caught on fire. As the battle turned and the retreat became a rout, Jackson came forward to the edge of the woods, gazed out at the disorder and confusion before him, and raised his hand in prayer. Some of Early's men, caught up in the sudden thrill of their success, chased the Union troops out onto the plain, only to be repulsed by stiff artillery fire and the fresh reserves Franklin should have sent up in support of Meade. The battle on the Confederate right was, for all intents and purposes, over. Meade's breakthrough had offered the brief illusion that Jackson could be broken on Prospect Hill when, in fact, the Federals never had much of a chance—not attacking with single divisions, anyway.

Franklin wired Burnside at two fifteen, via battlefield telegraph, to say that his men had been driven back. When Burnside later ordered him to advance his right, Franklin said it was impossible. Jackson spent the next hour shifting his lines, partly to bait Franklin into another attack. But to no avail. Jackson wanted to attack, and even had D. H. Hill's division make preparations, but the orders miscarried. And he soon realized anyway that he did not stand a chance against the massed Union artillery on Stafford Heights.[45] He had suffered more than 3,400 casualties, most of those in A. P. Hill's division. The Union had sustained nearly 5,000.

The fight on the Confederate right paled in comparison to the bloody human destruction on the left. At about 11:00 a.m., with artillery from Jackson's fight booming in the distance, Union forces advanced against Longstreet. William H. "Blinky" French was ordered to advance his division and take Marye's Heights, a task that turned out to be impossible.[46] Emerging from the town's ravaged streets, French's men had to advance across an open plain with almost no cover against a stacked and virtually impregnable defensive line. In front of them lay three thousand Confederates arrayed three deep in the Sunken Road behind the stone wall. Forty to fifty feet above them on the heights were more infantry. These two positions created, in effect, two front lines, which together brought six thousand rifles to bear simultaneously across a six-hundred-yard front. The Confederate artillery was stacked, too. Edward Porter Alexander, Longstreet's chief of artillery and a man not prone to exaggeration, told his commander that "we cover that ground now so well that we will comb it as with a fine-tooth comb. A chicken could not live on that field when we open on it."

What happened over the next six hours was something close to butchery, one of the war's worst and bloodiest examples. French's men were cut to pieces. Two of his brigades suffered 50 percent casualties within minutes. Whole regiments melted away before the unceasing rolling crash of guns and muskets and the flashes of white fire inside a wall of smoke. The Union boys never got to the wall. Most never got within a hundred yards of it. After French's division came Hancock's, attacking brigade by brigade just as French had, and then Howard's, Wilcox's, Sturgis's, and Griffin's, and so on, all fed by the stubborn Burnside into the killing machine at the top of the hill. The pattern of the attack would change hardly at all. There was no art to what was happening on either side: the men went up the hill, were cut down where they stood, and the survivors fell back while their comrades advanced over all that human wreckage—almost eight thousand casualties against less than a thousand for Longstreet's men. There was no glory on Marye's Heights either, just men killing men in a terrible and systematic way. Seven full Union divisions were sent in, one brigade at a time in fourteen different assaults against six thousand rebels. Porter Alexander, who spent the afternoon amusing himself with his spyglass by spotting men who had sought the almost nonexistent shelter, then blasting them from their cover, wrote later that "Fredericksburg was the easiest battle we ever fought."[47] Lee commented that "the attack on the 13th had been so easily repulsed, and by so small a part of our army, that it was not supposed that the enemy would limit his efforts to an attempt which . . . seemed so comparatively insignificant."[48]

Yet that is what happened. The last of the Federal assaults on the heights ended the Battle of Fredericksburg. The Union had suffered 12,653 killed and wounded, the Confederacy 5,309. Ambrose Burnside, stubborn till the end, wanted to personally lead an attack of his 9th Corps the next day, but was talked out of it by his generals. Though he has gone down in history as an incompetent field commander for his tactics at Fredericks-burg, in fact there was often a fine line in the Civil War between tenacity and foolishness. At Gaines's Mill, Lee spent more than five hours assault-ing uphill against a phenomenally strong Federal position, and lost nearly 8,000 men in the process. Yet because his final charges, by Hood in partic-ular, won the day, the battle is remembered as a glorious victory. Because Burnside sacrificed all those men in a losing cause, he is often seen as inept and mindlessly obstinate.[49] Though Lee, Jackson, and Longstreet expected the attacks to resume, they never did. The Union troops stayed in place on December 14, and on December 15 they retreated across the river. Soon Burnside's pontoon bridges were gone, too, and the Federals were back in their camps along the high riverbank, nursing their wounded.

Both armies ended the battle in the same place they started it, but this time there were no debates about who had won. Burnside wired the president the next morning with the disingenuously hopeful news that his men held "the first ridge outside of town" and that they intended "to carry the crest today." But news of heavy casualties soon cast the outcome in a different light. That evening a reporter for the *New York Tribune* who had covered the battle met with Lincoln and gave him the unvarnished version: Fred-ericksburg was a disaster, the worst defeat ever suffered by the Army of the Potomac.[50] By December 15 much of the Northern press, so recently proclaiming the glory of the impending victory, fully understood that it would be impossible to spin the results into anything but a crushing defeat. The *New York Times* called it "a black day in the calendar of the Republic." The *Cincinnati Commercial* wrote, "It can hardly be in human nature for men to show more valor or generals to manifest less judgment, than were perceptible on our side that day." Senator Zachariah Chandler, a radical Republican, wrote, "The President is a weak man, too weak for the occa-sion, and those fool or traitor generals are wasting time and yet more pre-cious blood in indecisive battles and delays." Lincoln soon faced a full-scale mutiny from the Senate Republican caucus, which in effect demanded Sec-retary of State William Seward's head in compensation for the loss. Though the president famously outmaneuvered the senators—and Seward kept his job—the shocking loss on the battlefield once again suggested a rudderless, divided country fighting a war with no clear end in sight.

The South, meanwhile, was giddy. Jefferson Davis, who had been feeling political heat for everything from the plunging value of Confederate currency to the impressment of supplies, the ragged condition of his army, and its failures in the western theater, rode the wave of victory. He claimed that the Federal defeat demonstrated yet again "the impossibility of subjugating a people determined to be free" and spoke of his "profound contempt" for the "impotent rage" of the Emancipation Proclamation.[51]

Jackson, meanwhile, expressed only regret that he had not hit his adversaries harder. Looking out over the corpse-strewn battlefield, he said, in a tone of resignation, "I did not think that a little red earth would have frightened them. I am sorry that they are gone. I am sorry I fortified."

As always, such hard-heartedness was leavened with occasional kindness. During Meade's attack Brigadier General Maxcy Gregg had been severely wounded. Gregg, a bookish and slightly deaf South Carolina aristocrat with a strong sense of right and wrong, had once called Jackson "tyrannical and unjust." The two men had clashed on a number of occasions, once when Jackson had arrested Gregg's regimental colonels for allowing men to break ranks, and once when he arrested them for allowing the men to remove fences for firewood. Jackson and Gregg had exchanged heated words, and Gregg at one point had preferred charges against Jackson, prompting Lee to intervene, saying that "he desired the matter to go no further."[52]

At about 4:00 a.m. Jackson, who had been awake in his tent reading the Bible, sent a messenger to inquire about Gregg's condition. The answer: he was dying. There was no hope. The messenger said that General Gregg "wishes to tell you that he regrets having sent you the note he did the day before yesterday, as he has since discovered that you were right and he mistaken."[53] The note has been lost, and in any case Jackson did not remember it. But he rode through the early-morning darkness with his aide James Power Smith to visit Gregg. When he arrived he found him fully conscious and in great pain. Jackson took Gregg's hand, and in a voice filled with emotion said, "The doctor tells me that you have not long to live. Let me ask you to dismiss this matter from your mind and turn your thoughts to God and to the world to which you go." Gregg, with tears in his eyes, mumbled thanks. He died a day later of his wounds.

On the way back to headquarters Jackson, riding now with McGuire and Smith, said nothing until they neared their camp, when he suddenly said, "How horrible is war."

"Horrible, yes," McGuire replied. "But we have been invaded. What can we do?"

"Kill them, sir," Jackson said. "Kill every man."[54]

• • •

Burnside would make one last attempt at Lee, more than a month later, on January 20. By this time many of his own generals, led by ringleaders William F. "Baldy" Smith and William B. Franklin, were in open revolt against him, undercutting him both in Washington and with his own troops. Smith, in fact, was demoted for doing so. Hooker was running down Burnside in press interviews. They were upset by what they saw as the needless butchery at Fredericksburg and by the appalling demoralization in the ranks. There were even cries for McClellan's restoration.

In part to prove his critics wrong, Burnside now launched a campaign "to strike a mortal blow to the rebellion." The plan was to cross the Rappahannock upstream of Fredericksburg and try to get behind Lee's position on Marye's Heights. Once again, the plan looked reasonable on paper. But then a cold, wind-driven rain started falling, which turned into a howling nor'easter. Soon the army, trudging upstream along the Rappahannock, found itself in what one soldier called "a complete sea of mud." Wagons sank to their hubs, horses to their fetlocks. Mules sank completely out of sight in the middle of the road. There was obviously no way to continue, so Burnside called it off, ending once and for all his abortive winter campaign against Robert E. Lee.

But he was just beginning his campaign to punish his own generals for their insubordination and conspiracy against him. He drew up formal dismissals of the offending officers, including Hooker, Smith, and Franklin. Since he had to get presidential approval for such an action, he traveled to Washington, where he told Lincoln, in effect, fire them or accept Burnside's resignation. Lincoln chose the latter. He relieved Burnside and gave the command to Hooker, about whom he had reservations. "Hooker does talk badly," he said, "but the trouble is, he is stronger with the country to-day than any other man."[55]

PART FIVE

ALL THAT IS EVER GIVEN TO A MAN

CHAPTER FORTY-THREE

WINTER OF DREAMS

❖

Eighteen months after the first shot at Fort Sumter, there were certain truths that the soldiers had come to know. Death in war was neither picturesque nor peaceful, and dying bravely didn't make you any less dead, or mean that you would not be dumped into the cold earth of a mass grave with everyone else, brave and not brave. Nor was there likely to be anyone to hear your last miserable words. People of the era cherished the idea of a "good death"—a peaceful, dignified passing wherein God was embraced and sins repented and salvation attained, preferably in your own bed with your family gathered devotedly around to hear your last murmurs of Christian resignation. War made a mockery of all that.[1] War made a mockery of the idea of a benevolent God. It replaced the family home with the rank, powder-scorched horrors of the battlefield. These were the new truths. In war you lived outdoors like a wild animal. You lived in blistering heat, drenching rains, and knifelike cold. You were exposed and vulnerable. The majority of men who died did not even have the honor of dying in a fight. Two out of three were carried away by diseases that killed them just as surely as minié balls. Those who survived did so on a quarter pound of bacon and eighteen ounces of flour a day—one-third the regular meat ration—with the infrequent small issue of rice, molasses, or sugar.[2] (The rice ration was an ounce.) Men lived without shoes or coats or blankets. Food was short all over the South. Soldiers hunted up sassafras buds and wild onions to ward off scurvy.[3] Horses died for lack of forage. In Richmond, where much of the eastern army's fare was gathered and transshipped, there were bread riots.[4]

In spite of these hardships, which seemed to multiply as the war dragged on, many of the men in the Confederate States Army remembered the winter of 1862–63 as one of the most extraordinary times of their lives. After the Battle of Fredericksburg they went into winter quarters on the right bank of the Rappahannock. They did not break camp until four and a half months later. In this period of sudden and miraculous leisure, free of fighting and marching, but with sharp, fresh memories of death and hardship, they experienced their own lives more keenly than ever before. As artillerist Edward Porter Alexander wrote later, echoing the sentiments of many of his comrades, it was "one of the happiest periods of all my life."[5] That happiness took many forms: in the joyous Christian revivals that continued to sweep through the army; in singing and band concerts and social visits and elaborately staged shows and snowball fights, and quiet evenings before fires smoking pipes and talking about the battles they had fought, the comrades who had died, and this extraordinary war to decide the fate of the nation that they found themselves in the middle of. It was a time to take inventory of oneself and one's life, a time when men could dream again about something more than surviving to fight the next battle.

For Jackson and his 2nd Corps this unusual interlude began at a place called Moss Neck, one of the most magnificent estates in Virginia. They had stumbled into it in darkness, about eight miles south of where they had fought: a newly constructed brick mansion in the Greek Revival style measuring 250 feet from wing to wing, trimmed out with teak and mahogany and ornate plaster carvings, and elevated on a picture-book knoll that overlooked the Rappahannock valley. His staff made inquiries: the place belonged to the Corbin family. Though the man of the house, twenty-nine-year-old Richard Corbin, was off fighting with the 9th Virginia Cavalry, the house had six occupants: Richard's twenty-seven-year-old wife, Roberta ("Bertie"), and their five-year-old daughter, Jane Wellford Corbin ("Janie"); his twenty-three-year-old sister, Catherine ("Kate") Corbin; and his other sister, twenty-four-year-old Netty Corbin Dickinson and her children, Jane Parke (four) and Gardiner (two).[6]

The Corbins invited Jackson to stay with them and make his headquarters there. He declined, but was persuaded to accept the offer of an outbuilding 130 feet from the house, used by the family as an office. There was a small lobby in front; a closet for wood; a narrow staircase to the attic; and a fireplace with a cot on one side and a table, chair, and stools on the other. In the manner of Virginia country homes, the main room was festooned with paintings and engravings of racehorses and hunting dogs. Here Jackson would spend the winter.

Christmas dinner at Moss Neck offered a glimpse of the pleasantly aberrant season to come. The affair took place in Jackson's office and was attended by Generals Robert E. Lee, Jeb Stuart, and William Pendleton along with select members of their staffs—ten guests in all. Considering the privations of war that were visible all around them, the meal Jackson's new aide, James Power Smith, put on was extraordinary. Almost all of the foods were gifts: three turkeys, a ham, a bucket of oysters, a box of fine foods sent by ladies from Staunton, pickled vegetables, and even a bottle of wine. Jackson's servant Jim baked some white biscuits from regular rations. There was a plate of butter in the table's center bearing the ornate imprint of a fighting cock.[7] To serve it all, in this room festooned with images of the sporting life of upper-class Virginia, was a slave named John who was assigned to Jackson's staff, turned out in a white apron.

The effect was startling. Lee and Stuart both reacted by making jokes at Jackson's expense. Lee said that Jackson and his staff were merely playing at being soldiers; they should come to Lee's headquarters to see how soldiers *really* lived. Stuart, pretending that Jackson himself had chosen the office decor, launched an attack on the general's questionable taste. As Smith recalled it, Stuart toured the room, commenting on the paintings in solemn tones, saying that he "wished to express his astonishment and grief at the display of General Jackson's low tastes" and that it would be "a sad disappointment to the old ladies of the country, who thought that Jackson was a good man." He concluded by pointing to the chanticleer-imprinted butter, thundering, "If there is not the crowning evidence of our host's sporting tastes! He even puts his favorite gamecock on his butter!"[8] Throughout Stuart's tirade Jackson grinned and blushed. He liked Stuart immensely and never minded being teased by him. (The next day Stuart led one of his trademark raids that had made him for many Southerners and Northerners alike the most glamorous officer in the war. He crossed the Rappahannock upstream with 1,800 horsemen and four guns and struck a supply depot twenty miles into Yankee-held territory. Facing stiff resistance, he turned *north* instead of south, captured a Union telegraph office just fifteen miles from Washington, and sent a wire to Union quartermaster Montgomery Meigs complaining that the substandard mules he was capturing were not up to the job of pulling all the provisions he was stealing. He returned to Fredericksburg on New Year's Day with two hundred prisoners, two hundred captured horses, a hundred arms, and twenty wagons stuffed with loot.[9])

While the generals feasted in the office, Bertie Corbin threw a sumptuous party in the parlors of the main house. The featured attraction was her unmarried and very engaging sister-in-law Kate. Several of Jackson's younger staffers, including Clement Fishburne and Sandie Pendleton, were already falling for her. Fishburne later wrote that he was "very nearly in love," but "discovered, before I became hopelessly gone, that my friend Col. A. S. Pendleton . . . was likely to be a successful applicant." He also noted that several other officers "were further gone than I was," and that some of them actually proposed.[10]

Moss Neck became the center of life in Jackson's corps that winter. In the army's camps that spread outward from the estate, men quickly learned to build wooden huts against the unusually cold Virginia weather. Bertie Corbin wrote one of the best descriptions of life there. "Thousands of soldiers in sight," she recalled,

> the hills echoing with noises of army life, fife and drum, brisk tattoo and reveille, the sound of many axes, the crashing of great trees as they fell—all became our daily fare of strange experience. The great forests surrounding Moss Neck were literally mowed down. Almost instantly there sprang into life settlements of wooden huts. . . . How the sounds of camp life haunt me still! The hum of voices, the music of the bands, especially the "Stonewall Brigade Band," stationed right in front of the house.[11]

Hers was not the only Virginia estate watching its forests razed to the ground. By one estimate, fully thirty square miles of timber on both sides of the Rappahannock were clear-cut by the armies.[12]

While Jackson enjoyed cordial relations with the older Corbins and was a frequent social guest at the main house, he developed a very special friendship with five-year-old Janie, who visited him in his quarters in the afternoon. She was a bright, attractive child, with large eyes and light blond hair. She was very much taken with the kind general. She would spend hours cutting out paper soldiers and parading them on his table.[13] He always had a present for her when she came: an apple or orange, a piece of candy, or a bright print.[14] One day he discovered that she had lost the comb that normally kept her long hair in place. He took his lieutenant general's hat in hand—the one Anna had given him—and with a penknife carefully removed the band of gold braid that encircled it and bound it around her head. Then, taking her head in his hands, he asked her to wear it for him. He later explained to Anna, "I became so ashamed of the broad gold lace that was on the cap you sent me, as to induce me to take it off. I like simplicity."

Janie came often, and the stern general and the golden-haired girl passed the time happily together, and this continued through the winter. On one occasion Jackson was standing with several subordinates in the yard when the little girl emerged from the house, ran across the lawn, and clasped her arms around his leg, crying, "General Jackson, kiss me please!" Though his staff had seen him kiss her before, the public setting embarrassed him and he declined.[15] On March 16, the day he left Moss Neck for new headquarters, Jackson learned that Janie and her two young cousins were ill with scarlet fever. Before he left he called on Bertie Corbin to express his concern. She told him that Janie appeared to be out of danger.[16] A day later she was dead. Her cousins died within a few days. He heard the news with "an outburst of tears and a convulsed frame."[17] He perhaps felt her death even more deeply because Anna had written him that his own daughter was ill.

Though there were duties to keep the men busy that winter—drilling, as always, the occasional review, the building of defensive works on the high ground of the south bank, and the usual run of camp chores—there was also a good deal of free time. The winter at Moss Neck was a time for those rarest of wartime pursuits: reading and meditation. Jackson did a good deal of both. He devoted large chunks of the Sabbath to quiet prayer. He and his staff discovered the Corbins' library. Jackson especially liked Henry Hunter's *Life of Moses*. He wrote Anna that it was "a delightful book. I feel more improved reading it than by an ordinary sermon."[18] His staff plunged into Shakespeare, Thackeray, Hugo, Dickens, Tennyson, and Browning.[19] The very idea that there would be leisure time to read was new to them. Jackson's adjutant Sandie Pendleton not only found time to read, he also courted and won Kate Corbin, whom he would soon marry.

But mostly that winter there was just talking, a lot of it, in the tents, around campfires, on long walks and rides that their lessened duties now afforded them. Jackson demonstrated that he could actually participate in light conversation. He welcomed a number of English visitors, holding forth at length on his favorite topic of medieval cathedrals, especially York Minster and Westminster Abbey. He sat before campfires with his staff, especially Hotchkiss and McGuire, and listened to and told stories. One night he spoke of his life as a teacher, saying that he had been very fond of it. He spoke, too, of his love of the Spanish language and of certain idioms of both the Spanish and English languages. He even talked about his childhood and his family, especially about his beloved mother.

Such conversation was without precedent at Stonewall Jackson's headquarters. He was clearly more relaxed, as was everyone else, including Robert E. Lee. In this more casual world of the winter camp, Lee, too, teased Jackson, once facetiously introducing him to two ladies as "the most cruel and inhuman man you have ever seen." When one of the ladies protested that she considered Jackson a Christian soldier, Lee replied, shaking his head, "Why, when we had the battle up at Fredericksburg, do you know . . . that it was as much as we could do to prevent him from taking his men, with bayonets on their guns and driving the enemy to the river?"[20] Jackson's staff even persuaded him to play a prank on General Jubal Early, who had taken to commandeering ambulances for social outings with lady friends. Over Jackson's signature, a note to Early demanded to know why ambulances were being deployed for frivolous purposes. "Great and hilarious was the merriment when [Early's] long report came," wrote James Power Smith later.[21]

Private soldiers seemed just as swept up in this new, lighthearted feeling. In December they built a theater out of logs and clapboard and staged amazingly elaborate performances every night, a combination of variety shows and burlesques on officers, quartermasters, and commissaries. In one a soldier is told that his head wound would require his head to be amputated. He replies that at least then he will be able to get a furlough, only to be told that his headless body is needed as a decoy to fool the enemy.[22]

The grandest show of all took place in February, put on by the Washington Artillery with music by the 12th and 16th Mississippi Regiments. Programs were printed in Richmond, and people came from twenty miles around to see it. Though Lee sent a letter of regret, Longstreet and other generals attended in full dress. The main feature was titled *Pocahontas or Ye Gentle Savage*, which brought the house down several times. The show concluded with a thumping rendition of "Bonnie Blue Flag."[23] (A month later a group of soldiers quartered near Fredericksburg put on an all-male burlesque in which one of the principal actors completely disrobed.[24])

Probably the most fun the soldiers had that winter were the snowball fights. Many of them had never seen snow before. Now there was lots of it, and they knew just what to do. Every time it snowed—which was frequently—there were battles, usually involving small groups of soldiers. But on at least one occasion they mounted a fight on a massive scale. Two armies were formed, of 2,500 men each, complete with authentic generals, colors, signal corps, fifers and drummers beating the long roll, couriers, and cavalry. They conducted head-on assaults and flank attacks. There were formal demands under flags of truce, and fortifications everywhere. "It was probably the greatest snowball battle ever fought," wrote one participant, "and showed that 'men are but children of larger growth. . . . ' If all battles would terminate that way it would be a great improvement on the old slaughtering plan."[25] Robert E. Lee, who came out to observe the battle, was struck by several snowballs.[26] The Richmond newspapers each devoted several columns to accounts of the fight.

The sweetest and saddest moment of this dreamy season came one evening when several Union bands appeared on the northern bank of the Rappahannock to play some favorites, songs such as "When This Cruel War Is Over" (by far the most popular), "Tenting Tonight on the Old Campground," "John Brown's Body," and "The Battle Cry of Freedom." Thousands of soldiers in groups on the hillside sang along while the rebels listened. Finally the Confederates called out across the river, "Now play one of ours!" Without missing a beat the Yankee bands pitched into "Dixie," "The Bonnie Blue Flag," and "Maryland, My Maryland." They ended the concert by playing "Home Sweet Home," with 150,000 men on both sides choking up as they sang it.[27]

Before the war Jackson had said on several occasions how much he admired the ministry as a profession, and how deeply he was drawn to it. He understood, at the same time, that he was unsuited for it. He was a poor public speaker. He was shy. Thus what almost certainly would have been his principal calling in life became his avocation, from his work as a deacon at the Presbyterian church in Lexington and his management of the Sunday school to his behind-the-scenes efforts to promote religion in the ranks. But at no time in his life was he more actively involved in these Christian pursuits than during the winter at Moss Neck. And at no time did he have so large an effect on the religious life of the Confederate army. Perhaps his most ardent desire, after peace itself, was to lead what he often called a "converted army."[28]

His efforts were rooted in his own reluctance to make his feelings and beliefs public, though he felt considerable pressure to do so. "You suggest that I give my views and wishes in such form and extent as I am willing should be made public," he wrote Reverend White in Lexington. "This

I shrink from doing, because it looks like presumption in me, to come before the public and even intimate what course I think should be pursued by the people of God."[29] He preferred to push privately, and push he did, hard, starting with what he saw as the main problem: the lack of chaplains in the army. He had discovered that more than half of the regiments in his 2nd Corps had no chaplains at all. He aimed to fix that. His first move was to bring his friend B. Tucker Lacy into camp. Lacy was six years older than Jackson, and for the years immediately before the war had been pastor of a Presbyterian church in Frankfort, Kentucky. He was a strong and inspirational speaker, with a gift for organization. Though he had arrived at Moss Neck in the expectation of being a regimental chaplain, Jackson, who contributed $700 of his own money to Lacy's support, soon made him, in effect, the religious overseer of his entire corps.[30] Jackson housed him in his personal residence and gave him one of his horses to use.

The Lacy-Jackson plan to help promote religious awakening in the army had two parts. First, chaplains had to be recruited, and money had to be found to pay them, which included lobbying Richmond. The effort was entirely nondenominational. Jackson insisted that no sectarian distinctions be drawn. "As a general rule," he wrote Reverend White, "I do not think that a chaplain who would preach denominational sermons should be in the army."[31] Jackson had already done some of this work, but the effort was now much more ambitious and more systematic. He spent considerable time writing recruitment letters. At one point he found two soldiers who had gone into the army just before they had finished their theological courses at seminary. Jackson offered them leave to get their licenses, and then found places for them as regimental pastors.[32] He also allowed his name to be used by his friends quietly in their own efforts to lobby the General Assembly of the Presbyterian Church, which soon began dispatching ministers to the camps.

Second, the chaplains were formed into a tightly organized association, run by Lacy, which held weekly meetings, the main point of which was to extend religious services to as many parts of the corps as possible. Though Jackson in his own words "did not wish to provoke any criticism by being personally prominent," he kept a tight rein on Lacy and the committee's activities. "Now come and report," he would tell Lacy after each meeting.[33] Jackson himself contributed $300 to pay for Bibles and other religious reading, and was instrumental in recruiting prominent ministers as guest preachers.[34]

Jackson's work paid off quickly. Services grew in number and size and soon were being conducted all over his corps. On March 27, designated by Jefferson Davis as a national day of prayer, more than fifty sermons were preached in the corps.[35] The Stonewall Brigade built its own chapel out of logs. Other regiments and brigades followed. In late spring a large open-air chapel capable of holding two thousand or more soldiers was built near Hamilton's Crossing. Jackson, whose headquarters was nearby, was a constant presence at the services there, as were other generals, including Robert E. Lee. Wrote Robert Lewis Dabney, "The example of so famous a warrior . . . the curiosity to see him and the galaxy of celebrities who came to worship with him . . . soon drew a vast congregation to this spot."[36] That winter Jackson also led informal prayer meetings with his staff during their mess.

Still, Jackson worried about the godliness of his country and his army. He wanted more than just a Great Awakening in his camps. In a letter to his old friend and business partner—and Maggie's husband—J. T. L. Preston, he wanted the Southern nation itself to officially embrace God. Saying that he thought the United States had taken unnecessarily extreme means to separate church and state, he wrote, "Let our Government acknowledge the God of the Bible as its God, and we may expect soon to be a happy and independent people."[37]

Though there was no fighting that winter, Jackson was caught up, like everyone else, in the great political and administrative swirl that was the Army of Northern Virginia. There was the huge backlog in the courts-martial to attend to, including death sentences that Jackson as usual upheld, though President Davis managed to commute some of them. There were battle reports to file stretching back a year, the writing of which Jackson delegated to his new chief of staff, former congressman and minister to France Charles Faulkner. The "severe Roman simplicity" that Jackson insisted on, plus Faulkner's inexperience, made the reports often maddeningly incomplete.[38] Jackson also had to navigate the usual political intrigues that surrounded staff promotions and transfers, which included the departure of his brother-in-law D. H. Hill for the western theater. The prickly Hill had clashed with his superiors, including Lee, and though Jackson tried he had been unable to patch it up.

As usual, Jackson was forced to grapple with the other Hill—the brilliant, stubborn, and recalcitrant A.P.—who continued to insist, over Lee's objections, on the resolution of the charges pending against him. While the controversy smoldered, and accusations and counteraccusations flew, a more serious confrontation occurred. On March 8, Hill filed his report on the Battle of Cedar Mountain, offering explanations for his slow marches that were the cause of his arrest in the first place. Hill not only denied any delinquency, but also accused Jackson of giving conflicting orders. Jackson was furious. Instructing his staff to collect every possible piece of evidence, he wrote an unusually long comment on Hill's report that rebutted, point by point, everything Hill had said.[39] Now it was A. P. Hill's turn to explode in anger. The feud simmered on into April with a dispute over an order from Hill to a staff member that countermanded one of Jackson's orders. That was the end of Jackson's patience. He immediately forwarded charges and specifications against Hill for the Cedar Mountain incidents—all of which seem petty enough today ("failed to move as directed from Orange Courthouse towards Culpeper Courthouse on Aug. 8"[40])—but on April 24 submitted a new and startling request of Lee: "When an officer orders in his command such disregard for the orders of his superiors I am of the opinion that he should be relieved from duty with his command, and I respectfully request that Genl. Hill be relieved from duty in my corps."[41] Jackson was asking Lee to dismiss the commander of the finest division in his army. Lee, exasperated that he could not contain this feud between his talented generals, took no immediate action. A postscript to the affair was written later by Jed Hotchkiss, whose accounts of the war were generally accurate, fair, and reasonable. A. P. Hill, he wrote, "found in every order that was issued to him something to complain of. . . . Only a surly obedience was rendered by Hill and his subordinates to orders from corps headquarters."[42]

All of this was more or less business as usual in Jackson's army. What was not at all usual was the visit, on April 20, of Anna Jackson and her five-month-old daughter, Julia. Jackson had always wanted them to come, but the baby was still very young and had been sick several times, once with a severe case of chicken pox, and the trip from North Carolina would be long and hard.[43] Jackson missed them terribly, and wrote a series of long, affectionate letters to Anna to that effect over the winter. "How much I do want to see you and our darling baby!" he wrote on January 5.

But I don't know when I shall have this happiness, as I am afraid, since hearing so much about the little one's health, that it would be imprudent to bring it upon a journey, so I must just content myself. Mrs. General

Longstreet, Mrs. General A. P. Hill, and Mrs. General Rodes have all been to see their husbands. Yesterday I saw Mrs. Rodes at church, and she looked so happy that it made me wish I had Mrs. Jackson here too; but whilst I cannot see my wife and baby, it is a great comfort to know that you have a darling little pet to keep you company in my absence.[44]

In other letters he told her that he missed their home, missed gardening and preparing his "hot-beds," and described some of the gifts he received from as far away as London.[45] In February he wrote, "If you could hear me talking to my *esposa* in the mornings and evenings, it would make you laugh, I'm sure. It is the funny way I talk to her when she is hundreds of miles away."[46] Though we do not have Anna's own letters, by her own account they were full of love, hope, and a deep desire to see her family reunited.

Mother and baby arrived by train at midday at Guiney's Station, south of Jackson's camp. It was raining. Jackson leaped aboard the train in his dripping raincoat, pushed his way through the crowd, and finally found them. "His face was all sunshine and gladness," wrote Anna, "and after greeting his wife, it was a picture, indeed, to see his look of perfect delight and admiration as his eyes fell upon that baby!" Cheers erupted from the soldiers on the railroad platform, while Jackson and his family boarded their carriage and rode away to their lodgings at a brick estate known as Belvoir. Once inside, Jackson took off his wet coat and held his daughter in his arms. During the visit he would hold her as often as he could, walking to and fro with her, holding her up to the mirror—"Now, Miss Jackson, look at yourself!"—and kneeling over her cradle when she slept.[47] Three days later, on her five-month birthday, Julia Laura Jackson was baptized by the Reverend Tucker Lacy, with a small crowd of raptly attentive officers in attendance.

Anna and the baby were wildly popular among the soldiers, who ventured great distances just to get a look at them. It did not hurt that the thirty-one-year-old Anna was slim, good-looking, and, unlike her reserved husband, extremely outgoing. She and "Little Miss Stonewall," as one officer called the baby, received many social calls from officers, including one from General Lee, who stopped by with several members of his staff to pay their respects. Troops would be brought near the house for parade and review, and the baby would be taken out so that everybody could get a look. Mainly the men were just curious to see the stern, unemotive taskmaster in this nearly unimaginable role as doting father and husband. Douglas thought him "the model of a quiet, well-behaved, first father."[48] On a pleasant and breezy April 26, Jackson and Anna attended religious services at the open-air chapel near Jackson's headquarters, where two thousand men heard Tucker Lacy preach a sermon on the parable of Lazarus and the dead man, which Anna found "earnest and edifying." The two spent that afternoon together talking. "His conversation was more spiritual than I had ever observed before," Anna wrote later.[49]

The Jacksons were thrilled to be together again. Anna had never seen him healthier or as handsome. Though he worked most of the day at his headquarters, he would come home in the afternoon and devote the rest of his time to his wife and baby. He even showed off for them. He arrived one morning mounted on a splendid bay horse he had received as a gift. He let everyone look at the horse, then remounted, spun around, and galloped away at such a speed that his hat fell off. He did not stop to pick it up. Anna was duly impressed with her war-hero husband. "As far as he could be seen," she wrote, "he was flying like the wind—the impersonation of fearlessness and manly vigor."[50]

Then, quite abruptly, their domestic happiness ended. Sometime before dawn Jubal Early's adjutant galloped into the yard at Belvoir and knocked loudly on the door. Early's division held Jackson's left flank. The news the adjutant carried was that Joseph Hooker, now in command of the Union army, was on the move. His troops had been spotted fording the river, in heavy fog, two miles below the town. The war was on again. Anna and the baby must hurry to Richmond. Jackson kissed them good-bye, mounted Little Sorrel, and rode away. Anna packed quickly, and soon Reverend Lacy arrived with an ambulance wagon, saying that General Jackson had sent him to take them to the train station. He carried a note from Jackson invoking God's blessing and telling Anna and Julia that he loved them. The visit had lasted exactly nine days. As they left, Hooker's big guns were already thundering from the riverbank, rattling the windows of the house.[51] The spring campaign had begun.

CHAPTER FORTY-FOUR

COMETH THE HOUR, COMETH THE MAN

Sometime deep in the afternoon of April 30, 1863, Robert E. Lee and his staff rode to the top of a high promontory near Fredericksburg known as Telegraph Hill.[1] From its ramparts—cleared of trees by his orders—Lee had directed the Battle of Fredericksburg four and a half months earlier. From here he had watched the seemingly endless waves of blue-uniformed men crash on the killing grounds below the Sunken Road. He had watched Jackson's bloody rout of Meade and Gibbon, which had prompted him to comment, "It is well that war is so terrible, or we would grow too fond of it."[2] Today he had come not to see men fight but to try to understand his enemy's mind. Though he had grown accustomed to thwarting the well-laid plans of his Union counterparts, he had been caught off guard by large Federal troop movements in the preceding two days. Now it was his turn to be puzzled. From the hilltop he watched the Federals intently for some time. Then he closed his glass, turned to a staff officer, and said, "The main attack will come from above." By "above" he meant to the west, upstream on the Rappahannock, where a large chunk of the Union army had suddenly materialized a dozen miles due west of his main force in Fredericksburg—*behind him.* Lee was right, and he knew it, even though most of his officers did not agree with him.[3] But this was not exactly good news. It meant that his adversary Major General Joseph Hooker, known fondly to his men as Fighting Joe and referred to contemptuously by Lee as Mr. F. J. Hooker, had stolen a march on him.

It was that very contempt that had gotten Lee into this trouble. Hooker, as it turned out, was not at all like the man he replaced. Though the forty-eight-year-old general was seen in the army as a pushy, self-promoting opportunist who happily disparaged others to advance himself and was fonder of strong drink than he ought to be, he was also an aggressive fighter and, to everyone's surprise, a talented administrator.[4] He had inherited a demoralized army from Ambrose Burnside and in three and a half months given it back its snap. He replaced incompetent officers and reduced absenteeism. He streamlined operations and improved food, sanitation, campsites, and even clothing. Hospitals were cleaned up. Pay arrived on time.[5] There was order and clarity and purpose in the camps, and the men could feel it. There was a sense, too, reminiscent of the old McClellan days, that the high command cared once again about the fate of the ordinary soldier. One of Hooker's most important moves was to revamp his intelligence service, now known as the Bureau of Military Information. Unlike the bizarrely incompetent Allan Pinkerton, the BMI delivered consistently accurate estimates of rebel troop strength. Hooker, who had 159,329 men in his army (of whom roughly 135,000 were infantry, cavalry, and artillery), knew for a fact that Robert E. Lee had roughly 55,000 infantry available to fight.[6] For the first time in the war, a Union commander had a clear picture, literally brigade by brigade and general by general, of his enemy's strength.

Hooker, moreover, had a plan, and it was a good one, and it did not depend on reckless and sacrificial assaults on entrenched Confederate positions. He had put it in motion on Sunday, April 27, with elaborate secrecy, while Anna and Thomas Jackson were listening to Reverend Lacy preach at the open-air church at Hamilton's Crossing. That day Hooker launched his "flying column"—three full army corps, stripped to the bare essentials of fighting, carrying eight days' rations—on a march that covered more than thirty miles for some units around the rebel army's extended left flank. Brilliantly executed and completely unknown to Lee—who had been fooled by a simple ruse of the Union signal corps into deploying his intelligence-gathering cavalry too far upstream—forty thousand men, nine batteries, and their assorted trains had tramped off to the west and south, crossed both the Rappahannock and the Rapidan, then swung east toward Lee's flank and rear. By April 30, the Union flanking column—the 5th Corps under George G. Meade, the 12th Corps under Henry W. Slocum, and the 11th under Oliver O. Howard—were all camped in the vicinity of a little crossroads called Chancellorsville. They were soon joined by Darius Couch's 2nd Corps.

What Lee had finally understood, squinting through his telescope that afternoon, was that the threat to his army's existence came not from the 1st and 6th Corps sitting in front of Jackson—though they were forty thousand strong—but from this massive turning movement to his west. The 1st and the 6th were merely there to hold the Confederate army in place while Hooker's main column rolled up its flank. Lee was still unaware of the third and equally menacing component of Hooker's plan: a cavalry strike at his supply line between Richmond and Fredericksburg. The previous day Jackson's quiet West Point roommate George Stoneman and ten thousand Union horsemen had taken off on a long, looping ride far above the Confederate left. Their mission was to destroy Lee's railroad link to Richmond and thus the line by which all of his supplies moved. By these movements Hooker planned to force Lee out of his entrenchments and into the open, where he would either have to fight or retreat on Richmond. By April 30, everything was going exactly as planned.

Robert E. Lee, meanwhile, the great strategic and tactical genius, had failed to anticipate any of this.[7] The best evidence of this failure was that, as Hooker's men were marching, fully a quarter of Lee's army was running an errand some eighty miles away in southeastern Virginia. Two crack divisions under James Longstreet—John Bell Hood's and George Pickett's—had been dispatched in February to blunt a suspected movement toward Richmond by the Union 9th Corps. When that threat failed to materialize, the Confederate force stayed to gather much-needed food and forage for the army—shipping it up on rail lines through Richmond—and to try to capture the Union garrison at Suffolk. Longstreet was busy laying siege to that town when he received Lee's call for help, sent on April 29 and received on April 30. But Lee had already waited too long. Longstreet would not be able to even start north until May 3. Lee would have to fight Hooker's army with what he had.

But before he did anything else, Lee had to throw something in the way of Hooker's oncoming legions. He had already ordered Major General Richard H. Anderson to fall back from the river with his nine thousand men and establish a defensive line east of Chancellorsville. Now he summoned Jackson. Jackson, predictably, had wanted to attack the Federal troops who had crossed the Rappahannock on the foggy morning of April 29 and were now in his front. (It was the sound of the guns covering their crossing that had awakened him and led to Anna's hasty departure.) Lee, who did not agree with Jackson, had nevertheless indulged this idea. But having studied the enemy's dispositions, Jackson now told Lee he concurred that "It would be inexpedient to attack there." By that he meant that massed Federal artillery on Stafford Heights would blast him out of existence if he tried.

Instead, Lee now ordered a massive shift to his left, sending most of Lafayette McLaws's division plus three of Jackson's divisions (under Robert Rodes, Raleigh Colston, and A. P. Hill) to join Anderson east of Chancellorsville. He left only a single division, plus one attached brigade, of twelve thousand men under Jubal Early, to defend the heights west and south of Fredericksburg. Lee thus committed four-fifths of his available army, under Jackson's command, to stopping Hooker's flanking column.[8] Jackson was thrilled with the prospect. He was always in high mood before battle, but today—whether it was due to Anna's visit or the long lapse in fighting—he was as animated as his staff had ever seen him. "I well remember the elation of Jackson," wrote his ordnance officer William Allan. "He seemed full of life & joy. His whole demeanor was cheerful & lively compared with his usual quiet manner."[9]

Back in Chancellorsville the Union command was indulging in a small orgy of self-congratulation. They had been outmaneuvered, outflanked, outmarched, and outgamed so many times by Lee and Jackson that they could scarcely believe this new scheme was working so well. Hooker had earlier boasted to a group of officers, "My plans are perfect, and when I start to carry them out, may God have mercy on General Lee, for I will have none." Which might have seemed more of that standard-issue, high-command Union bloviation, familiar from the days of Pope and McClellan, except that the plan *had* worked perfectly so far. They *had* outfoxed the master. Three army corps had executed a difficult and nearly flawless sequence of maneuvers that had surprised Lee and placed them squarely on his flank. Now they were being reinforced. Full of confidence and pride, Hooker issued a general order to his army that read,

> It is with heartfelt satisfaction that the commanding general announces to the army that the operations of the last three days have determined that our enemy must either ingloriously fly, or come out from behind his defenses and give us battle on our own ground, where certain destruction awaits him.

The order was greeted with cheers. Except for the bit about "certain destruction," everything Hooker said was accurate.[10]

• • •

Chancellorsville was not really a town at all. It was not even a hamlet. It was barely a crossroads. The place consisted of a single large two-and-a-half-story brick house with a columned porch and a couple of outbuildings. The house was the residence of the widow Fanny Chancellor, her young son, and seven good-looking daughters, plus a handful of local refugees. Partly on the strength of the comely daughters, it had become a sort of social center during that extended, languorous Confederate winter. Dinner guests included Generals Dick Anderson and Jeb Stuart and the dashing Mississippi brigadier Carnot Posey.[11] The girls loved Stuart above all, with his perfect manners, his plumed hat, and his perpetual good humor. The fun and ringing laughter had ended with the arrival of the Yankees, who took over the house for use as Hooker's headquarters, including all of its most comfortable rooms, consigning the unhappy residents to one crowded wing.

More important for the two hundred thousand men who were about to fight here was the peculiar terrain surrounding the Chancellor house. People called it the Wilderness of Spotsylvania or just the Wilderness. The name was well chosen. It was a dense tangle of forest that spread twelve miles long and six miles deep on the flanks of the Rappahannock. There had been an iron industry here since colonial times, and the trees had all been cut down to make charcoal for furnaces and foundries. The vegetation that had grown back was a stunted, thorny snarl of dwarf pine, cedar, hickory, scrub oak, and assorted brambles. Though the woodland was pierced here and there by a few roads, much of it was indeed dark, impenetrable, trackless, labyrinthine, and often swampy wilderness. In all of its more than seventy square miles there were only a few cleared areas, most of which lay athwart the two main east-to-west roads that ran through it: the Orange Turnpike, and the looping and intermittent Orange Plank Road. The largest of these was a seventy-acre open area around the Chancellor house. There was nothing pretty or pleasant about the Wilderness. It would soon become apparent to many soldiers that, as a place to fight a battle, these dark woods were something out of a nightmare.

Jackson's men marched from their camps below Fredericksburg in the light of a brilliant moon that yielded in the early dawn to a thick, watery mist. They left quietly, all twenty-four thousand of them, and headed west.[12] By 11:00 a.m. on May 1 most of them had reached General Anderson's division, which was busily digging in along a ridge about three and a

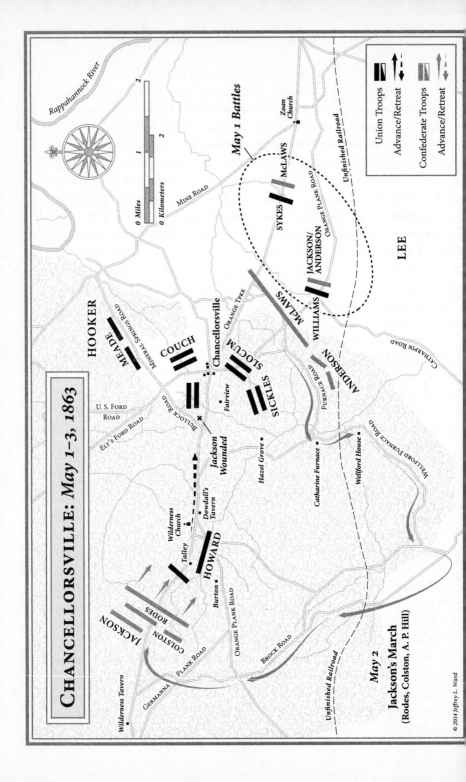

CHANCELLORSVILLE: *May 1–3, 1863*

Rappahannock River

MINE ROAD

May 1 Battles

Zoan Church

McLAWS

SYKES

JACKSON/ANDERSON

ORANGE PLANK ROAD

WILLIAMS

McLAWS

Unfinished Railroad

LEE

HOOKER

MINERAL SPRINGS ROAD

MEADE

COUCH

Chancellorsville

ORANGE TPKE

SLOCUM

Fairview

SICKLES

ANDERSON

CATHARPIN ROAD

U. S. FORD ROAD

ELY'S FORD ROAD

BULLOCK ROAD

Jackson Wounded

FURNACE ROAD

Hazel Grove

Catharine Furnace

WELLFORD FURNACE ROAD

Wellford House

Wilderness Church

Talley

Dowdall's Tavern

HOWARD

JACKSON

COLSTON

RODES

Burton

ORANGE PLANK ROAD

BROCK ROAD

Wilderness Tavern

GERMANNA PLANK ROAD

Unfinished Railroad

May 2
Jackson's March
(Rodes, Colston, A. P. Hill)

0 Miles   1   2

0 Kilometers   1   2

	Union Troops		Confederate Troops
	Advance/Retreat		Advance/Retreat

© 2014 Jeffrey L. Ward

half miles east of Chancellorsville that crossed both the Orange Turnpike and the Orange Plank Road. There they confronted Hooker's army and braced themselves for the inevitable attack. Lee's trust in Jackson was such, by this point in the war, that he had given him only the broadest guidelines for action: "Make arrangements to repulse the enemy," he had said, which allowed Jackson to handle the problem as he saw fit. Jackson knew, at the same time, that it was Lee's ultimate desire to drive Hooker back across the Rapidan. That suited him just fine. And so, upon assuming command near the Zoan Church, he told the troops under Anderson and McLaws to put down their picks and spades, climb out of their trenches, and prepare to attack.

There is no way to know Jackson's thought process as he prepared to engage the Union army in front of him. He knew very little about it and certainly he had no idea that, at the moment he ordered his men to advance, he was actually outnumbered five to one. But it was characteristic of the man that his means of determining the enemy's strength was to hit the enemy in the face and then see what happened. Typical, too, was his impatience to fight. As at Port Republic, he chose to attack before his full force had arrived.

Hooker, meanwhile, a few miles to the west, was unaware that Jackson himself had taken the field against him. Jackson's movements, under cover of night and fog, had gone completely undetected, and Hooker's latest intelligence still placed the entire 2nd Corps on the heights below Fredericksburg. The Union commander thus believed he was facing only the divisions of Lafayette McLaws and Richard Anderson. They would be dug in, he believed, and he expected them to fight a defensive battle. With his superior numbers, he would spread their flanks and make short work of them. At roughly 10:30 a.m. Hooker signaled the start of a three-pronged advance, stacked north to south: George Meade with two divisions on the River Road, George Sykes with one division on the Orange Turnpike, and Henry Slocum on the Plank Road with another two divisions. They would move forward, link up, and, if all went well, carry the heights of Fredericksburg by 2:00 p.m.

At almost exactly the same moment, Jackson signaled his own advance. To the amazement of the Union command, which had not expected to be attacked, his rapidly advancing columns slammed into the two lower prongs of Hooker's attacking force. Jackson not only had the element of pure surprise, but also, by hitting the Federal columns head-on and hitting them early, he deprived them of their ability to communicate with one another and, as they had planned, to join forces. Meade's two 5th Corps divisions in the north were isolated from their comrades and out of the fight, while McLaws hit Sykes in the center with superior numbers and Jackson stopped Slocum cold almost before he got started. By 1:00 p.m. Hooker knew that his plan had gone badly awry. So had his strategy at Fredericksburg. He had ordered John Sedgwick to "threaten an attack in full force" below the town, but Sedgwick had done nothing at all. That was because, due to faulty telegraphs, Sedgwick would not even receive those orders until almost 5:00 p.m.[13]

By now Hooker was beginning to understand what was happening to him. He received more bad news: a large Confederate force had detached from Fredericksburg and marched west. Thus his opponent on the field was almost certainly not Richard Anderson but Stonewall Jackson himself. And so when Union general George Sykes, fighting astride the Orange Turnpike, reported that he was heavily outnumbered and that his flanks were being turned, this information took on new meaning. Sykes not only could not be rescued easily, but also, with *Jackson* on the field, the divisions under Meade and Slocum might be threatened, too. At about 2:00 p.m. Hooker issued orders to all three columns to withdraw. Jackson, as always, pursued. But the Federals managed disciplined countermarches under fire, and Jackson's last-ditch attempt at a flank attack was repulsed by Hooker's heavy artillery. In spite of his natural predatory instincts, Jackson knew that a frontal assault on Hooker's entrenched, U-shaped defensive position at Chancellorsville would have been suicidal. The day ended with Hooker's troops in exactly the same position they had been in at dawn. Jackson's men were two miles in advance of Anderson's entrenchments. Jackson had won the day: Hooker's huge army was suddenly penned up in dense thickets, where its numbers meant far less than they would have on open ground.

In spite of his repulse, and his failure to take the high ground at Zoan Church, which should have been readily his, Hooker was undaunted. He believed he had accomplished his main purpose—flushing Lee from his defensive position and out into the open—and that he was now in a position to fight a defensive battle "on my own ground."[14] That was how he saw it, anyway. He was, moreover, expecting word from George Stoneman any minute that the rebels' railroad supply line had been cut.[15] What he did not comprehend was that, while his individual decisions may have been perfectly rational, and while he held, technically speaking, one of the stoutest defensive positions of the war, he had also surrendered the initiative to Robert E. Lee and Stonewall Jackson. And that was a very dangerous thing to do.

Just how important Jackson's presence was in Hooker's decision to withdraw is impossible to know. But it likely loomed large. Hooker later explained his retreat by saying that he believed he "was hazarding too much to continue the movement" and that because of the difficulty of deploying his troops in the wooded terrain he "was apprehensive about being whipped in detail." Both statements might have referred to Jackson.[16] Jackson's name alone may not have been worth two divisions, as an observer once suggested, but it was still enough to inspire prudence and caution in even a hard-fighting man like Joe Hooker, whom Jackson had fought to a bloody standstill in the cornfield at Antietam and who had been fully present for Jackson's tactical masterstroke at Second Manassas.

Whatever Hooker's thoughts, Jackson by this point in his meteoric and still ascendant career cast a large shadow, far larger than the sum of his flesh-and-blood parts. There was something fateful about him, something foreordained, as though he had been born to occupy precisely this moment in time and space, as though his strange and mystical communion with God had granted him special power over both his own men and his enemies. His personal oddities now fueled the legend. Though James Longstreet was a good general and a resolute fighter, he was a prosaic and somewhat colorless human being. Jackson, by contrast—remote, silent, eccentric, and reserved, his hand raised in prayer in the heat of battle—suggested darkness and mystery and magic. Longstreet inspired respect; Jackson, fear and awe. There are several remarkable accounts of him by his own men as he rode to battle on that day, men trying to put into words what it was like to see the living myth as he passed by. North Carolina colonel R. T. Bennett described seeing Jackson on his way to Tabernacle Church that morning, surrounded by the booming cheers of the men. "Suddenly the sound of a great multitude who had raised their voices in accord came over the tips of the bayonets," he wrote. "The very air of heaven seemed agitated. . . . The horse and his rider cross our vision. The simple Presbyterian Elder, anointed of God, with clenched teeth, a very statue, passes to his transfiguration."[17] Other descriptions of him have this same oddly mystical cast. ("The people of the Confederate states had begun to regard this immortal leader as above the reach of fate," wrote John Esten Cooke in his 1863 biography.[18]) Later that day Edward Porter Alexander watched Jackson and

Lee ride by together at the head of a column of men, to more wild cheering. His brief description of Jackson in that moment was one of the most memorable of the war. "As a fighter and a leader," Alexander wrote of the once scorned college professor, "he was all that can ever be given to a man to be."[19]

While Joe Hooker attended to his troop dispositions in the comfort of the Chancellor house that evening, and put the final touches on his prodigious defensive lines, Robert E. Lee and Stonewall Jackson were sitting on a log near the intersection of the Orange Plank and Catharine Furnace Roads, talking. They had met at about 7:00 p.m., after Jackson had called off his attack, and had made their way to a sheltered clearing on the northwest quadrant of the intersection to avoid Federal sharpshooters. Their conference lasted several hours. Staff officers and various generals came and went. Gunshots from the front lines sputtered and finally died out. Darkness fell. Later on, when those observers understood the full historic significance of this conversation, they would strain to remember something—anything—about what they had seen or heard.

The meeting began with a discussion of the day's battle. Jackson told Lee in detail what he had seen, and expressed his surprise at "the ease with which [the enemy] had been driven back to Chancellorsville," as Fitzhugh Lee remembered the conversation.[20] Jackson believed that Hooker would withdraw by morning. Lee had a different idea. As he saw it, Hooker's quick retreat simply meant that he wanted to fight a defensive battle. Instead of withdrawing, he was digging in, and daring Lee to attack. Lee was right, as it turned out, and he fully intended to oblige his adversary.

The question was how. As the two generals conversed, Confederate reconnaissance parties were scouting the margins of the Union position, probing for weakness. Hooker's center was almost absurdly strong, unassailable. There were five army corps on the Chancellorsville front, arrayed in a convex, six-mile-long line manned by nearly two-thirds of the Army of the Potomac and supported by 184 pieces of artillery. Thanks to the abundance of wood, and plenty of leisure time to cut and haul it, Union lines bristled with field fortifications, abatis, and obstructions of various designs, a defender's dream. The army's left, in the form of George Meade's tough 5th Corps, was anchored stoutly on the Rappahannock, which meant that it could not be turned.

Thus Lee looked to the Union right, where he soon found exactly what he was looking for. Jeb Stuart's subordinate, Brigadier General Fitzhugh Lee, whose cavalry had been doing the main reconnaissance, had discovered something extraordinary out there: rebel horsemen controlled virtually all the roads on the Confederate left, right up to the Federal picket lines, and thus the "eyes and ears" on Hooker's right flank belonged entirely to the Confederacy. This was partly—though not entirely—because much of the Union cavalry corps was off with its commander George Stoneman trying to disrupt Confederate supply lines. Stoneman's expedition would turn out to be an epic failure and one of the worst tactical mistakes of the war. But no one knew that yet; no one in the Union high command, in fact, had heard anything from Stoneman. Lee knew only that he was abroad with his troopers making mischief somewhere in central Virginia. But Lee now knew for certain that Hooker had left himself virtually blind in the west. Seeking advice on the terrain, Lee and Jackson summoned Reverend Tucker Lacy, whose family owned land in the area. Lacy explained that a marching column looping to the south and west could trace a long arc from Catharine Furnace that would reach the Orange Turnpike at Wilderness Tavern, about five miles west of Chancellorsville.[21] This confirmed what Lee and Jackson had heard from Stuart and Fitzhugh Lee, and would put the Confederate troops well beyond Hooker's right wing. Robert E. Lee soon made his decision: he would send Jackson on a march around the Union right. Though he did not know exactly where that was, he had a clear enough idea from what Fitzhugh Lee had told him. He would leave the details of the flanking movement, and subsequent attack, up to Jackson.[22] Jeb Stuart and his cavalry would screen his movements. Lee issued marching orders for the next day. Then the two generals made a simple camp in the pine woods. They spread saddle blankets on the ground, covered themselves with their overcoats, and used their saddles as pillows.

Sometime after midnight, Tucker Lacy, who had camped near Jackson and Lee, awoke to find a small fire burning, and Jackson sitting alone in front of it on a Union hardtack box. "Sit down," Jackson said. "I want to talk to you." He explained that he needed more information about the roads west of Catharine Furnace. Jackson was worried that the route Lacy had suggested might bring his column too near the Federal pickets. Wasn't there a way farther to the south that would make them less visible?[23] Lacy said he did not know but he did know someone who could plot such a route: Charles C. Wellford, the proprietor of Catharine Furnace, the only operating ironworks in the area. Jackson roused his mapmaker Hotchkiss and dispatched him and Lacy to the Wellford house, two miles away. There Wellford indeed suggested a better way—a road through the thickets that he had recently reopened to haul wood and iron ore—that would be invisible to just about anyone in the area. Wellford volunteered his son as a guide. Hotchkiss and Lacy galloped back to camp with the news, where they found Lee and Jackson both awake and sitting on hardtack boxes by the fire. Hotchkiss pulled up a third box and spread his map out on it, showing the generals this secret passage to the enemy's rear.

As Hotchkiss recalled, when he had finished his presentation, Lee turned to Jackson.

"General Jackson, what do you propose to do?" Lee asked.

"Go around here," Jackson replied, pointing to Wellford's suggested route on the map.

"What do you propose to make the movement with?"

"With my whole command."

"What will you leave me?"

"The divisions of Anderson and McLaws."

There was a pause as Lee reflected on the high-risk plan they were so calmly discussing. He had divided his army once in February, sending Longstreet south. He had divided it again the previous day, leaving Jubal Early with his single division on the heights of Fredericksburg. Now he had decided not only to divide his army a third time, but also to march the largest part of it directly across his enemy's front, roughly similar to what Edwin Sumner and John Sedgwick had done with the Union 2nd Corps at Antietam, where Jackson had slaughtered them like animals. Lee was betting—it was one of the most daring and perilous bets of the war—that Hooker would wait to be attacked.

"Well, go ahead," Lee said.

And that was all there was to it. Lee made some final notes for the orders he would have to issue. Then Jackson saluted and said, "My troops will move at once, sir."[24]

Moving at once was actually impossible, considering how much work it was going to take to get three divisions all marching and pointed in the same direction. At about seven o'clock on the chilly morning of May 2 the lead elements of the 2nd Corps crossed the narrow Plank Road on their way to Catharine Furnace and beyond. General Lee sat on his horse by the side of the road, watching. When Jackson rode up, the two men conversed briefly—whatever they said is lost to history—then Jackson pointed toward the enemy's lines and rode on. With him went 29,400 men along with 27 batteries with 108 guns. Riding on his flank were three and a half regiments of Jeb Stuart's cavalry. In all Jackson had 33,000 men. By agreement, he had left Lee with a meager 15,000 to face the bulk of Hooker's army. Jackson's corps was stripped down for combat. It carried only ammunition wagons and ambulances, no baggage or commissary wagons. The men marched at a rate that would cover a mile in twenty-five minutes, resting ten minutes each hour. As a North Carolina private recalled,

> We went swiftly forward through the Wilderness, striking now and then a dim path or road. Strict silence was enforced, the men only being allowed to speak in whispers. Occasionally a courier would spur his tired horse past us as we twisted through the bush. For hours at a time we neither saw nor heard anything.[25]

The column wound forward along narrow paths that had been cut through the dense woods, an enormous, silent body of men making its way west. Jackson, riding at the head of the column, stopped to pick up his guide, Charles Wellford. When he galloped past his men he did so with his cap held high, while his men all raised theirs in silent tribute. It was not an easy march. Temperatures rose, and the length and narrowness of the column meant that every piece of uneven terrain and every mudhole would cause it to string out, leading to endless halting and starting, halting and starting.[26] The last of Jackson's troops, under A. P. Hill, did not leave until eleven o'clock. Still, they pressed forward with minimal straggling: Jackson had made sure of that by placing his regimental commanders in the rear.

As the hours passed, Jackson was mostly silent. But he would occasionally join the conversation of the officers who rode with him. One of them noted how many former VMI faculty and students were with the 2nd Corps on its march. Division commanders Robert Rodes and Raleigh Colston had both been professors there. Rodes, a VMI graduate, had left his teaching job there when the full professorship he wanted was given to newcomer Thomas J. Jackson in 1851. Colston had accompanied Jackson and his cadets when they traveled to Richmond in April 1861. Artillery chief Stapleton Crutchfield had been a student of Jackson's. Cavalry colonel Tom Munford had been the ranking cadet at VMI when Jackson had first arrived, had treated the odd new professor kindly, and the two had become friends. Brigadier General James H. Lane had been a student of

Jackson's and later taught mathematics at VMI. There were, in fact, twenty brigadiers and colonels of line and staff that day who were VMI graduates. Jackson, pleased with this notion, turned to Munford and said, "Colonel, the Institute will be heard from today." At about 2:30 p.m. the head of Jackson's column came to a halt at the Orange Plank Road, three miles west of Chancellorsville.

May 2 was an odd day for Joseph Hooker, as much for what did not happen as for what did. He remained supremely confident in his position, had passed this confidence on to his general officers, and they all agreed that their success was virtually guaranteed. For once they had reliable estimates of rebel troop strength and knew they held better than a two-to-one advantage over Lee. They knew that Longstreet was too far away to make any difference. They held immensely strong defensive positions that extended all the way to the Rappahannock and shielded their own supply lines. Hooker's main concern was Stoneman, riding with ten thousand men somewhere in the rebel rear but unheard from for four days. Hooker expected he would hear very soon that his cavalry commander had succeeded and that the rebel communications had been cut, which meant that Fighting Joe once again held both the initiative and the upper hand.

For the moment he could only do his best to shore up his position. That meant strengthening his right, which consisted of O. O. "Otis" Howard's 11th Corps, a weak fighting force full of German-speaking Germans. He was known as the "Christian General," a man who, like Jackson, prayed before and during battle, and spoke of war in religious terms. Unlike Jackson, he was an ineffectual commander. It was no accident that Hooker had stationed him well west of Chancellorsville in what must have seemed to him the middle of nowhere and certainly far from whatever fighting was likely to take place. Still, he had taken pains to strengthen this wing of his army. At about 1:00 a.m. he had sent an order to General John Reynolds, in command of the 1st Corps and still deployed on the Fredericksburg front. Reynolds was to move before daylight and march his entire 16,900-man force upriver, past Chancellorsville, and take a new position on the right rear of the 11th Corps. They would arrive by midafternoon on May 2. This meant that the questionable Howard would be well backed up. It also meant that the Union right, instead of being in the air, where it now was, would be strongly anchored on the Rapidan River three miles west of its confluence with the Rappahannock.[27]

This was a very good idea, especially since Hooker's troops in Fredericksburg had clearly failed to hold the Confederate forces there in place. But Hooker was once again the victim of the inept and inconsistent Union Signal Corps. Reynolds did not receive his telegraph until daylight, which meant that his men would not be in place in Chancellorsville until very late afternoon or evening. Hooker's chief of staff, Dan Butterfield, called this lapse "one of the most unfortunate that has occurred."

Another, even more damaging mistake would be made that morning. Starting at about 8:00 a.m., Union observers sitting in tall trees began reporting an unusual and unanticipated event taking place behind rebel lines: the apparent movement south and west of a large Confederate column, complete with artillery and trains. Though most of Jackson's route of march was cloaked even from these treeborne scouts, there was one section of road that ran along high, open ground just east of Catharine Furnace where the column became briefly visible. The reports were passed quickly up the line. An hour and a half later, 3rd Corps commander Major General Daniel Sickles personally observed the column through field glasses and secured permission from Hooker to open fire on it with his artillery. Taking no chances, Hooker sent a message to Otis Howard, saying, "we have good reason to suppose that the enemy is moving to our right" and observing that "the disposition you have made of your corps has been with a view to a front attack by the enemy. If he should throw himself on your flank . . . determine upon the position you will take in that event." He reminded Howard to keep reserves "well in hand to meet this contingency." Howard read the order, discussed it briefly with one of his generals, then more or less disregarded it. He sent an officer from the Signal Corps a mile to the west but did not reposition any of his troops. His feeling, shared by others, was that the density of the Wilderness around him would be defense enough.

Sickles, meanwhile, wanted to know more about this odd troop movement. At midday he asked for and received permission from Hooker to attack the Confederate column with infantry. Actually this was the *tail* of Jackson's column, which had been swinging past Catharine Furnace for more than five hours. Jackson had had the foresight to leave the 23rd Georgia Regiment behind to secure this vulnerable, open area, and now the Georgians collided with Sickles's attacking force. There was a sharp, extended fight near the Catharine Furnace in which 296 of the Georgians were taken prisoner. But they did the job Jackson had intended them to do, which was to keep the Union forces away from the marching column.

Except for one broken-down caisson, every piece of Jackson's force passed unscathed.

Even better for the success of Lee's plan was the conclusion that Sickles drew from his engagement with the 23rd Georgia. At about 1:30 p.m. he reported that what he was witnessing was actually a rebel *retreat*. The enemy's troops, after all, were seen moving in a southerly direction, and had their trains with them. It only made sense. Sickles's message got to Hooker's headquarters at about 2:00 p.m., at which point the Union high command, too, became convinced that Lee was retreating toward Gordonsville. (Maybe this was because Lee's supply lines had been cut, Hooker fantasized, and his enemy was marching to the Orange and Alexandria line to restore them.) Further evidence to support this interpretation were reports of Jubal Early's sudden disengagement from the Fredericksburg front. They happened to be true, though the movement was entirely unintentional. As it turned out, Lee's chief of staff, Robert Chilton, had misinterpreted Lee's wishes. Lee had wanted Early to watch the Federals closely, and if they seemed to be departing for Chancellorsville, he was to leave a small holding force in place and join Lee. The orders were discretionary. But what Early got from Chilton was a peremptory directive to immediately fall back, even though the 6th Corps was still in front of him. By 4:45 p.m. the Union command knew for certain that Early was leaving, which seemed to be final, conclusive proof of the rebel withdrawal. Orders had already gone out alerting Union commanders to replenish food and ammunition and to be ready to pursue the retreating rebel army the next morning. Now there was no doubt at all.

Lee also benefited from the eventual escalation of the fight Sickles had started at Catharine Furnace. It soon drew in not only elements from Richard Anderson's Confederate divisions but also, more important, involved some twenty-five thousand Federal troops, many of whom had been stripped from the Union left, leaving a mile-wide gap in the line just east of Howard's 11th Corps. Though the fighting involved advances and retreats, much pounding of artillery, and expenditure of powder and bullets, nothing much came of it. But it had the effect of leaving Otis Howard, late that afternoon, quite isolated and alone on the Union right.

Jackson's column had moved resolutely forward, in secret and in silence, cutting an elliptical arc around the Union right. The 2nd Corps had taken the Catharine Furnace Road, then the Wellfords' road, then a series of narrow byways that had finally rejoined the Brock Road, which had put their lead at the Orange Plank Road in midafternoon. Except for the open area near the furnace, they had remained unseen and undetected. Every path and byway that went off to the right had been sealed off by Stuart's horsemen. According to the plan Lee and Jackson had developed, the column would turn right at the intersection of the Brock and Plank Roads. From there the Union right was supposed to be about two miles to the east. To see if this was true, the 2nd Virginia Cavalry, under Tom Munford, conducted a reconnaissance up the Plank Road. They soon found a piece of high ground from which a Confederate captain saw a view rarely afforded to any scout. He galloped back to find Fitzhugh Lee, who saw it, too, then himself galloped back to find Jackson, who was riding at the head of Robert Rodes's column.

Lee drew rein, and said, "General, if you will ride with me, halting your column here . . . I will show you the enemy's right." Minutes later Jackson was gazing down upon a major piece of the Union army, not seven hundred yards away. This was Howard's 11th Corps, though Jackson had no way of knowing that. But it was clearly the terminus of the Union right. From the spot where the Orange Plank Road intersected the Orange Turnpike, Jackson could see roughly half a mile of open space on either side. As Fitzhugh Lee recalled,

> Below and but a few hundred yards distant ran their line of battle, with abatis in front and long lines of stacked arms in the rear. Cannon in position were visible, and the soldiers were in groups, chatting, smoking, and playing cards, while the ones in the rear were driving up and butchering beeves.[28]

Jackson could also see that the Union line was facing *south*. He thus understood, when it was pointed out to him, that an attack up the Plank Road would amount to a frontal assault. An advance eastward on the Orange Turnpike, on the other hand, which intersected Brock Road a mile and a half to the north, would mean that his own battle line would be almost perfectly perpendicular to the Union line. He turned to Fitzhugh Lee and said, "Tell General Rodes to move across the Plank Road and halt when he gets to the old turnpike. I will join him there."[29] Rodes did just that. He turned to the east on the turnpike, continued for a mile to a four-hundred-yard-wide clearing at the farm of John Luckett, and then stopped, unnoticed and unmolested by anyone in a blue coat.

At about 3:00 p.m. Jackson wrote out a brief dispatch in his clumsy scrawl for General Lee: "The enemy has made a stand at Chancellor's which is about 2 miles from Chancellorsville. I hope as soon as practicable to attack. I trust that an ever kind Providence will bless us with great success. Respectfully, T. J. Jackson." He then added a postscript that read, with more of his usual deadpan understatement, "The leading division is up & the next two appear to be well closed."[30]

Though the marching had indeed been disciplined, it still took a long time to convert the elongated column to a battle line. It was even harder because most of that line had to assemble in the supposedly impenetrable woods. Over the next two hours Jackson labored to place 21,800 infantry and 8 pieces of artillery into position. This would be his attacking force. The rest would follow behind, in reserve. He had plenty of daylight to work with and was able to pay attention to the smallest details. He had never had this luxury before. Roughly half a mile ahead of him, his foes went about their business, suspecting nothing. When Jackson had finished, his battle line was two miles long, aimed directly at a Union army corps that was in most places only a few men deep, facing south.

At 5:30 p.m. Jackson was sitting on his horse on the Orange Turnpike next to General Robert Rodes. His lines were formed and waiting. Though the men had marched some twelve miles and they were in high, fighting spirits, they were as yet unaware of exactly what was going to happen. Jackson's veterans knew by now that long marches preceded spectacular events. After surveying his battle lines he turned to his fellow rider and said, "Are you ready, General Rodes?" "Yes, sir!" came the enthusiastic response. Jackson then said quietly, "You may go forward, then."

A bugle call rang through the woods, followed by responses from bugles on the left and right, and suddenly the woods were alive with fast-moving Confederates.[31] As they quick-stepped forward through the tangled undergrowth, which didn't seem to dampen their enthusiasm, the wild, eerie, corkscrewing sound of the rebel yell swept down the ranks. In minutes they were in range of the Union lines. Though the rough terrain broke up Jackson's neat battle lines, the men did not stop to re-form but pushed forward, singly and in groups. Jackson rode close behind his men, shouting, "Press forward! Press forward!"

The speed and direction of the Confederate attack took the 11th Corps completely by surprise. Because of an acoustical anomaly in the forest, they had heard none of the bugle calls. They had been enjoying a moment of drowsy calm and seemingly perfect security. Men were fixing dinner and taking naps or relaxing, listening to the distant music of a regimental band, or perhaps discussing the Confederate retreat, when suddenly all nature seemed to rise up in revolt around them. Through their camps rushed frantic rabbits, deer, quail, and wild turkeys, then there was an odd silence, and then Jackson's massive, screaming, onrushing wall of gray was upon them. It was so sudden and so overwhelming that men who were there later used storm or avalanche metaphors to describe it. There was very little they could do about it, except to drop what they had and run for their lives. There was an effort made here and there by Union infantry to form and make some sort of fight, but the shock of the assault was too much for most of them. "The surprise was complete," wrote Confederate artillery officer David Gregg McIntosh:

A bolt from the sky would not have startled [brigade commander Leopold] Von Gilsa's men half so much as the musket shots in the thicket, and the sight of their flying comrades, followed by a straggling line of skirmishers, and then by a solid wall of gray. . . . The resistance offered was speedily beaten down. There was nothing left to do but lay down their arms and surrender, or flee. . . . Arms, knapsacks, clothing, equipage, everything, was thrown aside and left behind. The camp was in wild confusion. Men lost their heads in terror, the road and the woods on both sides were filled with men, horses and cattle, in one mad flight. The rebel yells added terror to the situation.[32]

The victory was fast and complete. In an hour and a half Jackson had shattered the 11th Corps and driven forward a full mile and a quarter to a point less than two miles from Hooker's headquarters. The 11th Corps had suffered 2,400 casualties out of 11,000 men, including 1,000 captured. Jackson lost only 800 men.[33] Former VMI professors Rodes and Colston had led the attack. The dashing Rodes in particular was a brilliant presence on the field, exhorting his men with his long mustaches flying. Jackson personally congratulated him on his gallant performance. Indeed, Jackson's men had never seen their leader quite so thrilled with a victory. "He was in unusually fine spirits," wrote one Confederate captain, "and every time he heard the cheering of ourselves which was the signal of victory he raised his right hand a few seconds as if in acknowledgment of the blessing and to return thanks to God for the victory."[34] One Georgian remembered that even after the fighting had died down the ground seemed "to tremble as if shaken by an earthquake, the cheering is so tremendous, caused by Gen. Jackson riding along the line."[35]

Like the hapless Otis Howard, Hooker had also been taken completely by surprise. He had been busy planning a full-scale pursuit of Lee's supposedly retreating army for the following morning. He had certainly been curious about various Confederate advances on the turnpike and the Plank Road east of Chancellorsville at about five thirty—which was actually Lee demonstrating loudly to cover Jackson's attack. He had had trouble getting Sedgwick to advance, as ordered, on Fredericksburg. And he still had not heard from George Stoneman. But he was not terribly worried. He would work these things out. At about 6:30 p.m., as he was conversing with two captains on his staff on the porch of the Chancellor house, he heard a sudden noise from the road. One of the captains stepped off the porch, looked through his glass, and shouted, "My God, here they come!" Hooker and his staff rode westward on the road to see what was happening, and immediately encountered the men, horses, and wagons of the 11th Corps in wild panic and full flight. Many had no weapons, hats, haversacks, or coats. They demanded, wild-eyed, to know how to get to the bridges, so they could cross the river to safety.[36] Because almost half of them were German, and shouting in their native language, it was hard to tell at first what was going on. (Hooker's staffers may have learned at that moment that *"Alles ist verloren!"* meant "All is lost!") But soon enough they understood that the 11th had been routed, and the Union flank shattered beyond repair. Hooker himself did not panic. He acted quickly. He brought up artillery and pointed it west instead of south, pulled other troops back from the furnace to the turnpike and faced them the same way, and shifted Meade's 5th Corps to protect his lines to the river. He went to work constructing a new west-facing line three-quarters of a mile east of his headquarters. Orders went out that the high ground near the Chancellor house—the center of the army's position—was to be held at all costs. In minutes, Hooker's attitude had changed from serene self-confidence to fear for the safety of his army. He was right to be alarmed. To the west, through the descending darkness, Stonewall Jackson was planning to cut off his retreat and smash him yet again that very night.

CHAPTER FORTY-FIVE

"An Iron Sabre Vowed to an Iron Lord"[1]

⬦⬦⬦

Jackson was waiting. Though he had already engineered one of the most stunning attacks of the war, and its most brilliant single march, he was not satisfied with the ground he had won, or that he had driven the 11th Corps clear through the center of Hooker's army and out the other side. He wanted more. He wanted to hit the Yankee defenses on the Plank Road and around the Orange Turnpike, smash through them, and join forces with McLaws and Anderson, while his left swept the Union flank and cut off its main escape route at US Ford.[2] The fact that darkness was falling and night attacks had proved difficult to manage (as at Second Manassas) did not seem to trouble him. Because the divisions of Rodes and Colston that had made the attack were now badly disorganized and commingled, the advance would be led by five fresh regiments from A. P. Hill's division under Brigadier General James H. Lane, a former student of Jackson's and colleague on the VMI faculty. In the weirdly still night air pierced occasionally by the shouts of Union soldiers, Jackson was waiting—he was actually riding restlessly back and forth in the rear of Lane's brigade—for Lane to shake out his regiments into a line of battle.[3]

He soon encountered A. P. Hill and some of his staff and asked his West Point classmate how long it would be before he was ready to move. A few minutes, Hill replied, the time it would take to finish bringing his men forward of Rodes's troops. Jackson assigned his chief engineer, Keith Boswell, to Hill as a guide, then said, "General Hill, as soon as you are ready push right forward. Allow nothing to stop you. Press on to the United States

Ford." Jackson rode forward on the Orange Plank Road, then shifted slightly north to the parallel Mountain Road. He was now in front of the men of the 18th North Carolina, in the margin between the Confederate lines and Lane's skirmishers, who were deployed several hundred yards ahead. Such personal reconnaissance was an old habit of Jackson's. He liked to scout the battlefield from as far forward as possible. Though this exasperated his staff, who feared for his safety, he persisted in doing it. With him were eight other riders, including his signal officer, Captain Richard Eggleston Wilbourn, his brother-in-law and aide-de-camp Lieutenant Joseph G. Morrison, a couple of Signal Corps enlisted men, and several couriers. One of them, who lived in the immediate neighborhood and knew the road and terrain well, served as guide. Following them eastward was another mounted group of nine riders with A. P. Hill. In all, nineteen riders went forward into that uneasy, moonlit darkness.[4] Hill, who was following mainly out of military etiquette, lagged about fifty yards behind Jackson. In a remarkable lapse of communication, neither Brigadier General Lane nor the men in his regiments knew that Jackson and Hill were in front of them.

Jackson and his fellow riders continued forward, almost to where the skirmishers of the 33rd North Carolina were posted, where they could hear the sounds of Federal soldiers frantically felling trees to build obstructions to slow the rebel advance. To Jackson this would have been useful intelligence. Jackson listened for a time, then turned back toward the Confederate lines. At that point he was about 120 yards from his own infantry. It was after 9:00 p.m. A. P. Hill, still on the Plank Road, was now about 60 yards behind Jackson on a diagonal line. What happened next happened very quickly. A single shot, fired by a Confederate skirmisher, rang out well to the south of the Plank Road. Skirmishers on both sides took up the firing and it rolled in a northerly direction, and several hundred muskets were discharged in short order. Some of the men in the main Confederate line fired, too, which meant they were firing at the backs of their own skirmishers. Just as this small-scale firefight reached the center of the Confederate line around the Plank Road, the men of the 18th North Carolina, who occupied that position, saw what looked like enemy cavalry closing on them from short range. This was Hill, Boswell, and the rest of their group, returning to their lines. The infantry, of course, had no idea that there were Confederate horsemen in front of them, least of all A. P. Hill and Stonewall Jackson, and they knew that the mounted figures could not possibly have been their own footbound skirmishers. The 18th North Carolina opened fire.[5]

Their volleys tore through both Jackson's and Hill's parties. Since Hill was closest to the firing, his group suffered the worst. Two men were shot dead (including Jackson's engineer, Boswell, shot twice through the heart), one mortally wounded, one shot twice in the face, and another severely injured when his horse was killed. The horses of two others were shot and carried their riders helplessly into Union lines, where they became prisoners. Only two staffers were neither killed nor injured, but both of their horses were killed. Hill escaped harm only by lying facedown on the ground. Farther off in the darkness, where the bullets found Jackson's group, the damage was less severe to individuals and horses, but devastating to the Confederacy and its chances of winning the war. Six of the nine riders with him were untouched by bullets. One of the couriers was killed, another wounded and carried by his horse into Union lines.

Then there was Jackson himself, whose astonishing good luck on the battlefield had just run out. He was hit by three bullets. One, a smoothbore round, entered above the base of his right thumb, broke two fingers, and buried itself under the skin on the back of his hand. The other two hit his left arm and were far more destructive. One entered an inch below his elbow and exited just above the wrist. The other hit him three inches below the shoulder and completely shattered the bone. His signal officer, Richard Wilbourn, seeing that he was hit, managed to rein in the frantic Little Sorrel, who had initially taken off toward enemy lines, then helped his wounded general to the ground.[6] Soon A. P. Hill arrived, and the two men ripped through Jackson's jacket, pulled off his blood-filled gloves, tied handkerchiefs above and below his shoulder wound, and made a sling for his right arm.[7]

The problem was how to get him back to safety. The firing now became more widespread, and Union artillery opened on the suspected rebel advance. With more than a dozen men attending him at various times, Jackson was alternately supported while he walked and carried in a litter. Twice while being carried he fell to the ground: once when one of the litter bearers was shot, again when one tripped and fell. Both falls landed him on his shattered arm, which caused him excruciating pain. He groaned loudly. "At this moment the scene was a fearful one," wrote Hunter McGuire. "The air seemed to be alive with the shrieks of shells and the whistling of bullets; horses, riderless and mad with fright, dashed in every direction."[8]

According to Jackson's aide James Power Smith, the men were so frightened by the barrage of shell and shrapnel that "we were obliged to lay the litter and its burden down, as the litter-bearers ran for the cover of the trees."[9] Smith himself lay down next to Jackson, covering him with his own body. At one point the group encountered Brigadier General Dorsey Pender, who was shocked to see Jackson and told him he was worried about the damage the Federal barrage was doing to his brigade. Jackson, defiant in spite of his wounds, pushed aside the men who were helping support him, raised himself up to his full height, and said in a weak voice, "General Pender, you must hold on to the field; you must hold out to the last."

Once behind Confederate lines, Jackson was taken to the ambulance wagon Hunter McGuire had brought up.

"I hope you are not badly hurt, General," McGuire said when he saw his pale general.

"I am badly injured, Doctor," Jackson replied in a calm but feeble voice. "I fear I am dying." After a pause he went on, "I am glad you have come. I think the wound in my shoulder is still bleeding."

It was. Jackson in fact had lost a good deal of blood. His clothes were saturated with it. He had a very faint pulse. McGuire stopped the bleeding, administered some whiskey and morphine, and the ambulance rolled westward toward the field hospital that had been set up half a mile in the rear at Wilderness Tavern. Riding with Jackson in the bed of the wagon was his artillery chief, Colonel Stapleton Crutchfield, who had been wounded in the leg.[10] Jackson was quite concerned about Crutchfield, and according to McGuire "expressed, very feelingly, his sympathy" for his former VMI student. At one point Jackson reached up and pulled McGuire down to him and asked quietly if Crutchfield was severely injured. "No, only painfully hurt," replied McGuire. "I am glad it is no worse," said Jackson. A few minutes later Crutchfield did exactly the same thing, and asked McGuire the same question about Jackson. When McGuire told him that the lieutenant general was "very seriously wounded," Crutchfield groaned and cried out, "Oh, my God!" Jackson, mistaking this for an expression of agony, ordered the ambulance to stop to see if something could be done to ease his comrade's pain.[11]

Two and a half hours later, Jackson's pulse was finally strong enough to allow McGuire to examine the wounds. Before anesthetizing his patient with chloroform, McGuire told Jackson that his left arm would probably need to be amputated, and asked if, in the event that it was necessary, it should be done immediately. "Yes, certainly, Dr. McGuire," Jackson replied. "Do for me whatever you think best." Jackson was resolutely polite throughout his ordeal. McGuire took off the arm just below the shoulder.

At 3:30 a.m., while Jackson was recuperating, and with news of his injury pulsing through the ranks, his assistant adjutant, Sandie Pendleton, arrived at the Wilderness Tavern hospital with an urgent question. After Jackson was wounded, command had passed to A. P. Hill. But Hill himself had been hit in the legs a few minutes later by a shell fragment from the Federal artillery barrage triggered by the volleys that wounded Jackson. Hill could not walk or ride, so he had turned over temporary command to Robert Rodes. But he believed that the command should go to Jeb Stuart—the only other major general left in the 2nd Corps. Since Lee was too far away to receive a message quickly, Hill dispatched a courier to Stuart with orders to take over. At about midnight the latter reached the battlefield, where Hill, lying under a blanket on the Orange Plank Road with his wounded legs bandaged, told him what little he knew about Jackson's battle plan. Jackson, typically, had given him only the barest outline. That left Stuart in a quandary. With part of A. P. Hill's division poised for attack, what should he do? He sent Pendleton on an urgent mission to find out.

Though McGuire was at first reluctant to let Pendleton see Jackson, he relented when Pendleton explained the seriousness of the crisis. When he entered the tent, Jackson was awake.

"Well, Major, I am glad to see you," he said to his favorite staff member. "I thought you were killed."

Pendleton then explained the problem and Stuart's request to know how to proceed. What followed was very likely the product of Jackson's severe trauma and injury, major surgery, and the aftereffects of the chloroform, but it was shocking just the same. In McGuire's description,

General Jackson was at once interested, and asked in his quick, rapid way several questions. When they were answered he remained silent for a moment, evidently trying to think; he contracted his brow, set his mouth, and for some moments was obviously endeavoring to concentrate his thoughts. For a moment it was believed he had succeeded, for his nostrils dilated, and his eye flashed its old fire, but it was only for a moment; his face relaxed again, and presently he answered very feebly and sadly, "I don't know, I can't tell; say to General Stuart he must do what he thinks best."[12]

Pendleton saluted, left the tent, and wept freely, while McGuire tried to comfort him.

The next morning Jackson was feeling better. He dispatched Anna's brother Joseph Morrison to Richmond to arrange for her to come. James Power Smith read him a message from General Lee. "I have just received your note, informing me that you were wounded," Lee wrote. "I cannot express my regret at the occurrence. Could I have directed events, I should have chosen, for the good of the country, to have been disabled in your stead. I congratulate you upon the victory, which is due to your skill and energy." Jackson listened, then said, "General Lee is very kind, but he should give the praise to God."

His mental clarity seemed to return, too. He wanted to know the details of the battle, how individual brigades or officers had performed, and was pleased to learn that his old Stonewall Brigade had fought gallantly. "The men of that brigade will some day be proud to say 'I was one of the Stonewall Brigade,'" he said, insisting at the same time that the famous nickname "belongs to the brigade, and not to me."[13] That same day he told Tucker Lacy that, in spite of what had happened, he was perfectly content with his situation. "You find me severely wounded," Jackson said, "but not unhappy or depressed. I believe that it has been done according to the will of God; and I acquiesce entirely in His holy will. It may appear strange, but you never saw me more perfectly contented than I am today, for I am sure my heavenly father designs this affliction for my own good."[14] Later that day Jackson told Lacy that he had experienced a moment of revelation on the battlefield. "I thought, after I fell from the litter, that I would die upon the field," he said, "and I gave myself up into the hands of my heavenly father without fear. I was in the possession of perfect peace."[15] He also spoke about the battle. He said that Hooker had had a good plan, "But he shouldn't have sent away his cavalry; that was his great blunder." Of his flank march, he said, "Our movement yesterday was a great success; I think the most successful military movement of my life. But I expect to receive far more credit for it than I deserve. Most men will think I had planned it all from the first; but it was not so. I simply took advantage of circumstances as they were presented to me in the providence of God."[16]

Because Lee worried that Jackson might be captured, he ordered his wounded general transported from the hospital at Wilderness Tavern to a private home near Guiney's Station, the railroad depot south of Fredericksburg. By now everyone in the Army of Northern Virginia and in the surrounding areas knew what had happened to him. As he traveled, lying on a mattress in the wagon bed, rough-hewn teamsters stood by the roadside with their hats off, weeping. At Spotsylvania Courthouse and along the entire route, men and women rushed to the ambulance and with tears in their eyes blessed him and prayed for his recovery.[17] The most common sentiment was the one expressed in Lee's note: "I wish it was me, sir."[18]

Meanwhile, miles behind him, the battle that he had so brilliantly begun raged through the day. Jackson would have been proud of his men, many of whom cried, "Remember Stonewall Jackson!" or "Revenge Jackson!" as they advanced against their more numerous enemies.[19] The Confederate attack resumed at five thirty the next morning. By 10:00 a.m. Hooker, who had been knocked briefly unconscious when an artillery projectile struck his headquarters, had fallen back to the north, allowing the two halves of Lee's army to unite and ceding critical high ground to the Confederate artillery under Porter Alexander. Soon the Union army was conducting a fighting retreat to defensive positions near US Ford on the Rappahannock. While this was happening, four Union divisions under John Sedgwick broke through Confederate defenses under Jubal Early at Fredericksburg, took Marye's Heights and the Sunken Road, and advanced west toward Chancellorsville to join Hooker. At 3:30 p.m. Sedgwick attacked and was repulsed by a small Confederate force under Lafayette McLaws. The following morning Early reoccupied Fredericksburg, and on May 4, Confederate forces under McLaws, Early, and Anderson attacked Sedgwick. Though these attacks were repulsed in the late afternoon, Sedgwick had had enough. He retreated across the river that night. On May 5 Hooker ordered the rest of the army to withdraw to the north side of the Rappahannock. The Battle of Chancellorsville, from Jackson's stunning flank attack to the withdrawal of the immense Union army under cover of darkness, is considered Robert E. Lee's greatest victory. He had won it without Longstreet and with less than half as many soldiers as his enemy. But at terrible cost. There were 30,500 casualties in all in three days of fighting: 17,197 Union and 13,303 Confederate. And the indomitable Jackson was convalescing miles behind the lines. "Jackson has lost his left arm," Lee told Lacy. "But I my right arm."[20] Fifty miles away, in Washington, Lincoln's reaction to Hooker's defeat was, "My God, my God, what will the country say?"

• • •

Jackson was taken to a large house known as Fairfield, the residence of the Chandler family, where he was lodged in a tidy, whitewashed outbuilding that looked a good deal like his winter quarters at Moss Neck. Not far away was the bustling Guiney's Station, the depot on the Richmond, Fredericksburg, and Potomac Railroad that handled supplies coming north from Richmond and had become a collection point for more than four thousand captured Union soldiers. Jackson arrived with a cavalry escort at about 8:00 p.m. after a harrowingly bumpy twenty-seven-mile ride through the Virginia outback. When he was greeted by the proprietor, Thomas Chandler, Jackson said in a tired voice, "I am sorry I cannot shake hands with you, but one arm is gone and my right hand is wounded." Jackson was placed in a double, rope-trellis bed, ate some bread and drank tea, and fell asleep. Thanks to orders from Lee, Hunter McGuire, one of the finest medical officers in the war, had been released from his other duties to tend Jackson full-time. He, James Power Smith, Joseph Morrison, and Jackson's servant Jim Lewis would be the only other occupants of the house.

For the next two days—Tuesday, May 5, and Wednesday, May 6 (he was wounded the night of May 2)—Jackson's condition stabilized, then improved. McGuire was pleased with his progress. On Wednesday Jackson ate heartily and was, in McGuire's words, "uniformly cheerful." In his immobilized state, without immediate purpose in his life and free of the usual pull of duty, he became uncharacteristically talkative. He chatted with Lacy, Smith, and McGuire on a range of religious topics that included discussion of how every aspect of a man's religious life should be a self-conscious religious act. While washing oneself, one might imagine the cleansing blood of Christ; while dressing, one might pray to be cloaked in the Savior's righteousness; while eating, to be feeding on the bread of heaven. Jackson had long lived this way, consecrating even his most trivial actions to God. Now he had leisure time to discuss his beliefs in detail. He asked his aide Lieutenant Smith, a former theological student, where the Bible gives generals models for their official battle reports. Smith replied, laughing, that he would never have thought to find such a thing in Scripture. "Nevertheless," said Jackson, "there are such, and excellent models too. Look, for instance, at the narrative of Joshua's battle with the Amalekites. . . . It has clearness, brevity, fairness, modesty, and it traces the victory to its right source—the blessing of God."[21] He asked James Power Smith, "What were the headquarters of Christianity after the crucifixion?" and asked McGuire if he thought that diseased people who had been healed by Jesus's touch ever suffered again from the same malady.[22] Thus the unusually chatty lieutenant general passed the first days of his recovery.

In the early morning of Thursday, May 7, Jackson's condition suddenly worsened. When McGuire examined him at dawn he complained of a sharp pain in his side. He had difficulty breathing. His diagnosis: pneumonia, probably brought on by a "contusion of the lung" produced by the fall from the litter.[23] Up to this point, plans had been under way to move Jackson to Richmond for the rest of his recovery. Now all that changed. Whether McGuire was right is still a matter of debate: some present-day doctors think his diagnosis likely, others think sepsis produced by severe infection was the cause, others pulmonary emboli that damaged his lungs.[24] But this was the diagnosis in 1863, confirmed by other doctors summoned by McGuire, and that was what Jackson would be treated for. Pneumonia was a major killer in the Civil War: some thirty-seven thousand soldiers on both sides would die of it.[25] Jackson wasn't going to Richmond. He would have to fight for his life in place at Guiney's Station.

Joseph Morrison's assigned task—retrieving his sister Anna—was not as easy as it might have seemed. George Stoneman's ten thousand riders were roaming between Fredericksburg and Richmond relatively unchallenged, which meant that Confederate soldiers traveling in that corridor were in automatic danger. Morrison had been forced to hide in the woods and had narrowly escaped capture. It wasn't until the early evening of Tuesday, May 5, nearly three days after he had set out, that he finally arrived at the house where his sister was staying. Though she had been told of her husband's wounding, she had received conflicting reports of his condition. Now her brother reported the devastating news that his arm had been amputated. But he was alive and in cheerful spirits, he told her. Unfortunately, what little damage Stoneman's cavalry had inflicted on the RF&P Railroad had just occurred, and all passenger trains had been stopped. Since it was far too dangerous to travel north in a private coach, Anna was forced to wait until Thursday morning, May 7, and even then had to board an armed train that in her words "was prepared to fight its way through."[26] She traveled with her brother; her five-and-a-half-month-old daughter, Julia; the wife of the Presbyterian pastor in Richmond; and Hetty, the Jacksons' slave who had been Anna's own nurse from infancy.[27]

When she arrived at the Chandler house at noon, Anna was told she could not see her husband right away because the doctor was dressing his wound. Frustrated, she was "walking off" her "impatience" near the house when she saw a coffin being exhumed from the ground for reburial elsewhere. She inquired about it, only to be told, to her horror, that it was the body of her Lexington neighbor thirty-five-year-old Frank "Bull" Paxton, commander of the Stonewall Brigade, who had been shot in the chest and killed on the second day of battle. Anna remembered watching Paxton's young wife weep bitterly when he left home in the early days of the war; now he would be returning to her in Lexington as a corpse in a wooden box.[28]

When she was finally ushered into the sickroom, Anna was appalled by what she saw. Only eight days earlier she had seen a man, in her own words, "in the full flush of vigorous manhood . . . I never saw him look so handsome, so happy, or so noble."[29] Now she saw a flushed, gaunt figure in a morphine stupor with sunken eyes and a mutilated body. His face bore "angry scars" of hitting tree branches after Little Sorrel had bolted. He had trouble breathing. Nothing had prepared her for his appearance, which she said "wrung my soul with such grief and anguish as it had never before experienced." He had to be roused to speak to her, and though he "expressed much joy and thankfulness" at seeing her he quickly lapsed back into his opiated sleep.

She stayed with him for the next several days, leaving only to see her baby. He was now in a semiconscious state. When awakened, he was able to recognize people in the room, and would speak coherently for a few minutes before lapsing into unconsciousness again. "My darling, you must cheer up," he said, "and not wear a long face. I love cheerfulness and brightness in a sickroom." He always had something nice to say to her when he woke up: "My darling, you are very much loved," or "You are one of the most precious little wives in the world." He refused to see his daughter Julia, saying, "Not yet; wait til I feel better." Sometimes when he was still asleep he spoke as if still in battle: "Tell Major Hawks to send forward provisions to the men," or "Order A. P. Hill to prepare for action."[30]

He was no better on Friday or Saturday, though by now no fewer than eight doctors had been brought to consult, including Dr. S. B. Morrison, a cousin of Anna's and a surgeon in Jubal Early's division. Jackson was getting the best medical treatment available, which included drawing blood from his chest, applying mustard plasters, and regular doses of laudanum (a mixture of opium and whiskey). On Saturday he began to speak more about the possibility of his own death. "I see from the number of physicians that you think my condition dangerous," he said to McGuire, "but I thank God, if it is his will, that I am ready to go."[31] Still, he wasn't sure he wanted to depart just yet. "I do not believe I shall die at this time," he told Anna after she said she was worried his illness might be fatal. "I am persuaded the Almighty has yet a work for me to perform. I am not afraid to die. I am willing to abide [by] the will of my heavenly father."

He was fading fast. On Saturday night he asked Anna and her brother Joseph to sing hymns. They sang several, including one of his favorites, "Harwell":

> King of glory! Reign forever—
> Thine an everlasting crown;
> Nothing from thy love shall sever
> Those whom thou has made thine own;
> Happy objects of thy grace,
> Destined to behold thy face.
> Hallelujah! Hallelujah! Hallelujah!

Sunday morning, May 10, 1863, was bright and still. If there had been fleeting moments of hope for Jackson in the last few days, now there were none at all. His illness was crushing him. Doctors McGuire and Morrison examined him, agreed that he did not have long to live, and told Anna, who went into the sickroom to tell Jackson the news. He had told her earlier that, though he was ready to die whenever God might call him, he would prefer to have a few hours to prepare himself for the moment. It was a difficult task. Jackson had never believed that he was really going to die.

"Do you know that doctors say you must very soon be in heaven?" she asked. She repeated words to that effect several times, with no response. Then she said, "Do you not feel willing to acquiesce in God's allotment, if He wills you to go today?"

"I prefer it," he said in a weak voice, and then louder, "I prefer it."

"Well, before this day closes, you will be with the blessed Savior in His glory," Anna said.

Jackson replied, "I will be an infinite gainer to be translated."[32]

But he still struggled to accept his own death. Later Anna told him again that he would soon be in Paradise, to which he replied, "Oh, no! You are frightened, my child. Death is not so near. I may yet get well." Anna, who until now had mostly maintained a stolidly cheerful manner—at Jackson's request—now broke down sobbing. Jackson suddenly snapped out of his drug-induced daze and into focus. He called for Dr. McGuire, who came immediately to his bed. "Doctor," he said, "Anna informs me that you have told her that I am to die to-day. Is it so?" McGuire told him it was. Jackson stared at him for a moment, then said, "Very good, very good. It is all right."[33]

Still, there were matters to settle in the time he had left, and Anna did her best. She asked him where he wanted to be buried and he said, "Lexington, in my own plot." He told her he preferred that she live with her father in North Carolina. Finally she had the nurse Hetty bring his daughter, Julia, in to see him. In Anna's words,

As soon as they entered the door, he looked up, his countenance brightened with delight, and he never smiled more sweetly as he exclaimed: "Little darling! Sweet one!" She was seated on the bed by his side, and after watching her intently, with radiant smiles, for a few moments, he closed his eyes as if in prayer.[34]

Jackson slept. When he awoke, at about 1:00 p.m., he received a visit from Sandie Pendleton. The two men had a very close, almost father-son relationship. Jackson asked him who was preaching at headquarters that day, the Sabbath, May 10. Pendleton, barely in control of his emotions, told him that Reverend Lacy was. Jackson had forgotten that he had asked Lacy to do that, rather than stay with him. Then Pendleton said, in a wavering voice, "The whole army is praying for you, General." "Thank God," Jackson replied. "They are very kind." That included Robert E. Lee, who had attended the services and asked about Jackson. Lacy said that he was nearly hopeless. "Surely Jackson must recover," Lee replied. "God will not take him from us now that we need him so much." After the service, Lee approached Lacy again and said, "When a suitable occasion arises, tell him I prayed for him last night as I never prayed, I believe, for myself." Then he turned away, overcome by emotion.[35]

Jackson's mind now began to fail as the last of his strength ebbed. Sometimes he would awaken and seem to be clear in his mind. Sometimes he gave orders, as though on the battlefield again. During a moment of apparent clarity, McGuire offered him some brandy and water. He declined it, saying, "It will only delay my departure, and do no good; I want to preserve my mind, if possible, to the last." At one thirty he was told he had a few hours to live, and he replied, again, "Very good, it is all right."

Shortly after 3:15 p.m. he awoke in a delirium, crying, "A. P. Hill to prepare for action! Pass the infantry to the front rapidly. Tell Major Hawks . . ." Then he went abruptly silent. Soon "a smile of ineffable sweetness" came across his face and he said, "Let us cross over the river and rest under the shade of the trees." Then, without pain or struggle, McGuire wrote, "his spirit passed from the earth to the God who gave it."

CHAPTER FORTY-SIX

IMMORTALITY

⁓⁂⁓

Even before Lee's official announcement of Jackson's death, the news was surging through the camps of the Army of Northern Virginia. It did not seem possible that, just as the Confederacy was celebrating its greatest victory—indeed, the high-water mark of its existence—the great warrior was gone. The jolt was crueler because, until the moment of his death, the news coming from the sickroom at Guiney's Station had been uniformly good: Jackson was recovering. He would live to fight again. "The announcement of the death of General Jackson followed frequent assurances that he was doing well," a shaken Jefferson Davis wired Lee, "and though the loss was one which would have been deeply felt under any circumstances, the shock was increased by its suddenness." Davis, the man who had once disliked and distrusted Jackson and had actively worked to undermine his authority at Romney, now proclaimed his passing "a great national calamity."[1]

It was that, and more. In the camps "the sounds of merriment died away as if the Angel of Death himself had flapped his muffled wings over the troops," wrote Raleigh Colston. "A silence profound, mournful, stifling and oppressive as a funeral pall succeeded to the voices of cheerfulness."[2] Jackson, whose most notable personal attribute was his silence, now inspired a wave of deep, despairing quiet throughout the army and the Southern nation.

At the Chandler house, Anna Jackson could see or feel little of this. She could only observe the soldiers who had collected in the yard, hundreds of them with their hats off, many weeping openly. On the afternoon of his death Jackson was laid out on a table in the Chandlers' parlor. Because his uniform had been badly torn to treat his wounds, he had been dressed in an ordinary suit and dark military coat. His face was noticeably thinner than it had been in life, but it bore no trace of suffering. Anna found his appearance "more natural than I had dared hope."[3] She spent a sleepless night, with daughter Julia by her side, and later wrote of "the agony and anguish of those silent midnight hours, when the terrible reality of my loss and the desolation of widowhood forced itself upon me."[4] The next morning she came downstairs to find Jackson in an open pine coffin covered with lilies of the valley. As she gazed on his lifeless face, a distraught Sandie Pendleton came up and stood beside her and said, "God knows I would have died for him."[5]

Meanwhile, the official machinery of death was grinding into gear. The previous day Lee had sent a formal note to Confederate secretary of war James Seddon: "It becomes my melancholy duty to announce to you the death of General Jackson. He expired at 3:15 p.m. today. His body will be conveyed to Richmond in the train tomorrow, under charge of Major Pendleton. . . . Please direct an escort of honor to meet it at the depot, and that suitable arrangement be made for its disposition."[6] That morning a locomotive with a single car departed Guiney's Station for Richmond, forty-five miles distant. It contained Jackson's body, his wife, Anna, and daughter, Julia, the nurse, Hetty, Anna's friends Mrs. Chandler and Mrs. Hoge, and some of Jackson's staff. To spare herself the anguish of having to face crowds, Anna disembarked outside the city, where the wife of Virginia governor John Letcher conveyed her privately to the governor's mansion.

She was wise to have departed the train. By the time it entered the outskirts of Richmond, an immense crowd had gathered, the largest in the history of the city. The train slowed to a crawl, then proceeded ahead for two miles to the station, surrounded by thousands of bareheaded men and weeping women. Church bells tolled and minute guns split the air. Somewhere a band played a military dirge. All businesses in the city were closed. Black crape hung everywhere in the city. Even the mastheads of newspapers were draped in black.[7]

At the train depot Jackson's coffin was wrapped in a flag, in keeping with military tradition. But this was no ordinary flag. The Confederate Congress had recently authorized a new national flag consisting of the familiar crossed bars of the Army of Northern Virginia's battle flag superimposed on a pure white background. (The old "Stars and Bars"—the first Confederate national flag—was considered too easily mistaken for the Stars and Stripes in battle.) The first such flag had just been delivered, and was meant to fly from the roof of the capitol. But by Davis's orders it now became the shroud over Jackson's coffin. The coffin was transferred to a raven-plumed hearse drawn by two white horses, under military escort, to the governor's mansion. Jackson was embalmed, placed in a sealed metal casket with a glass panel so that his face could be seen, and laid out in the governor's reception room for viewing by friends, family, army officers, and official Richmond. There Anna saw her husband for the last time, and found this sealed-up version of him "disappointing and unsatisfactory." Outside, the bells of the city's churches tolled until sundown, while many citizens remained in the streets. "We have never before seen such an exhibition of heartfelt and general sorrow," wrote the *Richmond Dispatch*.[8] One of Jackson's chief mourners was Robert E. Lee, who could not be in Richmond because he believed Hooker might attack again. "It is a terrible loss," he told his son Custis. "I am grateful to Almighty God for having given us such a man." When he tried to tell W. N. Pendleton how he felt, he broke down in tears.

Among the many soldiers who came to pay their respects that evening was Richard B. Garnett, brigadier general of Longstreet's 1st Corps, who arrived at about midnight. Jackson had brought Garnett up on charges of retreating without orders at the Battle of Kernstown, and because the court-martial had never concluded, the stain on Garnett's reputation and career had remained. Jackson's treatment of Garnett was perhaps his worst moment, the charges he brought his least forgivable act. Yet now the brigadier stood before Jackson's casket with tears in his eyes. He turned to Pendleton and Douglas and said, "You know of the unfortunate breach between General Jackson and myself. I can never forget it, nor cease to regret it. But I do wish here to assure you that no one can lament his death more sincerely than I do. I believe that he did me a great injustice, but I believe also that he acted from the purest motives. He is dead. Who can fill his place?" Touched by Garnett's words, Pendleton asked him to be one of the pallbearers the next day. Garnett eagerly accepted.[9]

At eleven the next morning, while field artillery detonated and a band played the haunting "dead march" from Handel's oratorio *Saul*, Stonewall Jackson's funeral procession began. Once again the streets were dense with people, many of whom had been waiting for hours. The procession was led by a large column of soldiers, with reversed arms, then a battery with six cannons, the 44th Virginia Cavalry, and the band.[10] Then came the hearse with Jackson's coffin, drawn by four white horses, and flanked by generals serving as pallbearers: Richard S. Ewell, George E. Pickett, Richard B. Garnett, George H. Steuart, John H. Winder, Montgomery D. Corse, James L. Kemper, and Rear Admiral French Forrest,[11] and Jackson's riderless horse (not Little Sorrel), with boots reversed in the stirrups and tended by his loyal servant Jim Lewis.[12] Behind them followed the carriage bearing Anna, Julia, and Jefferson Davis, so disconsolate that he would apologize to a friend later that day for being so distracted: "You must forgive me," he said. "I am still staggering from a dreadful blow. I cannot think." Behind them were Jackson's staff officers (McGuire, Pendleton, Smith, Douglas, Morrison, Hawks, and Bridgford), then a vast contingent of official Richmond, including the governor, cabinet officers, congressmen, and local dignitaries.[13]

The procession moved slowly in a large rectangle through the city streets, starting at the Governor's Mansion and ending at the Confederate House of Representatives (the old Virginia Senate chamber) on Capitol Square. The coffin was placed on a bier in front of the Speaker's chair. That day more than twenty thousand people filed past it. After the doors had finally closed, a Confederate veteran arrived, demanding to be admitted. With tears in his eyes, he pointed to his amputated stump of an arm and said loudly, "By this arm which I lost for my country, I demand the privilege of seeing my General once more!" Governor Letcher, who happened to be standing nearby and heard the ruckus, let the man pass.[14]

When it was over, and the doors had shut, and the minute guns and bells had stopped sounding, people there spoke of an even worse feeling, of despondency and loss. "Officers and soldiers gathered to do last honors to their dead comrade and chieftain seemed suddenly to realize that they were to see 'Stonewall' Jackson no more forever, and fully to measure the great misfortune that had come upon them," wrote James Longstreet in his war memoir. "And as we turned away, we seemed to face a future bereft of much of its hopefulness."[15] A young woman who was visiting Richmond wrote simply, "I never saw human faces show such grief, almost despair."[16]

Elsewhere in the South there were similar public outpourings of sorrow and loss. "Everyone feels as though he had sustained a personal bereavement," wrote the *Courier* in Charleston, South Carolina, voicing a common feeling. "In the agony of this overwhelming sorrow we exclaim, 'Would God I had died for thee.'" In Knoxville, Tennessee, the *Register* said that "for the first time since the war began this whole nation weeps as one man. . . . There lives not a leader whose memory shall be cherished more sacredly than that of Stonewall Jackson and not one whose loss we could have borne with less fortitude." In Lexington, Jackson's great friend Maggie Junkin Preston, who had kept in close touch with him during the war (though none of Jackson's correspondence with her survives), wrote in her diary on May 12: "The grief in this community is intense; everybody is in tears. . . . How fearful the loss to the Confederacy! The people made an idol of him, and God has rebuked them. . . . Who thinks or speaks of victory? The word is scarcely ever heard. Alas! Alas! When is the end to be?"[17]

If Southerners were feeling a strange and unsettling emptiness that seemed to transcend the mere death of their beloved general, there was good reason. The country—North or South—had never in its short history experienced anything quite like the death of Stonewall Jackson. There had been a few big funeral processions: Benjamin Franklin drew twenty thousand in Philadelphia in 1790. About a hundred thousand came out in Washington after the death of sitting president Zachary Taylor in 1850. But neither death bore the urgency or meaning of Jackson; neither person was considered vital at the moment of his death to the survival of the country. By the time he died at eighty-four, Franklin was a sick, obese old man who had rarely been seen in public since he signed the Constitution in 1787. His great work in life was long finished. Zachary Taylor was an authentic war hero, but his passing had more effect on sectional politics than on anything vital to the fate of his country. Washington died at sixty-seven and was buried quietly and with no fanfare in 1799, as was Jefferson (eighty-three) in 1826. John Adams, who died at ninety the same year, drew four thousand to a church in Quincy, Massachusetts. William Henry Harrison, also a war hero, was the first sitting president to die in office and the first to get a state funeral. But it was a quiet, small-scale affair. None of these men died on the battlefield or during a war at the height of his fame with the very survival of his nation on the line. The closest parallel might have been George Washington's death on the battlefield at Yorktown in 1781. Like Jackson's death, it would have shattered the country's emotions and encouraged its enemies. Washington, of course, died in his bed at home eighteen years later. Though history seems to have forgotten it—in part because the Confederacy exists no more and in part because Northerners never counted it as a "nation" anyway—the fact is that Jackson triggered the first great national outpouring of grief for a fallen leader in the country's history.

In his 1865 biography of Jackson, the Reverend Robert Lewis Dabney, one of the South's leading theologians and Jackson's former chief of staff, reviewed the events in Richmond after his beloved general's death and concluded: "No such homage was ever paid to an American."[18] He was speaking strictly of May 12, 1863, the day when the long procession wound through the streets of Richmond and Jackson lay in state while thousands of people streamed by his coffin. What he meant by "homage" was not just the pageantry and ceremony but the pure depth of feeling, the great and overwhelming sorrow that everyone he saw felt. Of course, the feeling was the same throughout the Confederacy, as the large crowds that greeted Jackson's train en route to Lexington testified. Jackson's death touched the heart of every household in the South.

It was also overshadowed in history by another, more momentous passing almost exactly two years later: that of President Abraham Lincoln. The similarities between the two are striking, starting with their symbolism. All that wild grief was not just for the two leaders. Their deaths embraced the deaths of all soldiers on battlefields far away; their bodies became the bodies of young men who would never come home; their funerals stood in for the hundreds of thousands of funerals of dead soldiers that would never take place.[19] They were vessels into which the vast, pent-up heartache of the American nation, North and South, could be poured. The great effusions of anguish and sorrow were for the war itself, for the totality of its sadness and affliction. "We were not in any sense spectators," wrote Maggie's step-daughter of the crowd at the Lexington funeral, but she might have been speaking for the entire South. "We were heart-broken mourners, a clan bereft of its chieftain, a country in peril." Drew Gilpin Faust called Lincoln's procession "the national funeral." In Confederate terms, Jackson's was, too.[20]

There were other striking similarities. Both men died at the height of their power and achievement, and also at the high-water marks of their respective countries in the Civil War. Both men were transported back home—another idea fraught with emotional symbolism in a geographically dislocating war—by trains that wound through the countryside while grieving Americans clustered around and threw flowers. The scale, of course, was vastly different. The South did not have the concentrated populations the North did. New York was not the same as Lynchburg. In New York alone seventy-five thousand people followed Lincoln's cortege. But the ideas and feelings were the same. Both men were Christian heroes who believed that God was with them and against their enemies, and to their followers and supporters they seemed to be evidence that God, in fact, *was* on their side.

Though the manner of Lincoln's death was widely condemned in the South by everyone from Richard Ewell to John Singleton Mosby's troopers and the *Raleigh Standard*, much of the Southern reaction to his death had to do with fear of reprisals. Most Southerners believed, with good reason, that Lincoln would have treated them more fairly and more decently than Andrew Johnson and the radical Republicans.[21] Most still disliked or hated the man. But in the North there was widespread admiration for Jackson, for both his Christian piety and his warrior prowess. *Harper's Weekly* described him as "an honorable and conscientious man" who had hesitated to take sides until secession forced his hand. British author and America watcher Catherine Cooper Hopley wrote that Northerners "pride themselves that he was a fellow citizen of the republic, an *American*, independent of northern or southern birth."[22]

There were signs everywhere of the immense respect people of the North had for Jackson's bravery and skill as a soldier. "I rejoice at Stonewall Jackson's death as a gain to our cause," wrote Union brigadier general Gouverneur K. Warren, soon to be a hero of the Battle of Gettysburg, "and yet in my soldier's heart I cannot but see him as the best soldier of all this war, and grieve at his untimely end."[23] Wrote Union veteran and historian Charles Francis Adams Jr., "I am sure as Americans this [Union] army takes a pride in 'Stonewall' second only to that of the Virginians and Confederates. To have fought against him is next to having fought under him."

Northern feelings about Jackson were perhaps best summarized by John W. Forney, the prominent editor of the *Washington Chronicle*. "Stonewall Jackson was a great general, a brave soldier, a noble Christian, and a pure man. May God throw these great virtues against the sins of the secessionist, the advocate of a great national crime."[24] (Lincoln wrote Forney immediately to compliment him on the "excellent and manly" article in the *Chronicle* on "Stonewall" Jackson.[25]) Jackson's beloved, estranged father-in-law George Junkin, who had embraced the Union cause and moved north, voiced some of the same feelings. "I was completely unmanned," he wrote, of hearing the news of Jackson's death.

> I sought my state-room, to weep there. Is it wrong, is it treason, to mourn for a good and great, though clearly mistaken man? I cannot feel it to be so. I loved him dearly—but now—he is with *dear, dear* Ellie and the rest!

Oh, God! Oh give us grace to acquiesce in these terrible mysteries of Thy providence.[26]

It is curious that, though many Northerners could not forgive him for fighting, as they perceived it, to protect the institution of slavery, the Northern newspaper the *Independent*, edited by archabolitionist clergyman Henry Ward Beecher, voiced no such qualms. It said simply that Jackson was "Quiet, modest, brave, noble, honorable, and pure. He fought neither for reputation now, nor for future personal advancement."[27]

The most famous Northern view of Jackson came from the celebrated poet John Greenleaf Whittier, whose poem "Barbara Frietchie," published in 1864, became a national sensation. It described an almost entirely mythological incident from September 1862, when Jackson's troops were passing through Frederick, Maryland, on their way to the battles of Harpers Ferry and Antietam. As Whittier told it, after Jackson's troops had taken down all the American flags, the elderly Frietchie had retrieved one and flown it from her attic window. Seeing it, Jackson ordered his men to shoot it down, but Frietchie caught it as it fell and held it forth, crying, "Shoot, if you must, this old gray head / But spare your country's flag." Jackson's reaction followed:

> A shade of sadness, a blush of shame,
> Over the face of the leader came;
>
> The nobler nature within him stirred
> To life at that woman's deed and word:
>
> "Who touches a hair of yon gray head
> Dies like a dog! March on!" he said.
>
> All day long through Frederick street
> Sounded the tread of marching feet:
>
> All day long that free flag tost
> Over the heads of the rebel host.
>
> Ever its torn folds rose and fell
> On the loyal winds that loved it well;

> And through the hill-gaps sunset light
> Shone over it with a warm good-night.

None of this ever happened. But to the Northern nation—the *wartime* nation—the incident was as good as documented fact. What it said to them was that Jackson was a gentleman and a Christian and a decent person in spite of his role in killing and maiming tens of thousands of their young men. But it also said that he was, fundamentally, an *American*. It was his *Americanness* that had "stirred" in him and redeemed him.

The effect of Jackson's death on the fate of the Confederacy itself is harder to measure. There were many, such as historian John Esten Cooke, writing in 1865, who believed that "with his disappearance from the scene, the fortunes of the South, like her banner, began to droop." Jed Hotchkiss said that "nearly all regarded [Jackson's death] as the beginning of the end," a feeling that was reinforced by the disastrous Confederate loss at Gettysburg only two months later. For some this went beyond the unsettling feeling that the Confederate star of destiny had dimmed. One soldier in the 13th Virginia Regiment wrote that "men who had fought without flinching up to this time became timid and fearful of success."[28] Such feelings were by no means universal, and there was optimism still left in the South, though in shorter supply. But the great emotional lifts of Second Manassas and Chancellorsville would never be repeated. Lee would never again divide his army in that spectacular way, there would be no more flashing flank marches. Robert E. Lee would never again be quite so brilliant. After the war he commented only once on what might have happened if Jackson had lived. He was talking about Gettysburg. "Jackson would have held the heights which Ewell took on the first day," he told his brother. By that he meant that Jackson would have seized the high ground where the Union made its famous defensive stands: Cemetery Ridge, Big and Little Round Tops. There would have been no Pickett's charge because Jackson would have held that ground before the battle started. It's all hypothesis. We will never know.

At eight o'clock on the morning of May 13, 1863, a train on the Virginia Central Railroad carrying Jackson's remains left Richmond for the journey back to his final resting place in Lexington. At Gordonsville the cars were shifted to the Orange and Alexandria line. At every stop along the way, large, silent crowds came out to meet the train. Many of the people wept quietly; others handed flowers through the windows of the train, and there were soon enormous heaps and mounds of flowers and wreaths around the casket. In the days since Jackson's death, an interest bordering on obsession had developed to see the general's baby daughter. She not only had to be seen by the mourners, but touched and handled as well. Her presence seemed to make them feel better. This phenomenon had begun in Richmond while Jackson lay in state in the capitol and Anna received visitors in a darkened room in the Governor's Mansion. "So numerous were the requests to see her," wrote Anna, "that Hetty, finding the child growing worried at so much notice and handling, sought a refuge beyond the reach of the crowd . . . bewailing that 'people would give her baby no rest.' "[29] Now, on the train, which stopped only for fuel and water and not to embark or disembark passengers, the clamoring was so loud that, in Anna's words, little Julia "was handed in and out of the car windows to be kissed."[30]

At Lynchburg, where the traveling party left the train and boarded a canal boat for Lexington, citizens once again thronged to see Jackson's casket. The city mounted a full tribute. As in Richmond, minute guns fired and bells tolled, and thousands of people came forward and silently offered flowers. Fifteen hundred convalescent soldiers limped forth to join the procession that followed the casket to the James River. The boat headed upstream at a laborious pace, with two mules pulling it along from the bank, picked up the North Fork of the James, and finally arrived in Lexington at sunset on May 14, where the entire corps of cadets from the Virginia Military Institute was there, in full dress, to meet it.

Jackson's body was taken by artillery caisson to the VMI barracks, where he was laid out in his old lecture room, near his old chair and the cases containing his scientific teaching equipment.[31] Superintendent Francis H. Smith ordered the lecture room draped in mourning for six months, and half-hour guns to be fired throughout the next day. Far into that evening, men, women, and children from the town and country came to visit Jackson for the last time. That night cadets stood guard over his casket. The next day, May 15, his remains were taken in another long procession to the First Presbyterian Church, where he had been a deacon and had run the black Sunday school. There, before an overflow crowd of more than four thousand—the wartime population of the town was less than two thousand—Jackson's old friend and mentor Dr. William S. White conducted the memorial service. He read from First Corinthians—"The last enemy that shall be destroyed is death"—and then gave a sermon based on letters he had received from Jackson during the war, in particular one after White's son's death. "The death of your noble son and my much esteemed friend, Hugh, must have been a severe blow to you," Jackson had written, "yet we have the sweet assurance that, whilst we mourn his loss to the country, to the church, and to ourselves, all has been gain for him . . . that inconceivable glory to which we are looking forward is already his."[32] It was as though Jackson were telling his country, from beyond the grave, how to think about his own death. From the church the procession re-formed and, led by eight companies of VMI cadets, with Jackson's tearful servant Jim Lewis leading the riderless horse, moved to the Lexington graveyard, where Jackson was buried next to his and Anna's daughter Mary Graham and close to his first wife, Ellie, and their stillborn son. In life he had known the place well. He had gone there countless times after Ellie's death, racked by grief and hopelessness and feeling that God "had left me to mourn in human desolation." He had wanted desperately to join her. He believed she was in a better place, a place where they would both be granted what he had once called "an unending immortality of happiness."[33]

ACKNOWLEDGMENTS

I would like to express my gratitude and appreciation for the help given me on this manuscript by Peter Cozzens, John Hennessy, and Robert K. Krick. I admire them greatly as historians and writers and they have been more than generous in helping me avoid many of the pitfalls and traps that await novice Civil War historians. The book is much better for their help. I would also like to thank H. W. Brands for his advice on researching the Civil War era. It was invaluable and saved me much time. Drury Wellford, former photo archivist for the Museum of the Confederacy—and an old *Time* magazine colleague—brought wonderful expertise to the task of finding photographs and images for the book. Finally, I would like to thank battlefield scout Peter Maratta, who helped me understand the terrain and troop movements at the battles of First and Second Manassas and Antietam.

OTHER LIVES, OTHER DESTINIES

Jackson touched many lives during the war, from his immediate family to his students at VMI, the residents of Lexington, and friends and colleagues in the army. Many of these people never lived to see the end of the war; some lived well into the twentieth century. Here is what became of them.

FAMILY AND FRIENDS

ANNA AND JULIA JACKSON

Following her husband's death Anna lived in Lincoln County, North Carolina, northwest of Charlotte, with her parents. She later moved to Charlotte and Baltimore, where her daughter, Julia, received formal schooling. Anna lived in Richmond and spent summers in Lexington (though not in the Washington Street house) and eventually settled in Charlotte, where she lived out her life as the Widow of the Confederacy, a highly visible and beloved figure in the South who attended many Confederate reunions and dedications of monuments, including several to her husband. She was awarded a pension by the North Carolina legislature in 1907, which she used to start a school for wayward boys. In response to a request from her daughter, Julia, she wrote a comprehensive biography of her husband (with help from friends), which stands today as one of the best sources on the subject. Anna died in Charlotte in 1915 at age eighty-three. Julia—who changed her middle name from "Laura" to "Thomas"—married William Christian in 1885 and had two children, a daughter and a son. She died tragically of typhoid fever at age twenty-six in 1889. Her daughter—Stonewall Jackson's granddaughter—Julia Jackson Christian Preston, died in 1991 at age 104.

LAURA JACKSON ARNOLD

Laura remained a strong Unionist and kept her distance from the Jackson family for the rest of her life. She was one of two women awarded membership in a Union veterans association known as the Grand Army of the Republic. Anna wrote to her after her brother Thomas's death, but we know nothing of any other contact. She divorced her Confederate-leaning husband in 1870. Because of poor health she spent nearly thirty years in a private sanatorium near Columbus, Ohio. She died at age eighty-five at the home of her daughter-in-law in Buckhannon, West Virginia, in 1911.

MARGARET JUNKIN PRESTON

Maggie had a happy marriage to John T. L. Preston and went on to become one of the most prominent poets in the South, male or female. She maintained friendships and literary correspondence with Robert Browning, Alfred Lord Tennyson, Henry Wadsworth Longfellow, and Christina Rossetti, among others. She published prose and poetry mostly in magazines, including *Harper's* and the *Southern Literary Messenger*. She wrote both prose and poetry about her beloved friend Thomas Jackson. She became blind in her old age and died in Baltimore in 1897 at seventy-six.

GEORGE JUNKIN

The father of Ellie and Maggie Junkin had been the first president of Lafayette College in Easton, Pennsylvania, and president of Miami University in Oxford, Ohio, before assuming the post of president of Washington College in 1848. He left that job in May 1861 at age seventy-one amid controversy over his pro-Union and anti-secession views. He moved to Philadelphia and wrote several tracts attacking secession. He was heartbroken over the death of his former son-in-law Thomas, who was also his close friend. He died in Philadelphia in 1868.

JIM LEWIS

Devastated by Jackson's death, Lewis went to work for Sandie Pendleton and served him until Pendleton's death in 1864. He returned to his hometown of Lexington—where he was believed to have attended Jackson's Sunday school—and died there.

THE REVEREND DR. WILLIAM S. WHITE

White continued as pastor of the Presbyterian church in Lexington until his retirement in 1866. Upon his death at seventy-three in 1873, Maggie Preston wrote a memorial poem for him.

STAFF

SANDIE PENDLETON AND KATE CORBIN

After Jackson's death, Pendleton served under Richard Ewell and eventually as chief of staff to Jubal Early. In December 1863 he married Kate Corbin at Moss Neck Manor. He was with Early when the latter was defeated by Union general Phil Sheridan at the Third Battle of Winchester on September 19, 1864, in the Shenandoah Valley. In a follow-up battle, Pendleton was fatally wounded in the abdomen. He died on September 23, 1864. A month later, Kate gave birth to a son, who died of diphtheria in 1865. Kate later remarried. Kate, Sandie, and their child are buried in the cemetery at Lexington near Jackson.

HUNTER MCGUIRE

McGuire rose to become the most prominent physician in Virginia, where he founded a number of hospitals, including what would become the Medical College of Virginia in Richmond. He was president of the American Medical Association. After the war he wrote articles and gave speeches about Jackson, for whom he was a staunch advocate. There is a statue of McGuire on the grounds of the Virginia state capitol. He died in 1900.

ALEXANDER ROBINSON BOTELER

Boteler returned to his farm near Shepherdstown, now West Virginia, and combined a life of farming with public service, which included appointments to the 1876 Centennial Commission, the Tariff Commission, and to a post as assistant attorney in the Justice Department. He was a beloved and colorful figure in his hometown. He died in 1892.

HENRY KYD DOUGLAS

Douglas later served as chief of staff and assistant adjutant general to Generals Edward Johnson, John B. Gordon, Jubal Early, J. H. Pegram, and John A. Walker. As a colonel with the 13th and 49th Virginia Regiments, he was wounded six times. After being severely wounded at Gettysburg, he was captured and imprisoned until March 18, 1864, when he was paroled. He was treasurer of a committee of the Stonewall Brigade that raised more than $6,000 to erect a monument to Stonewall Jackson. After the war he practiced law in Winchester, Virginia, and later in Hagerstown, Maryland. He died in 1903 at sixty-five years of age. Douglas noted in his memoir that Jackson "while living, never had a staff member killed or wounded until Chancellorsville, where he fell, and as he had never spared them or himself it was often remarked upon." But when the "protection of his presence" was removed, all that changed. Douglas listed the following present or former staff subsequently killed or wounded: J. K. Boswell, Stapleton Crutchfield, E. F. Paxton, W. S. H. Baylor, Edward Willis, J. R. Jones, A. J. Jackson, Sandie Pendleton, Joseph G. Morrison, and Charles Marshall.

JAMES POWER SMITH

Jackson's young aide returned to the Union Theological Seminary and was ordained a Presbyterian minister. He served as pastor at the Presbyterian church in Fredericksburg for twenty-three years. He later shared in the dedication of the large Jackson Monument in Richmond. He also dedicated a site on the Lacy farm near Chancellorsville, where the resourceful Tucker Lacy had buried Jackson's arm after it was amputated. (The "grave" can be visited today.) Smith died in 1923 at eighty-six, the last surviving member of Jackson's staff.

ROBERT L. DABNEY

Dabney's first project after the war was a biography of Stonewall Jackson, which he published in 1865. Though he was deeply biased in favor of his beloved general, the book is full of useful material and is still in print today. After the war Dabney remained one of the most prominent intellectuals in Southern Presbyterianism. He taught at Union Theological Seminary in Virginia and later at the University of Texas. He continued to hold pro-slavery opinions, and spoke widely on Jackson and the Confederacy. He died in 1898 at age seventy-seven.

JOSEPH GRAHAM MORRISON

Anna Jackson's brother served in the 57th North Carolina Infantry and was promoted to captain. He was wounded and lost a foot after the Battle of Petersburg. He contracted tuberculosis and after the war spent four years recuperating in California. He returned to build a successful career as a planter in North Carolina, where he also ran the Mariposa Cotton Mills. He eventually reclaimed the family home where he and his sister Anna had grown up. He died in 1906 at age sixty-three.

CONFEDERATE GENERALS

ROBERT E. LEE

Lee became president of Washington College (now Washington and Lee) in Lexington in October 1865 and held that position until his death from pneumonia, following a stroke, in 1870, at age sixty-three. His famous name helped him raise funds and transform Washington into one of the South's leading colleges. As president he lived in the same magnificent Greek Revival mansion where Jackson and his first wife, Ellie—the daughter of the college's then president George Junkin—resided during their marriage. It is now known as the Lee-Jackson House. Lee, like Jackson, is buried in Lexington. Though he had applied for a pardon and restoration of his citizenship after the war, it was never granted to him. William Seward, who had no intention of approving Lee's request, had given Lee's application to a friend as a souvenir, and thus it disappeared for more than a hundred years. In 1970 Lee's "Amnesty Oath" was discovered and in 1975 President Gerald Ford finally restored Lee's full status as an American citizen.

A. P. HILL

Hill was promoted to lieutenant general after Jackson's death and commanded the Army of Northern Virginia's 3rd Corps in the Gettysburg campaign. He was killed during the Union offensive at the Third Battle of Petersburg in April 1865.

D. H. HILL

The prickly, hypercritical Hill was not given a corps command in the reorganization that followed Jackson's death. In 1863 he played an important role in the Confederate triumph at Chickamauga, after which he was openly critical of General Braxton Bragg for failing to exploit the victory. His criticism landed him on the sidelines for the rest of the war. In postbellum years Jackson's brother-in-law was quite successful. He edited the popular magazine *The Land That We Love*, and served as the first president of the University of Arkansas, from 1877 to 1884. He then became president of Middle Georgia Military and Agricultural College (now called Georgia Military College), where he served for five years. He died in Charlotte in 1889 at age sixty-eight and was buried at Davidson College, where his father-in-law, Robert Hall Morrison—father of both Isabella Hill and Mary Anna Jackson—had been the institution's first president.

JEB STUART

The magical early days of his dominance over the Union cavalry ended at the Battle of Brandy Station on June 9, 1863, when he was barely able to hold the field against the Union force under Alfred Pleasonton in what amounted to the largest mounted battle in American history. Less than a month later, Stuart fell out of touch with headquarters in the crucial days leading to the Battle of Gettysburg. He arrived late on that battle's second day and was repulsed by Union cavalry on the third. He fought his final battle on May 11, 1864, successfully checking Union general Philip Sheridan's advance toward the city of Richmond. Stuart was shot by a dismounted Michigan cavalryman with a pistol and died the day after the battle, May 12. He was thirty-one years old.

RICHARD B. GARNETT

Garnett served as a pallbearer in Jackson's procession in Richmond. Two months later, he was killed commanding a brigade in George Pickett's famous charge at the Battle of Gettysburg on July 3, 1863, at age forty-five.

RICHARD S. EWELL

Ewell did not fare nearly so well after he lost Jackson. In the wake of the latter's death, he was promoted to lieutenant general in charge of most of Jackson's old corps, making him the third-ranking officer in the army after Lee and Longstreet. Though Ewell performed well at the beginning of the Gettysburg campaign, winning the Second Battle of Winchester and capturing a garrison of four thousand men, he did poorly at Gettysburg. After a victory on the battle's first day, he declined to press his advantage, which meant that the Union forces ended up holding the key high-ground positions south of town, which eventually included Cemetery Ridge, Little Round Top, and Big Round Top. Jackson, in a similar situation, likely would have taken that ground, which would have radically changed what happened on the battlefield the next day. Lee later said as much. Ewell led his corps in the Battle of the Wilderness and performed well, but lapsed again at the Battle of Spotsylvania Courthouse. Lee reassigned him to the garrison of Richmond. He surrendered that force a few days before Lee surrendered at Appomattox. After the war he turned to farming at his wife's property near Spring Hill, Tennessee, and leased a successful cotton plantation in Mississippi. He was president of the board of trustees of the Columbia Female Academy. He doted on his grandchildren. He died of pneumonia at age fifty-four in 1872.

JAMES LONGSTREET

Though Longstreet strenuously objected to Lee's tactics at Gettysburg, it was his men who mounted the unsuccessful attack on the Confederate left on day two (including Little Round Top) and his men who went forward in Pickett's famous charge, the doomed offensive that resulted in a Confederate defeat. Longstreet later fought well in the Confederate victory at the Battle of Chickamauga, and was seriously wounded during the Battle of the Wilderness in 1864. After the war his criticism of Lee's tactics and his support of the Republican Party—especially the 1868 presidential campaign of Ulysses S. Grant—led to attacks on his character in the South by such "Lost Cause" proponents as Jubal Early and W. N. Pendleton. Grant appointed him surveyor of customs for New Orleans. He wrote an eight-hundred-page memoir of the war, published in 1895. He later served as US ambassador to Turkey and railroad commissioner before his death in 1904. His second, much younger, wife, Helen, died in 1962.

JUBAL EARLY

Early fought at Gettysburg, the Shenandoah Valley, Spotsylvania Courthouse, and Cold Harbor. He emerged as one of Lee's better generals. When the Army of Northern Virginia surrendered on April 9, 1865, Early escaped to Texas, then proceeded to Mexico, Cuba, and eventually to Toronto, Canada, where he briefly settled and wrote a memoir of the war. Pardoned in 1868, he returned to Virginia to practice law and soon became the most vocal of the unreconstructed rebels. His writing helped launch the so-called Lost Cause movement, whose main tenets were that the North had beaten the South not by military skill but because it was able to field vastly more men and weaponry; that the war was about defending states' rights against Northern aggression; that slavery was a benign institution; that Reconstruction was an attempt to destroy the Southern way of life; and that the leaders of the Confederate armies were principled, Christian men in contrast to Union leaders such as Grant, Sherman, and Sheridan, who showed their low moral character in their brutally destructive marches through Georgia, South Carolina, and the Shenandoah Valley. The principal heroes of the Lost Cause were Robert E. Lee and Stonewall Jackson; its principal villain was James Longstreet. Early died in 1894 at age seventy-seven after falling down a flight of stairs in Lynchburg, Virginia.

UNION GENERALS

GEORGE MCCLELLAN

After being relieved of command by Lincoln in November 1862, McClellan entered politics and in 1864 won the Democratic nomination for president. He ran against Lincoln on an antiwar platform and lost. Following the war he worked at various engineering jobs, including as chief engineer for the New York City Department of Docks. He was president of a railroad. In 1878 he was elected governor of New Jersey, a position he held for a single term, until 1881. He spent much of his last years traveling and writing his memoirs, which were published posthumously. He died unexpectedly of a heart attack in Orange, New Jersey, in 1885 at age fifty-eight.

AMBROSE BURNSIDE

Burnside's war career after his defeat at Fredericksburg was spotty. Exiled to the Department of the Ohio, he engineered the successful defense of Knoxville. He commanded the Union 9th Corps in the overland campaign, which included the Battles of the Wilderness, Spotsylvania Courthouse, North Anna, and Cold Harbor. At the siege of Petersburg he famously approved a plan for Union coal miners to tunnel under a Confederate fort and blow it up. Though the mine's explosion indeed blew a huge hole in the Confederate lines, Burnside's men were unable to take advantage of it, a failure for which he was unfairly blamed. After the war he did rather well. He was president of three railroads and served three one-year terms as governor of Rhode Island. He was elected a US senator in 1874 and served until 1881, when he died suddenly of angina at age fifty-seven.

WILLIAM H. FRENCH

Old Blinky—Jackson's nemesis in Florida and beyond—served in the Gettysburg campaign. His reputation was ruined for good in the Mine Run campaign in November 1863 when he was harshly criticized by General George Meade for being too slow to pursue an advantage. Though he saw no more combat, he remained with the army, serving on various military boards in Washington. From 1865 to 1872 he commanded artillery on the Pacific Coast. In 1875 he was appointed commander of Fort McHenry. He retired in 1880 and died in 1881 at age sixty-six.

JOSEPH HOOKER

After his defeat at Chancellorsville, Hooker moved the Army of the Potomac north to block Lee's invasion of Maryland and Pennsylvania. When he impulsively offered his resignation after a minor squabble, Lincoln and Stanton were quick to accept it, replacing him with the man they preferred anyway, George Meade. Hooker was transferred to the western theater, where he saw success at the Battle of Lookout Mountain. Later he served well in Sherman's 1864 Atlanta campaign. From 1864 until his retirement from the army in 1868, Hooker served as commander of various Federal departments. He suffered from poor health in the postwar years and was partially paralyzed by a stroke. He died in 1879 at age sixty-four.

IRVIN MCDOWELL

After the defeat at Second Manassas, McDowell spent two years in effective exile from Union military leadership. He remained in the army, and spent the years from 1864 to his retirement in 1882 in a series of regional army commands that included the Department of the Pacific, the Departments of the East and South, and the Division of the Pacific. In 1879 a presidential board of review issued a report on the Battle of Second Manassas, recommending a pardon for General Fitz John Porter. The report was harshly critical of McDowell, arguing, among other points, that he had failed to forward information to either Pope or Porter about James Longstreet's position. After his retirement, McDowell became parks commissioner in San Francisco, helping to lay out parts of Golden Gate Park. He died in 1885 at age sixty-six.

JOHN POPE

Pope's Civil War career did not end with the fiasco at Second Manassas, nor did it suffer over the long term. He spent the remainder of the war fighting Indians, first in the Department of the Northwest. In 1864 he became commander of the Department of Missouri, and by war's end the Military

Division of the Missouri, the largest geographical command in the United States. He was a prominent departmental commander during the Indian Wars. Like Irvin McDowell, he rose to the rank of major general in the Regular Army, of which there were only six. His final posting was in California in the Division of the Pacific. Also like McDowell, his reputation was damaged in 1879 by the federal report on the Battle of Second Manassas that concluded that he and not Fitz John Porter bore most of the blame for the defeat. He retired in 1886 and died in 1892 at the Ohio Soldiers' Home near Sandusky at the age of seventy.

NATHANIEL BANKS

Banks's military career continued to sputter after Second Manassas. He was briefly given command of defense forces in Washington, then shipped south to New Orleans to assume command of the Department of the Gulf. There he performed poorly in several military campaigns, though he did have the distinction of commanding the first African-American troops in combat. In 1864 he was sent back to Washington for the rest of the war. He spent the rest of his life doing what he always did best: politics. He served in Congress from 1865 to 1879, then as US marshal for Massachusetts—a patronage job—until 1888, and again in Congress for a single term, from 1888 to 1890. He died in September 1894 at age seventy-eight. His death made national headlines.

MISCELLANY

LITTLE SORREL

Lost after the Battle of Chancellorsville, the horse Jackson called "Fancy" was eventually recovered by a Confederate soldier and sent to Virginia governor John Letcher, who in turn sent him to live with Anna Jackson in North Carolina. The horse became a much-loved pet, famous for using his mouth to lift latches and let himself out of his stable. In Anna Jackson's memoir she wrote that he would "go deliberately to the doors of all the other horses and mules, liberate each one, and then march off with them all behind him . . . to the green fields of grain around the farm." Fences proved no obstacle to him, either. He would use his mouth and muzzle to lift off fence rails until the fence was low enough to jump over. He later lived at VMI, where he grazed on the parade ground and was a favorite of cadets, and spent his last days at the Old Confederate Soldiers' Home. His hide was stuffed and mounted and can be seen today at VMI.

SHENANDOAH VALLEY

What Sherman's men did to Georgia is more famous, but what happened to the lovely Shenandoah Valley was just as horrific, and a great deal more systematic. The valley's unfortunate location made it an almost continuous battleground. It was the scene of three major campaigns and some twenty-three battles. Winchester alone changed hands an estimated seventy-two times. The worst of it came in the fall of 1864, when Union general Philip Sheridan's army embarked on a deliberate campaign to destroy the valley's food-producing capacity during what was a bumper year. In a two-week period Sheridan's soldiers burned barns, mills, and standing crops. They burned at least fifty houses to the ground. They rounded up livestock and killed them or drove them away. Much of the devastation wrought by Sherman's soldiers on his march to the sea was haphazard or accidental. Here it was all quite deliberate, and every bit as destructive. By the end of it much of the valley was a smoking ruin.

VMI

On May 15, 1864, the cadet corps from VMI fought as a unit for the first time, at the Battle of New Market in the Shenandoah Valley. Ten were killed and forty-seven wounded. Less than a month later, the institute was shelled and burned by Union troops under David Hunter. Destroyed were the barracks where Stonewall Jackson taught, the mess hall, two faculty residences, and the library—all but two buildings. The cadets were relocated to Richmond. A total of 1,800 VMI cadets fought in the war (16 for the North), and of them 250 were killed.

STONEWALL BRIGADE

Jackson's most famous brigade later fought in the Gettysburg, Mine Run, and Wilderness campaigns. When its commander Colonel James Walker was wounded at Spotsylvania, the brigade was disbanded and dispersed to other units. They continued to fight in the Shenandoah Valley Campaign of 1864, at Petersburg, and at Appomattox. By the war's end only 210 of the 6,000 men who had served in the brigade during the war were still under arms.

NOTES

PROLOGUE: LEGENDS OF SPRING

1. A. R. Boteler, "Stonewall Jackson in Campaign of 1862," *Southern Historical Society Papers,* September 1915, vol. 40, p. 176.
2. Ibid., p. 177.
3. Ibid., p. 176.
4. Gary Ecelbarger, *Three Days in the Shenandoah,* p. 3; he notes that the army was the largest in the Western Hemisphere.
5. Douglas Southall Freeman, *R. E. Lee: A Biography.*
6. James McPherson, *Crossroads of Freedom: Antietam* (Oxford, New York: Oxford University Press, 2002), p. 32.
7. Allan Nevins, *War for the Union: 1862–1863,* vol. 2, p. 108.
8. Ibid., p. 32.
9. Ibid., p. 39.
10. Ibid.
11. Boteler, "Stonewall Jackson in Campaign of 1862," p. 177.
12. Henry A. Chambers diary, June 19, 1862, North Carolina Department of Archives and History. Cited in James I. Robertson, *Stonewall Jackson: The Man, the Legend, the Soldier,* p. 459.
13. Biographical Sketch in Alexander Robinson Boteler Papers, Duke University.
14. Boteler, "Stonewall Jackson in Campaign of 1862," p. 177.
15. Ibid.
16. Chambers diary.
17. Ibid.
18. Letter from Jackson to Thomas Taylor Munford, June 17, 1862. Manuscript in Huntington Library, Pasadena, CA.
19. J. William Jones, "Reminiscences of the Army of Northern Virginia," *Southern Historical Society Papers,* vol. 9, p. 364.
20. Letter from Edwin Stanton to George McClellan, June 25, 1861; cited in Jubal A. Early, *War Memoirs,* p. 75; Stanton had reports placing Jackson at four locations, one of which was Gordonsville with forty thousand men.
21. Jedediah Hotchkiss Papers, Library of Congress, Washington, DC. Anecdote by J. William Jones, former chaplain in Jackson's army.
22. Hunter McGuire, "1897 Address to R. E. Lee Camp," *Southern Historical Society Papers,* June 23, 1897.
23. Drew Gilpin Faust, *This Republic of Suffering,* p. 3.
24. *Richmond Whig,* June 11, 1862, and June 12, 1862.

25. "A Great General," *Richmond Daily Dispatch*, June 18, 1862.
26. Douglas Southall Freeman, *Lee's Lieutenants*, vol. 1, p. 303.
27. Allen C. Redwood, "With Stonewall Jackson," *Scribner's Monthly* 18, no. 2 (June 1879).

CHAPTER ONE: AWAY TO RICHMOND

1. Lenoir Chambers, *Stonewall Jackson*, p. 22.
2. Napier Bartlett, *A Soldier's Story of the War*, p. 16.
3. G. H. M. Cloverlick Recollection, February 16, 1880, *Southern Historical Society Papers*, vol. 9, 1881, pp. 44–45.
4. Ibid.
5. Dabney Herndon Maury, "General T. J. Jackson: Incidents in the Remarkable Career of the Great Soldier," *Richmond Times*, January 23, 1898.
6. Board of Visitors Minutes, VMI Archive.
7. Raleigh Colston, *Reminiscences*, Raleigh Edward Colston Papers, Southern Historical Collection, University of North Carolina.
8. Colonel William Couper, *One Hundred Years at V.M.I.*, vol. 2, p. 98.
9. "Recollections of Charles Copland Wight, 1841–1897," manuscript, Wight Papers, Virginia Historical Society.
10. Sherman, on hearing that South Carolina had seceded in December 1860, remarked to a Southern friend: "You people of the South don't know what you are doing. This country will be drenched in blood, and God only knows how it will end. . . . You people speak so lightly of war; you don't know what you're talking about. War is a terrible thing!"
11. Mary Anna Jackson, *Memoirs of Stonewall Jackson*, p. 143.
12. Thomas Jackson Arnold, *Early Life and Letters of General Thomas J. Jackson* (London and Edinburgh: Fleming H. Revell Company, 1916), p. 294.
13. Jackson, *Memoirs of Stonewall Jackson*, p. 141.
14. Ibid.
15. Margaret J. Preston, "Reminiscences of Stonewall Jackson," *Century Magazine*, October 1886, pp. 927–936.
16. Robert L. Dabney, *Life and Campaigns of Lieutenant-General Thomas J. Stonewall Jackson*, p. 154.
17. Ibid.
18. Jackson, *Memoirs of Stonewall Jackson*, p. 144.
19. January 26, 1861, letter from Thomas J. Jackson to Thomas Jackson Arnold, in Thomas Jackson Arnold, *The Early Life and Letters of General Thomas J. Jackson*, p. 294; Jackson papers, West Virginia University.
20. Ibid.

CHAPTER TWO: THE IMPERFECT LOGIC OF WAR

1. The acquisitions stack up as follows: the Louisiana Purchase—828,000 square miles; the Mexican Cession—525,000 square miles; the annexation of the Oregon Territory—260,000-plus square miles.
2. Mary Anna Jackson, *Memoirs of Stonewall Jackson*, pp. 139–140. Anna wrote of Jackson, "In politics he had always been a Democrat, but he was never a very strong partisan, and took no part in the political contest of 1860 except to cast his vote for John C. Breckenridge. . . ."; Robertson, *Stonewall Jackson*, p. 197. Here Robertson makes the point that "Jackson was aware of the growing schism between North and South. He was a Democrat with inherent respect for states' rights. . . . That is probably as much thought as Jackson

gave to the national picture. Marriage, the loss of another child, a new home, persistent illnesses, business ventures, renewed church activities—these were matters of greater concern to the major."

3. Allan Nevins, *The War for the Union,* vol. 1, *The Improvised War, 1861–1862,* p. 10.

4. Jackson's view of this was expressed in his January 26, 1861, letter to his nephew Thomas Jackson Arnold. "If the free states . . . should endeavor to subjugate us, and thus *excite our slaves to servile insurrection in which our Families will be murdered without quarter or mercy . . .*" (italics mine). The reference is to Brown's raid. Like many Southerners, this was how Jackson saw it.

5. U.S. Census shows 490,865 slaves in Virginia in 1860, and a free population of 1,105,453.

6. William Couper, *One Hundred Years at V.M.I.,* vol. 2, p. 17.

7. Ibid., p. 11.

8. Dispatch from Charleston of November 26, 1859, *Richmond Daily Dispatch.*

9. Letter from Thomas Jonathan Jackson to Mary Anna Jackson, November 28, 1859, in Jackson, *Memoirs of Stonewall Jackson,* p. 130.

10. Couper, *One Hundred Years at V.M.I.,* vol. 2, p. 15.

11. Letter from Jackson to his wife, December 2, 1861, in Jackson, *Memoirs of Stonewall Jackson,* p. 131.

12. For an excellent treatment of the John Brown material, see Robert E. McGlone, *John Brown's War Against Slavery.*

13. James M. McPherson, *Battle Cry of Freedom,* p. 208.

14. *New York Herald Tribune,* November 3, 1859; report of Brown's courtroom speech.

15. McPherson, *Battle Cry of Freedom,* p. 210, citing other sources.

16. Robert Lewis Dabney, *The Life and Campaigns of Lieutenant-General Thomas J. Stonewall Jackson,* p. 144.

17. Henry Kyd Douglas, *I Rode with Stonewall,* p. 3.

18. McPherson, *Battle Cry of Freedom,* p. 211.

19. Susan Leigh Blackford and Charles Minor Blackford, *Letters from Lee's Army, or Memoirs of Life In and Out of the Army in Virginia During the War Between the States,* pp. 2–3.

20. Couper, *One Hundred Years at V.M.I.,* vol. 2, pp. 78–79; James I. Robertson, *Stonewall Jackson: The Man, the Legend, the Soldier,* p. 208.

21. Robertson, *Stonewall Jackson,* p. 213, citing David X. Junkin, *The Reverend George Junkin,* pp. 518–526.

22. *Recollections of Charles Copland Wight, 1841–1897.* Manuscript at the Virginia Historical Society, Wight Papers, Richmond, VA.

23. Couper, *One Hundred Years at V.M.I.,* vol. 2, p. 79.

24. In his 1939 history of VMI, Couper cites a story in the *Valley Star* newspaper of April 18, 1861, that lists "Maj. Colston," "J.W. [sic] Brockenbrough," and "J.W. Massie" as speakers. Colston taught French at VMI, Massie taught math at VMI, and Brockenbrough was a state judge.

25. Couper, *One Hundred Years at V.M.I.,* vol. 2, p. 81. As Couper points out in his voluminous note on this subject, there are so many accounts of the cadet riot that it is difficult to tell what actually happened. Charles Copland Wight, who was there (see his manuscript at the Virginia Historical Society, Wight Papers), left a fair account; Couper did by far the best research. It remains a bit confusing.

26. Wight Recollections, manuscript.

27. William S. White, *Rev. William S. White, D.D., and His Times,* p. 173.

28. Randolph Barton, "Stonewall Jackson," *Southern Historical Society Papers,* vol. 38, p. 273.

29. *Official Records*, Series 3, vol. 1, pp. 67–78.
30. Letter from Thomas B. Webber to his mother, June 15, 1861; also cited by Shelby Foote in *The Civil War*, p. 65, and by James McPherson in *Battle Cry of Freedom*, p. 311.
31. William Thomas Poague, *Gunner with Stonewall*, p. 4.

CHAPTER THREE: FATE INTERVENES

1. G.F.R. Henderson, *Stonewall Jackson and the American Civil War*, p. 105; for a good general description of the early recruits at Richmond, see also Bell Irvin Wiley, *The Life of Johnny Reb*, pp. 110–111.
2. Robert Lewis Dabney, *Life and Campaigns of Lieutenant-General Thomas J. Stonewall Jackson*, p. 179.
3. Colonel William Couper, *One Hundred Years at V.M.I.*, vol. 2, p. 101.
4. Ibid., p. 105.
5. Henderson, *Stonewall Jackson and the American Civil War*, p. 104.
6. Dabney, *Life and Campaigns of Lieutenant-General Thomas J. Stonewall Jackson*, p. 183–184.
7. James I. Robertson, *Stonewall Jackson: The Man, the Soldier, the Legend*, p. 218.
8. Couper, *One Hundred Years at V.M.I.*, vol. 2, p. 101.
9. Charles W. Turner, *A Reminiscence of John Newton Lyle of the Liberty Hall Volunteers*, Roanoke, Virginia, Lithograph and Graphics, 1987 (in VMI archives).
10. Henry Kyd Douglas, *I Rode with Stonewall*, p. 21.
11. Letter to Mary Anna Jackson, April 25, 1861, in Jackson, *Memoirs of Stonewall Jackson*, p. 149.
12. Ibid., p. 150.
13. Ibid.
14. Mrs. Jackson's comment was that he was upset "because he felt that he could not render as much service in it [the engineers] as by more active service in the field," ibid.
15. *Official Records*, Series 1, vol. 2, pp. 784–785.
16. Jackson's comment in a letter he wrote to Anna after reaching Harpers Ferry was: "I am very gratified with my command, and would rather have this post than any other in the state." Jackson, *Memoirs of Stonewall Jackson*, p. 151.
17. *Official Records*, Series 1, vol. 2, pp. 784–785.

CHAPTER FOUR: DISCIPLINE AND OTHER NOVEL IDEAS

1. Henry Kyd Douglas, *I Rode with Stonewall*, p. 6.
2. James I. Robertson, *Stonewall Jackson: The Man, the Legend, the Soldier*, p. 222. Robertson also cites Charles Grattan's excellent account of the state of affairs at Harpers Ferry when Jackson arrived.
3. William C. Chase, *Story of Stonewall Jackson*, p. 222.
4. John D. Imboden, "Jackson at Harper's Ferry in 1861," in Robert Underwood Johnson and Clarence Clough Buel, eds., *Battles and Leaders*, vol. 1, pp. 111–125.
5. Ibid.
6. Douglas Southall Freeman, *Lee's Lieutenants*, vol. 1, p. xxiii.
7. Robert Lewis Dabney, *Life and Campaigns of Lieutenant-General Thomas J. Stonewall Jackson*, p. 189.
8. John G. Gittings, *Personal Recollections of Stonewall Jackson*, p. 22.
9. Robertson, p. 222, citing Charles Grattan's account.
10. Imboden, "Jackson at Harper's Ferry in 1861."
11. Dennis Frye, "Stonewall Jackson at Harper's Ferry."

12. Ibid.

13. G.F.R. Henderson, *Stonewall Jackson and the American Civil War*, vol. 1, p. 122.

14. Reference to "elegant mansion" in letter to Anna dated May 8, 1861; Jackson, *Memoirs of Stonewall Jackson*, p. 151.

15. *Official Records*, Series 1, vol. 2, p. 822.

16. *Official Records*, Series 1, vol. 2, p. 861, report of Inspector Lieutenant Colonel General George Deas, dated May 21, 1861, and May 23, 1861.

17. Kirby Smith Papers, University of North Carolina.

18. *Official Records*, Series 1, vol. 2, pp. 976–977.

19. Deas's report dated May 21, 1861.

20. Jackson, *Memoirs of Stonewall Jackson*, p. 158.

21. Letter to Anna dated May 8, 1861; Jackson, *Memoirs of Stonewall Jackson*, p. 152.

22. *Official Records*, Series 1, vol. 2, p. 809.

23. Lee's letter to Jackson dated May 9, 1861, *Official Records*, Series 1, vol. 2, p. 822.

24. Frye, "Stonewall Jackson at Harper's Ferry," p. 3.

25. Letter to Lee dated May 7, 1861, *Official Records*, Series 1, vol. 2, p. 814.

26. Ibid., p. 825.

27. The *Daily South Carolinian*, February 6, 1864. Letcher remembered that Jackson "had urged on him the policy of flying the black flag, proposing to set the example himself."

28. Dabney, *Life and Campaigns of Lieutenant-General Thomas J. Stonewall Jackson*, p. 192.

29. For an excellent, book-length treatment of these ideas, see Charles Royster's *The Destructive War*.

CHAPTER FIVE: A BRILLIANT RETREAT

1. *Official Records*, Series 1, vol. 2, p. 907.

2. Richard Taylor, *Destruction and Reconstruction*, p. 41.

3. *Official Records*, Series 1, vol. 2, p. 185.

4. Ibid., p. 186.

5. Ibid.

6. Byron Farwell, *Stonewall: A Biography of Thomas J. Jackson*, p. 169.

7. Letter to Anna dated July 4, 1861; Mary Anna Jackson, *Memoirs of Stonewall Jackson*, p. 166.

8. *Official Records*, Series 1, vol. 2, p. 186.

9. Ibid.

10. Letter to Anna; Jackson, *Memoirs of Stonewall Jackson*, p. 167.

11. William C. Oates, *War Between the Union and the Confederacy*, pp. 186–187.

CHAPTER SIX: MANEUVERS, LARGE AND SMALL

1. William W. Blackford, *War Years with Jeb Stuart*, p. 15.

2. *Report of the Joint Committee on the Conduct of the War, Part II, Bull Run and Ball's Bluff*, p. 122.

3. G.F.R. Henderson, *Stonewall Jackson and the American Civil War*, p. 130.

4. Drew Gilpin Faust, *This Republic of Suffering*, p. 4.

5. The 10 percent number comes from Chimborazo Hospital, the largest in the city.

6. Cited in James I. Robertson, *Stonewall Jackson: The Man, the Legend, the Soldier*, p. 247. The soldier is Captain James J. White.

7. Mary Anna Jackson, *Memoirs of Stonewall Jackson*, p. 170.

8. Ibid., p. 168.

9. Alfred Roman, *The Military Operations of General Beauregard,* vol. 1, pp. 52ff.

10. John Esten Cooke, *The Wearing of the Gray,* pp. 83ff.

11. James Barnet Fry, *McDowell and Tyler in the Campaign of Bull Run, 1861,* p. 62.

12. James Harrison Wilson, *Under the Old Flag,* vol. 1, p. 66.

13. Jackson, who knew Scott in Mexico, found that he was engaging when it came to talking strictly military affairs, but that in casual conversation he was vain and conceited.

14. Edward Porter Alexander, July 5, 1861, letter to his wife, Bessie, E. P. Alexander Papers, Southern Historical Collection, University of North Carolina.

15. William C. Davis, *Battle at Bull Run,* p. 41.

16. Commissioner of Public Buildings in Interior Department Report, November 30, 1861.

17. *Report of the Joint Committee on the Conduct of the War, Part II, Bull Run and Ball's Bluff,* p. 81.

18. Ibid., p. 82.

19. *Official Records,* Series 1, vol. 2, pp. 168–169.

20. Ibid., p. 172.

21. Robertson, *Stonewall Jackson,* p. 254.

22. *Official Records,* Series 1, vol. 2, p. 172.

23. Jackson, *Memoirs of Stonewall Jackson,* p. 175.

24. John Overton Casler, *Four Years in the Stonewall Brigade,* p. 22.

CHAPTER SEVEN: ALL GREEN ALIKE

1. Daniel Burr Conrad, *History of the First Fight and Organization of the Stonewall Brigade,* p. 471.

2. When Union brigadier general Samuel Heintzelman first saw the 33rd Virginia, on Jackson's left on the top of Henry Hill during the battle of First Manassas, he described them as dressed entirely in civilian clothes. That was his impression, which suggests at least a large component of civilian dress in that regiment.

3. John Hennessy, *The First Battle of Manassas: An End to Innocence,* p. 3.

4. Joseph E. Johnston, *Narrative of Military Operations,* p. 38.

5. Jubal Anderson Early, *War Memoirs: Autobiographical Sketches and Narrative of the War Between the States,* pp. 10–11.

6. Ibid.

7. Ibid., p. 11.

8. The plan is nicely summarized in a letter from Beauregard's aide-de-camp James Chestnut to Beauregard, dated July 16, 1861, and reprinted in Alfred Roman, *The Military Operations of General Beauregard,* pp. 85–87.

9. *Report of the Joint Committee on the Conduct of the War, Part II, Bull Run and Ball's Bluff,* McDowell's testimony, p. 38.

10. Hennessy, *The First Battle of Manassas,* p. 7.

11. McDowell gives an interesting account of these problems in testimony before the Joint Committee on the Conduct of the War, *Part II, Bull Run and Ball's Bluff,* p. 39.

12. Martin D. Hayes, *History of the Second Regiment New Hampshire Volunteers in the War of the Rebellion,* p. 21; cited in Hennessy, *The First Battle of Manassas,* p. 8.

13. William C. Davis, *Battle at Bull Run,* pp. 157–158.

CHAPTER EIGHT: THE BULLET'S SONG

1. Edward Porter Alexander, *Fighting for the Confederacy: The Personal Recollections of General Edward Porter Alexander,* p. 124.

2. Alfred Roman, *Military Operations of General Beauregard,* p. 98. Beauregard had based this partly on Union troop movements, partly on the Blackburn's Ford fight. Roman wrote, "As General Beauregard believed that the repulse of the 18th would deter the Federal general from another attack on the centre, these facts, in his opinion, pointed to a movement against the left flank."

3. Ibid. Though the words are technically Roman's, the book amounts to a personal memoir by Beauregard himself. It was closely edited and supervised by the Creole, who approved every word written.

4. Douglas Southall Freeman, *Lee's Lieutenants,* vol. 1, p. 50. Freeman's account of Beauregard's problematic orders is the best I have read.

5. Roman, *Military Operations of General Beauregard,* vol. 1, appendix, pp. 447–448.

6. Jackson letter to Colonel J. M. Bennett, July 28, 1861, in John Esten Cook, *Stonewall Jackson: A Military Biography,* p. 30; in it, he summarized the confusing orders. See also Robertson, *Stonewall Jackson,* p. 260.

7. Through most of the war, the wigwag system used a binary code, forming letters by using combinations of the numerals 1 and 2 (2122 might be "B," 2211 "D," and so on). The number 1 was made by moving the flag from the vertical to the sender's left, for example.

8. John Hennessy, *The First Battle of Manassas,* p. 40.

9. Alexander, *Fighting for the Confederacy,* p. 50.

10. Ibid. Alexander's comment was: "I had heard stories about reconnoitering officers seeing a little & reporting a great deal so I determined to be very exact in my reports."

11. Edward Porter Alexander, "The Battle of Bull Run," *Scribner's Magazine* 41 (1907), pp. 87–88.

12. Mary Anna Jackson, *Memoirs of Stonewall Jackson,* pp. 166–167.

13. This idea of a struggle within Jackson was first articulated by his brother-in-law D. H. Hill, whose analysis of Jackson was always perceptive. Jackson was a profoundly ambitious man, and it collided with his ideas of humility.

14. To those readers for whom the notion that "God is on our side" has a hollow or self-serving ring, I would point out how common this belief has been in American history. It is fair to say that in World War II, to take one recent example, most Americans believed that God was on their side against the Germans, Italians, and Japanese and therefore that He looked favorably on the killing or wounding of millions of American enemies. Many Christian sermons and prayers petitioned God for help in gaining victory. Franklin D. Roosevelt, the president of the country, routinely invoked God in his public speeches on the war. In a lengthy prayer written by Roosevelt and read to the nation on radio on the evening of D-Day, June 6, 1944, he affirmed his belief that God favored the American side: "We know that by Thy grace, and by the righteousness of our cause, our sons will triumph." Leaders on both sides of the American Civil War, including, most famously, Lincoln, firmly believed that God was on their side. This may seem obvious enough, but much has been made of Jackson's belief that God was on the side of the Confederacy, and it has been suggested that this was part of his religious "fanaticism." There is nothing necessarily fanatical about such a belief.

15. The Bible, English Standard Version, Psalm 118, verses 6 and 7.

16. Charles W. Squires, *The Last of Lee's Battle Line: The Autobiography of Charles W. Squires of the Confederate States Army and of the National Guard of Missouri,* Manuscript in Library of Congress.

17. C. A. Fonderden, *A Brief History of the Military Career of Carpenter's Battery,* p. 7.

18. John Lyle, *Sketches Found in a Confederate's Desk,* p. 202.

19. DeWitt Boyd Stone, *Wandering to Glory,* p. 6.

20. Letter from an unknown member of the 4th Alabama to his brother, dated July 23; source: "Bullrunnings" website.

21. William C. Davis, *Battle at Bull Run,* p. 194. Davis has unusually good coverage of the actions of Hampton's Legion.

CHAPTER NINE: SCREAM OF THE FURIES

1. John Lyle, *Sketches from a Confederate's Desk,* p. 202.

2. Charles Copland Wight, *The Recollections of Charles Copland White, 1841–1897,* manuscript at the Virginia Historical Society, Wight Papers.

3. One of Wade Hampton's men, arriving at the field near noon, said of the Federals on Matthews Hill, "Their bayonets flashed like silver in the bright sunshine." John Coxe, "The Battle of First Manassas," *Confederate Veteran,* cited in John Hennessy, *The First Battle of Manassas,* p. 65.

4. John D. Imboden, "Incidents of the First Bull Run," in Robert Underwood Johnson and Clarence Clough Buel, eds., *Battles and Leaders,* vol. 1, pp. 229–239. Imboden spoke of Union infantry "massing" near the Stone House.

5. Ibid.

6. Ibid.

7. Ibid.

8. Both Johnston and Beauregard would praise Jackson's choice of terrain in their battle reports.

9. Lyle, *Sketches from a Confederate's Desk.*

10. Wight, *The Recollections of Charles Copland Wight.*

11. Pierre Beauregard, "The First Battle of Bull Run," in Johnson and Buel, *Battles and Leaders,* vol. 1, p. 210.

12. Tedford Barclay, letter to his mother dated July 27, 1861, Barclay papers, Library of Virginia.

13. Captain Randolph C. Barton, "Stonewall Jackson," *Southern Historical Society Papers,* vol. 38, p. 280.

14. Imboden, "Incidents of the First Bull Run," p. 236.

15. William W. Blackford, *War Years with Jeb Stuart,* p. 30.

16. There are four and only four eyewitness accounts to Bee's use of the term "stone wall" to describe Jackson, and they all corroborate the fact that it happened later in the afternoon and not, as most historical accounts have it, around the time of Bee's retreat in the late morning. The usual description situates Bee's "They are driving us" comment close to his "stone wall" comment and thus close to his own death. Based on the course of the battle, such a sequence makes no sense at all. His first comment came just as the two-hour "lull" went into effect. The correct sequence of events disproves once and for all the theory that Bee had used the term "stone wall" to criticize Jackson for not coming to his aid on Matthews Hill. That could not possibly have happened. At the time Bee said it, Jackson was wounded and at the very center of the white-hot fight on Henry Hill. For by far the best analysis of what happened and the sequence of events, see John Hennessy's excellent and definitive "Stonewall Jackson's Nickname" in *The Civil War: Magazine of the Civil War Society* 7, no. 2 (April 1990). As Hennessy points out, all four eyewitnesses place the movement forward of Bee with his one hundred men at the same moment that Jackson is moving his artillery back, an event that happened quite late in the battle.

17. Jack Coggins, *Arms and Equipment of the Civil War*, p. 62.

18. James M. McPherson, *Battle Cry of Freedom*, p. 345.

19. For many decades, historians considered that the rebel yell, one of the most important sounds of the war, was lost forever. Reenactors and other enthusiasts invariably tried it, but the sound they produced never equaled the blood-curdling qualities that Union soldiers ascribed to it. But recent research by the Museum of the Confederacy in Richmond has led to the rediscovery of the sound itself. Starting with the recording of a single member of the 37th North Carolina Infantry giving the yell, the museum then used a modern sound studio to replicate and layer the sound to create the effect of large numbers of men doing it simultaneously. The yell consists of a three-part cadence: a short, high-pitched yelp that sounds something like the bark of a fox; a short, lower-pitched yelp; and then a long, high-pitched yelp. The product of the sound-studio work is astounding. The noise produced is indeed feral, nightmarish, unearthly—everything the Yankee soldiers said it was. The museum confirmed its discovery by finding another recording of a single Confederate soldier from another state, recorded at a different time, giving a nearly identical yell. In 2009 a group of four hundred reenactors, trained to do the three-part yell, themselves reproduced a sound that was nearly identical to the studio version. This material is available from the Museum of the Confederacy on a CD entitled "The Rebel Yell Lives."

20. William Thomas Poague, *Gunner with Stonewall*, p. 11.

21. John Overton Casler, *Four Years in the Stonewall Brigade*, p. 29.

22. Beauregard, "The First Battle of Bull Run," in Johnson and Buel, *Battles and Leaders*, vol. 1, p. 212.

23. The observation is from Roman, but it comports with other accounts of the breadth of the Federal battle line. Alfred Roman, *Military Operations of General Beauregard*, p. 108.

24. Irvin McDowell, official report on the Battle of Bull Run, August 4, 1861.

25. Congressman Albert Riddle, quoted in Samuel S. Cox, *Three Decades of Federal Legislation 1855–1885*, p. 158.

26. Hunter McGuire,, "Address to the Robert E. Lee Camp Veterans," *Southern Historical Society Papers*, vol. 25, June 23, 1897.

CHAPTER TEN: GLORY AND DARKNESS

1. Both citations from Allan Nevins, *War for the Union: 1861–1862*, pp. 221–222.

2. Cited in James McPherson, *Battle Cry of Freedom*, p. 346.

3. Civil War casualty estimates vary widely due to faulty or incomplete reporting, especially of mortal wounds. These estimates are from McPherson, *Battle Cry of Freedom*, p. 347.

4. Robert Manson Myers, ed., *Children of Pride: The True Story of Georgia and the Civil War*, pp. 720–721.

5. Letter from Greeley to Lincoln, July 29, 1861, Library of Congress, Washington, DC.

6. "Victory at Bull's Run—Sumter Avenged," *New York Times*, July 22, 1861, in Harold Holzer and Craig Symonds, eds., *The New York Times Complete Civil War 1861–1865*. On July 26, the benighted *Times* was still saying that it was impossible to tell who really won the battle.

7. Douglas Southall Freeman, *Lee's Lieutenants*, vol. 1, p. 81.

8. *Official Records*, Series 1, vol. 2, p. 500.

9. The section containing praise of Jackson sits in a very long catalog of officer evaluations in Beauregard's battle report, just after Bee.

10. Mary Anna Jackson, *Memoirs of Stonewall Jackson,* letter dated July 22, 1861, pp. 177–178.

11. Ibid., p. 180.

12. Mary Boykin Chestnut, *A Diary from Dixie,* p. 89.

13. *Charleston Mercury,* July 25, 1861.

14. John D. Imboden, "Incidents of the First Bull Run," in Robert Underwood Johnson and Clarence Clough Buel, eds., *Battles and Leaders,* vol. 1, p. 238.

15. Ulysses S. Grant, *Personal Memoirs of U. S. Grant,* vol. 1, p. 41.

16. Daniel H. Hill, "The Real Stonewall Jackson," *Century Magazine* 47, February 1894, p. 623.

17. Ibid.

18. Ibid.

19. Cited in James I. Robertson, *Stonewall Jackson: The Man, the Myth, the Soldier,* p. 54.

20. Lenoir Chambers, *Stonewall Jackson and the Virginia Military Institute,* p. 90.

21. Cited in Roberston, *Stonewall Jackson,* p. 63.

22. Hunter McGuire and George L. Christian, *The Confederate Cause and Conduct in the War Between the States,* p. 207.

23. Letter to Laura dated October 26, 1847, in Thomas Jackson Arnold, *The Early Life and Letters of General Thomas J. Jackson,* pp. 128–129.

24. Ibid., p. 130.

25. Robertson, *Stonewall Jackson,* pp. 68–69; this sequence of events is covered in all the major biographies of Jackson, starting with Robert Lewis Dabney, *Life and Campaigns of Lieutenant-General Thomas J. Stonewall Jackson.* The Colston Reminiscences, cited widely in Robertson, give it added depth.

26. Margaret Junkin Preston, "Personal Reminiscences of Stonewall Jackson," *Century Magazine* 32 (1886), p. 929.

CHAPTER ELEVEN: A VERY SMALL, VERY BITTER FIGHT

1. Letters from Jackson to Laura Arnold, July 2, 1849, and March 8, 1850, in Thomas Jackson Arnold, *The Early Life and Letters of General Thomas J. Jackson,* pp. 154–160.

2. His comment to his sister, Laura, was "I like scouting very much as it gives me a relish for everything; but it would be still more desirable if I could have an occasional encounter with Indian parties." Ibid., p. 170.

3. Letter from French to Everett, February 26, 1851, Selected Letters Received, Department of Florida, Relating to Majors T. J. Jackson and W. H. French, 1851, Records of the War Department, U.S. Army Commands, National Archives (hereafter Jackson-French Papers).

4. French to Captain J. M. Brannan, April 16, 1851, Jackson-French Papers.

5. Jackson to Everett, March 23 and March 26, 1851, Jackson-French Papers.

6. Everett to Jackson, March 29, 1851, Jackson-French Papers.

7. D. H. Hill, "The Real Stonewall Jackson," *Century Magazine* 47 (1893–1894), pp. 624–625.

8. He had not yet adopted his practice of refusing to write, read, or post letters on Sunday.

9. French to Brannan, April 14, 1851, Jackson-French Papers, National Archives.

10. Twiggs to Secretary of War Charles M. Conrad, March 6, 1852, National Archives.

11. James I. Robertson, *Stonewall Jackson: The Man, the Legend, the Soldier,* p. 103.

12. Robert Lewis Dabney, *Life and Campaigns of Lieutenant-General Thomas J. Stonewall Jackson,* p. 62.

CHAPTER TWELVE: A HIGHLY UNUSUAL MAN

1. Robert Lewis Dabney, *Life and Campaigns of Lieutenant-General Thomas J. Stonewall Jackson*, p. 79.
2. Thomas Munford, *How I Came to Know Major Thomas J. Jackson*, memoir at Duke University, Munford Papers.
3. William S. White and H. M. White, eds., *Rev. William S. White, D.D., and His Times: An Autobiography*, p. 160.
4. Megan Haley, "The African American Experience in Thomas 'Stonewall' Jackson's Lexington," paper for graduate fellowship, Stonewall Jackson House, Lexington, Virginia, p. 10.
5. D. X. Junkin, *Biography of Dr. George Junkin*, p. 493.
6. Elizabeth Preston Allan, *The Life and Letters of Margaret Junkin Preston*, p. 49. In a letter written in 1850, Maggie Junkin (later Preston) noted that "sociality . . . is the atmosphere in which Southern people live, move and have their being" and called her new neighbors "the *visiting* Virginians" (italics hers).
7. Margaret J. Preston, "Reminiscences of Stonewall Jackson," *Century Magazine* (October 1886), p. 929.
8. Ibid., p. 928.
9. Ibid., p. 929.
10. Ibid.
11. Elizabeth Preston Allan, *Life and Letters*, p. 83.
12. George Winfred Hervey, *The Principles of Courtesy*. This book, published in 1852, was among the most heavily underlined in Jackson's personal, 122-volume library.
13. James I. Robertson, *Stonewall Jackson: The Man, the Legend, the Soldier*, pp. 154–156.
14. Dabney, *Life and Campaigns of Lieutenant-General Thomas J. Stonewall Jackson*, p. 73.
15. D. H. Hill, "The Real Stonewall Jackson," *Century Magazine* 47 (1893–1894), p. 625.
16. Mary Anna Jackson, *Memoirs of Stonewall Jackson*, p. 61. This is her reconstruction of these events, many years later.
17. Ibid., p. 62.
18. Elizabeth Preston Allan, *Life and Letters*, p. 82.
19. Ibid.
20. Hill, "The Real Stonewall Jackson," p. 625.
21. His brother-in-law D. H. Hill considered him to be a hypochondriac.
22. Jackson letter to Laura Arnold, April 4, 1855, in Thomas Jackson Arnold, *The Early Life and Letters of General Thomas J. Jackson*, p. 223.
23. Henry Kyd Douglas, *I Rode with Stonewall*, p. 122.
24. Jackson letter to Laura Arnold, June 19, 1858, in Arnold, *Early Life and Letters*, p. 264.
25. Jackson letter to Laura Arnold, February 1853, in ibid., p. 195.
26. Jackson letter to Laura Arnold, August 10, 1850, in ibid., p. 164.
27. Dabney Herndon Maury, *Recollections of a Virginian in the Mexican, Indian, and Civil Wars*, p. 71.
28. James H. Lane, *General James H. Lane's Reminiscences of Gen. Thomas "Stonewall" Jackson, ca. December 1888*, manuscript in Auburn University Archives and Manuscripts Department.

CHAPTER THIRTEEN: THE EMBATTLED PROFESSOR

1. G.F.R. Henderson, *Stonewall Jackson and the American Civil War*, vol. 1, p. 58.
2. Rev. J. C. Hiden, "Stonewall Jackson: Reminiscences of Him as a Professor in the Virginia Military Institute," *Montgomery* (Alabama) *Advertiser*, November 27, 1892.

3. James H. Lane, *Reminiscences re: Stonewall Jackson, ca. December 1888,* Auburn University Archives and Manuscripts Department.

4. Cited in James I. Robertson, *Stonewall Jackson: The Man, the Legend, the Soldier,* p. 120.

5. Lane, *Reminiscences re: Stonewall Jackson.*

6. Raleigh Colston, *Reminiscences,* Raleigh Edward Colston Papers, University of North Carolina, Southern Historical Collection.

7. John G. Gittings, *Personal Recollections of Stonewall Jackson,* p. 19.

8. Ibid., p. 18.

9. John Esten Cooke, *Stonewall Jackson: A Military Biography,* p. 25.

10. William Couper, *One Hundred Years at V.M.I.,* p. 168.

11. Lane, *Reminiscences re: Stonewall Jackson,* p. 11.

12. Willie Walker Caldwell, *Stonewall Jim,* p. 3.

13. Lenoir Chambers, *Stonewall Jackson and the Virginia Military Institute: The Lexington Years,* p. 61.

14. Hiden, "Stonewall Jackson: Reminiscences of Him."

15. D. H. Hill, "The Real Stonewall Jackson," *Century Magazine* 47 (February 1894), p. 627.

16. Couper, *One Hundred Years at V.M.I.,* vol. 3, p. 187.

17. Cadet James McCabe, cited in Robertson, *Stonewall Jackson,* p. 123.

18. Chambers, *Stonewall Jackson and the Virginia Military Institute: The Lexington Years,* p. 59.

19. Robertson, *Stonewall Jackson,* p. 122, citing Thomas Boyd.

20. Lane, *Reminiscences re: Stonewall Jackson,* p. 15.

21. Jennings Cropper Wise, *The Military History of the Virginia Military Academy, 1839–1865,* p. 89. Wise does not mention the specific incident that Lane talks about, but the two accounts would appear to coincide.

22. Couper, *One Hundred Years at V.M.I.,* vol. 3, p. 179.

23. Caldwell, *Stonewall Jim,* p. 83.

24. Ibid., p. 3.

25. Robertson, *Stonewall Jackson,* p. 170. Robertson gives an excellent and detailed version of this event, the best in any Jackson biography.

26. Mary Anna Jackson, *Memoirs of Stonewall Jackson,* p. 57.

CHAPTER FOURTEEN: DELIBERATELY AND INGENIOUSLY CLOAKED

1. James I. Robertson, *Stonewall Jackson: The Man, the Legend, the Soldier,* p. 6.

2. The material for this brief section on Jackson's childhood is drawn from several different sources: G.F.R. Henderson, Thomas Jackson Arnold, Roy Bird Cook, Robert Lewis Dabney, Mary Anna Jackson, Lenoir Chambers, and James I. Robertson. As with many other aspects of Jackson's life, the Robertson material is the most comprehensive. A significant part of the research in this short section is from secondary sources. Because of the brevity of the treatment, I have not provided exhaustive notes.

3. Roy Bird Cook, *The Family and Early Life of Stonewall Jackson,* p. 21.

4. Ibid., p. 49. Many of Jackson's biographers seem to strain to make his childhood more exceptional than it really was. Cook's comment was: "For twelve years the boyhood of the future general was spent at the Jackson homestead, an existence not unlike that of many others of the same period."

5. Her obviously hurt feelings surfaced when she was not told of or invited to his first wedding, and later when Jackson and his second wife did not visit her the summer they were married. See Jackson's letter to Laura, November 30, 1853, regarding her silence after his wedding; see Anna's letter to Laura, September 27, 1857, acknowledging that she and

Thomas were "sorry to learn from your letters that you feel so hurt . . ." (letter cited in Cook, *Family and Early Life of Stonewall Jackson*, pp. 146–147).

6. Jackson letter to Laura, February 1, 1853, in Thomas Jackson Arnold, *The Early Life and Letters of General Thomas J. Jackson*, pp. 194–196.

7. Jackson letter to Laura, April 1, 1853, in ibid., p. 197.

8. Jackson letter to Laura, April 15, 1853, in ibid., p. 199.

9. After the war, Robert E. Lee became president of the college, which later changed its name to Washington and Lee.

10. D. X. Junkin, *George Junkin, D.D., LL.D.: A Historical Biography*, p. 494.

11. Ibid., p. 504.

12. Ibid., p. 492.

13. D. H. Hill, "The Real Stonewall Jackson," *Century Magazine* 47 (February 1894), p. 625.

14. Mary P. Coulling, *Margaret Junkin Preston*, p. 66.

15. Elizabeth Preston Allan, *Margaret Junkin Preston: Life and Letters*, p. 60.

16. Ibid., p. 61.

17. Coulling, *Margaret Junkin Preston*, pp. 168ff.

18. Letter written by an unnamed Dickey cousin, cited in ibid., p. 66.

19. Hill, "The Real Stonewall Jackson," p. 627.

20. Poem by Margaret Junkin, "To my Sister," undated, typed copy in Thomas J. Jackson Papers, Southern Historical Collection, University of North Carolina.

21. Letter from Maggie to Ellie, undated, Margaret Preston Junkin Papers, Southern Historical Collection, University of North Carolina.

22. Margaret Junkin Preston, "Personal Reminiscences of Stonewall Jackson," *Century Magazine* 32 (1886) p. 932.

23. Ibid.

24. Junkin, *George Junkin*, p. 504.

25. Elizabeth Preston Allan,, *Margaret Junkin Preston: Life and Letters*, p. 62.

26. Jackson letter to Laura, March 4, 1854, in Arnold, *Early Life and Letters*, pp. 208–10.

27. James Power Smith, "The Religious Character of Stonewall Jackson," Address at the VMI, *Union Seminary Review*, vol. 25, 1898.

28. Mary Anna Jackson, *Memoirs of Stonewall Jackson*, pp. 72–73.

29. Robertson, *Stonewall Jackson*, p. 157, citing a previously unpublished letter from Jackson to William E. "Grumble" Jones, March 24, 1855.

30. Raleigh Colston, *Reminiscences*, manuscript in Raleigh Edward Colston Papers, Southern Historical Collection, University of North Carolina.

31. Robertson, *Stonewall Jackson*, p. 158, citing a previously unpublished letter from Jackson to Laura, October 23, 1854, at Jackson archives, USMA.

32. Letter from Jackson to Maggie, February 14, 1855, cited in Allan, *Margaret Junkin Preston*, p. 74.

33. Hill, "The Real Stonewall Jackson," p. 625.

34. Letter from Jackson to Laura, June 1, 1855: "Had I one request on earth to ask in accordance with my own feelings and apart from duty, it would be that I might join her before the close of another day." In Arnold, *Early Life and Letters*, p. 224.

35. Letter from Jackson dated February 6, 1855, cited in Allan, *Margaret Junkin Preston*, p. 72.

36. Manuscript letter from Jackson to Maggie, February 14, 1855, in Margaret Junkin Preston papers, Southern Historical Collection, University of North Carolina.

37. Letter from Jackson to Maggie, August 16, 1855, in ibid.

38. Preston, "Personal Reminiscences of Stonewall Jackson," *Century Magazine*, p. 932.

39. Ibid., p. 933.
40. Ibid., p. 927.
41. Letter from Jackson to Maggie dated May 31, 1856, Preston Papers, University of North Carolina.

CHAPTER FIFTEEN: AN UPRIGHT CITIZEN

1. Jackson had planned such a trip five years earlier, but his job offer at VMI precluded it.
2. Mary Anna Jackson, *Memoirs of Stonewall Jackson*, pp. 85–86; she used the term "rapturous" to describe his reaction.
3. Ibid., p. 99.
4. Mary P. Coulling, *Margaret Junkin Preston: A Biography*, p. 97.
5. Jackson, *Memoirs of Stonewall Jackson*, p. 110; the account of Jackson's daily routine comes from her, pp. 109ff.
6. Ibid., pp. 109, 121.
7. Ibid., p. 128.
8. Ibid., p. 122.
9. James I. Robertson, *Stonewall Jackson: The Man, the Legend, the Soldier*, p. 193.
10. William S. White and H. M. White, eds., *Rev. William S. White, D.D., and His Times*, p. 139.
11. Letter from Robert I. White to Jackson, dated January 27, 1863; Thomas J. Jackson Papers, Southern Historical Collection, University of North Carolina.
12. Mark A. Snell, "Bankers, Businessmen and Benevolence: An Analysis of the Antebellum Finances of Thomas J. Jackson," typed manuscript, Stonewall Jackson House Graduate Student Fellow, 1989, Virginia Historical Society.
13. Ibid.
14. Jackson, *Memoirs of Stonewall Jackson*, p. 115.
15. Ibid., p. 116.
16. After describing her slaves, Anna's precise words were: "The other animate possessions of the family were a good-looking horse (named for his color, Bay), two splendid milch cows, and a lot of chickens." Jackson, *Memoirs of Stonewall Jackson*, p. 119.
17. White, *Rev. William S. White*, p. 158.
18. Letter from Jackson to John Lyle Campbell, June 7, 1858 (no. 2); Stonewall Jackson Archives, VMI; in the letter Jackson outlines in great detail exactly how the school works and what its procedures are.
19. Letter from J. D. Davidson, Esq., to the *Lexington Gazette*, August 16, 1876, in *Southern Historical Society Papers*, vol. 9, pp. 46–47.
20. White, *Rev. William S. White*, p. 159.
21. White Narrative, Box 20, Dabney Papers, Southern Historical Collection, University of North Carolina.

CHAPTER SIXTEEN: WHERE IS THE THUNDER OF WAR?

1. François d'Orleans, Prince de Joinville, a French nobleman and former vice admiral, was quoted in the *Philadelphia Press* of November 23, 1861, saying that he "never saw anything that compared to it in the Old World."
2. The review took place at Bailey's Crossroads, a place that retains its name today but has been swallowed by suburban sprawl. The Baileys achieved notoriety for putting on circuses, and became famous as part of the Barnum and Bailey Circus and later the Ringling Brothers and Barnum and Bailey Circus.

3. Letter from Sergeant Oren M. Stephens, November 24, 1861.

4. The quote comes from Bayard Taylor's letter in the *New York Weekly Tribune* after an army review in September, September 24, 1861; the description of the cavalry escort and band is from the *Washington Evening Star*, November 21, 1861.

5. *New York Times*, November 21, 1861.

6. *Philadelphia Press*, November 21, 1861.

7. The reference is to the so-called Battle of Lewinsville in McClean, Virginia, on September 11. There were three Union casualties, four Union captured; the Confederates, under Jeb Stuart, took no casualties. Source: "All Not So Quiet on the Civil War," DC Lawyer on the Civil War blog; also Douglas S. Freeman, *Lee's Lieutenants*, p. 111.

8. On October 15, McClellan's rolls showed 152,501 soldiers, of whom realistically only 100,000 or so were available to actively campaign. The 41,000 or so under Johnston at Manassas were subject to the same deductions for sick, absent, confined, etc.

9. General James A. Wadsworth at Centreville used a sensible intelligence-gathering system based on Confederate fugitives and slave and freedmen spies. He estimated the Confederate forces at fifty thousand, which, including Jackson's and Hill's forces in the west, was remarkably accurate, and he begged McClellan to attack. Allan Nevins, *The War for the Union*, p. 301.

10. At Second Manassas, McClellan effectively withheld the main part of his army from General John Pope, famously suggesting that Lincoln "leave Pope to get out of his own scrape." See my later chapter on this.

11. William Howard Russell, *My Diary North and South*, p. 240.

12. McClellan letter to Samuel L. M. Barlow, November 8, 1861, in Stephen Sears, ed., *The Civil War Papers of George B. McClellan*, pp. 127–128.

13. McClellan to his wife, Mary Ellen McClellan, July 27, 1861, in ibid., p. 70.

14. McClellan to his wife, July 30, 1861, in ibid., p. 71.

15. McClellan letters to his wife, October 2, 7, 10; November 2, 17, 1861; selection of quotes comes from James McPherson, *Battle Cry of Freedom*, p. 364.

16. Letter from McClellan to his wife, November 2, 1861, in Sears, *Civil War Papers*.

17. Ethan Rafuse, *McClellan's War: The Failure of Moderation in the Struggle for the Union*, p. 390.

18. Peter Cozzens, *Shenandoah 1862: Stonewall Jackson's Valley Campaign*, p. 50.

19. James A. Morgan, "The Accidental Battle of Ball's Bluff," *Hallowed Ground Magazine*, Fall 2011.

20. Russell, *My Diary North and South*, p. 398.

CHAPTER SEVENTEEN: A PRETERNATURAL CALM

1. G.F.R. Henderson, *Stonewall Jackson and the American Civil War*, p. 174.

2. W. J. Wood, *Civil War Generalship: The Art of Command*, p. 12; Wood wrote, "American generals of 1861 studied Jomini [Précis de l'Art de la Guerre] in the misguided faith that they were studying Napoleon. They marched against strategic points—Corinth, Richmond, Atlanta—content to let Confederate armies escape to fight again, so long as they could occupy real estate."

3. Henry Kyd Douglas, *I Rode with Stonewall*, p. 30.

4. Douglas Southall Freeman, *Lee's Lieutenants*, vol. 1, p. 104.

5. Jackson letter to Anna, October 1, 1861, in Anna Jackson, *Memoirs of Stonewall Jackson*, p. 194.

6. Ibid.

7. James I. Robertson, *Stonewall Jackson: The Man, the Legend, the Soldier,* p. 278. Robertson makes the case for Davis's impression of Jackson as a "fanatic." The future event referred to is Davis overriding Jackson's orders and recalling General William W. Loring from Romney in January 1862.

8. G. W. Smith gave this account to early Jackson biographer G.F.R. Henderson; see Henderson, *Stonewall Jackson and the American Civil War,* pp. 174–175.

9. Sheridan's army spent the last week of September and the first week of October 1864 burning buildings, farms, mills, houses, and any public buildings that had survived the previous valley campaigns. "Such as cannot be consumed, destroy" were his orders.

10. Ibid., p. 176.

11. Douglas, *I Rode with Stonewall,* p. 30.

12. Bell Irvin Wiley, *The Life of Johnny Reb: The Common Soldier of the Confederacy,* pp. 248–250.

13. Mary Anna Jackson, *Memoirs of Stonewall Jackson,* pp. 188–189.

14. The material concerning Anna's visit comes from her own descriptions; ibid., pp. 188–191.

15. Ibid., p. 206.

16. Douglas, *I Rode with Stonewall,* p. 14.

17. Ibid.

CHAPTER EIGHTEEN: A SEASON OF STORMS

1. The Virginia Central Railroad ran from Staunton in the southern valley through Rockfish Gap to Charlottesville, Gordonsville, and Richmond beyond.

2. Peter Cozzens, *Shenandoah 1862: Stonewall Jackson's Valley Campaign,* p. 51.

3. Cited in William Allan, *History of the Campaign of Gen. T. J. (Stonewall) Jackson in the Shenandoah Valley of Virginia,* p. 16.

4. James I. Robertson, *Stonewall Jackson: The Man, the Legend, the Soldier,* p. 841, note 30.

5. Mary Anna Jackson, *Memoirs of Stonewall Jackson,* pp. 218ff.

6. Jedediah Hotchkiss, letter to Fitzhugh Lee, October 22, 1891, Hotchkiss Papers, Library of Congress.

7. William B. Taliaferro, "Some Personal Reminiscences of Lt.-Gen. Thos J. (Stonewall) Jackson," in Jackson, *Memoirs of Stonewall Jackson,* p. 510.

8. Letter from W. L. Jackson to Thomas J. Jackson, November 23, 1861; Thomas J. Jackson Papers, Southern Historical Collection, University of North Carolina.

9. Letter from John Preston to Maggie, December 5, 1861, in Elizabeth Preston Allan, *Margaret Junkin Preston: Life and Letters,* p. 123.

10. Robertson, *Stonewall Jackson,* p. 306.

11. Charges and specifications against Gilham can be found in Thomas J. Jackson Papers, Southern Historical Collection, University of North Carolina.

12. Letter from William Gilham to Jedediah Hotchkiss, November 25, 1866, Hotchkiss Papers, Library of Congress.

13. Harman cited in Cozzens, *Shenandoah 1862,* pp. 84–85.

14. John H. Worsham, *One of Jackson's Foot Cavalry,* p. 63.

15. Henry Kyd Douglas, *I Rode with Stonewall,* p. 24.

16. William Thomas Poague, *Gunner with Stonewall,* p. 17.

17. John Overton Casler, *Four Years in the Stonewall Brigade,* p. 63.

18. Letter from Jackson to Benjamin, January 20, 1862, cited in Allan, *History of the Campaign of Gen. T. J. (Stonewall) Jackson in the Shenandoah Valley of Virginia,* p. 28.

19. Taliaferro, "Some Personal Reminiscences of Lt.-Gen. Thos. J. (Stonewall) Jackson," in Jackson, *Memoirs of Stonewall Jackson,* p. 511.

20. Jackson letter to Boteler, January 29, 1862, Alexander R. Boteler, "Stonewall Jackson's Discontent," *Philadelphia Weekly Times,* June 2, 1877, in Robert Underwood Johnson and Clarence Cough Buel, eds., *Battles and Leaders,* vol. 6, pp. 102ff.

21. Cozzens, *Shenandoah 1862,* p. 103. Cozzens does a superb job of sorting out the Union side of the Romney fiasco, including Lander's aborted advance.

22. Hunter McGuire to Jedediah Hotchkiss, November 8, 1897, Hotchkiss Papers, Library of Congress.

23. *Official Records,* Series 1, vol. 5, pp. 1041–1042.

24. Alexander R. Boteler, "Stonewall Jackson's Discontent," *Philadelphia Weekly Times,* June 2, 1877, in Johnson and Buel, *Battles and Leaders,* vol. 6, pp. 102ff.

25. Ibid., p. 106.

26. Letter from Taliaferro to Loring, January 29, 1862, Roy Bird Cook Papers, West Virginia University.

27. Douglas Southall Freeman, *Lee's Lieutenants,* vol. 1, p. 116.

28. Ibid.

29. Joseph E. Johnston, *Narrative of Military Operations,* p. 89.

30. Robertson, *Stonewall Jackson,* p. 314; draft of report on the winter campaign, Dabney Papers, Southern Historical Collection, University of North Carolina.

31. Boteler, "Stonewall Jackson's Discontent," p. 107.

32. Ibid., pp. 107–108.

33. Letter from Rev. Francis McFarland to Jackson, February 5, 1862, Dabney-Jackson Collection, Library of Virginia, Series II.

34. Col. S. Bassett French, cited in Robertson, *Stonewall Jackson,* p. 320.

35. Rev. James R. Graham, "Reminiscences of Gen. T.J. ("Stonewall") Jackson," in Jackson, *Memoirs of Stonewall Jackson,* pp. 496–497.

36. Boteler, "Stonewall Jackson's Discontent," p. 108.

37. Charges and specifications against Loring in Dabney Papers, Southern Historical Collection, University of North Carolina.

38. McClellan's troop estimates were, as usual, well in excess of everyone else's. Around this time Pinkerton reported that Johnston had seventy-five thousand *fresh* troops, ready to attack Washington, which was a wholesale fabrication.

39. The local Union commanders, as it turned out, had been anxious to attack Jackson. In mid-November, General Nathaniel Banks, in possession of remarkably accurate information about the Confederate forces facing him, had asked McClellan for permission "to make the expedition to Winchester." McClellan had refused, ordering Banks into winter headquarters. On December 19, Banks had put forth another proposal, this time to move in force across the Potomac and take Martinsburg, a mere fifteen miles north of Winchester. McClellan had again turned him down flat. In January, Brigadier General Frederick Lander, in Hancock, just across the Potomac from Bath, had asked for permission to cross the river and pursue Jackson. He, too, was turned down. Finally, Lander, sputtering with anger and frustration, was ordered by McClellan to go to Romney and retreat northward with the Union army to the Baltimore and Ohio Railroad. Jackson's boldness may not have frightened Nathaniel Banks, but it had absolutely scared the timorous George McClellan. The rest did not matter.

40. H. W. Brands, *The Man Who Saved the Union: Ulysses S. Grant in War and Peace,* pp. 167–169.

CHAPTER NINETEEN: A LOOMING PERIL

1. Peter Cozzens, *Shenandoah 1862: Stonewall Jackson's Valley Campaign*, p. 115.
2. David Hunter Strother, *A Virginia Yankee in the Civil War*, pp. 10ff.
3. Richard R. Duncan, *Beleaguered Winchester: A Virginia Community at War, 1861–1865*, p. 40.
4. *Richmond Whig*, February 15, 1862.
5. James McPherson, *Battle Cry of Freedom*, p. 428, citing various published sources.
6. Elizabeth Preston Allan, *The Life and Letters of Margaret Junkin Preston*, pp. 134–135.
7. John Harman, letter to David Harman, February 18, 1862, in Hotchkiss Papers, Box 38, Library of Congress.
8. Gary Ecelbarger, *"We are in for it!" The First Battle of Kernstown*, p. 38.
9. John Harman, letter to David Harman, March 7, 1862, Hotchkiss Papers, Library of Congress.
10. The aggregate Union forces number comes from Ecelbarger, *"We are in for it!,"* p. 38; the number for Banks alone is from Cozzens, *Shenandoah 1862*, p. 121.
11. Ecelbarger, *"We are in for it!,"* p. 45; the information about weaponry came from a Private Jacob Poisel, a Confederate deserter whose information confirmed what other spies, slaves, and deserters had told Banks.
12. Letter from Jackson to Letcher, March 1862; Thomas T. Munford Papers, Duke University.
13. LTC (ret.) Joe Griffin, "Joe Brown's Pikes: Southern Cold Steel in Close Quarters," *Journal of the Historical Society of the Georgia National Guard* 8, no. 2, Fall 2000.
14. Jackson's own estimates were not as accurate at Banks's. He thought Banks had somewhat more troops than he actually had. It was a mismatch either way.
15. *Official Records*, Series 1, vol. 5, pp. 1083–1084; Cozzens, *Shenandoah 1862*, p. 115.
16. John Harman letter to David Harman, February 26, 1862, Hotchkiss Papers, Library of Congress.
17. Michael Fellman, "Sherman's Demons," *New York Times*, November 11, 2011.
18. Mary Anna Jackson, *Memoirs of Stonewall Jackson*, p. 210.
19. Rev. James R. Graham, "Reminiscences of General T. J. 'Stonewall' Jackson," in Jackson, *Memoirs of Stonewall Jackson*, pp. 488–490.
20. Jackson, *Memoirs of Stonewall Jackson*, pp. 214–215.
21. Ibid., p. 159. Jackson first reports his good health to Anna in April 1861; she observes it in the Winchester winter, and after her departure he confirms it again in a letter to her.
22. James G. Hollandsworth, *Pretense of Glory: The Life of General Nathaniel P. Banks*, p. 19.
23. Ibid., p. 3.
24. W. J. Wood, *Civil War Generalship: The Art of Command*, pp. 46ff.
25. Ecelbarger, *"We are in for it!,"* pp. 44–45.
26. Cited in ibid., p. 47.
27. Joseph E. Johnston, *Narrative of Military Operations*, p. 106.
28. Hunter McGuire, "General T. J. ("Stonewall") Jackson: His Career and Character," an address; *Southern Historical Society Papers*, vol. 25, p. 97.
29. Bayard Taylor, *New York Tribune*, March 13, 1862.
30. Lincoln to McClellan, April 9, 1862, *Official Records*, Series 1, vol. 5, p. 74.

CHAPTER TWENTY: THE REALM OF THE POSSIBLE

1. Clarence Thomas, *General Turner Ashby: Centaur of the South*, p. 68.
2. Letter from McClellan to Banks, March 16, 1862; *Official Records*, Series 1, vol. 5, p. 56.
3. Peter Cozzens, *Shenandoah 1862: Stonewall Jackson's Valley Campaign*, pp. 134–136.

4. Gary L. Ecelbarge, *"We are in for it!" The First Battle of Kernstown*, p. 52.

5. David Hunter Strother, *A Virginia Yankee in the Civil War*, p. 18.

6. Ibid., p. 16.

7. Ibid., p. 17; "ridiculous distance" was his comment.

8. Ecelbarger, *"We are in for it!,"* p. 66.

9. Jack Coggins, *Arms and Equipment of the Civil War*, pp. 47ff.

10. Dee Brown, "War On Horseback," *The Image of War 1861–1865*, vol. 4, *Fighting for Time*, National Historical Society.

11. Ibid.

12. P. S. Carmichael, "Turner Ashby's Appeal," essay in Gary W. Gallagher, ed., *The Shenandoah Campaign of 1862*, pp. 145ff.

13. Henry Kyd Douglas, *I Rode with Stonewall*, p. 82.

14. Carmichael, "Turner Ashby's Appeal," p. 151, citing quote from Brigadier General John W. Geary.

15. Letter from Ashby to Dorothea Farrar (Ashby) Moncure, September 6, 1861; cited in Carmichael, "Turner Ashby's Appeal," p. 152.

16. Dabney Herndon Maury, *Recollections of a Virginian in Mexican, Indian, and Civil Wars*, p. 49.

17. Nominally the advantage was three to one, but thanks to Gary Ecelbarger's statistical work, we know that Union effectives were far less than the paper force. Two to one is not precise, but a good guideline.

CHAPTER TWENTY-ONE: A JAGGED LINE OF BLOOD

1. George Neese, part of Preston Chew's battery under Ashby, cited in Gary L. Ecelbarger, *"We are in for it!" The First Battle of Kernstown*.

2. *Official Records*, Series 1, vol. 12, pt. 1, p. 340.

3. Testimony of General J. C. Sullivan, May 22, 1862, before the *Report of the Joint Committee on the Conduct of the War*, p. 408.

4. *Official Records*, Series 1, vol. 12, pt. 3, p. 836.

5. Peter Cozzens, *Shenandoah 1862: Stonewall Jackson's Valley Campaign*, p. 161.

6. Letter from Jackson to Anna, April 11, 1862; Mary Anna Jackson, *Memoirs of Stonewall Jackson*, p. 249.

7. Ecelbarger, *"We are in for it!,"* p. 95.

8. Ibid., p. 110.

9. Ibid., p. 107.

10. Jack Coggins, *Arms and Equipment of the Civil War*, pp. 61ff.

11. Ibid., p. 63. He makes the point that both sides misused artillery tactically; until 1863 "both the confederacy and the western armies of the Union assigned a battery to each infantry brigade." The advantages gained by massing, on the other hand, were "painfully evident at Malvern Hill when an almost continuous battery of 60 pieces directed by Gen. Henry J. Hunt beat down every Confederate attack and smashed one southern battery after another."

12. Cozzens makes this astute observation in *Shenandoah 1862*, p. 177.

13. Virgil Smalley of the 7th Ohio, cited in Cozzens, *Shenandoah 1862*, p. 179.

14. Letter from Jackson to A. W. Harman, March 28, 1862, *Southern Historical Society Papers*, vol. 19 (1891), p. 318.

15. William S. Young, "Shenandoah Valley: Criticizing General Capehart's Article on That Campaign," *National Tribune*, April 18, 1889.

16. While it is true that at a range of one hundred yards or less smoothbores lost many of their disadvantages, part of this battle took place at ranges of up to two hundred yards or more. There is no question that the Federal weaponry was superior.

17. Ecelbarger, *"We are in for it!,"* p. 249.

18. Cited in ibid., p. 149.

19. Private letter from Alexander R. Boteler Jr., dated March 26, 1862, published in the *Richmond Daily Dispatch,* April 3, 1862.

20. John Overton Casler, *Four Years in the Stonewall Brigade,* p. 67.

21. William Thomas Poague, *Gunner with Stonewall,* p. 20.

22. Private letter from Alexander R. Boteler Jr., dated March 26, 1862, published in the *Richmond Daily Dispatch,* April 3, 1862.

23. John H. Worsham, *One of Jackson's Foot Cavalry, His Experiences and What He Saw During the War,* p. 69. Many Confederate soldiers blamed the retreat on lack of ammunition. In his battle report, Lieutenant Colonel Andrew Grigsby wrote: "The position was held until the Reg't was ordered to retire, which order was received after the men had fired their last round of cartridge."

24. "The Battle of Kernstown: An Interesting Narrative," *Richmond Dispatch,* March 28, 1862.

25. Jedediah Hotchkiss, note appended in Casler, *Four Years in the Stonewall Brigade,* p. 68.

26. Letter from Jackson to Anna, March 28, 1862; Jackson, *Memoirs of Stonewall Jackson,* p. 247.

27. Cozzens, *Shenandoah 1862,* p. 214.

28. Sergeant John C. Marsh, of the 29th Ohio, cited in ibid., p. 211.

29. Ecelbarger, *"We are in for it!,"* p. 249.

30. Letter from James Shields to Assistant Adjutant General, Army of the Potomac, May 25, 1862; *Official Records,* Series 1, vol. 12, ch. 24, pt. 1; Shields also cites this same number in his March 27 correspondence ("The rebels admitted they had 11,000 in the field").

31. William J. Miller, "Such Men as Shields, Banks, and Frémont," essay in Gallagher, *The Shenandoah Valley Campaign of 1862,* p. 50.

32. Cozzens, *Shenandoah 1862,* p. 228.

CHAPTER TWENTY-TWO: THE SHOOTING WAR

1. Ulysses S. Grant, *Memoirs and Selected Letters,* p. 66.

2. "The Rifle-Musket and the Minie Ball," *Civil War Times,* June 12, 2006.

3. Bevin Alexander, *Lost Victories: The Military Genius of Stonewall Jackson,* p. 3.

4. Jack Coggins, *Arms and Equipment of the Civil War,* p. 23.

5. Mark Grimsley, "How to Read a Civil War Battlefield," www.cohums.ohio-state.edu/history/people/grimsley.1/tour/default.htm.

6. Ibid.

7. Pat Leonard, "The Bullet That Changed History," *New York Times,* August 31, 2012.

8. Bruce Catton, *Mr. Lincoln's War,* p. 198.

9. John Worsham, *One of Jackson's Foot Cavalry,* p. 106.

10. Ibid., p. 60.

11. Edward Porter Alexander, *Fighting for the Confederacy,* p. 122.

12. Keith S. Bohannon, "Placed on the Pages of History in Letters of Blood: Reporting on and Remembering the 12th Georgia Infantry in the 1862 Valley Campaign," essay in Gary W. Gallagher, ed., *The Shenandoah Valley Campaign of 1862,* p. 120.

13. Bell Irvin Wiley, *The Life of Johnny Reb,* p. 290.

14. It is worth noting that the bullet that hit him at Chancellorsville from a Confederate musket was a *smoothbore* round.

CHAPTER TWENTY-THREE: A FOOL'S PARADISE

1. McClellan's orders to Banks were, "If [Jackson] be in force, drive him from the Valley."
2. We do not have Laura's letters to her brother; his letters to her stop on April 6.
3. Letter from Jackson to Laura, April 6, 1861, in Thomas Jackson Arnold, *The Early Life and Letters of General Thomas J. Jackson*, pp. 295–297.
4. James I. Robertson, *Stonewall Jackson: The Man, the Legend, the Soldier*, p. 690.
5. Ibid., p. 691.
6. David Hunter Strother, *A Virginia Yankee in the Civil War: The Diaries of David Hunter Strother*, p. 21.
7. Ibid., p. 9.
8. Ibid., p. 22.
9. Jonathan M. Berkey, "In the Very Midst of the War Track: The Valley's Civilians and the Shenandoah Campaign," essay in Gary W. Gallagher, ed., *The Shenandoah Valley Campaign of 1862*, p. 91.
10. Ibid.
11. Ibid., p. 92.
12. Ibid.
13. Ibid., p. 94.
14. Jackson letter to Anna, May 5, 1862; on April 16, describing a slightly more northern part of the valley, he had written: "This country is one of the most beautiful that I ever beheld."
15. Robertson, *Stonewall Jackson*, p. 363.
16. Jackson's army would increase somewhat from this level during this period, at least on paper.
17. Though the conscription law would not be passed by the Confederate legislature until April 16, Virginia governor John Letcher, in anticipation of it, had called up active militia into the volunteer army.
18. Jedediah Hotchkiss, *Make Me a Map of the Valley*, pp. 19ff; both sides obviously had to deal with the same weather.
19. William J. Miller, "Such Men as Shields, Banks, and Frémont," essay in Gallagher, *The Shenandoah Valley Campaign of 1862*, p. 52.
20. Peter Cozzens, *Shenandoah 1862: Stonewall Jackson's Valley Campaign*, p. 242. He quotes General Alpheus Williams saying, "It was a splendid spectacle, the finest military show I have seen in America."
21. Hotchkiss, *Make Me a Map of the Valley*, pp. 26ff.
22. Robert G. Tanner, *Stonewall in the Valley*, p. 156.
23. *Official Records*, Series 1, vol. 12, pp. 446ff.
24. Cozzens, *Shenandoah 1862*, p. 255. Not all of Banks's officers seem to have believed that Jackson had fled the valley. His division commander, Alpheus Williams, wrote his sister on April 29 that Jackson was "fifteen to twenty miles distant on the slopes of the Blue Ridge," which was substantially correct. It is unclear whether Williams was outvoted by other officers, or whether he kept his own counsel. In any case, the Union commanders had to sift and sort through many different types of intelligence.
25. *Official Records*, Banks to Stanton, April 30, 1862.
26. Cozzens, *Shenandoah 1862*, p. 254.

27. *Official Records,* Stanton to Banks, May 1, 1862.
28. *Official Records,* Series 1, vol. 12, pt. 3, pp. 859ff.
29. Ibid.
30. Jackson's force left Elk Run Valley for Port Republic on April 30; Lee's wire saying he had reviewed the three plans and was leaving the choice to Jackson was dated May 1 (*Official Records*).
31. Jackson's report, *Official Records,* Series 1, vol. 12, pt. 1, p. 470: "The positions of these armies were such that left unmolested they could readily form a junction on the [Harrisonburg and Warm Springs Turnpike] and move with their force against Staunton."
32. Cited in Robertson, *Stonewall Jackson,* p. 367.
33. Richard Taylor, *Destruction and Reconstruction,* p. 34; the description is probably a bit extreme, but the substance of it seems right based on other accounts.
34. John Brown Gordon, *Reminiscences of the Civil War,* p. 38.
35. William Allan, interview with Robert E. Lee, March 3, 1868, William Allan Papers, Southern Historical Collection, University of North Carolina.
36. The description of the valley as seen by Ewell's troops on April 30 comes from Taylor, *Destruction and Reconstruction,* p. 43.
37. Henry Kyd Douglas, *I Rode with Stonewall,* p. 47.
38. Robertson, *Stonewall Jackson,* p. 369.
39. Civilwaracademy.com.
40. John D. Imboden, "Stonewall Jackson in the Shenandoah," in Robert Underwood Johnson and Clarence Clough Buel, eds., *Battles and Leaders of the Civil War,* vol. 2, pp. 282ff.
41. John Overton Casler, *Four Years in the Stonewall Brigade,* p. 73.
42. Imboden, "Stonewall Jackson in the Shenandoah," pp. 282ff.
43. The preceding dispatches concerning Jackson's whereabouts are all found in *Official Records,* Series 1, vol. 12, pt. 3.
44. Hotchkiss, *Make Me a Map of the Valley,* p. 36.
45. Robertson, *Stonewall Jackson,* p. 370, citing *Official Records.*
46. *Official Records,* Banks to Stanton, May 5, 1862, from New Market: "Yesterday the forces were withdrawn from Harrisonburg to this place."
47. Jackson letter to Colonel Francis H. Smith, April 30, 1862, Sara (Henderson) Smith Papers, Virginia Historical Society.
48. Milroy to Schenck, May 7, *Official Records,* Series 1, vol. 12, pt. 3.
49. Robert C. Schenck, "Notes on the Battle of McDowell," in Johnson and Buel, *Battles and Leaders of the Civil War,* vol. 2, p. 298.
50. Ibid.
51. Ibid.
52. Cozzens, *Shenandoah 1862,* p. 265.
53. Keith S. Bohannon, "Placed on the Pages of History in Letters of Blood," essay in Gallagher, *The Shenandoah Valley Campaign of 1862,* p. 120,
54. Ibid.
55. Letter from S. G. Pryor to his wife, May 18, 1862, cited in Bell Irvin Wiley, *The Life of Johnny Reb,* p. 32.
56. Jackson's battle report, *Official Records,* Series 1, vol. 12, pt. 1, pp. 471ff.
57. Ibid.
58. Cited in Robertson, *Stonewall Jackson,* p. 375.
59. Jackson's battle report, *Official Records,* Series 1, vol. 12, pt. 1, pp. 471ff.
60. Imboden, "Stonewall Jackson in the Shenandoah," pp. 282ff.

CHAPTER TWENTY-FOUR: HAZARDS OF COMMAND

1. Jedediah Hotchkiss, *Make Me a Map of the Valley,* p. 21.
2. Henry Kyd Douglas, *I Rode with Stonewall,* p. 40.
3. Hotchkiss, *Make Me a Map of the Valley,* p. 20.
4. Jackson letter to Anna, April 11, 1862, Mary Anna Jackson, *Memoirs of Stonewall Jackson,* p. 249.
5. A. Cash Koeniger, "Prejudices and Partialities: The Garnett Controversy Revisited," essay in Gary W. Gallagher, ed., *The Shenandoah Valley Campaign of 1862,* p. 220.
6. Charges and specifications in Thomas J. "Stonewall" Jackson Collection, Eleanor S. Brockenbrough Archives, Museum of the Confederacy.
7. Douglas, *I Rode with Stonewall,* p. 37.
8. Letter from Richard B. Garnett to Hon. R.M.T. Hunter, April 1862, Thomas J. "Stonewall" Jackson Collection, Eleanor S. Brockenbrough Archives, Museum of the Confederacy.
9. Cited in Peter Cozzens, *Shenandoah 1862: Stonewall Jackson's Valley Campaign,* p. 221.
10. John Worsham, *One of Jackson's Foot Cavalry,* p. 91.
11. Peter S. Carmichael, "Turner Ashby's Appeal," essay in Gallagher, *The Shenandoah Valley Campaign of 1862,* pp. 154ff.
12. Douglas, *I Rode with Stonewall,* pp. 40–41.
13. Ibid.
14. D. H. Hill, "The Real Stonewall Jackson," *Century Magazine* (February 1894), pp. 623–627.
15. Quote from William McDonald, cited in Cozzens, *Shenandoah 1862,* p. 253.
16. Letter from John Harman to W. A. Harman, April 25, 1862, Hotchkiss Papers, Box 38, Library of Congress, Washington, DC.
17. Jackson to Harman, April 14, 1862, Hotchkiss Papers, Library of Congress, Washington, DC.
18. Harman to his brother, May 15 and May 18, 1862, Hotchkiss Papers, Library of Congress, Washington, DC.
19. Robert L. Dabney, *The Life and Campaigns of Lieutenant-General Thomas J. Stonewall Jackson,* p. 354.
20. Douglas, *I Rode with Stonewall,* pp. 42ff.
21. Gary Ecelbarger, *Three Days in the Shenandoah: Stonewall Jackson at Front Royal and Winchester,* p. 33.
22. Hotchkiss, *Make Me a Map of the Valley,* p. 10.

CHAPTER TWENTY-FIVE: HUNTER AS PREY

1. J. William Jones, "Reminiscences of the Army of Northern Virginia," *Southern Historical Society Papers,* vol. 9, p. 364.
2. Thomas T. Munford, "Reminiscences of Jackson's Valley Campaign," *Southern Historical Society Papers,* vol. 7, pp. 523ff; there is another version of this story, similar in substance, in Willie Walker Caldwell, *Stonewall Jim,* pp. 38–40; and yet another in Douglas Southall Freeman, *Lee's Lieutenants.*
3. Munford, "Reminiscences of Jackson's Valley Campaign," pp. 523ff.
4. Ibid.
5. Cited in Lenoir Chambers, *Stonewall Jackson: The Legend and the Man,* vol. 1, p. 509.
6. Dispatch from Taylor (for Lee) to Jackson, May 14, *Official Records,* Series 1, vol. 12, pt. 3, p. 887.
7. William Allan, *History of the Campaign of General T. J. (Stonewall) Jackson;* Jedediah Hotchkiss, *Campaign of Jackson in the Shenandoah Valley,* p. 87.

8. Letter from Johnston to Ewell dated May 13, 1862, *Official Records,* Series 1, vol. 12, pt. 3, p. 888.

9. Peter Cozzens, *Shenandoah 1862: Stonewall Jackson's Valley Campaign,* pp. 276ff. Cozzens offers an excellent account and analysis of this game of dispatches, which I have largely followed here.

10. Ewell to Jackson and Jackson to Ewell, May 18, 1862, *Official Records,* Series 1, vol. 12, pt. 3, p. 897.

11. Henry Kyd Douglas, *I Rode with Stonewall,* p. 93.

12. Jackson to Lee, May 20, 1862, *Official Records,* Series 1, vol. 12, pt. 3, p. 898.

13. James I. Robertson, *Stonewall Jackson: The Man, the Legend, the Soldier,* p. 388.

14. Williams to his daughter, May 17, 1862; cited in Cozzens, *Shenandoah 1862,* p. 279.

15. J. William Miller, "Such Men as Shields, Banks, and Frémont," essay in Gary W. Gallagher, ed., *The Shenandoah Campaign of 1862,* p. 54.

16. Banks to Stanton, May 22, 1862, *Official Records,* Series 1, vol. 12, pt. 1, p. 524.

17. This description comes in part from David Hunter Strother's account of a May 18 meeting with Banks. Strother, *A Virginia Yankee in the Civil War,* p. 36.

18. Lanty Blackford to his mother, cited in Cozzens, *Shenandoah 1862,* p. 289.

19. *Official Records,* Series 1, vol. 12, pt. 1, p. 701.

CHAPTER TWENTY-SIX: THE PROFESSOR'S TIME/SPEED/DISTANCE EQUATION

1. Peter Cozzens, *Shenandoah 1862: Stonewall Jackson's Valley Campaign,* p. 278. As Cozzens points out, there were mixed feelings among the troops, but the prevailing sentiment seemed to be that the war would end without them.

2. George H. Gordon, *Brook Farm to Cedar Mountain,* p. 190.

3. David Hunter Strother, *A Virginia Yankee in the Civil War,* pp. 38–40.

4. *Official Records,* Series 1, vol. 12, pt. 1, p. 546.

5. Strother, *A Virginia Yankee in the Civil War,* p. 39.

6. Ibid.

7. *Official Records,* Series 1, vol. 12, pt. 1, p. 546.

8. Jedediah Hotchkiss, *History of the Campaign of Stonewall Jackson in the Shenandoah Valley,* p. 109.

9. Fulkerson to his sister, May 16, 1862, Fulkerson Papers, VMI, cited in Gary Ecelbarger, *Three Days in the Shenandoah,* p. 35.

10. Ecelbarger, *Three Days in the Shenandoah,* p. 34.

11. Ibid.

12. Ibid., p. 58.

13. Ibid., pp. 86–88; Ecelbarger gives an excellent account of the final cavalry attack.

14. Donald Pfanz, *Richard S. Ewell: A Soldier's Life,* pp. 185–186.

CHAPTER TWENTY-SEVEN: A LETHAL FOOTRACE

1. Banks's report; *Official Records,* Series 1, vol. 12, pt. 1, p. 546.

2. Cited in Peter Cozzens, *Shenandoah 1862: Stonewall Jackson's Valley Campaign,* p. 316.

3. Banks to his wife, May 24, 1862, cited in Gary Ecelbarger, *Three Days in the Shenandoah,* p. 103.

4. Cited in Ecelbarger, *Three Days in the Shenandoah,* p. 123.

5. *Official Records,* Series 1, vol. 12, pt. 1, pp. 575–577.

6. Robert L. Dabney, *The Life and Campaigns of Lieutenant-General Thomas J. Stonewall Jackson,* p. 372.

7. Jackson's comment in his official report was that Ashby's men "deserted their colors and abandoned themselves to pillage to such an extent as to make it necessary for that gallant officer to discontinue further pursuit." *Official Records,* Series 1, vol. 12, pt. 1, p. 704.

8. Henry Kyd Douglas, *I Rode with Stonewall,* p. 57.

9. Ecelbarger, *Three Days in the Shenandoah,* p. 155.

10. McDowell to Lincoln, May 24, 1862; *Report of the Joint Committee on the Conduct of the War,* 1863, p. 274.

11. Stephen W. Sears, ed., *The Civil War Papers of George B. McClellan: Selected Correspondence 1860–1865,* p. 275.

CHAPTER TWENTY-EIGHT: THE TAKING OF WINCHESTER

1. Banks to Lincoln, May 24, *Official Records,* Series 1, vol. 12, pt. 1, p. 527.

2. Peter Cozzens, *Shenandoah 1862: Stonewall Jackson's Valley Campaign,* p. 360.

3. Gary Ecelbarger, *Three Days in the Shenandoah,* p. 185.

4. J. William Jones, "Reminiscences of the Army of Northern Virginia," *Southern Historical Society Papers,* vol. 9, p. 235.

5. Richard Taylor, *Destruction and Reconstruction,* p. 60.

6. Ibid., p. 61.

7. Alpheus S. Williams, *From the Cannon's Mouth: The Civil War Letters of General Alpheus S. Williams,* p. 81.

8. Jedediah Hotchkiss, "Memoranda—Valley Campaign of 1861," unpublished ms. At the New-York Historical Society, cited in James I. Robertson, *Stonewall Jackson: The Man, the Legend, the Soldier,* p. 407.

9. Henry Kyd Douglas, *I Rode with Stonewall,* p. 59.

10. Cozzens, *Shenandoah 1862,* p. 369.

11. David Hunter Strother, *A Virginia Yankee in the Civil War,* p. 42.

12. Robert L. Dabney, *The Life and Campaigns of Lieutenant-General Thomas J. Stonewall Jackson,* p. 380.

13. Letter from Jackson to Anna, May 26, 1862; Mary Anna Jackson, *Memoirs of Stonewall Jackson,* p. 265.

14. Cited in Robertson, *Stonewall Jackson,* p. 410.

15. Ecelbarger, *Three Days in the Shenandoah,* p. 215.

16. Robertson, *Stonewall Jackson,* p. 410.

17. Williams, *From the Cannon's Mouth,* p. 84.

18. Ibid., p. 85.

19. Banks's report to Stanton, *Official Records,* Series 1, vol. 12, pt. 1, pp. 551ff.

CHAPTER TWENTY-NINE: LINCOLN'S PERFECT TRAP

1. Gary W. Gallagher, "You Must Either Attack Richmond or Give Up the Job and Come to the Defence of Washington: Lincoln and the 1862 Shenandoah Valley Campaign," essay in Gary W. Gallagher, ed., *The Shenandoah Campaign of 1862,* p. 8.

2. Ibid. Gallagher makes a solid case that Lincoln, instead of panicking, sought to use Jackson to help persuade McClellan to act. He also saw Jackson's position north of Winchester as a golden opportunity to destroy him, and gave orders accordingly.

3. Exchange of wires between Lincoln and McClellan, May 25, 1862; George Brinton McClellan, *Report Upon the Organization of the Army of the Potomac and Its Campaigns: From July 26, 1861, to November 7, 1862,* p. 65.

4. Peter Cozzens, *Shenandoah 1862: Stonewall Jackson's Valley Campaign,* p. 398.

5. Letters from John Harman to W. A. Harman, May 9 and May 27, 1862, Hotchkiss Papers, Box 38, Library of Congress, Washington, DC.

6. Cited in Cozzens, *Shenandoah 1862*, p. 393.

7. *Richmond Dispatch,* May 27, 1862.

8. *Southern Literary Messenger* 34 (May 1862), p. 327.

9. Henry Kyd Douglas, *I Rode with Stonewall,* p. 66.

10. In one account of Jackson's meeting with Winder, he was said to have deeply insulted Brigadier General Arnold Elzey. The story goes as follows: Jackson had been chatting with Winder and Elzey, a hero of Manassas. Winder reported that the enemy had been heavily reinforced, and Elzey, agreeing with Winder, stated that the Union had "heavy guns on Maryland Heights." Jackson then asked him: "General Elzey, are you afraid of heavy guns?" Elzey blushed but said nothing. This, of course, was a serious breach of etiquette, uncommon during the war (though James Longstreet did it at least twice). The account comes from a memoir by McHenry Howard (*Recollections of a Maryland Confederate Soldier and Staff Officer Under Johnston, Jackson, and Lee,* pp. 114–115). Because this seems to be the only source of the story, and because it is so utterly out of character for Jackson to have so gratuitously embarrassed a fellow general in public, I have not placed the incident in the main narration but in the notes instead. Jackson was very tough on generals, but never in that particular way.

11. Alexander R. Boteler, "Stonewall Jackson in Campaign of 1862," *Southern Historical Society Papers,* New Series, vol. 2, Richmond, September 1915.

12. Ibid.

13. Ibid.

14. This account was pieced together from both Boteler's narrative (per above) and that of Jedediah Hotchkiss in his *Make Me a Map of the Valley,* pp. 49–50.

15. This comes from two different accounts of the story, one from Hotchkiss (*Make Me a Map of the Valley,* p. 50) and the other from Wells J. Hawks's letter to Hotchkiss of January 17, 1866.

16. Boteler, "Stonewall Jackson in Campaign of 1862."

17. William J. Miller, "Such Men as Shields, Banks, and Frémont," essay in Gallagher, *The Shenandoah Valley Campaign of 1862,* p. 66.

18. Hotchkiss, *Make Me a Map of the Valley,* p. 44.

19. Letter from Henry Kyd Douglas to Tippie Boteler, July 24, 1862, Douglas Papers, Duke University.

20. Boteler, "Stonewall Jackson in Campaign of 1862."

21. Miller, "Such Men as Shields, Banks, and Frémont," p. 74.

22. *Official Records,* Series 1, vol. 12, pt. 3, pp. 290–306, correspondence to and from Stanton, Lincoln, McDowell, Shields, Geary, and McCall.

23. Cozzens, *Shenandoah 1862,* p. 408.

24. Shields to Secretary of War Stanton, June 2, 1862, *Official Records,* Series 1, vol. 12, pt. 3, p. 322; there is also a good account of this in Miller, "Such Men as Shields, Banks, and Frémont," p. 74.

25. *Official Records,* Series 1, vol. 12, pt. 3, p. 322.

26. Miller, "Such Men as Shields, Banks and Fremont," essay in Gallagher, *The Shenandoah Valley Campaign of 1862,* p. 69.

27. McHenry Howard, *Recollections of a Maryland Confederate Soldier and Staff Officer Under Johnston, Jackson, and Lee,* p. 117.

28. Douglas, *I Rode with Stonewall,* p. 70.

29. Randolph H. McKim, *A Soldier's Recollections: Leaves from the Diary of a Young Confederate*, p. 108.
30. Cited in Cozzens, *Shenandoah 1862*, p. 412.

CHAPTER THIRTY: A STRANGE FONDNESS FOR TRAPS

1. Shields to Carroll, June 1, 1862, *Official Records*, Series 1, vol. 12, pt. 3, pp. 316–317.
2. Shields's note to Carroll was sent at 8 p.m. on June 1, ordering him to leave at 4 a.m. on June 2 (*Official Records*, Series 1, vol. 12, pt. 3, p. 316) on a fifty-mile trip that was expected to take two days. Though Shields ordered Carroll to impress horses if necessary, he also encumbered him with four pieces of artillery. Jackson gave orders on June 1 to Coyne and his cavalry to burn the bridges, and they reached them by dawn on June 2. Jackson not only thought of the idea first, but by dispatching cavalry he made it impossible for Carroll to win the race.
3. Jackson was casually brilliant at choosing defensive terrain, starting with the backside of Henry Hill at First Manassas, and continuing through Port Republic and Second Manassas.
4. James I. Robertson, *Stonewall Jackson: The Man, the Legend, the Soldier*, p. 428.
5. James Dinwiddie of the Charlottesville Artillery, cited in Cozzens, *Shenandoah 1862*, p. 426.
6. Samuel V. Fulkerson to unknown addressee, June 14, 1862; cited in Robertson, *Stonewall Jackson*, pp. 451–452.
7. Henry Kyd Douglas, *I Rode with Stonewall*, p. 75.
8. A. S. Pendleton to his mother, June 7, 1862, in W. G. Bean, *Stonewall's Man: Sandie Pendleton*, p. 364.
9. Robert K. Krick, *Conquering the Valley: Stonewall Jackson at Port Republic*, pp. 69–71.
10. Robert K. Krick gives an insightful, detailed account of the question of the burning of the bridge, which became the subject of a huge controversy in which Carroll was pilloried for what looked like pure stupidity. A number of eyewitnesses said later that Union soldiers had attempted to burn the bridge. The truth, as Krick sorts it out, was that "The considerable, if conflicting, testimony suggests that the Truth About The Bridge is that: Shields ordered Carroll to save it; in case destruction became necessary, a detachment ready to attempt that went along; in the frenzied excitement as events unfolded, no one had much chance to think about burning, and surely no time to accomplish it." *Conquering the Valley,* p. 62.
11. Peter Cozzens, *Shenandoah 1862: Stonewall Jackson's Valley Campaign,* p. 444.
12. Ibid., p. 445, citing Kimball's postwar letter.
13. C. W. Rossiter, "Orders Disobeyed: Had the bridge been burned, Stonewall Jackson would have been annihilated," *National Tribune*, September 2, 1915; Cozzens, *Shenandoah 1862*, p. 445.
14. James McPherson, *Battle Cry of Freedom*, p. 330.
15. Peter S. Carmichael, "Turner Ashby's Appeal," essay in Gary W. Gallagher, ed., *The Shenandoah Campaign of 1862*, pp. 155ff.
16. Krick, *Conquering the Valley*, p. 25, citing Parmeter diary.
17. Jackson's battle report; *Official Records*, Series 1, vol. 12, pt. 1, p. 712.
18. Cozzens, *Shenandoah 1862*, p. 467.
19. Bruce Catton, *Mr. Lincoln's War*, p. 201; Catton has a nice meditation on this idea of how Civil War battles were won or lost on the front lines. Overwhelming firepower will almost always produce a retreat. But what happens with a single regiment against a single

regiment, facing each other across 250 yards of open meadow? How does one side "win" the engagement? It's a provocative question, not always easy to answer.

20. Robert L. Dabney, *The Life and Campaigns of Lieutenant-General Thomas J. Stonewall Jackson*, p. 415.

21. Douglas, *I Rode with Stonewall*, p. 89.

CHAPTER THIRTY-ONE: SLAUGHTER IN A SMALL PLACE

1. Jackson's Official Report, *Official Records*, Series 1, vol. 12, pt. 1, p. 714.

2. Jackson stated to Colonel John M. Patton that "I hope to be back [at Cross Keys] by ten o'clock." He clearly believed he would be fully engaged in battle with Frémont before noon.

3. The story combines two accounts, both from Munford. One is from the Thomas T. Munford manuscript in the Munford-Ellis Papers at Duke University; the other is from General T. T. Munford, "Reminiscences of Jackson's Valley Campaign," *Southern Historical Society Papers*, vol. 7, p. 530.

4. In addition to describing Jackson's eyes, "Old Blue Light" may also have been a reference to "Blue Light Presbyterians," notable as conservatives in the church.

5. Peter Cozzens, *Shenandoah 1862: Stonewall Jackson's Valley Campaign*, p. 488.

6. Robert K. Krick, *Conquering the Valley*, p. 407; see also Jackson's battle report (*Official Records*, Series 1, vol. 9, p. 293); one of the best primary source accounts of this battle is Henry B. Kelly, *Port Republic* (New York: J. B. Lippincott, 1886).

7. Richard Taylor, *Destruction and Reconstruction*, p. 81.

8. Cited from Cozzens, *Shenandoah 1862*, p. 493.

9. Taylor, *Destruction and Reconstruction*, p. 81.

10. J. William Jones, "Reminiscences of the Army of Northern Virginia," *Southern Historical Society Papers*, vol. 9, p. 362.

11. Cited in William J. Miller, "Such Men as Shields, Banks, and Frémont," essay in Gary W. Gallagher, ed., *The Shenandoah Valley Campaign of 1862*, p. 79.

12. Jedediah Hotchkiss, *Make Me a Map of the Valley*, p. 57.

CHAPTER THIRTY-TWO: ACCLAIM, AND A NEW MISSION

1. Gary Ecelbarger notes that even the nickname Stonewall was not much known before Kernstown, and that one Northern soldier wrote home that he had fought "members of the famous Stone Fence Brigade." Presented at the Valley Campaign Conference, March 3, 2012, in Winchester, Virginia; Robert G. Tanner in his book *Stonewall in the Valley* also cites a story of a drunk who asked the general, "Are you the stone, stone, the stone, are you Stone Fence Jackson?" (p. 39).

2. "A Great General," *Richmond Dispatch*, June 13, 1862.

3. "The Achievements of Stonewall Jackson," *Richmond Whig*, June 18, 1862 (story also appeared in the *Charleston Mercury*); it is noteworthy that at least one Southern general, Lafayette McLaws, believed that Richmond papers reserved most of their praise for Virginians, and only grudgingly wrote nice things about people from other states (Charles Royster, *The Destructive War*, p. 69).

4. *New Era*, June 4, 1862.

5. "What Is Thought in Washington," *New York Times*, May 27, 1862; and "What Stonewall Jackson has done for the Union," *New York Times*, May 30, 1862, in Harold Holzer and Craig Symonds, eds., *The New York Times Complete Civil War, 1861–1865*, pp. 160–161.

6. Robert K. Krick, "The Metamorphosis of Stonewall Jackson's Public Image," essay in Gary W. Gallagher, ed., *Shenandoah Valley Campaign of 1862*, p. 24.

7. Ibid., pp. 28–30; Robert K. Krick analyzed extensive correspondence from Northern and Southern soldiers, cited here.

8. Edward Porter Alexander, *Fighting for the Confederacy*, p. 94.

9. The estimate of one-third of the force gone comes from Peter Cozzens, *Shenandoah 1862: Stonewall Jackson's Valley Campaign*, p. 508.

10. D. H. Hill, "The Real Stonewall Jackson," *Century Magazine* (February 1894), pp. 623–627.

11. William S. White Statement, Dabney Papers, Southern Historical Collection, University of North Carolina.

12. Robert L. Dabney, *Life and Campaigns of Lieutenant-General Thomas J. Stonewall Jackson*, p. 739.

13. Hunter McGuire, "Career and Character of General T. J. 'Stonewall' Jackson," *Southern Historical Society Papers*, vol. 25, p. 91.

14. William B. Taliaferro, "Some Personal Reminiscences of Lt.-Gen. Thos. J. (Stonewall) Jackson," essay in Mary Anna Jackson, *Memoirs of Stonewall Jackson*, p. 513.

15. Allan Nevins, *The War for the Union*, vol. 2, *1862–1863*, p. 132.

16. D. H. Hill, "Lee's Attacks North of the Chickahominy," in Robert Underwood Johnson and Clarence Clough Buel, eds., *Battles and Leaders*, vol. 2, pp. 347–362.

17. Armistead Lindsay Long and Marcus Joseph Wright, *Memoirs of Robert E. Lee*, p. 283.

CHAPTER THIRTY-THREE: THE HILLJACK AND THE SOCIETY BOY

1. Though the idea of fame is a highly relativistic concept, especially as it applies to Civil War generals, at this point in the war the better-known generals had fought in the eastern theater. Grant's star was certainly rising in the west and his "unconditional surrender" demand at Fort Donelson had made him that theater's first big hero. But his stock had fallen somewhat after Shiloh, when he was criticized for the heavy Union casualties. (See Allan Nevins, *War for the Union, 1862–1863*, vol. 2, pp. 109–111.) David Farragut, in a daring maneuver for which he was promoted to rear admiral, had taken New Orleans, but his larger fame was yet to come. In any case, it would take some time before the western battles began to rival the likes of First and Second Manassas, Seven Days, Antietam, etc., in the public imagination. As noted earlier, Beauregard, the biggest star of the early war, was already in eclipse. Joe Johnston, now wounded, and having won no victories since July 1861, was not nearly the hero, at this moment, that Jackson was. Lee had just been given command of the Army of Northern Virginia.

2. Dabney Herndon Maury, *Recollections of a Virginian in the Mexican, Indian, and Civil Wars*, pp. 22–23.

3. Dabney Herndon Maury, "General T. J. 'Stonewall' Jackson: Incidents in the Remarkable Career of a Great Soldier," *Southern Historical Society Papers*, vol. 25, pp. 309–310.

4. Stephen W. Sears, *George B. McClellan: The Young Napoleon*, p. 2.

5. Ibid., p. 4.

6. Ibid., p. 3.

7. Maury, *Recollections of a Virginian*, p. 22.

8. James I. Robertson, *Stonewall Jackson: The Man, the Legend, the Soldier*, p. 32.

9. Thomas Jackson Arnold, *The Early Life and Letters of General Thomas J. Jackson*, p. 66.

10. Ulysses S. Grant, *Memoirs and Selected Letters*, pp. 166–167.

11. John C. Waugh, *Class of 1846*, p. 65; Robertson, *Stonewall Jackson*, pp. 42–43.

12. G.F.R. Henderson, *Stonewall Jackson and the American Civil War*, vol. 1, p. 20.

13. Eugene C. Tidball, *No Disgrace to My Country: The Life of John C. Tidball*, pp. 29–30.
14. Ibid.
15. Robertson, *Stonewall Jackson*, p. 37.
16. Waugh, *The Class of 1846*, p. 35.
17. Robertson, *Stonewall Jackson*, p. 44, citing Maury and others.
18. Maury, "General T. J. 'Stonewall' Jackson," p. 310.
19. Henderson, *Stonewall Jackson and the American Civil War*, vol. 1, p. 19.
20. Sears, *George B. McClellan*, p. 8.
21. Ibid.
22. Ibid., p. 7.
23. Robertson, *Stonewall Jackson*, p. 92.
24. Letter from Jackson to Laura, January 28, 1844; Arnold, *The Early Life and Letters of General Thomas J. Jackson*, p. 64.
25. John Gibbon, "Stonewall Jackson," manuscript in Hotchkiss Papers at the Library of Congress, letter to Hotchkiss dated November 10, 1893.
26. Waugh, *The Class of 1846*, p. 46.
27. Ibid., p. 50.
28. Cited in ibid., p. 67.
29. Ibid., p. 54.

CHAPTER THIRTY-FOUR: THE DEFENSE OF RICHMOND

1. Alexander Hunter, *Johnny Reb and Billy Yank*, p. 170; the moment comes from the afternoon at Gaines's Mill, when word came that Jackson had arrived. Kyd Douglas describes it thus: "A staff officer dashed along Longstreet's wearied lines, crying out 'Stonewall's at them!' and was answered with yell after yell of joy, which added a strange sound to the din of battle." (*I Rode with Stonewall*, p. 103); I have taken this slightly out of sequence here but the sentiments are all correct.
2. Brian K. Burton, *Extraordinary Circumstances: The Seven Days Battles*, p. 31.
3. This simple but revealing notion comes from William J. Miller's 2013 essay in Civil War Trust, "The Seven Days Battles."
4. Clifford Dowdey, *The Seven Days: The Emergence of Robert E. Lee*, p. 77.
5. Allan Nevins, *The War for the Union*, vol. 2, *1862–1863*, p. 119.
6. Robert L. Dabney, *The Life and Campaigns of Lieutenant-General Thomas J. Stonewall Jackson*, p. 436; Nevins, *The War for the Union*, vol. 2, pp. 118–199.
7. This included a division under General George McCall that had been detached from Irvin McDowell.
8. Edward Porter Alexander, *Fighting for the Confederacy*, p. 95.
9. Letter from McClellan to Stanton, June 25; Stephen W. Sears, ed., *The Civil War Papers of George B. McClellan*, p. 309.
10. Burton, *Extraordinary Circumstances*, pp. 15 and 56.
11. Ibid.
12. Ibid., p. 51.
13. Letter from George McClellan to Mary Ellen McClellan, Sears, *The Civil War Papers*, p. 306.
14. Lee to Jackson, June 25, cited in James I. Robertson, *Stonewall Jackson: The Man, the Legend, the Soldier*, p. 469.
15. Robert Dabney to Jedediah Hotchkiss, September 12, 1896, Hotchkiss Papers, Library of Congress.

16. Dabney, *Life and Campaigns of Lieutenant-General Thomas J. Stonewall Jackson*, p. 440.

17. After the Battle of Malvern Hill, Jackson wrote Anna: "During the past week I have not been well, have suffered from fever and debility, but through the blessing of an ever kind Providence am better today." Thus he was ill, though we don't know exactly which day he first fell sick. It could well have been as early as June 26, when he was already clearly in a state of exhaustion; his physical condition had everything to do with the events of the week; Mary Anna Jackson, *Memoirs of Stonewall Jackson*, p. 302.

18. McClellan to Stanton, June 25, 1862, Sears, *The Civil War Papers*, p. 312.

19. Stephen W. Sears, *To the Gates of Richmond*, p. 199.

20. Alexander, *Fighting for the Confederacy*, p. 99.

21. Allen C. Redwood, "The Confederate in the Field," chapter in *The Photographic History of the Civil War in Ten Volumes*, vol. 8, p. 155.

22. Alexander, *Fighting for the Confederacy*, p. 100.

23. Judkin Browning, *The Seven Days' Battles*, p. 53; Burton, *Extraordinary Circumstances*, p. 74.

24. McClellan to Stanton, June 26, 1862; Sears, *The Civil War Papers*, p. 317.

25. Richard Taylor, *Destruction and Reconstruction*, p. 93.

26. The definitive study of Jackson's role in the Seven Days is to be found in Brian K. Burton's superb 2001 book *Extraordinary Circumstances: The Seven Days Battles*. His analysis of Jackson's actions has largely been adopted as my framework here. James I. Robertson Jr. also offers a well-researched and highly readable analysis in his 1997 biography, *Stonewall Jackson: The Man, the Soldier, the Legend*. Its conclusions comport largely with those in Burton's book.

27. Sears, *To the Gates of Richmond*, p. 210.

28. Ibid.

CHAPTER THIRTY-FIVE: VICTORY BY ANY OTHER NAME

1. Stephen W. Sears, *To the Gates of Richmond*, p. 214.

2. Robert L. Dabney, *The Life and Campaigns of Lieutenant-General Thomas J. Stonewall Jackson*, p. 443.

3. Ibid., p. 444.

4. Cited in Sears, *To the Gates of Richmond*, p. 233.

5. *Chasseur* is French for "hunter."

6. John Esten Cooke, *Outlines from the Outpost*, pp. 50–51.

7. Interview with Bobby Krick, "The Battle of Gaines's Mill: Then and Now," Civil War Trust.

8. Cited in Brian K. Burton, *Extraordinary Circumstances*, p. 154.

9. Cited in Judkin Browning, *The Seven Days' Battles: The War Begins Anew*, p. 78.

10. Heros Von Borcke, *Memoirs of the Confederate War for Independence*, vol. 1, p. 60.

11. Edwin K. Gould, *Major-General Hiram Berry: His career as a contractor, bank president, politician, and major-general of volunteers in the Civil War*, p. 172.

12. Browning, *The Seven Days' Battles*, p. 86.

13. McClellan to Stanton, June 28, 1862, 12:20 a.m., Stephen W. Sears,, ed., *The Civil War Papers of George B. McClellan*, p. 323.

14. Burton, *Extraordinay Circumstances*, pp. 206–207.

15. James I. Robertson, *Stonewall Jackson: The Man, the Legend, the Soldier*, p. 488; Robertson first uncovered the communiqué, which changed historians' views of Jackson's behavior.

16. D. H. Hill, "McClellan's Change of Base and Malvern Hill," in Robert Underwood John-

son and Clarence Clough Buel, eds., *Battles and Leaders of the Civil War*, vol. 2, pp. 383–395.

17. Dabney, *The Life and Campaigns of Lieutenant-General Thomas J. Stonewall Jackson*, p. 460.

18. John Overton Casler, *Four Years in the Stonewall Brigade*, p. 94.

19. Letter to Anna, June 30, "Near White Oak Swamp Bridge," Mary Anna Jackson, *Memoirs of Stonewall Jackson*, p. 297.

20. W. W. Blackford MS. Memoir cited in Douglas Southall Freeman, *Lee's Lieutenants*, vol. 1, p. 656.

21. Sears, *To the Gates of Richmond*, p. 280.

22. Testimony of Samuel Heintzelman before the Joint Committee on the Conduct of the War, cited in William Swinton, ed., *The "Times" Review of McClellan: His Military Career Reviewed and Exposed*, p. 24.

23. Robert Stiles, Address at the Dedication of the Monument of Confederate Dead, University of Virginia, June 7, 1893.

24. Ibid.; the other account was from John Wallace McCreery, one of Jackson's couriers; Burton, *Extraordinary Circumstances*, p. 231.

25. Note that Jackson biographer James I. Robertson believes that Stiles's account is a fabrication, for various reasons, including that Jackson's uniform would have been rain-drenched and not dusty, that there would have been no dust on the ground to mark on, etc. Brian K. Burton says that the McCreery account corroborates the Stiles account except in the identification of the drawer of the diagram.

26. Edward Porter Alexander, *Fighting for the Confederacy*, p. 109.

27. Jackson, *Memoirs of Stonewall Jackson*, p. 297.

28. Ibid.

29. Cited in Browning, *The Seven Days' Battles*, p. 112.

30. Robertson, *Stonewall Jackson*, p. 495.

31. General William B. Franklin, "Rear Guard Fighting During the Change of Base," in Underwood and Buel, *Battles and Leaders*, vol. 2, pp. 377–382; General A. R. Wright, whom Lee sent to join Jackson, actually found this ford, though he did not manage to inform Jackson of that. Still, the charge is valid; the evidence is clear Jackson was not aggressively searching out fords and crossings that day.

32. Alexander, *Fighting for the Confederacy*, p. 96.

33. Robertson, *Stonewall Jackson*, p. 499.

34. Hill, "McClellan's Change of Base and Malvern Hill."

35. Jackson's report on Seven Days, February 20, 1863; *Official Records*, Series 1, vol. 11, ch. 2.

36. Hill, "McClellan's Change of Base and Malvern Hill."

37. Henry Kyd Douglas, *I Rode with Stonewall*, p. 108.

38. William Thomas Poague, *Gunner with Stonewall*, p. 29.

39. Robertson, *Stonewall Jackson*, p. 501.

40. Burton, *Extraordinary Circumstances*, p. 330.

41. Hunter McGuire, "General T. J. ("Stonewall") Jackson, Confederate States Army: His Career and Character, an Address by Hunter McGuire, M.D., LL.D.," *Southern Historical Society Papers*, vol. 25, p. 91.

42. James M. McPherson, *Battle Cry of Freedom*, p. 470.

CHAPTER THIRTY-SIX: IN WHICH EVERYTHING CHANGES

1. James M. McPherson, *Battle Cry of Freedom*, pp. 494–495.
2. Ibid., p. 496; Allan Nevins, *War for the Union*, vol. 2, *1862–1863*, pp. 137–138.
3. McClellan to Lincoln, July 7, 1862, Stephen W. Sears, ed., *The Civil War Papers of George B. McClellan*, pp. 344–345.
4. Brian K. Burton, *Extraordinary Circumstances: The Seven Days Battles*, pp. 397–398.
5. Clifford Dowdey, *The Seven Days: The Emergence of Robert E. Lee*, p. 14.
6. Shelby Foote, *The Civil War: A Narrative*, p. 524.
7. James I. Robertson, *Stonewall Jackson: The Man, the Legend, the Soldier*, p. 505, citing William W. Blackford, *War Years with Jeb Stuart*.
8. Letter from Hunter McGuire to Jedediah Hotchkiss, May 28, 1896, Hotchkiss Collection, Library of Congress.
9. Dr. Hunter McGuire, "General Thomas J. Jackson: Reminiscences of the Famous Leader by Dr. Hunter McGuire," originally in *Richmond Dispatch*, July 19, 1891; also *Southern Historical Society Papers*, vol. 19, p. 298.
10. Alexander Boteler, "Stonewall Jackson's Campaign of 1862," account in *Philadephia Weekly Times*, February 11, 1892; also in *Southern Historical Society Papers*, vol. 40, pp. 180–181.
11. Susan Leigh Blackford and Charles Minor Blackford, *Letters From Lee's Army*, p. 89.
12. Ibid.
13. Allen C. Redwood, "With Stonewall Jackson," *Scribner's Monthly* 18, no. 2 (June 1879).
14. Charles Royster, *The Destructive War*, pp. 43–45.
15. Kenneth Hall, *Stonewall Jackson and Religious Faith in Military Command*, p. 56.
16. Ibid.
17. Henry Kyd Douglas, *I Rode with Stonewall*, p. 114.
18. Ibid., pp. 113–114.
19. One win—Gaines's Mill; two losses—Mechanicsville and Malvern Hill; three draws—Oak Grove, Savage's Station, Glendale.
20. William Thomas Poague, *Gunner with Stonewall*, p. 32.
21. John Worsham, *One of Jackson's Foot Cavalry*, p. 60.
22. Letter from Jackson to Ewell, July 12, 1862; manuscript in Huntington Library.
23. Douglas, *I Rode with Stonewall*, p. 119.
24. McGuire, "General Thomas J. Jackson: Reminiscences"; this story is a blend of the accounts of Hunter McGuire and Henry Kyd Douglas.
25. Douglas, *I Rode with Stonewall*, p. 119.
26. Blackford, *Letters from Lee's Army*, p. 86.
27. Douglas Southall Freeman, *Lee's Lieutenants*, vol. 1, pp. 610–613.

CHAPTER THIRTY-SEVEN: NO BACKING OUT THIS DAY

1. Frémont resigned rather than serve under McDowell.
2. Louis-Philippe-Albert D'Orleans, Comte de Paris, *History of the Civil War in America*, p. 245.
3. *Official Records*, Series 1, vol. 12, pt. 3, pp. 473–474.
4. Richard Taylor, *Destruction and Reconstruction*, p. 105.
5. Letter from Fitz John Porter to J.C.G. Kennedy, July 17, 1862; Porter Papers, Massachusetts Historical Society.
6. Quote from *Cornhill Magazine*, cited in Robert K. Krick, *Stonewall Jackson at Cedar Mountain*, p. 4.

7. Eliza Amelia Dwight, *Life and Letters of Wilder Dwight, Lieut. Col., Second Massachusetts Infantry Volunteers*, p. 233.

8. John Hennessy, *Return to Bull Run*, pp. 21–22.

9. James I. Robertson, *Stonewall Jackson: The Man, the Legend, the Soldier*, p. 514.

10. The *Richmond Dispatch* of August 5, 1862, quoted a letter to the *Philadelphia Inquirer*, in which the writer said: "The men are in the best of spirits and the issuing of the recent orders by Gen. Pope have cheered up the drooping hearts of many a weary and foot sore patriot, who . . . has been compelled to mount guard over rebel commissary stores, while Jackson's crew were refreshing themselves with sleep. . . . "

11. Hennessy, *Return to Bull Run*, p. 15. In *Return to Bull Run*, his definitive book on Second Manassas, Hennessy provides an excellent analysis of Pope's front-man role.

12. Ed Bonekemper, "General Disobedience: 'Little Mac' Let John Pope Twist in the Wind," *Civil War Times*, December 2010.

13. *Official Records*, Series 1, vol. 12, pt. 3, p. 527.

14. Jedediah Hotchkiss, *Make Me a Map of the Valley*, p. 62.

15. Letter from Anna to Dr. McGuire, August 4, 1862, McGuire Papers, Virginia Historical Society.

16. Letter from Jackson to Anna, sent from Gordonsville, July 28, 1862, Mary Anna Jackson, *Memoirs of Stonewall Jackson*, p. 310.

17. Robertson, *Stonewall Jackson*, p. 519.

18. Robert K. Krick, *Stonewall Jackson at Cedar Mountain*, p. 48.

19. John Pope, *The Military Memoirs of John Pope*, Notes, p. 271; Pope and his courier (Lee's nephew) both challenged Banks's version, saying that Pope never intended for Banks to attack Jackson's entire army single-handedly.

20. Testimony of Nathaniel Banks before the Joint Committee on the Conduct of the War, Dec. 14, 1864, in *Report of the Joint Committee, Second Session, 38th Congress*, Washington, 1865.

21. Krick, *Stonewall Jackson at Cedar Mountain*, p. 45. This is Krick's estimate of the men who actually fought on August 9, not the total number of effectives present.

22. Ibid., p. 106, citing John Blue's memoir, *Hanging Rock Rebel*, p. 119; also cited in Robertson, *Stonewall Jackson*, p. 528.

23. Sam Smith, "Jackson Is With You! The Battle of Cedar Mountain," Civil War Trust website.

24. Blue, *Hanging Rock Rebel*, p. 121.

25. The best evidence for this is the absence of any follow-up to Crawford's attack. No regiments came up behind him; no effort was made to consolidate his gains; he was more or less left alone on the field, and he was bitter about it.

26. George Henry Gordon, *Brook Farm to Cedar Mountain, 1861–2*, p. 294.

27. John Worsham, *One of Jackson's Foot Cavalry*, p. 112.

28. Gordon, *Brook Farm to Cedar Mountain*, p. 295.

29. Krick, *Stonewall Jackson at Cedar Mountain*, p. 186, citing Susan Leigh Blackford and Charles Minor Blackford, *Letters from Lee's Army*.

30. Krick, *Stonewall Jackson at Cedar Mountain*, p. 204.

31. Blackford and Blackford, *Letters From Lee's Army*, p. 105.

32. William B. Taliaferro, "Some Personal Reminiscences of Lt.-Gen. Thos. J. (Stonewall) Jackson," essay in Jackson, *Memoirs of Stonewall Jackson*, pp. 517–518.

33. Ibid., p. 105.

34. Hotchkiss, *Make Me a Map of the Valley*, p. 67.

35. S. W. Crawford, quoted in Robert Underwood Johnson and Clarence Clough Buel, eds., *Battles and Leaders,* vol. 2, p. 459.
36. Krick, *Stonewall Jackson at Cedar Mountain,* pp. 367–376.
37. Ibid., p. 328.
38. Lee to Jackson, August 12, 1862; *Official Records,* Series 1, vol. 12, pt. 2, p. 185.
39. Letter from Jackson to Anna, August 11, 1862, Jackson, *Memoirs of Stonewall Jackson,* p. 312.
40. Blackford and Blackford, *Letters from Lee's Army,* entry for August 17, 1862, p. 108.

CHAPTER THIRTY-EIGHT: THE HUM OF A BEEHIVE

1. Description of plunder of local farms, "From the Rappahannock Lines," *Richmond Dispatch,* August 25, 1862: "Many a family has been left in a condition verging upon absolute want and starvation."
2. Peter S. Carmichael, "So Far From God and So Close To Stonewall Jackson," *Virginia Magazine of History and Biography* 111, no. 1 (2003), pp. 33–66.
3. Ibid.
4. Ibid.
5. John Overton Casler, *Four Years in the Stonewall Brigade,* pp. 100–101.
6. Samuel Basset French, *Centennial Tale,* pp. 15ff; see also James I. Robertson, *Stonewall Jackson: The Man, the Legend, the Soldier,* pp. 542–544; and Carmichael, "So Far From God."
7. Carmichael, "So Far From God."
8. William C. Oates, *The War Between the Union and the Confederacy,* p. 131.
9. John Hennessy, *Return to Bull Run,* pp. 28–29; Hennessy points out what most historians do not, that Cedar Mountain produced an immediate shift in Union attitudes.
10. *Official Records,* Series 1, vol. 12, pt. 3, p. 132; Hennessy has a good summary of this change of heart; see his *Return to Bull Run,* pp. 29, 40.
11. *Official Records,* Series 1, vol. 12, pt. 3, pp. 560ff.
12. Robertson, *Stonewall Jackson,* p. 546.
13. Hennessy, *Return to Bull Run,* p. 92.
14. Henry Kyd Douglas, *I Rode with Stonewall,* p. 132.
15. G.F.R. Henderson, *Stonewall Jackson and the American Civil War,* vol. 2, pp. 123–124. McGuire said he recalled seeing the two "the day before we started to march," which would have been Sunday the 24th, and thus presumably the same meeting—there was only one as far as we know—that ended with Jackson saying, per Douglas, "I will be moving within an hour." McGuire's account varies a bit from Douglas's, but this would seem to be a function of the passage of time: McGuire was remembering events of thirty-five years before.
16. Douglas, *I Rode with Stonewall,* p. 133. Jackson, in fact, got his troops moving out of their positions along the river that evening. But he would not be able to leave until morning.
17. Hennessy, *Return to Bull Run,* p. 94.
18. William B. Taliaferro, "Jackson's Raid Around Pope," in Robert Underwood Johnson and Clarence Clough Buel, eds., *Battles and Leaders,* vol. 2, p. 501.
19. Casler, *Four Years in the Stonewall Brigade,* p. 107; "We had started with three days' rations, and if we had failed to make those captures we would have been in a barren country without rations."
20. Taliaferro, "Jackson's Raid Around Pope," p. 501.
21. Oates, *The War Between the Union and the Confederacy,* p. 133.

22. Gen. James H. Lane, *Reminiscences re: General Thomas "Stonewall" Jackson*, p. 28.

23. William Thomas Poague, *Gunner with Stonewall*, pp. 34–35.

24. *Official Report of General Thomas J. Jackson* on operations from August 15, 1862, to September 3, 1862, *Official Records*, Series 1, vol. 12, pt. 2, p. 643.

25. Robert L. Dabney, *Life and Campaigns of Lieutenant-General Thomas J. Stonewall Jackson*, pp. 516–517; Samuel D. Buck, *With the Old Confeds*, p. 51.

26. Allen C. Redwood, "With Stonewall Jackson," *Scribner's Monthly* 18, no. 2 (June 1879).

27. Hennessy, *Return to Bull Run*, p. 103.

28. Ibid.

29. I have chosen not to repeat here what seems to be an apocryphal story of Stuart and Jackson meeting and having a jolly exchange about Stuart's theft of Pope's overcoat. Jeffry D. Wert, *Cavalryman of the Lost Cause: A Biography of J. E. B. Stuart*, p. 131.

30. William W. Blackford, *War Years with Jeb Stuart*, pp. 112–113.

31. Hennessy, *Return to Bull Run*, p. 117.

32. Ibid., p. 118.

33. Jedediah Hotchkiss, *Make Me a Map of the Valley*, p. 130, journal entry for April 15, 1863.

34. "Official Report of Thomas Jackson," *Official Records*, Series 1, vol. 12, pt. 2, p. 643.

35. Oates, *The War Between the Union and the Confederacy*, p. 135.

36. Hennessy, *Return to Bull Run*, p. 130.

37. William W. Blackford, *War Years with Jeb Stuart*, pp. 116–118.

CHAPTER THIRTY-NINE: AT BAY ON HIS BAPTISMAL SOIL

1. John Hennessy, *Return to Bull Run*, p. 162.

2. Kearny was so put out by it that he delayed his march against Jackson the next morning, assuming it was yet another of Pope's wild-goose chases.

3. William W. Blackford, *War Years with Jeb Stuart*, p. 118.

4. William J. K. Beaudot and Lance J. Hergeden, eds., *An Irishman in the Iron Brigade: The Civil War Memoirs of James P. Sullivan*.

5. Ibid., p. 44.

6. Allen C. Redwood, "With Stonewall Jackson," *Scribner's Monthly* 18, no. 2 (June 1879).

7. Doubleday is often mistakenly credited with inventing the game of baseball.

8. From *Campbell Brown's Civil War*, cited in Hennessy, *Return to Bull Run*, p. 182.

9. William B. Taliaferro, "Jackson's Raid Around Pope," in Robert Underwood Johnson and Clarence Clough Buel, eds., *Battles and Leaders*, vol. 2, p. 510.

10. Like many hard-fighting brigades in the war the Stonewall Brigade's numbers had been almost shockingly depleted. By the end of Second Manassas, it was the size of a single, modest regiment.

11. Hennessy, *Return to Bull Run*, p. 188.

12. George F. Noyes, *The Bivouac and the Battlefield: Campaign Sketches in Virginia and Maryland*, p. 119.

13. John Gibbon, *Personal Recollections of the Civil War*, p. 56.

14. *Official Records*, Series 1, vol. 12, pt. 1.

15. Hennessy, *Return to Bull Run*, p. 196; the author offers a cogent analysis of the idea that Pope was drawn into a battle he did not need to fight.

16. Carl Schurz, *The Reminiscences of Carl Schurz*, vol. 2, *1852–1863*, pp. 364–365.

17. Jeffry Wert, "Union Major General John Pope Was No Match for Robert E. Lee," *America's Civil War Magazine*, November 1997.

18. Hennessy, *Return to Bull Run*, p. 272.

19. Ibid., p. 273.

20. Henry Kyd Douglas, *I Rode with Stonewall*, p. 138.

21. Ibid.

22. Hennessy, *Return to Bull Run*, p. 283.

23. For more on this see Curt Anders, *Injustice on Trial*.

24. John Pope, "The Second Battle of Bull Run," Johnson and Buel, *Battles and Leaders*, vol. 2, pp. 449–494.

25. Hunter McGuire, "General T. J. 'Stonewall' Jackson, Confederate States Army, His Career and Character," *Southern Historical Society Papers*, vol. 25, p. 91.

26. Stephen W. Sears, ed., *The Civil War Papers of George B. McClellan: Selected Correspondence 1860–1865*, p. 368.

27. Ibid., p. 389.

28. Peter Cozzens, *General John Pope: A Life for the Nation*, pp. 107–134; Cozzens makes a persuasive argument that Halleck shared considerable blame for the failure of Franklin and/or Sumner to advance to Pope's aid. Most historians have hung it squarely on McClellan.

29. Ibid., pp. 159–163; I am following Cozzens's arguments closely here on the subject of McClellan's supposed treachery.

30. James Longstreet, "Our March Against Pope," in Johnson and Buel, *Battles and Leaders*, vol. 2., p. 520; in the full quote Longstreet refers to the "Confederate left" as the location of the battle. He obviously meant the Confederate right.

31. Jackson's report of operations from August 15 to September 5, 1862, *Official Records*, Series 1, vol. 12, pt. 2, pp. 641ff.

32. Hennessy, *Return to Bull Run*, p. 351; Hennessy provides the best analysis I have found of the Confederate use of artillery in Porter's attack.

33. Jackson's battle report, *Official Records*, Series 1, vol. 12, pt. 2, p. 643.

34. Schurz, *The Reminiscences of Carl Schurz*, p. 372.

35. James Longstreet, *From Manassas to Appomattox: Memoirs of the Civil War in America*, p. 188.

36. Scott C. Patchan, *Second Manassas: Longstreet's Attack and the Struggle for Chinn Ridge*, p. 125.

37. Charles Walcott of the 21st Massachusetts, cited in Hennessy, *Return to Bull Run*, p. 437.

38. William Thomas Poague, *Gunner with Stonewall*, p. 40.

39. Bruce Catton, *Mr. Lincoln's Army*, p. 49.

40. Hennessy, *Return to Bull Run*, p. 451.

41. Stephen W. Sears, *George B. McClellan: The Young Napoleon*, p. 262, citing Jacob D. Cox, *Military Reminiscences of the Civil War*.

CHAPTER FORTY: THE MONGREL, BAREFOOTED CREW

1. Gary W. Gallagher, "The Most Propitious Time . . . for the Confederacy to Enter Maryland," Civil War Trust (online).

2. Ibid.

3. Major General John G. Walker, "Jackson's Capture of Harper's Ferry," in Robert Underwood Johnson and Clarence Clough Buel, eds., *Battles and Leaders*, vol. 2, p. 605.

4. The Lee/Jackson relationship prefigures in some ways the Grant/Sherman partnership that would have such a large effect on the latter part of the war.

5. "Jackson Wounded," *Richmond Whig*, May 9, 1863, editorial.

6. Jedediah Hotchkiss, *Make Me a Map of the Valley*, p. 80; James I. Robertson, *Stonewall Jackson: The Man, the Legend, the Soldier*, p. 597, citing John Newton Lyle, *Sketches Found in a Confederate Veteran's Desk*, manuscript, Washington and Lee University, Lexington, Virginia.

7. Henry Kyd Douglas, *I Rode with Stonewall*, p. 149, also Henry Kyd Douglas, "Stonewall Jackson in Maryland," in Johnson and Buel, *Battles and Leaders*, vol. 2, p. 621.

8. Heros Von Borcke, *Memoirs of the Confederate War*, p. 190.

9. Robertson, *Stonewall Jackson*, p. 605.

10. James M. McPherson, *Crossroads of Freedom: Antietam*, p. 94.

11. My translation of "*Demandez au gouvernement anglais s'il ne croit pas le moment venu de reconnaître le sud.*"

12. James M. McPherson, *Battle Cry of Freedom*, p. 554.

13. Richard Wheeler, ed., *Lee's Terrible Swift Sword: From Antietam to Chancellorsville*, pp. 54–55.

14. Bell Irvin Wiley, *The Life of Johnny Reb: The Common Soldier of the Confederacy*, p. 118.

15. Keith S. Bohannon, "Confederate Logistical Problems," in Gary W. Gallagher, ed., *The Antietam Campaign*, p. 102.

16. Ibid., p. 103.

17. Ibid.

18. Gary W. Gallagher, *Antietam: Essays on the 1862 Maryland Campaign*, p. 10.

19. Ibid., p. 11.

20. Walker, "Jackson's Capture of Harper's Ferry," p. 605 (footnote).

21. Cited in Jack Coggins, *Arms and Equipment of the Civil War*, p. 10.

22. John Worsham, *One of Jackson's Foot Cavalry*, p. 82.

23. Douglas Southall Freeman, *Lee's Lieutenants*, vol. 2, p. 154.

24. William A. Blair, "Maryland Our Maryland: Or How Lincoln and His Army Helped to Define the Confederacy," essay in Gallagher, *The Antietam Campaign*, pp. 74–75.

25. James Longstreet, "The Invasion of Maryland," in Johnson and Buel, *Battles and Leaders*, vol. 2, p. 606.

26. John Gibbon, *Recollections of the Civil War*, p. 73.

27. Jeffry D. Wert, *Cavalryman of the Lost Cause: A Biography of J. E. B. Stuart*, pp. 146–148.

28. Walker, "Jackson's Capture of Harper's Ferry," p. 606.

29. D. H. Hill, "The Battle of South Mountain," in Johnson and Buel, *Battles and Leaders*, vol. 2, p. 560.

30. *Official Records*, Series 1, vol. 19, pt. 2, pp. 289 and 294–295.

31. Walker, "Jackson's Capture of Harper's Ferry," p. 609.

32. Stephen W. Sears, *Landscape Turned Red*, p. 144.

33. Walker, "Jackson's Capture of Harper's Ferry," p. 611.

34. *Official Records*, Series 1, vol. 19, pt. 1, p. 951.

35. Robertson, *Stonewall Jackson*, p. 606.

36. Ibid.

37. Sears, *Landscape Turned Red*, p. 166.

38. Von Borcke, *Memoirs of the Confederate War*, p. 221.

39. Freeman, *Lee's Lieutenants*, vol. 2, p. 200.

40. William W. Blackford, *War Years with Jeb Stuart*, p. 144.

41. Ibid., p. 145.

CHAPTER FORTY-ONE: THE BLOOD-WASHED GROUND

1. Edward Porter Alexander, *Fighting for the Confederacy*, p. 146.

2. Ibid.

3. Ibid.
4. Stephen T. Whitman, *Antietam 1862*, p. 101.
5. Stephen W. Sears, *Landscape Turned Red*, p. 173.
6. Richard Slotkin, *The Long Road to Antietam: How the Civil War Became a Revolution*, p. 226.
7. William Thomas Poague, *Gunner with Stonewall*, p. 44.
8. Henry Kyd Douglas, *I Rode with Stonewall*, pp. 146–147. Douglas's comment was that on several occasions "Hill had exhibited a provoking want of promptness in spite of orders and it became necessary for the General to teach him one lesson at least."
9. Douglas, *I Rode with Stonewall*, p. 167.
10. Slotkin, *The Long Road to Antietam*, p. 225.
11. Sears, *Landscape Turned Red*, p. 141.
12. This involved knocking the powder cartridge off against the hub of a wheel, and placing that cylinder in the barrel after the charged one. The effect was like discharging both barrels of a double-barreled shotgun. John Gibbon, *Recollections of the Civil War*, p. 83.
13. Ibid., p. 81.
14. Sears, *Landscape Turned Red*, p. 200.
15. Slotkin, *The Long Road to Antietam*, p. 266. Here I have followed Richard Slotkin's excellent analysis of this phenomenon, which was not limited to the Battle of Antietam.
16. Sears, *Landscape Turned Red*, p. 202.
17. *Official Records*, Series 1, vol. 19, pt. 1, p. 218.
18. Sears, *Landscape Turned Red*, p. 213; Slotkin, *The Long Road to Antietam*, p. 277; movement of Stuart's artillery from Jackson's official report of the battle.
19. Early was his other reserve, but was occupied in the early morning in support of Stuart's artillery on Nicodemus Hill; Jackson later moved him into the West Woods.
20. This offers a classic example of the value of "interior lines." Sedgwick's division had to take "the long way around" from its position behind Antietam Creek. Lee's troops could move in straight lines, over shorter distances.
21. In his 2002 book *Disaster in the West Woods*, Marion Armstrong argues that Sumner's decision to march for the Confederate flank was supported by his own reconnaissance, and not necessarily the foolish decision it is often portrayed to be. He thought he knew where Jackson's men were; he did not. His choice of marching order is less defensible, as was his decision to have a single untested regiment protect his left.
22. Francis Winthrop Palfrey, *The Antietam and Fredericksburg*, p. 83.
23. Sears, *Landscape Turned Red*, p. 224.
24. Gibbon, *Recollections of the Civil War*, p. 88.
25. Sears, *Landscape Turned Red*, pp. 230, 248–249.
26. Jackson's official report of the battles of Harpers Ferry and Antietam.
27. James I. Robertson, *Stonewall Jackson: The Man, the Legend, the Soldier*, p. 616.
28. Ibid., p. 614.
29. Douglas Southall Freeman, *Lee's Lieutenants*, p. 202; Freeman's assessment of Jackson's performance was "shrewd, vigorous and free of mistakes," p. 240.
30. "Jackson and Ewell: The Latter's Opinion of His Chief—Interview with Col. Benjamin Ewell," *Southern Historical Society Papers*, vol. 20, p. 30.
31. Hunter McGuire to Jedediah Hotchkiss, March 30, 1896; cited in Robertson, *Stonewall Jackson*, p. 617.
32. George F. Noyes, *Bivouac and the Battlefield*, p. 196.
33. Ibid.

34. Stephen W. Sears, *Chancellorsville,* p. 326.
35. Slotkin, *The Long Road to Antietam,* p. 310.
36. Ibid., pp. 319–320.
37. Freeman, *Lee's Lieutenants,* p. 221.
38. Sears, *Landscape Turned Red,* p. 292.
39. James I. Robertson Jr., *Stonewall Jackson,* pp. 290–291.
40. Ibid., p. 155.
41. Douglas, *I Rode with Stonewall,* p. 179.
42. *Official Records,* Series 1, vol. 19, pt. 1, pp. 32, 65.
43. McClellan to his wife, September 20, 1862; Stephen W. Sears, *The Civil War Papers of George B. McClellan,* p. 473.
44. Report of Lieutenant General Jackson of operations September 5–27, 1862, *Official Records,* Series 1, vol. 9, p. 580.
45. James M. McPherson, *Crossroads of Freedom: Antietam,* pp. 136–137.
46. Ralph Waldo Emerson, "The President's Proclamation," *Atlantic,* November 1862.
47. *Official Records,* Series 1, vol. 24, pt. 3, p. 157.

CHAPTER FORTY-TWO: STONEWALL JACKSON'S WAY

1. Lenoir Chambers, *Stonewall Jackson,* vol. 2, p. 314; in camp, Jackson was generally in the habit of "receiving, each morning, for reports and plans, his quartermaster, commissary, ordnance, and medical officers."
2. Colonel Garnet Wolseley, "A Month's Visit to the Confederate Headquarters," *Blackwood's Edinburgh Magazine,* January 1863.
3. Chambers, *Stonewall Jackson,* p. 338.
4. James I. Robertson, *Stonewall Jackson: The Man, the Legend, the Soldier,* p. 633.
5. Wolseley, "A Month's Visit to the Confederate Headquarters."
6. Mary Anna Jackson, *Memoirs of Stonewall Jackson,* p. 358.
7. Ibid., p. 411.
8. Chambers, *Stonewall Jackson,* p. 311. Chambers states that the only other known illness during the war was an ear problem of some sort in December 1862 after the battle at Fredericksburg; he mentions his eyes once and his ears once in letters to Anna but these did not seem to be significant problems and in any case nothing like what he experienced before the war.
9. Robertson, *Stonewall Jackson,* p. 628, citing David Ballenger letter, October 24, 1862.
10. Henry Kyd Douglas, *I Rode with Stonewall,* pp. 197–198.
11. Ibid.
12. Jackson, *Memoirs of Stonewall Jackson,* p. 349.
13. Robertson, *Stonewall Jackson,* p. 629.
14. Ibid., p. 635.
15. Susan Leigh Blackford and Charles Minor Blackford, *Letters from Lee's Army,* pp. 130–131.
16. Douglas, *I Rode with Stonewall,* p. 196.
17. Heros Von Borcke, *Memoirs of the Confederate War,* vol. 1, pp. 295–296; G.F.R. Henderson, *Stonewall Jackson and the American Civil War,* vol. 2, pp. 282–283.
18. Von Borcke, *Memoirs of the Confederate War,* vol. 1, pp. 295–296; Robertson, *Stonewall Jackson,* p. 630, citing September 30, 1862, Jackson letter to Stuart, J. E .B. Stuart Papers, Huntington; Jeffry Wert, *Cavalryman of the Lost Cause,* p. 165.
19. Douglas, *I Rode with Stonewall,* p. 186.

20. Ibid.

21. *Official Records*, Series 1, vol. 19, pt. 1, Report of Major General Henry W. Halleck of operations September 3–October 24, 1862.

22. Stephen W. Sears, ed., *The Civil War Papers of George B. McClellan*, p. 500.

23. John Hay and John G. Nicolay, *Abraham Lincoln: A History*, vol. 7, p. 363.

24. Sears, *The Civil War Papers*, pp. 481, 514, 515.

25. Ibid., p. 521, McClellan to Mary B. Burnside, November 8, 1862.

26. George C. Rable, *Fredericksburg! Fredericksburg!*, p. 90.

27. Letter from Sandie Pendleton to "Mary," November 9, 1862; Southern Historical Collection, University of North Carolina.

28. Jackson, *Memoirs of Stonewall Jackson*, p. 352.

29. Wolseley, "A Month's Visit to the Confederate Headquarters."

30. Jackson, *Memoirs of Stonewall Jackson*, pp. 360–361.

31. Ibid., p. 361.

32. Ibid., pp. 361–362.

33. Ibid., p. 377.

34. Blackford and Blackford, *Letters from Lee's Army*, p. 146.

35. Alan T. Nolan, "Confederate Leadership," essay in Gary W. Gallagher, ed., *The Fredericksburg Campaign: Decision on the Rappahannock*, pp. 37–38.

36. Rable, *Fredericksburg! Fredericksburg!*, 162.

37. Edward Porter Alexander, *Fighting for the Confederacy*, p. 170.

38. Rable, *Fredericksburg! Fredericksburg!*, p. 164.

39. Alexander, *Fighting for the Confederacy*, p. 171.

40. Douglas, *I Rode with Stonewall*, p. 205.

41. Von Borcke, *Memoirs of the Confederate War*, vol. 2, p. 213.

42. Henderson, *Stonewall Jackson and the American Civil War*, vol. 2, p. 313.

43. Jackson made it clear in his battle report that the gap, a small piece of his two-mile front that he likely was not aware of, was Hill's responsibility. Jackson refers to "the interval which he [Hill] had left between Archer and Lane." Nolan, "Confederate Leadership," p. 40.

44. Rable, *Fredericksburg! Fredericksburg!*, p. 206.

45. Ibid., p. 253.

46. Eric J. Wittenberg, David J. Petruzzi, and Michael F. Nugent, *One Continuous Fight*.

47. Alexander, *Fighting for the Confederacy*, p. 185.

48. Nolan, "Confederate Leadership," p. 42.

49. William Marvel, "The Making of a Myth," essay in Gallagher, *The Fredericksburg Campaign*, p. 23.

50. Rable, *Fredericksburg! Fredericksburg!*, p. 324.

51. Ibid., p. 387.

52. Alexander, *Fighting for the Confederacy*, p. 158.

53. Alexander Robinson Boteler, "At Fredericksburg With Stonewall," *Philadelphia Weekly Times*, August 6, 1881.

54. There are several different accounts of this nighttime visit to Gregg, including two versions by McGuire himself. Boteler also has an account from his perspective, as a guest in Jackson's tent that night. Boteler, "At Fredericksburg With Stonewall"; for a listing of the other accounts, see Robertson's note 148 on p. 906 of *Stonewall Jackson*.

55. Stephen W. Sears, *Chancellorsville*, p. 24.

CHAPTER FORTY-THREE: WINTER OF DREAMS

1. Drew Gilpin Faust, *This Republic of Suffering*, pp. 23ff.
2. Stephen W. Sears, *Chancellorsville*, p. 36.
3. James M. McPherson, *Battle Cry of Freedom*, p. 638.
4. Ibid., p. 617.
5. Edward Porter Alexander, *Fighting for the Confederacy*, p. 188.
6. Robert K. Krick, "Janie Corbin, Stonewall Jackson, and the Famous Gold Braid," privately published booklet, 2007.
7. Lenoir Chambers, *Stonewall Jackson*, p. 334.
8. James Power Smith, "Stonewall Jackson in Winter Quarters at Moss Neck," speech given at Winchester, VA, January 19, 1898, manuscript, in Hotchkiss Papers, Library of Congress; Robert Lewis Dabney, *Life and Campaigns of Lieutenant-General Thomas J. Stonewall Jackson*, p. 638.
9. Sears, *Chancellorsville*, pp. 47–48.
10. Krick, "Janie Corbin, Stonewall Jackson, and the Famous Gold Braid."
11. Mrs. Roberta Cary Corbin Kinsolving, "Stonewall Jackson in Winter Quarters: Memories of Moss Neck in the Winter of 1862-3," *Confederate Veteran*, vol. 20, January 1912.
12. Sears, *Chancellorsville*, p. 76.
13. James Power Smith, "The Religious Character of Stonewall Jackson: Delivered at the Inauguration of the Stonewall Jackson Memorial Building, VMI, June 23, 1897."
14. Dabney, *Life and Campaigns of Lieutenant-General Thomas J. Stonewall Jackson*, p. 639.
15. Krick, "Janie Corbin, Stonewall Jackson, and the Famous Gold Braid," citing Hunter McGuire letter to Lieutenant William McWillie.
16. Mary Anna Jackson, *Memoirs of Stonewall Jackson*, p. 396.
17. Smith, 1897 address.
18. Jackson, *Memoirs of Stonewall Jackson*, p. 401.
19. Henry Kyd Douglas, *I Rode with Stonewall*, p. 209.
20. James I. Robertson, *Stonewall Jackson: The Man, the Legend, the Soldier*, p. 682, citing Hotchkiss letter to Sara Hotchkiss, January 23, 1863.
21. Smith, 1898 address.
22. John Overton Casler, *Four Years in the Stonewall Brigade*, pp. 202ff.
23. Bell Irvin Wiley, *The Life of Johnny Reb: The Common Soldier of the Confederacy*, p. 60.
24. Ibid., p. 53, citing letter from W. C. McClellan to his sister, March 1863.
25. Casler, *Four Years in the Stonewall Brigade*, pp. 202ff; see also Chambers, *Stonewall Jackson*, p. 333.
26. Sears, *Chancellorsville*, p. 39.
27. Bruce Catton, *Mr. Lincoln's Army*, pp. 181–182.
28. Jackson, *Memoirs of Stonewall Jackson*, p. 395.
29. Jackson to White, March 9, 1863, in Dabney, *Life and Campaigns of Lieutenant-General Thomas J. Stonewall Jackson*, pp. 645–646.
30. "Beverly Tucker Lacy's Narrative of His War Experiences," Dabney Collection, Southern Historical Collection, University of North Carolina.
31. Ibid.
32. Chambers, *Stonewall Jackson*, p. 353.
33. Ibid., p. 352.
34. Lacy narrative.
35. Jedediah Hotchkiss, *Make Me a Map of the Valley*, p. 123.
36. Dabney, *Life and Campaigns of Lieutenant-General Thomas J. Stonewall Jackson*, p. 649.

37. Ibid., p. 644.
38. Hotchkiss, *Make Me a Map of the Valley*, p. 124; Douglas goes into some detail about the poor quality of the battle reports, and resentment that Sandie Pendleton was both passed over for chief of staff and not allowed to write the reports. Douglas, *I Rode with Stonewall*, p. 210.
39. Hotchkiss, *Make Me a Map of the Valley*, p. 126.
40. Jackson's Charges and Specifications against A. P. Hill, Thomas J. Jackson Papers, Southern Historical Collection, University of North Carolina.
41. Douglas Southall Freeman, *Lee's Lieutenants*, vol. 2, p. 514.
42. Hotchkiss memo on A. P. Hill in Hotchkiss Papers, Library of Congress, Reel 49.
43. Jackson, *Memoirs of Stonewall Jackson*, p. 397.
44. Ibid., pp. 397–398.
45. Jackson letters to Anna of February 7 and 14, 1863, Jackson, *Memoirs of Stonewall Jackson*, pp. 26–28.
46. Jackson letter to Anna, February 7, 1863, Jackson, *Memoirs of Stonewall Jackson*, p. 402.
47. Jackson, *Memoirs of Stonewall Jackson*, p. 409.
48. Douglas, *I Rode with Stonewall*, p. 218.
49. Jackson, *Memoirs of Stonewall Jackson*, p. 411.
50. Ibid., p. 413.
51. Ibid., p. 416.

CHAPTER FORTY-FOUR: COMETH THE HOUR, COMETH THE MAN

1. Soon to be known as "Lee's Hill." But in 1862 it was known by its original name. Park Service notes, Fredericksburg and Spotsylvania National Military Park.
2. Edward Porter Alexander, *Fighting for the Confederacy*, p. 302.
3. Fitzhugh Lee, "Address at the 9th Annual Reunion of the Virginia Division of the Army of Virginia Association" (1879), in T.M.R. Talcott, "General Lee's Strategy at Chancellorsville," *Southern Historical Society Papers*, vol. 34, 1906, p. 13.
4. John Hennessy, "We Shall Make Richmond Howl," essay in Gary W. Gallagher, ed., *Chancellorsville: The Battle and Its Aftermath*, p. 7.
5. Ibid., pp. 10–11.
6. Stephen W. Sears, *Chancellorsville*, pp. 132, 151.
7. Ibid., p. 168.
8. Ibid., p. 189.
9. W. G. Bean, *Stonewall's Man: Sandie Pendleton*, p. 109.
10. Sears, *Chancellorsville*, p. 192.
11. Posey would be promoted to brigadier general that spring, with date of rank November 1, 1862.
12. James Power Smith, "Stonewall's Last Battle," *Century Magazine* 32, no. 6 (1886).
13. Sears, *Chancellorsville*, p. 210.
14. Ibid., p. 212.
15. Ibid., p. 211.
16. Edward Longacre, *The Commanders of Chancellorsville*, p. 173.
17. R. T. Bennett, "With Glowing Apostrophe to General T. J. Jackson," An Address Before the Ladies Memorial Association, Charlotte, North Carolina, May 10, 1906, in *Southern Historical Society Papers*, vol. 34, p. 55.
18. John Esten Cooke, *The Life of Stonewall Jackson*, p. 7.
19. Edward Porter Alexander, *Fighting for the Confederacy*, p. 196.

20. Lee, "Address at the 9th Annual Reunion of the Virginia Division of the Army of Virginia Association."

21. Sears, *Chancellorsville*, p. 233.

22. Much has been written of this conference, specifically focusing on whose idea the flanking march was. Lee and Jackson were always intensely collaborative, and this meeting was no exception. By his own later description, Lee had first proposed this movement to Jackson, and Jackson had heartily agreed. What remained was to work out the details of the march, the Union position, and so forth, and this was presumably what they spent so much time doing that evening and then later the following morning. Lee gave a good accounting in a January 25, 1866, letter to Anna Jackson after he had read a draft of Dabney's biography giving credit to Jackson for the idea. "I am misrepresented at the Battle of Chancellorsville in proposing an attack in front," Lee wrote. ". . . On the contrary, I decided against it, and stated to General Jackson, we must attack on our left as soon as practicable; and the necessary movement of the troops began immediately. In consequence of a report received about that time from General Fitzhugh Lee describing the position of the federal army, and the roads which he held with his army leading to its rear, General Jackson, after some inquiry concerning the roads leading to the furnace, undertook to throw his command entirely in Hooker's rear, which he accomplished with equal skill and boldness." The usually reliable Jed Hotchkiss concluded that the marching orders had not been given until near dawn on May 2, when in fact Lee gave them the preceding evening. See the account of this historical dispute in T.M.R. Talcott, "General Lee's Strategy at Chancellorsville," *Southern Historical Society Papers*, vol. 34, 1906.

23. "Beverly Tucker Lacy's Narrative of His War Experiences," Dabney Collection, Southern Historical Collection, University of North Carolina.

24. G.F.R. Henderson, *Stonewall Jackson and the American Civil War*, vol. 2, pp. 431ff.

25. James I. Robertson, *Stonewall Jackson: The Man, the Legend, the Soldier*, p. 717.

26. Alexander, *Fighting for the Confederacy*, p. 201.

27. Sears, *Chancellorsville*, p. 228.

28. Fitzhugh Lee, *General Lee*, p. 248.

29. Ibid.

30. Jackson dispatch to Lee, May 2, 1862, 3 p.m. (original in Virginia Historical Society, Henry Brainerd McClellan Papers).

31. James Power Smith, "Stonewall's Last Battle."

32. David Gregg McIntosh, *The Campaign of Chancellorsville*, p. 76.

33. Sears, *Chancellorsville*, p. 286.

34. Captain Richard Eggleston Wilbourn, letter to Charles J. Faulkner, May 1863, Virginia Historical Society, Faulkner Papers.

35. Robert K. Krick, "The Smoothbore Volley That Doomed the Confederacy," essay in Gallagher, *Chancellorsville: The Battle and Its Aftermath*, p. 108.

36. Sears, *Chancellorsville*, p. 284.

CHAPTER FORTY-FIVE: "AN IRON SABRE VOWED TO AN IRON LORD"

1. From the description of Stonewall Jackson in Stephen Vincent Benet's epic poem "John Brown's Body."

2. Stephen W. Sears, *Chancellorsville*, p. 290.

3. Robert K. Krick, "The Smoothbore Volley That Doomed the Confederacy," essay in Gary W. Gallagher, ed., *Chancellorsville: The Battle and Its Aftermath*, p. 111.

4. Ibid., p. 113.

5. Ibid. Though much historical ink has been used up trying to figure out what happened and who was to blame, Krick's meticulous 1996 account of these events is the best I have read and I am largely following his analysis here.
6. Letter from Richard Eggleston Wilbourn to Colonel Charles Faulkner, May 1863, Virginia Historical Society.
7. Krick, "The Smoothbore Volley That Doomed the Confederacy," pp. 129–130.
8. Hunter McGuire, "The Death of Stonewall Jackson," in *Southern Historical Society Papers*, vol. 14, p. 155.
9. James Power Smith, "Stonewall's Last Battle," *Century Magazine* 32, no. 6 (1886).
10. Ibid.
11. Ibid.
12. Ibid.
13. McGuire, "The Death of Stonewall Jackson."
14. "Beverly Tucker Lacy's Narrative of His War Experiences," Dabney Collection, Southern Historical Collection, University of North Carolina.
15. Ibid.
16. Mary Anna Jackson, *Memoirs of Stonewall Jackson*, pp. 443–444.
17. McGuire, "The Death of Stonewall Jackson."
18. Lacy narrative.
19. James I. Robertson, *Stonewall Jackson: The Man, the Legend, the Soldier*, p. 739.
20. Lacy narrative.
21. Robert Lewis Dabney, *Life and Campaigns of Lieutenant-General Thomas J. Stonewall Jackson*, pp. 714–715.
22. Jackson, *Memoirs of Stonewall Jackson*, p. 446; Lacy narrative.
23. McGuire, "The Death of Stonewall Jackson."
24. "Surgeon: Pneumonia Likely Killed 'Stonewall' Jackson," Associated Press, May 10, 2013.
25. Source: CivilWarAcademy.com
26. Jackson, *Memoirs of Stonewall Jackson*, p. 449.
27. Hetty had been given along with two other slaves to the Jacksons as a wedding gift from Anna's father. She had then accompanied Anna to North Carolina after the war started.
28. Jackson, *Memoirs of Stonewall Jackson*, p. 450.
29. Ibid., p. 451.
30. Ibid., p. 452.
31. McGuire, "The Death of Stonewall Jackson."
32. "Translated" in Christian terms means "passing on" or "entering paradise." The sentence means, simply, that he will be much better off in the presence of God.
33. Ibid.
34. Jackson, *Memoirs of Stonewall Jackson*, p. 456.
35. Lacy narrative.

CHAPTER FORTY-SIX: IMMORTALITY

1. Davis to Lee, May 11, 1863, *Official Records*, Series 1, vol. 25, pt. 2.
2. Raleigh Colston, "Address of General R. E. Colston Before the Ladies' Memorial Assoc. at Wilmington, NC, May 10, 1870," *Southern Historical Society Papers*, vol. 21, p. 45.
3. Mary Anna Jackson, *Memoirs of Stonewall Jackson*, p. 458; Jackson's death mask, at the Valentine Museum in Richmond, shows how thin his face had become, especially when contrasted with the photograph taken of him a few months before.

4. Ibid., p. 459.

5. Cited in James I. Robertson, *Stonewall Jackson: The Man, the Legend, the Soldier,* p. 755.

6. Lee to Seddon, May 10, 1863, *Official Records,* Series 1, vol. 25, pt. 2, p. 791.

7. Drew Gilpin Faust, *This Republic of Suffering,* p. 155.

8. Cited in Lenoir Chambers, *Stonewall Jackson,* vol. 2, pp. 451–452.

9. Henry Kyd Douglas, *I Rode with Stonewall,* p. 38.

10. Chambers, *Stonewall Jackson,* vol. 2, p. 453.

11. There are various versions of this list of generals serving as pallbearers. This one, from Robertson, seems to be the most reasonable.

12. Little Sorrel had bolted through Union lines and was a captive. He would later be returned.

13. "Funeral procession of Lieut. Gen. Thos. J. Jackson," *Richmond Dispatch,* May 13, 1863; "The death of General Jackson and Funeral ceremonies," *Richmond Dispatch,* May 12, 1863. Note that I have left off Longstreet as a pallbearer, as did the *Dispatch* in its several articles that listed in detail the participants in the procession. Though some books have included Longstreet in the list, it would seem impossible for the leading local paper to have missed the presence as pallbearer of the second most prominent soldier in the Confederacy.

14. Jackson, *Memoirs of Stonewall Jackson,* p. 461; Robert Lewis Dabney, *Life and Campaigns of Lieutenant-General Thomas J. Stonewall Jackson,* p. 731.

15. James Longstreet, *From Manassas to Appomattox: A Memoir of the Civil War in America,* p. 332.

16. Robertson, *Stonewall Jackson,* p. 756.

17. Elizabeth Preston Allan, *The Life and Letters of Margaret Junkin Preston,* p. 165.

18. Dabney, *Life and Campaigns of Lieutenant-General Thomas J. Stonewall Jackson,* p. 731.

19. Faust, *This Republic of Suffering,* p. 156. Faust makes some of these points in regard to Lincoln's death. I am extending her point to include Jackson since the two are so obviously similar. The comparison is mine, not hers.

20. Ibid.

21. Thomas Reed Turner, *Beware the People Weeping: Public Opinion and the Assassination of Abraham Lincoln,* p. 91.

22. Charles Royster, *The Destructive War,* p. 45.

23. Robert K. Krick, "The Smoothbore Round That Doomed the Confederacy," essay in Gary W. Gallagher, ed., *Chancellorsville: The Battle and Its Aftermath,* p. 133.

24. *Chronicle,* May 13, 1863.

25. Chambers, *Stonewall Jackson,* vol. 2, p. 459.

26. D. X. Junkin, *George Junkin, D.D., LL.D.: A Historical Biography,* pp. 551–552.

27. Royster, *The Destructive War,* p. 213.

28. Ibid., pp. 227–228.

29. Jackson, *Memoirs of Stonewall Jackson,* p. 463.

30. Ibid.

31. "The Funeral of Stonewall Jackson," *Lexington Gazette,* May 20, 1863; VMI archives online.

32. Chambers, *Stonewall Jackson,* vol. 2, p. 457.

33. Letter from Jackson to his sister, Laura, March 4, 1854, commenting on his mother-in-law's passing: "Her death was no leaping into the dark. She died with the bright hope of an unending immortality of happiness."

BIBLIOGRAPHY

BIBLIOGRAPHICAL NOTE

In writing this book I have not attempted to be comprehensive in reporting the details of Jackson's life. I leave that to such admirable biographers as
Lenoir Chambers, James I. Robertson Jr., and G.F.R. Henderson. Instead
of putting in everything known about Jackson, my approach has been to
include facts and analysis that I feel *best illuminate my subject.* Thus, if there
are twelve recorded incidents of Jackson raising his hand in prayer during
battle, the reader will see only three or four of them, with an explanation
that this is what he generally does. Jackson mentions his relationship with
God frequently in letters to his wife, Anna, and his sister, Laura, but here
the reader will find only a fraction of those cited, with the idea that they
are representative of his behavior. The book is thus highly selective, and I
will leave it to the reader to decide if I have chosen the facts that best bring
the man into focus. I offer *Rebel Yell* as a biographical work, but not as a
full-scale, A-to-Z biography.

I have consulted a variety of sources. My main reliance has been on the
truly astounding quantity of published primary sources available on the
Civil War and on Jackson's life, including much material that is now available online from various collections. I have tried to base my own analysis
and conclusions as much as possible on documents of the era, from the
Official Records and the *Report of the Committee on the Conduct of the War*
to letters, memoirs, diaries, battle reports, and other contemporaneous
observations. I have also made use of various library collections of manuscripts and other materials, as noted below. Another hallmark of Civil War
research is the tremendous amount of secondary material, including eight
significant biographies of Jackson since 1864. One of the burdens of this
sort of research is that one has to be familiar with the work that has gone
before, and there is a fair amount of it.

I have relied on some very fine monographs or microhistories—detailed, well-researched books focused on single battles or campaigns. I would like to acknowledge my debt to Peter Cozzens for his definitive work on the valley campaign, *Shenandoah 1862: Stonewall Jackson's Valley Campaign;* John Hennessy for his two equally definitive works on the Manassas battles: *First Battle of Manassas: An End to Innocence* and *Return to Bull Run: The Campaign and Battle of Second Manassas;* Robert K. Krick for his excellent analysis of two valley battles, *Conquering the Valley: Stonewall Jackson at Port Republic* and *Stonewall Jackson at Cedar Mountain,* plus a number of good essays, including the definitive studies of Jackson's death and his time at Moss Neck plus his generally encyclopedic knowledge of Stonewall Jackson; Gary Ecelbarger's solid research in *Three Days in the Shenandoah: Stonewall Jackson at Front Royal and Winchester* and *We Are in for It! The First Battle of Kernstown;* Brian K. Burton for his exhaustive *Extraordinary Circumstances: The Seven Days Battles;* and finally Stephen W. Sears for his superb works on two battles, *Chancellorsville* and *Landscape Turned Red: The Battle of Antietam.* Though I cannot possibly match the depth of their research (without writing a five-thousand-page biography), I can use them as one might use a wise and experienced guide through dense forest. They have my gratitude.

COLLECTIONS/MANUSCRIPTS

(as cited in the text)
Auburn University, Auburn, Alabama
Duke University/Rubinstein Library, Durham, North Carolina
Henry E. Huntington Library, Pasadena, California
Library of Congress, Washington, DC
Library of Virginia, Richmond, Virginia
Museum of the Confederacy/Eleanor S. Brockenbrough Collection, Richmond, Virginia
National Archives, Washington, DC
North Carolina Office of Archives and History, Raleigh, North Carolina
Stonewall Jackson House, Lexington, Virginia
Tulane University, New Orleans, Louisiana
University of North Carolina/Southern Historical Collection, Chapel Hill, North Carolina
Valentine Museum, Richmond, Virginia
Virginia Historical Society, Richmond, Virginia
Virginia Military Institute, Lexington, Virginia
Washington and Lee University, Lexington, Virginia
West Virginia University, Morgantown, West Virginia

NEWSPAPERS

Berkshire Eagle (Pittsfield, Mass.)
Charleston Mercury
Clarksburg News

Daily Evening Bulletin (Philadelphia)
Daily South Carolinian
London Times
Courier-Journal (Louisville, KY)
Macon Daily Telegraph
Montgomery Advertiser (Alabama)
National Tribune
New York Herald Tribune
New York Times
New York Weekly Tribune
Philadelphia Inquirer
Philadelphia Press
Philadelphia Weekly Times
Richmond Dispatch
Richmond Enquirer
Richmond Examiner
Richmond Times
Richmond Whig
Washington Evening Star
Washington Post

MAGAZINES

America's Civil War Magazine
Blackwood's Edinburgh Magazine
Blue and Gray
Century Magazine
Civil War: Magazine of the Civil War Society
Civil War Times
Confederate Veteran
Cornhill Magazine
Hallowed Ground Magazine
Harper's
Land That We Love
Scribner's Monthly
Southern Literary Messenger
The Independent (New York)
Union Seminary Review

GOVERNMENT DOCUMENTS

U.S. Senate, 37th Congress, *Report of the Joint Committee on the Conduct of the War,* 10 volumes.
U.S. War Department, *The War of the Rebellion: A Compilation of the Official Records of the Union and Confederate Armies,* 128 volumes, Washington, DC, 1880–1901 (referred to throughout as *Official Records*).

GENERAL CONTEMPORANEOUS SOURCES

Battles and Leaders of the Civil War, volumes 1–3.
Confederate Veteran, 40 volumes.
Southern Historical Society Papers, 52 volumes; DVD published by Eastern Digital Resource.

MISCELLANEOUS SOURCES

Boteler, Alexander R. Speech to House of Representatives, January 25, 1860, West Virginia State Archives, Boyd F. Stutler Collection, John Brown Pamphlets, vol. 12.

Brown, Dee. "War on Horseback," *The Image of War 1861–1865,* Volume 4; *Fighting for Time,* National Historical Society.

Haley, Megan. "The African American Experience in Thomas 'Stonewall' Jackson's Lexington," paper for graduate fellowship, Stonewall Jackson House, Lexington, Virginia.

McGuire, Dr. Hunter. *Career and Character of Stonewall Jackson,* Address on June 23, 1897, at the dedication of the Jackson Memorial Hall in Lexington, Virginia, and later to the R. E. Lee Camp Confederate Veterans, Richmond, July 2, 1897.

Smith, James Power. "The Religious Character of Stonewall Jackson: Delivered at the Inauguration of the Stonewall Jackson Memorial Building, VMI, June 23, 1897," Lynchburg, Virginia, J. P. Bell, 1897.

———. *Stonewall Jackson and Chancellorsville: A Paper read before the Military Historical Society of Massachusetts on the First of March, 1904.* Published by R. E. Lee Camp, no. 1, Confederate Veterans, Richmond, Virginia.

Snell, Mark A. "Bankers, Businessmen and Benevolence: An Analysis of the Antebellum Finances of Thomas J. Jackson," typed manuscript. Stonewall Jackson House Graduate Student Fellow, 1989, Virginia Historical Society.

INTERNET SOURCES

CivilWarAcademy.com

Frye, Dennis, "Stonewall Jackson at Harper's Ferry," Historynet.com

Grimsley, Mark, "How to Read a Civil War Battlefield," www.cohums.ohio-state.edu/history/people/grimsley.1/tour/default.htm

Krick, Bobby, interview with, "The Battle of Gaines's Mill: Then and Now," Civil War Trust

Miller, William J., "The Seven Days Battles," 2013 essay in Civil War Trust.

Pittman, Rickey E., "Stonewall Jackson's Black Sunday School," reviewed in *Black History Month* magazine, February 24, 2010.

"The Rifle-Musket and the Minié Ball," History.net, June 12, 2006.

Smith, Sam, "Jackson Is With You! The Battle of Cedar Mountain," Civil War Trust website.

Taylor, Lonn, "Blue Light Presbyterians," online posting, Texas History Forum, August 15, 1998.

"War on Horseback," civilwarhome.com

Wilbourn, Captain Richard Eggleston, letter to Charles J. Faulkner, May 1863, Virginia Historical Society, Faulkner Papers (online).

BOOKS

Alexander, Bevin. *Lost Victories and the Military Genius of Stonewall Jackson.* New York: Henry Holt, 1992.

Alexander, Edward Porter. *Fighting for the Confederacy: The Personal Recollections of General Edward Porter Alexander.* Edited by Gary Gallagher. Chapel Hill: University of North Carolina Press, 1989.

Allan, Elizabeth Preston. *The Life and Letters of Margaret Junkin Preston.* Boston and New York: Houghton Mifflin and Company, 1903.

Allan, William. *History of the Campaign of Gen. T. J. (Stonewall) Jackson in the Shenandoah Valley of Virginia from November 4, 1861, to June 17, 1862.* Dayton, Ohio: Morningside House, 1987.

Allen, Ujanirtus. *Campaigning with "Old Stonewall": Confederate Captain Ujanirtus Allen's Letters to His Wife.* Edited by Randall Allen and Keith Bohannon. Baton Rouge: Louisiana State University Press, 1998.

Armstrong, Marion. *Disaster in the West Woods: General Edwin V. Sumner and the II Corps at Antietam.* Sharpsburg, Md.: Western Independent Interpretive Assn., 2002.

Arnold, Thomas Jackson. *Early Life and Letters of General Thomas J. Jackson.* New York: Fleming H. Revell Company, 1914.

Austin, Aurelia. *Georgia Boys with "Stonewall" Jackson: James Thomas Thompson and the Walton Infantry.* Athens: University of Georgia Press, 1967.

Bartlett, Napier. *A Soldier's Story of the War, Including the Marches and Battles of the Washington Artillery.* New Orleans, 1874.

Bean, W. G. *Stonewall's Man: Sandie Pendleton.* Wilmington, N.C.: Broadfoot Publishing Co., 1987 (originally published 1959).

Beaudot, William J. K., and Lance J. Herdegen, eds. *An Irishman in the Iron Brigade: The Civil War Memoirs of James P. Sullivan, Sergt., Company K, 6th Wisconsin Volunteers.* New York: Fordham University Press, 1993.

Benet, Steven Vincent. *Selected Works of Steven Vincent Benet.* New York: Farrar and Rinehart, 1942.

Bennett, William. *A Narrative of the Great Revival which Prevailed in the Southern Armies.* Philadelphia: Claxton, Remsen, and Haffelfinger, 1877.

Bierce, Ambrose. *The Collected Works of Ambrose Bierce.* New York: The Neale Publishing Co., 1909.

Blackford, Susan Leigh, and Charles Minor Blackford. *Letters from Lee's Army, or Memoirs of Life in and out of the Army in Virginia During the War Between the States.* New York: Charles Scribner's Sons, 1947.

Blackford, William W. *War Years with Jeb Stuart.* New York: Charles Scribner's Sons, 1945.

Blue, John. *Hanging Rock Rebel: Lt. John Blue's War in West Virginia and the Shenandoah Valley.* Shippensburg, Pa.: Burd Street Press, 1994.

Brands, H. W. *The Man Who Saved the Union: Ulysses S. Grant in War and Peace.* New York: Doubleday, 2012.

Browning, Judkin. *The Seven Days' Battles: The War Begins Anew.* Santa Barbara, Calif.: Praeger, 2012.

Buck, Samuel D. *With the Old Confeds: Actual experiences of a captain in the line.* Gaithersburg, Md.: Butternut Press, 1983.

Burton, Brian K. *Extraordinary Circumstances: The Seven Days Battles.* Bloomington: Indiana University Press, 2001.

Caldwell, Willie Walker. *Stonewall Jim: A Biography of General James A. Walker, CSA.* Elliston, Va.: Northcross House, 1990.

Casler, John Overton. *Four Years in the Stonewall Brigade,* 2nd ed. Revised, corrected, and improved by Major Jed Hotchkiss. Girard, Kans.: Appeal Publishing Company, 1906; Guthrie, Okla.: State Capital Printing Co., 1893.

Catton, Bruce. *Civil War Trilogy: "The Coming Fury," "Terrible Swift Sword," and "Never Call Retreat."* London: Phoenix Press, 1963.

———. *Mr. Lincoln's War.* New York: Pocket Books, 1964.

———. *A Stillness at Appomattox.* Garden City, N.Y.: Doubleday, 1953.

———. *This Hallowed Ground: The Story of the Union Side in the Civil War.* New York: Doubleday, 1956.

Chambers, Lenoir. *Stonewall Jackson,* 2 vols. New York: William Morrow, 1959.

———. *Stonewall Jackson and the Virginia Military Institute: The Lexington Years.* Lexington, Va.: Garland Gray Memorial Research Center, Stonewall Jackson House, 1959.

Chase, William C. *Story of Stonewall Jackson.* Atlanta: D. E. Luther, 1913.

Chestnut, Mary Boykin. *A Diary From Dixie, as Written by Mary Boykin Chestnut, Wife of James Chestnut, Jr., U.S. Senator from South Carolina, 1859–61, and afterward an Aide to Jefferson Davis and a Brigadier-General in the Confederate Army.* Edited by Isabella D. Martin and Myrta Lockett Avary. New York: D. Appleton and Co., 1905.

———. *Mary Chestnut's Civil War.* Edited by C. Vann Woodward. New Haven: Yale University Press, 1981.

Cockrell, Monroe F., ed. *Gunner with Stonewall: Reminiscences of William Thomas Poague.* Jackson, Tenn.: McCowat-Mercer Press, 1957.

Coggins, Jack. *Arms and Equipment of the Civil War.* Garden City N.Y.: Dover Press, 2004 (originally published by Doubleday, 1962).

Conrad, Daniel Burr. *History of the First Fight and Organization of the Stonewall Brigade.* The United Service, 1892.

Cook, Roy Bird. *The Family and Early Life of Stonewall Jackson.* Richmond, Va.: Old Dominion Press, 1924.

Cooke, John Esten. *Life of Stonewall Jackson from Official Papers, Contemporary Narratives, and Personal Acquaintance, by a Virginian.* Richmond, Va.: Ayres and Wade Presses, 1863; later republished as *Stonewall Jackson: A Military Biography.* New York: D. Appleton and Co., 1866.

———. *Outlines from the Outpost.* Chicago: Lakeside Press, 1961.

———. *The Wearing of the Gray.* Gaithersburg, Md.: Old Soldier Books, 1988.

Coulling, Mary Price. *Margaret Junkin Preston: A Biography.* Winston-Salem, N.C.: John F. Blair, Publisher, 1993.

Couper, Colonel William. *One Hundred Years at V.M.I.,* 3 volumes. Richmond, Va.: Garrett and Massie, 1939.

Cox, Samuel S. *Three Decades of Federal Legislation, 1855–1885.* Providence, 1885.

Cozzens, Peter. *General John Pope: A Life for the Nation.* Urbana and Chicago: University of Illinois Press, 2000.

———. *Shenandoah 1862: Stonewall Jackson's Valley Campaign.* Chapel Hill: University of North Carolina Press, 2008.

Dabney, Robert Lewis. *Life and Campaigns of Lieutenant-General Thomas J. Stonewall Jackson.* New York: Blalock and Co., 1866.

Davis, William C. *Battle at Bull Run: A History of the First Major Campaign of the Civil War.* Garden City, N.Y.: Doubleday, 1977.

Detzer, David. *Donnybrook: The Battle of Bull Run, 1861.* New York: Harcourt, 2004.

Dooley, John. *Confederate Soldier, His War Journal.* Washington, D.C.: Georgetown University Press, 1945.

D'Orleans, Louis-Philippe-Albert, Comte de Paris. *History of the Civil War in America.* Philadelphia: Porter and Coates, 1876.

Doubleday, Abner. *Chancellorsville and Gettysburg.* New York: Da Capo Press, 1994 (first published in 1882).

———. *My Life in the Old Army: The Reminiscences of Abner Doubleday from the Collections of the New-York Historical Society.* Fort Worth: Texas Christian University Press, 1998.

Douglas, Henry Kyd. *I Rode with Stonewall.* Chapel Hill: University of North Carolina Press, 1940.

Dowdey, Clifford. *The Seven Days: The Emergence of Robert E. Lee.* Wilmington, N.C.: Broad-foot Publishing Co., 1988.

Duncan, Richard R. *Beleaguered Winchester: A Virginia Community at War, 1861–1865.* Baton Rouge: Louisiana State University Press, 2007.

Dwight, Eliza Amelia. *Life and Letters of Wilder Dwight, Lieut. Col., Second Massachusetts Infantry Volunteers.* Boston: Ticknor and Fields, 1868.

Early, Jubal Anderson. *War Memoirs: Autobiographical sketches and narrative of the War Between the States.* Bloomington: Indiana University Press, 1960 (originally published 1912).

Eby, Cecil D., Jr. *A Virginia Yankee in the Civil War: The Diaries of David Hunter Strother.* Chapel Hill: University of North Carolina Press, 1961.

Ecelbarger, Gary L. *Frederick W. Lander: The Great Natural American Soldier.* Baton Rouge: Louisiana State University Press, 2001.

———. *Three Days in the Shenandoah: Stonewall Jackson at Front Royal and Winchester.* Norman: University of Oklahoma Press, 2008.

———. *"We are in for it!"—The First Battle of Kernstown.* Shippensburg, Pa.: White Man Publishing Co., 1997.

Farwell, Byron. *Stonewall: A Biography of Thomas J. Jackson.* New York: W. W. Norton and Co., 1992.

Faust, Drew Gilpin. *This Republic of Suffering: Death and the American Civil War.* New York: Vintage Books, 2008.

Fields, Barbara Jean. *Slavery and Freedom on the Middle Ground: Maryland During the Nine-teenth Century.* New Haven: Yale University Press, 1985.

Fonderden, C. A. *A Brief History of the Military Career of Carpenter's Battery.* New Market, Va.: Henkel and Co., 1911.

Foote, Shelby. *The Civil War, A Narrative,* 3 volumes. New York: Random House, 1958.

Freeman, Douglas Southall, ed. *Lee's Dispatches: Unpublished letters of General Robert E. Lee to Jefferson Davis and the War Department of the Confederate States of America.* Baton Rouge: Louisiana State University Press, 1994 (originally published by G. P. Putnam's Sons in 1957).

———. *Lee's Lieutenants,* 3 volumes. New York: Charles Scribner's Sons, 1942–1944.

———. *R. E. Lee,* 4 volumes. New York: Charles Scribner's Sons, 1935.

French, Samuel Bassett. *Centennial Tale.* New York: Carlton Press, 1962.

Fry, James Barnet. *McDowell and Tyler in the Campaign of Bull Run, 1861.* New York: D. Van Nostrand, 1884.

Furgurson, Ernest B. *Chancellorsville 1863: The Souls of the Brave.* New York: Alfred A. Knopf, 1992.

Gallagher, Gary W. *Antietam: Essays on the 1862 Campaign.* Kent, Ohio: Kent State University Press, 1989.

———. *The Confederate War.* Cambridge, Mass.: Harvard University Press, 1997.

———. *Lee and His Army in Confederate History.* Chapel Hill: University of North Carolina Press, 2001.

———. *Lee and His Generals in War and Memory.* Baton Rouge: Louisiana State University Press, 1998.

———, ed., *The Antietam Campaign.* Chapel Hill: University of North Carolina Press, 1999.

———, ed. *Chancellorsville: The Battle and Its Aftermath.* Chapel Hill: University of North Carolina Press, 1996.

———, ed., *The Fredericksburg Campaign: Decision on the Rappahannock.* Chapel Hill: University of North Carolina Press, 1995.

———, ed., *The Shenandoah Campaign of 1862.* Chapel Hill: University of North Carolina Press, 2003.

———. *The Union War.* Cambridge, Mass.: Harvard University Press, 2011.

Gibbon, John. *Personal Recollections of the Civil War.* New York: G. P. Putnam's Sons, 1928.

Gittings, John G. *Personal Recollections of Stonewall Jackson.* Cincinnati: The Editor Publishing Company, 1899 (Huntington Library collection).

Goldfield, David. *America Aflame: How the Civil War Created a Nation.* New York: Bloomsbury Press, 2011.

Gordon, George Henry. *Brook Farm to Cedar Mountain: In the War of the Great Rebellion 1861–2.* Boston: Houghton Mifflin and Company, 1885.

Gordon, John Brown. *Reminiscences of the Civil War.* New York: Charles Scribner's Sons, 1904.

Gould, Edwin K. *Major-General Hiram Berry: His career as a contractor, bank president, politician, and major-general of volunteers in the Civil War.* Rockland, Maine: Press of the Courier-Gazette, 1899.

Grant, U. S. *Memoirs and Selected Letters.* New York: Library of America, 1990 Edition.

Greene, A. Wilson. *Whatever You Resolve to Be: Essays on Stonewall Jackson.* Baltimore: Butternut and Blue, 1992.

Hall, Kenneth E. *Stonewall Jackson and Religious Faith in Military Command.* Jefferson, N.C.: McFarland and Co., 2005.

Hamlin, Percy Gatlin. *"Old Bald Head" and the Making of a Soldier: Letters of General R. S. Ewell.* Gaithersburg, Md.: Ron R. Van Sickle Military Books, 1988.

Hay, John, and John G. Nicolay. *Abraham Lincoln: A History,* volume 7. New York: The Century Co., 1890.

———, eds. *Abraham Lincoln, Complete Works.* New York:, The Century Co., 1920.

Haynes, Martin A. *History of the Second Regiment New Hampshire Volunteers in the War of the Rebellion.* Lakeport, N.H.: 1896.

Henderson, G.F.R. *Stonewall Jackson and the American Civil War,* two volumes. London: Longmans, Green and Co., 1898.

Hennessy, John J. *First Battle of Manassas: An End to Innocence.* Lynchburg, Va.: H. E. Howard, 1989.

———. *Return to Bull Run: The Campaign and Battle of Second Manassas.* New York: Simon & Schuster, 1993.

Hervey, George Winfred. *The Principles of Courtesy.* New York: Harper and Bros., 1852.

Hettle, Wallace. *Inventing Stonewall Jackson: A Civil War Hero in History and Memory.* Baton Rouge: Louisiana State University Press, 2011.

Heysinger, Captain Isaac W. *Antietam and the Maryland and Virginia Campaigns of 1862.* New York: The Neale Publishing Company, 1912.

Hollandsworth, James G. *Pretense of Glory: The Life of General Nathaniel P. Banks.* Baton Rouge: Louisiana State University Press, 1998.

Holzer, Harold, and Craig L. Symonds, eds. *The New York Times Complete Civil War 1861–1865.* New York: Black Dog and Leventhal Publishers, 2010.

Hotchkiss, Jedediah. *Make Me a Map of the Valley: The Civil War Journal of Stonewall Jackson's Topographer.* Dallas: Southern Methodist University Press, 1973.

Howard, McHenry. *Recollections of a Maryland Confederate Soldier and Staff Officer Under Johnston, Jackson, and Lee.* Baltimore: Williams & Wilkins, 1914.

Hunter, Alexander. *Johnny Reb and Billy Yank.* New York: Konecky and Konecky, 1904.

Jackson, Mary Anna. *Memoirs of Stonewall Jackson.* Louisville, Ky.: The Prentice Press, 1895.

Jewett, Robert. *Captain America Complex.* Philadelphia: Westminster, 1973.

Johnson, Robert Underwood, and Clarence Clough Buel, eds. *Battles and Leaders of the Civil War,* volumes 1 and 2. New York: Castle, 1982.

Johnston, Joseph E. *Narrative of Military Operations.* Bloomington: Indiana University Press (Civil War Centennial Series), 1959 (originally published in New York by D. Appleton in 1874).

Johnston, R. M. *Bull Run: Its Strategy and Tactics.* Boston and New York: Houghton Mifflin Co., 1913.

Junkin, David X. *The Reverend George Junkin, D.D., LL.D.: A Historical Biography.* Philadelphia: J. B. Lippincott & Co., 1871.

Kelly, Henry B. *Port Republic.* New York: J. B. Lippincott, 1886.

Krick, Robert K. *Conquering the Valley: Stonewall Jackson at Port Republic.* New York: William Morrow and Co., 1996.

———. *Janie Corbin, Stonewall Jackson, and the Famous Gold Braid,* privately published booklet, 2007.

———. *The Smoothbore Volley That Doomed the Confederacy: The Death of Stonewall Jackson and Other Chapters on the Army of Northern Virginia.* Baton Rouge: Louisiana State University Press, 2002.

———. *Stonewall Jackson at Cedar Mountain.* Chapel Hill: University of North Carolina Press, 1990.

Lee, Fitzhugh. *General Lee.* New York: The University Society, 1905.

Long, Armistead Lindsay, and Marcus Joseph Wright. *Memoirs of Robert E. Lee.* London: Sampson, Low, Marston, Searle and Rivington, 1886.

Longacre, Edward G. *The Commanders of Chancellorsville.* Nashville, Tenn.: Rutledge Hill Press, 2005.

Longstreet, James. *From Manassas to Appomattox: Memoirs of the Civil War in America.* Philadelphia: J. B. Lippincott, 1896.

Lonn, Ella. *Desertion During the Civil War.* New York: The Century Co., 1928.

Luvaas, Dr. Jay, and Col. Harold W. Nelson, eds. *The U.S. Army War College Guide to the Battle of Antietam: The Maryland Campaign of 1862.* Carlisle, Pa.: South Mountain Press, 1987.

———, eds. *The U.S. Army War College Guide to the Battles of Chancellorsville and Fredericksburg.* Carlisle, Pa.: South Mountain Press, 1988.

Maury, Dabney Herndon. *Recollections of a Virginian in the Mexican, Indian, and Civil Wars.* New York: Charles Scribner's Sons, 1894. (Electronic Edition: UNC-CH digitization project: Documenting the American South, docsouth.unc.edu.)

McClellan, George Brinton. *Report Upon the Organization of the Army of the Potomac and Its Campaigns: From July 26, 1861, to November 7, 1862.* Boston: Boston Courier, 1864.

McClellan, H. B. *The Life and Campaigns of Major General J. E. B. Stuart.* Little Rock, Ark.: Eagle Press, 1987.

McGlone, Robert E. *John Brown's War Against Slavery.* New York: Cambridge University Press, 2009.

McGuire, Hunter, and George L. Christian. *The Confederate Cause and Conduct in the War Between the States.* Richmond, Va., 1907.

McIntosh, David Gregg. *The Campaign of Chancellorsville.* Richmond, Va.: Wm. Ellis Jones' Sons, 1915.

McKim, Randolph Harrison. *A Soldier's Recollections: Leaves from the Diary of a Young Confederate, with an Oration on the Motives and Arms of the Soldiers of the South.* New York: Longman's, 1911.

McPherson, James M. *Battle Cry of Freedom.* New York: Oxford University Press, 1988.

———. *Crossroads of Freedom: Antietam.* New York: Oxford University Press, 2002.

———, ed. *The Most Fearful Ordeal: Original Coverage of the Civil War.* New York: St. Martin's Press, 2004.

Moore, Edward A. *The Story of a Cannoneer Under Stonewall Jackson.* New York: The Neale Publishing Co., 1907.

Myers, Robert Manson, ed. *Children of Pride: The True Story of Georgia and the Civil War.* New Haven: Yale University Press, 1972.

National Park Service, U.S. Dept. of the Interior. *Study of Civil War Sites in the Shenandoah Valley of Virginia,* September 1992, www.nps.gov/history/hps/abpp/shenandoah/svs0-1.html.

Nevins, Allan. *Ordeal of the Union,* volumes 4–6 (1947–1971). New York: Scribner, 1992.

———. *The War for the Union,* 4 volumes, New York: Scribner's, 1959.

Noyes, George F. *Bivouac and the Battlefield or Campaign Sketches in Virginia and Maryland.* New York: Harper & Brothers, 1864.

Oates, William C. *War Between the Union and the Confederacy.* New York and Washington, D.C.: The Neale Publishing Co., 1905.

Opie, John N. *A Rebel Cavalryman with Lee, Stuart and Jackson.* Chicago: W. B. Conkey, 1899.

Palfrey, Gen. Francis W. *The Antietam and Fredericksburg.* New York: Da Capo, 1996 (originally published by Scribner in 1882).

Patchan, Scott C. *Second Manassas: Longstreet's Attack and the Struggle for Chinn Ridge.* Washington, D.C.: Potomac Books, 2011.

Pearson, Johnnie Perry. *Lee and Jackson's Bloody Twelfth.* Knoxville: University of Tennessee Press, 2010.

Pfanz, Donald. *Richard S. Ewell: A Soldier's Life.* Chapel Hill: University of North Carolina Press, 1998.

Poague, William Thomas. *Gunner with Stonewall.* Wilmington, N.C.: Broadfoot Publishing, 1987 (written for his children in 1903).

Pope, John. *The Military Memoirs of John Pope.* Edited by Peter Cozzens and Robert I. Girardi. Chapel Hill: University of North Carolina Press, 1998.

Rable, George C. *Fredericksburg! Fredericksburg!* Chapel Hill: University of North Carolina Press, 2002.

Rafuse, Ethan S. *A Single Grand Victory: The First Campaign and Battle of Manassas.* Wilmington, Del.: SR Books, 2002.

———. *McClellan's War: The Failure of Moderation in the Struggle for the Union.* Bloomington: Indiana University Press, 2005.

Redwood, Allen C., et al., eds. *The Photographic History of the Civil War,* volume 8. New York: Review of Reviews Co., 1911.

Rhodes, James Ford. *History of the Civil War, 1861–1865.* New York: Macmillan Company, 1917.

———. *History of the United States from the Compromise of 1850 to the Restoration of Home Rule at the South,* 7 volumes. Chicago: University of Chicago Press, 1892–1906.

Robertson, James I. *The Stonewall Brigade.* Baton Rouge: Louisiana State University Press, 1963.

———. *Stonewall Jackson: The Man, the Legend, the Soldier.* New York: Macmillan, 1997.

Roman, Alfred. *The Military Operations of General Beauregard,* volume I. New York: Da Capo Press, 1994 (originally published 1884).

Royster, Charles. *The Destructive War.* New York: Vintage Books, 1993.

Russell, Frederick H. *Just War in the Middle Ages.* Cambridge, Eng.: Cambridge University Press, 1975.

Russell, William Howard. *My Diary North and South.* London: Bradbury and Evans, 1865.

Schultz, Duane. *The Fate of War: Fredericksburg 1862.* Yardley, Pa.: Westholme Publishing, 2011.

Schurz, Carl. *The Reminiscences of Carl Schurz,* volume 2, 1852–1863. New York: The McClure Company, 1907.

Sears, Stephen W. *Chancellorsville.* Boston: Houghton Mifflin, 1996.

————. *George B. McClellan: The Young Napoleon,* New York: Ticknor and Fields, 1988.

————. *Landscape Turned Red: The Battle of Antietam.* New Haven, Conn.: Ticknor and Fields, 1983.

————, ed. *The Civil War: The Second Year Told by Those Who Lived It.* New York: Library of America, 2012.

————, ed., *The Civil War Papers of George B. McClellan: Selected Correspondence 1860-1865,* New York: Da Capo Press, 1992.

————. *To the Gates of Richmond: The Peninsula Campaign.* New York: Ticknor and Fields, 1992.

Selby, John. *Stonewall Jackson as Military Commander.* London and Princeton, N.J.: Van Nostrand, 1968.

Silver, James W. *Confederate Morality and Church Propaganda.* New York: W. W. Norton, 1967.

Slotkin, Richard. *The Long Road to Antietam: How the Civil War Became a Revolution.* New York: Liveright Publishing Corporation, 2012.

Spruill, Matt, III, and Matt Spruill IV. *Echoes of Thunder: A Guide to the Seven Days' Battles.* Knoxville: University of Tennessee Press, 2006.

Stiles, Robert. *Address at the Dedication of the Monument of Confederate Dead, University of Virginia, June 7, 1893.* Richmond, Va.: Taylor and Taylor, 1893 (booklet).

————. *Four Years Under Marse Robert.* New York: The Neale Publishing Co., 1903.

Stoddard, Brooke C., and Daniel P. Murphy. *The Everything Civil War Book.* New York: Everything Books, 2009.

Stone, DeWitt Boyd. *Wandering to Glory: Confederate Veterans Remember Evans' Brigade.* Columbia: University of South Carolina Press, 2002.

Sutherland, Daniel E. *Fredericksburg and Chancellorsville.* Lincoln: University of Nebraska Press, 1998.

Tanner, Robert G. *Stonewall in the Valley.* New York: Doubleday, 1976.

Taylor, Richard. *Destruction and Reconstruction: Personal Experiences of the Late War.* New York: Appleton and Co., 1879.

Thomas, Clarence. *General Turner Ashby: Centaur of the South.* Winchester, Va.: Eddy Press, 1907.

Thorpe, Francis Newton. *Constitutional History of the United States, 1765–1895,* volume 1. Clark, N.J.: Lawbook Exchange Ltd., 2008.

Tidball, Eugene C. *No Disgrace to My Country: The Life of John C. Tidball.* Kent, Ohio: Kent State University Press, 2002.

Turner, Thomas Reed. *Beware the People Weeping: Public Opinion and the Assassination of Abraham Lincoln.* Baton Rouge: Louisiana State University Press, 1991.

Vandiver, Frank E. *Mighty Stonewall.* College Station: Texas A&M Press, 1989 (originally published by McGraw-Hill in 1957).

Von Borcke, Heros. *Memoirs of the Confederate War for Independence,* volume 1. New York: Peter Smith, 1938.

Wagner, Margaret E., Gary W. Gallagher, and Paul Finkelman, eds. *Civil War Desk Reference.* New York: Grand Central Press, 2002.

Warden, Robert. B. *An Account of the Private Life and Public Service of Salmon Portland Chase.* Cincinnati: Wilstach, Baldwin and Co., 1874.

Warner, Ezra J. *Generals in Blue: Lives of the Union Commanders.* Baton Rouge: Louisiana State University Press, 1964.

———. *Generals in Gray: Lives of the Confederate Commanders.* Baton Rouge: Louisiana State University Press, 1959.

Waugh, John C. *The Class of 1846: From West Point to Appomattox: Stonewall Jackson, George McClellan and Their Brothers.* New York: Ballantine Books, 1999 (originally published by Warner Books, 1994).

Wert, Jeffry D. *A Brotherhood of Valor: The Common Soldiers of the Stonewall Brigade, C.S.A., and the Iron Brigade, U.S.A.* New York: Simon & Schuster, 1999.

———. *Cavalryman of the Lost Cause: A Biography of J. E. B. Stuart.* New York: Simon & Schuster, 2008.

———. *General James Longstreet, The Confederacy's Most Controversial Soldier: A Biography.* New York: Simon & Schuster, 1993.

Wheeler, Richard, ed. *Lee's Terrible Swift Sword: From Antietam to Chancellorsville.* New York: HarperCollins, 1992.

White, William S. *Rev. William S. White, D.D., and His Times.* Richmond, Va.: Presbyterian Committee of Publication, 1891.

Whitman, T. Stephen. *Antietam: Gateway to Emancipation* (Battles and Leaders of the Civil War series). Santa Barbara, Calif.: Praeger, 2012.

Wiley, Bell Irvin. *The Life of Johnny Reb: The Common Soldier of the Confederacy.* Baton Rouge: Louisiana State University Press, 1943.

Williams, Alpheus S. *Letters From the Cannon's Mouth: The Civil War Letters of General Alpheus S. Williams.* Lincoln: University of Nebraska Press, 1995 (first published in 1959).

Wilson, James Harrison. *Under the Old Flag,* volume 1. New York and London: D. Appleton and Co., 1912.

Wise, Jennings Cropper. *The Military History of the Virginia Military Institute from 1839 to 1865.* Lynchburg, Va.: J. P. Bell, 1915.

Wise, John S. *The End of an Era.* New York and Boston: Houghton Mifflin, 1899.

Wittenberg, Eric J., J. David Petruzzi, and Michael F. Nugent. *One Continuous Fight: The Retreat from Gettysburg and the Pursuit of Lee's Army of Northern Virginia, July 4–14, 1863.* New York: Savas Beatie, 2008.

Wood, W. J. *Civil War Generalship: The Art of Command.* Westport, Conn.: Greenwood Press, 1997.

Worsham, John H. *One of Jackson's Foot Cavalry.* New York: Neale Publishing Co., 1912.

INSERT PHOTOGRAPH CREDITS

1. Courtesy of the Virginia Military Institute Archives
2. Courtesy of the Virginia Military Institute Archives
3. Courtesy of the Virginia Military Institute Archives
4. Courtesy of the Virginia Military Institute Archives
5. Courtesy of the Rockbridge Historical Society Collections, Special Collections, Washington and Lee University
6. Courtesy of the Virginia Military Institute Archives
7. Courtesy of the Virginia Military Institute Archives
8. Michael Miley Collection, Special Collections and Archives, James G. Leyburn Library, Washington and Lee University
9. Courtesy of the Virginia Military Institute Archives
10. Courtesy of the Virginia Military Institute Archives
11. National Archives (111B5153)
12. National Park Service
13. Prints & Photographs Division, Library of Congress, LCB8177649
14. Prints & Photographs Division, Library of Congress, LC-DIG-cwpb-04402
15. Virginia Historical Society
16. The Museum of the Confederacy, Richmond, Virginia
17. Prints & Photographs Division, Library of Congress, LCBH83616
18. Fred Barr Collection, Stewart Bell, Jr., Archives Room, Handley Regional Library, Winchester, Virginia.
19. Jedediah Hotchkiss Papers, 18451905, Accession #2822, University of Virginia Library, Charlottesville
20. Prints & Photographs Division, Library of Congress, LCDIGcwpb02017
21. National Archives (111B1782)
22. Virginia Historical Society
23. Cook Collection, Valentine Richmond History Center
24. National Park Service
25. Prints & Photographs Division, Library of Congress, LCDIGppmsca32887
26. Prints & Photographs Division, Library of Congress, LCDIGstereo1s02842
27. Prints & Photographs Division, Library of Congress, LCB8136383
28. Prints & Photographs Division, Library of Congress, LCppmsca19389
29. Prints & Photographs Division, Library of Congress, LCDIGcwpb04325
30. Prints & Photographs Division, Library of Congress, LCDIGcwpb00487
31. Prints & Photographs Division, Library of Congress, LCB8131630
32. Prints & Photographs Division, Library of Congress, LCUSZ61985
33. Goodhart Collection

34. Virginia Historical Society
35. National Archives (111B3569)
36. National Archives (111B1867)
37. Prints & Photographs Division, Library of Congress, LC-DIG-ppmsca-35125
38. The Valentine Richmond History Center

Opening and closing endpapers: Frank Leslie Famous Leaders and Battle Scenes of the Civil
War (New York, N.Y.: Mrs. Frank Leslie, 1896), couresy of the private collection of Roy
Winkelman, Florida Center for Instructional Technology

INDEX

ABOUT THE AUTHOR

S. C. Gwynne is the author of the *New York Times* bestseller *Empire of the Summer Moon,* which was a finalist for the Pulitzer Prize and the National Book Critics Circle Award. He is an award-winning journalist whose work has appeared extensively in *Time,* for which he worked as bureau chief, national correspondent, and senior editor from 1988 to 2000, and in *Texas Monthly,* where he was executive editor. His work has also appeared in *Outside* magazine, the *New York Times,* the *Dallas Morning News,* the *Los Angeles Times,* the *Los Angeles Herald Examiner, Harper's,* and *California* magazine. He lives in Austin, Texas, with his wife, the artist Katie Maratta, and daughter, Maisie.